Dewey Decimal Classification and Relative Index

Dewey Decimal Classification and Relative Index

Devised by Melvil Dewey

EDITION 21

Edited by

Joan S. Mitchell, Editor

Julianne Beall, Assistant Editor

Winton E. Matthews, Jr., Assistant Editor

Gregory R. New, Assistant Editor

VOLUME 3

Schedules 600–999

FOREST PRESS

A Division of
OCLC Online Computer Library Center, Inc.
ALBANY, NEW YORK
1996

Library of Congress Cataloging-in-Publication Data
Dewey, Melvil, 1851-1931.
    Dewey decimal classification and relative index / devised by
Melvil Dewey. -- Ed. 21 / edited by Joan S. Mitchell, Julianne Beall,
Winton E. Matthews, Jr., Gregory R. New.
    p.   cm.
    Contents: v. 1. Introduction. Tables --v. 2-3. Schedules --v. 4. Relative
index. Manual.
    ISBN 0-910608-50-4 (set : alk. paper)
    1. Classification, Dewey decimal. I. Mitchell, Joan S. II. Beall,
Julianne, 1946-   . III. Matthews, Winton, E. IV. New, Gregory R. V.
Forest Press. VI. Title.
Z696.D52   1996   96-7393
025.4'31--dc20   CIP

The paper used in this publication meets the requirements of ANSI/NISO
Z39.48-1992 (Permanence of Paper).

ISBN: (set) 0-910608-50-4; v. 1 0-910608-51-2; v. 2 0-910608-52-0;
v. 3 0-910608-53-9; v. 4 0-910608-54-7

 Recycled paper

Contents

Volume 1

Contents

Schedules

Use of the Schedules

Full instructions on the use of the schedules are found in the Introduction to the Dewey Decimal Classification in volume 1.

The first three digits of a DDC number are found in the number column, or at the top of the page.

Numbers in square brackets [ ] are not used. Numbers in parentheses ( ) are options to standard usage.

600

600 Technology (Applied sciences)

See also 303.483 for technology as a cause of cultural change, 306.46 for sociology of technology, 338.1–338.4 for economic aspects of industries based on specific technologies, 338.926 for technology transfer, 338.927 for appropriate technology

See Manual at 300 vs. 600; also at 500 vs. 600

SUMMARY

601	Philosophy and theory
602	Miscellany
603	Dictionaries, encyclopedias, concordances
604	Technical drawing, hazardous materials technology, history and description with respect to kinds of persons
605	Serial publications
606	Organizations
607	Education, research, related topics
608	Inventions and patents
609	Historical, geographic, persons treatment
610	Medical sciences Medicine
.1–.9	[Standard subdivisions, medical personnel, nursing]
611	Human anatomy, cytology (cell biology), histology (tissue biology)
612	Human physiology
613	Promotion of health
614	Forensic medicine, incidence of disease, public preventive medicine
615	Pharmacology and therapeutics
616	Diseases
617	Miscellaneous branches of medicine Surgery
618	Other branches of medicine Gynecology and obstetrics
619	Experimental medicine
620	Engineering and allied operations
.001–.009	Standard subdivisions and general topics of engineering
.1–.8	[Engineering mechanics and materials, vibrations, engineering for geographic environments, fine particle and remote control technology, surface engineering, nanotechnology, human factors and safety engineering]
621	Applied physics
622	Mining and related operations
623	Military and nautical engineering
624	Civil engineering
625	Engineering of railroads and roads
627	Hydraulic engineering
628	Sanitary and municipal engineering Environmental protection engineering
629	Other branches of engineering

630	**Agriculture and related technologies**
.1–.9	Standard subdivisions
631	Specific techniques; apparatus, equipment, materials
632	Plant injuries, diseases, pests
633	Field and plantation crops
634	Orchards, fruits, forestry
635	Garden crops (Horticulture) Vegetables
636	Animal husbandry
637	Processing dairy and related products
638	Insect culture
639	Hunting, fishing, conservation, related technologies
640	**Home economics and family living**
.1–.9	Standard subdivisions and specific aspects of household management
641	Food and drink
642	Meals and table service
643	Housing and household equipment
644	Household utilities
645	Household furnishings
646	Sewing, clothing, management of personal and family living
647	Management of public households (Institutional housekeeping)
648	Housekeeping
649	Child rearing; home care of persons with illnesses and disabilities
650	**Management and auxiliary services**
.01–.09	Standard subdivisions
.1	Personal success in business
651	Office services
652	Processes of written communication
653	Shorthand
657	Accounting
658	General management
659	Advertising and public relations
660	**Chemical engineering and related technologies**
.01–.09	Standard subdivisions
.2–.7	[General topics in chemical engineering, biotechnology, industrial stoichiometry]
661	Technology of industrial chemicals
662	Technology of explosives, fuels, related products
663	Beverage technology
664	Food technology
665	Technology of industrial oils, fats, waxes, gases
666	Ceramic and allied technologies
667	Cleaning, color, coating, related technologies
668	Technology of other organic products
669	Metallurgy
670	**Manufacturing**
.1–.9	Standard subdivisions and special topics
671	Metalworking processes and primary metal products
672	Iron, steel, other iron alloys
673	Nonferrous metals
674	Lumber processing, wood products, cork
675	Leather and fur processing
676	Pulp and paper technology
677	Textiles
678	Elastomers and elastomer products
679	Other products of specific kinds of materials

680	Manufacture of products for specific uses
681	Precision instruments and other devices
682	Small forge work (Blacksmithing)
683	Hardware and household appliances
684	Furnishings and home workshops
685	Leather and fur goods, and related products
686	Printing and related activities
687	Clothing and accessories
688	Other final products, and packaging technology

690	Buildings
.01–.09	Standard subdivisions
.1–.8	[Structural elements, general activities, specific types of buildings]
691	Building materials
692	Auxiliary construction practices
693	Construction in specific types of materials and for specific purposes
694	Wood construction Carpentry
695	Roof covering
696	Utilities
697	Heating, ventilation, air-conditioning engineering
698	Detail finishing

601 Philosophy and theory

602 Miscellany

[.72] Patents

Do not use; class in 608

.75 Trademarks and service marks

Class here comprehensive works on trademarks generally used for products rather than services

Class interdisciplinary works on trademarks and service marks in 929.95

.9 **Commercial miscellany**

Class commercial miscellany of products and services used in individual and family living in 640.29; class commercial miscellany of manufactured products in 670.29; class interdisciplinary commercial miscellany in 380.1029

603 Dictionaries, encyclopedias, concordances

604 Technical drawing, hazardous materials technology, history and description with respect to kinds of persons

.2 **Technical drawing**

Class here engineering graphics, drafting illustrations

For architectural drawing, see 720.284. For drafting illustrations in a specific subject, see the subject, plus notation 0221 from Table 1, e.g., map drawing 526.0221, drafting in electronics 621.3810221

See also 006.6 for computer graphics

.22 Arrangement and organization of drafting rooms, preservation and storage of drawings

.24 Specific drafting procedures and conventions

.242 Production illustration

Nontechnical graphic representations

.243 Dimensioning; lettering, titling; shades, shadows

.245 Projections

Including isometric, orthographic, spherical projections; perspectives

.25 Preparation and reading of copies

Standard subdivisions are added for either or both topics in heading

Including blueprints, photostats

See also 686.42 for printing blueprints

.7 Hazardous materials technology

Methods of extracting, manufacturing, processing, utilizing, handling, transporting, storing solids, liquids, gases of corrosive, explosive, flammable, infectious, radioactive, toxic nature

Class interdisciplinary works on hazardous materials in 363.17. Class technology of a specific hazardous material with the technology, e.g., explosives 662.2; class safety techniques for a specific application of hazardous materials with the application outside 300, plus notation 0289 from Table 1, e.g., safety techniques in working with hazardous paving materials 625.80289 (*not* 363.179)

See Manual at 363.176 vs. 604.7; also at 604.7 vs. 660.2804

.8 History and description with respect to kinds of persons

Add to base number 604.8 the numbers following —08 in notation 081–089 from Table 1, e.g., women 604.82

605 Serial publications

606 Organizations

[.8] Management

Do not use; class in 658

607 Education, research, related topics

.01–.03 Education, research, related topics in areas, regions, places in general; in ancient world

Add to base number 607.0 notation 1–3 from Table 2, e.g., technical training in ancient Rome 607.0376

[.04–.09] Education, research, related topics in specific continents, countries, localities in modern world

> Do not use; class in 607.4–607.9

.1 **Education**

.2 **Research; statistical methods**

> Class here industrial, products research; historical, descriptive, experimental research
>
> Class product planning in management in 658.5038; class management of research for new and improved products in 658.57

[.201–.209] Geographic treatment of research; statistical methods

> Do not use; class in 607.21–607.29

.21–.29 Geographic treatment of research; statistical methods

> Do not use for historical, descriptive, experimental research or statistical methods when not limited by geographic area; class in 607.2
>
> Add to base number 607.2 notation 1–9 from Table 2, e.g., products research in China 607.251

.3 **Other aspects of education and research**

> Add to base number 607.3 the numbers following —07 in notation 074–079 from Table 1, e.g., fairs and exhibitions 607.34
>
> Class commercial aspects of fairs and exhibitions in 381.1; class interdisciplinary works on fairs and exhibitions in 907.4

.4–.9 **Education, research, related topics in specific continents, countries, localities in modern world**

> Add to base number 607 notation 4–9 from Table 2, e.g., education and research in Japan 607.52

608 Inventions and patents

> Do not use for history and description of technology with respect to kinds of persons; class in 604.8
>
> *See Manual at 608 vs. 609*

[.09] Historical, geographic, persons treatment

> Do not use; class in 608.7

.7 **Historical, geographic, persons treatment of inventions and patents**

> Add to base number 608.7 notation 01–9 from Table 2, e.g., patents from Brazil 608.781
>
> *For history of inventions, see 609*

609 Historical, geographic, persons treatment

Class here history of inventions, technological aspects of industrial archaeology

Class historical and geographic treatment of production and economic aspects of industrial archaeology in 338.09; class historical aspects of industrial archaeology in 900

See Manual at 300 vs. 600: Interdisciplinary works; also at 608 vs. 609

610 Medical sciences   Medicine

Class home care of persons with illnesses and disabilities in 649.8

For veterinary medicine, see 636.089

See Manual at 362.1–362.4 vs. 610; also at 571–573 vs. 610; also at 610 vs. 362.17; also at 610 vs. 616

SUMMARY

610.1–.9	[Standard subdivisions, medical personnel, nursing]
611	**Human anatomy, cytology (cell biology), histology (tissue biology)**
.001–.009	Standard subdivisions
.01	Anatomic embryology, cytology (cell biology), histology (tissue biology)
.1	Cardiovascular organs
.2	Respiratory organs
.3	Digestive tract organs
.4	Lymphatic and glandular organs
.6	Urogenital organs
.7	Musculoskeletal system, integument
.8	Nervous system Sense organs
.9	Regional and topographical anatomy
612	**Human physiology**
.001–.009	Standard subdivisions
.01–.04	[Biophysics, biochemistry, control processes, tissue and organ culture, physiology of specific activities]
.1	Blood and circulation
.2	Respiration
.3	Digestion
.4	Secretion, excretion, related functions
.6	Reproduction, development, maturation
.7	Musculoskeletal system, integument
.8	Nervous functions Sensory functions
.9	Regional physiology

613	**Promotion of health**
.04	Promotion of health of specific sex and age groups
.1	Environmental factors
.2	Dietetics
.4	Personal cleanliness and related topics
.5	Artificial environments
.6	Special topics of health and safety
.7	Physical fitness
.8	Substance abuse (Drug abuse)
.9	Birth control, reproductive technology, sex hygiene
614	**Forensic medicine, incidence of disease, public preventive medicine**
.1	Forensic medicine (Medical jurisprudence)
.4	Incidence of and public measures to prevent disease
.5	Incidence of and public measures to prevent specific diseases and kinds of diseases
.6	Disposal of the dead
615	**Pharmacology and therapeutics**
.1	Drugs (Materia medica)
.2	Inorganic drugs
.3	Organic drugs
.4	Practical pharmacy
.5	Therapeutics
.6	Methods of administering medication
.7	Pharmacodynamics
.8	Specific therapies and kinds of therapies
.9	Toxicology
616	**Diseases**
.001–.009	Standard subdivisions
.01–.09	[General topics of diseases]
.1	Diseases of cardiovascular system
.2	Diseases of respiratory system
.3	Diseases of digestive system
.4	Diseases of blood-forming, lymphatic, glandular systems Diseases of endocrine system
.5	Diseases of integument, hair, nails
.6	Diseases of urogenital system Diseases of urinary system
.7	Diseases of musculoskeletal system
.8	Diseases of nervous system and mental disorders
.9	Other diseases
617	**Miscellaneous branches of medicine Surgery**
.001–.008	Standard subdivisions of surgery
.01–.09	[General topics of surgery and historical, geographic, persons treatment]
.1	Injuries and wounds
.2	Results of injuries
.4	Surgery by systems
.5	Regional medicine Regional surgery
.6	Dentistry
.7	Ophthalmology
.8	Otology and audiology
.9	Operative surgery and special fields of surgery

618		**Other branches of medicine Gynecology and obstetrics**
	.01–.09	**Standard subdivisions and special topics of gynecology and obstetrics**
	.1	**Gynecology**
	.2	**Obstetrics**
	.3	**Diseases and complications of pregnancy**
	.4	**Childbirth (Parturition) Labor**
	.5	**Complicated labor (Dystocia)**
	.6	**Normal puerperium**
	.7	**Puerperal diseases**
	.8	**Obstetrical surgery**
	.9	**Pediatrics and geriatrics**
619		**Experimental medicine**
	.5	**Birds**
	.7	**Dogs**
	.8	**Cats**
	.9	**Other mammals**

[.23]   Medicine as a profession, occupation, hobby

> Do not use; class in 610.69

.28   Auxiliary techniques and procedures; apparatus, equipment, materials

> Class here comprehensive works on biomedical engineering

> *For biological aspects of biomedical engineering, see 570.28*

.6   Organizations, management, professions

.65   Group practice

> Class economics of group practice in 338.7–338.8

.69   Medical personnel

> Class nature of duties, characteristics of profession, relationships of medical personnel (other than nurses) of a specific specialty with the specialty, plus notation 023 from add tables under 616.1–616.9, 617, 618, e.g., obstetricians 618.2023; class critical appraisal and description of work, individual and collected biographies with the specialty, plus notation 092 from Table 1, e.g., biography of coroners 614.1092, of psychiatrists 616.890092

> *See Manual at 610.69*

.695   Specific kinds of medical personnel

> Nature of duties, characteristics of professions

> Class here medical missionaries

> Class medical records librarians in 651.504261; class medical secretaries in 651.3741

> *For nursing personnel, see 610.73069*

.695 2   Physicians

.695 3   Medical technicians and assistants

> Standard subdivisions are added for either or both topics in heading

.696	Medical relationships

Including relationships between medical personnel and patients, between medical personnel and the public, within medical professions

.7   Education, research, nursing, related topics

.724	Experimental research

Class experimental medicine in 619

.73	Nursing and services of medical technicians and assistants

Class here general medical nursing

Class patient education by nurses in 615.507

See Manual at 610.73

.730 1	Philosophy and theory of nursing
.730 2	Miscellany of nursing
[.730 23]	Nursing as a profession, occupation, hobby

Do not use; class in 610.73069

.730 3–.730 5	Standard subdivisions of nursing
.730 6	Nursing organizations and personnel
[.730 68]	Management of services of nurses

Do not use; class in 362.173068

.730 69	Nursing personnel

Nature of duties, characteristics of the profession, relationships

See Manual at 610.69

.730 692	Professional nurses and nursing

Standard subdivisions are added for either or both topics in heading

Including associate-degree nurses and nursing, nurse practitioners

.730 693	Practical nurses and nursing

Standard subdivisions are added for either or both topics in heading

Including registered nursing assistants (Canada)

.730 698	Auxiliary personnel

Including aides, attendants, orderlies, volunteers

.730 699	Relationships of nurses

Including relationships between nurses and patients, between nurses and the public, within nursing profession

.730 7–.730 9   Standard subdivisions of nursing

>   610.732–610.736   Nursing

Class comprehensive works in 610.73

.732   Private duty nursing

.733   Institutional nursing and ward management

Standard subdivisions are added for either or both topics in heading

Class nonmedical aspects of ward management in 362.173068

.734   Public health nursing

Class here Red Cross nursing

.734 3   Community and district nursing

Standard subdivisions are added for either or both topics in heading

Including work of visiting nurses

.734 6   Occupational health nursing (Industrial nursing)

.734 9   Disaster nursing

.736   Specialized nursing

Unless other instructions are given, observe the following table of preference, e.g., pediatric surgical nursing 610.73677 (*not* 610.7362):

Surgical, obstetrical, gynecologic nursing	610.7367
Pediatric nursing	610.7362
Geriatric nursing	610.7365
Nursing with respect to specific diseases	610.7369
Psychiatric and neurological nursing	610.7368
Intensive (Critical), emergency, long-term, terminal care nursing	610.7361

For public health nursing, see 610.734

.736 1   Intensive (Critical), emergency, long-term, terminal care nursing

.736 2   Pediatric nursing

.736 5   Geriatric nursing

.736 7   Surgical, obstetrical, gynecologic nursing

See also 618.2 for midwifery

.736 77   Surgical nursing

Including ophthalmic nursing, orthopedic nursing

Class nursing for obstetrical and gynecologic surgery in 610.73678; class nursing for cancer surgery in 610.73698

.736 78	Obstetrical and gynecologic nursing
.736 8	Psychiatric and neurological nursing
	Including nursing of persons with mental retardation
.736 9	Nursing with respect to specific diseases
	For psychiatric and neurological nursing, see 610.7368
.736 91	Cardiovascular diseases
.736 92	Respiratory diseases
.736 98	Cancer
.736 99	Communicable diseases
.737	Services of medical technicians and assistants
	Standard subdivisions are added for either or both topics in heading
[.737 023]	Work of medical technicians and assistants as a profession, occupation, hobby
	Do not use; class in 610.6953

.9   Historical, geographic, persons treatment

See Manual at 610.9

611   Human anatomy, cytology (cell biology), histology (tissue biology)

Standard subdivisions are added for human anatomy, cytology (cell biology), histology together; for human anatomy alone

For pathological anatomy, see 616.07

See Manual at 599.94 vs. 611; also at 612 vs. 611

SUMMARY

611.001–.009	**Standard subdivisions**
.01	**Anatomic embryology, cytology (cell biology), histology (tissue biology)**
.1	**Cardiovascular organs**
.2	**Respiratory organs**
.3	**Digestive tract organs**
.4	**Lymphatic and glandular organs**
.6	**Urogenital organs**
.7	**Musculoskeletal system, integument**
.8	**Nervous system Sense organs**
.9	**Regional and topographical anatomy**

.001–.009	Standard subdivisions
.01	Anatomic embryology, cytology (cell biology), histology (tissue biology)
	Class here specific systems, organs, regions

.013	Anatomic embryology
.018	Cytology (Cell biology) and histology (tissue biology)
.018 1	Cytology (Cell biology)
.018 15	Pathology (Cytopathology)
.018 16	Physiological genetics

Including nucleic acids [*formerly also* 612.01579]

>   611.018 2–611.018 9   Histology (Tissue biology)

Class here histogenesis, histophysiology, histopathology, tissue regeneration

Class comprehensive works in 611.018

.018 2	Connective tissue

Including adipose, areolar, collagenous, elastic, reticular tissues; pigmented cells; fibers, ground substances

For cartilaginous tissue, see 611.0183; for osseous tissue, see 611.0184

.018 3	Cartilaginous tissue

Including elastic, fibrous, hyaline cartilage

.018 4	Osseous (Bone) tissue

Including spongy and compact bone tissues, endosteum, periosteum; red and yellow bone marrow (medulla)

.018 5	Blood and lymph elements

Including blood plasma, red corpuscles (erythrocytes), white corpuscles (leukocytes), platelets (thrombocytes), lymph plasma, lymphocytes

.018 6	Muscular tissue

Including smooth (nonstriated, involuntary), skeletal (striated, voluntary), cardiac (striated, involuntary) muscle tissues

.018 7	Epithelial tissue

Including serous and mucous membranes; simple columnar, simple squamous, stratified squamous epithelia

.018 8	Nerve tissue

Including neurons, interstitial nerve tissue (neuroglia, neurilemma, satellite cells), meninges, sheaths

.018 9   Histology (Tissue biology) of specific systems, organs, regions

> Add to base number 611.0189 the numbers following 611 in 611.1–611.9, e.g., histology of thymus gland 611.018943; however, for specific tissues of specific systems, organs, regions, see 611.0182–611.0188

\>   **611.1–611.9 Gross anatomy**

Class here comprehensive works on gross anatomy and tissue structure

Class tissue structure in 611.0182–611.0189; class comprehensive works in 611

See Manual at 612.1–612.8

.1   **Cardiovascular organs**

.11   Pericardium

.12   Heart

> Including ventricles, auricles, endocardium, myocardium
>
> *For pericardium, see 611.11*

.13   Arteries

> Class here comprehensive works on blood vessels
>
> *For veins, see 611.14; for capillaries, see 611.15. For blood vessels of a specific system or organ, see the system or organ, e.g., cerebral blood vessels 611.81*

.14   Veins

.15   Capillaries

.2   **Respiratory organs**

.21   Nose and nasal accessory sinuses

.22   Larynx

> Including epiglottis, glottis, laryngeal muscles

.23   Trachea and bronchi

.24   Lungs

.25   Pleura

.26   Diaphragm

.27   Mediastinum

.3   **Digestive tract organs**

.31	Mouth
.313	Tongue
.314	Teeth
.315	Palate
.316	Salivary glands
.317	Lips
.318	Cheeks
.32	Pharynx, tonsils, esophagus
.33	Stomach

> Including pylorus
>
> Class here comprehensive works on gastrointestinal organs
>
> *For intestine, see 611.34*

.34	Intestine
.341	Small intestine

> Including duodenum, jejunum, ileum

.345	Cecum, vermiform appendix
.347	Large intestine

> Including sigmoid flexure (sigmoid colon)
>
> Class here colon
>
> *For cecum, vermiform appendix, see 611.345; for rectum, see 611.35*

.35	Rectum and anus

> *See also 611.96 for perineum*

.36	Biliary tract

> Including liver, gallbladder, bile ducts

.37	Pancreas and islands of Langerhans
.38	Peritoneum

> Including mesentery, omentum

.4   Lymphatic and glandular organs

> *For glandular organs of a specific system, see the system, e.g., salivary glands 611.316*

.41	Spleen

Class here comprehensive works on anatomy of blood-forming (hematopoietic or hemopoietic) system

For bone marrow, see 611.0184

.42	Lymphatic system

For lymphatic glands, see 611.46

.43	Thymus gland
.44	Thyroid and parathyroid glands
.45	Adrenal glands
.46	Lymphatic glands
.47	Carotid, pituitary, pineal glands
.49	Breasts
.6	**Urogenital organs**
.61	Kidneys and ureters

Standard subdivisions are added for kidneys and ureters together, for kidneys alone

Class here comprehensive works on anatomy of urinary organs

For bladder and urethra, see 611.62

.62	Bladder and urethra
.63	Testicles, prostate, scrotum

Class here comprehensive works on male genital organs

For penis, see 611.64

.64	Penis
.65	Ovaries and fallopian tubes

Class here comprehensive works on female genital organs

For uterus, see 611.66; for vagina, hymen, vulva, see 611.67

.66	Uterus

Including cervix of uterus

.67	Vagina, hymen, vulva
.7	**Musculoskeletal system, integument**
.71	Bones

For ossicles, see 611.85

.711	Bones of spinal column
.712	Bones of chest

Including ribs

For sternum, see 611.713

.713	Sternum
.715	Bones of brainpan

For mastoid processes, see 611.85

.716	Bones of face
.717	Bones of upper extremities

Including scapulas, clavicles, humeri, radii, ulnas, carpal and metacarpal bones, phalanges and sesamoid bones of hands

Class comprehensive works on bones of extremities in 611.718

.718	Bones of lower extremities

Including hip bones, femurs, patellas, tibias, fibulas, tarsal and metatarsal bones, phalanges and sesamoid bones of feet

Class here comprehensive works on bones of extremities

For bones of upper extremities, see 611.717

.72	Articulations (Ligaments and joints)
.73	Muscles

For muscles of a specific system or organ, see the system or organ, e.g., heart muscles 611.12

.731	Muscles of back
.732	Muscles of head
.733	Muscles of neck
.735	Muscles of chest
.736	Muscles of abdomen and pelvis
.737	Muscles of upper extremities

Including muscles of shoulders, arms, forearms, hands

Class comprehensive works on muscles of extremities in 611.738

.738	Muscles of lower extremities

Including muscles of hips, buttocks, thighs, legs, feet

Class here comprehensive works on muscles of extremities

For muscles of upper extremities, see 611.737

.74 Connective tissue

Including tendons, fasciae

For ligaments, see 611.72; for bursae, sheaths of tendons, see 611.75

.75 Bursae, sheaths of tendons

.77 Integument

For hair and nails, see 611.78

.78 Hair and nails

Including hair follicles

.8 **Nervous system   Sense organs**

Class here neuroanatomy

.81 Brain

Class here central nervous system

For spinal cord, see 611.82

.82 Spinal cord

.83 Nerves and ganglia

Class nerves of a specific system or organ with the system or organ, e.g., optic nerves 611.84

.84 Eyes

Class here orbits

.85 Ears

Including mastoid processes, ossicles

.86 Olfactory organs

.87 Gustatory organs

.88 Tactile organs

.9 **Regional and topographical anatomy**

Including back

Class specific systems or organs in a region in 611.1–611.8

.91 Head

For face, see 611.92

.92 Face

See also 611.317 for lips, 611.318 for cheeks

.93 Neck

.94	Thorax

.95 Abdomen

Epigastric through lumbar regions

.96 Perineum and pelvic region

.97 Upper extremities

Class comprehensive works on extremities in 611.98

.98 Lower extremities

Class here comprehensive works on extremities

For upper extremities, see 611.97

612 Human physiology

Class here comprehensive works on anatomy and physiology

Class physiological psychology in 152

For human anatomy, cytology (cell biology), histology (tissue biology), see 611; for pathological physiology, see 616.07

See Manual at 612 vs. 611; also at 616 vs. 612

SUMMARY

612.001–.009	**Standard subdivisions**
.01–.04	**[Biophysics, biochemistry, control processes, tissue and organ culture, physiology of specific activities]**
.1	**Blood and circulation**
.2	**Respiration**
.3	**Digestion**
.4	**Secretion, excretion, related functions**
.6	**Reproduction, development, maturation**
.7	**Musculoskeletal system, integument**
.8	**Nervous functions Sensory functions**
.9	**Regional physiology**

.001–.009 Standard subdivisions

.01 Biophysics and biochemistry

.014 Biophysics

.014 2 Physical phenomena in humans

Including human aura when scientifically considered

See also 133.892 for the aura as a manifestation of psychic power

.014 21 Bioenergetics

For body heat, see 612.01426; for bioelectricity, see 612.01427

.014 26	Body heat
	Including regulation
	Class here production, maintenance
.014 27	Bioelectricity
	Including electrophysiology
.014 4	Effects of terrestrial agents .
	Including aerospace physiology
	Class space physiology in 612.0145
.014 41	Mechanical forces
.014 412	Gravitational forces
.014 414	Acceleration and deceleration
	Standard subdivisions are added for either or both topics in heading
.014 415	Pressure
	Including submarine physiology
.014 42	Electricity and magnetism
.014 44	Visible light
.014 45	Sound and related vibrations
.014 452	Subsonic vibrations
.014 453	Sound
.014 455	Ultrasonic vibrations
.014 46	Thermal forces
.014 462	Heat and high temperatures
	Standard subdivisions are added for either or both topics in heading
.014 465	Cold and low temperatures
	Standard subdivisions are added for either or both topics in heading
	For cryogenic temperatures, see 612.014467
.014 467	Cryogenic temperatures

.014 48	Radiation (Radiobiology)

Class here dosimetry

Class comprehensive medical works on radiation sickness and injuries in 616.9897

For visible light, see 612.01444. For a specific application of dosimetry, see the application, e.g., dosimetry in radiotherapy 615.842

.014 481	Radio waves and microwaves

Standard subdivisions are added for either or both topics in heading

.014 482	Infrared radiation
.014 484	Ultraviolet radiation
.014 485	X rays
.014 486	Particle radiations

Including cosmic rays [*formerly* 612.014487], beta, gamma, neutron radiations

For X rays, see 612.014485

[.014 487]	Cosmic rays

Relocated to 612.014486

.014 5	Extraterrestrial biophysics

Class here bioastronautics, space physiology

Class aerospace physiology in 612.0144; class space medicine in 616.980214

.014 53	Effects of mechanical forces

Add to base number 612.01453 the numbers following 612.01441 in 612.014412–612.014415, e.g., gravity 612.014532

[.014 54–.014 57]	Effects of sound and related vibrations, of radiations, of thermal forces, of electricity and magnetism

Numbers discontinued; class in 612.0145

.015	Biochemistry

Class metabolism in 612.39

For physiological genetics, see 611.01816

.015 01	Philosophy and theory

Class theoretical biochemistry in 612.01582

.015 02	Miscellany

.015 028	Auxiliary techniques and procedures; apparatus, equipment, materials
	Class analytical biochemistry in 612.01585
.015 1	Enzymes
	Add to base number 612.0151 the numbers following 572.7 in 572.75–572.79, e.g., saccharolytic enzymes 612.015156, lipolytic enzymes 612.015157
.015 2	Fluids, inorganic constituents, pigments
.015 22	Fluids
	Including electrolytic balance, fluid balance, water
	Class here fluid metabolism
	See Manual at 612.01522 vs. 612.3923, 616.3992
.015 24	Inorganic constituents
	Including minerals
	Class inorganic fluids in 612.01522; class inorganic pigments in 612.01528
.015 28	Pigments
	Class biochemistry of skin pigmentation in 612.7927
.015 4	Biosynthesis
[.015 43–.015 47]	Lipids, carbohydrates, proteins, pigments
	Numbers discontinued; class in 612.0154
.015 7	Organic compounds
	Add to base number 612.0157 the numbers following 547.7 in 547.72–547.78, e.g., carbohydrates 612.01578; however, for enzymes, see 612.0151; for vitamins, see 612.399; for hormones, see 612.405
	For organic fluids, see 612.01522; for organic pigments, see 612.01528
[.015 79]	Nucleic acids
	Relocated to 611.01816
.015 8	Theoretical, physical, analytical biochemistry
	Class physical, theoretical, analytical biochemistry of a specific constituent with the constituent, e.g., physical chemistry of carbohydrates 612.01578
.015 82	Theoretical biochemistry
.015 83	Physical biochemistry

.015 85	Analytical biochemistry
.02	Control processes and tissue and organ culture
.022	Control processes

Including biological rhythms, homeostasis

.028	Tissue and organ culture
.04	Physiology of specific activities

Class here comprehensive works on the physiology of physical movements in relation to multiple physiological systems

For physiology of physical movements in relation to a specific system, see the system, e.g., musculoskeletal system 612.76

.042	Work
.044	Exercise and sports

Standard subdivisions are added for either or both topics in heading

Including walking

Class here recreation

For physiology of exercise on the job, see 612.042

> **612.1–612.8 Specific functions, systems, organs**

Class comprehensive works in 612

See Manual at 612.1–612.8

.1   Blood and circulation

For lymph and lymphatics, see 612.42. For circulation in a specific system or organ, see the system or organ, e.g., brain 612.824

.11	Blood

Class spleen in 612.41; class bone marrow in 612.491

For blood chemistry, see 612.12

.111	Red corpuscles (Erythrocytes)
.111 1	Biochemistry

Including hemoglobins

.111 2	Counts and counting
.112	White corpuscles (Leukocytes)
.112 1	Biochemistry
.112 2	Biophysics

.112 7	Counts and counting
.115	Coagulation (Clotting)

Including role of fibrin, fibrinoplastin, plasma, thrombin in clotting

.116   Plasma

For role of plasma in clotting, see 612.115

.117   Platelets and hemoconia

.118   Biophysics and biological properties

.118 1   Biophysics

Physical properties and phenomena, effect of physical agents

Including hemorrheology (study of blood flow)

For biophysics of a specific component or function, see the compound or function in 612.111–612.117, e.g., biophysics of platelets 612.117

.118 2   Biological properties

.118 25   Blood types and typing (Blood groups and grouping)

Standard subdivisions are added for any or all topics in heading

.12   Blood chemistry

Including carbohydrates, cholesterol, enzymes, lipids, minerals

Class biological properties in 612.1182

For chemistry of a specific component or function, see the component or function in 612.111–612.117, e.g., chemistry of coagulation 612.115

.13   Blood vessels and vascular circulation

Standard subdivisions are added for either or both topics in heading

For vasomotors, see 612.18

.133   Arteries and arterial circulation

Standard subdivisions are added for either or both topics in heading

.134   Veins and venous circulation

Standard subdivisions are added for either or both topics in heading

.135   Capillaries and capillary circulation

Standard subdivisions are added for either or both topics in heading

.14   Blood pressure

.17   Heart

.171	Biophysics

    Including contraction and dilation of heart cavities, valvular activity, recording methods

    For blood pressure, see 612.14

.173	Biochemistry
.178	Innervation
.18	Vasomotors

    Nerves causing dilation (vasodilators) and constriction (vasoconstrictors) of blood vessels

.2   **Respiration**

    Including comprehensive works on physiology of the nose

    Class physiology of the nose as an olfactory organ in 612.86

.21	Biophysics

    Including respiratory movements, rhythm, sounds

.22	Biochemistry

    Including oxygen supply, gas exchange, carbon dioxide removal

.26	Tissue (Internal) respiration
.28	Innervation of respiratory apparatus

.3   **Digestion**

    Class here nutrition

    Class dietetics and applied nutrition in 613.2

.31	Mouth and esophagus

    Standard subdivisions are added for mouth and esophagus together, for mouth alone

    Including ingestion and start of digestion

.311	Teeth

    Including mastication

.312	Tongue and tonsils

    Class here comprehensive works on physiology of tongue

    For physiology of tongue as a gustatory organ, see 612.87

.313	Salivary glands and saliva

    Standard subdivisions are added for salivary glands and saliva together, for salivary glands alone

.315   Esophagus

.32   Stomach and gastric secretions

Standard subdivisions are added for stomach and gastric secretions together, for stomach alone

Class here comprehensive works on gastrointestinal organs and secretions

For intestine and intestinal secretions, see 612.33

.33   Intestine and intestinal secretions

Standard subdivisions are added for intestine and intestinal secretions together, for intestine alone

For large intestine, see 612.36

.34   Pancreas and pancreatic secretions

Standard subdivisions are added for pancreas and pancreatic secretions together, for pancreas alone

.35   Biliary tract

Including liver, gallbladder, bile and bile ducts

.36   Large intestine and defecation

Standard subdivisions are added for large intestine and defecation together, for large intestine alone

.38   Absorption

Transfer of digested food from alimentary canal into blood stream

Class absorption in a specific part of the alimentary canal with the part, e.g., intestine 612.33

.39   Metabolism

For biosynthesis, see 612.0154; for metabolism of drugs, see 615.7; for metabolism of toxic substances, see 615.9. For metabolism within a specific function, system, or organ, see the function, system, or organ, e.g., metabolism of plasma 612.116

.391   Hunger and thirst mechanisms

.392   Metabolism of inorganic substances

Class here minerals

.392 3   Water

See Manual at 612.01522 vs. 612.3923, 616.3992

.392 4   Elements

Including iron, phosphorus, sulfur

.392 6	Compounds other than water

Including salts

.396	Carbohydrate metabolism
.397	Lipid metabolism

Including fats

.398	Protein metabolism
.399	Vitamins

.4   Secretion, excretion, related functions

Class here endocrine system

For glands and glandular activity in a specific system or organ, see the system or organ, e.g., salivary glands 612.313, mammary glands and lactation 612.664

.400 1–.400 9	Standard subdivisions
.405	Hormones
.41	Spleen

Class here comprehensive works on blood-forming (hematopoietic or hemopoietic) system

For physiology of bone marrow, see 612.491

.42	Lymph and lymphatics
.43	Thymus gland
.44	Thyroid and parathyroid glands
.45	Adrenal glands
.46	Excretion

Class here urinary system

For defecation, see 612.36

.461	Urine
.463	Kidneys
.467	Ureters, bladder, urethra
.49	Bone marrow and carotid, pituitary, pineal glands
.491	Bone marrow
.492	Carotid, pituitary, pineal glands

.6   **Reproduction, development, maturation**

Class here comprehensive medical works on sex

Class interdisciplinary works on sex in 306.7

For a specific aspect of sex, see the aspect, e.g., sexual disorders 616.69

.600 1–.600 9   Standard subdivisions

.61   Male reproductive system

Including function in sexual activity

For climacteric, see 612.665

.62   Female reproductive system

Including function in sexual activity

For pregnancy and childbirth, see 612.63; for menstruation, see 612.662; for climacteric, see 612.665

.63   Pregnancy and childbirth

Including placenta

Class comprehensive works on pregnancy and childbirth in 618.2

For physiology of embryo and fetus, see 612.64

.64   Physiology of embryo and fetus

Class here comprehensive works on embryology

For anatomic embryology, see 611.013

.640 01–.640 09   Standard subdivisions

.640 1   Development of specific systems, organs, regions

Add to base number 612.6401 the numbers following 611 in 611.1–611.9, e.g., development of the eye 612.640184

.646   Development of embryo

.647   Development of fetus

> 612.65–612.67 Postnatal development

Class comprehensive works in 612.6

For postnatal development of a specific system, organ, region, see the system, organ, region, e.g., postnatal development of teeth 612.311

.65   Child development

.652   Development of newborn (neonate)

First month of postnatal development

.654   Development from infancy to beginning of puberty

> From second month of postnatal development

.66   Adult development and maturity

> *For aging, see 612.67*

.661   Puberty and development prior to attainment of full maturity

.662   Menstruation

> Including menarche

.663   Full maturity

.664   Mammary glands and lactation

.665   Climacteric

> Including menopause

.67   Aging

> Class here physical gerontology
>
> *See also 616.078 for death*

.68   Longevity factors

.7   **Musculoskeletal system, integument**

.74   Muscles

> Class locomotion, exercise, rest in 612.76. Class muscles of a specific system or organ with the system or organ, e.g., eye muscles 612.846

.741   Biophysics

> Including contractions, elasticity, irritability, tonus

.743   Innervation

.744   Biochemistry

> Including fatigue products

.75   Bones, joints, connective tissues

> Class bone marrow in 612.491; class locomotion, exercise, rest in 612.76
>
> *For mastoid processes, ossicles, see 612.854*

.76   Locomotion, exercise, rest

> Including body mechanics
>
> Class the total physiology of physical movements (including muscle contractions, breathing, blood flow, digestion during exercise) in 612.04

.78   Voice and speech

Standard subdivisions are added for either or both topics in heading

Including neurolinguistics

Class here organs of speech

.79   Integument   Skin

.791   Biophysics of skin

Including absorbency, contractions, irritability, resistivity, tonus

.792   Biochemistry of skin

.792 1   Glands and glandular secretions

Standard subdivisions are added for glands and glandular secretions together, for glands alone

Including perspiration

.792 7   Pigmentation

.798   Innervation of skin

.799   Hair and nails

.8   Nervous functions   Sensory functions

Class here neurophysiology, psychophysiology

See Manual at 612.8 vs. 152

.804   Special topics

.804 2   Neurochemistry

Including cerebrospinal fluid

.804 3   Biophysics of nervous system

.81   Nerves and nerve fibers

Standard subdivisions are added for nerves and nerve fibers together, for nerves alone

Class here peripheral nervous system

For autonomic nervous system, see 612.89. For innervation and neural activity in a specific system or organ, see the system or organ, e.g., heart innervation 612.178

.811   Motor and sensory nerves

.813   Biophysics

Including electrophysiology

For irritability, see 612.816. For biophysics of a specific kind of nerve, see the nerve, e.g., biophysics of cranial nerves 612.819

.814   Biochemistry

> *For biochemistry of a specific kind of nerve, see the nerve, e.g., biochemistry of motor nerves 612.811*

.816   Irritability

.819   Cranial and spinal nerves

.82   Brain

Class here central nervous system; physiology of memory, of thinking

> *For spinal cord, see 612.83*

> *See also 153.12 for psychology of memory, 153.42 for psychology of thinking*

.821   Sleep phenomena

Physiology of brain during sleep and dreams

> *See Manual at 612.821 vs. 154.6*

.822   Biochemistry and biophysics

> *For biochemistry and biophysics of a specific part of brain, see the part, e.g., biophysics of cerebrum 612.825*

.824   Circulation

> *For circulation in a specific part of brain, see the part, e.g., circulation in cerebellum 612.827*

.825   Cerebrum

Including cerebral hemispheres, convolutions, corpus striatum, cortex, rhinencephalon

Class here prosencephalon (forebrain)

> *For cerebral commissures and peduncles, see 612.826; for diencephalon, see 612.8262*

.825 2   Localization of motor functions

.825 5   Localization of sensory functions

.826   Diencephalon and brain stem

Including cerebral commissures and peduncles

> *For medulla oblongata, see 612.828*

.826 2   Diencephalon

Including geniculate bodies, hypothalamus, thalamus

.826 4   Mesencephalon (Midbrain)

Including corpora quadrigemina

.826 7	Pons Variolii
.827	Cerebellum
.828	Medulla oblongata
.83	Spinal cord

>   **612.84–612.88 Sense organs and sensory functions**

      Class comprehensive works in 612.8

.84   **Eyes and vision**

      Standard subdivisions are added for either or both topics in heading

      Class here physiological optics, eyeballs

.841   **Fibrous tunics, conjunctivas, anterior chambers**

        Including corneas, scleras

.842   **Uveas**

        Including choroids, ciliary bodies, irises

.843   **Optic nerves and retinas**

.844   **Aqueous humors, crystalline lenses, vitreous bodies**

.846   **Movements**

        Class here ocular neuromuscular mechanism

.847   **Eyelids and tear ducts**

        Class conjunctivas in 612.841

.85   **Ears and hearing**

      Standard subdivisions are added for either or both topics in heading

.851   **External ears**

.854   **Middle ears**

        Including eustachian tubes (auditory tubes), mastoid processes, ossicles, tympanic membranes

.858   **Internal ears**

        Including cochleas, labyrinths, semicircular canals, vestibules

.86 Nose and smelling

 Standard subdivisions are added for either or both topics in heading

 Class here chemical senses

 Class comprehensive works on physiology of nose in 612.2

  For tasting, see 612.87

.87 Tongue and tasting

 Standard subdivisions are added for either or both topics in heading

 Class comprehensive works on physiology of the tongue in 612.312

.88 Other sense organs and sensory functions

 Including sense of movement (motion), tactile and proprioceptive organs and senses

 Including pain sensations and reactions

.89 Autonomic nervous system

 Including sympathetic and parasympathetic nervous systems

.9 **Regional physiology**

 Including back

 Add to base number 612.9 the numbers following 611.9 in 611.91–611.98, e.g., physiology of face 612.92

 Class physiology of specific systems and organs in specific regions in 612.1–612.8

613 **Promotion of health**

 Including inherited diseases as a factor

 Class here measures to promote health and prevent disease taken by individuals and their medical advisers, comprehensive medical works on personal and public measures to promote health and prevent disease

 For public measures to promote health and prevent disease, see 614; for personal preventive measures applied to specific diseases or groups of diseases, see 616–618

 See Manual at 613 vs. 615.8

SUMMARY

613.04	**Promotion of health of specific sex and age groups**
.1	**Environmental factors**
.2	**Dietetics**
.4	**Personal cleanliness and related topics**
.5	**Artificial environments**
.6	**Special topics of health and safety**
.7	**Physical fitness**
.8	**Substance abuse (Drug abuse)**
.9	**Birth control, reproductive technology, sex hygiene**

.04 Promotion of health of specific sex and age groups

.042 Promotion of health of specific sex groups

.042 3 Males

.042 32 Boys under twelve

.042 33 Males twelve to twenty

.042 34 Adult men

.042 4 Females

.042 42 Girls under twelve

.042 43 Females twelve to twenty

.042 44 Adult women

.043 Promotion of health of specific age groups

Class promotion of health of specific age groups of specific sexes in 613.042

.043 2 Infants and children

Through age eleven

Class here pediatric preventive measures

.043 3 Young people twelve to twenty

.043 4 Mature adults

Including college-age, middle-aged persons

For persons in late adulthood, see 613.0438

.043 8 Persons in late adulthood

Class here geriatric preventive measures

[.081–.084] Persons of specific sex and age groups

Do not use; class in 613.04

.1	**Environmental factors**

Class here acclimation

For artificial environments, see 613.5

.11	Weather and climate

Standard subdivisions are added for either or both topics in heading

For seasonal changes, see 613.13; for humidity, see 613.14

[.110 911]	Weather and climate in frigid zones

Do not use; class in 613.111

[.110 913]	Weather and climate in torrid zone (tropics)

Do not use; class in 613.113

.111	Cold weather and climate

Standard subdivisions are added for either or both topics in heading

Including arctic climate

.113	Hot weather and climate

Standard subdivisions are added for either or both topics in heading

Including tropical climate

.12	Physiographic and other regions

Including mountains, seashore

.122	Health resorts
.13	Seasonal changes
.14	Humidity
.19	Air and light
.192	Breathing
.193	Sun bathing
.194	Nudism

.2 **Dietetics**

Class here beverages [*formerly* 613.3], applied nutrition [*formerly also* 641.1], comprehensive works on nutritive values of beverages [*formerly* 641.2], guides to nutritional aspects of food, comprehensive works on personal health aspects of food

Class human nutritional requirements considered in relation to physiological processes and the role of nutrients in the body in 612.3; class diet therapy in 615.854; class nutritive values of specific beverages in 641.2; class nutritive values of specific foods in 641.33–641.39; class personal aspects of preventing alcohol abuse in 613.81; class comprehensive works on diet and physical fitness in 613.7; class interdisciplinary works on food safety in 363.192. Class diets to prevent a specific disease with the disease, plus notation 05 from the tables under 616.1–616.9, 617, 618.1–618.8, e.g., diets to prevent hypertension 616.13205

See also 616.39 for conditions resulting from nutritional deficiencies, 641.563 for cooking for preventive and therapeutic diets

See Manual at 363.8 vs. 613.2, 641.3

.208 2 Women

Class dietetics for nursing women in 613.269; class dietetics for pregnant women in 618.24

.208 3 Young people

Class home economics and child-rearing aspects of feeding children, interdisciplinary works on feeding children in 649.3

.208 32 Infants

Class breast feeding in 613.269

.208 5 Relatives   Parents

.208 52 Mothers

Class dietetics for nursing mothers in 613.269

.23 Calories

Class here calorie counters

Class high-calorie diets in 613.24; class low-calorie diets in 613.25

.24 Weight-gaining diets

.25 Weight-losing diets

.26 Specific dietary regimens

Including raw food diet, regimens involving specific foods

For weight-gaining diets, see 613.24; for weight-losing diets, see 613.25; for regimens involving specific nutritive elements, see 613.28

[.260 1–.260 9]	Standard subdivisions
	Do not use; class in 613.201–613.209
.262	Vegetarian diets
.263	High-fiber and low-fiber diets
	Class vegetarian diets in 613.262
.264	Macrobiotic diet
.269	Human breast milk diet

Class here nutritional and general health aspects of breast feeding for both mother and infant, comprehensive medical works on breast feeding

Class interdisciplinary works on breast feeding in 649.33

For a specific medical aspect of breast feeding not provided for here, see the aspect, e.g., prolactin and physiology of human lactation 612.664

See Manual at 649.33 vs. 613.269

.28   Specific nutritive elements

Class calories in 613.23; class weight modification diets involving specific nutritive elements in 613.24–613.25; class high-fiber and low-fiber diets in 613.263

[.280 1–.280 9]	Standard subdivision
	Do not use; class in 613.201–613.209
.282	Proteins
.283	Carbohydrates
.284	Fats and oils

Standard subdivisions are added for either or both topics in heading

.285   Minerals

Including calcium, iron, sodium

.286	Vitamins
.287	Water

[.3]   **Beverages**

Relocated to 613.2

.4   **Personal cleanliness and related topics**

Class personal grooming in 646.7

.41   Bathing

.48	Clothing and cosmetics
.482	Clothing
.488	Cosmetics

.5   Artificial environments

In enclosed spaces

Including homes, offices; indoor temperatures and air conditioning

.6   Special topics of health and safety

Class here personal safety

For personal safety in a specific field, see the field, plus notation 0289 from Table 1, e.g., personal safety in welding 671.520289

.62   Industrial and occupational health

Standard subdivisions are added for either or both topics in heading

See Manual at 363.11 vs. 613.62

.66   Self-defense

.67   Military and camp health

Standard subdivisions are added for either or both topics in heading

.68   Travel health

Including shipboard health

.69   Survival

After accidents and disasters, in other unfavorable circumstances

For self-defense, see 613.66

.7   Physical fitness

Class here comprehensive works on diet and physical fitness

For breathing, see 613.192; for diet, see 613.2

.704   Special topics

> 613.704 2–613.704 5 Specific age and sex groups

Class physical yoga of specific age and sex groups in 613.7046; class comprehensive works in 613.704

.704 2   Physical fitness of children

.704 3   Physical fitness of young people twelve to twenty

.704 4   Physical fitness of adults

Class physical fitness of adult women in 613.7045

.704 46	Physical fitness of persons in late adulthood
	Class physical fitness of men in late adulthood in 613.70449

.704 49   Physical fitness of adult men

Class here physical fitness of males

> *For physical fitness of boys under twelve, see 613.7042; for physical fitness of young men twelve to twenty, see 613.7043*

.704 5   Physical fitness of adult women

Class here physical fitness of females

> *For physical fitness of girls under twelve, see 613.7042; for physical fitness of young women twelve to twenty, see 613.7043*

.704 6   Physical yoga

Class here hatha yoga

Class exercises from the martial arts traditions in 613.7148

[.708 1–.708 4]   Persons of specific sex and age groups

Do not use; class in 613.7042–613.7045

.71   Exercise and sports activities

Standard subdivisions are added for exercise and sports activities together, for exercise alone

Class here aerobic exercise, comprehensive works on exercise and sports activities for fitness and for improvement in the shape of the body

Class physical yoga in 613.7046; class exercises to aid childbirth in 618.24; class parental supervision of children's exercise and sports activities in 649.57

> *For exercise and sports activities to improve the shape of the body, see 646.75*

See Manual at 613.71 vs. 646.75, 796

[.710 247 96]   For persons occupied with athletics and sports

Do not use; class in 613.711

[.710 887 96]   Treatment with respect to persons occupied with athletics and sports

Do not use; class in 613.711

.711	Fitness training for sports

Including fitness training for specific sports not provided for in 613.713–613.717, e.g., football

Class here promotion of health of athletes

Class a specific kind of fitness training with the kind, e.g., weight lifting 613.713; class fitness training for a specific sport listed in 613.713–613.717 with the sport, e.g., swimming 613.716

.713	Weight lifting
.714	Calisthenics and isometric exercises

Standard subdivisions are added for calisthenics and isometric exercises together, for calisthenics alone

Class here gymnastic exercises

See also 613.713 for weight lifting, 613.715 for aerobic dancing, 613.716 for aquatic exercises

.714 8	Exercises from the martial arts traditions

Including aikido, karate exercises

Class here T'ai chi ch'üan [*formerly also* 796.8155], fitness training for the martial arts

See also 796.815 for jujitso and related martial arts as sports

.714 9	Isometric exercises
.715	Aerobic dancing
.716	Aquatic exercises and swimming
.717	Running and walking
.717 2	Running
.717 6	Walking
.78	Correct posture
.79	Relaxation, rest, sleep
.8	**Substance abuse (Drug abuse)**

Limited to personal preventive aspects

Including abuse of analgesics, depressants, inhalants, sedatives, tranquilizers

Class here appeals to the individual to avoid substance abuse for health reasons

Class comprehensive medical works on addictive and disorienting drugs in 615.78; class comprehensive medical works on substance abuse as a disease in 616.86; class interdisciplinary works on substance abuse in 362.29

.81	Alcohol

.83   Narcotics, hallucinogens, psychedelics, cannabis

.835   Cannabis

> Class here specific kinds of cannabis, e.g., hashish, marijuana

.84   Stimulants and related substances

> Standard subdivisions are added for stimulants and related substances together, for stimulants alone

> Including amphetamine, ephedrine; cocaine

> Class nicotine in 613.85

.85   Tobacco

.9   Birth control, reproductive technology, sex hygiene

> Including sexual abstinence as a method of birth control and disease prevention

> Class sexual abstinence for birth control in 613.94; class sexual abstinence for disease prevention in 613.95

.907   Education, research, related topics

> Class sex education of children in the home in 649.65

.94   Birth control and reproductive technology

> Standard subdivisions are added for birth control and reproductive technology together, for birth control alone

> Including artificial insemination, measures to increase the likelihood of having a child of the desired sex

> Class here family planning

> Class interdisciplinary works on birth control and family planning in 363.96

.942   Surgical methods of birth control

> Limited to personal health aspects

> Including tubal sterilization, vasectomy

> Class comprehensive works on surgical methods of birth control for males in 617.463; class comprehensive works on surgical methods of birth control for females in 618.1

.943   Chemical, rhythm, mechanical methods of birth control

.943 2   Chemical methods of birth control

> Limited to personal health aspects

> Including pills (oral contraceptives)

> Class the pharmacodynamics of chemical contraceptives in 615.766

.943 4   Rhythm method of birth control

.943 5 Mechanical methods of birth control

Including intrauterine devices, comprehensive works on condoms

For use of condoms for disease prevention, see 613.95

.95 Sex hygiene

Including use of condoms for prevention of disease

Class manuals of sexual technique in 613.96

[.950 81–.950 84] Sex hygiene of specific age and sex groups

Do not use; class in 613.951–613.955

.951 Sex hygiene of young people

To age twenty

For sex hygiene of males to age twenty, see 613.953; for sex hygiene of females to age twenty, see 613.955

.952 Sex hygiene of adult men

Class here sex hygiene of males

For sex hygiene of males to age twenty, see 613.953

.953 Sex hygiene of males to age twenty

.954 Sex hygiene of adult women

Class here sex hygiene of females

For sex hygiene of females to age twenty, see 613.955

.955 Sex hygiene of females to age twenty

.96 Manuals of sexual technique

614 Forensic medicine, incidence of disease, public preventive medicine

Class social provision for public health services other than those concerned with incidence and prevention of disease in 362.1; class public safety programs and social provision for prevention of injuries in 363.1; class environmental problems and services in 363.7

SUMMARY

614.1	Forensic medicine (Medical jurisprudence)
.4	Incidence of and public measures to prevent disease
.5	Incidence of and public measures to prevent specific diseases and kinds of diseases
.6	Disposal of the dead

.1 Forensic medicine (Medical jurisprudence)

Including determination of time and cause of death; determination of cause, nature and extent of injury; forensic dentistry, psychiatry, toxicology

.4   **Incidence of and public measures to prevent disease**

Class here epidemiology

For incidence of and public measures to prevent specific diseases and kinds of diseases, see 614.5

See also 353.59 for registration and certification of births and deaths

See Manual at 614.4; also at 614.4–614.5 vs. 362.1–362.4

.409   Historical, geographic, persons treatment of epidemiology

For geographic treatment of incidence of diseases, see 614.42; for history of epidemics, see 614.49

.42   Incidence

Rate, range, or amount of occurrence

Class here health surveys, medical geography

.422   Treatment by areas, regions, places in general

Add to base number 614.422 the numbers following — 1 in notation 11–19 from Table 2, e.g., diseases in the tropics 614.4223

.423–.429   Treatment by specific continents, countries, localities

Add to base number 614.42 notation 3–9 from Table 2, e.g., diseases in the United States 614.4273

.43   Disease carriers (Vectors) and their control

Standard subdivisions are added for either or both topics in heading

Class diseases transmitted by vertebrates other than humans in 614.56

.432   Insects

.432 2   Flies

.432 3   Mosquitoes

.432 4   Fleas and lice

Standard subdivisions are added for either or both topics in heading

.433   Arachnids

Including mites, ticks

.434   Birds

.438   Rodents

.44   Public preventive medicine

For specific preventive measures, see 614.45–614.48

> 614.45–614.48   Specific preventive measures

Class comprehensive works in 614.44

.45   Isolation

Prevention of spread of disease in homes, hospitals, schools, public places through isolation

For quarantine, see 614.46

.46   Quarantine

Isolation procedures at frontiers and ports of entry

Class comprehensive works on isolation in 614.45

.47   Immunization

Public measures for preventing disease through protective inoculation

.48   Disinfection, fumigation, sterilization

Standard subdivisions are added for any or all topics in heading

.49   History of epidemics

Add to base number 614.49 notation 1–9 from Table 2, e.g., history of epidemics in the United Kingdom 614.4941

.5   Incidence of and public measures to prevent specific diseases and kinds of diseases

Class incidence of and public measures to prevent mental and emotional illnesses and disturbances in 362.2

See Manual at 614.5; also at 614.4–614.5 vs. 362.1–362.4

SUMMARY

614.51	**Salmonella and bacillary diseases, cholera, dysentery, epidemic diarrhea, influenza**
.52	**Eruptive diseases (Exanthems) and rickettsial diseases**
.53	**Protozoan diseases**
.54	**Miscellaneous diseases**
.55	**Parasitic diseases**
.56	**Zoonoses**
.57	**Bacterial and viral diseases**
.59	**Diseases of regions, systems, organs; other diseases**

.51   Salmonella and bacillary diseases, cholera, dysentery, epidemic diarrhea, influenza

.511   Salmonella diseases

.511 2   Typhoid fever (Enteric fever)

.511 4   Paratyphoid fever

.512		Bacillary diseases

For bacillary dysentery, see 614.516

.512 3		Diphtheria
.512 5		Botulism
.512 8		Tetanus
.514		Cholera

See Manual at 616.932 vs. 616.33

.516		Amebic and bacillary dysentery
.517		Epidemic diarrhea
.518		Influenza

Including acute influenzalike diseases in epidemic form

.52	Eruptive diseases (Exanthems) and rickettsial diseases
.521	Smallpox (Variola major) and attenuated forms

Standard subdivisions are added for smallpox and attenuated forms together, for smallpox alone

Including cowpox (variola vaccinia)

.522	Scarlet fever (Scarlatina)
.523	Measles (Rubeola)
.524	German measles (Rubella)
.525	Chicken pox (Varicella)
.526	Rickettsial diseases

Add to base number 614.526 the numbers following 616.922 in 616.9222–616.9226, e.g., Q fever 614.5265

.53	Protozoan diseases

Add to base number 614.53 the numbers following 616.936 in 616.9362–616.9364, e.g., malaria 614.532

For amebic dysentery, see 614.516

.54	Miscellaneous diseases

Limited to the diseases provided for below

.541	Yellow fever
.542	Tuberculosis
.543	Whooping cough (Pertussis)

| .544 | Mumps (Epidemic parotitis) |
| .545 | Puerperal septicemia and pyemia |

> Standard subdivisions are added for puerperal septicemia and pyemia together, for puerperal septicemia alone

> Class comprehensive works on incidence of and public measures to prevent septicemia and pyemia in 614.577

| .546 | Leprosy (Hansen's disease) |
| .547 | Sexually transmitted diseases |

> Former heading: Venereal diseases

> Class Acquired Immune Deficiency Syndrome (AIDS) in 614.599392

.547 2	Syphilis
.547 8	Gonorrhea
.549	Poliomyelitis
.55	Parasitic diseases

> Add to base number 614.55 the numbers following 616.96 in 616.962–616.969, e.g., schistosomiasis 614.553; however, for trichinosis, see 614.562

| .56 | Zoonoses |

> Class incidence of and public measures to prevent a specific zoonotic disease not provided for here with the disease, e.g., Q fever 614.5265

| .561 | Anthrax |

> Variant names: charbon, splenic fever

> Including Woolsorters' disease

.562	Trichinosis
.563	Rabies (Hydrophobia)
.564	Glanders (Equinia)
.565	Undulant fever (Brucellosis)
.566	Psittacosis (Parrot fever)
.57	Bacterial and viral diseases

> Standard subdivisions are added for bacterial and viral diseases together, for bacterial diseases alone

> Class specific bacterial diseases not provided for here with the diseases, e.g., Rickettsial diseases 614.526

| .571 | Dengue fever |

.573–.575 Viral and specific bacterial viral diseases

> Add to base number 614.57 the numbers following 616.92 in 616.923–616.925, e.g., tularemia 614.5739

.577 Bacterial blood diseases

> Including erysipelas, pyemia, septicemia
>
> Class puerperal septicemia and pyemia in 614.545

.59 Diseases of regions, systems, organs; other diseases

.591–.598 Diseases of regions, systems, organs

> Add to base number 614.59 the numbers following 616 in 616.1–616.8, e.g., heart disease 614.5912, nutritional diseases 614.5939; however, for mental and emotional illnesses, see 362.2; for epidemic diarrhea, see 614.517; for allergies affecting specific regions, systems, organs, see 614.5993; for tumors (neoplasms) of regions, systems, organs, see 614.5999
>
> *See Manual at 363.82 vs 614.5939*

.599 Other diseases

.599 2 Gynecological, obstetrical, pediatric, geriatric disorders

> Add to base number 614.5992 the numbers following 618 in 618.1–618.9, e.g., pediatric disorders 614.599292; however, for puerperal septicemia and pyemia, see 614.545

.599 3 Diseases of immune system

> Class here allergies, failures of immunity
>
> Add to base number 614.5993 the numbers following 616.97 in 616.973–616.979, e.g., acquired immune deficiency syndrome (AIDS) 614.599392

.599 6 Dental diseases

> Including fluoridation of water supply

.599 7 Eye diseases

.599 8 Ear diseases

.599 9 Tumors (Neoplasms)

> Benign and malignant

.599 94 Cancers

> Add to base number 614.59994 the numbers following 616.994 in 616.9941–616.9949, e.g., breast cancer 614.5999449
>
> Class public programs to control cancer-causing agents in 363.179; class public programs to control carcinogens in food in 363.192

.6 **Disposal of the dead**

Class social aspects and services in 363.75

615 Pharmacology and therapeutics

See Manual at 615

SUMMARY

.1 **Drugs (Materia medica)**

Substances used for diagnosis, cure, mitigation, treatment, or prevention of disease

Class here pharmacology

Class drug therapy in 615.58

For specific drugs and groups of drugs, see 615.2–615.3; for practical pharmacy, see 615.4; for physiological and therapeutic action of drugs, see 615.7

See Manual at 615.1 vs. 615.2–615.3; also at 615.1 vs. 615.4; also at 615.1 vs. 615.7

.11 Pharmacopoeias

[.110 93–.110 99] Treatment by specific continents, countries, localities

Do not use; class in 615.113–615.119

.113–.119 Specific continents, countries, localities

Add to base number 615.11 notation 3–9 from Table 2, e.g., pharmacopoeias of Japan 615.1152

.13 Formularies

Class here dispensatories

[.130 93–.130 99] Treatment by specific continents, countries, localities

Do not use; class in 615.133–615.139

.133–.139 Specific continents, countries, localities

Add to base number 615.13 notation 3–9 from Table 2, e.g., formularies of United States 615.1373

.14   Posology

Including incompatibilities

Class here dosage determination, prescription writing

.18   Drug preservation technique

Class here packaging designed to preserve drug quality and potency

.19   Pharmaceutical chemistry

Development, manufacture, analysis of drugs

.190 01   Philosophy and theory

.190 02   Miscellany

[.190 028 7]   Testing and measurement

Do not use; class in 615.1901

.190 03–.190 09   Standard subdivisions

.190 1   Analysis

>   **615.2–615.3   Specific drugs and groups of drugs**

Including pharmaceutical chemistry, preservation, general therapeutics

Class a specific drug or group of drugs affecting a specific system in 615.7; class comprehensive works in 615.1

See Manual at 615.1 vs. 615.2–615.3; also at 615.2–615.3 vs. 615.7

.2   **Inorganic drugs**

Add to base number 615.2 the numbers following 546 in 546.2–546.7, e.g., calomel (mercurous chloride) 615.2663

Class radiopharmacy (the use of radioactive medicines) in 615.842

.3   **Organic drugs**

See Manual at 615.2–615.3

.31   Synthetic drugs

Add to base number 615.31 the numbers following 547.0 in 547.01–547.08, e.g., sulfonamides 615.3167

Class a specific synthetic drug not provided for here with the drug, e.g., synthetic vitamins 615.328

.32   Drugs derived from plants and microorganisms

Class enzymes of plant origin in 615.35

.321	Pharmacognosy

Class here herbals, minimally processed alkaloids; comprehensive works on crude drugs and simples (products that serve as drugs with minimal processing, e.g., medicinal teas, baking soda, royal jelly)

For drugs derived from specific plants, see 615.322–615.327

.322	Drugs derived from bryophytes

Add to base number 615.322 the numbers following 588 in 588.2–588.3, e.g., drugs derived from Musci 615.3222

.323–.327	Drugs derived from specific plants

Add to base number 615.32 the numbers following 58 in 583–587, e.g., belladonna 615.323952

For drugs derived from bryophytes, see 615.322; for drugs derived from fungi and algae, see 615.329

.328	Vitamins

Including synthetic vitamins, vitamins of animal origin

Class here vitamin therapy

.329	Drugs derived from microorganisms, fungi, algae

Class here antibiotics

Add to base number 615.329 the numbers following 579 in 579.2–579.8, e.g., streptomycin 615.329378

.34	Fish-liver oils
.35	Enzymes

Including chymotrypsin, diastase, papain, pepsin, trypsin

.36	Drugs of animal origin

Class here hormones

Class a drug of animal origin not provided for here with the drug, e.g., fish-liver oils 615.34

.362	Thyroid and parathyroid extracts
.363	Pituitary hormones

Including ACTH (adrenocorticotrophic hormone)

.364	Adrenal hormones

Including adrenalin, aldosterone, cortisone

For sex hormones, see 615.366

.365	Insulin

.366	Sex hormones
.367	Liver extracts
.37	Serums and immunological drugs
.372	Vaccines, bacterins, serobacterins
.373	Toxins and toxoids

> Standard subdivisions are added for either or both topics in heading

.375	Antitoxins, toxin-antitoxins, convalescent serums
.39	Human blood products and their substitutes

> Standard subdivisions are added for human blood products and their substitutes together, for human blood products alone

> Including gamma globulins, plasma substitutes; blood and blood plasma transfusion

> *For convalescent serums, see 615.375*

> *See also 362.1784 for blood and blood plasma banks*

.4 **Practical pharmacy**

Preparing prescriptions and dispensing drugs

> *See Manual at 615.1 vs. 615.4*

.42 Solutions and extracts

> Including collodions, decoctions, elixirs, glycerites, infusions, syrups, tinctures

.43 Pills, capsules, tablets, troches, powders

.45 Ointments and emulsions

.5 **Therapeutics**

Class here comprehensive works on iatrogenic diseases, patient compliance, placebo effect

Class therapies applied to specific diseases or groups of diseases in 616–618

> *For specific therapies and kinds of therapies, see 615.8; for emergency care, see 616.025; for intensive care, see 616.028. For a specific occurrence of iatrogenic diseases, patient compliance, placebo effect, see the occurrence, e.g., drug interactions not anticipated by a doctor 615.7045, surgical complications and sequelae 617.01*

.507 1 Education

Class here comprehensive works on patient education

> *For patient education on a specific topic, see the topic, plus notation 071 from Table 1, e.g., patient education about diabetes mellitus 616.4620071*

.53 General therapeutic systems

Including eclectic and botanic medicine

Class here Ayurveda ("Hindu medicine")

Class drug therapy regardless of system in 615.58

See also 615.32 for botanic remedies

See Manual at 615.53

.530 28 Auxiliary techniques and procedures; apparatus, equipment, materials

Class methods of administering medication in 615.6

.531 Allopathy

System of therapy based on the theory that the best cure is a treatment having effects that are opposite to the effects of the disease

Class allopathy as a synonym for orthodox or standard medical practice in 610

.532 Homeopathy

.533 Osteopathy

As a therapeutic system

Class comprehensive works on osteopathy as a medical science in 610. Class a specific application of osteopathy with the application, e.g., osteopathic discussion of thyroid diseases 616.44

.534 Chiropractic

See Manual at 615.534

.535 Naturopathy

.54 Pediatric and geriatric therapeutics

.542 Pediatric therapeutics

For a specific aspect of pediatric therapeutics, see the aspect, plus notation 083 from Table 1, e.g., medical gymnastics as therapy for children 615.824083

.547 Geriatric therapeutics

For a specific aspect of geriatric therapeutics, see the aspect, plus notation 0846 from Table 1, e.g., acupuncture as therapy for persons in late adulthood 615.8920846

.58 Drug therapy

Class here chemotherapy

Class general therapeutics of a specific drug or group of drugs in 615.2–615.3

For methods of administering medication, see 615.6

.6   **Methods of administering medication**

Limited to works that focus narrowly on methods of administering medication

Including external, inhalatory, oral, rectal methods; parenteral methods (e.g., intra-arterial, intradermal, intramuscular, intravenous, subcutaneous injections); administering medication through serous and mucous membranes

Class general works on a specific type of therapy with the therapy, e.g., drug therapy 615.58, inhalatory therapy 615.836

> *For methods of administering a specific drug or group of drugs, see 615.2–615.3*

.7   **Pharmacodynamics**

Physiological and therapeutic action of drugs

Class here pharmacokinetics

> *For toxicology, see 615.9*

> *See Manual at 612.1–612.8; also at 615.1 vs. 615.7; also at 615.2–615.3 vs. 615.7; also at 615.7 vs. 615.9; also at 616–618 vs. 615.7*

.704   Special effects and actions of drugs

Class here adverse reactions, toxic reactions

Class drug allergies in 616.9758

.704 2   Side effects

.704 5   Interactions

.71   Drugs affecting cardiovascular system

.711   Heart stimulants

.716   Heart depressants

.718   Drugs affecting blood and blood-forming organs

.72   Drugs affecting respiratory system

Including cough remedies, expectorants

.73   Drugs affecting digestive system and metabolism

Standard subdivisions are added for drugs affecting digestive system and metabolism together, for drugs affecting digestive system alone

.731   Emetics

.732   Cathartics (Laxatives, Purgatives)

.733   Anthelmintics

.734   Digestants

.735   Demulcents

.739	Drugs affecting metabolism
.74	Drugs affecting lymphatic and glandular systems
.75	Antipyretics (Febrifuges)
.76	Drugs affecting urogenital system
.761	Drugs affecting urinary system

> Including diuretics, antidiuretics

.766	Drugs affecting reproductive system
.77	Drugs affecting musculoskeletal system, integument
.771	Drugs affecting bones
.773	Drugs affecting muscles
.778	Drugs affecting integument

> *For drugs affecting nails and hair, see 615.779*

.779	Drugs affecting nails and hair
.78	Drugs affecting nervous system

> Class here addictive and disorienting drugs, psychopharmacology

> Class personal aspects of preventing drug addiction in 613.8; class drug therapy for mental disorders in 616.8918; class comprehensive medical works on addictions as diseases in 616.86; class interdisciplinary works on drug addiction in 362.29

> *For antipyretics, see 615.75*

> *See also 178 for the ethics of using addictive and disorienting drugs*

.781	Anesthetics
.782	Sedative-hypnotic drugs

> Including barbiturates

.782 2	Narcotics
.782 7	Cannabis

> Including marijuana

.782 8	Alcohol
.783	Analgesics

> Including comprehensive works on drugs used as both analgesics and antipyretics

> *For antipyretic use, see 615.75*

.784	Antispasmodics (Anticonvulsants)

.785	Stimulants
.788	Psychotropic drugs
.788 2	Tranquilizers
	Including chlorpromazine, diazepam, meprobamate
.788 3	Hallucinogenic and psychedelic drugs
	Standard subdivisions are added for either or both topics in heading

.8   Specific therapies and kinds of therapies

Class comprehensive works in 615.5

For drug therapy, see 615.58; for surgery, see 617

See Manual at 615.8; also at 613 vs. 615.8

.804	Special topics
.804 3	Therapies directed toward a specific objective
	Including resuscitation
.82	Physical therapies

Class here physiotherapy, therapeutic manipulations and exercises

For therapies of light, heat, sound, climate, air, inhalation, see 615.83; for radiotherapy and electrotherapy, see 615.84; for hydrotherapy and balneotherapy, see 615.853

.822	Mechanotherapy and therapeutic massage
	Including acupressure
	Class here interdisciplinary works on massage
	For reducing and slenderizing massage, see 646.75
.824	Medical gymnastics
.83	Therapies of light, heat, sound, climate, air, inhalation
	Including ultrasonic therapy
.831	Phototherapy
	Including color therapy
.831 4	Heliotherapy
.831 5	Ultraviolet-radiation therapy
.832	Thermotherapy
.832 2	Infrared-radiation therapy
.832 3	Diathermy (Thermopenetration)
.832 5	Fever therapy

.832 9	Cryotherapy
.834	Climatotherapy
.836	Aerotherapy and inhalation therapy

> Standard subdivisions are added for either or both topics in heading
>
> Including oxygen and carbon dioxide therapies, pneumatotherapy

.84	Radiotherapy and electrotherapy
.842	Radiotherapy (Radiation therapy, Actinotherapy)

> *For phototherapy, see 615.831*

.842 2	X-ray therapy
.842 3	Radium therapy
.842 4	Radioactive isotope therapy

> Class radium therapy in 615.8423

.845	Electrotherapy and magnetotherapy

> Standard subdivisions are added for electrotherapy and magnetotherapy together, for electrotherapy alone
>
> Including electronic therapy

.85	Miscellaneous therapies

> Limited to the therapies provided for below

.851	Mental and activity therapies

> *For faith healing, see 615.852*

.851 2	Hypnotherapy (Suggestion therapy)
.851 5	Activity (Occupational) therapies

> *For bibliotherapy and educational therapies, see 615.8516*

.851 53	Recreational therapy
.851 54	Music therapy
.851 55	Dance therapy
.851 56	Art therapy
.851 6	Bibliotherapy and educational therapies

.852   Religious and psychic therapy

> Standard subdivisions are added for religious and psychic therapy together, for religious therapy alone
>
> Including spiritualistic surgery
>
> Class here faith healing
>
> *See Manual at 615.852 vs. 291.31, 234.131*

.853   Hydrotherapy and balneotherapy

> Standard subdivisions are added for either or both topics in heading

.854   Diet therapy

> *See Manual at 615.854*

.855   Parenteral therapy

> *For a specific kind of parenteral therapy, see the kind, e.g., parenteral drug therapy 615.58, parenteral feeding 615.854*

.856   Controversial and spurious therapies

> Standard subdivisions are added for either or both topics in heading
>
> Class here quackery
>
> *For a specific controversial or spurious therapy, see the therapy, e.g., controversial diet therapy 615.854*

.88   Empirical and historical remedies

> Standard subdivisions are added for either or both topics in heading
>
> Class here home remedies
>
> *For ancient and medieval remedies, see 615.899*

.880 9   Historical, geographic, persons treatment of empirical and historical remedies

> *See Manual at 615.8809*

.882   Folk medicine

> *See Manual at 615.882; also at 398.27, 398.353 vs. 615.882; also at 615.8809*

.886   Patent medicines

.89   Other therapies

.892   Acupuncture

> Class here comprehensive works on acupuncture and acupressure
>
> *For acupressure, see 615.822*

.899	Ancient and medieval remedies

> *See Manual at 615.8809*

.9   **Toxicology**

Class here poisons and poisoning

Class forensic toxicology in 614.1; class effects of poisons on specific systems and organs in 616–618

> *See Manual at 615.7 vs. 615.9*

.900 1	Philosophy and theory
.900 2	Miscellany
[.900 287]	Testing and measurement

> Do not use; class in 615.907

.900 3–.900 9	Standard subdivisions
.902	Industrial toxicology

Including toxicology of pollution

Class here environmental toxicology

> *For toxic reactions and interactions of drugs, see 615.704; for toxicology of food additives, see 615.954*

.905	Prevention of poisoning
.907	Tests, analysis, detection of poisons and poisoning

Class here diagnoses and prognoses of poisoning

Topics listed under 616.075 Diagnoses and prognoses are all included here

.908	Treatment of poisoning
.91	Gaseous poisons

Including asphyxiating gases

Class here lethal gases

.92	Inorganic poisons

> *For gaseous inorganic poisons, see 615.91; for radiation poisoning, see 616.9897*

.921	Acids

> *For specific acids, see 615.925*

.922	Alkalis

> *For specific alkalis, see 615.925*

.925   Specific inorganic poisons

       Add to base number 615.925 the numbers following 546 in 546.2–546.7, e.g., mercurial poisons 615.925663

.94   Animal poisons

.942   Venoms

       Including bee, scorpion, snake, spider venoms

.945   Poisonous food animals

       Including poisonous fishes; mammalian organs; food animals made poisonous by microorganisms, e.g., shellfish made poisonous by red tides

.95   Organic poisons

       Class gaseous organic poisons in 615.91

       For animal poisons, see 615.94

.951   Synthetic and manufactured poisons

       Add to base number 615.951 the numbers following 547.0 in 547.01–547.08, e.g., ethers 615.95135

       Subdivisions are added for either or both topics in heading

.952   Plant and microorganism poisons, poisons derived from plants and microorganisms

       Standard subdivisions are added for all topics in heading together, for plant poisons, for poisons derived from plants

       Class food animals made poisonous by plants and microorganisms in 615.945

.952 3–.952 8   Specific plant poisons, poisons derived from specific plants

       Add to base number 615.952 the numbers following 58 in 583–588, e.g., opium 615.952335

        For fungi and algae poisons, poisons derived from fungi and algae, see 615.9529

.952 9   Microorganism, fungi, algae poisons; poisons derived from microorganisms, fungi, algae

       Add to base number 615.9529 the numbers following 579 in 579.2–579.8, e.g., bacterial food poisons 615.95293

.954   Food poisons

       Including toxicology of food additives

       Class poisonous food animals in 615.945. Class a specific plant poison and poisons derived from specific plants and microorganisms with the poison in 615.952, e.g., bacterial food poisons 615.95293

616   Diseases

Class here internal medicine

For incidence of and public measures to prevent disease, see 614.4; for therapeutics, see 615.5; for wounds and injuries, surgical treatment of diseases, diseases by body region, diseases of teeth, eyes, ears, see 617; for gynecological, obstetrical, pediatric, geriatric diseases, see 618

See Manual at 610 vs. 616; also at 616–618 vs. 615.7; also at 616 vs. 612; also at 616 vs. 616.07; also at 616 vs. 616.075; also at 616 vs. 617.4; also at 616 vs. 618.92; also at 617 vs. 616

SUMMARY

616.001–.009	**Standard subdivisions**
.01–.09	**[General topics of diseases]**
.1	**Diseases of cardiovascular system**
.2	**Diseases of respiratory system**
.3	**Diseases of digestive system**
.4	**Diseases of blood-forming, lymphatic, glandular systems Diseases of endocrine system**
.5	**Diseases of integument, hair, nails**
.6	**Diseases of urogenital system Diseases of urinary system**
.7	**Diseases of musculoskeletal system**
.8	**Diseases of nervous system and mental disorders**
.9	**Other diseases**

> 616.001–616.009   Standard subdivisions

Class comprehensive works in 616

See Manual at 610 vs. 616: Standard subdivisions

.001   Philosophy and theory

.002   Miscellany

[.002 3]   Work with diseases as a profession, occupation, hobby

Do not use; class in 610.69

.002 8   Auxiliary techniques and procedures; apparatus, equipment, materials

[.002 87]   Testing and measurement

Do not use; class in 616.075

.003–.006   Standard subdivisions

.007   Education, research, related topics

[.007 24]   Experimental research

Relocated to 619

.008   History and description with respect to kinds of persons

.008 3	Young people

For diseases of infants and children up to puberty, comprehensive works on child and adolescent medicine, see 618.92

.008 4	Persons in specific stages of adulthood
[.008 46]	Persons in late adulthood

Do not use; class in 618.97

.009	Historical, geographic, persons treatment
.009 2	Persons

Class life with a physical disease in 362.19. Class life with a mental disorder with the disorder in 616.85–616.89, plus notation 0092 from table under 616.1–616.9, e.g., life with manic-depressive disorder 616.8950092

SUMMARY

616.01	**Medical microbiology**
.02	**Special topics**
.04	**Special medical conditions**
.07	**Pathology**
.08	**Psychosomatic medicine**
.09	**Case histories**

> 616.01–616.02   Medical microbiology, special topics

Class medical microbiology and special topics applied to special medical conditions in 616.04; class comprehensive works in 616

.01	Medical microbiology

Study of pathogenic microorganisms and their relation to disease

Class here drug resistance in microorganisms

Class resistance to specific drugs in 615; class comprehensive works on etiology of diseases in 616.071

See Manual at 579.165 vs. 616.01; also at 616.9 vs. 616.01

.014	Bacteria

Add to base number 616.014 the numbers following 579.3 in 579.32–579.39, e.g., Enterobacteriaceae 616.0144

For rickettsiae, see 616.0192

.015	Fungi
.016	Protozoa
.019	Ultramicrobes

.019 2	Rickettsiae
.019 4	Viruses

.02   Special topics

.024   Domestic medicine

Diagnosis and treatment of ailments without direction of physician

Including advice on when to go to a doctor

For first aid, see 616.0252

.025   Medical emergencies

Class here comprehensive works on emergency therapy

For intensive care, see 616.028. For a specific kind of emergency therapy, see the therapy in 615, e.g., oxygen therapy 615.836

.025 2   First aid

.028   Intensive (Critical) care

For a specific kind of intensive care therapy, see the therapy in 615, e.g., oxygen therapy 615.836

.029   Terminal care

For a specific kind of terminal care therapy, see the therapy in 615, e.g., drug therapy 615.58

.04   Special medical conditions

.042   Genetic (Hereditary) diseases

Class here genetic aspects of diseases with complex causation, medical genetics

Class immunogenetics in 616.0796; class prenatal procedures to diagnose genetic diseases (e.g., amniocentesis and chorionic villus biopsy) in 618.3204275

.043   Congenital diseases

Including teratology

Class congenital diseases of genetic origin in 616.042

.044   Chronic diseases

Class chronic fatigue syndrome in 616.0478

.047   **Manifestations of disease**

Symptoms and general pathological processes as problems in their own right

Including edema, fever, gangrene, infections, shock

Class here pathology, diagnosis, treatment of symptoms of various etiologies; symptomatology

Class interpretation of symptoms for diagnosis and prognosis in 616.075. Class symptoms and pathological processes of a specific disease or class of diseases with the disease, e.g., symptoms of heart diseases 616.12

.047 2   **Pain**

Class headaches in 616.8491

.047 3   **Inflammation**

.047 8   **Chronic fatigue syndrome**

Class chronic fatigue syndrome discussed as a specific kind of disease with the disease, e.g., chronic fatigue syndrome discussed as a disease of immune system 616.97

See also 616.044 for chronic diseases

\>   **616.07–616.09   Pathology, psychosomatic medicine, case histories**

Class pathology, psychosomatic medicine, case histories applied to special medical conditions in 616.04; class comprehensive works in 616

.07   **Pathology**

For cytopathology, see 611.01815; for histopathology, see 611.0182–611.0189; for forensic pathology, see 614.1; for medical microbiology, see 616.01; for manifestations of disease, see 616.047

See Manual at 616 vs. 616.07

.071   **Etiology**

Class social factors contributing to spread of a disease in 362.1042; class genetic diseases, genetic aspects of diseases with complex causation in 616.042

For microbiological causes of disease, see 616.01

.075   **Diagnosis and prognosis**

Standard subdivisions are added for diagnosis and prognosis together, for diagnosis alone

Class here differential diagnosis

Class nonprofessional diagnosis in 616.024

See Manual at 616 vs. 616.075

.075 1	Medical history taking
.075 4	Physical diagnosis

Including thermography

Class here comprehensive works on diagnostic imaging

> *For radiological diagnosis, see 616.0757*
>
> *See Manual at 616.0757 vs. 616.0754, 616.07572*

.075 43	Ultrasonic diagnosis

Class here sonography (echography)

Class comprehensive works on tomography in 616.0757

.075 44	Sound
.075 45	Optical diagnosis

Class here endoscopy

Class microscopy in 616.0758

.075 47	Electrical diagnosis
.075 48	Magnetic diagnosis

Class here magnetic resonance imaging (MRI)

Class comprehensive works on tomography in 616.0757

.075 6	Chemical diagnosis

Including diagnostic serology, immunodiagnosis

Class here clinical chemistry, laboratory diagnosis

> *For radioimmunoassay, see 616.0757; for microscopy in diagnosis, see 616.0758*

.075 61	Blood analysis

Including phlebotomy

> *See also 616.15075 for diagnosis of diseases of blood*

.075 63	Analysis of gastroenteric contents

> *See also 616.3075 for diagnosis of diseases of digestive system*

.075 66	Urinalysis

Class radioscopic urinalysis in 616.0757; class urinary manifestations of diseases of urogenital system in 616.63

> *See also 616.6075 for diagnosis of diseases of urogenital system*

.075 7   **Radiological diagnosis**

Diagnosis involving use of X-rays, radioactive materials, other ionizing radiations

Including radioimmunoassay, radioscopic urinalysis

Class here comprehensive works on tomography, on medical radiology

> *For radiotherapy, see 615.842; for magnetic resonance imaging, see 616.07548*

> *See Manual at 616.0757 vs. 616.0754, 616.07572*

.075 72   **Radiography (Roentgenology, X-ray examination)**

Including computerized axial tomography (CAT scan, CT), fluoroscopy

> *See Manual at 616.0757 vs. 616.0754, 616.07572*

.075 75   **Radioisotope scanning (Radionuclide imaging)**

Often called nuclear medicine

Including positron emission tomography (PET), single-photon emission-computed tomography (SPECT)

> *See also 616.07548 for nuclear magnetic resonance imaging*

.075 8   **Microscopy in diagnosis**

Class here biopsies

.075 81   **Bacteriological examination**

.075 82   **Cytological examination**

.075 83   **Histological and histochemical examination**

.075 9   **Autopsy (Post-mortem examination)**

Class forensic autopsy in 614.1

.078   **Death**

Class interdisciplinary works on human death in 306.9

.079   **Immunity**

Class here disease resistance, immune system, immunochemistry, immunology, leukocytes, lymphocytes

Class immunological drugs in 615.37; class diagnostic immunochemistry, immunodiagnosis in 616.0756; class diseases of immune system in 616.97

> *See Manual at 616.079 vs. 571.96*

>   616.079 1–616.079 6   Immunochemistry

        Class comprehensive works in 616.079. Class applications of immunochemistry to a specific type of cell or to reactions associated with a specific type of cell with the cell or reaction in 616.0797–616.0799, e.g., immunochemistry of antigen-antibody reactions 616.07987

.079 1   Interferons

.079 2   Antigens

[.079 3]   Antibodies (Immunoglobulins)

                Relocated to 616.0798

.079 5   Immune response

                Including clonal selection

                Class here antigen recognition, comprehensive works on serology

                Immune reactions associated with specific types of cells relocated to 616.0797–616.0799

                For diagnostic serology, see 616.0756

.079 6   Immunogenetics

>   616.079 7–616.079 9   T cells, B cells, phagocytes, complement

        Class here immune reactions associated with specific types of cells [*formerly* 616.0795]

        Class comprehensive works in 616.079

.079 7   T cells (T lymphocytes)

                Class here cell-mediated (cellular) immunity, cytotoxic T cells

                See also 616.0799 for killer cells

.079 8   B cells (B lymphocytes)

                Class here antibodies (immunoglobulins) [*formerly* 616.0793]

                For antibody-dependent immune mechanisms, see 616.0799

.079 87   Antigen-antibody reactions

.079 9   Phagocytes and complement

> Standard subdivisions are added for phagocytes and complement together, for phagocytes alone
>
> Including granulocytes, killer cells
>
> Class here antibody-dependent immune mechanisms, reticuloendothelial system
>
> *See also 616.0796 for cytotoxic T cells*

.079 95   Macrophages

.079 97   Complement

> Class activation of macrophages by complement in 616.07995

.08   Psychosomatic medicine

> This number is largely limited to psychosomatic aspects of diseases defined in 616.1–616.7, 616.9
>
> Class psychosomatic symptoms considered as problems in their own right in 616.047; class neuroses and their somatic manifestation in 616.852; class disorders of personality, intellect, impulse control and their somatic manifestation in 616.858; class mental disorders and their somatic manifestation in 616.89; class diseases caused by stress in 616.98; class comprehensive works on psychological and psychosomatic aspects of disease in 616.0019

.09   Case histories

> ## 616.1–616.9   Specific diseases

All notes under 616.01–616.08 are applicable here

Except for modifications shown under specific entries, add to each subdivision identified by * as follows:

001	Philosophy and theory
002	Miscellany
[0023]	The specialty as a profession, occupation, hobby
	Do not use; class in 023
0028	Auxiliary techniques and procedure; apparatus, equipment, materials
[00287]	Testing and measurement
	Do not use; class in 075
003–006	Standard subdivisions
007	Education, research, related topics
[00724]	Experimental research
	Do not use; class in 027
008	History and description with respect to kinds of persons

(continued)

> **616.1–616.9 Specific diseases (continued)**

0083	Young people

> *For diseases of infants and children up to puberty, comprehensive works on child and adolescent medicine, see 618.92*

0084	Person in specific stages of adulthood
[00846]	Persons in late adulthood

> Do not use; class in 618.97

009	Historical, geographic, persons treatment
0092	Persons

> Class life with a physical disease in 362.19. Class life with a mental disease with the disease in 616.85–616.89, plus notation 0092, e.g., life with depression 616.85270092

>01–03	Medical microbiology, special topics, rehabilitation

> Class microbiology, special topics, rehabilitation applied to special classes of diseases in 04; class comprehensive works in 616 without adding from this table

01	Medical microbiology

> Add to 01 the numbers following 616.01 in 616.014–616.019, e.g., fungi 015
> When the cause of a disease or class of diseases is known to be a single type of microorganism, use 01 without further subdivision for works about the type of microorganism
> *See Manual at 616.1–616.9: Add table: 071 vs. 01*

02	Special topics
023	Personnel

> Nature of duties, characteristics of profession, relationships
> Do not use for technology of operations that personnel perform, e.g., techniques used by a cardiological paramedic 616.12 (*not* 616.120233)

0232	Physicians
0233	Technicians and assistants
024	Domestic medicine

> Class a specific kind of therapy with the therapy in 06, e.g., drug therapy 061
> *For first aid, see 0252*

025	Medical emergencies

> Class here comprehensive works on emergency therapy for specific diseases or kinds of diseases
> *For intensive care, see 028. For a specific kind of emergency therapy, see the therapy in 06, e.g., emergency drug therapy 061*

0252	First aid
027	Experimental medicine

(continued)

> **616.1–616.9 Specific diseases (continued)**

028   Intensive (Critical) care
             For a specific kind of intensive care therapy, see the
             therapy in 06, e.g., drug therapy 061
029   Terminal care
             For a specific kind of terminal care therapy, see the
             therapy in 06, e.g., drug therapy 061
03   Rehabilitation
             Restoration of a sick or disabled person by therapy and by
             training for participation in activities of a normal life within
             limitations of disabilities
             Class rehabilitative therapy in 06; class comprehensive works
             on rehabilitation in 617.03
04   Special classes of diseases
             Limited to the classes named below
042   Genetic (Hereditary) diseases
             Class here genetic aspects of diseases with complex
             causation, medical genetics
             When a specific type of genetic disease has an indirect
             etiology, class with the system showing the most visible
             manifestations, e.g., mental retardation caused by
             hereditary metabolic disorders 616.8588042, not 616.39042
0421–0423   Microbiology, special topics, rehabilitation
             Add to base number 042 the numbers following 0 in
             notation 01–03 from table under 616.1–616.9, e.g.,
             experimental medicine for genetic diseases 04227
0425–0429   Preventive measures, therapy, pathology, psychosomatic
             medicine, case histories
             Add to base number 042 the numbers following 0 in
             notation 05–09 from table under 616.1–616.9, e.g.,
             therapy for genetic diseases 0426
043   Congenital diseases
             Class congenital diseases of genetic origin in 042
0431–0433   Microbiology, special topics, rehabilitation
             Add to base number 043 the numbers following 0 in
             notation 01–03 from table under 616.1–616.9, e.g.,
             experimental medicine for congenital diseases 04327
0435–0439   Preventive measures, therapy, pathology, psychosomatic
             medicine, case histories
             Add to base number 043 the numbers following 0 in
             notation 05–09 from table under 616.1–616.9, e.g.,
             therapy for congenital diseases 0436

(continued)

> **616.1–616.9 Specific diseases (continued)**

>05–09	Preventive measures, therapy, pathology, psychosomatic medicine, case histories
	Class preventive measures, therapy, pathology, psychosomatic medicine, case histories applied to specific classes of diseases in 04; class comprehensive works in 616 without adding from this table
05	Preventive measures
	By individuals and by medical personnel
	Class public measures for preventing specific diseases in 614.5; class comprehensive works in 613
06	Therapy
	Class here rehabilitative therapy; specific kinds of therapy used in domestic medicine, medical emergencies, intensive care, terminal care
	Class comprehensive works on therapy in 615.5; class comprehensive works on therapy for specific diseases or kinds of diseases in domestic medicine in 024; class comprehensive works on therapy for specific diseases or kinds of diseases in medical emergencies in 025; class comprehensive works on therapy for specific diseases or kinds of diseases in intensive care in 028; class comprehensive works on therapy for specific diseases or kinds of diseases in terminal care in 029; class comprehensive works on rehabilitative therapy and training for persons with a specific disease or kind of disease in 03. Class comprehensive works on therapy and pathology (07) of a specific disease or kind of disease with the disease or kind of disease, without adding from add table, e.g., cause, course, and cure of heart disease 616.12 (*not* 616.1206)
061	Drug therapy
	See Manual at 616–618 vs. 615.7
062–069	Other therapies
	Add to 06 the numbers following 615.8 in 615.82–615.89, e.g., X-ray therapy 06422, rehabilitative activity therapies 06515
07	Pathology
	Add to 07 the numbers following 616.07 in 616.071–616.079, e.g., etiology 071, diagnosis 075
	Class social factors contributing to spread of a disease in 362.19
	See Manual at 616.1–616.9: Add table: 071 vs. 01; also at 616 vs. 616.07
08	Psychosomatic medicine
09	Case histories

Class comprehensive works in 616

See Manual at 612.1–612.8

> **616.1–616.8 Diseases of specific systems and organs**

Class comprehensive works in 616

For diseases of immune system, see 616.97; for tumors of specific systems and organs, see 616.992; for tuberculosis of specific systems and organs, see 616.995

See Manual at 616.1–616.8; also at 616.1–616.8 vs. 616.9

.1   ***Diseases of cardiovascular system**

Class here cardiopulmonary diseases

Class cardiopulmonary resuscitation (CPR) in 616.1025; class diseases of blood-forming system in 616.41

For pulmonary diseases, see 616.24

.11   ***Diseases of endocardium and pericardium**

.12   ***Diseases of heart**

Including cor pulmonale

Class here cardiology; necrosis and other degenerative diseases of heart

For diseases of endocardium and pericardium, see 616.11

.122   ***Angina pectoris**

.123   ***Coronary diseases (Ischemic heart diseases)**

Class works on heart attacks in sense of myocardial infarction in 616.1237; class comprehensive works on cardiac arrest, on heart attacks in 616.123025. Class cardiac arrest and heart attacks not caused by narrowing or blocking of coronary arteries with the cause, e.g., heart attacks caused by congestive heart failure 616.129025

For angina pectoris, see 616.122

.123 028   Intensive care

Number built according to instructions under 616.1–616.9

Class coronary care in sense of intensive care for any serious heart disease in 616.12028

.123 2   ***Coronary arteriosclerosis**

.123 7   ***Myocardial infarction**

.124   ***Myocarditis**

Class here comprehensive works on diseases of myocardium

For myocardial infarction, see 616.1237

---

*Add as instructed under 616.1–616.9

.125	*Valvular diseases
.127	*Rheumatic heart diseases

> *For rheumatic valvular diseases, see 616.125*

.128	*Arrhythmia

Including allorhythmia

Class implantation of heart pacers in 617.412059; class functioning of heart pacers in 617.4120645

.129	*Heart failure

Class here congestive heart failure

Class comprehensive works on cardiac arrest in 616.123025

.13	*Diseases of blood vessels

Including arterial occlusive diseases

Class here angiology; diseases of blood vessels in a specific region, e.g., abdominal and pelvic cavities

Class a specific arterial occlusive disease with the disease, e.g., arteriosclerosis 616.136; class diseases of blood vessels in a specific system or organ with the system or organ, e.g., cerebrovascular diseases 616.81

> *For diseases of veins and capillaries, see 616.14*

.131	*Peripheral vascular diseases

> 616.132–616.136 Hypertension, aneurysms, arterial embolisms and thromboses, arteriosclerosis

Class hypertension, aneurysms, embolisms, thromboses, arteriosclerosis of aorta in 616.138; class comprehensive works in 616.13

.132	*Hypertension

Essential and renal

.133	*Aneurysms
.135	*Arterial embolisms and thromboses

Class here comprehensive works on embolisms, on thromboses

> *For venous embolisms and thromboses, see 616.145; for pulmonary embolisms and thromboses, see 616.249*

.136	*Arteriosclerosis

Class here atherosclerosis

.138	*Diseases of aorta

*Add as instructed under 616.1–616.9

.14   *Diseases of veins and capillaries

> Subdivisions are added for diseases of veins and capillaries together, for diseases of veins alone

.142   *Phlebitis

> Including thrombophlebitis

.143   *Varicose veins (Varix)

.145   *Venous embolisms and thromboses

> Class thrombophlebitis in 616.142; class comprehensive works on embolisms, on thromboses in 616.135

.148   *Diseases of capillaries

> Including telangiectasis, telangitis

.15   *Diseases of blood

> Class here hematology
>
> *For bacterial blood diseases, see 616.94*
>
> *See also 616.07561 for use of blood analysis in diagnosis of diseases in general*

.151   *Diseases of erythrocytes

> Class here hemoglobin disorders
>
> *For anemia, see 616.152; for polycythemia, see 616.153*

.152   *Anemia

> Including thalassemia

.152 7   *Sickle cell anemia

.153   *Polycythemia

.154   *Diseases of leukocytes

> Including agranulocytosis

.156   *Reticulosis

.157   *Hemorrhagic diseases

> Including Von Willebrand's disease
>
> Class here comprehensive works on disorders of blood coagulation
>
> *For arterial embolisms and thromboses, see 616.135; for venous embolisms and thromboses, see 616.145*

.157 2   *Hemophilia

*Add as instructed under 616.1–616.9

.2   **Diseases of respiratory system**

Including apnea

Class here dyspnea

.200 1–.200 3   Standard subdivisions

As modified under 616.1–616.9

.200 4   Special topics

Add to base number 616.2004 the numbers following 0 in notation 01–09 from table under 616.1–616.9, e.g., diagnosis of respiratory diseases 616.200475

.200 5–.200 9   Standard subdivisions

As modified under 616.1–616.9

.201   *Croup

.202   *Respiratory allergies

Class here hay fever

Class asthma in 616.238

.203   *Influenza

.204   *Whooping cough (Pertussis)

.205   *Common cold

.208   *Hyperventilation

.21   *Diseases of nose, larynx, accessory organs

Class otorhinolaryngology, comprehensive works on diseases of eyes, ears, nose, throat in 617.51

For laryngology, see 616.22

.212   *Diseases of nose, nasopharynx, accessory sinuses

Standard subdivisions are added for diseases of nose, nasopharynx, accessory sinuses together; for diseases of nose alone

Class here rhinology

Class common cold in 616.205

.22   *Diseases of larynx, glottis, vocal cords, epiglottis

Standard subdivisions are added for diseases of larynx, glottis, vocal cords, epiglottis together; for diseases of larynx alone

Class here laryngology

*Add as instructed under 616.1–616.9

.23   *Diseases of trachea and bronchi

     Including bronchiectasis, tracheitis

     Class bronchopneumonia in 616.241

.234   *Bronchitis

.238   *Bronchial asthma

     Class here comprehensive works on asthma

     For cardiac asthma, see 616.12

.24   *Diseases of lungs

     Including chronic obstructive pulmonary disease

     Class here comprehensive works on diseases of lungs and bronchi

     Class cystic fibrosis in 616.37; class pulmonary tuberculosis in 616.995; class comprehensive works on cardiopulmonary diseases in 616.1

     For diseases of bronchi, see 616.23

.241   *Pneumonia

     Including Legionnaires' disease

     See also 616.245 for necropneumonia

.244   *Pneumoconiosis

     Diseases caused by dust and other particles

     Including asbestosis, black lung disease, byssinosis (brown lung disease), pulmonary abscesses, silicosis

.245   *Necropneumonia

.248   *Emphysema

.249   *Pulmonary embolisms and thromboses

     Class comprehensive works on embolisms, on thromboses in 616.135

.25   *Diseases of pleura

     Class pleural pneumonia in 616.241

.27   *Diseases of mediastinum

.3   ***Diseases of digestive system**

     Class allergies of digestive system in 616.975

     See also 616.07563 for use of analysis of gastroenteric contents in diagnosis of diseases in general

*Add as instructed under 616.1–616.9

SUMMARY

.31   *Diseases of mouth and throat

> Subdivisions are added for diseases of mouth and throat together, for diseases of mouth alone

> Class oral region (a broader concept than mouth as a digestive organ) in 617.522; class diseases of teeth and gums in 617.63

> *For laryngology, see 616.22; for diseases of pharynx, see 616.32*

.312   *Trench mouth (Vincent's angina)

.313   *Mumps (Epidemic parotitis)

.314   *Diseases of tonsils

.316   *Diseases of salivary glands

> *For mumps, see 616.313*

.32   *Diseases of pharynx and esophagus

> Including gastroesophageal reflux

.33   *Diseases of stomach

> Including gastroptosis

> Class here gastroenteritis, comprehensive works on gastroenterology (gastrointestinal diseases)

> Class gastroesophageal reflux in 616.32

> > *For diseases of the intestine, see 616.34; for typhoid fever, see 616.9272; for cholera, see 616.932; for dysenteries, see 616.935; for hiatal hernia, see 617.559*

> > *See Manual at 616.932 vs. 616.33*

.332   *Functional disorders

> Including disorders of secretion, dyspepsia, gastric indigestion

.333   *Gastritis

.334   *Gastric ulcers

> Class comprehensive works on ulcers in 616.343

---

*Add as instructed under 616.1–616.9

.34	*Diseases of intestine

Including appendicitis, giardiasis

For hernias, see 617.559

.342	*Functional disorders

Including irritable colon, obstructions

.342 3	*Malabsorption

Class a specific malabsorption disease with the disease in 616.39, e.g., lactose intolerance 616.3998

.342 7	*Diarrhea
.342 8	*Constipation
.343	*Peptic ulcers

Class here comprehensive works on gastric and peptic ulcers

For gastric ulcers, see 616.334

.343 3	*Duodenal ulcers
.343 4	*Gastrojejunal ulcers
.344	*Enteritis

Including duodenitis, jejunitis

Class here inflammatory bowel disease

.344 5	*Ileitis

Including Crohn's disease

.344 7	*Colitis
.35	*Diseases of rectum and anus

Including hemorrhoids

Class here proctology

.36	*Diseases of biliary tract
.362	*Diseases of liver

For Reye's syndrome, see 616.83

.362 3	*Hepatitis
.362 4	*Cirrhosis
.362 5	*Jaundice
.365	*Diseases of gallbladder and bile duct

Subdivisions are added for diseases of gallbladder and bile duct together, for diseases of gallbladder alone

*Add as instructed under 616.1–616.9

.37   *Diseases of pancreas

         Including cystic fibrosis

         Class diseases of pancreatic internal secretion in 616.46

.38   *Diseases of peritoneum

.39   *Nutritional and metabolic diseases

         Subdivisions are added for either or both topics in heading

         Class inborn (inherited) errors of metabolism in 616.39042. Class nutritional and metabolic diseases of a specific system or organ with the system or organ, e.g., metabolic bone diseases 616.716

         For endocrinology, see 616.4

>   616.392–616.396   Deficiency diseases

         Class comprehensive works in 616.39

.392   *Beriberi

.393   *Pellagra

.394   *Scurvy

.395   *Rickets

.396   Other deficiency diseases and states

         Including emaciation, fatty degeneration, kwashiorkor

         Class anorexia nervosa in 616.85262

         For multiple deficiency states, see 616.399

.398   *Obesity

         Including endocrinal obesity, nutritional obesity

         Class appetite and eating disorders as neuroses in 616.8526

.398 08   Psychosomatic medicine

         Number built according to instructions under 616.1–616.9

         Food addiction relocated to 616.8526

.399   Other nutritional and metabolic diseases

         Including multiple deficiency states, phenylketonuria, porphyria

.399 2   *Body fluid disorders

         Including acid-base imbalances

         Class here water-electrolyte imbalances

         See Manual at 612.01522 vs. 612.3923, 616.3992

*Add as instructed under 616.1–616.9

.399 5	*Diseases of protein metabolism
	Including amyloidosis
.399 7	*Diseases of lipid metabolism
.399 8	*Diseases of carbohydrate metabolism
	Including lactose intolerance
.399 9	*Gout

.4   ***Diseases of blood-forming, lymphatic, glandular systems**   **Diseases of endocrine system**

Class here endocrinology

Class endocrinal obesity in 616.398. Class diseases of glands in a specific system or organ with the system or organ, e.g., diseases of female sex glands 618.1

.41   *Diseases of blood-forming (hematopoietic) system

Spleen and bone marrow disorders

For anemia, see 616.152

.42   *Diseases of lymphatic system

Including lymphatitis, lymphomatosis

Class filiarial elephantiasis in 616.9652; class Hodgkin's disease in 616.99446

>   616.43–616.48   Diseases of endocrine system

Class comprehensive works in 616.4

.43   *Diseases of thymus gland

.44   *Diseases of thyroid and parathyroid glands

Subdivisions are added for diseases of thyroid and parathyroid glands together, for diseases of thyroid alone

.442   *Goiter

.443   *Hyperthyroidism

Including Graves' disease

.444   *Hypothyroidism

For myxedema, see 616.858848

.445   *Diseases of parathyroid glands

Including hyperparathyroidism, hypoparathyroidism

*Add as instructed under 616.1–616.9

.45   *Diseases of adrenal glands

> Including Addison's disease, Cushing's syndrome, hyperadrenalism, hypoadrenalism

.46   *Diseases of islands of Langerhans

.462   *Diabetes mellitus

> Class here comprehensive works on diabetes
>
> *For diabetes insipidus, see 616.47*

.466   *Hypoglycemia

.47   *Diseases of pituitary gland

> Including acromegaly, diabetes insipidus, pituitary dwarfism, pituitary gigantism, hypopituitarism, Simmond's disease

.48   *Diseases of other glands of endocrine system

> Including hyperpinealism, polyglandular disorders

.49   *Diseases of male breast

> Class comprehensive works on diseases of breast in 618.19

.5   *Diseases of integument, hair, nails

> Including photosensitivity diseases, sunburn
>
> Class here dermatology
>
> Subdivisions are added for diseases of integument, hair, nails together; for diseases of integument alone
>
> Class porphyria in 616.399
>
> > *For allergies of skin, see 616.973; for dermatological manifestations of food and drug allergies, see 616.975; for dermatological manifestations of physical allergies (including allergic reaction to light), see 616.977*

.51   *Papular eruptions

> Including urticaria (hives)
>
> Class here dermatitis
>
> > *For vesicular and pustular eruptions, see 616.52; for contact allergies, see 616.973*

.52   *Pustular and vesicular eruptions

> Including herpes simplex type 1 (cold sores, fever blisters)
>
> Subdivisions are added for either or both topics in heading
>
> Class herpes simplex type 2 (genital herpes) in 616.9518; class comprehensive works on herpesvirus diseases in 616.925

---

*Add as instructed under 616.1–616.9

.521	*Eczema
	Including atopic dermatitis
.522	*Shingles (Herpes zoster)
.523	*Boils and carbuncles
	Subdivisions are added for either or both topics in heading
.524	*Impetigo
.526	*Psoriasis
.53	*Diseases of sebaceous glands
	Including acne, blackheads, seborrhea, wens
.54	*Skin hypertrophies, scalp diseases, related disorders

For pigmentary changes, see 616.55

.544	*Skin hypertrophies

Including callosities, corns, ichthyosis, keratosis, scleroderma, warts (verrucae), xeroderma

.545	*Skin ulcerations

Including decubitus ulcers (bedsores)

.546	*Diseases of scalp, hair, hair follicles

Including baldness (alopecia), dandruff, excessive hairiness (hypertrichosis)

.547	*Diseases of nails
.55	*Pigmentary changes

Including albinism, moles, pigmentary nevi, vitiligo; comprehensive works on nevi

For capillary nevi, see 616.99315

.56	*Diseases of sweat glands

Including anhidrosis, heat rash, prickly heat

.57	*Parasitic skin diseases

Including athlete's foot, mange, ringworm, scabies, yaws

Class leishmaniasis in 616.9364

.58	Chapping, chilblains, frostbite

Standard subdivisions are added for any or all topics in heading

.6   ***Diseases of urogenital system**   **Diseases of urinary system**

Class here urology

*Add as instructed under 616.1–616.9

> 616.61–616.64 Diseases of urinary system

Class comprehensive works in 616.6

.61 *Diseases of kidneys and ureters

Class here nephrology

Subdivisions are added for kidneys and ureters together, for kidneys alone

Class renal hypertension in 616.132; class kidney dialysis in 617.461059

For kidney stones, see 616.622

.612 *Nephritis

Including Bright's disease, glomerulonephritis

.613 *Pyelitis (Pyelonephritis) and pyelocystitis

.614 *Renal failure

.62 *Diseases of bladder and urethra

Subdivisions are added for either or both topics in heading

For diseases of male urethra, see 616.64

.622 *Kidney stones (Urinary calculi)

Renal and vesical calculi

.623 *Cystitis

.624 *Urethritis

.63 *Urinary manifestations

Limited to manifestations of diseases of urogenital system

Including albuminuria, hematuria, proteinuria

Class interpretation of symptoms for diagnosis and prognosis of diseases of urogenital system in 616.6075. Class urinary manifestations of a specific disease or of disease in a specific organ with the disease or organ, e.g., urinary manifestations of renal failure 616.614, enuresis as a manifestation of neurological or mental disorders 616.849

See also 616.07566 for use of urinalysis to diagnose diseases in general

.633 *Pyuria

.635 *Uremia

.64 *Diseases of male urethra

*Add as instructed under 616.1–616.9

.65   *Diseases of genital system

> Class here diseases of male genital system, diseases of prostate gland

> *For sexual disorders, see 616.69; for diseases of female genital system, see 618.1. For diseases of a specific male genital organ not provided for here, see the organ, e.g., diseases of male urethra 616.64*

.66   *Diseases of penis

.67   *Diseases of scrotum

.68   *Diseases of testicles and accessory organs

> Subdivisions are added for diseases of testicles and accessory organs together, for diseases of testicles alone

.69   *Sexual disorders

> Class here male sexual disorders

> *For sexual personality disorders, see 616.8583; for female sexual disorders, see 618.17*

.692   *Impotence and infertility

> Class here comprehensive works on male and female infertility, on impotence

> *For impotence as a psychological disorder, see 616.85832; for female infertility, artificial insemination, see 618.178*

.692 06   Therapy

> Number built according to instructions under 616.1–616.9

> Class here comprehensive medical works on human reproductive technology

> *For human reproductive technology applied to female infertility, see 618.17806*

.693   *Male climacteric disorders

> Class comprehensive works on climacteric disorders in 618.175

.694   *Hermaphroditism

.7   *Diseases of musculoskeletal system

> Class here nonsurgical aspects of and comprehensive works on orthopedics [*both formerly* 617.3]

> *For orthopedic surgery of musculoskeletal system, see 617.47; for orthopedic regional surgery, see 617.5*

*Add as instructed under 616.1–616.9

.71   *Diseases of bones

            Class here chronic diseases of skeletal system

            Class pituitary gigantism, pituitary dwarfism in 616.47; class Marfan
            syndrome in 616.77

            For diseases of spine, see 616.73; for fractures, see 617.15

.712   *Osteitis

            Including osteitis deformans (Paget's disease of bone), osteochondritis,
            periostitis

.715   *Osteomyelitis

.716   *Disorders of metabolic origin

            Including osteoporosis

            For rickets, see 616.395

.72   *Diseases of joints

            For gout, see 616.3999

.722   *Arthritis

.722 3   *Osteoarthritis (Hypertrophic arthritis)

.722 7   *Rheumatoid arthritis

               Class ankylosing spondylitis in 616.73

.723   *Rheumatism

            Class here rheumatology

            *For a specific rheumatic disease, see the disease, e.g., rheumatoid
            arthritis 616.7227, rheumatic fever 616.991*

.73   *Diseases of spine

            Including ankylosing spondylitis

.74   *Diseases of muscles

            Including fibrositis, myalgia

            Class diseases of muscles in a specific system or organ with the system or
            organ, e.g., diseases of heart 616.12

.742   *Muscular rheumatism

.743   *Myositis

.744   *Neuromuscular diseases

            Class neuromuscular diseases resulting from disorders of central nervous
            system in 616.83

*Add as instructed under 616.1–616.9

.744 2	*Myasthenia gravis
.748	*Muscular dystrophy
.75	*Diseases of tendons and fasciae

> See also 616.76 for diseases of sheaths of tendons

.76	*Diseases of bursae and sheaths of tendons
.77	*Diseases of connective tissues

Including Ehlers-Danlos syndrome, Marfan syndrome, Sjögren's syndrome, systemic lupus erythematosus

Class here collagen diseases

Class carpal tunnel syndrome in 616.87

> For rheumatoid arthritis, see 616.7227; for diseases of tendons and fasciae, see 616.75

.8　　　Diseases of nervous system and mental disorders

Class here neuropsychiatry

SUMMARY

616.800 1–.800 9	**Standard subdivisions**
.801–.809	**Standard subdivisions and special topics of diseases of nervous system, of diseases of brain**
.81	**Cerebrovascular diseases**
.82	**Meningeal diseases**
.83	**Other organic diseases of central nervous system**
.84	**Manifestations of neurological diseases and mental disorders**
.85	**Miscellaneous diseases of nervous system and mental disorders**
.86	**Substance abuse (Drug abuse)**
.87	**Diseases of cranial, spinal, peripheral nerves**
.88	**Diseases of autonomic nervous system**
.89	**Mental disorders**

.800 1–.800 9	Standard subdivisions

> 　616.801–616.84　Diseases of nervous system　　Diseases of brain

Class here neurology

Class comprehensive works in 616.8. Class diseases of nerves needed to make a specific system or organ function properly with the system or organ, e.g., neuromuscular diseases 616.744, diseases of optic nerves 617.732

Diseases of nerves needed to make a region function properly are classed with diseases of the nerves, e.g., disease of peripheral nerves needed to make the hand function properly are classed with diseases of peripheral nerves in 616.87

> For diseases of cranial, spinal, peripheral nerves, see 616.87; for diseases of autonomic nervous system, see 616.88

*Add as instructed under 616.1–616.9

.801–.803	Standard subdivisions of diseases of nervous system, of diseases of brain

As modified under 616.1–616.9

.804   Special topics of diseases of nervous system, of diseases of brain

Add to base number 616.804 the numbers following 0 in notation 01–09 from table under 616.1–616.9, e.g., diagnosis of brain diseases 616.80475

Class manifestations of neurological diseases as problems in their own right in 616.84

.805–.809   Standard subdivisions of diseases of nervous system, of diseases of brain

As modified under 616.1–616.9

.81   *Cerebrovascular diseases

Including apoplexy (stroke)

.82   *Meningeal diseases

Including meningitis

.83   Other organic diseases of central nervous system

Including amyotrophic lateral sclerosis, Friedreich's ataxia, Reye's syndrome, tardive dyskinesia; comprehensive works on dementia

Class here diseases of basal ganglia, of spinal cord

Class phenylketonuria in 616.399

For chorea, see 616.851; for epilepsy, see 616.853. For a specific kind of dementia or dementia-causing disease, see the dementia or disease, e.g., dementia caused by cerebrovascular disease 616.81

.831   *Alzheimer's disease

.832   *Encephalitis

.833   *Parkinson's disease (Paralysis agitans)

.834   *Multiple sclerosis

.835   *Poliomyelitis

.836   *Cerebral palsy

.837   *Paraplegia

Neurological aspects only

Class comprehensive works on neurological and surgical aspects in 617.58

*Add as instructed under 616.1–616.9

.838 *Locomotor ataxia (Tabes dorsalis)

> Class general paresis in 616.892; class comprehensive works on syphilis in 616.9513

.84 Manifestations of neurological diseases and mental disorders

> Symptoms as problems in their own right

> Class here pathology, diagnosis, treatment of symptoms

> Class interpretation of symptoms for diagnosis and prognosis of neurological diseases in 616.80475; class interpretation of symptoms for diagnosis and prognosis of mental disorders in 616.89075. Class diagnostic and prognostic interpretation of symptoms of a specific disease or class of diseases with the disease, e.g., interpretation of symptoms of schizophrenia 616.8982075

.841 Dizziness and vertigo

> Standard subdivisions are added for either or both topics in heading

.842 Paralysis

.845 Convulsions

.849 Miscellaneous symptoms

> Limited to coma, enuresis, pain, reflex disturbances, and symptoms provided for below

.849 1 *Headaches

> Including cluster headaches, tension headaches

> *For migraine, see 616.857*

.849 8 Sleep disturbances

> Including insomnia

> Class sleep disturbances in relation to a specific system with the system, e.g., sleep apnea 616.2

.85 Miscellaneous diseases of nervous system and mental disorders

> Only those named below

SUMMARY

616.851	Chorea
.852	Neuroses
.853	Epilepsy
.855	Speech and language disorders
.856	Cutaneous sensory disorders
.857	Migraine
.858	Disorders of personality, intellect, impulse control

.851 *Chorea

*Add as instructed under 616.1–616.9

.852	†Neuroses

Class neurotic aspects of a specific disease with the disease, e.g., neurotic aspects of asthma 616.238

For speech and language disorders, see 616.855

See also 616.856 for cutaneous sensory disorders

.852 1	†Traumatic neuroses

Including compensation and occupation neuroses, posttraumatic stress disorder

.852 12	†War neuroses (Combat fatigue)
.852 2	†Anxiety, phobic, obsessive-compulsive neuroses
.852 23	†Anxiety neuroses

Including panic disorder

For phobic neuroses, see 616.85225

.852 25	†Phobic neuroses

Including agoraphobia

.852 27	†Obsessive-compulsive neurosis

Comprehensive works on compulsive behavior relocated to 616.8584; pathological gambling relocated to 616.85841

.852 3	†Dissociative disorders
.852 32	†Amnesia and fugue

Subdivisions are added for amnesia and fugue together, for amnesia alone

.852 36	†Dual and multiple personalities

Subdivisions are added for either or both topics in heading

.852 4	†Hysterical neuroses

For dissociative disorders, see 616.8523

.852 5	†Hypochondriacal neuroses
.852 6	†Eating disorders

Class here food addiction [*formerly also* 616.39808], appetite disorders

.852 62	†Anorexia nervosa
.852 63	†Bulimia

†Add as instructed under 616.1–616.9, except use 0651 also for psychotherapies

.852 7	†Depressive neuroses

Class here comprehensive works on depression

Class postpartum depression in 618.76

> For neurasthenia, see 616.8528; for manic-depressive psychoses, see 616.895

.852 8	†Neurasthenia (Asthenic reactions)

Chronic fatigue and depression

Class chronic fatigue syndrome in 616.0478; class comprehensive works on depression in 616.8527

.853	*Epilepsy
.855	†Speech and language disorders

Class here comprehensive works on communicative disorders, on voice disorders

Class comprehensive works on learning and communicative disorders in 616.85889

.855 2	*Neurological language disorders (Aphasias)

Diminution or loss of faculty of language in any of its forms due to cerebral lesions, e.g., agrammatism, apraxia of speech

Agraphia relocated to 616.8553

> For written language disorders, see 616.8553

.855 3	†Written language disorders

Including agraphia [formerly also 616.8552]

Class here dyslexia

.855 4	†Stammering and stuttering

Subdivisions are added for either or both topics in heading

.856	*Cutaneous sensory disorders
.857	*Migraine
.858	Disorders of personality, intellect, impulse control
.858 2	†Sociopathic personality disorders

Class here self-destructive behavior, violent behavior

Class sexual disorders in 616.8583; class substance abuse in 616.86

> For other sociopathic neuroses, see 616.8584. For a specific type of self-destructive behavior, see the behavior, e.g., suicide 616.858445

---

*Add as instructed under 616.1–616.9

†Add as instructed under 616.1–616.9, except use 0651 also for psychotherapies

.858 22	†Family violence and abuse
	Including spouse abuse
.858 223	†Child abuse
	Class incest involving children, sexual abuse of children in 616.85836; class abused children in 618.92858223
.858 223 9	†Adult victims of child abuse
	Class a specific problem of adult victims of child abuse with the problem, e.g., depression 616.8527
.858 3	†Sexual disorders
	Including homosexuality treated as a medical disorder
	Class interdisciplinary works on homosexuality in 306.766
	See Manual at 616.8583: Homosexuality
.858 32	†Frigidity and impotence
	Class comprehensive works on impotence in 616.692
.858 33	†Nymphomania and satyromania
	Subdivisions are added for either or both topics in heading
[.858 34]	Homosexuality
	Number discontinued; class in 616.8583
.858 35	†Sadism and masochism
.858 36	†Sexual abuse of children
	Class here incest
	Class sexually abused children in 618.9285836
.858 369	†Adult victims of childhood sexual abuse
	Class a specific problem of adult victims of childhood sexual abuse with the problem, e.g., multiple personality disorder 616.85236
.858 4	Other sociopathic neuroses, disorders of impulse control, suicidal behavior
	Including compulsive shopping
	Class here comprehensive works on compulsive behavior [*formerly* 616.85227]
	For obsessive-compulsive neurosis, see 616.85227; for compulsive eating disorders, see 616.8526; for compulsive sexual disorders, see 616.8583; for substance abuse, see 616.86
.858 41	†Pathological gambling [*formerly* 616.85227]

†Add as instructed under 616.1–616.9, except use 0651 also for psychotherapies

.858 42	†Kleptomania
.858 43	†Pyromania
.858 44	Homicidal and suicidal behavior
.858 445	†Suicidal behavior
.858 45	†Compulsive lying and defrauding

        Subdivisions are added for either or both topics in heading

.858 5	Borderline and narcissistic personality disorders
.858 52	†Borderline personality disorder
.858 8	*Mental retardation and learning disabilities
.858 84	Mental retardation and learning disabilities due to deformity, injury, disease

        Class phenylketonuria in 616.399

.858 842	*Down's syndrome
.858 843	*Hydrocephalus
.858 844	*Microcephaly
.858 845	*Cerebral sphingolipidosis

        Including Tay-Sachs disease

.858 848	*Myxedema

        Class congenital myxedema (cretinism) in 616.858848043

.858 89	*Learning disabilities

        Regardless of level of intelligence

        Class here comprehensive works on learning and communicative disorders

        Class learning disabilities associated with a specific disorder with the disorder, e.g., minimal brain dysfunction 616.8589

        For communicative disorders, see 616.855

.858 9	*Attention deficit disorder and hyperactivity (hyperkinesia)

        Class here minimal brain dysfunction

        Subdivisions are added for either or both topics in heading

*Add as instructed under 616.1–616.9

†Add as instructed under 616.1–616.9, except use 0651 also for psychotherapies

.86   ‡Substance abuse (Drug abuse)

> Including abuse of analgesics, depressants, inhalants, sedatives, tranquilizers
>
> Class here addiction, dependence, habituation, intoxication
>
> Class personal measures to prevent substance abuse in 613.8; class food addiction in 616.8526; class comprehensive medical works on addictive and disorienting drugs in 615.78; class interdisciplinary works on substance abuse in 362.29
>
> *See Manual at 616.86 vs. 158.1, 248.8629, 291.442, 362.29*

.861   ‡Alcohol

> Class here alcoholism

.861 9   †Effect of alcoholism on persons close to alcoholics

> Class here adult children of alcoholics, codependent spouses of alcoholics
>
> Class minor children of alcoholics in 618.928619. Class a specific problem of persons close to alcoholics with the problem, e.g., depression 616.8527

>   616.863–616.865   Substances other than alcohol

> Including effects on persons close to substance abusers
>
> Class minor children of substance abusers in 618.92863–618.92865; class comprehensive works in 616.86. Class a specific problem of persons close to substance abusers with the problem, e.g., depression 616.8527

.863   ‡Narcotics, hallucinogens, psychedelics, cannabis

.863 2   ‡Narcotics

> Opium and its derivatives and synthetic equivalents
>
> Class here specific narcotics, e.g., heroin, morphine

.863 4   ‡Hallucinogens and psychedelics

> Class here specific hallucinogens and psychedelics, e.g., LSD, mescaline, PCP
>
> Subdivisions are added for either or both topics in heading
>
> Class cannabis in 616.8635

.863 5   ‡Cannabis

> Class here specific kinds of cannabis, e.g., hashish, marijuana

----

†Add as instructed under 616.1–616.9, except use 0651 also for psychotherapies

‡Add as instructed under 616.1–616.9, except use 0651 also for psychotherapies and do not use 05; class prevention in 613.8 or its subdivisions

.864 ‡Stimulants and related substances

> Class here specific kinds of stimulants, e.g., amphetamine, ephedrine
>
> Subdivisions are added for stimulants and related substances together, for stimulants alone
>
> Class nicotine in 616.865

.864 7 ‡Cocaine

> Class here specific forms of cocaine, e.g., crack

.865 ‡Tobacco

.869 †Effect of substance abuse on persons close to substance abusers

> Class here adult children of substance abusers, codependent spouses of substance abusers
>
> Class minor children of substance abusers in 618.92869. Class effect of abuse of a specific substance on persons close to abusers with the abuse of the specific substance, e.g., effect of alcoholism on persons close to alcoholics 616.8619, effect of cocaine abuse on persons close to cocaine abusers 616.8647; class a specific problem of persons close to substance abusers with the problem, e.g., depression 616.8527

.87 *Diseases of cranial, spinal, peripheral nerves

> Including carpal tunnel syndrome, disorders of smell and taste, neuralgias, neuritis, polyradiculoneuritis, sciatica
>
> Class neurofibromatosis in 616.99383
>
> *For shingles, see 616.522; for cutaneous sensory disorders, see 616.856; for diseases of autonomic nervous system, see 616.88*

.88 *Diseases of autonomic nervous system

> Including parasympathetic nervous system, sympathetic nervous system

.89 *Mental disorders

> Class here abnormal and clinical psychologies, comparative abnormal behavior of animals, psychiatry
>
> Class manifestations of mental disorders when considered as symptoms so serious that they become problems in their own right in 616.84; class puerperal mental disorders in 618.76. Class physical manifestations of mental disorders involving a specific system with the system, plus 08 from table under 616.1–616.9, e.g., psychosomatic ulcers 616.34308
>
> *For neuroses, see 616.852; for disorders of personality, intellect, impulse control, see 616.858*
>
> *See Manual at 616.89 vs. 150.195*

---

*Add as instructed under 616.1–616.9

†Add as instructed under 616.1–616.9, except use 0651 also for psychotherapies

‡Add as instructed under 616.1–616.9, except use 0651 also for psychotherapies and do not use 05; class prevention in 613.8 or its subdivisions

.890 083 5	Young people aged twelve to twenty [*formerly* 616.89022]
[.890 22]	Mental disorders of young people aged twelve to twenty
	Relocated to 616.8900835
[.890 6]	Therapy
	Do not use; class in 616.891
.891	Therapy
.891 2	Shock therapy
	Including insulin and other drug shock therapies
.891 22	Electric shock therapy (Electroconvulsive therapy)
.891 3	Physical therapies
	For electric shock therapy, see 616.89122; for psychosurgery, see 617.481
.891 4	Psychotherapy
	For group and family psychotherapy, see 616.8915; for mental and activity therapies, see 616.8916; for psychoanalysis, see 616.8917
.891 42	Behavior therapy (Behavior modification therapy)
	Including cognitive therapy
.891 43	Gestalt therapy
.891 44	Milieu therapy
	Utilization of environment for treatment
.891 45	Transactional analysis
.891 5	Group and family psychotherapy
.891 52	Group psychotherapy
.891 523	Psychodrama
.891 56	Family psychotherapy
	Including marital psychotherapy
.891 6	Mental and activity therapies
	Add to base number 616.8916 the numbers following 615.851 in 615.8512–615.8516, e.g., hypnotherapy 616.89162
.891 7	Psychoanalysis
[.891 701 9]	Psychological principles
	Do not use for comprehensive works; class in 150.195. Do not use for applications to therapy; class in 616.8917

.891 8   Drug therapy

                                Class drug shock therapy in 616.8912

>   616.892–616.898 Psychoses

                Class here functional psychoses, organic psychoses

                Class comprehensive works in 616.89. Class a specific organic psychosis not
                provided for here with the psychosis, e.g., psychosis due to brain tumors
                616.99281

                    For puerperal psychoses, see 618.76

.892   *General paresis (Neurosyphilis)

                        Class locomotor ataxia in 616.838; class comprehensive works on
                        syphilis in 616.9513

.895   †Manic-depressive psychoses (Bipolar disorders)

                        Including depressive reactions, involutional psychoses

                        Class here manic and depressive psychoses, circular and alternating
                        manic-depressive psychoses

                        Class comprehensive works on depression in 616.8527

.897   †Paranoia and paranoid conditions

                        Subdivisions are added for either or both topics in heading

.898   Schizophrenia, autism, senile dementia

.898 2   †Schizophrenia and autism

                        Subdivisions are added for either or both topics in heading

.898 3   *Senile dementia

                        Class Alzheimer's disease in 616.831; class comprehensive works on
                        dementia in 616.83

.9   Other diseases

                See Manual at 616.9 vs. 616.01; also at 616.1–616.8 vs. 616.9

---

*Add as instructed under 616.1–616.9
†Add as instructed under 616.1–616.9, except use 0651 also for psychotherapies

SUMMARY

[.900 1–.900 9]   Standard subdivisions for other diseases

Do not use; class in 616.001–616.009

>   616.901–616.96   Communicable diseases

Class comprehensive works in 616.9

For a specific communicable disease not provided for here, see the disease, e.g., mumps 616.313

.901–.903   Standard subdivisions of communicable diseases

As modified under 616.1–616.9

.904   Special topics of communicable diseases

Add to base number 616.904 the numbers following 0 in notation 01–09 from table under 616.1–616.9, e.g., diagnosis of communicable diseases 616.90475

.905–.908   Standard subdivisions of communicable diseases

As modified under 616.1–616.9

.909   Historical, geographic, persons treatment of communicable diseases

[.909 11–.909 13]   Frigid, temperate, tropical zones

Do not use; class in 616.9881–616.9883

.91   *Eruptive diseases (Exanthems)

For eruptive fevers, see 616.9223

.912   *Smallpox (Variola major)

See also 616.913 for attenuated forms of smallpox

.913   *Attenuated forms of smallpox

Including alastrim (amaas, Cuban itch, variola minor), cowpox (variola vaccinia)

*Add as instructed under 616.1–616.9

.914	*Chicken pox (Varicella)
.915	*Measles (Rubeola)
.916	*German measles (Rubella)
.917	*Scarlet fever (Scarlatina)
.92	*Bacterial and viral diseases

Including chlamydia infections, Lyme disease, staphylococcal diseases, streptococcal diseases, toxic shock syndrome

Subdivisions are added for bacterial and viral diseases together, for bacterial diseases alone

Class a specific bacterial disease or group of bacterial diseases not provided for here with the disease or group of diseases, e.g., bacterial blood diseases 616.94

For lymphogranuloma venereum, see 616.9518

.921	*Dengue fever
.922	*Rickettsial diseases
.922 2	*Epidemic (Louse-borne) and murine (flea-borne) typhus

Including Brill's disease

| .922 3 | *Rickettsialpox and tick typhus |

Including boutonneuse fever

Class here eruptive fevers, spotted fevers

For North Queensland tick typhus, see 616.9226

.922 4	*Tsutsugamushi disease (Japanese river fever, Scrub typhus)
.922 5	*Q fever
.922 6	Bullis fever, North Queensland tick typhus, trench fever
.923	*Pasteurella and related diseases

Subdivisions are added for pasteurella and related diseases together, for pasteurella alone

.923 2	*Bubonic plague
.923 9	*Tularemia
.924	*Colorado tick fever and relapsing fevers
.924 2	*Colorado tick fever
.924 4	*Relapsing fevers

*Add as instructed under 616.1–616.9

.925	*Viral diseases

Including comprehensive works on herpesvirus diseases

> *For a specific viral disease or group of viral diseases, see the disease or group of diseases, e.g., shingles 616.522, herpes simplex 2 (genital herpes) 616.9518*

.927	*Salmonella diseases
.927 2	*Typhoid fever (Enteric fever)
.927 4	*Paratyphoid fever
.928	*Yellow fever
.93	Bacillary diseases, cholera, dysenteries, protozoan diseases
.931	*Bacillary diseases

> *For bacillary dysentery, see 616.9355*

.931 3	*Diphtheria
.931 5	*Botulism
.931 8	*Tetanus
.932	*Cholera

> *See Manual at 616.932 vs. 616.33*

.935	*Dysenteries
.935 3	*Amebic dysentery
.935 5	*Bacillary dysentery (Shigella diseases)
.936	*Protozoan diseases

Class giardiasis in 616.34

> *For amebic dysentery, see 616.9353*

.936 2	*Malaria
.936 3	*Trypanosomiasis

Including African sleeping sickness, e.g., Gambian and Rhodesian trypanosomiasis; Chagas' disease (South American trypanosomiasis)

.936 4	*Leishmaniasis

Including cutaneous leishmaniasis (oriental sores), mucocutaneous leishmaniasis (forest yaws), visceral leishmaniasis (kala-azar)

.94	*Bacterial blood diseases
.942	*Erysipelas
.944	*Septicemia and pyemia

> *For puerperal septicemia and pyemia, see 618.74*

*Add as instructed under 616.1–616.9

.95   Sexually transmitted diseases, zoonoses

.951   *Sexually transmitted diseases

         Former heading: Venereal diseases

         For acquired immune deficiency syndrome (AIDS), see 616.9792

.951 3   *Syphilis

         For locomotor ataxia, see 616.838; for general paresis (neurosyphilis), see 616.892

.951 5   *Gonorrhea

.951 8   Other sexually transmitted diseases

         Including chancroid, herpes simplex type 2 (genital herpes), lymphogranuloma venereum

         Class comprehensive works on chlamydia infections in 616.92; class comprehensive works on herpesvirus diseases in 616.925

         See also 616.52 for herpes simplex type 1 (cold sores, fever blisters)

.953   *Rabies (Hydrophobia)

.954   *Glanders (Equinia)

.956   *Anthrax

         Variant names: charbon, splenic fever

         Including woolsorters' disease

.957   *Undulant fever (Brucellosis)

.958   *Psittacosis (Parrot fever)

.959   *Zoonoses

         For a specific zoonotic disease, see the disease, e.g., Q fever 616.9225, tularemia 616.9239

.96   *Parasitic diseases

         Class here medical parasitology

         For parasitic skin diseases, see 616.57; for protozoan diseases, see 616.936

.962   *Diseases due to endoparasites

         For diseases due to worms, see 616.963–616.965

*Add as instructed under 616.1–616.9

> 616.963–616.965   Diseases due to worms

Class here medical helminthology

Class comprehensive works in 616.962

.963   *Diseases due to flukes (Trematoda)

Including schistosomiasis (bilharziasis)

.964   *Diseases due to tapeworms (Cestoda)

Including hydatid diseases (echinococcosis)

.965   *Diseases due to roundworms (Nematoda)

.965 2   *Diseases due to filariae

Including elephantiasis, onchocerciasis, wuchereriasis

Class here filariasis

.965 4   Diseases due to other nematodes

Including ascariasis, enterobiasis, hookworm infestations (ancyclostomiasis), trichinosis

.968   *Diseases due to ectoparasites

Class here medical entomology

For a specific entomological disease, see the disease, e.g., Colorado tick fever 616.9242

.969   *Diseases due to fungi

Including candidiasis, fungal allergies

Class here medical mycology

.97   *Diseases of immune system

Class here failures of immunity, comprehensive works on allergies

For a specific allergy not provided for here, see the allergy, e.g., hay fever 616.202

.973   *Contact allergies

Class here dermatological allergies

Class dermatological manifestations of food and drug allergies in 616.975; class physical allergies in 616.977

.975   *Food and drug allergies

Class here allergies of digestive system

Subdivisions are added for food and drug allergies together, for food allergies alone

*Add as instructed under 616.1–616.9

.975 8   *Drug allergies

.977   *Physical allergies

Hypersensitivity to physical agents, e.g., cold, heat, humidity, sunlight

.978   *Autoimmune diseases

Diseases caused by immune reactions to body's own tissues

Class here autoimmunity

For a specific autoimmune disease, see the disease, e.g., systemic lupus erythematosus 616.77

.979   *Immune deficiency diseases

.979 2   *Acquired immune deficiency syndrome (AIDS)

.98   Noncommunicable diseases and environmental medicine

Standard subdivisions are added for either or both topics in heading

Class here communicable diseases as part of environmental medicine, diseases due to stress

Class a specific noncommunicable or environmentally linked disease or type of disease provided for elsewhere with the disease or type of disease, e.g., mental disorders 616.89, malaria 616.9362, cancer 616.994

.980 01–.980 08   Standard subdivisions

.980 09   Historical, geographic, persons treatment

[.980 091 1–.980 091 3]   Frigid, temperate, tropical zones

Do not use; class in 616.9881–616.9883

.980 2   Specialized medical fields

Including travel medicine

For industrial and occupational medicine, see 616.9803; for sports medicine, see 617.1027

.980 21   Aerospace medicine

.980 213   Aviation medicine

.980 214   Space medicine

.980 22   Submarine medicine

Class diseases due to compression and decompression in 616.9894

.980 23   Military medicine

For naval medicine, see 616.98024

.980 24   Naval medicine

*Add as instructed under 616.1–616.9

.980 3	Industrial and occupational medicine
	Standard subdivisions are added for either or both topics in heading
	See also 613.62 for industrial and occupational health
.988	*Diseases due to climate and weather
	Class here medical climatology, medical meteorology
	Subdivisions are added for either or both topics in heading
.988 1–.988 3	Diseases of frigid, temperate, tropical zones
	Class here communicable diseases of frigid, temperate, tropical zones
	Add to base number 616.988 the numbers following —1 in notation 11–13 from Table 2, e.g., diseases due to tropical climate 616.9883
.989	*Diseases due to physical agents
	Including heat exhaustion, hypothermia
	Class physical allergies (hypersensitivity to physical agents) in 616.977; class comprehensive works on diseases due to light in 616.5
.989 2	*Diseases due to motion
.989 3	*Diseases due to altitude
	Including mountain sickness
.989 4	*Diseases due to compression and decompression
	Subdivisions are added for either or both topics in heading
.989 6	*Diseases due to sound and diseases due to other vibrations
	Subdivisions are added for diseases due to sound and diseases due to other vibrations together, for diseases due to sound alone
.989 7	*Diseases due to radiation
	Class here comprehensive medical works on radiation sickness and injuries
	Class comprehensive works on radiation dosimetry in 612.01448
	For surgical aspects of radiation sickness, of radiation injuries, see 617.124
.99	Tumors and miscellaneous communicable diseases
	Only those named below
[.990 1–.990 9]	Standard subdivisions
	Do not use; class in 616.99
.991	*Rheumatic fever

*Add as instructed under 616.1–616.9

.992 †Tumors

> Variant names: neoplasms, neoplastic diseases
>
> Medical and surgical treatment
>
> Class here oncology
>
>> *For benign tumors, see 616.993; for malignant tumors, see 616.994*
>>
>> *See Manual at 616.994 vs. 616.992*

.992 1–.992 9 Tumors of specific systems and organs

> Add to base number 616.992 the numbers following 611 in 611.1–611.9, e.g., brain tumors 616.99281; then add further as instructed under 618.1–618.8, e.g., surgery for brain tumors 616.99281059

.993 †Benign tumors

> Variant name: benign neoplasms
>
> Medical and surgical treatment
>
> Including adenomas

.993 1–.993 9 Benign tumors of specific systems and organs

> Add to base number 616.993 the numbers following 611 in 611.1–611.9, e.g., benign skin tumors 616.99377, neurofibromatosis (Recklinghausen's disease) 616.99383; then add further as instructed under 618.1–618.8, e.g., therapy for neurofibromatosis 616.9938306

.994 †Cancers

> Variant names: malignant neoplasms, malignant tumors
>
> Medical and surgical treatment
>
> Class here carcinomas
>
>> *See Manual at 616.994 vs. 616.992*

.994 1 †Cancers of cardiovascular organs and blood

.994 11–.994 15 Cancers of cardiovascular organs

> Add to base number 616.9941 the numbers following 611.1 in 611.11–611.15, e.g., cancer of heart 616.99412; then add further as instructed under 618.1–618.8, e.g., therapy for cancer of heart 616.9941206

.994 18 †Cancer of blood

> Including erythrocytes, plasma, platelets
>
>> *For cancer of leukocytes, see 616.99419*

.994 19 †Leukemia

> Cancer of leukocytes

---

†Add as instructed under 618.1–618.8

.994 2–.994 9   Cancers of other organs and of regions

> Add to base number 616.994 the numbers following 611 in
> 611.2–611.9, e.g., breast cancer 616.99449; then for organs, systems,
> regions having their own number add further as instructed under
> 618.1–618.8, e.g., surgery for breast cancer 616.99449059
>> Subdivisions are added for a specific type of cancer if
>> subdivisions are added for comprehensive works on cancer of the
>> organ or region, e.g., surgery for Hodgkin's disease (a cancer of
>> lymphatic glands) 616.99446059

.995   *Tuberculosis

> Class here pulmonary tuberculosis

.995 1   Tuberculosis of cardiovascular system

> Add to base number 616.9951 the numbers following 611.1 in
> 611.11–611.15, e.g., tuberculosis of heart 616.99512; then add
> further as instructed under 616.1–616.9, e.g., therapy for tuberculosis
> of heart 616.9951206

.995 2   Tuberculosis of respiratory system

.995 21–.995 23   Tuberculosis of nose and nasal accessory sinuses, of larynx, of
trachea and bronchi

> Add to base number 616.9952 the numbers following 611.2 in
> 611.2–611.23, e.g., laryngeal tuberculosis 616.99522; then add
> further as instructed under 616.1–616.9, e.g., therapy for laryngeal
> tuberculosis 616.9952206

[.995 24]   Pulmonary tuberculosis

> Number discontinued; class in 616.995

.995 25–.995 27   Tuberculosis of pleura, diaphragm, mediastinum

> Add to base number 616.9952 the numbers following 611.2 in
> 611.25–611.27, e.g., pleural tuberculosis 616.99525; then add
> further as instructed under 616.1–616.9, e.g., therapy for pleural
> tuberculosis 616.9952506

.995 3–.995 9   Tuberculosis of other specific systems and organs

> Add to base number 616.995 the numbers following 611 in
> 611.3–611.9, e.g., tuberculosis of bones 616.99571; then add further
> as instructed under 616.1–616.9, e.g., therapy for tuberculosis of
> bones 616.9957106

.998   *Leprosy (Hansen's disease)

---

*Add as instructed under 616.1–616.9

617   Miscellaneous branches of medicine   Surgery

Only those branches named below

Except where contrary instructions are given, all notes under 616.01–616.08 and in table under 616.1–616.9 are applicable here

Except for modifications shown under specific entries, add to each subdivision identified by * as follows:

001–007	Standard subdivisions
	As modified under 616.1–616.9
008	History and description with respect to kinds of persons
0083	Young people
	Notation 0083 is used for pediatric aspects of specific kinds of wounds and injuries, e.g., burns and scalds in children 617.110083; for surgery of a specific organ, system, disorder, e.g., brain surgery in children 617.4810083; for specific aspects of pedodontics, e.g., caries in children 617.670083
	Class comprehensive works on pedodontics in 617.645; class comprehensive works on surgery for infants and children up to puberty in 617.98; class comprehensive works on pediatrics in 618.92; class regional medicine, ophthalmology, otology, audiology for infants and children up to puberty in 618.92097
0084	Persons in specific stages of adulthood
00846	Persons in late adulthood
	Notation 00846 is used for geriatric aspects of specific kinds of wounds and injuries, e.g., burns and scalds in late adulthood 617.1100846; for surgery of a specific organ, system, disorder, e.g., heart surgery in late adulthood 617.41200846
	Class comprehensive works on geriatric surgery in 617.97; class comprehensive works on geriatrics in 618.97
0088	Occupational and religious groups
0088355	Military personnel
	Class military surgery in 617.99
[009]	Historical, geographic, persons treatment
	Do not use; class in 09
>01–03	Surgical complications and sequelae, special topics, rehabilitation
	Class surgical complications and sequelae, special topics, rehabilitation applied to special classes of diseases in 04; class comprehensive works in 617, without adding from this table
01	Surgical complications and sequelae
	Standard subdivisions are added for either or both topics in heading
	Including complicating preconditions, e.g., heart problems; surgical infections
02	Special topics
023	Personnel
	Nature of duties, characteristics of profession, relationships

(continued)

617   Miscellaneous branches of medicine   Surgery (continued)

0232	Physicians
0233	Technicians and assistants
	Standard subdivisions are added for either or both topics in heading
024	Domestic medicine
	For first aid, see 0262
026	Emergencies
0262	First aid
027	Experimental medicine
028	Intensive care
03	Rehabilitation
	Restoration of a sick or disabled person by therapy and by training for participation in activities of a normal life within limitations of disabilities
	Including self-help devices for persons with disabilities
	Class rehabilitative therapy in 06
04	Special classes of diseases
	Limited to the classes named below
042	Genetic diseases
0421–0423	Surgical complications and sequelae, special topics, rehabilitation
	Add to base number 042 the numbers following 0 in notation 01–03 from table under 617, e.g., experimental medicine for genetic diseases 04227
0425–0428	Preventive measures, surgery, therapy, pathology, psychosomatic medicine
	Add to base number 042 the numbers following 0 in notation 05–08 from table under 617, e.g., diagnosis of genetic diseases 04275
043	Congenital diseases
	Add to base number 043 the numbers following 042 in notation 0421–0428 from table under 617, e.g., experimental medicine for congenital diseases 04327
	Class congenital diseases of genetic origin in 042
044	Injuries and wounds
	Including results of injuries
	Add to base number 044 the numbers following 042 in notation 0421–0428 from table under 617, e.g., experimental medicine for injuries and wounds 04427
	Subdivisions are added for either or both topics in heading
>05–08	Preventive measures, surgery, therapy, pathology, psychosomatic medicine
	Class preventive measures, surgery, pathology, psychosomatic medicine applied to special classes of diseases in 04; class comprehensive works in 617, without adding from this table
05	Preventive measures and surgery

(continued)

617   Miscellaneous branches of medicine   Surgery (continued)

052		Preventive measures
		By individuals and by medical personnel
		Class public measures for preventing specific diseases in 614.5; class comprehensive works on prevention in 613
059		Surgery
		Limited to operative surgery
		Including surgery utilizing specific instruments or techniques, e.g., catheterization, cryosurgery, endoscopic surgery, laser surgery, microsurgery
		Class nonoperative physical procedures in 06
		For surgical complications and sequelae, see 01
0592		Cosmetic and restorative plastic surgery, transplantation of tissue and organs, implantation of artificial organs
06		Therapy
		Class here rehabilitative therapy
		Class comprehensive works on rehabilitative therapy and training for persons with a specific disease or kind of disease in 03
		For surgery, see 059
		See Manual at 617: Add table: 06
061		Drug therapy
062–069		Other therapies
		Add to 06 the numbers following 615.8 in 615.82–615.89, e.g., X-ray therapy 06422, rehabilitative activity therapies 06515
07		Pathology
		Add to 07 the numbers following 616.07 in 616.071–616.079, e.g., physical diagnosis 0754
08		Psychosomatic medicine
09		Historical, geographic, persons treatment
		Add to 09 notation 01–9 from Table 2, e.g., the subject in India 0954

Class comprehensive works on minor surgery in 617.024; class comprehensive works on major surgery in 617.025; class comprehensive works on emergency surgery in 617.026; class comprehensive works on surgery by instrument and technique in 617.05; class comprehensive works on surgical pathology in 617.07; class comprehensive works on operative surgery and special fields of surgery in 617.9

See Manual at 616–618 vs. 615.7; also at 617 vs. 616; also at 618.92097 vs. 617; also at 618.977 vs. 617

SUMMARY

617.001–.008	**Standard subdivisions of surgery**
.01–.09	**[General topics of surgery and historical, geographic, persons treatment]**
.1	**Injuries and wounds**
.2	**Results of injuries**
.4	**Surgery by systems**
.5	**Regional medicine Regional surgery**
.6	**Dentistry**
.7	**Ophthalmology**
.8	**Otology and audiology**
.9	**Operative surgery and special fields of surgery**

> ### 617.001–617.5 Surgery

Class comprehensive works in 617

> *For surgical treatment of tumors, see 616.992–616.994; for operative surgery and special fields of surgery, see 617.9*

.001   Philosophy and theory of surgery

.002   Miscellany of surgery

[.002 3]   Surgery as a profession, occupation, hobby

> Do not use; class in 617.023

[.002 8]   Auxiliary techniques and procedures; apparatus, equipment, materials

> Do not use; class in 617.9

[.002 87]   Testing and measurement

> Do not use; class in 617.075

.003–.007   Standard subdivisions of surgery

.008   History and description of surgery with respect to kinds of persons

.008 3   Young people

> *For surgery for infants and children up to puberty, see 617.98*

.008 4   Persons in specific stages of adulthood

[.008 46]   Persons in late adulthood

> Do not use; class in 617.97

.008 8   Occupational and religious groups

[.008 835 5]   Military personnel

> Do not use; class in 617.99

[.009]   Historical, geographic, persons treatment of surgery

> Do not use; class in 617.09

.01	Surgical complications and sequelae

Standard subdivisions are added for either or both topics in heading

Including complicating preconditions, e.g., heart problems; surgical infection

For surgical shock, see 617.21

.02	Special topics
.023	Personnel

Nature of duties, characteristics of profession, relationships

Do not use for technology of operations that personnel perform, e.g., physical diagnosis by surgeons 617.0754 (*not* 617.0232)

.023 2	Surgeons
.023 3	Surgical technicians and assistants

Standard subdivisions are added for either or both topics in heading

.024	Minor surgery

Class here outpatient surgery

.025	Major surgery
.026	Emergency surgery
.026 2	First aid
.03	Rehabilitation

Restoration of a sick or disabled person by therapy and by training for participation in activities of a normal life within limitations of disabilities

Including self-help devices for persons with disabilities

Class rehabilitative therapy in 617.06

For orthopedic self-help devices for persons with disabilities, see 617.9

.05	Surgery utilizing specific instruments and techniques or specific groups of instruments and techniques

Including cryosurgery, endoscopic surgery, laser surgery, microsurgery

.06	Nonsurgical therapy

Class here rehabilitative therapy

Add to base number 617.06 the numbers following 615.8 in 615.82–615.89, e.g., X-ray therapy 617.06422, rehabilitative activity therapies in 617.06515

Class comprehensive works on rehabilitative therapy and training in 617.03

.07	Pathology

Add to base number 617.07 the numbers following 616.07 in 616.071–616.079, e.g., physical diagnosis 617.0754

.08	Psychosomatic medicine
.09	Historical, geographic, persons treatment of surgery

> Add to base number 617.09 notation 01–9 from Table 2, e.g., collective biographies of surgeons 617.0922

.1   Injuries and wounds

> Standard subdivisions are added for injuries and wounds together, for injuries alone

> Class here traumatology

> Class results of injuries in 617.2

> *For injuries and wounds of specific systems, regions, organs, see 617.4–617.5, plus notation 044 from table under 617*

.100 1–.100 9	Standard subdivisions
.102	Special topics
.102 6	Emergencies
.102 62	First aid

> *For first aid for a specific type of injury or wound, see the type, e.g., first aid for crash wounds 617.1028*

.102 7	Athletic injuries

> Class here sports medicine

> Class a specific branch of sports medicine with the branch, e.g., promotion of health of athletes 613.711

.102 8	Crash injuries

> Injuries resulting from transportation accidents

.103	Rehabilitation

> Restoration of a sick or disabled person by therapy and by training for participation in activities of a normal life within limitations of disabilities

> Including self-help devices for persons with disabilities

> Class rehabilitative therapy in 617.106

.106	Nonsurgical therapy

> Class here rehabilitative therapy

> Add to base number 617.106 the numbers following 615.8 in 615.82–615.89, e.g., therapeutic massage 617.10622, rehabilitative activity therapies 617.106515

> Class comprehensive works on rehabilitative therapy and training in 617.103

.107   Pathology

> Add to base number 617.107 the numbers following 616.07 in 616.071–616.079, e.g., physical diagnosis 617.10754

.11   *Burns and scalds

> Subdivisions are added for either or both topics in heading

> Class burns and scalds resulting from injuries from electricity and radiation in 617.12

.12   *Injuries from electricity and radiation

.122   *Injuries from electricity

.124   *Injuries from radiation

> Class comprehensive medical works on radiation sickness and injuries in 616.9897

.13   *Abrasions and contusions

> Subdivisions are added for either or both topics in heading

.14   *Wounds

> *For abrasions and contusions, see 617.13*

.140 6   Therapy

> Number built according to instructions under 617

> Class removal of foreign bodies from wounds in 617.146

.143   *Incisions, lacerations, punctures

> Subdivisions are added for any or all topics in heading

.145   *Gunshot wounds

.146   Removal of foreign bodies from wounds

.15   Fractures

> Add to base number 617.15 the numbers following 611.71 in 611.711–611.718, e.g., fracture of femur 617.158

.16   *Dislocations

.17   *Sprains and strains

> Subdivisions are added for either or both topics in heading

.18   *Asphyxia

> Including drowning

.19   *Blast injuries

> *For specific kinds of blast injuries, see the kind of injury, e.g., fractures 617.15*

*Add as instructed under 617

.2   **Results of injuries**

For results of injuries of specific systems, regions, organs, see 617.4–617.5, plus notation 044 from table under 617

See also 617.103 for rehabilitation, 617.106 for rehabilitative therapy

.21   Traumatic and surgical shock

Standard subdivisions are added for either or both topics in heading

.22   Fever, infection, inflammation

[.3]   **Orthopedics**

Nonsurgical aspects of orthopedics and comprehensive works on orthopedics relocated to 616.7, orthopedic surgery of musculoskeletal system relocated to 617.47, orthopedic regional medicine and orthopedic regional surgery relocated to 617.5

[.307]   Orthopedic appliances

Relocated to 617.9

\> **617.4–617.5 Surgery by systems and regions**

Class here injuries and wounds of specific systems, regions, organs; surgery of specific organs

Class comprehensive works in 617

.4   **Surgery by systems**

For respiratory system, see 617.54

See Manual at 612.1–612.8; also at 616 vs. 617.4

.41   †Cardiovascular system

.412   †Heart

Class implantation of heart pacers in 617.412059; class functioning of heart pacers in 617.4120645

.413   †Arteries

Class here comprehensive works on surgery of blood vessels (vascular surgery)

Class surgery of blood vessels in a specific system or organ with the system or organ, e.g., cerebrovascular surgery 617.481

For veins, see 617.414; for capillaries, see 617.415

.414   †Veins

.415   †Capillaries

---

†Add as instructed under 617, except use 059 by itself only for surgery utilizing specific instruments or techniques and do not use 06 by itself

.43 †Digestive system

Including bariatric surgery

For surgery of specific organs of digestive system, see 617.5

.44 †Glands and lymphatic system

Including bone marrow

For surgery of a specific gland, see the gland, e.g., thyroid gland 617.539

.46 †Urogenital system

For gynecological and obstetrical surgery, see 618

.461 †Kidneys, adrenal glands, ureters

Class here comprehensive works on surgery of urinary organs

Subdivisions are added for kidneys, adrenal glands, ureters together, for kidneys alone

Class hemodialysis, peritoneal dialysis in 617.461059

For bladder and urethra, see 617.462

.462 †Bladder and urethra

.463 †Male genital organs

Including circumcision, vasectomy

.47 †Musculoskeletal system, integument

Class here orthopedic surgery of musculoskeletal system [*formerly* 617.3]

Subdivisions are added for musculoskeletal system and integument together, for musculoskeletal system alone

Class orthopedics of specific regions in 617.5

For amputations, see 617.58059

.471 †Bones

Class chronic diseases of skeletal system in 616.71

For skull, see 617.514; for jaws, see 617.522

See also 617.44 for bone marrow

.471 044 Injuries and wounds

Number built according to instructions under 617

For fractures, see 617.15

---

†Add as instructed under 617, except use 059 by itself only for surgery utilizing specific instruments or techniques and do not use 06 by itself

.472		†Joints

> *For jaws, see 617.522; for joints of extremities, see 617.58*
>
> *See also 616.72 for nonsurgical medical aspects of joints*

.472 044 — Injuries and wounds

> Number built according to instructions under 617
>
> *For dislocations, see 617.16*

.473 — †Muscles

.473 044 — Injuries and wounds

> Number built according to instructions under 617
>
> *For sprains and strains, see 617.17*

.474 — †Tendons

.475 — †Bursae

.477 — †Integument

> Class here surgery of skin

.477 9 — †Hair

> Including removal

.48 — †Nervous system

> Class here neurosurgery
>
> Class ophthalmological surgery in 617.71; class otological surgery in 617.81–617.88. Class surgery of nerves of a specific system or organ with the system or organ, e.g., neuromuscular surgery 617.473

.481 — †Brain

> Including psychosurgery

.481 03 — Rehabilitation

> Number built according to instructions under 617
>
> Class rehabilitation of brain-injured patients in 617.4810443

.482 — †Spinal cord

> Including surgical treatment of spina bifida

.483 — †Nerves

---

†Add as instructed under 617, except use 059 by itself only for surgery utilizing specific instruments or techniques and do not use 06 by itself

.5 **Regional medicine   Regional surgery**

> Class here orthopedic regional medicine, orthopedic regional surgery [*both formerly* 617.3]
>
> Class nonsurgical medicine of specific systems or organs in specific regions in 616; except as provided for below, class surgery of a specific system in a specific region in 617.4
>
> *See Manual at 617.5*

SUMMARY

617.51	Head
.52	Face
.53	Neck
.54	Thorax (Chest) and respiratory system
.55	Abdominal and pelvic cavities
.56	Back
.57	Upper extremities
.58	Lower extremities

.51   *Head

> Class here otorhinolaryngology, comprehensive works on diseases of eyes, ears, nose, throat
>
> *For face, see 617.52; for throat, see 617.531; for eyes, see 617.7; for ears, see 617.8*

.514   †Skull

> Limited to surgery

.52   *Face

> Class eyes in 617.7

.522   *Oral region

> Including lips, tongue, jaws, parotid gland
>
> Class mouth as a digestive organ in 616.31
>
> *For teeth, see 617.6*
>
> *See Manual at 617.605 vs. 617.522*

.522 5   *Palate

.523   *Nose

> Class here comprehensive works on nose and throat
>
> Class comprehensive works on diseases of eyes, ears, nose, throat in 617.51
>
> *For throat, see 617.531*

*Add as instructed under 617

†Add as instructed under 617, except use 059 by itself only for surgery utilizing specific instruments or techniques and do not use 06 by itself

| .53 | *Neck |
| .531 | *Throat |

For pharynx, see 617.532; for larynx and trachea, see 617.533

| .532 | †Pharynx |

Limited to surgery

Including tonsils

| .533 | †Larynx and trachea |

Limited to surgery

Including epiglottis, vocal cords

| .539 | †Thyroid and parathyroid glands |

Limited to surgery

| .54 | *Thorax (Chest) and respiratory system |

Regional medicine and surgery of thorax; surgery of respiratory system

Subdivisions are added for thorax and respiratory system together, for thorax alone

For surgery of heart, see 617.412; for surgery of nose, see 617.523; for surgery of larynx and trachea, see 617.533

| .542 | †Lungs |

Limited to surgery

| .543 | †Pleura |

Limited to surgery

| .544 | †Bronchi |

Limited to surgery

| .545 | †Mediastinum |

Limited to surgery

| .546 | †Thymus gland |

Limited to surgery

| .547 | †Diaphragm |

Limited to surgery

| .548 | †Esophagus |

Limited to surgery

---

*Add as instructed under 617

†Add as instructed under 617, except use 059 by itself only for surgery utilizing specific instruments or techniques and do not use 06 by itself

.549	†Male breast
	Limited to surgery
	Class comprehensive works on surgery of breast in 618.19059
.55	*Abdominal and pelvic cavities
	For urogenital system, see 617.46
.551	†Spleen
	Limited to surgery
.553	†Stomach
	Limited to surgery
	Including pylorus
.554	†Intestine
	Limited to surgery
.554 1	†Small intestine
	Limited to surgery
	Including duodenum, jejunum, ileum
.554 5	†Cecum, vermiform appendix
	Limited to surgery
.554 7	†Large intestine
	Limited to surgery
	Including sigmoid flexure (sigmoid colon)
	Class here colon
	For cecum and vermiform appendix, see 617.5545; for rectum, see 617.555
.555	†Rectum, anus, perineum
	Limited to surgery
.556	†Biliary tract
	Limited to surgery
.556 2	†Liver
	Limited to surgery
.556 5	†Gallbladder
	Limited to surgery

*Add as instructed under 617

†Add as instructed under 617, except use 059 by itself only for surgery utilizing specific instruments or techniques and do not use 06 by itself

.556 7		†Bile ducts
		Limited to surgery
.557		†Pancreas and islands of Langerhans
		Limited to surgery
.558		†Peritoneum
		Limited to surgery
		Including mesentery, omentum
.559		*Abdominal hernias
		Including hiatal hernia
.56	*Back	
		Class shoulders in 617.572; class hips in 617.581
.564	*Backache	
.57	*Upper extremities	
		Class here surgery of joints of upper extremities
		Class comprehensive works on extremities, on amputations, on surgery of joints of extremities in 617.58
.572	*Shoulders	
.574	*Arms, elbows, wrists	
		Subdivisions are added for arms, elbows, wrists together, for arms alone
.575	*Hands	
		Class carpal tunnel syndrome in 616.87
.58	*Lower extremities	
		Class here comprehensive works on extremities, on paraplegia
		For neurological aspects of paraplegia, see 616.837; for upper extremities, see 617.57
		See also 616.72 for nonsurgical medical aspects of joints
.580 59		Surgery
		Number built according to instructions under 617
		Class here comprehensive works on amputations, on surgery of joints of extremities
		For amputations of upper extremities, surgery of joints of upper extremities, see 617.57059. For surgery of a specific joint, see the joint, e.g., surgery of knees 617.582059

*Add as instructed under 617

†Add as instructed under 617, except use 059 by itself only for surgery utilizing specific
  instruments or techniques and do not use 06 by itself

.581	*Hips
.582	*Knees and thighs

Subdivisions are added for knees and thighs together, for knees alone

.584	*Legs and ankles

Leg: segment of inferior limb between knee and ankle

.585	*Feet

Class here podiatry (chiropody)

.6   *Dentistry

[.600 83]   Young people

Do not use; class in 617.645

.600 9   Historical, geographic, persons treatment

.601   Oral hygiene and preventive dentistry

Do not use for surgical complications and sequelae; class in 617.605

Standard subdivisions are added for either or both topics in heading

Class here dental hygiene

.605   Surgery

Do not use for preventive measures; class in 617.601

Including surgical complications and sequelae

For a specific kind of dental surgery, see the kind, e.g., extractions 617.66

See Manual at 617.605 vs. 617.522

[.609]   Historical, geographic, persons treatment

Do not use; class in 617.6009

.63   *Dental diseases

For tumors of teeth and surrounding tissues, see 616.992314; for tuberculosis of teeth and surrounding tissues, see 616.995314

.632   *Diseases of gums and tooth sockets

Including alveolar abscesses, gingivitis, periodontitis, pyorrhea

Class here periodontics

.634   *Diseases of tooth tissues

Including diseases of cementum, dentin, enamel

For cavities, see 617.67

*Add as instructed under 617

.634 2   *Diseases of dental pulp

                          Class here endodontics

.64   Orthodontics and pedodontics

.643   *Orthodontics

.645   *Pedodontics

                          Class a specific aspect of pedodontics, plus notation 0083 from table
                          under 617, with the aspect, e.g., periodontics for children 617.6320083

.66   *Extractions

                          Class here exodontics

.67   *Cavities (Caries)

.672   Preparation and treatment

.675   Fillings and inlays

                          Including metallic and ceramic fillings and inlays

.69   Prosthetic dentistry (Prosthodontics)

.690 284   Apparatus and equipment

                          Do not use for materials; class in 617.695

.692   Dentures, crowns, bridges

.695   Materials

.7   *Ophthalmology

             Treatment of ocular diseases, correction of refractive errors

             For tumors of eyes, see 616.99284; for tuberculosis of eyes, see 616.99584

[.704 4]   Injuries and wounds

                          Do not use; class in 617.713

[.705 9]   Surgical therapy

                          Do not use; class in 617.71

[.707]   Pathology

                          Do not use; class in 617.71

.71   Pathology and surgery of eyes

                          Class surgical complications and sequelae in 617.701. Class pathology and
                          surgery of specific diseases and parts of eyes with the disease or part, e.g.,
                          diagnosis of glaucoma 617.741075

---

*Add as instructed under 617

.712	*Loss of function

Blindness and partial blindness

See also 617.75 for disorders of refraction and accommodation, color blindness

.713	*Injuries and wounds

Subdivisions are added for either or both topics in heading

.715	Diagnosis and prognosis

Add to base number 617.715 the numbers following 616.075 in 616.0751–616.0759, e.g., physical diagnosis 617.7154

Subdivisions are added for diagnosis and prognosis together, for diagnosis alone

.719	*Diseases of corneas and scleras

Subdivisions are added for corneas and scleras together, for corneas alone

See also 362.1783 for eye banks

[.719 009]	Historical, geographic, persons treatment

Relocated to 617.71909

.719 09	Historical, geographic, persons treatment [*formerly* 617.009]
.72	*Diseases of uveas

Including diseases of choroids, ciliary bodies, irises

.73	*Diseases of optic nerves, of retinas
.732	*Diseases of optic nerves

Class diseases of ocular neuromuscular mechanism in 617.762

.735	*Diseases of retinas
.74	*Diseases of eyeballs

For diseases of corneas and scleras, see 617.719; for diseases of uveas, see 617.72; for diseases of retinas, see 617.735

.741	*Glaucoma
.742	*Diseases of crystalline lenses

Class here cataracts

.746	*Diseases of vitreous bodies
.75	Disorders of refraction and accommodation, color blindness

Class here optometry

See also 617.712 for blindness and partial blindness

*Add as instructed under 617

.752	Optical work

Setting and adjusting lenses, mechanical work of opticians

.752 2	Eyeglasses

Other than contact lenses, intraocular lenses

See also 617.7523 for contact lenses, 617.7524 for intraocular lenses

.752 3	Contact lenses
.752 4	Intraocular lenses
.755	Disorders of refraction and accommodation

Including astigmatism, hyperopia, myopia, presbyopia

For aniseikonia, see 617.758

.758	Aniseikonia
.759	Color blindness
.76	Diseases of ocular muscles and lacrimal apparatus
.762	*Diseases of ocular neuromuscular mechanism

Including binocular imbalance, diplopia, strabismus

Class here orthoptics

.764	*Diseases of lacrimal apparatus
.77	Diseases of eyelids and conjunctivas
.771	*Diseases of eyelids
.772	*Trachoma
.773	*Conjunctivitis

For trachoma, see 617.772

.78	*Diseases of orbits
.79	Prosthetic ophthalmology

Fitting of artificial eyes

.8	***Otology and audiology**

Class here loss and impairment of function (deafness and hearing impairment)

Subdivisions are added for either or both topics in heading

For tumors of ears, see 616.99285; for tuberculosis of ears, see 616.99585

.81	*Diseases of external ears

For diseases of auricles, see 617.82; for diseases of auditory canals, see 617.83

*Add as instructed under 617

.82   *Diseases of auricles

.83   *Diseases of auditory canals

.84   *Diseases of middle ears

> *For diseases of tympanic membranes, see 617.85; for diseases of eustachian tubes, see 617.86; for diseases of mastoid processes, see 617.87*

.842   *Diseases of ossicles

.85   *Diseases of tympanic membranes

.86   *Diseases of eustachian tubes (auditory tubes)

.87   *Diseases of mastoid processes

.88   *Diseases of internal ears and of aural nervous system

.882   *Diseases of internal ears

> Including Ménière's disease; diseases of cochleas (labyrinths), semicircular canals, vestibules

> Class vertigo as a symptom of neurological disease in 616.841; class motion sickness in 616.9892

.886   *Diseases of aural nervous system

> Including sensorineural deafness

.89   Correction of impaired hearing

> Including use of hearing aids

> Class treatment of diseases of specific parts of hearing apparatus in 617.81–617.88

.9   Operative surgery and special fields of surgery

> Class here orthopedic appliances [*formerly* 617.307]; auxiliary techniques and procedures; apparatus, equipment, materials; comprehensive works on surgical appliances, on prosthetic equipment

> Class comprehensive works on orthopedic and nonorthopedic self-help devices for persons with disabilities in 617.03

> *For a specific appliance or piece of equipment, see the use of the appliance or equipment, e.g., dentures 617.692*

>   617.91–617.96   Surgical techniques, procedures, apparatus, equipment, materials

> Class comprehensive works in 617.9. Except for anesthesiology, class techniques, procedures, apparatus, equipment, materials of surgery of a specific system, organ, region with the surgical therapy of the system, organ, or region, e.g., preoperative care in neck surgery 617.53059

*Add as instructed under 617

.91   Operative surgery

For anesthesiology, see 617.96

.910 01   Philosophy and theory

.910 02   Miscellany

[.910 028]   Auxiliary techniques and procedures; apparatus, equipment, materials

Do not use; class in 617.9178

.910 03–.910 09   Standard subdivisions

.910 1   Asepsis and antisepsis

Standard subdivisions are added for either or both topics in heading

Class here sterilization

.917   Operating room

.917 2   Preparation of operating room

.917 8   Surgical instruments, apparatus, equipment, materials

For surgical dressings, see 617.93

.919   Preoperative and postoperative care

.93   Surgical dressings

.95   Cosmetic and restorative plastic surgery, transplantation of tissue and organs, implantation of artificial organs

For plastic surgery and transplantation of tissue of specific systems, regions, organs, see the system, region, organ in 617.4–617.5, plus notation 0592 from table under 617, e.g., plastic surgery of face 617.520592; for transplantation of a specific organ and implantation of artificial substitutes for a specific organ, see the organ in 617.4, plus notation 0592 from table under 617, e.g., heart transplantation 617.4120592; for plastic surgery and transplantation of tissue and organs, implantation of artificial organs in gynecological and obstetrical surgery, see the tissue or organ in 618, plus notation 0592 from table under 618.1–618.8, e.g., breast implants 618.190592

See also 362.1783 for tissue and organ banks

[.950 01–.950 09]   Standard subdivisions

Relocated to 617.9501–617.9509

.950 1–.950 9   Standard subdivisions [*formerly* 617.95001–617.95009]

.96   Anesthesiology

Methods and techniques of inducing anesthesia, management of accidents and complications resulting from it

Class acupuncture as an anesthetic in 615.892

.960 4	Special topics
.960 41	Complications and sequelae

> Standard subdivisions are added for either or both topics in heading

.960 42	Emergencies

> Class resuscitology in 615.8043

> \>   **617.962–617.966   Types of anesthesia**

Class anesthesiology regardless of type for specific kinds of surgery in 617.967; class comprehensive works in 617.96

.962	General anesthesia

> Including inhalation, intravenous, rectal anesthesias

.964	Regional anesthesia

> Including caudal, epidural (peridural), saddle block, spinal anesthesias

.966	Local anesthesia
.967	Anesthesiology for specific kinds of surgery

> General, regional, local anesthesia
>
> Add to base number 617.967 the numbers following 617 in 617.1–617.9, e.g., dental anesthesia 617.9676
>
> *For anesthesiology for gynecology and obstetrics, see 617.968*

.968	Anesthesiology for gynecology and obstetrics
.968 1	Gynecology
.968 2	Obstetrics

> \>   **617.97–617.99   Special fields of surgery**

Class comprehensive works in 617.9. Class a specific surgical technique regardless of field with the technique in 617.9101–617.96, e.g., anesthesiology of children 617.96083; class surgery of a specific organ, system, disorder regardless of field with the organ, system, or disorder, e.g., brain surgery on children 617.4810083

.97	*Geriatric surgery
.98	*Pediatric surgery
.99	*Military surgery

*Add as instructed under 617

618   Other branches of medicine   Gynecology and obstetrics

See Manual at 616–618 vs. 615.7

SUMMARY

618.01–.09	**Standard subdivisions and special topics of gynecology and obstetrics**
.1	**Gynecology**
.2	**Obstetrics**
.3	**Diseases and complications of pregnancy**
.4	**Childbirth (Parturition) Labor**
.5	**Complicated labor (Dystocia)**
.6	**Normal puerperium**
.7	**Puerperal diseases**
.8	**Obstetrical surgery**
.9	**Pediatrics and geriatrics**

.01   Philosophy and theory of gynecology and obstetrics

.02   Miscellany of gynecology and obstetrics

[.028 7]   Testing and measurement

Do not use; class in 618.0475

.03   Dictionaries, encyclopedias, concordances of gynecology and obstetrics

.04   Special topics of gynecology and obstetrics

Add to base number 618.04 the numbers following 0 in notation 01–09 from table under 618.1–618.8, e.g., emergencies 618.0425; however, for gynecology and obstetrics as a profession, occupation, hobby, see 618.023

.05–.07   Standard subdivisions of gynecology and obstetrics

.08   History and description of gynecology and obstetrics with respect to kinds of persons

.083   Young people

For gynecology for girls up to puberty, see 618.92098

.084   Persons in specific stages of adulthood

[.084 6]   Persons in late adulthood

Do not use; class in 618.978

.09   Historical, geographic, persons treatment of gynecology and obstetrics

Class life with a disease in 362.198

>   **618.1–618.8   Gynecology and obstetrics**

Medical and surgical

Except where contrary instructions are given, all notes under 616.01–616.08 and in table under 616.1–616.9 are applicable here

Except for modifications shown under specific entries, add to each subdivision identified by * as follows:

001–007	Standard subdivisions
	As modified under 616.1–616.9
008	History and description with respect to kinds of persons
0083	Young people
	Class gynecology for girls up to puberty in 618.92098
0084	Persons in specific stages of adulthood
[00846]	Persons in late adulthood
	Do not use; class in 618.978
009	Historical, geographic, persons treatment
0092	Persons
	Class life with a disease in 362.198
01–03	Microbiology, special topics, rehabilitation
	Add to 0 the numbers following 0 in notation 01–03 from table under 616.1–616.9, e.g., experimental medicine 027
	Class microbiology, special topics, rehabilitation applied to special classes of diseases in 04
04	Special classes of diseases
	Limited to the classes named below
042	Genetic diseases
0421–0423	Microbiology, special topics, rehabilitation
	Add to base number 042 the numbers following 0 in notation 01–03 from table under 616.1–616.9, e.g., experimental medicine for genetic diseases 04227
0425–0429	Preventive measures, surgery, therapy, pathology, psychosomatic medicine, case histories
	Add to base number 042 the numbers following 0 in notation 05–09 from table under 618.1–618.8, e.g., therapy for genetic diseases 0426
043	Congenital diseases
	Add to base number 043 the numbers following 042 in notation 0421–0429 from table under 618.1–618.8, e.g., experimental medicine for congenital diseases 04327
	Class congenital diseases of genetic origin in 042
>05–09	Preventive measures, surgery, therapy, pathology, psychosomatic medicine, case histories
	Class preventive measures, surgery, therapy, pathology, psychosomatic medicine applied to special classes of diseases in 04; class comprehensive works in 618.1–618.8, without adding from this table
05	Preventive measures and surgery

(continued)

> **618.1–618.8 Gynecology and obstetrics (continued)**

052   Preventive measures
             By individuals and by medical personnel
             Class public measures preventing specific diseases in
             614.5992; class comprehensive works on prevention in 613

059   Surgery
             Including surgical complications and sequelae; surgery
             utilizing specific instruments or techniques, e.g.,
             catheterization, cryosurgery, laparoscopic surgery, laser
             surgery, microsurgery

0592   Cosmetic and restorative plastic surgery, transplantation of
             tissue and organs, implantation of artificial organs

06   Therapy
             Class here rehabilitative therapy
             Class comprehensive works on rehabilitative therapy and
             education for living with handicaps and disabilities in 03
             For surgery, see 059

061   Drug therapy

062–069   Other therapies
             Add to 06 the numbers following 615.8 in 615.82–615.89,
             e.g., X-ray therapy 06422

07   Pathology
             Add to 07 the numbers following 616.07 in 616.071–616.079,
             e.g., physical diagnosis 0754

08   Psychosomatic medicine

09   Case histories

Class comprehensive works in 618

.1   ***Gynecology**

Including endocrine gynecology, endometriosis

Class tumors of genital system in 616.99265

For puerperal diseases, see 618.7; for pediatric gynecology, see 618.92098

.11   *Diseases of ovaries

.12   *Diseases of Fallopian tubes (oviducts)

.13   *Diseases of perimetrium (Periuterine diseases)

.14   *Diseases of uterus

Class here diseases of uterine cervix

For diseases of perimetrium, see 618.13

[.140 59]   Surgery

Do not use; class in 618.145

*Add as instructed under 618.1–618.8

.142	*Infections

Including cervicitis, endometritis, pyometra

For leukorrhea, see 618.173

See also 618.1 for endometriosis

.143	*Erosions
.144	*Malformations

Including prolapse of uterus

.145	Surgery
.145 3	Hysterectomies
.145 8	Dilation and curettage

See also 618.88 for surgical abortion

.15	*Diseases of vagina

For leukorrhea, see 618.173

.16	*Diseases of vulva
.17	*Functional and systemic disorders
.172	*Menstruation disorders

Including amenorrhea, dysmenorrhea, menorrhagia, oligomenorrhea, premenstrual syndrome (PMS)

.173	*Leukorrhea
.175	*Menopause disorders

Class here comprehensive works on climacteric disorders

Class involutional psychoses in 616.895

For male climacteric disorders, see 616.693

.178	*Infertility

Including artificial insemination

Class comprehensive works on male and female infertility in 616.692

.178 059	Surgery

Number built according to instructions under 618.1–618.8

Including embryo transplant (test-tube baby)

*Add as instructed under 618.1–618.8

.178 06   Therapy

Number built according to instructions under 618.1–618.8

Class here human reproductive technology applied to female infertility

Class comprehensive works on human reproductive technology in 616.69206

For surgery, see 618.178059

.19   *Diseases of breast

Class here comprehensive works on diseases of male and female breast

For diseases of male breast, see 616.49; for tumors of breast, see 616.99249; for diseases of lactation, see 618.71

.190 59   Surgery

Number built according to instructions under 618.1–618.8

Class here comprehensive works on surgery of male and female breast

For surgery of male breast, see 617.549

.2   ***Obstetrics**

Class here midwifery, comprehensive works on pregnancy and childbirth

For physiology of pregnancy and childbirth, see 612.63; for diseases, disorders, management of pregnancy, parturition, puerperium, see 618.3–618.8

[.205 2]   Preventive measures

Do not use; class in 618.24

[.205 9]   Surgery

Do not use; class in 618.8

.207 5   Diagnosis [*formerly* 618.22]

Number built according to instructions under 618.1–618.8

To be classed here a work should be broader than diagnosis of diseases and complications of pregnancy; it should include also diagnosis of labor complications (618.5) or diagnosis of puerperal diseases (618.7075)

For diagnosis of diseases and complications of pregnancy, see 618.3075

[.22]   Diagnosis

Relocated to 618.2075

*Add as instructed under 618.1–618.8

.24   Prenatal care and preparation for childbirth

Including dietetics for pregnant women, exercises to aid childbirth

See also 641.563 for cooking for pregnant women

.25   *Multiple pregnancy and childbirth

Subdivisions are added for either or both topics in heading

>   **618.3–618.8   Diseases, disorders, management of pregnancy, parturition, puerperium**

Class comprehensive works in 618.2

.3   *Diseases and complications of pregnancy

.31   Extrauterine pregnancy (Ectopic pregnancy)

Including abdominal, tubal pregnancies

.310 01–.310 09   Standard subdivisions [*formerly* 618.3101–618.3109]

As modified under 618.1–618.8

.310 1–.310 9   Microbiology, special topics, rehabilitation, special classes of diseases, preventive measures, surgery, therapy, pathology, psychosomatic medicine, case histories

Add to base number 618.310 the numbers following 0 in notation 01–09 from table under 618.1–618.8, e.g., treatment of extrauterine pregnancies 618.3106

Standard subdivisions relocated to 618.31001–618.31009

.32   *Fetal disorders

Class here perinatal medicine (perinatology)

Class neonatal medicine in 618.9201

For childbirth, see 618.4

.320 75   Diagnosis

Number built according to instructions under 618.1–618.8

Class procedures to diagnose genetic diseases, e.g., amniocentesis and chorionic villus biopsy, in 618.3204275

.326   Diseases of specific systems and organs

[.326 001–.326 09]   Standard subdivisions, microbiology, special topics, rehabilitation, special classes of diseases, preventive measures, surgery, therapy, pathology, psychosomatic medicine, case histories

Numbers discontinued; class in 618.326

---

*Add as instructed under 618.1–618.8

.326 1	*Diseases of cardiovascular system
.326 8	*Diseases of nervous system
	Including drug dependence
.34	*Diseases of placenta and amniotic fluid

Subdivisions are added for diseases of placenta and amniotic fluid, for diseases of placenta alone

.39	Miscarriage, spontaneous abortion, premature delivery
.392	Miscarriage and spontaneous abortion

Standard subdivisions are added for either or both topics in heading

Before fetus is viable

.397	Premature delivery

After fetus is viable and before full term

.4   Childbirth (Parturition)   Labor

Class a specific aspect not provided for here with the aspect, e.g., Cesarean section 618.86

.42	Presentation

Position of fetal body during labor

.45	Natural childbirth

Childbirth without use of analgesics

.5   Complicated labor (Dystocia)

.51	Maternal complications

Difficult labor due to anomalies of expellant forces and mechanical obstructions

.53	Fetal complications

Difficult labor due to size of fetus

.54	Uterine hemorrhage
.56	Placental complications
.58	Umbilical cord complications

.6   Normal puerperium

Postpartum management and care

.7   *Puerperal diseases

Including Sheehan's syndrome

*Add as instructed under 618.1–618.8

.71	*Diseases of lactation
.73	*Puerperal metritis and peritonitis
.74	*Puerperal septicemia and pyemia

Subdivisions are added for puerperal septicemia and pyemia together, for puerperal septicemia alone

| .75 | *Puerperal eclampsia |
| .76 | *Puerperal mental disorders |

Including postpartum depression

| .77 | *Puerperal blood disorders |

Class puerperal septicemia, puerperal pyemia in 618.74

| .79 | Maternal death |
| **.8** | **Obstetrical surgery** |

Class embryo transplant in 618.178059

| .82 | Version and extraction |
| .83 | Embryotomy |

Including craniotomy

| .85 | Minor surgery |

Including episiotomy, symphyseotomy, vaginiperineotomy

.86	Cesarean section
.87	Surgical removal of placenta
.88	Surgical abortion

See also 615.766 for abortifacient drugs

| .89 | Asepsis and antisepsis |

Standard subdivisions are added for either or both topics in heading

| **.9** | **Pediatrics and geriatrics** |
| .92 | Pediatrics |

Diseases of infants and children up to puberty

Including sudden infant death syndrome (crib death, cot death)

Class medicine for young people who have reached puberty in 616.00835

For pediatric aspects of wounds and injuries, see 617.10083; for pediatric aspects of results of injuries, see 617.2083; for pedodontics, see 617.645; for pediatric surgery, see 617.98

See Manual at 616 vs. 618.92

*Add as instructed under 618.1–618.8

.920 001–.920 008	Standard subdivisions
	As modified under 616.1–616.9
.920 009	Historical, geographic, persons treatment
.920 009 2	Persons
	Class life with a physical disease in 362.19892. Class life with a mental disorder with the disorder in 618.9285–618.9289, e.g., life with depression 618.9285270092
.920 01–.920 09	General topics of pediatrics
	Add to base number 618.920 notation 01–09 from table under 616.1–616.9, e.g., diagnosis 618.920075; however, for pediatric preventive measures, see 613.0432; for pediatric therapeutics, see 615.542
.920 1	Newborn infants (Neonates)
	In first month after birth
	Class here neonatal medicine (neonatology)
	Class perinatal medicine (perinatology) in 618.32
.920 11	Premature infants
.920 12	Full-term infants
.920 9	Special branches of medicine
	Class pediatric sports medicine in 617.1027083; class pedodontics in 617.645; class pediatric surgery in 617.98
.920 97	Regional medicine, ophthalmology, otology, audiology
	See Manual at 618.92097 vs. 617
.920 975	Regional medicine
	Add to base number 618.920975 the numbers following 617.5 in 617.51–617.58, e.g., disorders of face 618.9209752
.920 977–.920 978	Ophthalmology, otology, audiology
	Add to base number 618.92097 the numbers following 617 in 617.7–617.8, e.g., trachoma in children 618.92097772
.920 98	Gynecology
.920 981	Specific diseases
	Add to base number 618.920981 the numbers following 618.1 in 618.11–618.19, e.g., diseases of uterus 618.9209814

.921–.929		Specific diseases

Add to base number 618.92 the numbers following 616 in 616.1–616.9, e.g., cardiac diseases in children 618.9212

For pediatric dental diseases, see 617.645; for pediatric regional medicine diseases, pediatric diseases of eyes and ears, pediatric gynecological diseases, see 618.9209

.97   *Geriatrics

Diseases of persons in late adulthood

[.970 5]   Preventive measures

Do not use; class in 613.0438

[.970 6]   Therapy

Do not use; class in 615.547

.976–.978   Specific diseases

Add to base number 618.97 the numbers following 61 in 616–618, e.g., geriatric mental illness 618.97689; however, for geriatric aspects of wounds and injuries, see 617.100846; for geriatric aspects of results of injuries, see 617.20846; for geriatric surgery, see 617.97

See Manual at 618.977 vs. 617

619   Experimental medicine

Class here experimental research on diseases [*formerly also* 616.00724]

Class animal experimentation with respect to anatomy and physiology in 571–573; class human experimentation with respect to anatomy in 611; class human experimentation with respect to physiology in 612; class experimental medicine with respect to pharmacology and therapeutics in 615; class experimental medicine with respect to specific diseases in 616–618

.5   **Birds**

.7   **Dogs**

.8   **Cats**

.9   **Other mammals**

.93   Rodents and rabbits

Including guinea pigs, hamsters, mice, rats

.98   Primates

Including apes, monkeys, humans

*Add as instructed under 616.1–616.9

620   Engineering and allied operations

Standard subdivisions are added for engineering and allied operations together, for engineering alone

Class here manufacturing of products of various branches of engineering

Class comprehensive works on manufacturing in 670

For chemical engineering, see 660

SUMMARY

624		**Civil engineering**
	.029 9	Estimates of labor, time, materials
	.1	Structural engineering and underground construction
	.2	Bridges
	.3	Specific types of bridges
	.4	Tubular and box-girder bridges
	.5	Suspension bridges
	.6	Arch bridges
	.7	Compound bridges
	.8	Movable bridges
625		**Engineering of railroads and roads**
	.1	Railroads
	.2	Railroad rolling stock
	.3	Inclined, mountain, ship railroads
	.4	Rapid transit systems
	.5	Cable and aerial railways
	.6	Surface rail and trolley systems
	.7	Roads
	.8	Artificial road surfaces
627		**Hydraulic engineering**
	.04	Special topics
	.1	Inland waterways
	.2	Harbors, ports, roadsteads
	.3	Port facilities
	.4	Flood control
	.5	Reclamation, irrigation, related topics
	.7	Underwater operations
	.8	Dams and reservoirs
	.9	Other hydraulic structures
628		**Sanitary and municipal engineering Environmental protection engineering**
	.1	Water supply
	.2	Sewers
	.3	Sewage treatment and disposal
	.4	Waste technology, public toilets, street cleaning
	.5	Pollution control technology and industrial sanitation engineering
	.7	Sanitary engineering for rural and sparsely populated areas
	.9	Other branches of sanitary and municipal engineering
629		**Other branches of engineering**
	.04	Transportation engineering
	.1	Aerospace engineering
	.2	Motor land vehicles, cycles
	.3	Air-cushion vehicles (Ground-effect machines, Hovercraft)
	.4	Astronautics
	.8	Automatic control engineering

.001   Philosophy and theory

.001 1   Systems

> Class design of engineering systems in 620.0042; class manufacturing systems in 670.11; class interdisciplinary works covering systems of agriculture, home economics, or management in addition to engineering in 601.1; class interdisciplinary works on systems in 003

.001 13	Computer modeling and simulation
	Class computer-aided design in 620.00420285
.001 5	Scientific principles
[.001 53]	Physical principles in engineering
	Do not use; class in 621
[.001 531]	Mechanical principles in engineering
	Do not use; class in 620.1
[.001 534]	Principles of sound and related vibrations in engineering
	Do not use; class in 620.2
.002	Miscellany
[.002 87]	Testing and measurement
	Do not use; class in 620.0044
[.002 88]	Maintenance and repair
	Do not use; class in 620.0046
[.002 89]	Safety measures
	Do not use; class in 620.86
.003	Dictionaries, encyclopedias, concordances
.004	Design, testing, measurement, quality, maintenance, repair
.004 2	Engineering design
.004 202 85	Data processing Computer applications
	Class here computer-aided design (CAD)
	Class comprehensive works on computer-aided design and computer-aided manufacturing (CAD/CAM) in 670.285
.004 4	Testing and measurement
	Including inspection, simulation
	Class interdisciplinary works on measurement in 530.8
.004 5	Quality
	Including interchangeability, maintainability, precision
	Class testing and measurement for quality in 620.0044; class maintenance in 620.0046
.004 52	Reliability
.004 54	Durability

.004 6	Maintenance and repair

Class here interdisciplinary works on maintenance and repair

For maintenance and repair in a specific subject, see the subject, plus notation 0288 from Table 1, e.g., clock and watch repair 681.110288

.005–.008	Standard subdivisions
.009	Historical, geographic, persons treatment
.009 1	Treatment by areas, regions, places in general

Class engineering to overcome problems of specific kinds of geographic environments in 620.41

.009 2	Persons

Class persons treatment of engineers known primarily as entrepreneurs in 338.76

[.009 99]	Treatment by extraterrestrial worlds

Do not use; class in 620.419

.1   Engineering mechanics and materials

Standard subdivisions are added for engineering mechanics and materials together, for engineering mechanics alone

SUMMARY

620.100 1–.100 9	Standard subdivisions
.103–.107	Engineering (Applied) mechanics
.11	Engineering materials
.12	Wood
.13	Masonry materials
.14	Ceramic and allied materials
.16	Metals
.17	Ferrous metals
.18	Nonferrous metals
.19	Other engineering materials

.100 1–.100 9	Standard subdivisions

>   620.103–620.107   Engineering (Applied) mechanics

Class comprehensive works in 620.1

For fine particle technology, see 620.43

See also 531 for mechanics as a subject in physics

See Manual at 530 vs. 621

.103　　　Applied statics

　　　　　　For applied solid statics, see 620.1053; for applied fluid statics, see 620.1063; for applied gas statics, see 620.1073

.104　　　Applied dynamics

　　　　　　For applied solid dynamics, see 620.1054; for applied fluid dynamics, see 620.1064; for applied gas dynamics, see 620.1074

.105　　　Applied solid mechanics

　　　　　Class structural theory in 624.17

　　　　　For mechanical vibration, see 620.3

　　　　　See also 621.811 for physical principles of machinery

.105 3　　Statics

.105 4　　Dynamics

.106　　　Applied fluid mechanics

　　　　　Class here applied hydromechanics, comprehensive works on fluid-power technology

　　　　　　For applied gas mechanics, see 620.107; for steam engineering, see 621.1; for hydraulic-power technology, see 621.2; for hydraulic engineering, see 627

.106 3　　Statics

.106 4　　Dynamics

　　　　　Including cavitation, pressure surge, water hammer

　　　　　Class here flow

　　　　　　See also 621.4022 for convective transport, heat convection

.107　　　Applied gas mechanics

　　　　　Class here applied aeromechanics

　　　　　　For steam engineering, see 621.1; for pneumatic and vacuum technology, see 621.5; for aeromechanics of flight, see 629.1323; for air-conditioning engineering, see 697.93

.107 3　　Statics

.107 4　　Dynamics

.11　　Engineering materials

　　　　　Class comprehensive works on materials, manufacture of materials in 670

　　　　　For specific kinds of materials, see 620.12–620.19

.110 287　　　Testing and measurement

　　　　　　Do not use for nondestructive testing; class in 620.1127

.112   **Properties of materials and nondestructive testing**

Standard subdivisions are added for properties of materials and nondestructive testing together, for properties of materials alone

Class here failure, resistance, strength of materials

Class properties and nondestructive testing of porous, organic, composite materials in 620.116–620.118

>   620.112 1–620.112 6   **Resistance to specific forces**

Class comprehensive works in 620.112

.112 1   Resistance to thermal forces

Class resistance to thermal radiation in 620.11228

See also 620.11296 for thermal properties

.112 15   Changes in temperature

.112 16   Low temperatures

Including cryogenic temperatures

.112 17   High temperatures

.112 2   Resistance to decay, decomposition, deterioration

Standard subdivisions are added for any or all topics in heading

Physicochemical actions not basically thermal or mechanical

Including action of pests

.112 23   Biodegradation, corrosion, weathering

Including rot, rust

.112 28   Resistance to radiations

.112 3   Resistance to mechanical deformation (Mechanics of materials)

For resistance to specific mechanical stresses, see 620.1124; for resistance to fracture, see 620.1126

.112 302 87   Testing and measurement

Including strain gauges

.112 32   Temporary deformation (Elasticity)

Including elastic limit

.112 33   Permanent deformation (Plasticity)

Including creep, plastic flow

For properties affecting permanent deformation, see 620.1125

.112 4	Resistance to specific mechanical stresses
	Class resistance to change of form, regardless of stress, in 620.1125; class resistance to fracture, regardless of stress, in 620.1126
.112 41	Tension
.112 42	Compression
.112 43	Torsion
.112 44	Flexure
.112 45	Shearing
.112 48	Vibrations
.112 5	Properties affecting permanent deformation
	Including impact strength, rigidity, shock resistance; ductility, malleability
.112 6	Resistance to fracture (Fracture mechanics)
	Including brittleness, hardness
	Class here crack resistance, resistance to penetration and breaking; fatigue; fatigue, fracture, rupture strength
.112 7	Nondestructive testing
.112 72	Radiographic testing
	Class here X-ray testing
.112 73	Tracer testing
.112 74	Ultrasonic testing
.112 78	Magnetic testing
.112 9	Other properties
.112 92	Mechanical properties
	Including adhesiveness, roughness, texture; friction and wear resistance
	Class comprehensive works on friction in 621.89
	See also 620.44 for surface technology
.112 94	Acoustical properties
.112 95	Optical properties
	Including luminescence, photoelasticity, refractivity
.112 96	Thermal properties
	Including heat conductivity
	See also 620.1121 for resistance to thermal forces

.112 97	Electrical, electronic, magnetic properties
.112 972	Semiconductivity
.112 973	Superconductivity
.112 99	Microphysical properties

Including crystallographic and molecular properties; microstructure

For electronic properties, see 620.11297

> **620.116–620.118 Porous, organic, composite materials**

Class comprehensive works in 620.11

For a specific kind of porous, organic, composite material, see 620.12–620.19

| .116 | *Porous materials |

Class porous organic materials in 620.117; class porous composite materials in 620.118

| .117 | *Organic materials |

Class organic composite materials in 620.118

| .118 | *Composite materials |

For a specific composite material, see the predominant component in 620.12–620.19, e.g., ferroconcrete 620.137

> **620.12–620.19 Specific kinds of materials**

Add to each subdivision identified by * as follows:
```
0287          Testing and measurement
                   Do not use for nondestructive testing; class in 7
1–9   Specific properties and nondestructive testing
       Add the numbers following 620.112 in 620.1121–620.1129, e.g.,
       nondestructive testing 7
```

Class comprehensive works in 620.11. Class manufacturing and chemical properties of a specific kind of material with the material, e.g., wood 674

For porous, organic, composite materials, see 620.116–620.118

| .12 | *Wood |

Including laminated wood

| .13 | Masonry materials |

For brick, terra-cotta, tile, see 620.142

---

*Add as instructed under 620.12–620.19

.130 287   Testing and measurement

> Do not use for nondestructive testing; class in 620.130427

.130 4   Special topics

.130 42   *Specific properties and nondestructive testing

.132   *Natural stones

.135   *Cement

> Class here masonry adhesives

.136   *Concrete

> *For reinforced and prestressed concrete, see 620.137; for concrete blocks, see 620.139*

.137   *Reinforced and prestressed concrete

> Subdivisions are added for either or both topics in heading

.139   Artificial stones

> Including cinder and concrete blocks

.139 028 7   Testing and measurement

> Do not use for nondestructive testing; class in 620.1390427

.139 04   Special topics

.139 042   *Specific properties and nondestructive testing

.14   Ceramic and allied materials

> Standard subdivisions are added for ceramic and allied materials together, for ceramic materials alone

> Class masonry materials in 620.13

.140 287   Testing and measurement

> Do not use for nondestructive testing; class in 620.140427

.140 4   Special topics

.140 42   *Specific properties and nondestructive testing

.142   Brick, terra-cotta, tile

.143   *Refractory materials

> Including fireclays

> Class refractory metals in 620.16

> *For asbestos, see 620.195*

.144   *Glass

> Including fiber glass

*Add as instructed under 620.12–620.19

.146		Enamel and porcelain
.16		*Metals

Class here alloys

For ferrous metals, see 620.17; for nonferrous metals, see 620.18

.17		*Ferrous metals

Class here iron, steel

.18		Nonferrous metals

Class here nonferrous alloys

.180 287		Testing and measurement

Do not use for nondestructive testing; class in 620.180427

.180 4		Special topics
.180 42		*Specific properties and nondestructive testing
.182		*Copper

Class here brass, Muntz metal; bronze, gunmetal; copper-aluminum alloys; copper-beryllium alloys

.183		*Lead
.184		Zinc and cadmium
.184 2		*Zinc

For brass, Muntz metal, see 620.182

.184 6		*Cadmium
.185		*Tin

For bronze, gunmetal, see 620.182

.186		*Aluminum

For copper-aluminum alloys, see 620.182

.187		*Magnesium
.188		*Nickel
.189		Other metals
.189 1		*Mercury
.189 2		Precious, rare-earth, actinide-series metals

Add to base number 620.1892 the numbers following 669.2 in 669.22–669.29, e.g., uranium 620.1892931

.189 3		Metals used in ferroalloys

For nickel, see 620.188

*Add as instructed under 620.12–620.19

.189 302 87	Testing and measurement
	Do not use for nondestructive testing; class in 620.18930427
.189 304	Special topics
.189 304 2	*Specific properties and nondestructive testing
.189 32	Titanium, manganese, vanadium
.189 322	*Titanium
.189 33	*Cobalt
.189 34	Chromium, molybdenum, tungsten
.189 35	Zirconium and tantalum
.189 352	*Zirconium
.189 4	*Beryllium
	For copper-beryllium alloys, see 620.182
.189 5	Antimony, arsenic, bismuth
.189 6	Alkali and alkaline-earth metals
.189 602 87	Testing and measurement
	Do not use for nondestructive testing; class in 620.18960427
.189 604	Special topics
.189 604 2	*Specific properties and nondestructive testing
[.189 9]	Miscellaneous rare metals
	Number discontinued; class in 620.189
.19	Other engineering materials
.191	Soils and related materials
	Standard subdivisions are added for soils and related materials together, for soils alone
	Including aggregates, clay, gravel, sand
	Class foundation soils in 624.151; class interdisciplinary works on soils in 631.4
.191 028 7	Testing and measurement
	Do not use for nondestructive testing; class in 620.1910427
.191 04	Special topics
.191 042	*Specific properties and nondestructive testing

*Add as instructed under 620.12–620.19

.192	Polymers

For elastomers, see 620.194

.192 028 7	Testing and measurement

Do not use for nondestructive testing; class in 620.1920427

.192 04	Special topics
.192 042	*Specific properties and nondestructive testing
.192 3	*Plastics

Class here plastic laminating materials

.192 4	*Gums and resins

Subdivisions are added for either or both topics in heading

.193	Nonmetallic elements

Including carbon, silicon

.193 028 7	Testing and measurement

Do not use for nondestructive testing; class in 620.1930427

.193 04	Special topics
.193 042	*Specific properties and nondestructive testing
.194	*Elastomers

Class here rubber

.195	Insulating materials

Including asbestos, corkboard, kapok, rock wool; dielectric materials

.195 028 7	Testing and measurement

Do not use for nondestructive testing; class in 620.1950427

.195 04	Special topics
.195 042	*Specific properties and nondestructive testing
.196	Bituminous materials

Including asphalt, tar

.196 028 7	Testing and measurement

Do not use for nondestructive testing; class in 620.1960427

.196 04	Special topics
.196 042	*Specific properties and nondestructive testing
.197	Organic fibrous materials

Including paper, paperboard, rope, textiles

*Add as instructed under 620.12–620.19

.197 028 7   Testing and measurement

> Do not use for nondestructive testing; class in 620.1970427

.197 04   Special topics

.197 042   *Specific properties and nondestructive testing

.198   Other natural and synthetic minerals

> Including corundum, feldspar, gems, graphite, oil, quartz, water

.199   Adhesives and sealants

> Class here comprehensive works on laminating materials

> *For masonry adhesives, see 620.135; for plastic laminating materials, see 620.1923*

.199 028 7   Testing and measurement

> Do not use for nondestructive testing; class in 620.1990427

.199 04   Special topics

.199 042   *Specific properties and nondestructive testing

.2   **Sound and related vibrations**

> Standard subdivisions are added for sound and related vibrations together, for sound alone

> Class here applied acoustics (acoustical engineering)

> *See also 534 for physics of sound*

> *See Manual at 530 vs. 621*

> 620.21–620.25   Applied acoustics (Acoustical engineering)

> Class electroacoustical communications in 621.3828; class engineering works on architectural acoustics in 690.2; class comprehensive works in 620.2; class interdisciplinary works on architectural acoustics in 729.29

.21   General topics of applied acoustics

> Including reflection and refraction of sound

.23   Noise and countermeasures

> Standard subdivisions are added for either or both topics in heading

.25   Acoustics in specific physical environments

> Including underwater acoustics

.28   Applied subsonics and ultrasonics

> *For ultrasonic testing of materials, see 620.11274*

---

*Add as instructed under 620.12–620.19

.3   **Mechanical vibration**

Class effects of vibrations on materials in 620.11248

For sound and related vibrations, see 620.2

.31   Generation and transmission

.37   Effects and countermeasures

Standard subdivisions are added for either or both topics in heading

.4   **Engineering for specific kinds of geographic environments, fine particle and remote control technology, surface engineering**

.41   Engineering for specific kinds of geographic environments

Class a specific technology with the technology, plus notation 091 from Table 1 when the environment is not inherent in the subject, e.g., ergonomics for deserts 620.8209154, nautical engineering 623.8

.411–.417   Specific kinds of terrestrial environments

Add to base number 620.41 the numbers following — 1 in notation 11–17 from Table 2, e.g., ocean engineering 620.4162; however, for engineering of estuaries, see 627.124

Class hydraulic engineering in 627

.419   Extraterrestrial environments

.43   Fine particle technology

Including dust, liquid particle technology

Class here powder technology

.44   Surface engineering

.46   Remote control and telecontrol

Standard subdivisions are added for either or both topics in heading

.5   **Nanotechnology**

Technology that manipulates matter on the atomic or molecular scale

Class a specific application of nanotechnology with the technology, e.g., nanotechnology used in manufacturing thin-film circuits 621.3815

.8   **Human factors and safety engineering**

Class here work environment engineering

Class a specific application with the application, e.g., engineering of the home kitchen work environment 643.3

See also 628 for environmental protection engineering

.82   Human factors engineering

Variant names: biotechnology, design anthropometry, ergonomics

.86 Safety engineering

> *For safety engineering of a specific technology, see the technology, plus notation 0289 from Table 1, e.g., safety in machine engineering 621.80289*

> *See Manual at 363.1065 vs. 620.86: Accident investigation*

621 Applied physics

Class here mechanical engineering

Class a specific application of applied physics with the application, e.g., military engineering 623

> *For engineering (applied) mechanics, see 620.1; for applied acoustics, see 620.2*

> *See Manual at 530 vs. 621*

SUMMARY

621.04		Special topics
	.1	Steam engineering
	.2	Hydraulic-power technology
	.3	Electrical engineering; lighting; superconductivity; magnetic engineering; applied optics; paraphotic technology; electronics; communications engineering; computers
	.4	Heat engineering and prime movers
	.5	Pneumatic, vacuum, low-temperature technologies
	.6	Blowers, fans, pumps
	.8	Machine engineering
	.9	Tools

.04 Special topics

.042 Energy engineering

Class here engineering of alternative and renewable energy sources

Class interdisciplinary works on energy in 333.79

.044 Plasma engineering

Class interdisciplinary works on plasma in 530.44

> **621.1–621.2 Fluid-power technologies**

Class comprehensive works in 620.106

.1 **Steam engineering**

> 621.15–621.16   Specific kinds of steam engines

Class comprehensive works in 621.1

*For marine steam engines, see 623.8722; for steam locomotives, see
625.261; for steam tractors and rollers, see 629.2292*

.15   Portable engines

Class comprehensive works on specific structural types of steam engines in
621.16

.16   Stationary engines

Class here comprehensive works on specific structural types of steam
engines

For portable engines of specific structural types, see 621.15

.164   Reciprocating engines

.165   Turbines

[.166]   Other stationary engines

Number discontinued; class in 621.16

.18   Generating and transmitting steam

Standard subdivisions are added for generating and transmitting steam
together, for generating steam alone

Class generating steam in specific kinds of steam engines in 621.15–621.16;
class generating steam in central stations in 621.19

> 621.182–621.183   Generating steam

Class comprehensive works in 621.18

.182   Fuels

.183   Boilers and boiler furnaces

Standard subdivisions are added for either or both topics in heading

Including chimneys, mechanical stokers

.185   Transmitting steam

Including insulation, pressure regulators, safety valves, steam pipes

.19   Central stations

.194   Boiler operations (Boiler-house practices)

.197   Accessories

Including condensers, cooling towers, superheaters

.199　　　　　　　Cogeneration of electric power and heat

> Class interdisciplinary works on cogeneration of electricity and heat in 333.793

.2　　　　Hydraulic-power technology

> Class hydraulic control in 629.8042

.204　　　　　　Special topics

.204 2　　　　　　Specific liquids

.204 22　　　　　　Water

.204 24　　　　　　Hydraulic fluids

> Other than water

.21　　　　　　Water mills

> Including waterwheels

.24　　　　　　Turbines

.25　　　　　　Pumps and accumulators

.252　　　　　　Pumps

> Class comprehensive works on pumps in 621.69

.254　　　　　　Accumulators

.26　　　　　　Hydraulic transmission

> Class specific liquids in hydraulic transmission in 621.2042
>
> *For rams, see 621.27*

.27　　　　　　Rams

.3　　　　Electrical engineering; lighting; superconductivity; magnetic engineering; applied optics; paraphotic technology; electronics; communications engineering; computers

> Standard subdivisions are added for electromagnetic engineering, for combined electrical and electronic engineering, for electrical engineering alone
>
> *See also 537 for physics of electricity and electromagnetism*

SUMMARY

.302 84   Apparatus, equipment, materials

> Do not use for electrical equipment; class in 621.31042

.302 87   Testing and measurement

> Do not use for electrical testing and measurement; class in 621.37

.31   Generation, modification, storage, transmission of electric power

Class here alternating current

SUMMARY

.310 4   Special topics

.310 42   Electrical machinery and equipment

> Standard subdivisions are added for either or both topics in heading

> Including eddy currents, shaft currents

> Class a specific application with the application, e.g., refrigerators 621.57

> *For electric motors, see 621.46*

.312   Generation, modification, storage

> *For equipment for generation, modification, control, see 621.313–621.317*

.312 1   Generation

> Class here central and auxiliary power plants, mechanical generation

> *For direct energy conversion, see 621.3124*

.312 13	Specific kinds of mechanical generation
[.312 130 1–.312 130 9]	Standard subdivisions

           Do not use; class in 621.312101–621.312109

.312 132   Steam-powered generation

         Class here comprehensive works on generation from fossil fuels

           For generation by internal-combustion engines, see 621.312133; for nuclear steam-powered generation of electricity, see 621.483

.312 133   Generation by internal-combustion engines

.312 134   Hydroelectric generation

         Including tidal generation

         Class engineering of dams for hydroelectric power in 627.8

.312 136   Wind-powered generation

.312 4   Direct energy conversion

         For direct nuclear generation, see 621.3125

.312 42   Electrochemical energy conversion

         Class here batteries

         Class comprehensive works on electrochemical engineering in 660.297

           For solar batteries, see 621.31244

.312 423   Primary batteries

.312 424   Secondary batteries (Storage batteries)

.312 429   Fuel cells

.312 43   Thermoelectric generation

         Including thermionic converters

         Class generation of electricity from solar radiation in 621.31244

.312 44   Generation of electricity from solar radiation

         Class here photovoltaic generation, use of solar batteries and cells

.312 45   Magnetohydrodynamic generation

.312 5   Direct nuclear generation

.312 6   Modification and storage

         Including operation of transformer, converter substations

           For storage of electrical energy by chemical methods, see 621.312424

> 621.313–621.317 Machinery and equipment for generation, modification, control

Class comprehensive works in 621.31042

.313 Generating machinery and converters

Standard subdivisions are added for either or both topics in heading

Class here comprehensive works on generators and motors

For details and parts of generators, see 621.316; for electric motors, see 621.46

.313 2 Direct-current machinery

Including converters to alternating current, dynamos

.313 3 Alternating-current machinery

Class here synchronous machinery

For synchronous generators, see 621.3134; for synchronous converters to direct current, see 621.3135; for asynchronous machinery, see 621.3136

.313 4 Synchronous generators

.313 5 Synchronous converters to direct current

For rectifiers, see 621.3137

.313 6 Asynchronous machinery

For rectifiers, see 621.3137

.313 7 Rectifiers

.314 Transformers

.315 Capacitors (Condensers)

.316 Details and parts of generators

Including armatures, brushes, commutators, contactors, electromagnets

For a specific part not provided for here, see the part, e.g., transformers 621.314

.317 Control devices

Including circuit breakers, fuses, grounding devices, lightning arresters, relays, rheostats

Class here power electronics, switching equipment

Class switches at service end of line in 621.31924

.319	Transmission
	Including power failure
	Class here electrification
	Class interdisciplinary works on electrification, on power failure in 333.7932
	For electric power transmission for railroads, see 621.33
[.319 011]	Systems
	Do not use; class in 621.3191
.319 1	Systems
	Class circuitry and lines in 621.3192
.319 12	Direct-current systems
.319 13	Alternating-current systems
	Including high-tension systems
.319 15	Composite current systems
	Direct and alternating currents combined
.319 16	Polycyclic current systems
.319 2	Networks (Circuitry and lines)
.319 21	Physical phenomena in circuits
	Including heat losses in lines, transients
.319 22	Overhead lines
.319 23	Underground lines
.319 24	Apparatus at service end of line
	Including extension cords, outlets, sockets, switches
	Class here interior wiring
	For exterior service wiring and its components, see 621.31925
.319 25	Exterior service wiring
.319 3	Equipment and components
	Class equipment for generation, modification, control in 621.313–621.317; class use of equipment and components in lines and circuitry in 621.3192
[.319 32]	Uninsulated wires
	Relocated to 621.31933
.319 33	Wires
	Class here uninsulated wires [*formerly* 621.31932], insulated wires

.319 34	Cables
.319 37	Insulators and insulation

> Standard subdivisions are added for either or both topics in heading

.32   Lighting

Class here electric lighting

.321   Principles of lighting

.321 1	Layouts, calculations, photometry
.321 2	Direct lighting
.321 3	Indirect and semi-indirect lighting

> Standard subdivisions are added for either or both topics in heading

.321 4	Floodlighting

Class here directed lighting

Class exterior floodlighting in 621.3229

.322   Lighting in specific situations

Class here interior lighting

Class specific forms of lighting in 621.323–621.327

For public lighting, see 628.95; for lighting of airports, see 629.1365

.322 01–.322 09	Standard subdivisions for interior lighting

> Do not use for comprehensive works on lighting in specific situations; class in 621.3201–621.3209

.322 5–.322 8	Interior lighting

> Add to base number 621.322 the numbers following 72 in 725–728, e.g., lighting for libraries 621.32278

.322 9	Exterior lighting

Including advertising and display lighting, garden and patio lighting

---

> **621.323–621.327   Specific forms of lighting**

Class comprehensive works in 621.32

.323   Nonelectrical lighting

Including candles, oil-burning devices, torches

For gas lighting, see 621.324

.324   Gas lighting

>   621.325–621.327   Electric lighting

           Class comprehensive works in 621.32

.325   Arc lighting

           Electric-discharge lighting in which light is produced by consumable electrodes or by vapors emanating from consumable electrodes

.326   Incandescent lighting

.327   Vapor (Luminous-tube) lighting

.327 3   Fluorescent lighting

.327 4   Mercury-vapor lighting

.327 5   Neon lighting

.327 6   Sodium-vapor lighting

.33   Electric power transmission for railroads

.34   Magnetic engineering

           Class here artificial magnets, electromagnets

           Class electromagnets as parts of generators in 621.316; class electromagnets as parts of electric motors in 621.46; class comprehensive works on electromagnetic technology in 621.3

           See also 538 for physics of magnetism, 538.4 for natural magnets

.35   Superconductivity

           Class here superconductors

           Class superconductor circuits in 621.3815

.36   Applied optics and paraphotic technology

           Standard subdivisions are added for either or both topics in heading

           Class manufacture of optical instruments in 681.4; class interdisciplinary works on photography in 770

           For lighting, see 621.32

           See also 535 for optics and light as subjects in physics

           See Manual at 621.36 vs. 621.381045, 621.3827

.361   Spectroscopy

.361 2   Infrared spectroscopy

.361 3   Light spectroscopy

           Including Raman spectroscopy

.361 4	Ultraviolet spectroscopy
.361 5	Microwave and radiofrequency spectroscopy
.361 6	Gamma-ray and X-ray spectroscopy
.361 7	Magnetic resonance spectroscopy

> 621.362–621.364 Paraphotic technology

Class paraphotic spectroscopy in 621.361; class paraphotic photography in 621.3672; class comprehensive works in 621.36

.362	Infrared technology
.364	Ultraviolet technology
.366	Lasers

For laser communications, see 621.3827

.366 1	Solid-state lasers
.366 2	Fluid-state lasers

For gaseous-state lasers, see 621.3663

.366 3	Gaseous-state lasers
.366 4	Chemical and dye lasers
.367	Technological photography and photo-optics

Standard subdivisions are added for either or both topics in heading

Including spectrography, stroboscopic photography

Class here image processing, optical data processing

For photoelectrical and photoelectronic devices, see 621.381542; for optical communications, see 621.3827

See Manual at 006.37 vs. 006.42, 621.367, 621.391, 621.399; also at 778.3 vs. 621.367

.367 2	Infrared and ultraviolet photography
.367 3	Radiography (Gamma-ray and X-ray photography)
.367 5	Holography
.367 8	Remote sensing technology

For photogrammetry, see 526.982

.369	Other branches of applied optics
.369 2	Fiber optics

See also 621.381045 for optoelectronics

.369 3	Integrated optics
.369 4	Nonlinear optics
.37	Testing and measurement of electrical quantities

Instruments and their use

For testing and measurement of a specific apparatus, part, or function, see the apparatus, part, or function, plus notation 0287 from Table 1, e.g., testing overhead lines 621.319220287

.372	Units and standards of measurement

Including calibration of electrical instruments

.373	Recording meters

Class meters recording specific electrical quantities in 621.374

.374	Instruments for measuring specific electrical quantities
[.374 01–.374 09]	Standard subdivisions

Do not use; class in 621.3701–621.3709

.374 2	Instruments for measuring capacitance, inductance, resistance

Including bridges, ohmmeters, resistance boxes, shunts; comprehensive works on electrical bridges (bridge circuits)

For frequency bridges, see 621.3747

.374 3	Instruments for measuring potential

Including electrometers, potentiometers, voltage detectors, voltmeters

.374 4	Instruments for measuring current

Including ammeters, ampere-hour meters, coulometers, galvanometers, milliammeters, voltameters

.374 5	Instruments for measuring energy

Including electric supply meters, watt-hour meters

.374 6	Instruments for measuring power

Including electrodynamometers, volt-ammeters, wattmeters

.374 7	Instruments for measuring frequency

Including frequency bridges, oscillographs

Class electric phasemeters in 621.3749

.374 9	Instruments for measuring phase

Including power-factor meters, synchroscopes

.38	Electronics, communications engineering

SUMMARY

621.381	**Electronics**
.382	**Communications engineering**
.383	**Telegraphy**
.384	**Radio and radar**
.385	**Telephony**
.386	**Telephone terminal equipment**
.387	**Telephone transmission and nonterminal equipment**
.388	**Television**
.389	**Security, sound recording, related systems**

.381   Electronics

Class here microelectronics

Class signal processing in 621.3822; class electronic noise and interference in 621.38224. Class a specific application of electronics with the application, e.g., laser technology 621.366, radio engineering 621.384

See also 537.5 for physics of electronics

SUMMARY

621.381 04	**Special topics**
.381 3	**Microwave electronics**
.381 5	**Components and circuits**

.381 04   Special topics

.381 044   Power and energy in electronic systems

.381 045   Optoelectronics

See also 621.3692 for fiber optics

See Manual at 621.36 vs. 621.381045, 621.3827

.381 046   Packaging

.381 3   Microwave electronics

.381 31   Wave propagation and transmission

Including interference

.381 32   Circuits

Add to base number 621.38132 the numbers following 621.38153 in 621.381532–621.381537, e.g., amplifiers 621.381325

.381 33   Components and devices

Standard subdivisions are added for either or both topics in heading

Class use of components in specific circuits in 621.38132

.381 331   Wave guides

.381 332	Cavity resonators
.381 333	Klystrons
.381 334	Magnetrons
.381 335	Traveling-wave tubes
.381 336	Masers
.381 5	Components and circuits

Standard subdivisions are added for either or both topics in heading

Class here analog, digital, integrated, microelectronic, semiconductor, superconductor, thin-film circuits; circuits and components common to electronics and communications engineering

Class microwave components and circuits in 621.3813; class components and circuits of a specific branch of communications engineering in 621.383–621.389; class very large scale integration in 621.395

[.381 502 87]   Testing and measurement

Do not use; class in 621.381548

> 621.381 51–621.381 52 Components

Class use of components in specific circuits in 621.38153; class devices not intrinsic to circuits in 621.38154; class comprehensive works in 621.3815

.381 51	Electronic tubes
.381 512	Vacuum tubes
.381 513	Gas tubes
.381 52	Semiconductors

Class here crystal devices, miniaturization, optoelectronic devices, thin-film technology

.381 522   Diodes

Including junction, light-emitting, tunnel (Esaki), Zener diodes; varactors

.381 528   Transistors and thyristors

Standard subdivisions are added for transistors and thyristors together, for transistors alone

Including phototransistors

Class here bipolar transistors

.381 528 2	Junction transistors
.381 528 4	Field-effect transistors

.381 528 7	Thyristors
.381 53	Printed circuits and circuits for specific functions
.381 531	Printed circuits
	Including microlithography

>   621.381 532–621.381 537 Circuits for specific functions

Class comprehensive works in 621.3815

.381 532	Converters (Rectifiers and inverters), filters, interference eliminators
.381 532 2	Converters (Rectifiers and inverters)
.381 532 4	Filters
.381 533	Oscillators
	Class use of oscillators in pulse circuits in 621.381534
.381 534	Pulse circuits
	Including counting circuits, pulse generators and processes
	Class modulation and demodulation (detection) of pulses in 621.3815365
.381 535	Amplifiers and feedback circuits
	Standard subdivisions are added for amplifiers and feedback circuits together, for amplifiers alone
	Class operational amplifiers in 621.395
.381 536	Modulators and demodulators (detectors)
	Class here modulation, demodulation (detection)
.381 536 2	Amplitude
	Including attenuators
.381 536 3	Frequency
	See also 621.3815486 for frequency synthesizers
.381 536 4	Phase
	Including phase-locked loops
.381 536 5	Pulse
.381 537	Switching, control, trigger circuits, relays
.381 537 2	Switching theory
	Class switching theory in logic circuit design in 621.395

.381 54	Supplementary components
	Devices not intrinsic to circuits
	Class here electronic instrumentation (applications of electronics)
	Class instrumentation in a specific field with the field, e.g., electronic control 629.89
.381 542	Photoelectric and photoelectronic devices
	Including electron-ray tubes; electric eyes; photoconductive, photoemissive, photovoltaic cells; photomultipliers; phototubes
	See also 621.367 for image processing, 621.381045 for optoelectronics
.381 542 2	Video display devices
	Including liquid crystal displays
.381 548	Testing and measuring components
	Including bridges (bridge circuits); signal, square-wave, sweep generators; thermistors
	Class here testing and measuring electronic circuits and components, instruments for testing and measuring electronic signals
	Class testing and measuring a specific circuit or component with the circuit or component, plus notation 0287 from Table 1, e.g., testing amplifiers 621.3815350287
.381 548 3	Oscilloscopes
	Including oscillographs
.381 548 6	Frequency synthesizers
.381 59	Analog-to-digital and digital-to-analog converters
	Standard subdivisions are added for either or both topics in heading
	Class analog-to-digital and digital-to-analog converters in data communications engineering in 621.39814

.382	Communications engineering

Class here analog, digital, electronic communications; telecommunications; comprehensive works on digital data and telecommunications engineering

Unless other instructions are given, class a subject with aspects in two or more subdivisions of 621.382 in the number coming last, e.g., signal processing in acoustical communications 621.3828 (*not* 621.3822)

Class a component or circuit common to electronics and communications engineering with the component or circuit in 621.3815, e.g., amplifiers 621.381535, switching circuits 621.381537

> *For specific communications systems, see 621.383–621.389; for data communications engineering, see 621.3981*

> *See Manual at 004.6 vs. 621.382, 621.3981*

[.382 028 546 2]	Communications networks protocols (standards)

Do not use; class in 621.38212

[.382 028 546 5]	Communications network architecture

Do not use; class in 621.38215

[.382 028 546 6]	Data transmission modes and data switching methods

Do not use; class in 621.38216

.382 1	Communications networks

> *For communications networks based on a specific technology, see the technology, e.g., telephone networks 621.385*

.382 12	Communications networks protocols (standards)
[.382 120 218]	Standards

Do not use; class in 621.38212

.382 15	Communications network architecture

Class here systems analysis, design, topology (configuration) of communications networks

.382 16	Data transmission modes and data switching methods

Including circuit and packet switching, multiplexing, asynchronous and synchronous transfer modes

.382 2	Signal processing

Class here information theory

Class interdisciplinary works on information theory in 003.54

.382 23	Signal analysis and theory

Standard subdivisions are added for either or both topics in heading

.382 24	Interference and noise
	Standard subdivisions are added for either or both topics in heading
	Class here electronic interference and noise
.382 3	Miscellaneous topics
	Limited to studios, transmission facilities, and the topics provided for below
.382 32	Power supply in communications systems
.382 34	Recording devices
	Use for works covering recording devices of two or more communications systems, e.g. video recorders and sound recorders
	Including discs, tapes
	Class video recorders in 621.38833; class sound recorders in 621.38932
.382 35	Facsimile transmission
	By wire or radio wave
	Class here telefacsimile
.382 38	Space communications
	See also 621.3825 for satellite relay
.382 4	Antennas and propagation
.382 5	Relay communication
	Class here satellite relay
.382 54	Satellite antennas and propagation
.382 7	Optical communications
	Transmission of sound, visual images, other information by light
	Including optical disc technology
	Class here laser communications
	Class optoacoustic communications in 621.3828
	See Manual at 621.36 vs. 621.381045, 621.3827
.382 75	Optical-fiber communication
	Class here guided-light communication

.382 8   Acoustical communications

                            Audio systems covering broadcasting and transmission as well as
                            recording and reproduction of sound

                            Including acousto-optical communications

                            Class here electroacoustical communications

                            Class audio systems limited to recording and reproduction of sound
                            in 621.3893

.382 84   Specific devices

                                Including microphones, speakers

                                Class antennas in 621.3824

> 　　　　　　621.383–621.389 Specific communications systems

                            Class comprehensive works in 621.382

.383   Telegraphy

                                For radiotelegraphy, see 621.3842

.384   Radio and radar

                            Standard subdivisions are added for radio and radar together, for radio
                            alone

                            Class here broadcasting stations, comprehensive engineering works on
                            radio and television

                            Class interdisciplinary works on radio and television in 384.5; class
                            interdisciplinary works on broadcasting stations in 384.5453

                                For television, see 621.388

.384 028 8   Maintenance and repair

                                    Class maintenance and repair of receiving sets in
                                    621.384187

> 　　　　　　621.384 1–621.384 5 Radio

                            Class comprehensive works in 621.384

.384 1   Specific topics in general radio

[.384 101–.384 109]   Standard subdivision

                                Do not use; class in 621.38401–621.38409

.384 11   Wave propagation and transmission

                            Including interference

                                See also 384.54524 for allocation of frequencies

.384 12	Circuits
	Including amplifiers, filters, interference eliminators, modulation circuits, oscillators, rectifiers
	Class a specific application of circuits with the application, e.g., receiving set circuits 621.38418
.384 13	Components and devices
	Standard subdivisions are added for either or both topics in heading
.384 131	Transmitters
.384 132	Tubes
	Class use of tubes in specific circuits in 621.38412
.384 133	Miscellaneous supplementary devices
	Limited to condensers (capacitors), grounding devices, inductors, microphones, resistors, testing equipment
.384 134	Semiconductor devices
	Class use of semiconductor devices in specific circuits in 621.38412
.384 135	Antennas
.384 15	Systems by wave type, satellite and relay systems
	Standard subdivisions are added for systems by wave type, satellite and relay systems together; for systems by wave type alone

---

>   621.384 151–621.384 153   Systems by wave type

Class relay and satellite systems of a specific wave type in 621.384156; class comprehensive works in 621.38415

.384 151	Shortwave systems
	Including ultrahigh frequency (UHF), very-high-frequency (VHF) systems
	For frequency-modulation systems, see 621.384152
.384 152	Frequency-modulation (FM) systems
.384 153	Long-wave systems
	Including amplitude modulation (AM), single-sideband, very-low-frequency (VLF) systems
.384 156	Relay and satellite systems

.384 16	Amateur (Ham) radio

Class here comprehensive works on amateur and citizens band radio

For citizens band radio, see 621.38454

See Manual at 621.38416 vs. 621.38454

.384 18	Radio receiving sets
[.384 180 288]	Maintenance and repair

Do not use; class in 621.384187

.384 187	Maintenance and repair
.384 19	Special developments
.384 191	Direction and position finding

Standard subdivisions are added for either or both topics in heading

Including loran, radio beacons, radio compasses

.384 196	Radio control

Variant names: remote control, telecontrol

.384 197	Space communication
.384 2	Radiotelegraphy
.384 5	Radiotelephony

Including portable radios, walkie-talkies

Class here mobile radio stations, comprehensive works on radio transmission in telephony

For radio relays, see 621.38782

See Manual at 621.3845 vs. 621.38782

.384 54	Citizens band radio

Class comprehensive works on amateur and citizens band radio in 621.38416

See Manual at 621.38416 vs. 621.38454

.384 56	Cellular telephone systems

Variant names: cellular radio, portable telephone systems

.384 8	Radar
.384 83	Specific instruments and devices

Including antennas

.384 85	Systems

Including continuous, monopulse, pulse-modulated systems

[.384 86–.384 88]	Stations and scanning patterns
	Numbers discontinued; class in 621.3848
.384 89	Special developments
.384 892	Racon
.384 893	Shoran
.385	Telephony

> Class here telephone systems based on wires, cables, lasers, optical fibers

> Class cellular telephone systems in 621.38456; class data communications engineering in 621.3981

> *For radiotelephony, see 621.3845; for telephone equipment and transmission, see 621.386–621.387*

.385 1	Network analysis
.385 7	Automatic and semiautomatic switching systems
	Including direct distance dialing

> 621.386–621.387 Telephone equipment and transmission

Class comprehensive works in 621.385

.386	Telephone terminal equipment
	Dialing, transmitting, receiving equipment
.386 7	Telephone answering and message recording devices
.386 9	Pay telephones
.387	Telephone transmission and nonterminal equipment
	Including switches
.387 8	Transmission
.387 82	Long-distance systems
	Including radio relays
	See Manual at 621.3845 vs. 621.38782
.387 83	Local systems
.387 84	Transmission lines and cables
.388	Television
.388 001	Philosophy and theory
.388 002	Miscellany

.388 002 88	Maintenance and repair
	Do not use for maintenance and repair of receiving sets; class in 621.38887
	Maintenance and repair covering broadcast and transmission equipment as well as receiving sets
.388 003–.388 009	Standard subdivisions
.388 02	Black-and-white television
.388 04	Color television
.388 1	Wave propagation and transmission
	Including interference
.388 3	Components and devices
	Standard subdivisions are added for either or both topics in heading
.388 31	Transmitters
.388 32	Semiconductors, transistors, tubes
.388 33	Video recorders and video recordings
	Standard subdivisions are added for video recorders and video recordings together, for video recorders alone
[.388 330 288]	Maintenance and repair
	Do not use; class in 621.388337
.388 332	Video recordings
	Including cassettes, discs
[.388 332 028 8]	Maintenance and repair
	Do not use; class in 621.388337
.388 337	Maintenance and repair of video recorders and video recordings
.388 34	Cameras and components
.388 35	Antennas
.388 5	Communication systems
.388 53	Satellite television
.388 57	Cable television
.388 6	Stations
[.388 62–.388 64]	Specific kinds of stations
	Numbers discontinued; class in 621.3886
.388 8	Television sets

[.388 802 88]	Maintenance and repair
	Do not use; class in 621.38887
.388 87	Maintenance and repair
.389	**Security, sound recording, related systems**
.389 2	Public address, security, related systems
	Including paging systems, sirens
.389 28	Security electronics
	Including surveillance systems, e.g., electronic eavesdropping devices
	Class here alarm systems
.389 3	Sound recording and reproducing systems
	Audio systems limited to recording and reproduction of sound
	Class comprehensive works on acoustical communications, on audio systems covering transmission as well as recording and reproduction in 621.3828; class telephone message recording in 621.3867
.389 32	Recorders and recordings
	Including compact discs
.389 324	Tape recorders and recordings
	Including cassettes
.389 33	Reproducers
	Including jukeboxes
	Class here phonographs
	Class combination recorders-reproducers in 621.38932
.389 332	High-fidelity systems (Hi-fi)
	For stereophonic systems, see 621.389334
.389 334	Stereophonic systems
	Including quadraphonic systems
.389 4	Language translators
.389 5	Sonar
.389 7	Audiovisual engineering

.39 Computer engineering

Class here electronic digital computers, central processing units, computer reliability, general computer performance evaluation

Unless other instructions are given, class a subject with aspects in two or more subdivisions of 621.39 in the number coming last, e.g., circuitry of computer internal storage 621.3973 (*not* 621.395)

Class selection and use of computer hardware, works treating both hardware and either programming or programs in 004. Class a specific application of computers with the application, e.g., use of computers to regulate processes automatically 629.895

See Manual at 004–006 vs. 621.39

[.390 287] Testing and measurement

Do not use; class in 621.392

.391 General works on specific types of computers

Including optical computers

Class here specific types of processors, e.g., multiprocessors

Class programmable calculators in 681.14

See Manual at 006.37 vs. 006.42, 621.367, 621.391, 621.399

> 621.391 1–621.391 6 Digital computers

Class comprehensive works in 621.39

See Manual at 004.11–004.16

.391 1 Digital supercomputers

.391 2 Digital mainframe computers

For digital supercomputers, see 621.3911

.391 4 Digital minicomputers

Class comprehensive works on digital minicomputers and microcomputers in 621.3916

.391 6 Digital microcomputers

Class here personal computers, comprehensive works on minicomputers and microcomputers

For minicomputers, see 621.3914

.391 9 Analog and hybrid computers

.392 Systems analysis and design, computer architecture

Including hardware description languages

See Manual at 004.21 vs. 004.22, 621.392

.395 Circuitry

Class here logic circuits, logic design of circuits, very large scale integration (VLSI)

.397 Storage

.397 3 Internal storage (Main memory)

Including magnetic-core memory

Class here random-access memory (RAM), read-only memory (ROM)

Class compact disc read-only memory (CD-ROM) in 621.3976

.397 32 Semiconductor memory

Class here bipolar, metal-oxide-semiconductor (MOS), thin-film memory

.397 6 External (Auxiliary) storage

Including floppy and hard disks; compact disc read-only memory (CD-ROM); magnetic tapes (cartridges, cassettes, reel-to-reel tapes), disk and tape drives

.397 63 Magnetic bubble memory

.397 67 Optical storage devices

Class storage of pictorial data in optical storage devices in 621.367

.398 Interfacing and communications devices, peripherals

.398 1 Interfacing and communications devices

Class here data communications engineering

See Manual at 004.6; also at 004.6 vs. 621.382, 621.3981

.398 14 Analog-to-digital and digital-to-analog converters

Standard subdivisions are added for either or both topics in heading

Including modems

.398 4 Peripherals

Class peripheral storage in 621.3976

For peripherals combining input and output functions, see 621.3985; for input peripherals, see 621.3986; for output peripherals, see 621.3987

.398 5 Peripherals combining input and output functions

Class here computer terminals

Class tape and disk devices in 621.3976

.398 6   Input peripherals

         Including card readers, keyboards

.398 7   Output peripherals

         Including monitors (video display screens)

         See also 621.399 for computer graphics

.399   Devices for special computer methods

         Including devices for computer graphics, pattern recognition

         See Manual at 006.37 vs. 006.42, 621.367, 621.391, 621.399

.4   **Heat engineering and prime movers**

         Class here engines, power plants, propulsion systems

         For steam engineering, see 621.1; for hydraulic-power technology, see 621.2

SUMMARY

621.400 1–.400 9	**Standard subdivisions**	
.402–.406	**[Heat engineering and turbines]**	
.42	**Stirling engines and air motors**	
.43	**Internal-combustion engines**	
.44	**Geothermal engineering**	
.45	**Wind engines**	
.46	**Electric and related motors**	
.47	**Solar-energy engineering**	
.48	**Nuclear engineering**	

.400 1–.400 9   Standard subdivisions

.402   Heat engineering

         Class a kind of heat engineering with the kind, e.g., geothermal engineering 621.44, heating buildings 697

         For low-temperature technology, see 621.56

         See also 536 for physics of heat

.402 1   Thermodynamics

.402 2   Heat transfer

         Including conduction, convection, heat exchange, radiation

.402 3   Fuels and combustion

         Class pollution by-products of combustion in 628.532

.402 4   Insulation

.402 5   Equipment

         Including furnaces, heat engines, heat exchangers, heat pumps

         Class solar furnaces in 621.477

.402 8   Specific heat systems

Not provided for elsewhere

Including distribution and storage systems; electric heating

Class a specific aspect of a specific heat system with the aspect, e.g., heat transfer in electric heating 621.4022

.406   Turbines

Class here turbomachines

.42   Stirling engines and air motors

For wind engines, see 621.45

.43   Internal-combustion engines

Class generation of electricity by internal-combustion engines in 621.312133

See Manual at 629.046 vs. 621.43

> 621.433–621.436   Specific internal-combustion engines

Class parts and accessories of specific engines in 621.437; class comprehensive works in 621.43

.433   Gas turbines and free-piston engines

Standard subdivisions are added for gas turbines and free-piston engines, for gas turbines alone

For turbojet engines, see 621.4352

.433 5   Free-piston engines

.434   Spark-ignition engines

Nondiesel piston engines

Including rotary spark-ignition engines

Class here reciprocating spark-ignition engines

.435   Jet and rocket engines

.435 2   Jet engines

Including turbojet engines

.435 6   Rocket engines

Class here interdisciplinary works on rocketry

For a specific aspect of rocketry, see the aspect, e.g., rocket weapons 623.4519, booster rockets 629.475

.436	Diesel and semidiesel engines
	Standard subdivisions are added for either or both topics in heading
	Class here compression-ignition engines
[.436 028 8]	Maintenance and repair
	Do not use; class in 621.4368
.436 1	General topics of diesel and semidiesel engines
	Including combustion
.436 2	Design and construction
.436 8	Operation, maintenance, repair
.437	Parts and accessories of internal-combustion engines
	Including carburetors, connecting rods, cylinders, governors, ignition devices, pistons, valves
.44	Geothermal engineering
	Including prospecting for sources of geothermal energy, utilization of differences in ocean temperature
.45	Wind engines
	Class wind-powered generation of electricity in 621.312136
.453	Windmills
.46	Electric and related motors
	Standard subdivisions are added for electric and related motors together, electric motors alone
.465	Ion motors
.466	Plasma motors
.47	Solar-energy engineering
	Class engineering of secondary sources of solar energy with the secondary source, e.g., generation of electricity from solar radiation 621.31244, wind energy 621.45
.471	General topics of solar-energy engineering
.471 2	Heat storage
.472	Solar collectors
.473	Solar engines
.477	Solar furnaces

.48　　　　　　Nuclear engineering

　　　　　　　　Fission and fusion technology

　　　　　　　　Class direct nuclear generation of electricity in 621.3125

　　　　　　　　See also 539.7 for nuclear physics

.483　　　　　Nuclear reactors, power plants, by-products

　　　　　　　　Standard subdivisions are added for nuclear reactors, power plants, by-products together; for nuclear reactors alone; for nuclear power plants alone

　　　　　　　　Class here fission reactors, nuclear steam-powered generation of electricity; comprehensive works on fission and fusion reactor, power plants, by-products

　　　　　　　　For fusion reactors, power plants, by-products, see 621.484

.483 015 3　　　　　Physical principles

　　　　　　　　　　Do not use for reactor physics; class in 621.4831

[.483 028 9]　　　　Safety measures

　　　　　　　　　　Do not use; class in 621.4835

.483 1　　　　Reactor physics

　　　　　　　　Including critical size

　　　　　　　　Class here physics of reactor cores

　　　　　　　　Class physics of a specific component, material, process with the component, material, or process, plus notation 0153 from Table 1, e.g., nuclear reactions in fuel elements 621.483350153976

.483 2　　　　Design, construction, shielding, siting

.483 23　　　Shielding

.483 3　　　　Materials

.483 32　　　Structural materials

.483 35　　　Fuel element materials

　　　　　　　　Fuels and cladding

.483 36　　　Coolants

.483 37　　　Moderators

.483 4　　　　Specific types of reactors

　　　　　　　　Classified by neutron energy, moderator, fuel and fuel conversion, coolant

　　　　　　　　Including breeder reactors

　　　　　　　　Class a specific aspect of a specific type with the aspect, e.g., shielding of fast reactors 621.48323

.483 5	Operation, control, safety measures

        See Manual at 363.1065 vs. 620.86: Accident investigation

.483 7	Radioactive isotopes

        Class here comprehensive technological works on radioisotopes

        For a specific application of radioisotopes, see the application, e.g., radioactive isotope therapy 615.8424

.483 8	Waste technology
.484	Fusion (Thermonuclear) reactors, power plants, by-products

        Standard subdivisions are added for fusion reactors, power plants, by-products together; for fusion reactors alone; for fusion power plants alone

        Including tokamaks

        Class comprehensive works on fission and fusion reactor, power plants, by-products in 621.483

.485	Nuclear propulsion
.5	**Pneumatic, vacuum, low-temperature technologies**
.51	Pneumatic technology

        Class here air compression technology, air compressors

        For compressed-air transmission, see 621.53; for pneumatic conveying and cleaning, see 621.54; for blowers, fans, pumps, see 621.6; for pneumatic control, see 629.8045

.53	Compressed-air transmission
.54	Pneumatic conveying and cleaning

        Including carriers, cleaners, sandblasters

.55	Vacuum technology

        Including vacuum pumps

        See also 533.5 for vacuum physics

.56	Low-temperature technology

        Class here refrigeration

        For freezers and refrigerators, see 621.57; for ice manufacture, see 621.58; for cryogenic technology, see 621.59

        See also 536.56 for physics of low temperatures

.563	Heat pumps
.564	Refrigerants

.57	Freezers and refrigerators
.58	Ice manufacture
.59	Cryogenic technology

Including liquefaction and solidification of gases having low boiling points

.6   Blowers, fans, pumps

.61   Blowers and fans

Standard subdivisions are added for either or both topics in heading

For rotary blowers and fans, see 621.62; for centrifugal blowers and fans, see 621.63

.62   Rotary blowers and fans

Standard subdivisions are added for either or both topics in heading

.63   Centrifugal blowers and fans

Standard subdivisions are added for either or both topics in heading

---

> 621.64–621.69   Pumps

Class hydraulic pumps in 621.252; class comprehensive works in 621.69

.64   Hand pumps

.65   Reciprocating pumps

.66   Rotary pumps

.67   Centrifugal pumps

.69   Pumps   Pneumatic pumps

For hydraulic pumps, see 621.252; for hand pumps, see 621.64; for reciprocating pumps, see 621.65; for rotary pumps, see 621.66; for centrifugal pumps, see 621.67

.691   Jet pumps

.699   Density and direct-fluid-pressure displacement pumps

.8   Machine engineering

Class a specific kind of machinery not provided for here with the kind, e.g., hydraulic machinery 621.2; class a specific use of machinery with the use, e.g., gears in clocks 681.112

[.801 53]   Physical principles

Do not use; class in 621.811

.802 87   Testing and measuring

Class here strength tests of mechanisms

[.802 88]		Maintenance and repair
		Do not use; class in 621.816
.81		General topics of machine engineering
.811		Physical principles
		Including vibration
.812		Power and speed control devices
.815		Machine design
.816		Maintenance and repair
		Including balancing
.82		Machine parts
		For gears, ratchets, cams, see 621.83; for valves, pistons, see 621.84
.821		Journals
.822		Bearings
		Including ball, roller, sliding bearings
		Class journals in 621.821
.823		Shafts
		Including axles
		Class bearings in 621.822
		For journals, see 621.821
.824		Springs
.825		Clutches, couplings, universal joints
.827		Connecting rods, cranks, eccentrics
.83		Gears, ratchets, cams
.833		Gears
		Class here gearing
.833 1		Spur gears
.833 2		Bevel and skew bevel gears
.833 3		Spiral and worm gears
.837		Ratchets
		Including ratchet wheels
.838		Cams

.84   Valves and pistons

         Standard subdivisions are added for valves and pistons, for valves alone

         Variant names for valves: cocks, faucets, taps

.85   Power transmission systems

         Class power transmission systems for materials-handling equipment in 621.86. Class a specific machine part of a transmission system with the part, e.g., shafts 621.823

.852   Power transmission by belt

.853   Power transmission by rope

.854   Power transmission by wire

.859   Power transmission by chain

.86   Materials-handling equipment

         For derricks, cranes, elevators, see 621.87

.862   Hoisting equipment

         For specific kinds of hoisting equipment, see 621.863–621.865

\>   621.863–621.865   Specific kinds of hoisting equipment

         Class comprehensive works in 621.862

.863   Chain hoists, fork lifts, tackles

.864   Capstans, winches, windlasses

.865   Power shovels

.867   Conveying equipment

         For telpherage, see 621.868

.867 2   Pipes

         Including pipe laying

         Class here pipelines

         Class coal pipelines in 662.624; class petroleum pipelines in 665.544; class industrial gases pipelines in 665.744. Class manufacturing pipes of a specific material with the material, e.g., metal pipes 671.832

.867 5   Belt conveyors

.867 6   Escalators

.868   Telpherage

> Including chair lifts, ski tows

> Class here comprehensive works on people movers

>> *For escalators, see 621.8676; for elevators, see 621.877*

.87   Derricks, cranes, elevators

.872   Derricks

> Class cranes in 621.873

.873   Cranes

.877   Elevators

> Including jacks

.88   Fasteners

> *See also 621.97 for fastening equipment*

.882   Bolts, nuts, screws

.883   Cotters

.884   Nails and rivets

.885   Sealing devices

.89   Tribology

> Including lubrication, lubricants, wear

> Class here friction

>> *For bearings, see 621.822*

.9   Tools

> Class here fabricating equipment

> Class a specific use with the use, e.g., lathes in woodworking 684.08

.900 1–.900 9   Standard subdivisions

.902   Machine tools

.902 3   Numerical control

.904   Pneumatic tools

.908   Hand tools

.91   .   Planing and milling tools

> *See also 671.35 for machining metal*

.912   Planers, shapers, slotters

.914	Crushing tools
.92	Abrading and grinding tools

Standard subdivisions are added for either or both topics in heading

.922	Lapping tools

Including buffing, polishing tools

.923	Emery wheels and grindstones
.924	Filing tools
.93	Cutting, disassembling, sawing tools

Including axes, crowbars, saws, shears, slicers, trimmers

.932	Knives
.94	Turning tools

Class turning tools used for perforating in 621.95

.942	Lathes
.944	Gear-cutting, pipe-threading, screw-cutting tools

For tapping tools, see 621.955

.95	Perforating and tapping tools

Standard subdivisions are added for perforating and tapping tools together, for perforating tools alone

For punching tools, see 621.96

.952	Drilling tools

Class here boring tools

.954	Broaching and reaming tools
.955	Tapping tools

See also 621.84 for taps (valves)

.96	Punching tools

Class die punches in 621.984

.97	Fastening and joining equipment

Standard subdivisions are added for either or both topics in heading

Class fasteners in 621.88

.972	Screwdrivers and wrenches
.973	Hand hammers
.974	Power hammers

.977	Soldering and welding equipment
.978	Riveting equipment
.98	Pressing, impressing, molding equipment

Standard subdivisions are added for pressing, impressing, molding equipment together; for pressing equipment alone

.982	Bending tools
.983	Straightening tools
.984	Impressing and molding equipment

Including dies, molds, stamps

.99	Other tools and equipment
.992	Guiding, holding, safety equipment

Including chucks, clamps, guards, jigs, shields, vises

622 Mining and related operations

Standard subdivisions are added for mining and related operations together, for mining alone

SUMMARY

622.1	Prospecting
.2	Excavation techniques
.3	Mining for specific materials
.4	Mine environment
.5	Mine drainage
.6	Mine transport systems
.7	Ore dressing
.8	Mine health and safety

[.028 9]	Safety measures

Do not use; class in 622.8

.1 Prospecting

Class here exploratory operations

> 622.12–622.17 General topics of prospecting

Class general topics of prospecting applied to specific materials in 622.18; class general topics of prospecting applied to treasure in 622.19; class comprehensive works in 622.1

.12	Surface exploration

Including biogeochemical, geobotanical, geological prospecting

.13	Geochemical prospecting

> Including mineral surveys (qualitative and quantitative measurement of mineral content)
>
> Class biogeochemical prospecting in 622.12

.14	Mine surveys

> Determination of size, depth, shape of mines

.15	Geophysical prospecting
.152	Gravitational prospecting
.153	Magnetic prospecting
.154	Electrical prospecting
.159	Other methods of prospecting

> Including gas-detection, geothermal, radioactivity prospecting

.159 2	Seismic prospecting

> Variant name: acoustical, vibration prospecting

.17	Underwater prospecting
.18	Prospecting for specific materials

> Add to base number 622.18 the numbers following 553 in 553.2–553.9, e.g., prospecting for petroleum 622.1828; however, for prospecting for water, see 628.11
>> Standard subdivisions are added for specific materials even if only one type of prospecting is used, e.g., seismic exploration for petroleum in Texas 622.182809764

.19	Prospecting for treasure

> Underground and underwater
>
> Class here treasure hunting
>
> Class archaeological methods and equipment in 930.1028

.2	**Excavation techniques**

> Class here underground (subsurface) mining
>
> Class extraction techniques for specific materials in 622.3
>
> *See also 622.4–622.8 for nonextractive mining technologies*

.202 89	Safety measures [*formerly* 622.8]

> 622.22–622.29 Specific excavation techniques

Class here safety measures for a specific excavation technique [*formerly* 622.8]

Class comprehensive works in 622.2

> 622.22–622.28 Underground mining

Class comprehensive works in 622.2

.22 In-situ processing

Class here leach mining wells, solution mining

See Manual at 622.22, 622.7 vs. 662.6, 669

.23 Underground blasting and drilling

.24 Underground boring

.25 Shaft sinking

Class here shafts

.26 Tunneling

Class here tunnels

.28 Supporting structures

Class here control of roof and wall failure (rock failure)

.29 Surface and underwater mining

.292 Surface mining

Class here open-pit and strip mining

Class reclamation after surface mining in 631.64

.292 7 Alluvial mining

Including hydraulic and placer mining

.295 Underwater mining

Class here off-shore mining, mineral extraction from ocean floor

.3 ***Mining for specific materials**

Class here extraction techniques of specific materials

Class prospecting for specific materials in 622.18. Class a nonextractive mining technology relating to specific materials with the technology in 622.4–622.8, e.g., ore dressing 622.7

For surface mining of specific materials, see 622.292

*Do not use notation 0289 from Table 1 for safety measures; class in 622.8

.33   *Carbonaceous materials

.331–.337   Coal, graphite, solid and semisolid bitumens

> Add to base number 622.33 the numbers following 553.2 in 553.21–553.27, e.g., coal 622.334; however, for safety measures, see 622.8

.338   *Oil, oil shales, tar sands, natural gas

> Use 622.338 for extraction of petroleum in the broad sense covering oil and gas, 622.3382 for petroleum in the narrow sense limited to oil

> Class comprehensive technical works on petroleum in 665.5; class interdisciplinary works on petroleum in 553.28

.338 1   *Drilling techniques

> Including use of drilling muds (drilling fluids)

.338 19   *Offshore drilling

> Class here comprehensive works on offshore petroleum extraction

> *For a specific aspect of offshore petroleum extraction, see the aspect, e.g., offshore enhanced oil recovery 622.3382*

.338 2   *Oil

> Including well blowouts

> Class here reservoir engineering; enhanced, secondary, tertiary recovery; well flooding

> Class techniques of drilling for oil in 622.3381

.338 27   *Specific enhanced oil recovery methods

> Including enhanced recovery by use of bacteria

.338 3   *Oil shale and tar sands

> Variant names for oil shale: bituminous and black shale; for tar sands: bituminous and oil sands

> Class extraction of oils from oil shale and tar sands in 665.4

.338 5   *Natural gas

> Class techniques of drilling for natural gas in 622.3381

.339   *Fossil resins and gums

> Standard subdivisions are added for fossil resins and gums together, for fossil resins alone

.34   *Metals

> Class here the ore of the metal

.341   *Iron

---

*Do not use notation 0289 from Table 1 for safety measures; class in 622.8

> 622.342–622.349 Nonferrous metals

Class comprehensive works in 622.34

.342 *Precious metals

.342 2 *Gold

.342 3 *Silver

.342 4 *Platinum

.343–.349 Other nonferrous metals

Add to base number 622.34 the numbers following 553.4 in 553.43–553.49, e.g., uranium ores 622.34932; however, for safety measures, see 622.8

.35–.39 Other materials

Add to base number 622.3 the numbers following 553 in 553.5–553.9, e.g., gem diamonds 622.382; however, for safety measures, see 622.8; for water, see 628.114

> **622.4–622.8 Nonextractive mining technologies**

Class here nonextractive mining technologies relating to specific materials

Class comprehensive works in 622

.4 Mine environment

For mine drainage, see 622.5; for mine health and safety, see 622.8

.42 Ventilation and air conditioning

For temperature control, see 622.43

.43 Temperature control

.47 Illumination

.473 Portable lamps

.474 Electric lighting systems

.48 Electricity

Class electricity applied to a specific operation with the operation, e.g., temperature control 622.43

.49 Sanitation

.5 Mine drainage

*Do not use notation 0289 from Table 1 for safety measures; class in 622.8

.6	**Mine transport systems**
	Haulage and hoisting
.65	Hand and animal haulage
.66	Mechanical haulage
	Including mine railroads
	Class vertical haulage in 622.68
.67	Direct-driven and gear-driven hoists
.68	Elevators
	Including skips
.69	Surface transportation
	Including loading, unloading, transshipment
.7	**Ore dressing**
	Class here dressing of specific mineral ores
	See Manual at 622.22, 622.7 vs. 662.6, 669
.73	Crushing and grinding
.74	Sizing
	Including screening

> 622.75–622.77 Ore concentration

Variant names: beneficiation, ore separation

Class comprehensive works in 622.7

.75	Mechanical separation
.751	Gravity concentration
.752	Flotation
.77	Electrostatic (Inductive charging) and magnetic separation
.79	Milling plants
	Class specific milling-plant operations in 622.73–622.77

.8   **Mine health and safety**

Standard subdivisions are added for either or both topics in heading

Comprehensive works on safety measures for excavation techniques relocated to 622.20289; safety measures for a specific excavation technique relocated to 622.22–622.29, plus notation 0289 from Table 1, e.g., safety measures in tunneling 622.260289

Class control of roof and wall failure (rock failure) in 622.28; class interdisciplinary works on mine safety in 363.119622

For sanitation, see 622.49

See Manual at 363.1065 vs. 620.86: Accident investigation

.82   **Control of gas and explosions**

Class here comprehensive works on fire control, on respiratory safety

For dust control, see 622.83

.83   Dust control

.89   Rescue operations

623   Military and nautical engineering

Standard subdivisions are added for military and nautical engineering together, for military engineering alone

See Manual at 355 vs. 623

SUMMARY

623.04	**Special topics**
.1	**Fortifications**
.2	**Mine laying and clearance, demolition**
.3	**Engineering of defense**
.4	**Ordnance**
.5	**Ballistics and gunnery**
.6	**Military transportation technology**
.7	**Communications, vehicles, sanitation, related topics**
.8	**Nautical engineering and seamanship**

.04   Special topics

.042   Optical and paraphotic engineering

.043   Electronic engineering

.044   Nuclear engineering

.045   Mechanical engineering

.047   Construction engineering

>   **623.1–623.7   Military engineering**

Class special topics of military engineering in 623.04; class naval engineering in 623.8; class comprehensive works in 623

.1   Fortifications

Class here forts and fortresses

Class artistic aspects in 725.18

.109   Historical and persons treatment

Do not use for geographic treatment; class in 623.19

.15   Temporary fortifications

.19   Geographic treatment

Add to base number 623.19 notation 1–9 from Table 2, e.g., forts in France 623.1944

.2   Mine laying and clearance, demolition

.26   Mine laying and clearance

Standard subdivisions are added for either or both topics in heading

See also 623.45115 for manufacture of mines

[.262–.263]   Land and water mines

Numbers discontinued; class in 623.26

.27   Demolition

.3   Engineering of defense

Class warning systems in 623.737

See also 623.4 for ordnance

.31   Defense against invasion

Including countermining, flooding, mechanical barriers, moats, traps

Class artistic aspects of moats in 725.98

For fortifications, see 623.1; for mine laying, demolition, see 623.2

.38   Protective construction

Including air raid shelters

.4   Ordnance

Class combat ships in 623.82

For combat vehicles, see 623.74

SUMMARY

623.41	**Artillery**
.42	**Specific pieces of artillery**
.43	**Gun mounts**
.44	**Small arms and other weapons**
.45	**Ammunition and other destructive agents**
.46	**Accessories**

.41   Artillery

> *For specific pieces of artillery, see 623.42; for artillery projectiles, see 623.4513*

.412   Field artillery

.417   Coast artillery

.418   Naval artillery

.419   Space artillery

.42   Specific pieces of artillery

> Including cannons, howitzers, mortars, crew-served rocket launchers

.43   Gun mounts

.44   Small arms and other weapons

> Standard subdivisions are added for small arms and other weapons together, for small arms alone
>
> Class here side arms
>
> Class artistic aspects of arms and armor in 739.7. Class vehicle-mounted small arms with the vehicle, e.g., armored cars 623.7475
>
> *See also 623.455 for small arms ammunition*

.441   Weaponry of prefirearm origin

> Including armor, bayonets, bows and arrows, catapults, knives, maces, shields, spears, swords, tomahawks

.442   Portable firearms

> *For handguns, see 623.443*

.442 4   Automatic firearms

> Including automatic rifles, machine and submachine guns
>
> Class automatic pistols and revolvers in 623.443

.442 5   Carbines, muskets, rifles

.442 6   Portable rocket launchers (Bazookas)

.443   Handguns

.443 2	Pistols
.443 6	Revolvers

.445   Chemical weapons

Including flame throwers; rifle attachments for launching smoke and gas canisters

Class artillery for launching chemical projectiles in 623.41; class chemical delivery devices in 623.4516

For chemical agents, see 623.4592

.446   Destructive radiation weapons

Including laser weapons, thermal weapons

.447   Destructive vibration weapons

Including ultrasonic weapons

.45   Ammunition and other destructive agents

Standard subdivisions are added for ammunition and other destructive agents together, for ammunition alone

.451   Charge-containing devices

Class here bombs, missiles, projectiles

For tactical rockets, see 623.4543

See also 623.455 for small arms ammunition

.451 1   Grenades, mines, nuclear weapons

Class grenades and mines with special types of charges in 623.4516–623.4518

.451 14   Grenades

Class here hand and rifle grenades

.451 15   Mines

Class mine laying and clearance in 623.26

.451 19   Nuclear weapons

Including artillery projectiles, bombs

For nuclear missiles, see 623.4519

.451 3   Artillery projectiles

Class artillery projectiles with special types of charges in 623.4516–623.4518; class nuclear artillery projectiles in 623.45119

.451 4   Antipersonnel devices

                 Including booby traps

                 Class here shrapnel devices

                     For a specific antipersonnel device other than booby traps, see the device, e.g., antipersonnel hand grenades 623.45114

>   623.451 6–623.451 8   Devices with special types of charges

               Class comprehensive works in 623.451

               For nuclear weapons, see 623.45119

.451 6   Chemical and biological devices

                 Projectiles and related devices containing incendiary materials, microbes, poison gas, smoke

                 Standard subdivisions are added for chemical and biological devices together, for chemical devices alone

                 Class chemical agents in 623.4592; class biological agents in 623.4594

.451 7   High-explosive devices

                 Including blockbusters, high-explosive-antitank (HEAT) projectiles, torpedoes

                     For bangalore torpedoes, see 623.4545

.451 8   Armor-piercing devices

.451 9   Guided missiles

                 Nuclear and nonnuclear missiles

                 Class here storage and launching equipment, launch vehicles; strategic missiles, comprehensive works on rocket weapons

                 Class comprehensive works on rocketry in 621.4356

                     For tactical rockets, see 623.4543

.451 91   Air-to-air guided missiles

.451 92   Air-to-surface guided missiles

.451 93   Air-to-underwater guided missiles

.451 94   Surface-to-air guided missiles

                     Class here antimissile missiles, interceptor missiles

.451 95   Ballistic missiles (Surface-to-surface guided missiles)

.451 952   Short-range ballistic missiles

.451 953   Intermediate-range ballistic missiles

.451 954   Long-range ballistic missiles

                               Class here intercontinental ballistic missiles

.451 96   Surface-to-underwater guided missiles

.451 97   Underwater guided missiles

                               Including underwater-to-air, underwater-to-surface, underwater-to-underwater missiles

.451 98   Space guided missiles

.452   **Explosives**

.452 6   Burning and deflagrating explosives

                               Including cordite, guncotton, gunpowder, smokeless powder

                               Class here propellant explosives

.452 7   High explosives

                               Including dynamite, nitroglycerin, TNT

.454   **Detonators, tactical rockets, demolition charges**

.454 2   Detonators

                               Including fuses, percussion caps, primers

.454 3   Tactical rockets

                               Unguided nuclear and nonnuclear rockets

                               Class comprehensive works on rocket weapons, on rocket-propelled guided missiles in 623.4519

.454 5   Demolition charges

                               Including bangalore torpedoes, destructors, shaped charges

                               Class shaped charges in bombs, missiles, projectiles in 623.451

.455   **Small arms ammunition**

                               Including bazooka rockets, bullets, cartridges

.459   **Nonexplosive agents**

                               Class here detection of nonexplosive agents

.459 2   Chemical agents

                               Including tear gas

                               Class here poisons and gases

.459 4   Biological agents

.46   **Accessories**

                         Including range finders, sighting apparatus

.5	**Ballistics and gunnery**
.51	Ballistics
.513	Interior ballistics

Motion of projectiles within the bore

.514	Exterior ballistics

Motion of projectiles after leaving gun tube

.516	Terminal ballistics

Effect of projectiles on targets

.55	Gunnery

For recoil, see 623.57

.551	Land gunnery
.553	Naval gunnery
.555	Aircraft gunnery
.556	Spacecraft gunnery
.557	Target selection and detection

Class range and sighting apparatus in 623.46; class application to specific types of gunnery in 623.551–623.556

.558	Firing and fire control

Standard subdivisions are added for either or both

Class application to specific types of gunnery in 623.551–623.556

For target selection and detection, see 623.557

.57	Recoil
.6	**Military transportation technology**

For vehicles, see 623.74

.61	Land transportation

For roads, see 623.62; for railroads, see 623.63; for bridges, see 623.67; for tunnels, see 623.68

.62	Roads
.63	Railroads
.631	The way

Earthwork and track

.633	Rolling stock

.64   Naval facilities

         Including artificial harbors, docks, naval bases

         Class artistic aspects of naval facilities in 725.34

.66   Air facilities

         Class here air bases, airports, comprehensive works on military aerospace engineering

         Add to base number 623.66 the numbers following 629.136 in 629.1361–629.1368, e.g., airstrips 623.6612

         Class artistic aspects of air facilities in 725.39

         For military astronautics, see 623.69; for aircraft, see 623.746

.67   Bridges

.68   Tunnels

.69   Space facilities

         Class here comprehensive works on military astronautics

         For spacecraft, see 623.749

.7   **Communications, vehicles, sanitation, related topics**

SUMMARY

623.71	**Intelligence and reconnaissance topography**
.72	**Photography and photogrammetry**
.73	**Communications technology**
.74	**Vehicles**
.75	**Sanitation and safety engineering**
.76	**Electrical engineering**
.77	**Camouflage and concealment**

.71   Intelligence and reconnaissance topography

         Standard subdivisions are added for intelligence and reconnaissance topography together, for intelligence alone

         Including sketching and map making

         For photography and photogrammetry, see 623.72

.72   Photography and photogrammetry

.73   Communications technology

         Class comprehensive works on military electronics in 623.043

.731   Visual signals

.731 2   Flag signals, heliographs, semaphores

.731 3   Pyrotechnical devices

.731 4		Electrooptical devices
.732		Telegraphy

For radiotelegraphy, see 623.7342

.733	Telephony

For radiotelephony, see 623.7345

.734	Radio and radar

Standard subdivisions are added for radio and radar together, for radio alone

.734 1	Shortwave radio
.734 2	Radiotelegraphy

Class shortwave radiotelegraphy in 623.7341

.734 5	Radiotelephony

Class shortwave radiotelephony in 623.7341

.734 8	Radar
.735	Television
.737	Warning systems

Class here air raid warning systems

.74	Vehicles

Support vehicles, combat vehicles and their ordnance

For railroad rolling stock, see 623.633; for nautical craft, see 623.82

See Manual at 629.046 vs. 388

.741	Lighter-than-air aircraft

For specific types of lighter-than-air aircraft, see 623.742–623.744

> **623.742–623.744 Specific types of lighter-than-air aircraft**

Class comprehensive works in 623.741

.742	Free balloons

Class here comprehensive works on military balloons

For barrage balloons, see 623.744

.743	Airships (Dirigibles)
.743 5	Rigid airships
.743 6	Semirigid airships

.743 7	Nonrigid airships
.744	Barrage balloons
.746	Aircraft Heavier-than-air aircraft

For lighter-than-air aircraft, see 623.741

.746 04	Special topics

> 623.746 042–623.746 047   General types of heavier-than-air aircraft

Class here piloting general types of heavier-than-air aircraft

Class comprehensive works in 623.746; class comprehensive works on piloting in 623.746048

.746 042	Propeller-driven airplanes
.746 044	Jet planes
.746 045	Rocket planes
.746 047	Vertical-lift (VTOL) aircraft
	Including helicopters
.746 048	Piloting

Class piloting of a specific type of heavier-than-air aircraft with the aircraft, e.g., piloting jet planes 623.746044, piloting fighters 623.7464

.746 049	Components

Including engines, escape equipment, instrumentation (avionics)

Class components of a specific type of aircraft with the aircraft, e.g., components of jet planes 623.746044, of fighters 623.7464

For aircraft ordnance, see 623.7461

.746 1	Aircraft ordnance

For charge-containing devices, see 623.451

> 623.746 2–623.746 7   Heavier-than-air aircraft for specific uses

Class here piloting heavier-than-air aircraft for specific uses

Class aircraft ordnance regardless of type of aircraft in 623.7461; class pilotless aircraft regardless of type in 623.7469; class comprehensive works in 623.746; class comprehensive works on piloting in 623.746048

.746 2	Trainers

.746 3	Bombers and fighter-bombers
	Standard subdivisions are added for either or both topics in heading
.746 4	Fighters
.746 5	Transport aircraft
	Cargo and personnel
.746 6	Rescue aircraft
.746 7	Reconnaissance aircraft
.746 9	Pilotless aircraft (Guided aircraft)
	Variant name: drones
	Reconnaissance and combat
.747	**Motor land vehicles**
.747 2	Motor land vehicles for transporting personnel
	Class armored personnel carriers in 623.7475
.747 22	Jeeps and similar vehicles
	Standard subdivisions are added for jeeps and similar vehicles together, for jeeps alone
.747 23	Buses
.747 24	Ambulances
.747 4	Motor land vehicles for transporting supplies
.747 5	Motor land vehicles for combat
	Including armored personnel carriers
.747 52	Tanks
.748	**Air-cushion vehicles**
.748 2	Overland air-cushion vehicles
.748 4	Overwater air-cushion vehicles
.748 5	Amphibious air-cushion vehicles
.749	**Spacecraft**
.75	**Sanitation and safety engineering**
	Class here health engineering
.751	Water supply
.753	Sewage treatment and disposal
.754	Garbage and refuse treatment and disposal

.76	Electrical engineering

.77	Camouflage and concealment

.8 **Nautical engineering and seamanship**

Nautical engineering: engineering of ships and boats and their component parts

Standard subdivisions are added for nautical engineering and seamanship together, for nautical engineering alone

Class here naval engineering, comprehensive works on military water transportation

Class harbors, ports, roadsteads in 627.2

For naval facilities, see 623.64

SUMMARY

623.81	Naval architecture
.82	Nautical craft
.83	Shipyards
.84	Hulls of nautical craft
.85	Engineering systems of nautical craft
.86	Equipment and outfit of nautical craft
.87	Power plants of nautical craft
.88	Seamanship
.89	Navigation

.81	Naval architecture

Variant names: marine architecture, naval design

.810 287	Testing [*formerly* 623.819] and measurement

.812	Design of craft

.812 04	Design of general types of craft

Add to base number 623.81204 the numbers following 623.820 in 623.8202–623.8205, e.g., design of submersible craft 623.812045

.812 1–.812 9	Design of specific kinds of craft

Add to base number 623.812 the numbers following 623.82 in 623.821–623.829, e.g., design of sailboats 623.81223

.817	Structural analysis and design

Add to base number 623.817 the numbers following 624.17 in 624.171–624.177, e.g., structural analysis 623.8171, wreckage studies 623.8176

Class structural analysis and design of general and specific kinds of craft in 623.812; class structural analysis and design of specific metals in 623.818

.818	Design in specific materials

Add to base number 623.818 the numbers following 624.18 in 624.182–624.189, e.g., design in steel 623.81821

Class design of general and specific kinds of craft in a specific material in 623.812

[.819]	Testing

Relocated to 623.810287

.82	Nautical craft

Class shipyards in 623.83; class overwater hovercraft in 629.324

For naval architecture, see 623.81; for parts and details of nautical craft, see 623.84–623.87

See Manual at 629.046 vs. 388

SUMMARY

623.820 01–.820 09	**Standard subdivisions**
.820 1–.820 7	**[Models and miniatures, general types of craft, craft of specific materials]**
.821	**Ancient and medieval craft**
.822	**Modern wind-driven ships**
.823	**Small and medium power-driven ships**
.824	**Power-driven merchant and factory ships**
.825	**Power-driven warships**
.826	**Support warships and other government ships**
.827	**Nonmilitary submersible craft**
.828	**Other power-driven ships**
.829	**Hand-propelled and towed craft**

.820 01	Philosophy and theory
.820 02	Miscellany
[.820 022 8]	Models and miniatures

Do not use; class in 623.8201

.820 03–.820 09	Standard subdivisions
.820 1	Models and miniatures

Class ships in bottles in 745.5928

.820 104	Models and miniatures of general types of craft

Add to base number 623.820104 the numbers following 623.820 in 623.8202–623.8205, e.g., models of sailing craft 623.8201043

.820 11–.820 19	Models and miniatures of specific types of craft

Add to base number 623.8201 the numbers following 623.82 in 623.821–623.829, e.g., models of battleships 623.820152

> .820 2–623.820 5　General types of craft

Class general types of craft in specific materials in 623.8207; class specific types of craft in 623.821–623.829; class comprehensive works in 623.82

.820 2　　　　　*Small craft

Class small sailing craft in 623.8203; class small submersible craft in 623.8205; class small power-driven craft in 623.823

.820 23　　　　　*Pleasure craft

Including yachts

.820 26　　　　　*Working craft

.820 3　　　　　*Sailing ships

.820 4　　　　　*Power-driven ships

Including hydrofoils, steamships

Class power-driven submersible craft in 623.8205; class small power-driven craft in 623.823

.820 5　　　　　*Submersible craft

.820 7　　　　　*Craft of specific materials

Class works limited to hulls of specific materials in 623.84

.821　　　　　*Ancient and medieval craft

Including biremes, caravels, galleys, triremes

> 623.822–623.829　Modern craft

Class comprehensive works in 623.82

.822　　　　　*Modern wind-driven ships

Including rotor ships

Class comprehensive works on ancient, medieval, and modern wind-driven ships in 623.8203

.822 3　　　　　*Pleasure craft

Including sailing yachts

.822 4　　　　　*Merchant ships

Including clipper ships

.822 5　　　　　*Warships

*Do not use notation 0228 from Table 1 for models and miniatures; class in 623.8201

.822 6	*Work ships

Including research ships

For merchant ships, see 623.8224

>   623.823–623.828   Power-driven craft

Class comprehensive works in 623.8204

.823	*Small and medium power-driven ships

For small and medium power-driven craft not provided for here, see 623.824–623.828

.823 1	*Motorboats

Class here speedboats

.823 13	*Outboard motorboats
.823 14	*Inboard motorboats

Including hydroplanes, motor yachts

.823 15	*Inboard-outboard motorboats
.823 2	*Tugboats and towboats
.823 4	*Ferryboats
.824	*Power-driven merchant and factory ships

Standard subdivisions are added for power-driven merchant and factory ships together, for power-driven merchant ships alone

Class trawlers in 623.828

.824 3	*Passenger ships

Class ferryboats in 623.8234

.824 32	*Ocean liners
.824 36	*Inland-waterway ships

Including river steamers

.824 5	*Cargo ships

Including bulk carriers, freighters, tankers

.824 8	*Factory ships

Including ship canneries, whaleboats

.825	*Power-driven warships

For support warships, see 623.826

---

*Do not use notation 0228 from Table 1 for models and miniatures; class in 623.8201

.825 1   Naval ordnance

Class here armor, weapons

For naval artillery, see 623.418; for charge-containing devices, see 623.451

> 623.825 2–623.825 8 Specific types of combat warships

Class naval ordnance in 623.8251; class comprehensive works in 623.825

.825 2   *Battleships

.825 3   *Cruisers

.825 4   *Destroyers and destroyer escorts

Standard subdivisions are added for destroyers and destroyer escorts together, for destroyers alone

.825 5   *Aircraft carriers

.825 6   *Landing craft

.825 7   *Submarines

Class comprehensive works on submersible craft in 623.8205

.825 72   *Diesel-engine and electric-motor powered submarines

.825 74   *Nuclear-powered submarines

.825 8   *Light combat craft

Including torpedo boats

.826   *Support warships and other government ships

.826 2   *Minelayers and minesweepers

.826 3   *Coast guard vessels, police boats, revenue cutters

.826 4   *Hospital ships and military transports

.826 5   *Military supply ships

.827   *Nonmilitary submersible craft

Including bathyscaphes, bathyspheres

Class comprehensive works on submersible craft in 623.8205

.828   *Other power-driven ships

Including dredgers, drilling ships, icebreakers, lightships, trawlers

.829   *Hand-propelled and towed craft

Including barges, canoes, coracles, lifeboats, rafts, rowboats, scows, towed canalboats

*Do not use notation 0228 from Table 1 for models and miniatures; class in 623.8201

.83   Shipyards

         Including dry docks, floating dry docks

\>   623.84–623.87   Parts and details of nautical craft

         Class here design

         Class comprehensive works in 623.82

.84   Hulls of nautical craft

         Class hydrodynamics of hulls in 623.812

.842   Lofting

.843   Metalwork

.843 2   Riveting and welding

.843 3   Ship fitting

.844   Carpentry

.845   Construction with ceramics, masonry, allied materials

         Add to base number 623.845 the numbers following 624.183 in 624.1832–624.1838, e.g., concrete hulls 623.8454

.848   Resistant construction

         Including corrosion-resistant, fire-resistant construction

.85   Engineering systems of nautical craft

         For power plants, see 623.87

.850 01–.850 09   Standard subdivisions

.850 1   Mechanical systems

.850 3   Electrical systems

.850 4   Electronic systems

.852   Electric lighting

.853   Temperature controls and air conditioning

         Standard subdivisions are added for temperature controls and air conditioning together, for temperature controls alone

.853 5   Cooling

         Including refrigeration

.853 7   Heating and air conditioning

.854   Water supply and sanitation

.854 2	Potable water
.854 3	Seawater

Used for fire fighting and sanitation

.854 6	Sanitation

Class seawater for sanitation in 623.8543

.856	Communication systems

Add to base number 623.856 the numbers following 623.73 in 623.731–623.737, e.g., flag systems 623.85612

.86	**Equipment and outfit of nautical craft**

Including flares, other portable lights

Class use of equipment and outfit in 623.88

.862	Gear and rigging

Including anchors, cordage, masts, rope, rudders, sails, spars

.863	Nautical instruments
.865	Safety equipment

Including fire fighting, lifesaving equipment

Class comprehensive works on marine safety technology in 623.888

.866	Furniture
.867	Cargo-handling equipment

Class cargo handling in 623.8881

For onshore cargo-handling equipment, see 627.34

.87	**Power plants of nautical craft**

Class here marine engineering

.872	Specific kinds of engines
[.872 01–.872 09]	Standard subdivisions

Do not use; class in 623.8701–623.8709

.872 2	Steam engines
.872 3	Internal-combustion engines

Class here inboard motors

Add to base number 623.8723 the numbers following 621.43 in 621.433–621.437, e.g., outboard motors 623.87234, diesel engines 623.87236

.872 6	Electric engines

.872 7	Solar engines
.872 8	Nuclear engines
.873	Engine auxiliaries

Including boilers, pipes, propellers, pumps, shafts

.874	Fuels
.88	Seamanship

For navigation, see 623.89

[.880 289]   Safety measures

Do not use; class in 623.888

.881   Ship handling

Class safety and related topics in handling craft in 623.888

For handling specific types of craft, see 623.882

.881 2–.881 5   Handling general types of craft

Add to base number 623.881 the numbers following 623.820 in 623.8202–623.8205, e.g., handling small craft 623.8812

.882   Handling various specific types of craft

Class safety and related topics in handling specific types of craft in 623.888

[.882 01–.882 09]   Standard subdivisions

Do not use; class in 623.88101–623.88109

.882 1–.882 9   Specific types of craft

Add to base number 623.882 the numbers following 623.82 in 623.821–623.829, e.g., handling power-driven merchant ships 623.8824

.888   Specific topics of seamanship

Class here marine safety technology

For safety equipment, see 623.865

[.888 01–.888 09]   Standard subdivisions

Do not use; class in 623.8801–623.8809

.888 1   Loading and unloading of nautical craft

Standard subdivisions are added for either or both topics in heading

Class here cargo handling

.888 2   Knotting and splicing ropes and cables

                          Class here interdisciplinary works on knotting and splicing

                          For a specific application of knotting and splicing, see the
                          application, e.g., knotting in camping 796.545

.888 4   Prevention of collision and grounding

                          Including rules of the road

.888 5   Wreckage studies

                          Class wreckage studies in marine architecture in 623.8176

                          See Manual at 363.1065 vs. 620.86: Accident investigation

.888 6   Fire fighting technology

                          See also 623.865 for manufacture of fire fighting equipment

.888 7   Rescue operations

.89   Navigation

                          Selection and determination of course

                          Class navigation procedures to prevent collision and grounding in 623.8884

.892   Geonavigation

                          For electronic aids to geonavigation, see 623.893

.892 021   Tabulated and related materials

                          Do not use for tide and current tables; class in 623.8949

.892 2   Piloting and pilot guides

                          Positioning craft by visual observation of objects of known position

                          Standard subdivisions are added for either or both topics in heading

                          For piloting in and pilot guides to specific marine harbors and
                          shores, see 623.8929

[.892 209 163–.892 209 167]   Treatment by specific oceans and seas

                          Do not use; class in 623.89223–623.89227

.892 209 168   Treatment by specific oceanographic forms

                          Do not use for inland seas; class in 623.89229

.892 209 169   Treatment by fresh and brackish waters

                          Do not use for specific inland waters; class in
                          623.89229

.892 23–.892 27	Piloting in and pilot guides to specific oceans and intercontinental seas

Add to base number 623.8922 the numbers following — 16 in notation 163–167 from Table 2, e.g., pilot guides to North Sea 623.8922336; however, for piloting in and pilot guides to specific marine harbors and shores, see 623.8929

.892 29 Piloting in and pilot guides to specific inland waters

Add to base number 623.89229 notation 4–9 from Table 2, e.g., pilot guides to Great Lakes 623.8922977; however, for piloting in and pilot guides to specific marine harbors and shores, see 623.8929

.892 3 Dead reckoning

.892 9 Piloting in and pilot guides to specific marine harbors and shores

Standard subdivisions are added for either or both topics in heading

Class here approach and harbor piloting and pilot guides

.892 909 Historical and persons treatment

Do not use for geographic treatment; class in 623.89291–623.89299

.892 91–.892 99 Geographic treatment

Add to base number 623.8929 notation 1–9 from Table 2, e.g., harbor piloting for Scandinavia 623.892948; however, for approach and harbor piloting and pilot guides dealing comprehensively with specific oceans and intercontinental seas, see 623.89223–623.89227

.893 Electronic aids to geonavigation

Class here comprehensive works on aids to geonavigation

For nonelectronic aids to geonavigation, see 623.894

> 623.893 2–623.893 3 Direction-finding and position-finding devices

Class comprehensive works in 623.893

.893 2 Radio aids

Including compasses, loran, radio

.893 3 Microwave aids

Including racon, radar, shoran

.893 8 Sounding devices

Including echo-ranging and sound-ranging devices, e.g., sonar

.894 Nonelectronic aids to geonavigation

.894 2	Lighthouses

Class construction of lighthouses in 627.922; class interdisciplinary works on lighthouses in 387.155

.894 3	Lightships

Class construction of lightships in 623.828

.894 4	Beacons, buoys, daymarks

Class construction of beacons, buoys, daymarks in 627.924

.894 5	Light lists

.894 9	Tide and current tables

Standard subdivisions are added for either or both topics in heading

624   Civil engineering

Including engineering of landscape architecture

Class here construction engineering

For military construction engineering, see 623.047. For a specific branch of civil engineering not provided for here, see the branch, e.g., construction of buildings 690

See Manual at 624 vs. 624.1; also at 624 vs. 690

SUMMARY

624.029 9	**Estimates of labor, time, materials**
.1	**Structural engineering and underground construction**
.2	**Bridges**
.3	**Specific types of bridges**
.4	**Tubular and box-girder bridges**
.5	**Suspension bridges**
.6	**Arch bridges**
.7	**Compound bridges**
.8	**Movable bridges**

.029 9	Estimates of labor, time, materials [*formerly* 624.1042]

Class interdisciplinary works on quantity surveying in 692.5

.1   Structural engineering and underground construction

Standard subdivisions are added for structural engineering and underground construction together, for structural engineering alone

Class a specific application with the application, e.g., structural engineering of dams 627.8

See Manual at 624 vs. 624.1

SUMMARY

.101   Philosophy and theory

> Class structural analysis and design in 624.17

.102   Miscellany

.102 99   Estimates of labor, time, materials [*formerly* 624.1042]

[.104]   Special topics

> Number discontinued; class in 624.1

[.104 2]   Estimates of labor, time, materials

> Estimates of labor, time, materials for civil engineering relocated to 624.0299; estimates of labor, time, materials for structural engineering and underground construction relocated to 624.10299

.15   Foundation engineering and engineering geology

> Standard subdivisions are added for foundation engineering and engineering geology together, for foundation engineering alone

.151   Engineering geology

> Class here properties of soils that support structures (foundation soils)

.151 09   Historical, geographic, persons treatment

> Class soil surveys in 624.1517

.151 3   Rock and soil mechanics

.151 32   Rock mechanics

.151 36   Soil mechanics

> Including drainage properties, permeability; permafrost

.151 362   Consolidation

.151 363   Stabilization

.151 4   Soil content analysis

.151 7   Soil surveys

> Class general soil surveys not focusing on engineering problems in 631.47

[.151 709 1–.151 709 9]   Geographic treatment

> Do not use; class in 624.15171–624.15179

.151 71–.151 79   Geographic treatment

> Add to base number 624.1517 notation 1–9 from Table 2, e.g., soil survey of Japan 624.151752

\>   624.152–624.158 Foundation engineering

Class engineering geology of foundations in 624.151; class comprehensive works in 624.15

.152   Excavation

Including blasting, shoring

Class here earthwork

Class embankments in 624.162

.153   Foundation materials

Add to base number 624.153 the numbers following 620.1 in 620.12–620.19, e.g., iron 624.1537

Class foundation materials for specific types of foundations in 624.154–624.158

\>   624.154–624.158 Specific types of foundations

Class comprehensive works in 624.15

.154   Pile foundations

.156   Floating foundations

Including cantilever and platform foundations

.157   Underwater foundations

Including caissons, cofferdams

See also 627.702 for underwater construction operations

.158   Pier foundations

.16   Supporting structures other than foundations

Including abutments, piers

.162   Embankments

.164   Retaining walls

.17   **Structural analysis and design**

Class here interdisciplinary works on structural analysis and design, structural theory

For a specific application of structural analysis and design, see the application, e.g., structural analysis of aircraft 629.1341

.171   **Structural analysis**

Class analysis of specific structural elements in 624.1772–624.1779

For loads, see 624.172; for stresses and strains, see 624.176

.171 2   Graphic statics

.171 3   Statically indeterminate structures

Including static determinacy and indeterminacy

.171 4   Deflections

.171 5   Moment distribution method

>   **624.172–624.176   Loads, stresses, strains**

Class loads, stresses, strains of specific structural elements in 624.1772–624.1779; class comprehensive works in 624.171

.172   **Loads**

For wind loads, see 624.175

.175   **Wind loads**

.176   **Stresses and strains (Deformation)**

Standard subdivisions are added for either or both topics in heading

Including blast-resistant construction

Class here wreckage studies

.176 2   Earthquake engineering

.177   **Structural design and specific structural elements**

Class analysis in 624.171

.177 1   Structural design

For design of specific structural elements, see 624.1772–624.1779; for design with materials, see 624.18

.177 13   Structural optimization

> 624.177 2–624.177 9   Specific structural elements

Class here specific structural elements in metal, design and construction

Class specific structural elements in materials other than metal in 624.18; class comprehensive works in 624.17

.177 2   Beams, girders, cylinders, columns, slabs

.177 23   Beams and girders

Standard subdivisions are added for either or both topics in heading

.177 3   Trusses and frames

Standard subdivisions are added for either or both topics in heading

.177 4   Cables, wires, bars, rods

.177 5   Arches and domes

.177 6   Shells and plates

.177 62   Shells

.177 65   Plates

.177 9   Sandwich and honeycomb constructions

Standard subdivisions are added for either or both topics in heading

Class specific sandwich and honeycomb constructions in 624.1772–624.1776

.18   Materials

Class here design and construction

.182   Metals

Class specific structural elements in metal in 624.1772–624.1779

.182 1   Iron and steel (Ferrous metals)

Standard subdivisions are added for either or both topics in heading

.182 2–.182 9   Nonferrous metals

Add to base number 624.182 the numbers following 620.18 in 620.182–620.189, e.g., construction in aluminum 624.1826

.183   Masonry, ceramic, allied materials

.183 2   Stone

Including artificial stone, e.g., concrete blocks

.183 3   Cement

.183 4	Concrete
	Class concrete and cinder blocks in 624.1832
	See also 721.0445 for visual concrete
.183 41	Reinforced concrete (Ferroconcrete)
	Class a specific concrete structural element of reinforced concrete in 624.18342–624.18349
.183 412	Prestressed concrete
.183 414	Precast concrete
.183 42–.183 49	Specific concrete structural elements
	Add to base number 624.1834 the numbers following 624.177 in 624.1772–624.1779, e.g., concrete shells 624.183462
.183 6	Brick and tile
.183 8	Glass
.184	Wood and laminated wood
	Standard subdivisions are added for wood and laminated wood together, for wood alone
.189	Other materials
	Add to base number 624.189 the numbers following 620.19 in 620.191–620.199, e.g., design in plastics 624.18923
.19	Underground construction
	Class here ventilation
	Class subsurface mining in 622.2
	For construction of underground waste disposal facilities, see 628.44566
.192	Mountain tunnels
.193	Tunnels
	Class artistic aspects in 725.98
	For military tunnel engineering, see 623.68; for mountain tunnels, see 624.192; for underwater tunnels, see 624.194
.194	Underwater tunnels
.2	**Bridges**
	Class artistic aspects in 725.98
	For military bridge engineering, see 623.67; for specific types of bridges, see 624.3
.202 88	Maintenance and repair [*formerly* 624.28]

.25   Structural analysis and design

.252   Loads, stresses, strains

> Class loads, stresses, strains of specific structural elements and materials in 624.257

.253   Floor systems

.254   Foundations

.257   Structural elements and materials

> *For floor systems, see 624.253; for foundations, see 624.254*

.28   Floor systems and foundations

> Use of this number for comprehensive works on construction discontinued; class in 624.2

> Comprehensive works on maintenance and repair relocated to 624.20288

.283   Floor systems

> Class here comprehensive works on floor systems of bridges

> *For structural analysis and design of floor systems, see 624.253*

.284   Foundations

> Class here comprehensive works on foundations of bridges

> *For structural analysis and design of foundations, see 624.254*

.3   **Specific types of bridges**

> *For tubular bridges, see 624.4; for arch bridges, see 624.6; for compound bridges, see 624.7; for movable bridges, see 624.8*

[.301–.309]   Standard subdivisions

> Do not use; class in 624.201–624.209

> 624.32–624.35   Long-span bridges

> Class comprehensive works in 624.3

> *For suspension bridges, see 624.5*

.32   Trestle bridges

.33   Continuous bridges

> Bridges consisting of beams, girders, or trusses extending uninterruptedly over more than two supports

> *For trestle bridges, see 624.32*

.35   Cantilever bridges

.37   Girder and beam bridges

> Standard subdivisions are added for either or both topics in heading
>
> Including covered-girder, lattice-girder, plate-girder bridges; Bailey bridges
>
> Class long-span girder and beam bridges in 624.32–624.35
>
> > *For box-girder bridges, see 624.4; for plate-girder suspension bridges, see 624.5*

.38   Truss bridges

> Class long-span truss bridges in 624.32–624.35; class truss arch bridges in 624.6

.4   **Tubular and box-girder bridges**

.5   **Suspension bridges**

> Including plate-girder suspension bridges

.6   **Arch bridges**

> Class here truss arch bridges

.63   Arch bridges of masonry

.67   Arch bridges of metal

.7   **Compound bridges**

> > *For a specific type of compound bridge, see the type, e.g., plate-girder suspension bridges 624.5*

.8   **Movable bridges**

.82   Bascule bridges

.83   Swing bridges

> Variant names: swing drawbridges, swivel bridges

.84   Vertical lift bridges

.86   Transporter bridges

.87   Pontoon bridges

625   Engineering of railroads and roads

> Class tunnel engineering in 624.193; class bridge engineering in 624.2

SUMMARY

.1   **Railroads**

Including comprehensive works on special-purpose railroads

Class here comprehensive works on broad-gage, narrow-gage, standard-gage railroads

Class electrification of railroads in 621.33; class interdisciplinary works on railroads in 385

> *For military railroad engineering, see 623.63; for railroad rolling stock, see 625.2; for special-purpose railroads, see 625.3–625.6*

.100 1   Philosophy and theory

.100 2   Miscellany

[.100 228]   Models and miniatures

Do not use; class in 625.19

.100 288   Maintenance and repair [*formerly* 625.17]

Including snow removal operations

.100 3–.100 9   Standard subdivisions

.103   Monorail railroads

> *For elevated monorail systems, see 625.44*

.11   Surveying and design

Including final location surveys; determination of grades, switchbacks, right-of-way

---

>   625.12–625.16   Permanent way

Class comprehensive works in 625.1

.12   Earthwork

.122   Engineering geology

Including rock and soil mechanics

Class here properties of soils that support structures (foundation soils)

.123	Roadbed preparation
	Including excavation
.13	Protective structures
	Including retaining walls, snow fences, snowsheds
.14	Track

For rails and rail fastenings, see 625.15; for track accessories, see 625.16

.141	Ballast
.143	Ties (Sleepers)
	Including tie plates
.144	Track laying

For laying of monorail tracks, see 625.146; for laying of tracks over ice, see 625.147

.146	Monorail tracks
.147	Tracks over ice
.15	Rails
	Including rail fastenings
.16	Track accessories
.163	Turnouts and crossings
	Including frogs, switches, sidings
.165	Control devices
	Including signals, signs
[.17]	Maintenance and repair
	Relocated to 625.100288
.18	Railroad yards
.19	Model and miniature railroads and trains

Standard subdivisions are added for either or both topics in heading

Class here models and miniatures of rolling stock for roads with two running rails [*formerly also* 625.21–625.26]

Class play with model railroads and trains in 790.133

For models and miniatures of monorail rolling stock, see 625.280228. For models and miniatures of a specific kind of special-purpose railroad, see the type in 625.3–625.6, plus notation 0228 from Table 1, e.g., models of subways 625.420228

.192–.194   Specific types of cars

> Add to base number 625.19 the numbers following 625.2 in 625.22–625.24, e.g., models of cabooses 625.192

.196   Locomotives

> Add to base number 625.196 the numbers following 625.26 in 625.261–625.266, e.g., models of steam locomotives 625.1961

.2   **Railroad rolling stock**

> Class here comprehensive works on specific types of cars, on rolling stock for roads with two running rails

> *For rolling stock for special-purpose railroads, see 625.3–625.6*

> *See Manual at 629.046 vs. 388*

[.202 28]   Models and miniatures

> Do not use; class in 625.19

>   625.21–625.26   Rolling stock for roads with two running rails

> Models and miniatures relocated to 625.19

> Class comprehensive works in 625.2

.21   *Running gear

> Including axles, bearings, springs, wheels

> Class here running gear for specific types of cars

>   625.22–625.24   Specific types of cars

> Class running gear for specific types of cars in 625.21; class accessory equipment for specific types of cars in 625.25; class comprehensive works in 625.2

.22   *Work cars (Nonrevenue rolling stock)

> Including cabooses, handcars, railroad snowplows

.23   *Passenger-train cars

> Including coaches; baggage, dining, sleeping cars

.24   *Freight cars

> Including boxcars, gondola cars, refrigerator cars, tank cars

.25   *Accessory equipment

> Including brakes, buffers, couplings

> Class here accessory equipment for specific types of cars

*Do not use notation 0228 from Table 1; class in 625.19

.26	*Locomotives

> Class running gear in 625.21; class accessory equipment in 625.25

.261	*Steam locomotives
.262	*Gas-turbine locomotives
.263	*Electric locomotives

> *For diesel-electric locomotives, see 625.2662*

.265	*Air-compression-powered locomotives
.266	*Diesel and semidiesel locomotives
.266 2	*Diesel-electric locomotives
.266 4	*Diesel-hydraulic locomotives
.27	Mechanical operation
.28	Monorail rolling stock

> **625.3–625.6   Special-purpose railroads**

> Class here roadbeds, tracks and accessories, rolling stock

> Class comprehensive works in 625.1

> *For mine railroads, see 622.66*

.3	**Inclined, mountain, ship railroads**
.32	Funicular railroads
.33	Rack railroads
.39	Ship railroads
.4	**Rapid transit systems**

> Including guided-way systems

> *For surface systems, see 625.6*

.42	Underground railways (Subways)
.44	Elevated railroads

> Including elevated monorail systems

.5	**Cable and aerial railways**

> *For funicular railroads, see 625.32*

---

*Do not use notation 0228 from Table 1; class in 625.19

.6   **Surface rail and trolley systems**

> Standard subdivisions are added for either or both topics in heading
>
> Light interurban and local

.65   Roadbeds, tracks, accessories

.66   Streetcars and trolleys

> Standard subdivisions are added for either or both topics in heading
>
> Including horse-drawn streetcars

.7   **Roads**

> Class here highways, streets
>
> Class grade crossings (road crossings of railroads) in 625.163; class interdisciplinary works on roads and highways in 388.1; class interdisciplinary works on urban roads and streets in 388.411
>
> > *For military road engineering, see 623.62; for artificial road surfaces, see 625.8; for forestry roads, see 634.93*

[.702 88]   Maintenance and repair

> Do not use; class in 625.76

.702 89   Safety measures [*formerly* 625.7042]

[.704]   Special topics

> Number discontinued; class in 625.7

[.704 2]   Safety engineering

> Relocated to 625.70289

.72   Surveying and design

.723   Surveying

> Class soil surveys in 625.732

.725   Design

> Including determination of bankings, grades

.73   Earthwork

.732   Engineering geology

> Including rock and soil mechanics
>
> Class here properties of soils that support structures (foundation soils)

.733   Foundation preparation

> Including excavation

.734	Drainage

Including conduits, dikes, ditches, gutters, pipes

.734 2	Culverts
.735	Subsurface highway materials
.74	Dirt roads

Stabilized and unstabilized

Including soil stabilization processes

For surfacing dirt roads, see 625.75

.75	Surfacing dirt roads
.76	Maintenance and repair

Class maintenance and repair of a specific kind of road or associated feature with the road or feature, plus notation 0288 from Table 1, e.g., maintenance of dirt roads 625.740288, of roadside areas 625.770288

.761	Damages and their repairs

Standard subdivisions are added for either or both topics in heading

Including resurfacing, shoulder maintenance

.763	Snow and ice control measures

Including use of snowplows, snow fences

.77	Roadside areas

Including parking turnouts, picnic areas, rest areas; planting and cultivation of roadside vegetation

.79	Ice crossings, traffic control equipment, protective roadside barriers

For public lighting for roads, see 628.95

.792	Ice crossings

Class here ice and snow-compacted roads

.794	Traffic control equipment

Including markings, signals, signs

.795	Protective roadside barriers

Including dividers, fences

Class snow fences in 625.763; class curbs in 625.888

.8	**Artificial road surfaces**

Class here comprehensive works on paving

For a paving surface not provided for here, see the surface, e.g., airport runways 629.13634

[.802 88]   Maintenance and repair

Do not use; class in 625.76

>   625.81–625.86   Pavements in specific materials

Class sidewalks in specific materials in 625.881–625.886; class comprehensive works in 625.8

.81   Flagstones

.82   Brick and stone

Including gravel and crushed stone pavements

For flagstones, see 625.81

.83   Wood

.84   Concretes

For asphalt concrete, see 625.85

.85   Bituminous materials

Including tar

Class here asphalt, asphalt concrete

For macadam, see 625.86

.86   Macadam and telford surfaces

.88   Sidewalks and auxiliary pavements

Standard subdivisions are added for sidewalks and auxiliary pavements together, for sidewalks alone

.881–.886   Sidewalks in specific materials

Add to base number 625.88 the numbers following 625.8 in 625.81–625.86, e.g., brick sidewalks 625.882

.888   Curbs

.889   Auxiliary pavements

Including driveways, parking aprons

For curbs, see 625.888

[626]   [Unassigned]

Most recently used in Edition 14

627 Hydraulic engineering

The branch of engineering dealing with utilization and control of natural waters of the earth

Class here hydraulic structures, water resource engineering

Class comprehensive works on ocean engineering in 620.4162

For water supply engineering, see 628.1

SUMMARY

627.04		Special topics
	.1	Inland waterways
	.2	Harbors, ports, roadsteads
	.3	Port facilities
	.4	Flood control
	.5	Reclamation, irrigation, related topics
	.7	Underwater operations
	.8	Dams and reservoirs
	.9	Other hydraulic structures

[.015 325]   Hydrodynamics

Do not use; class in 627.042

.04   Special topics

.042   Hydrodynamics of waterways and water bodies

Standard subdivisions are added for either or both topics in heading

.046   Recreational waters

.1   Inland waterways

For dredging and other underwater operations, see 627.7

.12   Rivers and streams

Standard subdivisions are added for either or both topics in heading

Class interdisciplinary works on rivers and streams in 551.483

For canalized rivers, see 627.13

[.120 153 25]   Hydrodynamics

Do not use; class in 627.125

.122   Sediment and silt

Standard subdivisions are added for either or both topics in heading

.123   Water diversion

Including construction of barrages

.124   Estuaries and river mouths

Standard subdivisions are added for either or both topics in heading

.125　　　　　　Applied hydrodynamics

.13　　　　Canals

Class here canalized rivers, comprehensive engineering works on canals

Class tunnels carrying canals in 624.193; class bridges carrying canals in 624.2; class interdisciplinary works on canals in 386.4

For irrigation canals, see 627.52

.130 288　　　　　　Maintenance and repair [*formerly* 627.136]

.131　　　　Surveying and design

[.132]　　　Earthwork

Number discontinued; class in 627.13

.133　　　　Bank protection and reinforcement

Standard subdivisions are added for either or both topics in heading

[.134]　　　Water supply for canals

Number discontinued; class in 627.13

.135　　　　Auxiliary devices

.135 2　　　　Gates, locks, sluices

.135 3　　　　Inclines, lifts, ramps

[.136]　　　Maintenance and repair

Comprehensive works on maintenance and repair of canals relocated to 627.130288; maintenance and repair of ship canals relocated to 627.1370288; maintenance and repair of barge canals relocated to 627.1380288

> 　　　627.137–627.138　Specific types of navigation canals

Class engineering and construction details of specific types of canals in 627.131–627.135; class comprehensive works in 627.13

.137　　　　Ship canals

.137 028 8　　　　　　Maintenance and repair [*formerly* 627.136]

.138　　　　Barge canals

.138 028 8　　　　　　Maintenance and repair [*formerly* 627.136]

.14　　　　Lakes

.2   Harbors, ports, roadsteads

Standard subdivisions are added for harbors, ports, roadsteads together; for harbors alone; for ports alone

Class interdisciplinary works on harbors, ports, roadsteads in 387.1

For port facilities, see 627.3; for dredging and other underwater operations, see 627.7

.22   Roadsteads, anchorages, mooring grounds

Standard subdivisions are added for any or all topics in heading

Including supertanker berthing areas

Class freestanding mooring and berthing structures in 627.32

.23   Channels

Class here fairways

.24   Protective structures

Including breakwaters, jetties, seawalls

Class comprehensive works on seawalls in 627.58

.3   Port facilities

Class architectural aspects in 725.34

For navigation aids, see 627.92

>   627.31–627.34   Specific types of structures and equipment

Class specific types of structures in marinas in 627.38; class comprehensive works in 627.3

.31   Docks

Class here piers, quays, wharves

.32   Freestanding mooring and berthing structures

[.33]   Port buildings

Number discontinued; class in 627.3

.34   Cargo-handling equipment

Class comprehensive works on cargo-handling equipment in 623.867

.38   Marinas

.4 **Flood control**

Including flood wreckage studies

Class here use of dams and reservoirs for flood control

Class construction of dams and reservoirs for flood control in 627.8. Class flood control for and wreckage studies of a specific type of structure with the structure, e.g., flood wreckage studies of bridges 624.2

.42 Flood barriers

Including seawalls

Class here embankments, levees; comprehensive works on dikes

Class comprehensive works on seawalls in 627.58

For dikes and seawalls in reclamation from sea, see 627.549

.44 Water impoundment

.45 Water diversion

.5 **Reclamation, irrigation, related topics**

Class here comprehensive technological works on erosion and its control

Class interdisciplinary works on erosion in 551.302; class interdisciplinary works on land reclamation in 333.73153

For erosion of agricultural soils and its control, see 631.45; for reclamation of agricultural soils, see 631.6; for revegetation and surface mine reclamation, see 631.64

.52 Irrigation

Class here construction and use of irrigation canals

Class construction of dams and reservoirs for irrigation in 627.8

For on-farm irrigation, see 631.587

.54 Drainage and reclamation from sea

Standard subdivisions are added for drainage and reclamation from sea together, for drainage alone

.549 Reclamation from sea

Including dikes

Class here polders

.56 Artificial recharge of groundwater

Class comprehensive works on engineering of groundwater in 628.114

.58   Shore protection

Including stabilization of coastal dunes by engineering means, comprehensive works on seawalls

Class here beach erosion and its control, shore reclamation, comprehensive works on coastal engineering

Class dune stabilization by revegetation, comprehensive works on dune stabilization in 631.64

> *For harbor seawalls, see 627.24; for seawalls as flood barriers, see 627.42. For a specific aspect of coastal engineering, see the aspect, e.g., reclamation from sea 627.549*

.7   Underwater operations

.700 1   Philosophy and theory

.700 2   Miscellany

.700 288   Maintenance and repair [*formerly* 627.705]

.700 3–.700 9   Standard subdivisions

>   627.702–627.704 General topics of underwater operations

Class comprehensive works in 627.7

.702   Underwater construction

.703   Salvage operations

.704   Research operations

[.705]   Maintenance and repair

Relocated to 627.700288

.72   Diving

Class here interdisciplinary works on diving

For diving sports, see 797.2

.73   Dredging

.74   Blasting

.75   Drilling

.8   Dams and reservoirs

Standard subdivisions are added for dams and reservoirs together, for dams alone

Class here construction of dams and reservoirs for specific purposes

Class a specific use of dams and reservoirs with the use, e.g., water storage and conservation 628.132

.802 84	Materials [*formerly* 627.81], apparatus, equipment
.81	Earthwork, planning, surveying

Class earthwork, planning, surveying for specific kinds of dams in 627.82–627.84; class earthwork, planning, surveying for reservoirs in 627.86; class earthwork, planning, surveying for ancillary structures in 627.88

Materials relocated to 627.80284

>   627.82–627.84   Specific kinds of dams

Class ancillary structures of specific kinds of dams in 627.88; class comprehensive works in 627.8

.82	Masonry dams
.83	Earth-fill and rock-fill dams

Standard subdivisions are added for either or both topics in heading

.84	Movable dams
[.85]	Metal dams

Number discontinued; class in 627.8

.86	Reservoirs

Including silting control

Class ancillary structures of reservoirs in 627.88

.88	Ancillary structures
.882	Gates, penstocks, sluices
.883	Spillways and weirs
.9	**Other hydraulic structures**
.92	Navigation aids

Class use of navigation aids in 623.894

.922	Lighthouses
.924	Light beacons, buoys, daymarks

Class lists of buoys, daymarks in 623.8944; class light lists in 623.8945

.98	Offshore structures

Class here artificial islands, drilling platforms

Class a specific use of offshore structures with the use, e.g., use of drilling platforms in petroleum extraction 622.33819

For freestanding mooring and berthing structures, see 627.32

628   Sanitary and municipal engineering   Environmental protection engineering

Standard subdivisions are added for any or all topics in heading

Class here environmental health engineering, public sanitation technology

Class interdisciplinary works on environmental protection in 363.7

For military sanitary engineering, see 623.75; for plumbing, see 696.1. For a specific aspect of municipal engineering not provided for here, see the aspect, e.g., road and street engineering 625.7, laying gas pipelines 665.744

See Manual at 300 vs. 600; also at 363

SUMMARY

628.1	**Water supply**
.2	**Sewers**
.3	**Sewage treatment and disposal**
.4	**Waste technology, public toilets, street cleaning**
.5	**Pollution control technology and industrial sanitation engineering**
.7	**Sanitary engineering for rural and sparsely populated areas**
.9	**Other branches of sanitary and municipal engineering**

[.091 734]   Treatment in rural regions

Do not use; class in 628.7

.1   Water supply

Class here comprehensive works on engineering of water supply, sewers, sewage treatment and disposal

Class interdisciplinary works on water supply in 363.61

For sewers, see 628.2; for sewage treatment and disposal, see 628.3; for water supply for rural and sparsely populated areas, see 628.72

SUMMARY

628.102 87	**Measurement**
.11	**Sources**
.13	**Storage and conservation**
.14	**Collection and distribution systems**
.15	**Water mains and service pipes**
.16	**Testing, analysis, treatment, pollution countermeasures**

.102 87   Measurement

Do not use for testing; class in 628.161

.11 Sources

Class here protection and engineering evaluation of sources

Class economic and social evaluation of adequacy, development requirements, conservation of sources in 333.91; class hydraulic engineering in 627; class interdisciplinary works on sources, on evaluation of sources in 553.7

See also 628.132 for reservoirs

.112 Lakes, rivers, springs

Class artesian wells in 628.114

.114 Groundwater

Including artesian wells, prevention of seawater intrusion, prospecting for water

Class here wells

.116 Seawater

Class desalinization in 628.167

.13 Storage and conservation

Standard subdivisions are added for either or both topics in heading

Including storage tanks, water towers

Class construction of dams for water storage and conservation in 627.8

.132 Reservoirs

Including evaporation control

Class engineering of reservoirs for water supply, comprehensive works on protection of reservoirs in 627.86

.14 Collection and distribution systems

For construction of dams and reservoirs, see 627.8; for storage and conservation, see 628.13; for water mains and service pipes, see 628.15

.142 Collection systems

.144 Distribution systems

.15 Water mains and service pipes

Class here aqueducts

.16 Testing, analysis, treatment, pollution countermeasures

See Manual at 363.61

.161 Testing and analysis

Class here testing and measurement of pollution

.162	Treatment

Class here treatment of sewage effluent for reuse; comprehensive engineering works on treatment of water supply and sewage

For mechanical treatment, see 628.164; for chemical treatment, see 628.166; for desalinization, see 628.167; for sewage treatment, see 628.3

.162 2	Coagulation (Flocculation), screening, sedimentation (settling)
.164	Mechanical treatment

Including filtration, membrane (osmotic) processes

Class membrane processes for desalinization in 628.1674

For screening, sedimentation, see 628.1622

.165	Aeration

Including deaeration

See also 628.1662 for ozone treatment

.166	Chemical treatment

For coagulation, see 628.1622; for aeration, see 628.165

.166 2	Disinfection

Including chlorination, copper sulfate treatment, ozone treatment, ultraviolet radiation

.166 3	Fluoridation

Class interdisciplinary works on fluoridation in 614.5996

.166 6	Demineralization

Including softening

For desalinization, see 628.167

[.166 7]	Defluoridation

Number discontinued; class in 628.166

.167	Desalinization
.167 2	Distillation
.167 23	Distillation using nuclear energy
.167 25	Solar desalinization
.167 3	Electrolysis
.167 4	Membrane processes
[.167 42]	Electrodialysis

Number discontinued; class in 628.1674

.167 44	Reverse osmosis
[.167 46]	Piezodialysis
	Number discontinued; class in 628.1674
[.167 5–.167 6]	Desalinization by freezing and use of gas hydrates
	Numbers discontinued; class in 628.167
.168	Pollution countermeasures

Class prevention of natural pollution of water sources in 628.11; class interdisciplinary works on water pollution countermeasures in 363.7394

For countermeasures that consist of routine water treatment, see 628.162; for countermeasures that consist of sewage treatment, see 628.3

[.168 028 7]	Testing and measurement
	Do not use; class in 628.161
.168 2	Countermeasures for domestic wastes and sewage
[.168 23]	Detergents
	Number discontinued; class in 628.1682
.168 25	Wastes in sanitary landfills
.168 3	Countermeasures for industrial wastes

For countermeasures for radioactive wastes, see 628.1685. For countermeasures in a specific technology, see the technology, plus notation 0286 from Table 1, e.g., pollution control in metallurgy plants 669.0286

.168 31	Thermal pollution
.168 32	Acid mine drainage
.168 33	Oil spills
.168 36	Wastes from chemical and related industries

Standard subdivisions are added for wastes from chemical and related industries together, for wastes from chemical industries alone

.168 37	Manufacturing wastes

Class thermal pollution from manufacturing processes in 628.16831

For wastes from chemical and related technologies, see 628.16836

.168 4	Countermeasures for agricultural wastes
.168 41	Soil improvement wastes

Including fertilizers, irrigation return flow

.168 42		Pesticides
.168 46		Animal wastes
		Class here feedlot runoff
.168 5		Countermeasures for radioactive wastes

.2   **Sewers**

Class road drainage in 625.734

.202 88	Maintenance and repair [*formerly* 628.24]

.21   Sewer systems for handling precipitation

Including overflows

Class here urban runoff

.212   Storm sewers

.214   Combined sewers

.23   Deodorization and ventilation of sewers

Including ventilators [*formerly* 628.25]

.24   Design and construction

Maintenance and repair relocated to 628.20288

.25   Appurtenances of sewers

Including catch basins, house connections, manholes

Ventilators relocated to 628.23

.29   Pumping stations

.3   **Sewage treatment and disposal**

Standard subdivisions are added for sewage treatment and disposal together, for sewage treatment alone

> *For unsewered sewage disposal, see 628.742. For treatment and disposal of sewage in a specific technology, see the technology, plus notation 0286 from Table 1, e.g., treatment of sewage from beverage plants by beverage makers 663.0286*

> *See Manual at 363.61*

>   628.32–628.35   Treatment

Class comprehensive works in 628.3

.32   Disinfection

.34   **Primary treatment**

Including primary sedimentation, screening

Class comprehensive works on a specific process used in both primary and secondary treatment in 628.351–628.354

.35   **Secondary and tertiary treatment**

Standard subdivisions are added for secondary and tertiary treatment together, for secondary treatment alone

Class here aeration, biological treatment

\>   **628.351–628.354 Secondary treatment**

Class comprehensive works in 628.35

.351   **Oxidation ponds**

Variant names: sewage lagoons, stabilization ponds

Including oxidation ditches

.352   **Filtration**

.353   **Secondary sedimentation**

.354   **Activated sludge process**

.357   **Tertiary treatment**

Including nitrogen removal

Class comprehensive works on a specific process used in both secondary and tertiary treatment in 628.351–628.354

For demineralization, see 628.358

.358   **Demineralization**

.36   **Disposal**

For disposal into water, see 628.39

.362   **Sewage effluent disposal**

For disposal by artificial recharge of groundwater, see 627.56; for treatment for reuse as water supply, see 628.162

.362 3   Sewage irrigation

.364   **Sewage sludge disposal**

Including sanitary landfills

For underground disposal of sludge other than in sanitary landfills, see 628.366; for incineration of sludge, see 628.37; for utilization of sludge, see 628.38

.366   Underground disposal of sludge

Other than in sanitary landfills

Including construction of facilities, storage

.37   Incineration of sludge

.38   Utilization of sludge

For a specific use of sludge, see the use, e.g., use as fertilizer 631.869

.39   Disposal of sewage, sewage effluent, sewage sludge into water

.4   Waste technology, public toilets, street cleaning

Standard subdivisions are added for waste technology, public toilets, street cleaning together; for waste technology alone

Class here industrial waste treatment and disposal

Class pollution from wastes in 628.5; class interdisciplinary works on wastes in 363.728

For gaseous wastes, see 628.53; for waste technology for rural and sparsely populated areas, see 628.74. For control and utilization of wastes in a specific technology, see the technology, plus notation 0286 from Table 1, e.g., waste technology in fuel processing 662.60286

.42   Hazardous and toxic wastes

Standard subdivisions are added for either or both topics in heading

Waste technology only

Class social services for hazardous and toxic wastes in 363.7287

For hazardous and toxic liquid wastes, see 628.43; for hazardous and toxic solid wastes, see 628.44; for hazardous and toxic gaseous wastes, see 628.53

.43   Liquid wastes

For liquid wastes released into bodies of water, see 628.168; for sewage treatment and disposal, see 628.3

.44   Solid wastes (Refuse)

[.440 4]   Special topics

Number and its subdivision discontinued; class in 628.44

.442   Collection

.445   Treatment and disposal

Standard subdivisions are added for either or both topics in heading

> 628.445 6–628.445 9   Disposal

Class comprehensive works in 628.445

.445 6   Disposal on land and underground

.445 62   Open dumps

.445 64   Sanitary landfills

.445 66   Underground disposal

Other than in sanitary landfills

Including construction of facilities, storage

.445 7   Incineration

.445 8   Conversion into useful products

Class here recycling technology

For a specific conversion technology, see the technology, e.g., converting garbage into fertilizer 668.6375

.445 9   Disposal into water

.45   Public toilets

.46   Street cleaning

.5   Pollution control technology and industrial sanitation engineering

Standard subdivisions are added for pollution control technology and industrial sanitation engineering together, for pollution control technology alone

Class here industrial pollution

Class interdisciplinary works on pollution in 363.73

For noise control, see 620.23; for water pollution control, see 628.168. For pollution control technology in a specific technology, see the technology, plus notation 0286 from Table 1, e.g., engineering to control pollution in fuel processing plants 662.60286

.51   Industrial sanitation engineering

Class here plant sanitation

.52   Specific kinds of pollutants

Class here movement through environment

Class specific kinds of pollutants in water in 628.168; class specific kinds of pollutants in air in 628.53; class specific kinds of pollutants in soil in 628.55

.529   Pesticides

.53	**Air pollution**

Class here gaseous wastes, dispersal of pollutants from source

Class air quality surveys in 363.73922

.532	Products of combustion

Class here smog

.535	Radioactive substances

Including radon

.536	Microorganisms
.55	Soil pollution
.7	**Sanitary engineering for rural and sparsely populated areas**

Standard subdivisions are added for either or both topics in heading

Class pollution in rural and sparsely populated areas in 628.5091734; class pest control in rural and sparsely populated areas in 628.96091734

See Manual at 628.7

.72	Water supply
.74	Waste technology
.742	Unsewered sewage disposal

Including septic tanks

.744	Solid waste technology

Class agricultural solid waste technology in 628.746

.746	Agricultural waste technology

Class water pollution from agricultural wastes in 628.1684

For utilization of agricultural wastes in a specific technology, see the technology, e.g., utilization for biogas 665.776

.746 6	Animal wastes

Class here animal manures

.9	**Other branches of sanitary and municipal engineering**
.92	Fire safety and fire fighting technology

Including general disaster and rescue technology

Class interdisciplinary works on fire hazards and their control in 363.37

For a specific disaster and rescue technology, see the technology, e.g., first aid 616.0252

.922   Fire safety technology

         Including fire escapes, rescue operations

         Class here fire prevention

.922 2   Flammability studies and testing

         Standard subdivisions are added for either or both topics in heading

         Class development of fire resistance in products in 628.9223

.922 3   Fireproofing and fire retardation

         Including fire doors, fire retardants

         For fireproofing a specific product, see the product, e.g., textiles 677.689, buildings 693.82

.922 5   Fire detection and alarms

.925   Fire fighting technology

         Class here use of equipment and supplies, comprehensive works on their manufacture

         For shipboard fire fighting technology, see 623.8886; for fire fighting technology in airports, see 629.1368; for forest fire technology, see 634.9618. For manufacture of a specific kind of equipment and supplies, see the kind, e.g., nautical fire fighting equipment 623.865, fire resistant clothing 687.16, fire stations 690.519

.925 2   Extinction with water

         Including hydraulic systems, sprinkler systems

.925 4   Extinction with chemicals

.925 9   Fire fighting vehicles

         Class here fire engines

         For construction of fire engines, see 629.225

.95   Public lighting

         Class lighting of airports in 629.1365

.96   Pest control

         Class here household pests, comprehensive works on pest control technology

         Class interdisciplinary works on pest control in 363.78

         For control of plant pests, see 628.97; for control of agricultural pests, see 632.6

[.963]   Aquatic invertebrates

         Number discontinued; class in 628.96

.964   Mollusks

      Class here slugs, snails

      Use of this number for molluscoids discontinued; class in 628.96

.965   Terrestrial invertebrates

.965 7   Insects

      Including ants, cockroaches, house flies, mosquitoes, termites

[.967]   Cold-blooded vertebrates

      Number discontinued; class in 628.96

.968   Birds

.969   Mammals

.969 3   Rodents

      Class here rat control

[.969 7]   Land carnivores

      Number discontinued; class in 628.969

.97   Control of plant pests

629   Other branches of engineering

SUMMARY

629.04		**Transportation engineering**
	.1	**Aerospace engineering**
	.2	**Motor land vehicles, cycles**
	.3	**Air-cushion vehicles (Ground-effect machines, Hovercraft)**
	.4	**Astronautics**
	.8	**Automatic control engineering**

.04   Transportation engineering

      Unless other instructions are given, class a subject with aspects in two or more subdivisions of 629.04 in the number coming last, e.g., land vehicles 629.049 (*not* 629.046)

      Class military transportation technology in 623.6; class operation of transportation equipment for recreational purposes in 796–797; class interdisciplinary works on transportation in 388. Class technical problems peculiar to transportation of a specific commodity with the commodity, e.g., slurry transportation of coal 662.624

.040 289   Safety measures [*formerly* 629.042]

      Including comfort equipment, e.g., air conditioning; control devices, e.g., markings, signals, signs

      See Manual at 363.1065 vs. 620.86: Accident investigation

[.042]	Safety measures	

Relocated to 629.040289

.045   Navigation

For celestial navigation, see 527

.046   Transportation equipment

Including remote-control vehicles

Class here vehicles

See Manual at 629.046 vs. 388; also at 629.046 vs. 621.43

.046 022 8   Models and miniatures

Class interdisciplinary works on remote-control models in 796.15

See Manual at 796.15 vs. 629.0460228

.047   Stationary transportation facilities

Class here trafficways

For transportation buildings, see 690.53

\>   629.048–629.049   Engineering of transportation in specific mediums

Class comprehensive works in 629.04

For aerospace engineering, see 629.1

.048   Water transportation engineering

For nautical engineering and seamanship, see 623.8; for inland waterways, see 627.1; for harbors, ports, roadsteads, see 627.2; for overwater air-cushion vehicles, see 629.324

.049   Land transportation engineering

For pipes and pipelines, see 621.8672; for railroads, roads, highways, see 625; for motor land vehicles, cycles, see 629.2; for overland air-cushion vehicles, see 629.322; for nonmotor land vehicles, see 688.6

.1   **Aerospace engineering**

Class military aerospace engineering in 623.66

For astronautics, see 629.4

SUMMARY

629.11	**Mechanics and operation of aerospace flight**
.12	**Aerospace vehicles and stationary facilities**
.13	**Aeronautics**
.14	**Portable flight vehicles**

.11   Mechanics and operation of aerospace flight

Class mechanics and operation of a specific type of aerospace flight with the type, e.g., astromechanics 629.411

.12   Aerospace vehicles and stationary facilities

Aerospace vehicles: vehicles that function equally well in the atmosphere and space

Class a specific facility with the facility, e.g., air-cushion vehicles 629.3

For vehicles that function primarily in the atmosphere, see 629.133; for vehicles that function primarily in space, see 629.47

.13   Aeronautics

See Manual at 629.046 vs. 388

SUMMARY

629.130 01–.130 09	**Standard subdivisions**
.130 1–.130 9	**Standard subdivisions of flight**
.132	**Mechanics of flight, flying and related topics**
.133	**Aircraft types**
.134	**Aircraft components and general techniques**
.135	**Aircraft instrumentation (Avionics)**
.136	**Airports**

.130 01–.130 09   Standard subdivisions

.130 1   Philosophy and theory of flight

[.130 153 36]   Aeromechanics of flight

Do not use; class in 629.1323

[.130 155 15]   Aviation meteorology

Do not use; class in 629.1324

.130 2–.130 8   Standard subdivisions of flight

.130 9   Historical, geographic, persons treatment of flight

Do not use for flight guides; class in 629.13254

Record of flying activities in all types of aircraft

.130 91   Transoceanic flights

Do not use for other regional treatment; class in 629.1309

Add to base number 629.13091 the numbers following 551.46 in 551.461–551.469, e.g., transpacific flights 629.130915

.130 92   Fliers

Class here pilots

.132   Mechanics of flight, flying and related topics

[.132 01–.132 09]	Standard subdivisions
	Do not use; class in 629.1301–629.1309
.132 2	Aerostatics
.132 3	Aerodynamics
	Including aircraft noise
	Class here comprehensive works on aeromechanics
	For aerostatics, see 629.1322; for weather aerodynamics, see 629.1324
.132 300 1–.132 300 9	Standard subdivisions
.132 303	Subsonic aerodynamics
.132 304	Transonic aerodynamics
	Including sonic booms
.132 305	Supersonic aerodynamics
.132 306	Hypersonic aerodynamics
.132 31	Gliding and soaring
	Standard subdivisions are added for either or both topics in heading
.132 32	Airflow
	Including turbulence
	For boundary layers, see 629.13237
.132 322	Incompressible airflow
.132 323	Compressible airflow
.132 327	Air pockets (Air holes)
.132 33	Lift and thrust
.132 34	Drag (Air resistance)
.132 35	Pressure distribution and aerodynamic load
	Standard subdivisions are added for either or both topics in heading
.132 36	Stability and control
.132 362	Aeroelasticity, flutter, vibration
.132 364	Moments of inertia
	Including pitch, roll, yaw; restoring torques and damping
.132 37	Boundary layers
.132 38	Propulsion principles

.132 4	Aviation meteorology
	Weather conditions and aerodynamics
	Class piloting in bad weather in 629.1325214
.132 5	Flying and related topics
	Class flying model airplanes in 796.154; class flying kites in 796.158; class air sports in 797.5
	For aviation meteorology, see 629.1324; for automatic control, see 629.1326
	See Manual at 796.15 vs. 629.0460228
[.132 509]	Historical, geographic, persons treatment of flight
	Do not use; class in 629.1309
.132 51	Navigation
.132 52	Piloting
	Class here comprehensive works on piloting and navigation, on piloting airplanes
	For navigation, see 629.13251
[.132 520 92]	Pilots
	Do not use; class in 629.13092
.132 521	General topics
	Unless other instructions are given, class a subject with aspects in two or more subdivisions of 629.132521 in the number coming first, e.g., landing during bad weather 629.1325213 (*not* 629.1325214)
	Class general topics of specific types of aircraft in 629.132522–629.132528
.132 521 2	Takeoff
.132 521 3	Landing
.132 521 4	Piloting under adverse conditions
	Including bad weather, disablement of craft, nighttime
	Class here instrument flying
.132 521 6	Piloting commercial craft
.132 521 7	Piloting private craft
.132 522	Piloting lighter-than-air aircraft

.132 523–.132 528   Piloting specific types of heavier-than-air aircraft

Add to base number 629.13252 the numbers following 629.1333 in 629.13333–629.13338, e.g., piloting helicopters 629.1325252; however, for comprehensive works on piloting airplanes, see 629.13252; for piloting commercial craft, see 629.1325216; for piloting private craft, see 629.1325217

Class hang gliding in 629.14

.132 54   Flight guides (Pilot guides)

Class here charts, logbooks, maps

[.132 540 91–.132 540 99]   Geographic treatment

Do not use; class in 629.132541–629.132549

.132 541–.132 549   Specific geographic areas

Add to base number 629.13254 notation 1–9 from Table 2, e.g., pilot guides to Spain 629.1325446

.132 55   Wreckage studies

See Manual at 363.1065 vs. 620.86: Accident investigation

.132 6   Automatic control

Manned and guided aircraft

See also 629.1352 for automatic pilots

.133   Aircraft types

Class components of specific aircraft types in 629.134

[.133 022 8]   Models and miniatures

Do not use; class in 629.1331

[.133 028 7]   Testing and measurement

Do not use; class in 629.1345

[.133 028 8]   Maintenance and repair

Do not use; class in 629.1346

.133 028 9   Safety measures

Class safety equipment in 629.13443

.133 1	Models and miniatures

Add to base number 629.1331 the numbers following 629.133 in 629.1332–629.1333, e.g., models of helicopters 629.1331352

Class flying model aircraft, interdisciplinary works on building and flying model aircraft in 796.154. Class models and miniatures of a specific aircraft component with the component in 629.134–629.135, plus notation 0228 from Table 1, e.g., models of turboprop engines 629.13435320228

See Manual at 796.15 vs. 629.0460228

.133 2	*Lighter-than-air aircraft
.133 22	*Free and captive balloons

Including hot air balloons

Class dirigible balloons in 629.13324

.133 24	*Airships (Dirigibles)

For specific types of airships, see 629.13325–629.13327

>	629.133 25–629.133 27	Specific types of airships

Class comprehensive works in 629.13324

.133 25	*Rigid airships
.133 26	*Semirigid airships
.133 27	*Nonrigid airships (Blimps)
.133 3	*Heavier-than-air aircraft
.133 32	*Kites

Class flying kites in 796.158

.133 33	*Gliders

Class hang gliders in 629.14

.133 34	Airplanes

For rocket planes, see 629.13338

[.133 340 228]	Models and miniatures

Do not use; class in 629.133134

[.133 340 287]	Testing and measurement

Do not use; class in 629.1345

[.133 340 288]	Maintenance and repair

Do not use; class in 629.1346

*Do not use notation 0228 from Table 1; class in 629.1331

.133 340 4	Special topics
.133 340 42	General topics
.133 340 422	*Private airplanes

Class private short takeoff and landing airplanes in 629.133340426

.133 340 423	*Commercial airplanes

Class commercial short takeoff and landing airplanes in 629.133340426

.133 340 426	*Short takeoff and landing (STOL) airplanes
.133 343	*Propeller-driven airplanes

Piston and turboprop

Including ultralight airplanes

Class propeller-driven seaplanes in 629.133347; class propeller-driven amphibious planes in 629.133348

.133 347	*Seaplanes
.133 348	*Amphibious planes
.133 349	*Jet airplanes

Class jet seaplanes in 629.133347; class jet amphibious planes in 629.133348

.133 35	*Vertical-lift (VTOL) craft

Including autogiros, convertiplanes, flying jeeps

.133 352	*Helicopters
.133 36	*Orthopters (Ornithopters)
.133 38	*Rocket planes
.134	Aircraft components and general techniques

For aircraft instrumentation, see 629.135

[.134 028 7]	Testing and measurement

Do not use; class in 629.1345

[.134 028 8]	Maintenance and repair

Do not use; class in 629.1346

.134 1	Analysis and design

Class analysis and design of parts in 629.1343; class analysis and design of interiors and special equipment in 629.1344

*Do not use notation 0228 from Table 1; class in 629.1331

.134 2	Manufacturing and assembling

Class manufacturing and assembling of parts in 629.1343; class manufacturing and assembling of interiors and special equipment in 629.1344

.134 3	Parts

Class here components

For interiors and special equipment, see 629.1344

.134 31	Airframes

Class a specific component part with the component, e.g., fuselages 629.13434

.134 32	Airfoils

Including wing accessories

Class here wings

For control surfaces, see 629.13433; for propellers, vertical lift rotors, see 629.13436

.134 33	Control surfaces

Including ailerons, flaps, rudders

.134 34	Fuselages
.134 35	Engines and fuels

Standard subdivisions are added for engines and fuels together, for engines alone

Including pollution control

See Manual at 629.046 vs. 621.43

.134 351	Fuels

Class here propellants

Class fuels and propellants for specific engines in 629.134352–629.134355

.134 352	Reciprocating and compound engines

Piston and compound piston-turbine engines

Class comprehensive works on reciprocating, compound, gas-turbine, jet engines in 629.13435

.134 353	Gas-turbine and jet engines

Standard subdivisions are added for either or both topics in heading

.134 353 2	Turboprop engines

.134 353 3	Turbojet engines
.134 353 4	Turboramjet engines
.134 353 5	Ramjet engines
.134 353 6	Pulse-jet engines
.134 353 7	Fan-jet engines
.134 354	Rocket engines
.134 355	Nuclear power plants
.134 36	Propellers and vertical lift rotors
.134 37	Rigging and bracing equipment

Standard subdivisions are added for either or both topics in heading

.134 38	Other equipment
.134 381	Landing gear

See also 678.32 for manufacture of tires

.134 386	Escape equipment

Including capsule cockpits, parachutes, pilot ejection seats

.134 4	Interiors and special equipment
.134 42	Comfort equipment

Including air conditioning, heating, pressurization, soundproofing, ventilating equipment

.134 43	Safety equipment

Including fire prevention equipment, life rafts, safety belts

.134 45	Interiors

Including cabins

.134 5	Tests and measurements

Standard subdivisions are added for either or both topics in heading

Aircraft and airplanes in general

Tests and measurements of specific types of aircraft other than airplanes in general relocated to the type of aircraft in 629.1332–629.1333, plus notation 0287 from Table 1, e.g., tests and measurements of dirigibles 629.133240287, of seaplanes 629.1333470287

Class wreckage studies in 629.13255. Class test and measurements of a specific part with the part, plus notation 0287 from Table 1, e.g., maintenance of interiors 629.134450287

.134 52	Ground tests and inspection
	Standard subdivisions are added for either or both topics in heading
	Including wind and shock tunnels
.134 53	Flight tests
[.134 57]	Measurements
	Number discontinued; class in 629.1345
.134 6	Maintenance and repair
	Standard subdivisions are added for either or both topics in heading
	Aircraft and airplanes in general
	Maintenance and repair of specific types of aircraft other than airplanes in general relocated to the type of aircraft in 629.1332–629.1333, plus notation 0288 from Table 1, e.g., maintenance and repair of dirigibles 629.133240288, of seaplanes 629.1333470288
	Class maintenance and repair of a specific part with the part, plus notation 0288 from Table 1, e.g., maintenance of interiors 629.134450288
.135	**Aircraft instrumentation (Avionics)**
.135 1	Navigation instrumentation
	Including landing and navigation lights
.135 2	Flight instrumentation
	Including accelerometers, altimeters, Machmeters; automatic pilots; air-speed, vertical-speed, turn and bank indicators; directional gyros, gyrohorizons
.135 3	Power-plant monitoring instrumentation
.135 4	Electrical systems
	Class electrical systems of a specific kind of instrumentation in 629.1351–629.1353
.135 5	Electronic systems
	Class electronic systems of a specific kind of instrumentation in 629.1351–629.1353
.136	**Airports**
	Class here commercial land airports
.136 1	Types other than commercial land airports
	Including floating airports (seadromes)
	Class details of airports in 629.1363–629.1368

| .136 12 | Airstrips |
| .136 16 | Heliports |

> 629.136 3–629.136 8 Details of airports

Class comprehensive works in 629.136

.136 3	Runways
.136 34	Pavements
.136 35	Drainage systems
.136 37	Snow removal and compaction
.136 5	Lighting systems
.136 6	Air traffic control systems

See Manual at 629.1366 vs. 387.740426

| .136 8 | Fire fighting equipment |
| .14 | Portable flight vehicles |

Units intended to be carried by a single person

Including hang gliders and gliding

Class hang gliding as a sport in 797.55

.2 Motor land vehicles, cycles

Class military motor land vehicles in 623.747

See Manual at 629.046 vs. 388

SUMMARY

629.201–.209	Standard subdivisions
.22	Types of vehicles
.23	Design, materials, construction
.24	Chassis
.25	Engines
.26	Bodies
.27	Other equipment
.28	Tests, driving, maintenance, repair
.29	Specialized land vehicles

| [.202 28] | Models and miniatures |

Do not use; class in 629.221

| .202 84 | Apparatus and equipment |

Do not use for materials; class in 629.232

| [.202 87] | Testing and measurement |

Do not use; class in 629.282

[.202 88]	Maintenance and repair
	Do not use; class in 629.287
.202 89	Safety measures
	Class safety engineering of motor land vehicles in 629.2042

.204 Special topics

.204 2 Safety engineering of motor land vehicles

Class here comprehensive works on motor land vehicle and highway safety engineering

For highway safety engineering, see 625.70289

.22 Types of vehicles

Class design, materials, construction of a specific type of vehicle in 629.23; class parts of a specific type of vehicle in 629.24–629.27; class driving a specific type of vehicle in 629.283; class nonsurface motor land vehicles, vehicles for extraterrestrial surfaces in 629.29

[.220 228]	Models and miniatures
	Do not use; class in 629.221
[.220 287]	Testing and measurement
	Do not use; class in 629.282
[.220 288]	Maintenance and repair
	Do not use; class in 629.287
.220 289	Safety measures
	Class safety accessories in 629.276
.220 4	Special topics
	Including three-wheel vehicles
.220 42	*Off-road vehicles
	Including all-terrain vehicles, snowmobiles
	For dune buggies, see 629.222
.220 43	*Natural gas vehicles

*Do not use notation 0228 from Table 1 for models and miniatures; class in 629.221. Do not use notation 0287 from Table 1 for testing and measurement; class in 629.282. Do not use notation 0288 from Table 1 for maintenance and repair; class in 629.287

.221   Models and miniatures

Including models and miniatures of off-road vehicles

Add to base number 629.221 the numbers following 629.22 in 629.222–629.229, e.g., models of racing cars 629.2218

Class operating remote-control models in 796.156

See Manual at 796.15 vs. 629.0460228

>   629.222–629.228   Gasoline-powered, oil-powered, man-powered vehicles

Class comprehensive works in 629.22

.222   *Passenger automobiles

Including dune buggies, minivans, station wagons

Class passenger automobiles rebuilt or modified for high speed in 629.2286

See also 629.2234 for vans

.222 1   *Sports cars

Class racing cars in 629.228

For specific named sports cars, see 629.2222

.222 2   Specific named passenger automobiles

Arrange alphabetically by name or make of car

[.222 201–.222 209]   Standard subdivisions

Do not use; class in 629.22201–629.22209

.222 3   *Passenger automobiles for public transportation

.222 32   *Taxicabs and limousines

.222 33   *Buses

.222 34   *Ambulances

.223   *Light trucks

.223 2   *Pickup trucks

.223 4   *Vans

See also 629.222 for minivans

.224   *Trucks (Lorries)

Class here tractor trailers

For light trucks, see 629.223

---

*Do not use notation 0228 from Table 1 for models and miniatures; class in 629.221. Do not use notation 0287 from Table 1 for testing and measurement; class in 629.282. Do not use notation 0288 from Table 1 for maintenance and repair; class in 629.287

.225   *Work vehicles

Including bulldozers, fire engines

For automotive materials-handling equipment, see 621.86; for trucks, see 629.224

.225 2   *Tractors

For steam tractors, see 629.2292

.226   *Campers, motor homes, trailers (caravans)

Standard subdivisions are added for any or all topics in heading

Class here comprehensive works on recreational vehicles (RVs)

Class construction of towed mobile homes in 690.879

For a specific kind of recreational vehicle not provided for here, see the vehicle, e.g., dune buggies 629.222

See also 629.224 for tractor trailers

See Manual at 643.2, 690.879, 728.79 vs. 629.226

.227   *Cycles

.227 1   *Monocycles

.227 2   *Bicycles

For mopeds and motor bicycles, see 629.2275; for tandem bicycles, see 629.2276

.227 3   *Tricycles

.227 5   *Motorcycles

Including minibikes, mopeds, motor bicycles

Class here motorscooters

.227 6   *Tandem bicycles

.228   *Racing cars

Conventional and converted

Including karts

.228 6   *Hot rods

.229   *Other types of vehicles

.229 2   *Steam-powered vehicles

Including steam tractors and steamrollers

Class comprehensive works on tractors in 629.2252

---

*Do not use notation 0228 from Table 1 for models and miniatures; class in 629.221. Do not use notation 0287 from Table 1 for testing and measurement; class in 629.282. Do not use notation 0288 from Table 1 for maintenance and repair; class in 629.287

.229 3	*Electric-powered vehicles
.229 4	*Air-compression-powered vehicles
.229 5	*Solar energy-powered vehicles
.229 6	*Nuclear-powered vehicles
.23	Design, materials, construction

Class materials for, design and construction of parts in 629.24–629.27

.231	Analysis and design

Standard subdivisions are added for either or both topics in heading

Including ergonomic and safety design

Class safety accessories in 629.276

.232	Materials
.234	Manufacturing techniques

Including factory inspection

>   629.24–629.27 Parts

Class comprehensive works in 629.2

.24	Chassis
.242	Supporting frames
.243	Springs and shock absorbers

Standard subdivisions are added for either or both topics in heading

.244	Transmission devices
.244 6	Automatic transmission devices
.245	Rear axles, differentials, drive shafts
.246	Brakes

Including brake fluids

.247	Front axles and steering gear
.248	Wheels
.248 2	Tires

See also 678.32 for manufacture of tires

---

*Do not use notation 0228 from Table 1 for models and miniatures; class in 629.221. Do not use notation 0287 from Table 1 for testing and measurement; class in 629.282. Do not use notation 0288 from Table 1 for maintenance and repair; class in 629.287

.25   **Engines**

Class here pollution control

Most works covering automobile engines as a whole focus on spark-ignition engines and are classed in 629.2504

.250 01–.250 09   Standard subdivisions

>   629.250 1–629.250 9   **Specific types of engines**

Class comprehensive works in 629.25

.250 1   Steam engines

.250 2   Electric engines

.250 3–.250 6   Internal-combustion engines

Add to base number 629.250 the numbers following 621.43 in 621.433–621.436, e.g., spark-ignition engines 629.2504

See Manual at 629.046 vs. 621.43

.250 7   Air-compression engines

.250 8   Solar engines

.250 9   Nuclear engines

>   629.252–629.258   **Parts and auxiliary systems of internal-combustion engines**

Class here comprehensive works on specific kinds of parts and auxiliary systems of automotive engines

Class comprehensive works in 629.25

For a specific part and auxiliary system of noninternal-combustion engines, see 629.25

.252   **Motor parts of internal-combustion engines**

Including mufflers (silencers)

.252 8   Emission control devices

.253   **Fuel systems and fuels of internal-combustion engines**

Standard subdivisions are added for fuel systems and fuels together; for fuel systems alone

Class here electronic fuel injection systems

.253 3   Carburetors

.253 8   Fuels

.254	Ignition, electrical, electronic systems of internal-combustion engines

> Standard subdivisions are added for ignition, electrical, electronic systems together; for ignition systems alone; for electrical systems alone

> Class specific uses of electrical and electronic systems with the use, e.g., electronic fuel injection 629.253, electric starters 629.257

.254 2   Batteries

.254 8   Auxiliary electrical systems

> *For lighting equipment, see 629.271*

.254 9   Electronic systems

.255   Lubricating systems of internal-combustion engines

> Class here lubricants

.256   Cooling systems of internal-combustion engines

> Including antifreeze solutions

.257   Starting devices of internal-combustion engines

.258   Throttles and spark control devices of internal-combustion engines

[.259]   Parts and auxiliary systems of other kinds of power plants

> Number and its subdivisions discontinued; class in 629.25

.26   Bodies

> Including convertible tops, doors, fenders, running boards, seats

.260 288   Maintenance and repair

> Class here bodywork

> Class comprehensive works on customizing and detailing in 629.287

.262   Decorations

.266   Windows and windshields

> Standard subdivisions are added for either or both topics in heading

.27   Other equipment

.271   Lighting equipment

.273   Panel instrumentation

.275   Hardware

> Including handles, hinges, locks

.276	Safety accessories
	Including air bags, bumpers, mirrors, seat belts, windshield wipers and washers
	Class comprehensive works on safety design in 629.231
.277	Comfort, convenience, entertainment equipment
	Including glove compartments, radios, tape players, telephones, televisions, two-way radios
.277 2	Heaters, ventilators, air-conditioners
.28	Tests, driving, maintenance, repair
.282	Tests and related topics
	Class testing and measurement of a specific part with the part, plus notation 0287 from Table 1, e.g., testing brakes 629.2460287
	For factory inspection, see 629.234
.282 4	Road tests (Performance tests)
.282 5	Periodic inspection and roadability tests
.282 6	Wreckage studies
	Determination of mechanical failure through examination of remains
	See Manual at 363.1065 vs. 620.86: Accident investigation
.283	Driving (Operation)
	Class here driving private passenger automobiles
	Class methods of driving a specific kind of vehicle with the vehicle, e.g., driving a truck safely 629.2844
	For driving vehicles other than internal-combustion passenger vehicles, see 629.284
.283 04	Special topics
	Including factors in safe driving
.283 042	Driving off-road vehicles
	Including all-terrain vehicles, snowmobiles
.283 3	Driving public transportation vehicles
.283 32	Taxicabs and limousines
.283 33	Buses
.283 34	Ambulances
.284	Driving vehicles other than internal-combustion passenger vehicles
	Add to base number 629.284 the numbers following 629.22 in 629.223–629.229, e.g., driving trucks 629.2844

.286   Services provided by garages and service stations

> *For maintenance and repair, see 629.287*

> *See also 690.538 for construction of garage and service stations*

.287   Maintenance and repair

Standard subdivisions are added for either or both topics in heading

Class here customizing, detailing

Add to base number 629.287 the numbers following 629.22 in 629.2204–629.229, e.g., repair of motorcycles 629.28775

Arrange alphabetically by trade name under each type of vehicle (Option: Arrange all vehicles regardless of type alphabetically by trade name)

Class works on car tune-ups limited to maintenance and repair of the engine in 629.250288. Class maintenance and repair of a specific part with the part, plus notation 0288 from Table 1, e.g., maintenance of bodies 629.260288

.29   Specialized land vehicles

> *For overland air-cushion vehicles, see 629.322*

.292   Nonsurface motor land vehicles

Including subterranean, ocean floor vehicles

.295   Vehicles for extraterrestrial surfaces

Including moon cars

.3   Air-cushion vehicles (Ground-effect machines, Hovercraft)

Class military air-cushion vehicles in 623.748

.31   General topics

Class general topics applied to specific types of vehicles in 629.32

.313   Lift systems

.314   Propulsion systems

.317   Structural analysis and design

.32   Types of vehicles

.322   Overland air-cushion vehicles

Class amphibious air-cushion vehicles in 629.325

.324   Overwater air-cushion vehicles

Class amphibious air-cushion vehicles in 629.325

.325   Amphibious air-cushion vehicles

.4   **Astronautics**

Class military astronautics in 623.69; class interdisciplinary works on space policy in 333.94

See also 500.5 for space sciences

See Manual at 629.046 vs. 388

SUMMARY

629.401–.409	**Standard subdivisions**
.41	**Space flight**
.43	**Unmanned space flight**
.44	**Auxiliary spacecraft**
.45	**Manned space flight**
.46	**Engineering of unmanned spacecraft**
.47	**Astronautical engineering**

[.401 521]   Astromechanics

Do not use; class in 629.411

.409 2   Astronautical engineers

Class astronauts in 629.450092

.41   Space flight

Class preparation for flight to a specific celestial body with the flight, e.g., preparation for manned lunar flight 629.454

For unmanned space flight, see 629.43; for manned space flight, see 629.45

.411   Astromechanics

.411 1   Gravitation

.411 3   Orbits

.415   Planetary atmospheres

Including reentry problems

.415 1   Aerodynamics

.415 2   Atmospheric thermodynamics

.416   Space phenomena and environments affecting flight

Standard subdivisions are added for either or both topics in heading

Including meteoroids, radiations

.418   Weightlessness

.43   Unmanned space flight

See Manual at 629.43, 629.45 vs. 919.904

.432	Launching
.433	Guidance and homing
.434	Flight of artificial satellites

> Class satellite flight for a specific purpose with the purpose, e.g., weather satellites 551.6354

.435	Astronautical exploratory and data-gathering flights
.435 2	Ionospheric and near-space flights

> Standard subdivisions are added for either or both topics in heading

.435 3	Lunar flights
.435 4	Planetary flights

> Add to base number 629.4354 the numbers following 523.4 in 523.41–523.48, e.g., Venusian probes 629.43542

.437	Communications and tracking
.44	Auxiliary spacecraft
.441	Space shuttles
.442	Space stations

> Class here space laboratories [*formerly* 629.445], space colonies

[.445]	Space laboratories

> Relocated to 629.442

.45	Manned space flight

> Class auxiliary spacecraft in 629.44
>
> *See Manual at 629.43, 629.45 vs. 919.904*

.450 01–.450 09	Standard subdivisions
[.450 1]	Projected accounts

> Relocated to 919.904

.450 7	Selection and training of astronauts

> Standard subdivisions are added for either or both topics in heading

.452	Launching and takeoff

> Standard subdivisions are added for either or both topics in heading

.453	Guidance, homing, navigation
.454	Circumterrestrial and lunar flights
[.454 2–.454 5]	Specific activities

> Numbers discontinued; class in 629.454

.455   Planetary flights

Class here flights to planetary satellites

Add to base number 629.455 the numbers following 523.4 in
523.41–523.48, e.g., flights to Mars 629.4553; then add further as
follows:
    001–009   Standard subdivisions
    [02–05]   Specific activities
                 Notation discontinued; class in base number

Projected accounts of planetary flights relocated to 919.9204

.457   Communications and tracking

.458   Piloting and related activities

.458 2   Piloting

.458 3   Rendezvous with other spacecraft

.458 4   Extravehicular activities

Including space walks

.458 5   Rescue operations

.458 8   Atmospheric entry and landing

.46   Engineering of unmanned spacecraft

Class here artificial satellites

Add to base number 629.46 the numbers following 629.47 in
629.471–629.478, e.g., environmental control 629.467

.47   Astronautical engineering

Class here comprehensive works on spacecraft

*For auxiliary spacecraft, see 629.44; for engineering of unmanned
spacecraft, see 629.46*

.471   Structural analysis and design of spacecraft

Standard subdivisions are added for either or both topics in heading

.472   Spacecraft materials and components

.473   Spacecraft construction

.474   Spacecraft engineering systems

*For propulsion systems, see 629.475; for life-support systems, see
629.477*

.474 2   Flight operations systems

Including guidance, homing, landing, navigation, piloting systems

.474 3   Communication and tracking systems

.474 4	Auxiliary power systems
.474 43	Nuclear power systems
.474 45	Electric and magnetohydrodynamic power systems
.475	Propulsion systems

Including fuels, auxiliary equipment and instrumentation

Class here booster rockets, engines

Class fuels, auxiliary equipment and instrumentation of a specific type of propulsion in 629.4752–629.4755; class comprehensive works on rocketry in 621.4356

See Manual at 629.046 vs. 621.43

.475 2	Chemical propulsion
.475 22	Liquid propellant
.475 24	Solid propellant
.475 3	Nuclear propulsion
.475 4	Photon propulsion
.475 5	Electric and magnetohydrodynamic propulsion

Including plasma and ion propulsion

| .477 | Environmental control and life-support systems |

Standard subdivisions are added for either or both topics in heading

.477 2	Space suits
.477 3	Food and water supply
.477 4	Sanitation and sterilization

Including control of wastes

| .477 5 | Control of temperature, humidity, air supply and pressure |
| .478 | Terrestrial facilities |

Including launch complexes, space ports; spacecraft maintenance, ground testing, repair facilities

| **.8** | **Automatic control engineering** |

Class here automatons that are not computer controlled

Class a specific application with the application, e.g., numerical control of machine tools 621.9023

See Manual at 003.5 vs. 629.8

| .801 | Philosophy and theory |

For control theory, see 629.8312

.804	Special topics
.804 2	Hydraulic control
	Class here fluidics
.804 3	Electric control
	Class computer control in 629.89
.804 5	Pneumatic control
.82	Open-loop systems
	Mechanisms in which outputs have no effect on input signals
	Including vending machines
	Class computer control of open-loop systems in 629.89
.83	Closed-loop (Feedback) systems
	Mechanisms which maintain prescribed relationships between the controlled outputs and the inputs
	Class computer control of closed-loop systems in 629.89
.830 1	Philosophy and theory
	For control theory, see 629.8312
.830 2	Miscellany
.830 288	Maintenance and repair [*formerly* 629.8318]
.831	General principles
	Class general principles of specific mechanisms and systems in 629.832–629.836
.831 2	Control theory
	Mathematical design, analysis, synthesis
	Including optimal control
	Class here comprehensive works on control theory
	Class interdisciplinary works on control theory in 003.5
	For control theory for open-loop systems, see 629.82; for computer control theory, see 629.89
.831 3	Circuitry
.831 4	Feedback characteristics
.831 5	System components
	Including error correctors, error detectors
.831 7	Construction and assembly

| [.831 8] | Maintenance and repair |
| | Relocated to 629.830288 |

> 629.832–629.836 Specific systems

Including components, circuitry

Class here mechanisms

Class comprehensive works in 629.83

.832 Linear systems

.832 3 Servomechanisms

.833 Multiple-loop systems

.836 Nonlinear systems

Including adaptive control systems

.89 Computer control

Class here electronic control, comprehensive works on computer control

Computer control of factory operations for manufacture of products listed in 670–680 is classed in 670.427

.892 Robots

Unless it is redundant, add to base number 629.892 the numbers following 00 in 004–006, e.g., use of digital microcomputers 629.892416, but use of digital computers 629.892 (*not* 629.8924)

.895 Computerized process control

Use of computers to keep conditions of continuous processes as close as possible to desired values or within a desired range by controlling continuous variables such as temperature or pressure

Unless it is redundant, add to base number 629.895 the numbers following 00 in 004–006, e.g., use of digital microcomputers 629.895416, but use of digital computers 629.895 (*not* 629.8954)

630 Agriculture and related technologies

Standard subdivisions are added for agriculture and related technologies together, for agriculture alone

Class here farming, farms, comprehensive works on plant crops

Class agricultural sociology in 306.349; class agricultural economics in 338.1

> See also 307.72 for rural sociology, 333.76 for agricultural land economics, 909.09734 for general works on rural conditions and civilization, 930–990 plus notation 009734 from table under 930–990 for rural conditions and civilization in specific areas
>
> See Manual at 571–575 vs. 630; also at 630 vs 579–590, 641.3

SUMMARY

630.1–.9	**Standard subdivisions**
631	**Specific techniques; apparatus, equipment, materials**
.2	Agricultural structures
.3	Tools, machinery, apparatus, equipment
.4	Soil science
.5	Cultivation and harvesting
.6	Clearing, drainage, revegetation
.7	Water conservation
.8	Fertilizers, soil conditioners, growth regulators
632	**Plant injuries, diseases, pests**
.1	Damages caused by environmental factors
.2	Galls
.3	Diseases
.4	Fungus diseases
.5	Weeds
.6	Animal pests
.7	Insect pests
.8	Viral and rickettsial diseases
.9	General topics of pest and disease control
633	**Field and plantation crops**
.01–.09	Standard subdivisions
.1	Cereals
.2	Forage crops
.3	Legumes, forage crops other than grasses and legumes
.5	Fiber crops
.6	Sugar, syrup, starch crops
.7	Alkaloidal crops
.8	Other crops grown for industrial processing

634	Orchards, fruits, forestry
.04	Cultivation, harvesting, related topics of orchards, of fruits, of trees
.1	Pomaceous fruits
.2	Drupaceous fruits
.3	Citrus and moraceous fruits
.4	Other fruits
.5	Nuts
.6	Tropical and subtropical fruits
.7	Berries and herbaceous tropical and subtropical fruits
.8	Grapes
.9	Forestry

635	Garden crops (Horticulture) Vegetables
.04	Cultivation, harvesting, related topics
.1	Edible roots
.2	Edible tubers and bulbs
.3	Edible leaves, flowers, stems
.4	Cooking greens and rhubarb
.5	Salad greens
.6	Edible garden fruits and seeds
.7	Aromatic and sweet herbs
.8	Mushrooms and truffles
.9	Flowers and ornamental plants

636	Animal husbandry
.001–.009	Standard subdivisions
.01–.08	[General topics in animal husbandry]
.1	Equines Horses
.2	Ruminants and Camelidae Bovidae Cattle
.3	Smaller ruminants Sheep
.4	Swine
.5	Poultry Chickens
.6	Birds other than poultry
.7	Dogs
.8	Cats
.9	Other mammals

637	Processing dairy and related products
.1	Milk processing
.2	Butter processing
.3	Cheese processing
.4	Manufacture of frozen desserts
.5	Egg processing

638	Insect culture
.1	Bee keeping (Apiculture)
.2	Silkworms
.5	Other insects

639	**Hunting, fishing, conservation, related technologies**	
.091 6	**Treatment in air and water**	
.1	**Hunting**	
.2	**Commercial fishing, whaling, sealing**	
.3	**Culture of cold-blooded vertebrates**	**Of fish**
.4	**Mollusk fisheries and culture**	
.5	**Crustacean fisheries**	
.6	**Crustacean culture**	
.7	**Harvest and culture of invertebrates other than mollusks and crustaceaens**	
.8	**Aquaculture**	
.9	**Conservation of biological resources**	

[.15]   Scientific principles

> Do not use; class in 630.21–630.29

.2   Miscellany and scientific principles

.201   Tabulated, illustrative, related materials; humorous treatment; audiovisual treatment

.201 1–.201 2   Tabulated, illustrative, related materials

> Add to base number 630.201 the numbers following —02 in notation 021–022 from Table 1, e.g., agricultural pictures 630.20122

.201 7   Humorous treatment

.201 8   Audiovisual treatment

.202   Synopses and outlines

.203–.209   Other miscellany

> Add to base number 630.20 the numbers following —02 in notation 023–029 from Table 1, e.g., directories 630.205; however, for apparatus, equipment, materials, see 631

.21–.29   Scientific principles

> Do not use for miscellany; class in 630.201–630.209

> Add to base number 630.2 the numbers following 5 in 510–590, e.g., agricultural meteorology 630.2515; however, for agricultural genetics, see 631.5233

.7   Education, research, related topics

.715   Adult education and on-the-job training

> Class here extension departments and services

> *For extension work for young people, see 630.717*

.717   Extension work for young people

631 Specific techniques; apparatus, equipment, materials

Topics common to plant and animal husbandry or limited to plant culture

Class comprehensive works on apparatus, equipment, materials used in a specific auxiliary technique or procedure in 630.208, e.g., computers 630.2085

> *For plant injuries, diseases, pests, see 632; for specific techniques, apparatus, equipment, materials for specific plant crops, see 633–635; for specific techniques, apparatus, equipment, materials for animal husbandry, see 636.08*

SUMMARY

631.2	Agricultural structures
.3	Tools, machinery, apparatus, equipment
.4	Soil science
.5	Cultivation and harvesting
.6	Clearing, drainage, revegetation
.7	Water conservation
.8	Fertilizers, soil conditioners, growth regulators

.2 Agricultural structures

Class construction of farm buildings and structures other than farmhouses in 690.892

.21 Farmhouses

Class construction of farmhouses in 690.86

.22 General-purpose buildings

Class here barns

> *For housing for domestic animals, see 636.0831*

.25 Machine and equipment sheds

.27 Fences, hedges, walls

Construction and use

.28 Roads, bridges, dams

Class construction of bridges in 624.2; class construction of farm roads in 625.74; class construction of dams in 627.8

.3 Tools, machinery, apparatus, equipment

Class manufacture of tools, machinery, apparatus, equipment in 681.763. Class manufacture of a specific article with the article, e.g., tractors 629.2252

> *See also 631.2 for agricultural structures*

.304 Workshops

.34 Equipment for care and shelter of plants

> *For equipment for a specific purpose, see the purpose, e.g., greenhouses 631.583*

.37	Power and power machinery

For a specific use of power and power machinery, see the use, e.g., use of combines 633.1045

.371	Kinds of power

Including human, animal, mechanical, electric power

.372	Tractors
.373	Transport equipment

Including trucks, wagons

.4   Soil science

Class here interdisciplinary works on soils

For a specific aspect of soils, see the aspect, e.g., soil formation 551.305, engineering use of soils 624.151

[.401 2]	Classification of soils

Do not use; class in 631.44

[.401 5]	Scientific principles

Do not use; class in 631.4

[.409]	Historical, geographic, persons treatment

Do not use; class in 631.49

.41	Soil chemistry

For soil fertility, acidity, alkalinity, see 631.42

.416	Inorganic chemistry

Including salinity

Class use of soil conditioners in 631.82

.417	Organic chemistry

Including humus

Class here soil biochemistry

.42	Soil fertility, acidity, alkalinity
.422	Soil fertility

Class use of fertilizers in 631.8

.43	Soil physics
.432	Moisture and hydromechanics

Standard subdivisions are added for either or both topics in heading

.433   Soil mechanics

    Including effect of gas content, micropedology

    Class here soil texture

    Class interdisciplinary works on soil mechanics in 624.15136

    For hydromechanics, see 631.432

.436   Soil temperature

.44   Soil classification

.45   Soil erosion

    Class here control of soil erosion, soil conservation, comprehensive agricultural works on soil and water conservation

    Class comprehensive technological works on soil erosion in 627.5; class interdisciplinary works on soil conservation in 333.7316; class interdisciplinary works on soil erosion in 551.302

    For revegetation, see 631.64; for water conservation, see 631.7

.451   Conservation tillage

    Including mulch tillage

    For tillage for water conservation, see 631.586

.452   Crop rotation and cover crops

    Class comprehensive works on crop rotation in 631.582

.455   Contouring and terracing

.456   Strip cropping

.46   Soil biology

    For soil biochemistry, see 631.417

.47   Soil and land-use surveys

    Standard subdivisions are added for either or both topics in heading

.470 01–.470 08   Standard subdivisions

[.470 09]   Historical, geographic, persons treatment

    Do not use; class in 631.4701–631.479

.470 1–.479   Historical, geographic, persons treatment

    Class here soil types in specific areas

    Add to base number 631.47 notation 01–9 from Table 2, e.g., soil survey of Gonzales County, Texas 631.47764257
        Subdivisions are added for either soil or land-use surveys or both together

    See Manual at 631.474–631.479 vs. 631.494–631.499

.49 Historical, geographic, persons treatment

Add to base number 631.49 notation 01–9 from Table 2, e.g., soil science in China 631.4951

For soil and land-use surveys, see 631.47

See Manual at 631.474–631.479 vs. 631.494–631.499

.5 **Cultivation and harvesting**

.51 Soil working (Tillage)

Before and after planting

Class here cultivation in the narrow sense as synonymous with tillage

Class soil working in special methods of cultivation in 631.58

For conservation tillage, see 631.451

.52 Production of propagational organisms and new varieties

Standard subdivisions are added for production of propagational organisms and new varieties together, for production of propagational organisms alone

Including domestication, plant selection, seedlings

Class here plant breeding [*formerly* 631.53], nursery practice

.521 Seeds

.523 Development of new varieties

Including plant introduction

Class here germ plasm, hybrids

Class interdisciplinary works on germ plasm in 333.9534

.523 3 Agricultural genetics

Class here genetic engineering

.526 Bulbs and tubers

Standard subdivisions are added for either or both topics in heading

.53 Plant propagation

Class here comprehensive works on plant propagation and nursery practice

Plant breeding relocated to 631.52

For nursery practice, see 631.52; for grafting, pruning, training, see 631.54

.531 Propagation from seeds (Sowing)

.532 Propagation from bulbs and tubers

Standard subdivisions are added for either or both topics in heading

.533   Propagation from suckers, runners, buds

> Class propagation from tubers in 631.532; class propagation from cuttings in 631.535

.534   Propagation by layering

.535   Propagation from cuttings and slips

.536   Transplanting

> Class here planting seedlings

.54   Grafting, pruning, training

> Most works on grafting and pruning will be classed in 634.044 and cognate numbers in 634.1–634.8 or in 635.9

.541   Grafting

.542   Pruning

.546   Training on poles, trellises, walls

.55   Harvesting

> Including mowing, reaping

> Class operations subsequent to harvesting in 631.56

.558   Yields

> *See Manual at 338.1 vs. 631.558*

.56   Operations subsequent to harvesting

> Including cleaning, husking, packing

.567   Grading

.568   Storage

.57   Varieties and kinds of organisms used in agriculture

> Class here description of cultivated organisms that contain little or no information on how to grow them

> Class biology of agricultural plants in 580

> *For development of new varieties, see 631.523*

.58   Special methods of cultivation

> Including double cropping, multiple cropping, permiculture

> Class special methods of cultivation as topics in land economics in 333.76; class special methods of cultivation as topics in agricultural economics in 338.162

.581   Reduced cultivation methods

> Class here minimum tillage, surface tillage

.581 2	Fallowing
.581 4	No-tillage
.581 8	Shifting cultivation (Slash-and-burn agriculture)
.582	Crop rotation

> *For crop rotation to control erosion, see 631.452*

.583   Controlled-environment agriculture

Including forcing, retarding, hotbeds, use of artificial light

Class here greenhouse agriculture

Most works on use of artificial light in agriculture will be classed in 635.0483 and 635.9826

> *For greenhouse gardening, see 635.0483*

.584   Organic farming

> *For organic gardening, see 635.0484. For a specific aspect of organic farming, see the aspect, e.g., compost 631.875*

.585   Soilless culture (Hydroponics)

Most works on soilless culture will be classed in 635.0485 and cognate numbers in 635.1–635.9

.586   Dry farming

Class here tillage for water conservation

.587   Irrigation

Use only for works describing what is done on the farm, e.g., installation and use of center-pivot sprinkler systems

Class digging wells in 628.114; class interdisciplinary works on technological aspects of irrigation, works on obtaining irrigation water from off-farm sources in 627.52; class interdisciplinary works on irrigation in 333.913

> *For sewage irrigation, see 628.3623*

.6   **Clearing, drainage, revegetation**

.61   Clearing

.62   Drainage

Class off-farm drainage projects, interdisciplinary works on technological aspects of drainage in 627.54

.64   Revegetation

Including inland dune stabilization, surface mine reclamation

Class reforestation in 634.956; class interdisciplinary works on technological aspects of reclamation in 627.5

.7   **Water conservation**

> *For tillage for water conservation, see 631.586*

.8   **Fertilizers, soil conditioners, growth regulators**

Standard subdivisions are added for fertilizers, soil conditioners, growth regulators together; for fertilizers alone

Class here interdisciplinary works on agricultural chemicals

Class comprehensive works on soil fertility in 631.422

> *For pesticides, see 632.95; for manufacture of agricultural chemicals, see 668.6*

.81   Nutritive principles, complete fertilizers, methods of application

> *For nutritive principles and methods of application of specific fertilizers, see 631.83–631.87*

.811   Nutritive principles

.813   Complete fertilizers

.816   Methods of application

.82   Soil conditioners

Including conditioners for control of salinity

.821   Acid-soil conditioners

Including lime

.825   Alkaline-soil conditioners

.826   Conditioners for soil texture

Including peat

>   631.83–631.87   Specific kinds of fertilizers

Class comprehensive works in 631.8

.83   Potassium fertilizers

.84   Nitrogen fertilizers

.841   Ammonium, cyanamide, urea fertilizers

> *For ammonium nitrate, see 631.842*

.842   Nitrate fertilizers

Including ammonium nitrate

.843   Slaughterhouse residues

> *For bone meal, see 631.85*

.847	Biological methods of soil nitrification

Use of nitrifying bacteria, nitrifying crops

.85	Phosphorus fertilizers

Including bone meal

.86	Organic fertilizers

Class here animal wastes

> For slaughterhouse residues, see 631.843; for vegetable manures and converted household garbage, see 631.87

.861	Farm manure
.866	Guano
.869	Sewage sludge
.87	Vegetable manures and converted household garbage

Standard subdivisions are added for vegetable manures and converted household garbage together, for vegetable manure alone

.874	Green manures
.875	Compost

Including converted household garbage [*formerly* 631.877]

[.877]	Converted household garbage

Relocated to 631.875

.89	Growth regulators

632   Plant injuries, diseases, pests

Standard subdivisions are added for plant injuries, diseases, pests together; for plant injuries alone

Class here pathology of agricultural plants; comprehensive works on plant and animal injuries, diseases, pests

Class use of agricultural plants in studies of basic pathological processes in 571.92; class interdisciplinary works on physiology and pathology of agricultural plants in 571.2

> For injuries, diseases, pests of specific plant crops, see 633–635; for veterinary medicine, see 636.089

.1	**Damages caused by environmental factors**

Class here damages caused by climatic change, by weather

.11	Frost injury

Including other low-temperature injuries

.12	Drought and heat damage
.14	Hail damage
.15	Lightning damage
.16	Wind and rain damage
.17	Flood damage
.18	Fire damage
.19	Pollution damages

Class here air pollution damages, diseases caused by pollution

Radiation injury relocated to 632.3

> ## 632.2–632.8 Specific diseases and pests

Class here control of specific diseases

Class comprehensive works on diseases and pests together in 632; class comprehensive works on diseases in 632.3; class comprehensive works on pests in 632.6; class comprehensive works on disease and pest control in 632.9

For pesticides regardless of disease or pest, see 632.95

See Manual at 632.2–632.8; also at 632.95 vs. 632.2–632.8

.2   Galls

Class here gall-producing organisms

Pathological development relocated to 632.3

.3   Diseases

Including radiation injury [*formerly* 632.19], pathological development [*formerly* 632.2], protozoan diseases [*formerly* 632.631]

Class here disease control

For diseases caused by pollution, see 632.19; for galls, see 632.2; for fungus diseases, see 632.4; for viral and rickettsial diseases, see 632.8; for pesticides used in disease control, see 632.95

.32   Bacterial diseases

For rickettsial diseases, see 632.8

.4   Fungus diseases

Add to base number 632.4 the numbers following 579.5 in 579.52–579.59, e.g., rusts 632.492, smuts 632.493

.5   **Weeds**

Including poisonous plants

Class here plant pests, weed control

For herbicides, see 632.954

.52   Parasitic weeds

Class parasitic microorganisms in 632.3

[.58]   Weeds

Number discontinued; class in 632.5

.6   **Animal pests**

Class here pests, control of specific animal pests

Add to base number 632.6 the numbers following 59 in 592–599, e.g., nematodes 632.6257, common rats 632.69352; however, protozoan diseases relocated from 632.631 to 632.3; for gall-producing animal peats, see 632.2; for insect pests, see 632.7

Class comprehensive works on agricultural pest control, on specific topics of pest control other than pesticides in 632.9; class interdisciplinary works on pest control technology in 628.96; class interdisciplinary works on pests, works on pest control services in 363.78

For weeds, see 632.5; for pesticides, see 632.95; for predator control in animal husbandry, see 636.0839

.7   **Insect pests**

Add to base number 632.7 the numbers following 595.7 in 595.72–595.79, e.g., locusts 632.726, beetles 632.76

.8   **Viral and rickettsial diseases**

.9   **General topics of pest and disease control**

Standard subdivisions are added for pest and disease control together, for pest control alone

Including genetic engineering for pest resistance

Class here control of animal pests, integrated pest management

For disease control, see 632.3; for weed control, see 632.5; for control of specific animal pests, see 632.6

.902 84   Apparatus and equipment

Do not use for materials; class in 632.95

.93   Plant quarantine

.94   Crop-dusting, fumigation, spraying

.940 284   Apparatus and equipment

                             Do not use for materials; class in 632.95

.95   Pesticides

             Including algicides

             Class here pesticides used to control animal pests

             Class chemicals used in biological control in 632.960284

             See Manual at 632.95 vs. 632.2–632.8

.950 4   Special topics

                             Including fumigants

.950 42   Undesired effects and their control

                             Including pesticide resistance

                             Class interdisciplinary works on environmental effects of
                             pesticides in 363.7384

.951   Pesticides used to control specific animal pests

             Class comprehensive works on pesticides used to control animal pests in
             632.95

             Including rodenticides, vermicides

.951 7   Insecticides

             Including DDT

             Class here pesticides used to control arthropods

.952   Fungicides

             Use of this number for algicides discontinued; class in 632.95

.953   Bactericides

.954   Herbicides

.96   Biological control

> ## 633–635 Specific plant crops

Add to each subdivision identified by * as follows:
1–6   Cultivation and harvesting
    Add the numbers following 631.5 in 631.51–631.56, e.g.,
    harvesting 5
    For special cultivation methods, see 8
7   Varieties and kinds
    Class specific techniques of cultivation and harvesting specific
    varieties in 1–6; class fertilizers, soil conditioners, growth
    regulators for specific varieties in 89; class injuries, pests,
    diseases of specific varieties in 9
8   Special cultivation methods; fertilizers, soil conditioners, growth
    regulators
81–87   Special cultivation methods
    Add to 8 the numbers following 631.58 in 631.581–631.587,
    e.g., irrigation 87
89   Fertilizers, soil conditioners, growth regulators
    Add to 89 the numbers following 631.8 in 631.81–631.89, e.g.,
    compost 8975
9   Injuries, diseases, pests
    Add to 9 the numbers following 632 in 632.1–632.9, e.g., insect
    pests 97

Class comprehensive works in 630

See Manual at 633–635

633   Field and plantation crops

Large-scale production of crops intended for agricultural purposes or industrial
processing other than preservation

Class truck farming in 635

*For a specific field or plantation crop not provided for here, see the crop, e.g.,
bananas 634.772*

SUMMARY

633.01–.09	Standard subdivisions
.1	Cereals
.2	Forage crops
.3	Legumes, forage crops other than grasses and legumes
.5	Fiber crops
.6	Sugar, syrup, starch crops
.7	Alkaloidal crops
.8	Other crops grown for industrial processing

[.001]   Philosophy and theory

Relocated to 633.01

[.002]	Miscellany
	Relocated to 633.02
[.003–.009]	Standard subdivisions
	Relocated to 633.03–633.09
.01	Philosophy and theory [*formerly* 633.001]
.02	Miscellany [*formerly* 633.002]
[.028]	Auxiliary techniques and procedures; apparatus, equipment, materials
	Do not use for auxiliary techniques and procedures; class in 630.208
[.028 4]	Apparatus, equipment, materials
	Do not use; class in 631
.03–.09	Standard subdivisions [*formerly* 633.003–633.009]
.1	**Cereals**
	Including grain amaranths
	For cereal crops grown for forage, see 633.25
.104	*Cultivation, harvesting, related topics
.11	*Wheat
.12	*Buckwheat
.13	*Oats
.14	*Rye
.15	*Corn
	Variant names: Indian corn, maize
	Class sweet corn in 635.672
	For popcorn, see 635.677
.16	*Barley
.17	Millets, grain sorghums, upland and wild rice
.171	*Millets (Panicum and related genera)
.174	*Grain sorghums
	Class sweet sorghums in 633.62
.178	*Wild rice
.179	*Upland rice

*Add as instructed under 633–635

.18   *Rice

Class here paddy rice

For upland rice, see 633.179

See also 633.178 for wild rice

.2   Forage crops

Class here forage grasses, Pooideae grasses

For forage crops other than grasses, see 633.3

.200 1–.200 9   Standard subdivisions

.202   Pastures and their grasses

Class here range management

Class pasture use of forests in 634.99; class comprehensive works on ranches and farms devoted to livestock in 636.01

For specific pasture grasses, see 633.21–633.28

.208   *Cultivation, harvesting, related topics of forage crops

.21   *Bluegrasses (Poa)

.22   *Orchard grass

Variant name: cocksfoot

.23   *Bent grasses (Agrostis)

.24   *Timothy

.25   Cereal grasses

Add to base number 633.25 the numbers following 633.1 in 633.11–633.18, e.g., rye grasses 633.254

.26   Sedges

.27   Panicoideae grasses

For corn, see 633.255; for millets, see 633.2571; for sorghums, see 633.2574

.28   Other Pooideae grasses

Including fescues (Festuca)

*Add as instructed under 633–635

.3	**Legumes, forage crops other than grasses and legumes**

Standard subdivisions are added for legumes and forage crops other than grasses and legumes together, for legumes alone

Class here comprehensive works on legumes [*formerly* 635.65], grain legumes, forage legumes

Class interdisciplinary works on legumes as food in 641.3565

For leguminous fruits, see 634.46; for garden legumes, see 635.65

.304	*Cultivation, harvesting, related topics
.31	*Alfalfa

Variant name: lucerne

.32	*Trifolium clovers

Class here trefoils [*formerly also* 633.374]

Class sweet clovers in 633.366

.33	*Cowpeas

Variant name: black-eyed peas

.34	*Soybeans

Variant names: sojas, soyas

.35	*Vetches
.36	Lespedeza, sweet clovers, lupines, peanuts, field peas
.364	*Lespedeza

Variant name: bush clover

.366	*Sweet clovers (Melilotus)

Variant name: lotus [*formerly also* 633.374]

.367	*Lupines
.368	*Peanuts

Variant name: groundnuts

.369	*Field peas (Pisum arvense)

Variant name: Austrian winter peas

.37	Other legumes
.372	*Kidney beans

Variant names: navy, pea beans

*Add as instructed under 633–635

[.374]	Trefoils and lotus
	Trefoils relocated to 633.32; lotus relocated to 633.366
.39	Forage crops other than grasses and legumes
.5	**Fiber crops**
	Class here soft-fiber crops
	Class fiber plants grown for paper pulp in 633.89

>	633.51–633.56 Soft fibers
	Class comprehensive works in 633.5
.51	*Cotton
.52	*Flax
.53	*Hemp (Cannabis sativa)
	See also 633.79 for marijuana
.54	*Jute
.55	*Ramie
.56	Other soft fibers
	Including kenaf
.57	Hard fibers
	For hard fibers not provided for below, see 633.58
.571	*Manila hemp
	Variant name: abaca
.576	*Pineapple fibers
.577	*Sisal (Agave fibers)
.58	Other hard fibers
	Including bamboo, rattan, other basketwork and wickerwork plants
.6	**Sugar, syrup, starch crops**
	Standard subdivisions are added for sugar, syrup, starch crops together; for sugar crops alone; for syrup crops alone
.61	*Sugar cane
.62	*Sorgo
	Variant name: sweet sorghums

*Add as instructed under 633–635

.63	*Sugar beets
.64	*Sugar maples
.68	Starch crops

Including arrowroot, sago, taro

Class a crop raised for starch and another product with the other product, e.g., potatoes 635.21

.682	*Cassava (Manioc)

.7 Alkaloidal crops

.71	*Tobacco
.72	*Tea
.73	*Coffee
.74	*Cacao
.75	*Poppies (Papaver somniferum)
.76	*Kola nuts (Cola nuts)
.77	*Maté

Variant name: Paraguay tea

.78	*Chicory
.79	*Marijuana

Class here hashish

See also 633.53 for hemp

.8 Other crops grown for industrial processing

.81	Perfume-producing plants
.82	Flavoring-producing plants

Including hops, mints, sassafras, vanilla, wintergreen

For spices, see 633.83; for alliaceous plants, see 635.26; for aromatic and sweet herbs, see 635.7

.83	Spices

Including allspice, cinnamon, clove, ginger, nutmeg

Class here sweet spices

For hot spices, see 633.84

.84	Hot spices

Including black pepper, chili, horseradish, mustard, paprika

*Add as instructed under 633–635

.85	Plants producing nonvolatile oils

> Class here oilseed plants
>
> *For coconuts, see 634.61; for olives, see 634.63*

.851	*Oil palms
.853	*Rapeseed
.86	Dye-producing plants
.87	Tannin-producing plants

> Including canaigre

.88	Medicine-producing plants

> Add to base number 633.88 the numbers following 58 in 583–588, e.g., ginsengs 633.88384; however, for a crop producing medicine as a secondary product, see the primary product, e.g., poppy 633.75

.89	Crops grown for other industrial purposes
.895	Rubber-producing and resin-producing plants
.895 2	*Rubber tree (Hevea brasiliensis)
.895 9	*Turpentine-producing plants
.898	Insecticide-producing plants

634   Orchards, fruits, forestry

> Fruits: reproductive bodies of seed plants having an edible more or less sweet pulp associated with the seed
>
> Standard subdivisions are added for orchards, fruits, forestry together; for orchards alone; for fruits alone
>
> Class here comprehensive works on tree crops
>
> *For trees grown for plantation crops, see 633; for pepos, see 635.61; for ornamental trees, see 635.977*

SUMMARY

634.04	**Cultivation, harvesting, related topics of orchards, of fruits, of trees**
.1	**Pomaceous fruits**
.2	**Drupaceous fruits**
.3	**Citrus and moraceous fruits**
.4	**Other fruits**
.5	**Nuts**
.6	**Tropical and subtropical fruits**
.7	**Berries and herbaceous tropical and subtropical fruits**
.8	**Grapes**
.9	**Forestry**

.04	*Cultivation, harvesting, related topics of orchards, of fruits, of trees

*Add as instructed under 633–635

> **634.1–634.6 Orchards and their fruits**

Class comprehensive works in 634

.1   **Pomaceous fruits**

.11   *Apples

.13   *Pears

         See also 634.653 for alligator pears

.14   *Quinces

.15   *Medlars (Mespilus germanica)

         See also 634.16 for Japanese medlars

.16   *Loquats

         Variant name: Japanese medlars

.2   **Drupaceous fruits**

.21   *Apricots

.22   *Plums

.23   *Cherries

.25   *Peaches

.257   Varieties and kinds

         Number built according to instructions under 633–635

         Including nectarines

.3   **Citrus and moraceous fruits**

.304   *Citrus fruits

         For specific citrus fruits, see 634.31–634.34

.31   *Oranges

.32   *Grapefruit

.33   Citron group

.331   *Citrons

.334   *Lemons

.337   *Limes

.34   *Kumquats

*Add as instructed under 633–635

.36	*Moraceous fruits

> *For figs, see 634.37; for mulberries, see 634.38; for breadfruit, see 634.39*

.37	*Figs
.38	*Mulberries
.39	*Breadfruit

.4   Other fruits

Class tropical and subtropical fruits not provided for here in 634.6

.41	Annonaceous fruits

Including papaws

.42	Myrtaceous and passifloraceous fruits
.421	*Guavas
.425	*Passion fruit
.43	Sapotaceous fruits
.44	Anacardiaceous fruits

Including mangoes

Class cashews in 634.573

.45	*Persimmons
.46	Leguminous fruits

Including carob

Class comprehensive works on legumes in 633.3

.5   Nuts

.51	*Walnuts
.52	*Pecans
.53	*Chestnuts
.54	*Filberts
.55	*Almonds
.57	Cashews, pistachios, Brazil nuts
.573	*Cashews
.574	*Pistachios
.575	*Brazil nuts

*Add as instructed under 633–635

.6	**Tropical and subtropical fruits**

Not provided for elsewhere

For herbaceous tropical and subtropical fruits, see 634.77

.61	*Coconuts
.62	*Dates
.63	*Olives
.64	*Pomegranates
.65	Papayas, avocados, mangosteens
.651	*Papayas
.653	*Avocados

Variant name: alligator pears

.655	*Mangosteens
.7	**Berries and herbaceous tropical and subtropical fruits**

Standard subdivisions are added for berries and herbaceous tropical and subtropical fruits together, for berries alone

Class here comprehensive works on small fruits

For a specific small fruit not provided for here, see the fruit, e.g., mulberries 634.38, grapes 634.8

.71	Cane fruits (Rubus)
.711	*Raspberries
.713	*Blackberries
.714	*Loganberries
.717	*Dewberries
.718	*Boysenberries
.72	Ribes
.721	*Currants
.725	*Gooseberries
.73	Huckleberries and blueberries
.732	*Huckleberries
.737	*Blueberries (Vaccinium)
.74	Other bush fruits

Including barberries, juneberries

*Add as instructed under 633–635

.75   *Strawberries

.76   *Cranberries

.77   Herbaceous tropical and subtropical fruits

> Class comprehensive works on tropical and subtropical fruits in 634.6

.772   *Bananas

.773   *Plantains

.774   *Pineapples

.775   Cactus fruits

.8   **Grapes**

> Class here viticulture

[.81]   Soil working

> Relocated to 634.881

.82   Injuries, diseases, pests

> Add to base number 634.82 the numbers following 632 in 632.1–632.9, e.g., fungus diseases 634.824

.83   Varieties and kinds

> Class a specific aspect of varieties and kinds with the aspect, e.g., fungus diseases of muscadines 634.824

.88   Cultivation and harvesting

> Add to base number 634.88 the numbers following 631.5 in 631.51–631.58, e.g., soil working 634.881 [*formerly* 634.81]; however, for varieties, see 634.83

.9   **Forestry**

SUMMARY

634.92	**Forest management**
.93	**Access and safety features**
.95	**Silviculture**
.96	**Injuries, diseases, pests**
.97	**Kinds of trees**
.98	**Forest exploitation and products**
.99	**Agroforestry**

[.906 85]   Management of production

> Do not use; class in 634.92

---

*Add as instructed under 633–635

>   634.92–634.96   General topics

Class general topics applied to a specific kind of tree in 634.97; class comprehensive works in 634.9

For exploitation and products, see 634.98

.92   Forest management

Class here production management in forestry

Class comprehensive works on management in forestry in 634.9068. Class production management of a specific aspect of forestry with the aspect, e.g., production management of logging 634.980685

.928   Production planning and mensuration

.928 3   Production planning

.928 5   Mensuration

Including estimation

.93   Access and safety features

Including lookout towers, roads

.95   Silviculture

.953   Forest thinning

Former heading: Maintenance cuttings

.955   Brush disposal

Including prescribed burning

.956   Forestation

Class here afforestation, reforestation, plant breeding

Class interdisciplinary works on afforestation in 333.75152; class interdisciplinary works on reforestation in 333.75153

.956 2   Seeds and seedlings

Seeding at permanent site relocated to 634.9565

.956 4   Nursery practice

For seeds and seedlings, see 634.9562

.956 5   Propagation at permanent site

Including seeding at permanent site [*formerly also* 634.9652]

.96   Injuries, diseases, pests

Add to base number 634.96 the numbers following 632 in 632.1–632.9, e.g., forest fire technology 634.9618

.97 Kinds of trees

Class here general topics of forestry applied to specific kinds of trees

Add to each subdivision identified by † as follows:
2–6   General topics
Add the numbers following 634.9 in 634.92–634.96, e.g., reforestation 56
For exploitation and products, see 8
7   Varieties and kinds
Class a specific general topic with respect to a specific variety or kind with the topic, e.g., reforestation of a variety 56
8   Exploitation and products
Standard subdivisions are added for either or both topics in heading
Class here logging, logs, lumbering
For minor products, see 634.985–634.987; for sawmill operations, see 674.2
83   Pulpwood

.972 Dicotyledons

Class here hardwoods

For other dicotyledons, see 634.973

.972 1 †Oaks

.972 2 †Maples

.972 3 †Poplars

Class aspens, cottonwoods in 634.97365

See also 634.97322 for yellow poplar (tulip tree)

.972 4 †Chestnuts

.972 5 †Beeches

.972 6 †Birches

.972 7 †Lindens

.972 77 Varieties and kinds

Number built according to instructions under 634.97

Including basswood (American linden), lime (European linden)

.972 8 †Elms

.973 Other dicotyledons

Add to base number 634.973 the numbers following 583 in 583.2–583.9, e.g., eucalyptus 634.973766

†Add as instructed under 634.97

.974 Monocotyledons

Class here palm forestry

See also 633.58 for rattan palms, 633.851 for oil palms, 634.61 for coconut palm, 635.97745 for ornamental palms

[.974 1–.974 9] Specific Monocotyledons

Numbers discontinued; class in 634.974

.975 Gymnosperms

> 634.975 1–634.975 8 Coniferous trees

Class comprehensive works in 634.975

For coniferous trees not provided for here, see 634.9759

.975 1 †Pines

Class dammar, huon pines in 634.97593

.975 2 †Spruces

.975 3 †Hemlocks

.975 4 †Firs

.975 5 †Cypresses

.975 6 †Cedars

.975 7 †Larches

.975 8 †Sequoias

.975 9 Other gymnosperms

Add to base number 634.9759 the numbers following 585 in 585.2–585.9, e.g., kauris (dammar pines) 634.97593

.98 Forest exploitation and products

Standard subdivisions are added for either or both topics in heading

Class here logging, logs, comprehensive works on lumbering

Class exploitation and products of specific kinds of trees in 634.97; class lumber in 674. Class trees cultivated for products other than lumber or pulp with the product, e.g., turpentine trees 633.8959, pecan trees 634.52

For sawmill operations, see 674.2

.983 Pulpwood

Class nonwoody plants grown for paper pulp in 633.89

†Add as instructed under 634.97

> 634.985–634.987   Exploitation of minor forest products

     Use only for products that have not been cultivated

     Class here minor products of specific kinds of trees

     Class comprehensive works in 634.987

.985   Bark

.986   Sap

.987   Minor forest products

     Including fruits, seeds, nuts

     For bark, see 634.985; for sap, see 634.986

.99   Agroforestry

     Forestry in combination with other farming

     Including farm forestry, woodlots

     Class a specific aspect of agroforestry with the aspect, e.g., logging 634.98

635   Garden crops (Horticulture)   Vegetables

Vegetables: crops grown primarily for human consumption without intermediate processing other than cooking and preservation

Class here home gardening, truck farming

Class orchards in 634

SUMMARY

635.04		**Cultivation, harvesting, related topics**
	.1	**Edible roots**
	.2	**Edible tubers and bulbs**
	.3	**Edible leaves, flowers, stems**
	.4	**Cooking greens and rhubarb**
	.5	**Salad greens**
	.6	**Edible garden fruits and seeds**
	.7	**Aromatic and sweet herbs**
	.8	**Mushrooms and truffles**
	.9	**Flowers and ornamental plants**

.04   *Cultivation, harvesting, related topics

> 635.1–635.8   **Edible garden crops**

     Class comprehensive works in 635

.1   **Edible roots**

     For cassava, see 633.682

*Add as instructed under 633–635

.11   *Beets

.12   Turnips, rutabagas, celeriac

.125   *Turnips

                    Class rutabagas in 635.126

.126   *Rutabagas

                    Variant names: Russian turnips, swedes, Swedish turnips

.128   *Celeriac

.13   *Carrots

.14   *Parsnips

.15   *Radishes

.16   *Salsify

.2   Edible tubers and bulbs

             Standard subdivisions are added for edible tubers and bulbs together, for edible tubers alone

             For taro, see 633.68

.21   *Potatoes

.22   *Sweet potatoes

.23   *Yams (Dioscorea)

.24   *Jerusalem artichokes

.25   *Onions

.26   Alliaceous plants

                    Including chives, garlic, leeks, shallots

                    For onions, see 635.25

.3   Edible leaves, flowers, stems

             For cooking greens and rhubarb, see 635.4; for salad greens, see 635.5

             See Manual at 635.3 and 635.4, 635.5

.31   *Asparagus

.32   *Artichokes

                    See also 635.24 for Jerusalem artichokes

*Add as instructed under 633–635

.34   *Cabbage

Class here comprehensive works on cultivation of Brassica oleracea

For cauliflower and broccoli, see 635.35; for Brussels sprouts, see 636.36

.347   Varieties and kinds

Number built according to instructions under 633–635

Including kale (collards)

.35   *Cauliflower and broccoli

Subdivisions are added for either or both topics in heading

.36   *Brussels sprouts

.4   Cooking greens and rhubarb

Standard subdivisions are added for cooking greens and rhubarb together, for cooking greens alone

See Manual at 635.3 and 635.4, 635.5

.41   *Spinach

.42   *Chard

.48   *Rhubarb

.5   Salad greens

See Manual at 635.3 and 635.4, 635.5

.51   *Dandelions

.52   *Lettuce

.53   *Celery

See also 635.128 for celeriac

.54   *Chicory

.55   *Endive

.56   Sorrel and cresses

.6   Edible garden fruits and seeds

.61   Pepos

Class here melons

For squashes and pumpkins, see 635.62; for cucumbers, see 635.63

.611   *Muskmelons

.615   *Watermelons

*Add as instructed under 633–635

.62	*Squashes and pumpkins

Subdivisions are added for either or both topics in heading

.63	*Cucumbers
.64	Other garden fruits
.642	*Tomatoes
.643	*Sweet peppers

Variant name: bell, green peppers

.646	*Eggplants
.648	*Okra
.65	Garden legumes

Comprehensive works on legumes relocated to 633.3

.651	*Broad beans
.652	*Kidney beans

Variant names: snap, string, wax beans

.653	*Lima beans
.655	*Soybeans

Variant names: sojas, soyas

.656	*Peas (Pisum sativum)

Variant name: English peas, garden peas

.657	*Chick-peas
.658	*Lentils
.659	Other garden legumes
.659 2	*Black-eyed peas

Variant name: cowpeas

.659 6	*Peanuts

Variant name: groundnuts

.67	Corn

Variant names: Indian corn, maize

.672	*Sweet corn
.677	*Popcorn

*Add as instructed under 633–635

.7   **Aromatic and sweet herbs**

> Standard subdivisions are added for either or both topics in heading
>
> Class here herb gardens

.8   **Mushrooms and truffles**

> Standard subdivisions are added for mushrooms and truffles together, for mushrooms alone

.9   **Flowers and ornamental plants**

> Standard subdivisions are added for either or both topics in heading
>
> Class here floriculture
>
> Class landscape architecture of flower gardens in 712
>
> > *For planting and cultivation of roadside vegetation, see 625.77*
> >
> > *See Manual at 635.9 vs. 582.1*

SUMMARY

635.91	Specific techniques; apparatus, equipment, materials	
.92	Injuries, diseases, pests	
.93	Groupings by life duration; taxonomic groupings	
.94	Plants propagated from bulbs and tubers	
.95	Groupings by environmental factors	
.96	Groupings for special areas and purposes	
.97	Other groupings of ornamental plants	
.98	Special methods of cultivation	

[.902 84]   Apparatus, equipment, materials

> Do not use; class in 635.91

.91   Specific techniques; apparatus, equipment, materials

> Add to base number 635.91 the numbers following 631 in 631.2–631.8, e.g., nursery practice 635.9152 [*formerly* 635.969], propagating ornamental plants by specific means other than bulbs and tubers 635.91532 [*formerly* 635.94]; however, for special methods of cultivation, see 635.98
>
> Class specific techniques, apparatus, equipment, materials of specific groupings of ornamental plants in 635.93–635.97

.92   Injuries, diseases, pests

> Add to base number 635.92 the numbers following 632 in 632.1–632.9, e.g., fungus diseases 635.924
>
> > *For injuries, diseases, pests of specific groupings of plants, see 635.93–635.97*

> 635.93–635.97 Groupings of plants

Unless other instructions are given, class a subject with aspects in two or more subdivisions of 635.93–635.97 in the number coming first in the schedule, e.g., succulent house plants 635.9525 (*not* 635.965)

Class comprehensive works in 635.9

.93 Groupings by life duration; taxonomic groupings

.931 Groupings by life duration

Class specific taxonomic kinds regardless of life duration in 635.933–635.938

For perennials, see 635.932

.931 2 *Annuals

.931 4 *Biennials

.932 *Perennials

.933–.938 Taxonomic groupings

Add to base number 635.93 the numbers following 58 in 583–588, e.g., cacti 635.93356, roses 635.933734, orchids 635.9344; however, for everlastings, see 635.973; for comprehensive works on dicotyledons, see 635.9; for taxonomic groupings of trees, see 635.9773–635.9775

.94 Plants propagated from bulbs and tubers

Standard subdivisions are added for either or both topics in heading

Class here propagating ornamental plants from bulbs, from tubers

Use of this number for comprehensive works on groupings by means of propagation discontinued; class in 635.9

Propagating ornamental plants by specific means other than bulbs and tubers relocated to 635.9153

[.942] Plants propagated from seeds

Number discontinued; class in 635.9

[.944] Plants propagated from bulbs and tubers

Number discontinued; class in 635.94

[.946–.948] Plants propagated by other means

Numbers discontinued; class in 635.9

.95 Groupings by environmental factors

*Add as instructed under 633–635

.951	Native habitats

Add to base number 635.951 notation 4–9 from Table 2, e.g., ornamentals native to Scotland 635.951411

.952	Groupings by climatic factors

Including arctic plants

Class comprehensive works on temperate-zone plants in 635.9

.952 3	*Tropical plants
.952 5	*Desert plants

Including drought-resistant plants

Class here succulent plants [*formerly* 635.955]

Class works on succulent plants emphasizing cactus in 635.93356

.952 8	*Alpine plants

Including alpine gardens [*formerly* 635.9672], high-altitude plants

Class "alpine gardens" in the sense synonymous with rock gardens (that is, as rock gardens with nonalpine as well as alpine plants) in 635.9672

.953	Groupings by seasonal and diurnal factors

Including winter-flowering plants, morning-blooming and night-blooming plants

.954	Groupings by natural light factors

Including plants favoring sunlight

See also 635.9826 for artificial-light gardening

.954 3	*Shade-tolerant plants
.955	Groupings by soil factors

Including plants favoring difficult, poorly-drained, sandy soils

Succulent plants relocated to 635.9525

Class plants suitable for rock gardens in 635.9672

.96	Groupings by special areas and purposes

Class comprehensive works on plants for all purposes in 635.9

For foliage plants, see 635.975; for butterfly gardening, see 638.5789

.962	*Flower beds
.963	*Borders and edgings

Subdivisions are added for either or both topics in heading

*Add as instructed under 633–635

.964	Ground cover
	Class here grass
.964 2	*Turf
	Class lawns in 635.9647
.964 7	*Lawns
.965	*House plants
	Class here indoor gardening in the home
	Window-box gardens relocated to 635.9678
	Class comprehensive works on container gardening in 635.986
	For bonsai, see 635.9772
.966	*Flowers for cutting
	Class flower arrangement in 745.92
.967	Special kinds of gardens
.967 1	Roof, balcony, patio gardens
	Class comprehensive works on container gardening in 635.986
.967 2	*Rock gardens
	Alpine gardens relocated to 635.9528
.967 4	*Water gardens
.967 6	*Wild-flower gardens
	Class wild flowers of a specific native habitat in 635.951
.967 8	*Window-box gardens [*formerly* 635.965]
.968	Plants grown for fragrance and color
[.969]	Nursery practice
	Relocated to 635.9152
.97	Other groupings of ornamental plants
.973	*Everlastings
.974	*Vines
	Class here climbing plants
.975	*Foliage plants
.976	*Shrubs and hedges
	Subdivisions are added for either or both topics in heading
	Class hedges used as fences in 631.27

*Add as instructed under 633–635

.977   Trees

              Class here urban forestry; potted, shade, street trees

              Including tree planting

              Class comprehensive works on container gardening in 635.986

.977 1   General kinds of ornamental trees

              Class general kinds of trees of a specific taxa in 635.9773–635.9775; class comprehensive works in 635.977

              For bonsai, see 635.9772

.977 13   *Flowering trees

.977 15   *Evergreen trees

              Class Christmas trees, evergreen trees in the sense of conifers in 635.9775

.977 2   *Bonsai

              Class here dwarf potted trees, miniature trees, penjing

              Class specific taxonomic kinds of bonsai in 635.9773–635.9775

.977 3–.977 5 Taxonomic groupings

              Add to base number 635.977 the numbers following 58 in 583–585, e.g., elms 635.977345; however, for comprehensive works on dicotyledonous trees, see 635.977

.98   Special methods of cultivation in floriculture

              Class special methods of cultivation of specific groupings of plants in 635.93–635.97; class comprehensive works on special methods of cultivating vegetables and ornamental plants in 635.048

.982   Controlled-environment gardening

              For bell-jar gardening, see 635.985

.982 3   *Greenhouse gardening

.982 4   *Terrariums

.982 6   *Artificial-light gardening

.985   *Bell-jar gardening

.986   *Container gardening

              Class here pot gardening

.987   Organic gardening

              Class a specific aspect of organic gardening in floriculture with the aspect in 635.91–635.98, e.g., compost 635.91875

*Add as instructed under 633–635

636   Animal husbandry

Class here interdisciplinary works on species of domestic mammals [*formerly* 599]

For culture of nondomesticated animals, see 639

See Manual at 800 vs. 398.245, 590, 636

SUMMARY

636.001–.009	**Standard subdivisions**
.01–.08	**[General topics in animal husbandry]**
.1	**Equines Horses**
.2	**Ruminants and Camelidae Bovidae Cattle**
.3	**Smaller ruminants Sheep**
.4	**Swine**
.5	**Poultry Chickens**
.6	**Birds other than poultry**
.7	**Dogs**
.8	**Cats**
.9	**Other mammals**

.001   Philosophy and theory

[.001 576 5]   Genetics

                    Do not use; class in 636.0821

.002   Miscellany

[.002 77]   Ownership marks

                    Do not use; class in 636.0812

.003–.006   Standard subdivisions

.007   Education, research, related topics

.007 9   Competitions, festivals, awards, financial support

                    Animal shows and related awards relocated to 636.0811

.008–.009   Standard subdivisions

.01   Ranches and farms

                    Range management relocated to 636.0845

                    Class feeding livestock in 636.084

.07   Young of animals

                    Class production and maintenance, rearing for specific purposes, veterinary medicine of young animals in 636.08

.08   Specific topics in animal husbandry

Unless other instructions are given, class a subject with aspects in two or more subdivisions of this schedule in the number coming last, e.g., care and maintenance of pets 636.0887 (*not* 636.083)

For ranches and farms, see 636.01; for young of animals, see 636.07

SUMMARY

636.081	**Selection, showing, ownership marks**
.082	**Breeding**
.083	**Care, maintenance, training**
.084	**Feeding**
.085	**Feeds and applied nutrition**
.086	**Field-crop feeds**
.088	**Animals for specific purposes**
.089	**Veterinary sciences Veterinary medicine**

[.080 1–.080 9]   Standard subdivisions

Do not use; class in 636.001–636.009

.081   Selection, showing, ownership marks

For selection in breeding, see 636.082

.081 1   Showing

Class here animal shows and related awards [*formerly also* 636.0079], show animals [*formerly* 636.0888], judging

.081 2   Ownership marks

Class here branding

.082   Breeding

Including breeding stock [*formerly* 636.0881], selection in breeding

.082 1   Genetics

Including germ plasm

Class here genetic engineering

Class interdisciplinary works on livestock genetic resources in 333.954

.082 2   Breeding records

Class here herdbooks, pedigrees, studbooks

.082 4   Breeding and reproduction methods

[.082 41–.082 43]   Specific methods of breeding

Numbers discontinued; class in 636.0824

.082 45   Artificial insemination

.083   **Care, maintenance, training**

Including transportation

Class here stable management

For feeding, see 636.084

.083 1   Housing

Including barns, cages, stockyards

Class waste management in 636.0838; class construction of housing for domestic animals in 690.892

See also 636.0843 for feedlot management

.083 2   Animal welfare

Including animal hospitals

Class here animal rescue, animal shelters, condition of livestock

Class veterinary care of animals in 636.089

See also 179.3 for ethical aspects of animal care

.083 3   Individual tending

Including dipping, shearing

Class here grooming

.083 5   Training

Class training for a specific purpose in 636.088

.083 7   Harnesses and accessories

Most works on harnesses and accessories will be classed under horses in 636.10837

.083 8   Animal waste management

.083 9   Predator control

For predator control in wildlife conservation, see 639.966

.084   **Feeding**

For feeds and applied nutrition, see 636.085

.084 3   Feedlot management

For feedlot waste management, see 636.0838

.084 5   Grazing

Class here range management [*formerly* 636.01], browsing, herding

For development of pasturage, see 633.202; for pasture use of forests, see 634.99

.085	Feeds and applied nutrition
.085 2	Applied nutrition
	Class here composition and food value
	For composition and food value of a specific feed, see the feed, e.g., food value of silage 636.0862
.085 21	Nitrogen
.085 22	Proteins
.085 27	Minerals
	Class here trace elements
.085 28	Vitamins
.085 5	Feeds
	Class here other specific feeds [*formerly* 636.087]
	Class growing forage crops in 633.2; class grazing in 636.0845
	For field-crop feeds, see 636.086
[.085 51]	Green fodder
	Relocated to 636.086
[.085 52]	Silage
	Relocated to 636.0862
[.085 54]	Dry fodder
	Relocated to 636.086
.085 56	Feed from wastes
	Class here feed from agricultural wastes
.085 57	Feed additives and formula feeds
.086	Field-crop feeds
	Including green fodder [*formerly* 636.08551], dry fodder [*formerly* 636.08554]
.086 2	Silage [*formerly* 636.08552]
[.087]	Other specific feeds
	Relocated to 636.0855
.088	Animals for specific purposes
	See Manual at 636.1–636.8 vs. 636.088
[.088 1]	Breeding stock
	Relocated to 636.082

.088 2	Draft animals (Beasts of burden)

Class comprehensive works on work animals in 636.0886

.088 3	Animals raised for food

For animals raised for eggs and milk, see 636.08842

.088 4	Animals raised for special products

For animals raised for food, see 636.0883

.088 42	Animals raised for eggs and milk

Class milk processing in 637.1; class egg processing in 637.5

See Manual at 636.1–636.8 vs. 636.088

.088 44	Animals raised for hide

Animals raised for fur (fur farming) relocated to 636.97

For hair, see 636.08845

.088 45	Animals raised for hair and feathers

Including bristles, wool

.088 5	Laboratory animals
.088 6	Work animals

Including animals used to guard and herd

Hunting animals relocated to 636.0888

For draft animals, see 636.0882; for sport and stunt animals, see 636.0888

.088 7	Pets

Class here obedience training

Class reminiscences about and true accounts of pets in 808.883. Class reminiscences about and true accounts of pets in a specific literature with the literature in 800, plus notation 803 from Table 3–B under the appropriate language, e.g., reminiscences in English about pets 828.03; class literary treatment of pets other than reminiscences with the appropriate literary form in 800, e.g., a late 20th century English novel about pets 823.914

See Manual at 800 vs. 398.245, 590, 636

.088 8	Sport and stunt animals

Including hunting animals [*formerly also* 636.0886]; circus, fighting, game, racing animals

Show animals relocated to 636.0811

Class comprehensive works on work animals in 636.0886

See also 636.0811 for exhibiting animals

.088 9   Zoo animals

.089   Veterinary sciences   Veterinary medicine

Add to base number 636.089 the numbers following 61 in 610–619, e.g., veterinary viral diseases 636.0896925

Class animal hospitals, animal welfare in 636.0832

>   **636.1–636.8   Specific kinds of domestic animals**

Except for modifications shown under specific entries, add to each subdivision identified by * as follows:

01	Philosophy and theory
[015765]	Genetics
	Do not use; class in 2
02–06	Standard subdivisions
07	Education, research, related topics
079	Competition, festivals, awards, financial support
	Do not use for animal shows and related awards; class in 1
08–09	Standard subdivisions
1	Showing
	Class here judging
2	Breeding
22	Breeding records
	Class here origin of the breed or breeds; herdbooks, pedigrees, studbooks
3	Care, feeding, training
35	Training
39	Veterinary care

Class comprehensive works in 636

See Manual at 636.1–636.8 vs. 636.088

.1   Equines   Horses

.100 1–.108   Standard subdivisions, specific topics in husbandry of horses

Add to base number 636.10 the numbers following 636.0 in 636.001–636.08, e.g., housing horses 636.10831; however, for racehorses, see 636.12; for riding horses, see 636.13; for draft horses, see 636.15

Class training of riders and drivers, comprehensive works on training horses and their riders and drivers in 798

.109   Miniature horses [*formerly* 636.11–636.17]

Regardless of breed

>   636.11–636.17   Specific breeds and kinds of horses

Miniature horses regardless of breed relocated to 636.109

Class comprehensive works in 636.1

.11   Oriental horses

.112   *Arabian horse

.12   *Racehorses

Trotters relocated to 636.175

For a specific breed of racehorse, see the breed, e.g., Thoroughbred horse 636.132

.13   Saddle (Riding) horses

Including American saddlebred, Tennessee walking horses; Appaloosa, mustang

For wild mustang, see 599.6655; for Oriental horses, see 636.11; for comprehensive works on racehorses, see 636.12

.132   *Thoroughbred horse

.133   *Quarter horse

.138   *Lippizaner horse

.14   *Carriage horses

Including Cleveland bay and Hackney horses

Class here coach horses, comprehensive works on harness horses (carriage horses and light harness horses)

Comprehensive works on harness and draft horses relocated to 636.15

For light harness horses, see 636.17

.15   *Draft horses

Including Belgian draft, Clydesdale, Shire horses

Class here comprehensive works on harness and draft horses [*formerly* 636.14]

For harness horses, see 636.14

.16   Ponies

Including Chincoteague, Iceland, Shetland, Welsh ponies

[.161]   Specific topics in husbandry of ponies

Number discontinued; class in 636.16

*Add as instructed under 636.1–636.8

.17	Light harness horses
.175	*Standardbred horse

Class here trotters [*formerly* 636.12]

.177	*Morgan horse
.18	Other equines

Including zebras

.182	*Donkeys (Burros)
.183	*Mules
.2	**Ruminants and Camelidae Bovidae Cattle**

For smaller ruminants, see 636.3

.200 1–.208   Standard subdivisions, specific topics on husbandry of ruminants and Tylopoda

Add to base number 636.20 the numbers following 636.0 in 636.001–636.08, e.g., heifers 636.207; however, for cattle for specific purposes, see 636.21

.21   Cattle for specific purposes

Class here production, maintenance, training

Add to base number 636.21 the numbers following 636.088 in 636.0882–636.0889, e.g., raising cattle for beef 636.213, for milk 636.2142

Class veterinary science in 636.2089; class specific breeds of cattle for specific purposes in 636.22–636.28; class milking and milk processing in 637.1

\>   636.22–636.28   Specific breeds of cattle

Class comprehensive works in 636.2

.22	British breeds of cattle
.222	English beef breeds

Including Hereford and Shorthorn cattle

.223	Scottish, Welsh, Irish beef breeds

Including Aberdeen Angus, Galloway, Highland cattle

.224	Channel Island dairy breeds

Including Guernsey and Jersey cattle

.225	Scottish and Irish dairy breeds

Including Ayrshire and Dexter cattle

*Add as instructed under 636.1–636.8

.226	Dual-purpose breeds

Including Devon, English Longhorn, Polled Shorthorn cattle

.23	German, Dutch, Danish, Swiss breeds of cattle
.232	Beef breeds
.234	Dairy breeds

Including Brown Swiss and Holstein-Friesian cattle

.236	Dual-purpose breeds
.24	French and Belgian breeds of cattle
.242	Beef breeds
.244	Dairy breeds
.246	Dual-purpose breeds
.27	Other European breeds of cattle
.28	Non-European breeds of cattle
.29	Other larger ruminants and Camelidae
.291	Zebus (Brahmans)
.292	Bison

Variant names: American buffalo, buffalo

See also 636.293 for water buffalo

.293	Other Bovoidea

Including water buffalo

.294	Cervidae and Giraffidae

Including deer, reindeer

.295	*Camels

Subdivisions are added for specific breeds

.296	Camelidae

Including vicuña

For camels, see 636.295

.296 6	*Llamas (Guanaco, Alpacas)

Subdivisions are added for specific breeds

.3	**Smaller ruminants**	**Sheep**

Class Tragulidae in 636.963

*Add as instructed under 636.1–636.8

.300 1–.308   Standard subdivisions, specific topics in husbandry of smaller ruminants

> Add to base number 636.30 the numbers following 636.0 in 636.001–636.08, e.g., sheep ranches 636.301; however, for sheep for specific purposes, see 636.31

.31   Sheep for specific purposes

Class here production, maintenance, training

Add to base number 636.31 the numbers following 636.088 in 636.0882–636.0889, e.g., raising sheep for mutton 636.313, for wool 636.3145

Class veterinary science in 636.3089; class specific breeds of sheep for specific purposes in 636.32–636.38

>   636.32–636.38   Specific breeds of sheep

Class comprehensive works in 636.3

.32   British breeds of sheep

.33   German, Dutch, Swiss breeds of sheep

.34   French and Belgian breeds of sheep

.35   Italian breeds of sheep

.36   Merino breeds

Class here Spanish breeds of sheep

.366   Spanish Merino breeds

.367   Other European Merino breeds

.368   Non-European Merino breeds

.37   Other European breeds of sheep

.38   Non-European breeds of sheep

For non-European Merino breeds, see 636.368

.381   American breeds

.385   Asian breeds

.386   African breeds

.39   Goats

.390 01–.390 8   Standard subdivisions, specific topics in husbandry of goats

> Add to base number 636.390 the numbers following 636.0 in 636.001–636.08, e.g., breeding 636.39082; however, for goats for specific purposes, see 636.391

.391   Goats for specific purposes

Class here production, maintenance, training

Add to base number 636.391 the numbers following 636.088 in 636.0882–636.0889, e.g., raising goats for hair 636.39145

Class veterinary science in 636.39089; class specific breeds of goats for specific purposes in 636.392–636.398

.392–.398   Specific breeds of goats

Add to base number 636.39 the numbers following 636.3 in 636.32–636.38, e.g., Angora goat 636.3985

.4   Swine

.400 1–.408   Standard subdivisions, specific topics in husbandry of swine

Add to base number 636.40 the numbers following 636.0 in 636.001–636.08, e.g., swine for specific purposes other than food 636.4088 [*formerly* 636.41]

Class swine for food in 636.4

[.41]   Swine for specific purposes other than food

Relocated to 636.4088

>   636.42–636.48 Specific breeds of swine

Class comprehensive works in 636.4

.42–.47   European breeds of swine

Add to base number 636.4 the numbers following 636.3 in 636.32–636.37, e.g., British breeds 636.42

.48   Non-European breeds of swine

.482   Poland China swine

.483   Duroc-Jersey swine

.484   American breeds

Including Cheshire, Chester White, Hampshire, Victoria swine

For Poland China swine, see 636.482; for Duroc-Jersey swine, see 636.483

.485   Asian breeds

.486   African breeds

.489   Pacific Ocean island breeds

.5   **Poultry   Chickens**

Class here interdisciplinary works on species of domestic birds [*formerly* 598], comprehensive works on raising birds

For birds other than poultry, see 636.6

.500 1–.508   Standard subdivisions, specific topics of husbandry of poultry

Add to base number 636.50 the numbers following 636.0 in 636.001–636.08, e.g., chicken breeding 636.5082; however, for poultry for specific purposes, see 636.51

.51   Poultry for specific purposes

Class here production, maintenance, training

Add to base number 636.51 the numbers following 636.088 in 636.0882–636.0889, e.g., raising chickens for meat 636.513, for eggs 636.5142

Class veterinary science in 636.5089; class specific breeds of chickens for specific purposes in 636.52–636.58; class poultry other than chickens for specific purposes in 636.59

>   636.52–636.58   Specific breeds of chickens

Class comprehensive works in 636.5

.52–.57   European breeds of chickens

Add to base number 636.5 the numbers following 636.3 in 636.32–636.37, e.g., Leghorn 636.55

For diminutive varieties of European breeds of chickens, see 636.587

.58   Non-European and diminutive breeds of chickens

.581   American breeds

For Plymouth Rock chicken, see 636.582; for Wyandotte chicken, see 636.583; for Rhode Island Red chicken, see 636.584; for diminutive varieties of American breeds, see 636.587

.582   Plymouth Rock chicken

.583   Wyandotte chicken

.584   Rhode Island Red chicken

.585   Asian breeds

For diminutive varieties of Asian breeds, see 636.587

.587   Diminutive varieties

.587 1   *Bantams

---

*Add as instructed under 636.1–636.8

.587 2		Cornish fowl
.59	Other poultry	
.592		Turkeys

.592 001–.592 08   Standard subdivisions, specific topics in husbandry of turkeys

> Add to base number 636.5920 the numbers following 636.0 in 636.001–636.08, e.g., raising turkeys for meat 636.5920883

.593	Guinea fowl
.594	Pheasants
.595	Peafowl
.596	*Pigeons

> Subdivisions are added for specific breeds

.597   *Ducks

> Subdivisions are added for specific breeds

.598   Geese

.6   Birds other than poultry

> Class comprehensive works on birds in 636.5

.61   Birds raised for feathers

> Ratites raised for feathers relocated to 636.69

.63   Game birds

.68   Song and ornamental birds

> Including mynas, toucans
>
> Class here aviary and cage birds
>
> *For peafowl, see 636.595*

.681   Swans

.686   Finches, parrots, hawks

.686 2   *Finches

.686 25   *Canaries

> Subdivisions are added for specific varieties

.686 4   *Budgerigars

> Variant names: lovebirds; grass, shell parrakeets
>
> Subdivisions are added for specific varieties
>
> Class comprehensive works on parrakeets in 636.6865

---

*Add as instructed under 636.1–636.8

.686 5		*Parrots

Including cockatoos, conures, lories, macaws, comprehensive works on parrakeets

For budgerigars (lovebirds), see 636.6864

.686 56   *Cockatiels

Subdivisions are added for specific varieties

.686 9   *Hawks

Class here falcons

Subdivisions are added for specific varieties

.69   Ratites

Including ratites raised for feathers [*formerly* 636.61]

.694   *Ostriches

.7   Dogs

.700 1–.708   Standard subdivisions, specific topics in husbandry of dogs

Add to base number 636.70 the numbers following 636.0 in 636.001–636.08, e.g., breeding 636.7082; however, for working dogs, see 636.73; for hunting and sporting dogs, see 636.75

.71   Breeds of dogs

For specific breeds, see 636.72–636.76

>   636.72–636.75   Specific breeds and groups of dogs

Class comprehensive works in 636.71

For toy dogs of any breed, see 636.76

See Manual at 636.72–636.75

.72   Nonsporting dogs

Including bichon frise, Boston terrier, bulldog, Chinese Shar-Pei, chow chow, Dalmatian, Finnish Spitz, French bulldog, Keeshond, Lhasa apso, Schipperke, Tibetan spaniel, Tibetan terrier

Class here utility breeds (United Kingdom)

Class comprehensive works on terriers in 636.755

.728   *Poodles

Class here miniature poodles

Subdivisions are added for specific breeds

---

*Add as instructed under 636.1–636.8

.73   Working and herding dogs

Standard subdivisions are added for working and herding dogs together, for working dogs alone

Including sled dogs, watchdogs (guard dogs)

Including akita, Alaskan Malamute, Bernese mountain dog, boxer, bullmastiff, Eskimo dogs, Great Dane, Great Pyrenee, Komondor, Kuvasz, mastiffs, Newfoundland, Portuguese water dog, Rottweiler, Saint Bernard, Samoyed, Schnauzers (standard and giant), Siberian husky

Class Finnish spitz in 636.72; class Norwegian elkhound in 636.753; class miniature Schnauzer in 636.755

.736   *Doberman pinscher

Class miniature pinscher in 636.76

.737   Herding dogs

Including Australian cattle dog, Belgian Malinois, Belgian Tervuren, Bouvier des Flandres, Briard, puli, Welsh corgis; sheep dogs other than collies and German shepherd dog

.737 4   *Collies

Subdivisions are added for specific breeds

.737 6   *German shepherd dog (German police dog)

.75   Sporting dogs, hounds, terriers

Class here hunting dogs, sporting dogs (United Kingdom)

.752   Sporting dogs

Class here bird dogs, gundogs (United Kingdom)

Including Brittany, Vizsla, Weimaraner, wirehaired pointing griffon

.752 4   *Spaniels

Subdivisions are added for specific breeds

See also 636.76 for Japanese spaniel (chin)

.752 5   *Pointers

Subdivisions are added for specific breeds

.752 6   *Setters

Subdivisions are added for specific breeds

.752 7   *Retrievers

Subdivisions are added for specific breeds

*Add as instructed under 636.1–636.8

.753 **Hounds**

Including Norwegian elkhound

See Manual at 636.72–636.75: Hounds

.753 2 Gazehounds (Sighthounds)

Including Ibizan hound, Saluki, Scottish deerhound, whippet

For Afghan hound, see 636.7533; for greyhound, see 636.7534; for Borzoi, Irish wolfhound, see 636.7535

.753 3 *Afghan hound

.753 4 *Greyhound

Class Italian greyhound in 636.76; class greyhound racing in 798.8

.753 5 *Wolfhounds

Including Borzoi, Irish wolfhound

.753 6 Scent hounds (Tracking hounds)

Including Basenji, basset hound, black and tan coonhound, bloodhound, foxhounds, harrier, otterhound, petit basset griffon vendéen, pharaoh hound, Rhodesian ridgeback

For beagle, see 636.7537; for dachshund, see 636.7538

.753 7 *Beagle

.753 8 *Dachshund

Class miniature dachshunds in 636.76

.755 **Terriers**

Including miniature Schnauzer

For Boston and Tibetan terriers, see 636.72; for toy terriers, see 636.76

.755 9 *Bull terriers

Class here pit bull terriers

Subdivisions are added for specific breeds

.76 **Toy dogs**

Including affenpinscher, Brussels griffon, Chihuahua, Chinese crested, English toy spaniel, Italian greyhound, Japanese chin, Maltese, Mexican hairless (Xoloizuintli), miniature dachshund, miniature pinscher, Papillon, Pekingese, Pomeranian, pug, shih tzu, silky terrier, toy Manchester terrier, toy poodle, Yorkshire terrier

Class miniature poodle in 636.72; class miniature Schnauzer in 636.755

.8 **Cats**

*Add as instructed under 636.1–636.8

.800 1–.808	Standard subdivisions, specific topics in husbandry of cats

Add to base number 636.80 the numbers following 636.0 in 636.001–636.08, e.g., breeding cats 636.8082, cats for specific purposes other than pets 636.8088

Class cats as pets in 636.8

>   636.82–636.83   Specific breeds and kinds of domestic cats

Class comprehensive works in 636.8

See Manual at 636.82–636.83

.82	Shorthair cats

Including Chartreaux, Russian blue cats

Class here foreign (Oriental) shorthair cats

.822	Common shorthair cats

Breeds of British Isles, Canada, United States

Including Manx cat [*formerly* 636.823]; Bengal, rex cats

[.823]	Manx cat

Relocated to 636.822

.824	*Burmese cat [*formerly* 636.825]

Subdivisions are added for specific varieties

.825	*Siamese cat

Subdivisions are added for specific varieties

Use of this number for comprehensive works on Asian shorthair cats discontinued; class in 636.82

Burmese cat relocated to 636.824

.826	*Abyssinian cat

Subdivisions are added for specific varieties

Use of this number for other shorthair cats discontinued; class in 636.82

.83	Longhair cats

Including Himalayan, Maine coon, Turkish Angora, Turkish Van cats

.832	*Persian cat

Subdivisions are added for specific varieties

.89	Nondomestic cats

Including cheetah, ocelot

*Add as instructed under 636.1–636.8

.9   **Other mammals**

[.91]   Marsupials and monotremes

> Marsupials relocated to 636.92, monotremes relocated to 636.929

.92–.99   Other specific mammals

> Add to base number 636.9 the numbers following 599 in 599.2–599.8, e.g., marsupials 636.92 [*formerly* 636.91], monotremes 636.929 [*formerly* 636.91], fur-bearing animals (fur farming) 636.97 [*formerly also* 636.08844], hamsters 636.9356; however, for Equidae, see 636.1; for ruminants other than Tragulidae, see 636.2; for Camelidae, see 636.296; for Felidae, see 636.8

637   Processing dairy and related products

> Class comprehensive works on dairy farming in 636.2142

.1   **Milk processing**

>   637.12–637.14   Cow's milk

> Class comprehensive works in 637.1

.12   Milking and inspection of cow's milk

.124   Milking

.124 028 4   Apparatus, equipment, materials

> Class here milking machinery and equipment [*formerly* 637.125]

[.125]   Milking machinery and equipment

> Relocated to 637.1240284

.127   Inspection and testing

> Standard subdivisions are added for either or both topics in heading

.127 6   Butterfat tests

.127 7   Bacterial counts

.14   Processing specific forms of cow's milk

> Use of this number for comprehensive works on processing cow's milk discontinued; class in 637.1

>   637.141–637.146   Whole milk

> Class comprehensive works in 637.1

.141 Fresh whole milk

Including comprehensive works on pasteurization, homogenization, vitamin D treatment

For pasteurization, homogenization, vitamin D treatment of products other than fresh whole milk, see the product, e.g., cream 637.148

.141 028 7 Measurement

Do not use for testing; class in 637.127

.142 Concentrated liquid forms of whole milk

.142 2 Evaporated milk

.142 4 Sweetened condensed milk

.143 Dried whole milk

.146 Cultured whole milk

.147 Skim milk

.147 3 Dried skim milk

.147 6 Cultured skim milk

Class here yogurt

.148 Cream

.17 Milk other than cow's milk

.2 Butter processing

.202 87 Testing and measurement

Including quality determinations [*formerly also* 637.22]

[.22] Quality determinations

Relocated to 637.20287

.24 By-products

Class here buttermilk

.3 Cheese processing

Including by-products

.302 87 Testing and measurement

Including quality determinations [*formerly also* 637.32]

[.32] Quality determinations

Relocated to 637.30287

.35 Varieties

.352	Cream cheese
.353	Ripened soft cheeses

Including Brie

.354	Hard cheeses

Including cheddar and Swiss cheeses

.356	Fresh cheeses

Including cottage cheese

For cream cheese, see 637.352

.358	Cheese foods

.4 **Manufacture of frozen desserts**

Class here ice cream

.5 **Egg processing**

Class raising hens for eggs in 636.5142; class raising poultry other than chickens for eggs in 636.59

.54	Dried eggs

Including dried egg whites and yolks

Use of this number for chicken eggs discontinued; class in 637.5

[.541]	Fresh chicken eggs

Number discontinued; class in 637.5

[.543–.548]	Dried eggs and their parts

Numbers discontinued; class in 637.54

[.59]	Eggs other than chicken eggs

Number discontinued; class in 637.5

638 **Insect culture**

.1 **Bee keeping (Apiculture)**

[.11]	Apiary establishment

Number discontinued; class in 638.1

.12	Varieties of bees

Class a specific aspect of a specific variety of bee with the aspect, e.g., pasturage 638.13

.13	Pasturage for bees
.14	Hive management

.140 284	Apparatus, equipment, materials [*formerly* 638.142]
[.142]	Apparatus, equipment, materials

Relocated to 638.140284

.144	Supplementary feeding of bees
.145	Queen rearing
.146	Swarming control
.15	Injuries, diseases, pests
.151–.157	Specific injuries, diseases, pests

Add to base number 638.15 the numbers following 632 in 632.1–632.8, e.g., diseases 638.154

For adverse effects of pesticides, see 636.159

.159	Adverse effects of pesticides
.16	Honey processing

Class here comprehensive works on hive products

For wax, see 638.17

.17	Wax
.2	**Silkworms**
[.3]	**Resin-producing and dye-producing insects**

Relocated to 638.5

.5	**Other insects**

Class here resin-producing and dye-producing insects [*formerly* 638.3]

.57	Specific insects

Add to base number 638.57 the numbers following 595.7 in 595.72–595.79, e.g., butterfly gardening 638.5789

639　　Hunting, fishing, conservation, related technologies

For sports hunting and fishing, see 799

SUMMARY

639.091 6	**Treatment in air and water**
.1	Hunting
.2	Commercial fishing, whaling, sealing
.3	Culture of cold-blooded vertebrates Of fish
.4	Mollusk fisheries and culture
.5	Crustacean fisheries
.6	Crustacean culture
.7	Harvest and culture of invertebrates other than mollusks and crustaceans
.8	Aquaculture
.9	Conservation of biological resources

.091 6 Treatment in air and water

Class aquaculture in 639.8

.1 Hunting

Class here trapping, subsistence hunting

Comprehensive works on commercial and sports hunting relocated to 799.2

.11 Hunting mammals

Add to base number 639.11 the numbers following 599 in 599.2–599.8, e.g., bison (buffalo) hunting 639.11643, hunting fur-bearing animals 639.117; however, for whaling, see 639.28; for sealing, see 639.29

Most works on trapping mammals are on fur trapping, and will be classed in 639.117

See also 333.9549 for resource economics of game mammals in general, 333.959 for resource economics of specific mammals, 636.97 for fur farming, 799.2 for sports hunting

.12 Hunting birds

Most works on hunting game birds will be classed in 333.958 (resource economics) or 799.24 (sports hunting)

[.122] Land birds

Number discontinued; class in 639.12

[.123] Shore birds

Relocated to 639.12833

[.124] Waterfowl

Relocated to 639.12841

.128 Specific kinds of birds

Add to base number 639.128 the numbers following 598 in 598.3–598.9, e.g., shore birds 639.12833 [*formerly also* 639.123], waterfowl 639.12841 [*formerly also* 639.124]

.13   Hunting amphibians

            See also 639.378 for amphibian farming

.14   Reptile hunting

            Add to base number 639.14 the numbers following 597.9 in 597.92–597.98,
            e.g., hunting alligators 639.148

            See also 639.39 for reptile farming

.2   Commercial fishing, whaling, sealing

            Standard subdivisions are added for commercial fishing, whaling, sealing
            together; for commercial fishing alone

            Class here works on fisheries encompassing culture as well as capture, on
            fisheries encompassing invertebrates as well as fish

            Class comprehensive works on aquaculture in 639.8

            For culture of fish, see 639.3; for fisheries for invertebrates, see 639.4

>   639.21–639.22   Fishing in specific types of water

            Class fishing for specific kinds of fish regardless of kind of water in 639.27;
            class comprehensive works in 639.2

.21   Fishing in fresh water

.22   Fishing in salt waters

            Including fishing in brackish waters

            Class here deep-sea fishing

.27   Fishing for specific kinds of fish

            Add to base number 639.27 the numbers following 597 in 597.2–597.7, e.g.,
            salmon fishing 639.2756

.28   Whaling

.29   Sealing

.3   Culture of cold-blooded vertebrates   Of fish

>   639.31–639.34   Fish culture

            Class comprehensive works in 639.3

            For culture of specific kinds of fish, see 639.372–639.377

.31   Fish culture in fresh water

            Class here fishponds, freshwater fish farming

            For fish culture in freshwater aquariums, see 639.34

.311   Fish hatcheries

Use of this number for comprehensive works on fish culture in natural and artificial ponds discontinued; class in 639.31

.312   Fish culture in lakes

.313   Fish culture in streams

Class here fish culture in rivers

.32   Fish culture in salt waters

Including fish culture in brackish waters

For fish culture in marine aquariums, see 639.342

.34   Fish culture in aquariums

Class here freshwater aquariums, home aquariums

Class interdisciplinary works on aquariums in 597.073

.342   Marine aquariums

.344   Institutional aquariums

Use of this number for comprehensive works on freshwater aquariums discontinued; class in 639.34

Class interdisciplinary works on educational and scientific aquariums in 597.073

For marine aquariums, see 639.342

.37   Culture of amphibians and specific kinds of fish

.372–.377   Culture of specific kinds of fishes

Add to base number 639.37 the numbers following 597 in 597.2–597.7, e.g., carp, koi 639.37483; goldfish 639.37484; Scopelomorpha, Paracanthopterygii, Acanthopterygii 639.376 [*formerly* 639.375]; Perciformes 639.377 [*formerly* 639.3758]; however, amphibian farming relocated from 639.376 to 639.378; Gymnophiona relocated from 639.377 to 639.3782

.378   Amphibian farming [*formerly* 639.376]

Add to base number 639.378 the numbers following 597.8 in 597.82–597.89, e.g., Gymnophiona 639.3782 [*formerly* 639.377], frog farming 639.3789

.39   Reptile farming

Add to base number 639.39 the numbers following 597.9 in 597.92–597.98, e.g., turtle farming 639.392

.4   Mollusk fisheries and culture

Standard subdivisions are added for either or both topics in heading

Class here Bivalvia; comprehensive works on harvest and culture of invertebrates, on shellfish fisheries and culture

> *For crustacean fisheries, see 639.5; for crustacean culture, see 639.6; for harvest and culture of invertebrates other than mollusks and crustaceans, see 639.7*

> **639.41–639.46   Bivalvia**

Class comprehensive works in 639.4

.41   Oysters

Class here edible oysters

.412   Pearl oysters

.42   Mussels

.44   Clams

.46   Scallops [*formerly* 639.4811]

.48   Mollusks other than Bivalvia

[.481 1]   Other Bivalvia

Use of this number for other Bivalvia discontinued; class in 639.4

Scallops relocated to 639.46

.482–.485   Specific kinds of mollusks other than Bivalvia

Add to base number 639.48 the numbers following 594 in 594.2–594.5, e.g., land snails 639.4838

.5   Crustacean fisheries

Class here comprehensive works on crustacean fisheries and culture

Crustacean culture relocated to 639.6

.54   Lobsters and crayfishes

Standard subdivisions are added for lobsters and crayfishes together, for lobsters alone

Use of this number for specific crustaceans other than decapods discontinued; class in 639.5

[.541]   Lobsters and crayfishes

Number discontinued; class in 639.54

[.542–.544]	Specific decapod crustaceans other than lobsters and crayfishes

> Relocated to 639.56–639.58

.56–.58	Specific decapod crustaceans other than lobsters and crayfishes [*formerly* 639.542–639.544]

> Add to base number 639.5 the numbers following 595.38 in 595.386–595.388, e.g., shrimps 639.58

.6　Crustacean culture [*formerly* 639.5]

> Add to base number 639.6 the numbers following 595.38 in 595.384–595.388, e.g., crayfish culture 639.64

.7　Harvest and culture of invertebrates other than mollusks and crustaceans

> Standard subdivisions are added for either or both topics in heading
>
> *For insect culture, see 638*

[.73]	Protozoa, Porifera, Cnidaria, Ctenophora, Echinodermata, Hemichordata

> Number discontinued; class in 639.7

.75	Worms

> Class here bait worm culture, earthworms (night crawlers), fishworms, worm farming

[.752–.758]	Specific kinds of worms

> Numbers discontinued; class in 639.75

.8　Aquaculture

> Class here mariculture
>
> Class aquaculture of specific animal with the animal, e.g., aquaculture of fishes 639.3

.89	Aquaculture of plants

> Class hydroponics in 631.585

.9　Conservation of biological resources

> Class here conservation of animals, game animals, mammals, vertebrates, wildlife; game protection
>
> Class interdisciplinary works on conservation of biological resources in 333.9516; class interdisciplinary works on conservation of animals, vertebrates, mammals in 333.95416
>
> *See also 636.0888 for raising warm-blooded game animals*

>   639.92–639.96   Specific topics in conservation

Class specific topics in conservation of specific kinds of animals in 639.97; class specific topics in conservation of plants in 639.99; class comprehensive works in 639.9

.92   Habitat improvement

.93   Population control

.95   Maintenance of reserves and refuges

Standard subdivisions are added for either or both topics in heading

.96   Control of injuries, diseases, pests

.964   Diseases

.966   Pests

Class here predator control

Class comprehensive works on pest control in agriculture in 632.6; class comprehensive works on predator control in agriculture in 636.0839

.969   Adverse effects of pesticides

.97   Specific kinds of animals

Other than vertebrates taken as a whole, mammals taken as a whole

[.970 1–.970 9]   Standard subdivisions

Do not use; class in 639.901–639.909

.972–.978   Specific kinds of animals other than mammals

Add to base number 639.97 the numbers following 59 in 592–598, e.g., attracting birds 639.978

See also 598.07234 for bird watching, 638.5789 for butterfly gardening, 639.3 for raising game fishes, 690.8927 for building bird houses

.979   Specific kinds of mammals

Use of this number for comprehensive works on mammals discontinued; class in 639.9

[.979 01–.979 09]   Standard subdivisions

Do not use; class in 639.901–639.909

.979 2–.979 8   Subdivisions for specific kinds of mammals

Add to base number 639.979 the numbers following 599 in 599.2–599.8, e.g., habitat improvement for deer 639.97965

.99   Plant conservation

640   Home economics and family living

Class here management of home and personal life, domestic arts and sciences

Class personal health in 613

SUMMARY

640.1–.9	Standard subdivisions and specific aspects of household management
641	Food and drink
642	Meals and table service
643	Housing and household equipment
644	Household utilities
645	Household furnishings
646	Sewing, clothing, management of personal and family living
647	Management of public households (Institutional housekeeping)
648	Housekeeping
649	Child rearing; home care of persons with illnesses and disabilities

[.288]   Maintenance and repair

> Do not use; class in 643.7

[.297]   Evaluation and purchasing manuals

> Do not use; class in 640.73

.4   **Specific aspects of household management**

> Class comprehensive works on household management in 640

.41   Helpful hints and miscellaneous recipes

.42   Management of money

> Including records of household expenditures
>
> Class here accounting, budgeting, expenditure control
>
> Class evaluation and purchasing guides in 640.73
>
> *See Manual at 332.024 vs. 640.42*

.43   Management of time

.46   Household employees

> Duties, hours, selection, training
>
> Class management of institutional household employees in 647.2

.49   Survival housekeeping

> Housekeeping in presence of unfavorable circumstances and provisioning in anticipation of disaster, e.g., earthquakes
>
> Class personal survival after accidents, disasters, other unfavorable circumstances in 613.69

[.68] Household management

> Do not use for comprehensive works; class in 640. Do not use for specific aspects; class in 640.4

.7 **Education, research, related topics; evaluation and purchasing guides**

.73 Evaluation and purchasing guides

> Class here consumer education for home and personal needs

> Class interdisciplinary evaluation and purchasing guides and works on consumer education in 381.33; class comprehensive works on managing household money in 640.42. Class evaluation and purchasing guides for a specific product or service with the product or service, plus notation 0297 from Table 1, e.g., manual on evaluating automobiles 629.2220297

641 Food and drink

> *For meals and table service, see 642*

SUMMARY

641.013	Value
.2	Beverages (Drinks)
.3	Food
.4	Food preservation and storage
.5	Cooking
.6	Cooking specific materials
.7	Specific cooking processes and techniques
.8	Cooking specific kinds of composite dishes

.013 Value

> Class here gastronomy, pleasures of eating

[.1] **Applied nutrition**

> Relocated to 613.2

.2 **Beverages (Drinks)**

> Class here interdisciplinary works on beverages

> Comprehensive works on nutritive values of beverages relocated to 613.2

> Class nutritive values of specific beverages with the beverage, e.g., nutritive value of wine 641.22

> *For a specific aspect of beverages, see the aspect, e.g., manufacture (commercial preparation) 663*

.21 Alcoholic beverages

> *For wine, see 641.22; for brewed and malted beverages, see 641.23; for distilled liquor, see 641.25*

.22	Wine

Class here grape wine

See also 641.23 for sake (rice wine)

.222	Kinds of grape wine
[.222 01–.222 09]	Standard subdivisions

Do not use; class in 641.2201–641.2209

.222 2–.222 4	Specific kinds of grape wine

Add to base number 641.222 the numbers following 663.22 in 663.222–663.224, e.g., champagne 641.2224

.229	Nongrape wine

Including cider

.23	Brewed and malted beverages

Including pulque, sake

Class here beer, ale

Class malt whiskey in 641.252

.25	Distilled liquor

Including mescal, potato whiskey, tequila, vodka

.252	Whiskey

Class potato whiskey in 641.25

.253	Brandy
.255	Compound liquors

Including absinthe, cordials, gin, liqueurs

.259	Rum
.26	Nonalcoholic beverages

For specific nonalcoholic beverages and kinds of beverages, see 641.3

.3	**Food**

Class here interdisciplinary works on food

Class interdisciplinary works on composite dishes in 641.8

For a specific aspect of food, see the aspect, e.g., manufacture (commercial preparation) 664

See Manual at 363.8 vs. 613.2, 641.3; also at 630 vs. 579–590, 641.3

.300 1	Philosophy and theory
.300 2	Miscellany

| [.300 297] | Evaluation and purchasing manuals |
| | Do not use; class in 641.31 |

.300 3–.300 9   Standard subdivisions

.302   Health foods

Including organically grown foods

.303   Food from plants

For specific food from plant crops, see 641.33–641.35

.306   Food from animals

For specific food from animals, see 641.36–641.39

[.309]   Mineral food

Number discontinued; class in 641.3

.31   Evaluation and purchasing manuals

Class applied nutrition in 613.2; class evaluation and purchasing manuals of specific food in 641.33–641.39

.33–.35   Specific food from plant crops

Class here nutritive values

Add to base number 641.3 the numbers following 63 in 633–635, e.g., flavorings 641.3382, legumes 641.3565

Class comprehensive works on food from plants in 641.303

\>   641.36–641.39 Specific food from animals

Class here nutritive values

Class comprehensive works on food from animals in 641.306

.36   Meat

Add to base number 641.36 the numbers following 636 in 636.1–636.8, e.g., chicken meat 641.365

For game and seafood, see 641.39

.37   Dairy and related products

Add to base number 641.37 the numbers following 637 in 637.1–637.5, e.g., skim milk 641.37147

.38   Honey

.39   Game and seafood

Add to base number 641.39 the numbers following 641.69 in 641.691–641.696, e.g., oysters 641.394

> ### 641.4–641.8   Food preservation, storage, cooking

Class comprehensive works in 641.3

.4   Food preservation and storage

Class interdisciplinary works on food preservation in 664.028

> 641.41–641.47   Preservation techniques for fruit and vegetables, for food as a whole

Class comprehensive works in 641.4

For preservation techniques for meat and allied food, see 641.49

.41   Preliminary treatment

.42   Canning

.44   Drying and dehydrating

       Including freeze-drying

.45   Low-temperature techniques

.452   Cold storage

.453   Deep freezing

       For freeze-drying, see 641.44

.46   Brining, pickling, smoking

.47   Use of additives

.48   Storage

.49   Meat and allied food

       Class storage of meat and allied food in 641.48

.492   Red meat

       Add to base number 641.492 the numbers following 641.4 in 641.41–641.47, e.g., canning red meat 641.4922

.493   Poultry

       Add to base number 641.493 the numbers following 641.4 in 641.41–641.47, e.g., freezing poultry 641.49353

.494   Seafood

       Add to base number 641.494 the numbers following 641.4 in 641.41–641.47, e.g., brining seafood 641.4946

.495   Other animal flesh

                Including frogs, insects, snails, turtles

.5   **Cooking**

                Preparation of food with and without use of heat

                Unless other instructions are given, observe the following table of preference, e.g., outdoor cooking for children 641.5622 (*not* 641.578):

Cooking for special situations, reasons, ages	641.56
Quantity, institutional, travel, outdoor cooking	641.57
Money-saving and timesaving cooking	641.55
Cooking with specific appliances, utensils, fuels	641.58
Cooking specific meals	641.52–.54
Cooking by specific types of persons	641.51
Cooking characteristic of specific geographic environments, ethnic cooking	641.59

                Class menus and meal planning in 642

                For cooking specific materials, see 641.6; for specific cooking processes and techniques, see 641.7; for cooking specific kinds of composite dishes, see 641.8

SUMMARY

641.501–.509	**Standard subdivisions**
.51	**Cooking by specific types of persons**
.52	**Breakfast**
.53	**Luncheon, brunch, elevenses, tea, supper, snacks**
.54	**Dinner**
.55	**Money-saving and timesaving cooking**
.56	**Cooking for special situations, reasons, ages**
.57	**Quantity, institutional, travel, outdoor cooking**
.58	**Cooking with specific fuels, appliances, utensils**
.59	**Cooking characteristic of specific geographic environments, ethnic cooking**

[.502 4]   Cooking for users in specific occupations

                Do not use; class in 641.51

.508 3   Cooking by young people

                Do not use for cooking by children; class in 641.5123. Do not use for cooking for young people; class in 641.5622

.508 4   Cooking by persons in specific ages of adulthood

                Do not use for cooking for persons in specific ages of adulthood; class in 641.562

.508 7   Persons with disabilities; gifted persons

                Do not use for persons with illnesses; class in 641.5631

[.508 82]	Cooking with respect to religious groups
	Do not use; class in 641.567
[.508 9]	Cooking with respect to racial, ethnic, national groups
	Do not use; class in 641.592
.509	Historical, geographic, persons treatment

> Do not use for cooking characteristic of specific geographic environments; class in 641.59

> Class here collections of recipes from specific restaurants

.51	Cooking by specific types of persons
.512	Beginner cooking

> Easy dishes

.512 3	Children's cooking

> Class cooking of food for consumption by children in 641.5622

.514	Gourmet cooking

> 641.52–641.54 Cooking specific meals

Class comprehensive works in 641.5

.52	Breakfast
.53	Luncheon, brunch, elevenses, tea, supper, snacks
.54	Dinner
.55	Money-saving and timesaving cooking
.552	Money-saving cooking

> Including leftovers [*formerly* 641.6]

.555	Timesaving cooking

> Class here make-ahead meals

.56	Cooking for special situations, reasons, ages
.561	Cooking for one or two persons
.562	Cooking for persons of specific ages
.562 2	Young people

> Including baby food

> Class here cooking for children

> Class cooking by children in 641.5123

.562 7	Persons in late adulthood

.563   **Cooking for health, appearance, personal reasons**

Including cooking for pregnant women

Unless other instructions are given, class a subject with aspects in two or more subdivisions of 641.563 in the number coming first, e.g., low-carbohydrate, low-calorie cooking for persons with diabetes 641.56314 (*not* 641.5635 or 641.5638)

.563 1   Cooking for persons with illnesses

Class here cooking to prevent illness

Class cooking for overweight persons in 641.5635

.563 11   Persons with heart disease

.563 14   Persons with diabetes

.563 2   Cooking with specified vitamin and mineral content

Including salt-free cooking

.563 4   High-calorie cooking

.563 5   Low-calorie cooking

Class here cooking for overweight persons

.563 6   Vegetarian cooking

See also 641.65 for cooking vegetables

.563 7   Health-food cooking

Class comprehensive works on health cooking in 641.563

.563 8   Carbohydrate, fat, protein cooking

Including low-carbohydrate, low-cholesterol, low-fat cooking

.564   **Cooking for various specific times of year**

Class here seasonal cooking

Class cooking for special occasions in 641.568

.566   **Cooking for Christian church limitations and observances**

Including Lent

Class here cooking for Christian groups

Cooking for Christmas relocated to 641.568

| .567 | Cooking for religious limitations and observances |

Class here cooking for days of feast and fast, cooking with respect to religious groups

Add to base number 641.567 the numbers following 29 in 292–299, e.g., Jewish cooking 641.5676

For cooking for Christian church limitations and observances, see 641.566

| .568 | Cooking for special occasions |

Including Christmas [*formerly also* 641.566], birthdays, celebrations, holidays, parties

Class cooking for special religious occasions in 641.567

| .57 | Quantity, institutional, travel, outdoor cooking |

Including cooking for armed services

Class here short-order cooking

| .571 | School cooking |

| .572 | Hotel and restaurant cooking |

| .575 | Travel cooking |

Including airline, bus, camper (caravan) cooking

For cooking for railroad dining cars, see 641.576

| .575 3 | Shipboard cooking |

| .576 | Dining car cooking |

| .577 | Canteen cooking |

Temporary or mobile facilities for serving food

| .578 | Outdoor cooking |

Class here cookouts

Class cooking in campers (caravans) in 641.575

| .578 2 | Camp cooking |

| .578 4 | Cooking at an outdoor grill |

Class here cooking at outdoor barbecues

Class comprehensive works on techniques of barbecuing in 641.76

| .579 | Cooking for medical facilities |

Class here cooking for hospitals

.58   Cooking with specific fuels, appliances, utensils

            Including convection-oven cooking, wood-stove cooking

            Class outdoor cooking in 641.578

[.583]   Oil

            Number discontinued; class in 641.58

.584   Gas

.585   Alcohol-based fuels

            Class here cooking with chafing dishes

.586   Electricity

            Cooking with electric ranges and appliances, e.g., skillets, frying pans,
            roasters, grills, toasters, waffle irons

            Class convection-oven cooking in 641.58; class microwave cooking in
            641.5882; class electric slow cooking in 641.5884

.587   Steam and pressure cooking

            Standard subdivisions are added for either or both topics in heading

.588   Slow and fireless cooking

.588 2   Microwave cooking

.588 4   Electric slow cooking

.589   Specific utensils

            Including blenders, foils, specially coated utensils

            Class cooking with specific utensils using specific fuels in
            641.584–641.588

.59   Cooking characteristic of specific geographic environments, ethnic
            cooking

            Including international cooking

            Class historical and geographic treatment of general cooking in 641.509

            See also 641.509 for collections of recipes from specific restaurants

.591   Cooking characteristic of areas, regions, places in general

            Add to base number 641.591 the numbers following — 1 in notation
            11–19 from Table 2, e.g., arctic and cold-weather cooking 641.5911,
            tropical and hot-weather cooking 641.5913

.592   Ethnic cooking

            Add to base number 641.592 notation 03–9 from Table 5, e.g., African
            American cooking 641.59296073; however, for Jewish cooking, see
            641.5676; for cooking of ethnic groups dominant in their areas, see
            641.593–641.599

.593–.599	Cooking characteristic of specific continents, countries, localities

Add to base number 641.59 notation 3–9 from Table 2, e.g., Southern cooking 641.5975

Class ethnic cooking of nondominant aggregates in 641.592

.6	**Cooking specific materials**

Leftovers relocated to 641.552

Class specific kinds of composite dishes featuring specific materials in 641.8

.61	Cooking preserved foods

Add to base number 641.61 the numbers following 641.4 in 641.42–641.46, e.g., cooking using frozen foods 641.6153

Class home preservation in 641.4; class cooking using specific preserved foods in 641.63–641.69

.62	Cooking with beverages and their derivatives

Including vinegar

Class home preparation of beverages in 641.87. Class cooking with a specific nonalcoholic beverage with the product from which it is derived, e.g., cooking with chocolate 641.6374, with apple juice 641.6411

.622	Wine
.623	Beer and ale

Standard subdivisions are added for either or both topics in heading

.625	Spirits

> 641.63–641.69 Specific food

Class comprehensive works in 641.6

.63–.67	Cooking food derived from plant crops and domesticated animals

Add to base number 641.6 the numbers following 63 in 633–637, e.g., flavorings 641.6382, legumes 641.6565, meat 641.66, chicken meat 641.665; however, for ices and sherbets, see 641.863

Class vegetarian cooking in 641.5636; class comprehensive works on cooking with beverages in 641.62

For cooking with honey, see 641.68

.68	Cooking with honey
.69	Cooking game and seafood
.691	Game

.692	Fish

Class here seafood

For mollusks, see 641.694; for crustaceans, see 641.695

.694	Mollusks

Including clams, mussels, octopuses, oysters, snails, squid

Class here shellfish

For crustaceans, see 641.695

.695	Crustaceans

Including crabs, lobsters, shrimp

.696	Amphibians, insects, reptiles

Including frogs, snakes, turtles

.7	**Specific cooking processes and techniques**

Class specific processes applied to specific materials in 641.6; class specific processes applied to specific kinds of composite dishes in 641.8

.71	Baking and roasting
.73	Boiling, simmering, steaming, stewing
.76	Broiling, grilling, barbecuing

Class here comprehensive works on techniques of barbecuing

For cooking at outdoor grills, see 641.5784

.77	Frying, sautéing, braising
.79	Preparation of cold dishes

Including chilled dishes

.8	**Cooking specific kinds of composite dishes**

Class here interdisciplinary works on composite dishes

For food technology of composite dishes, see 664.65

.81	Side dishes and sauces

Other than those listed in 641.83–641.86

Including fondues, garnishes

.812	Appetizers, hors d'oeuvres, pâtés, relishes, savories, tapas
.813	Soups
.814	Sauces and salad dressings

.815   Breads and bread-like foods

Including biscuits (United States), crackers, crepes, hot cakes, pancakes, rolls, waffles

Class here comprehensive works on baked goods

Class main dishes based on breads and bread-like foods in 641.82; class sandwiches in 641.84

For pastries, see 641.865

.82   Main dishes

Including quiches, soufflés

.821   Casserole dishes

.822   Pasta dishes

.823   Stews

Class here chili

.824   Meat and cheese pies

Including pizza, meat loaf

Class cooking sausage in 641.66

.83   Salads

.84   Sandwiches

Including submarine sandwiches

.85   Preserves and candy

.852   Jams, jellies, marmalades, preserves

Standard subdivisions are added for any or all topics in heading

.853   Candy

Variant name: sweets (United Kingdom)

.86   Desserts

Class here comprehensive works on candies and desserts

For preserves and candy, see 641.85

.862   Ice cream

Including frozen yogurt, ice milk

.863   Ices and sherbet

Variant name: water ices

.864   Gelatins and puddings

.865 Pastries

Class comprehensive works on baked goods in 641.815

.865 2 Pies and tarts

.865 3 Cakes

Including cake decoration

See also 641.8659 for coffee cakes

.865 4 Cookies

Variant name: biscuits (United Kingdom)

.865 9 Danish, French, related pastries

Including coffee cakes, cream puffs, eclairs

.87 Beverages

Class interdisciplinary works on beverages in 641.2

.872 Wine

.873 Alcoholic brewed beverages

Class here beer, ale

.874 Alcoholic beverages

Including bartenders' manuals

Class here comprehensive works on mixed drinks

For wine, see 641.872; for alcoholic brewed beverages, see 641.873; for bottled and canned mixed drinks, see 663.1

.875 Nonalcoholic beverages

Including carbonated and malted drinks, juices, punches

For nonalcoholic brewed beverages, see 641.877

.877 Nonalcoholic brewed beverages

Including cocoa, coffee, teas; concentrates and substitutes

642 Meals and table service

> **642.1–642.5 Meals in specific situations**

Class here menus, menu cookbooks, comprehensive works on meals and table service in specific situations

Class comprehensive works in 642

For table service in specific situations, see 642.6

.1 **Meals for home and family**

Including packaged, prepared meals

.3 **Meals for camp, picnic, travel**

.4 **Meals for social and public occasions**

Including banquets, box lunches, catered meals

Class here meals and catering for social and public occasions

Class picnics in 642.3; class catering which includes restaurant operation in 647.95

.5 **Meals in public and institutional eating places**

Including meals in cafeterias, hospitals, schools

Class here meals in restaurants and hotels

Class meals for social and public occasions in 642.4; class operation of public eating places in 647.95

> **642.6–642.8 Table service**

Class here table service in specific situations

Class comprehensive works on meals and table service in specific situations in 642.1–642.5; class comprehensive works in 642.6

.6 **Serving at table**

Including place setting, seating guests, carving

Class here comprehensive works on table service

For table furnishings, see 642.7; for table decorations, see 642.8

.7 **Table furnishings**

Including dinnerware, glassware, silverware, table linens; napkin folding

For table decorations, see 642.8

.8 **Table decorations**

643 Housing and household equipment

Works for owner-occupants or renters covering activities of members of household

[.028 8]   Maintenance and repair

Do not use; class in 643.7

.1 **Housing**

> *For special kinds of housing, see 643.2*
>
> *See also 690.8 for construction of houses, 728 for comprehensive works on design and construction of houses*
>
> *See Manual at 363.5 vs. 643.1*

[.102 88]   Maintenance and repair

> Do not use; class in 643.7

[.102 97]   Evaluation and purchasing manuals

> Do not use; class in 643.12

.12   Selecting, renting, buying homes

> Including site selection, supervision of construction
>
> Class here evaluation and purchasing guides; home inspection
>
> Class moving in 648.9
>
> > *See also 333.338 for economics of home acquisition, 346.043 for law of real property*

.16   Household security

> Including burglarproofing

.2 **Special kinds of housing**

> Including apartments, condominiums, houseboats, mobile homes, modular and prefabricated houses, vacation homes
>
> Class single-family houses in 643.1. Class a specific aspect of a special kind of housing with the aspect, e.g., renovating vacation homes 643.7
>
> > *See also 388.346 for motorized homes*
> >
> > *See Manual at 643.2, 690.879, 728.79 vs. 629.226*

> **643.3–643.5**   **Specific areas and their equipment**

> Class household utilities in 644; class household furnishings in 645; class home construction of household articles made of fabric in 646.21; class manufacture of household appliances in 683.8; class manufacture of household furnishings in 684; class home workshops in 684.08; class comprehensive works in 643.1

.3   **Kitchens and their equipment**

> Standard subdivisions are added for kitchens and their equipment together, for kitchens alone
>
> Including kitchen linen
>
> Class use of food storage and preparation equipment in 641.4–641.8

.4 **Eating and drinking areas and their equipment**

Standard subdivisions are added for eating and drinking areas and their equipment together, for eating and drinking areas together, for eating areas alone

Including dining rooms, breakfast rooms, bars

Class table furnishings in 642.7

.5 **Other areas and their equipment**

Including attics, basements, storage areas

.52 Bathrooms

.53 Bedrooms

Including bedclothing, e.g., blankets

.54 Living rooms

.55 Recreation areas

Indoor and outdoor

Including patios, porches, swimming pools

.58 Study and work areas

Including dens

.6 **Appliances and laborsaving installations**

Standard subdivisions are added for either or both topics in heading

Class here maintenance and repair by members of household

Class appliances and installations for specific areas in 643.3–643.5. Class appliances and installations for a specific purpose with the purpose, e.g., sewing machines 646.2044

.7 **Renovation, improvement, remodeling**

Class here do-it-yourself work; comprehensive works on maintenance and repair in home economics, on maintenance and repair by members of household

Class renovation, improvement, remodeling of specific areas and their equipment in 643.3–643.5

For maintenance and repair of a specific topic in home economics, see the topic, plus notation 0288 from Table 1, e.g., repair of appliances 643.60288

See Manual at 690 vs. 643.7

644 Household utilities

Works for owner-occupants or renters covering activities by members of household

Class here home energy conservation

See Manual at 647 vs. 647.068, 658.2, T1—0682

.1 Heating

.3 Lighting

Class lighting fixtures as furnishings in 645.5

.5 Ventilation and air conditioning

.6 Water supply

645 Household furnishings

Works for owner-occupants or renters covering activities by members of household

Class here comprehensive works on household furnishings and interior decoration of residential buildings

For home construction of fabric furnishings, see 646.21

See also 684 for construction in wood and metal

[.029 7]   Evaluation and purchasing manuals

Do not use; class in 645.042

.04   Special topics

.042   Evaluation and purchasing manuals

Class selection and purchase of fabrics for furnishings in 645.046. Class evaluation and purchasing manuals for specific kinds of furnishings with the kind, plus notation 0297 from Table 1, e.g., purchasing manuals for lighting fixtures 645.50297

.046   Fabrics

Description, selection, purchase, care, use

> **645.1–645.6 Interior furnishings**

Class comprehensive works in 645

> **645.1–645.5 Specific kinds of interior furnishings**

Class comprehensive works in 645

.1   **Floor covering**

Including carpets, rugs, linoleum

.2   **Wall and ceiling coverings**

Standard subdivisions are added for wall and ceiling coverings together, for wall coverings alone

Including hangings, paint, paneling, wallpaper

.3   **Curtains and related furnishings**

Including draperies, shades, blinds, their accessories

Class wall hangings in 645.2

.4   **Furniture and accessories**

Including upholstery, slipcovers; arrangement for convenience and efficiency

Class artistic aspects of furniture and accessories in 749

.5   **Lighting fixtures**

.6   **Furnishings for specific rooms**

Class interior furnishings of specific kinds regardless of room in 645.1–645.5

.8   **Outdoor furnishings**

Including furnishings for balconies, courts, gardens, patios, roofs

646   Sewing, clothing, management of personal and family living

SUMMARY

646.1	Sewing materials and equipment
.2	Sewing and related operations
.3	Clothing and accessories
.4	Clothing and accessories construction
.5	Construction of headgear
.6	Care of clothing and accessories
.7	Management of personal and family living Grooming

.1   **Sewing materials and equipment**

Standard subdivisions are added for sewing materials and equipment together, for sewing materials alone

Including leathers and furs

See also 646.3028 for materials, equipment used for clothing

.11   Fabrics

Class here comprehensive works on fabrics in the home

For fabrics for a specific use, see the use, e.g., use in furnishings 645.046

.19   Sewing equipment, fasteners

Standard subdivisions are added for either or both topics in heading

Including needles, pins, scissors and shears, thimbles, thread

Class here notions

For sewing machines, see 646.2044

.2   Sewing and related operations

Standard subdivisions are added for sewing and related operations together, for sewing alone

Class here mending, sewing for the home

Class clothing construction in 646.4; class mending of clothing in 646.6

For knitting, crocheting, tatting, see 746.43; for embroidery, see 746.44

[.202 84]   Apparatus, equipment, materials

Do not use; class in 646.1. Do not use for sewing machines; class in 646.2044

.204   Basic sewing operations

Class here darning

.204 2   Sewing by hand

.204 4   Sewing by machine

Including serging

.21   Construction of home furnishings

Including making bedclothes, curtains, hangings, slipcovers, table linens, towels

Use of this number for comprehensive works on sewing for the home discontinued; class in 646.2

Class basic sewing operations in 646.204; class artistic and decorative aspects of construction of interior furnishings in 746.9

.25   Reweaving

.3   Clothing and accessories

Standard subdivisions are added for clothing and accessories together, for clothing alone

Description, selection, purchase of clothing and accessories for utility, quality, economy, appearance, style

Class interdisciplinary works on clothing and accessories in 391

For clothing and accessories construction, see 646.4; for care of clothing and accessories, see 646.6

See Manual at 391 vs. 646.3, 746.92

[.302 88]	Maintenance and repair
	Do not use; class in 646.6
[.308 1–.308 2]	Clothing for men and women
	Do not use; class in 646.32–646.34
.308 3	Clothing for young people
	Do not use for children under twelve; class in 646.36
.308 351	Clothing for young men twelve to twenty
	Comprehensive works on clothing for young adult men relocated to 646.32
.308 352	Clothing for young women twelve to twenty
	Comprehensive works on clothing for young adult women relocated to 646.34
.308 4	Clothing for persons in specific stages of adulthood
	Do not use for clothing for men in specific stages of adulthood; class in 646.32. Do not use for clothing for women in specific stages of adulthood; class in 646.34
.308 7	Clothing for gifted persons
	Do not use for clothing for persons with disabilities and illnesses; class in 646.31
.31–.36	Clothing for persons with disabilities and illnesses; men, women, children

Add to base number 646.3 the numbers following 646.40 in 646.401–646.406, e.g., comprehensive works on clothing for young adult men 646.32 [*formerly* 646.308351], comprehensive works on clothing for young adult women 646.34 [*formerly* 646.308352]; however, for clothing for males twelve to twenty, see 646.308351; for clothing for females twelve to twenty, see 646.308352

.4　　　　**Clothing and accessories construction**

Standard subdivisions are added for clothing and accessories construction together, for clothing construction alone

Class here casual clothes, sports clothes

Class commercial manufacture of clothing in 687

For construction of headgear, see 646.5

.400 1–.400 7	Standard subdivisions
.400 8	Clothing with respect to specific kinds of persons
[.400 81]	Clothing for men
	Do not use; class in 646.402

[.400 82]	Clothing for women
	Do not use; class in 646.404
.400 83	Clothing for young people
	Do not use for children under twelve; class in 646.406
.400 835 1	Clothing for young men twelve to twenty
	Comprehensive works on clothing for young adult men relocated to 646.402
.400 835 2	Clothing for young women twelve to twenty
	Comprehensive works on clothing for young adult women relocated to 646.404
.400 84	Clothing of persons in specific stages of adulthood
	Do not use for clothing for men in specific stages of adulthood; class in 646.402. Do not use for clothing for women in specific stages of adulthood; class in 646.404
.400 87	Clothing for gifted persons
	Do not use for persons with disabilities and illnesses; class in 646.401
.400 9	Historical, geographic, persons treatment
.401	**Clothing for persons with disabilities and illnesses**

> 646.402–646.406 Clothing for men, women, children

Class construction of clothing for persons with disabilities and illnesses regardless of age or sex in 646.401; class patterns regardless of kind of persons in 646.407; class fitting and alterations regardless of kind of persons in 646.408; class comprehensive works in 646.4

.402	**Men's clothing**
	Including comprehensive works on clothing for young adult men [*formerly* 646.4008351]
.404	**Women's clothing**
	Including comprehensive works on clothing for young adult women [*formerly* 646.4008352]
.406	**Children's clothing**
.407	**Patterns**
	Including selection, purchase, use
.407 2	**Pattern design and patternmaking**
	Standard subdivisions are added for either or both topics in heading

.408	Fitting and alterations

Standard subdivisions are added for either or both topics in heading

---

>	646.42–646.48 Specific kinds of clothing

Add to each subdivision identified by * the numbers following 646.4 in 646.4001–646.406, e.g., construction of the kind of clothing for persons with disabilities

Class comprehensive works in 646.4

.42	*Underwear and hosiery

Subdivisions are added for underwear and hosiery together, for underwear alone

.43	*Specific kinds of garments

Not provided for elsewhere

.432	*Dresses

.433	*Suits, trousers, jackets

Subdivisions are added for any or all topics in heading

For outdoor jackets, see 646.45

.435	*Shirts, blouses, tops

Subdivisions are added for any or all topics in heading

.437	*Skirts

.45	*Outer coats, sweaters, wraps

Class here comprehensive works on coats

Class outdoor athletic wear, e.g., ski clothing, in 646.47

For suit coats, see 646.433

See also 646.47 for evening wear

.452	*Overcoats

Including topcoats

.453	*Raincoats

.454	*Sweaters

.457	*Cloaks, jackets, stoles

Subdivisions are added for any or all topics in heading

Class suit jackets in 641.433

*Add as instructed under 646.42–646.48

.47   *Garments for special purposes

> Including athletic garments, evening and formal dress, maternity garments, wedding clothes
>
> Class accessories for special purposes in 646.48
>
> *See also 646.4 for casual and sports clothes*

.475   *Nightclothes

.478   *Costumes

> Including party, period costumes
>
> Class here theatrical costumes

.48   Accessories

> Including aprons, belts, gloves and mittens, handkerchiefs, neckwear, scarves
>
> Class hosiery in 646.42; class headgear in 646.5; class boots and shoes in 685.31; class handcrafted costume jewelry in 745.5942

.5   Construction of headgear

.500 1–.500 7   Standard subdivisions

.500 8   History and description with respect to kinds of persons

[.500 81]   Men

> Do not use; class in 646.502

[.500 82]   Women

> Do not use; class in 646.504

[.500 83]   Young people

> Do not use; class in 646.506

.500 84   Persons in specific stages of adulthood

> Do not use for headgear for men in specific stages of adulthood; class in 646.502. Do not use for headgear for women in specific stages of adulthood; class in 646.504

.500 9   Historical, geographic, persons treatment

.502   Men's headgear

.504   Women's headgear

> Class here millinery

.506   Young people's headgear

> Class here children's headgear

---

*Add as instructed under 646.42–646.48

.6   Care of clothing and accessories

> Standard subdivisions are added for clothing and accessories together, for clothing alone
>
> Including mending, reweaving; packing, storage
>
> *For laundering and related operations, see 648.1*

.7   Management of personal and family living   Grooming

> Class here interdisciplinary works on success, successful living
>
> Class interdisciplinary works on success in business and other public situations in 650.1
>
> > *For parapsychological and occult means for achievement of well-being, happiness, success, see 131; for psychological means for achievement of personal well-being, happiness, success, see 158; for etiquette (manners), see 395*
> >
> > *See also 362.82 for social services to families*

.700 1–.700 7   Standard subdivisions of management of personal and family living

.700 8   Management of personal and family living with respect to kinds of persons

[.700 846]   Management of personal and family living for persons in late adulthood

> Do not use; class in 646.79

.700 9   Historical, geographic, persons treatment of personal and family living

.701–.703   Standard subdivisions of grooming

.704   Grooming for women, men, young people

.704 2   Grooming for women

.704 4   Grooming for men

.704 6   Grooming for young people

> Class here grooming for children

.705–.707   Standard subdivisions of grooming

.708   Grooming for specific kinds of persons

[.708 1–.708 3]   Grooming for men, women, young people

> Do not use; class in 646.704

.708 4   Grooming for persons in specific stages of adulthood

> Do not use for grooming for women in specific stages of adulthood; class in 646.7042. Do not use for grooming for men in specific stages of adulthood; class in 646.7044

.709   Historical, geographic, persons treatment of grooming

>   646.71–646.75   Grooming

Class clothing selection and dressing with style in 646.3; class training children in grooming in 649.63; class comprehensive works in 646.7

See also 646.76 for charm

.71   Cleanliness

Including bathing, showering

.72   Care of hair, face, skin

Class here cosmetology

.724   Care of hair

Including braiding, care of beards, dyeing, hairweaving, permanent waving, relaxing, shaving

Class here barbering, haircutting, hairdressing, hairstyling

[.724 2]   Hairdressing

Number discontinued; class in 646.724

[.724 5]   Hairstyling

Number discontinued; class in 646.724

.724 8   Wigs

Including cleaning, dyeing, selection, styling

.726   Care of face, skin

Standard subdivisions are added for either or both topics in heading

Including care of eyes, lips

Class manicuring and pedicuring in 646.727

.727   Manicuring and pedicuring

Standard subdivisions are added for either or both topics in heading

.75   Physique and form

Reducing, slenderizing, bodybuilding

Including massage, sauna, Turkish baths

See also 613.25 for reducing diets, 613.7 for physical fitness

See Manual at 613.71 vs. 646.75, 796

.76   Charm

.77 Dating and choice of mate

Standard subdivisions are added for either or both topics in heading

.78 Family living

Class here guides to harmonious family relations

For child rearing, see 649.1

.79 Guides for persons in late adulthood

Class here guides to retirement

Class family living in 646.78

> *See also 362.6 for social services to persons in late adulthood, 646.7008 for guides to management of personal and family living for other age brackets*

647 Management of public households (Institutional housekeeping)

See Manual at 647 vs. 647.068, 658.2, T1—0682

.068 Management

See Manual at 647 vs. 647.068, 658.2, T1—0682

[.068 3] Personnel management (Human resource management)

Do not use; class in 647.2

> ### 647.2–647.6 Employees

Class comprehensive works on household employees in 640.46; class comprehensive works on public household employees in 647.2

.2 **Indoor employees**

Class here personnel management, comprehensive works on public household employees

For outdoor employees, see 647.3; for hours and duties, see 647.6

.3 **Outdoor employees**

For hours and duties, see 647.6

.6 **Employee hours and duties**

.9 **Specific kinds of public households and institutions**

Class a specific aspect of public households and institutions with the aspect, e.g., laundering 648.1

See Manual at 647 vs. 647.068, 658.2, T1—0682

.92   Multiple dwellings for long-term residents

Including apartments, apartment hotels, flats, tenements

For boarding and rooming houses, see 647.94

.94   Multiple dwellings for transient residents

See Manual at 913–919: Add table: 04: Guidebooks

[.940 253–.940 259]   Directories of specific continents, countries, localities

Do not use; class in 647.943–647.949

[.940 93–.940 99]   Treatment by specific continents, countries, localities

Do not use; class in 647.943–647.949

.943–.949   Treatment by specific continents, countries, localities

Class here directories

Add to base number 647.94 notation 3–9 from Table 2, e.g., multiple dwellings for transients in Canada 647.9471; then add further as follows:

001–009	Standard subdivisions
01	Hotels, inns, resorts
02	Motels
03	Bed and breakfast establishments
	Class here boarding and rooming houses
05	Clubs
06	Hostels
	For youth hostels, see 07
07	Youth hostels
08	Trailer camps
09	Campsites

.95   Eating and drinking places

Standard subdivisions are added for either or both topics in heading

See Manual at 913–919: Add table: 04: Guidebooks

[.950 253–.950 259]   Directories of specific continents, countries, localities

Do not use; class in 647.953–647.959

[.950 93–.950 99]   Treatment by specific continents, countries, localities

Do not use; class in 647.953–647.959

.953–.959   Treatment by specific continents, countries, localities

Class here directories, operation of catering establishments

Add to base number 647.95 notation 3–9 from Table 2, e.g., restaurants of Hawaii 647.95969

> 647.96–647.99   Institutional households not primarily used for residence, eating, drinking

> Class comprehensive works in 647

.96   Miscellaneous institutional households

> Not provided for elsewhere

> Add to base number 647.96 the numbers following 725 in 725.1–725.9, e.g., office buildings 647.9623

.98   Religious institutions

> Add to base number 647.98 the numbers following 726 in 726.1–726.9, e.g., monasteries 647.987

.99   Educational and research institutions

> Add to base number 647.99 the numbers following 727 in 727.1–727.9, e.g., libraries 647.998

648   Housekeeping

Class here household sanitation

Class works about "housekeeping" in the sense of running the home, e.g., preparing meals and doing routine repairs as well as cleaning in 640

See Manual at 647 vs. 647.068, 658.2, T1—0682

.1   Laundering and related operations

> Including bleaching, drying, dyeing, pressing, spot removal

> Class dry cleaning in 667.12

.5   Housecleaning

> Class here cleaning floors, furnishings

[.56]   Dishwashing

> Number discontinued; class in 648.5

.7   Pest control

.8   Storage

.9   Moving

649   Child rearing; home care of persons with illnesses and disabilities

.1   **Child rearing**

Class here training, supervision

Unless other instructions are given, observe the following table of preference, e.g., infant boys 649.122 (*not* 649.132):

Exceptional children	649.15
Children of specific status, type, relationships	649.14
Children of specific age groups	649.12
Children of specific sexes	649.13

Class specific elements of home care of children regardless of age, sex, or other characteristics in 649.3–649.7

.102 4   Works for specific types of users

Do not add as instructed in Table 1

.102 42   Works for expectant parents

.102 43   Works for single parents

.102 45   Works for older children in family

.102 48   Works for babysitters

.108   Child care with respect to kinds of persons

Do not use for care of specific kinds of children; class in 649.12–649.15

.12   Children of specific age groups

.122   Infants

Children from birth through age two

.123   Children three to five

Class here preschool children

.124   Children six to eleven

Class here comprehensive works on school children to age fourteen

For school children over eleven, see 649.125

.125   Young people twelve to twenty

.13   Children of specific sexes

.132   Boys

.133   Girls

.14   Children of specific status, type, relationships

Add to base number 649.14 the numbers following 155.44 in 155.442–155.446, e.g., the only child 649.142

.15   Exceptional children; children distinguished by social and economic levels, by level of cultural development, by racial, ethnic, national origin

> Standard subdivisions are added for all topics in heading together, for exceptional children alone

.151–.155   Exceptional children

> Add to base number 649.15 the numbers following 371.9 in 371.91–371.95, e.g., home care of gifted children 659.155

> Class comprehensive works on home care of exceptional children in 649.15

.156   Children distinguished by social and economic levels, by level of cultural development

[.156 2]   Upper classes

> Number discontinued; class in 649.156

.156 7   Socially and culturally disadvantaged children

[.156 75]   Migrant children

> Number discontinued; class in 649.1567

.157   Children distinguished by racial, ethnic, national origin

.157 001–.157 009   Standard subdivisions

.157 03–.157 9   Specific racial, ethnic, national groups

> Add to base number 649.157 notation 03–9 from Table 5, e.g., Japanese children 649.157956, Japanese-American children 649.157956073

>   **649.3–649.7   Specific elements of home care of children**

> Class comprehensive works in 649.1

.3   **Feeding**

.33   Breast feeding

> Class nutritional aspects of breast feeding in 613.269

> *See Manual at 649.33 vs. 613.269*

.4   **Clothing and health**

> Class feeding in 649.3; class home care of children with illnesses and disabilities in 649.8

.5   **Activities and recreation**

.51   Creative activities

> Including modeling, music, painting, paper work

.55 Play with toys

> Including dolls, games
>
> Class sports games in 649.57

.57 Exercise, gymnastics, sports

.58 Reading and related activities

> Standard subdivisions are added for reading and related activities together, for reading alone
>
> Including storytelling, reading aloud to children, supervision of children's reading, listening; home teaching of reading
>
> Reading instruction in home schools at elementary level relocated to 372.4

.6 Training

> Class religious training in 291.44; class Christian religious training in 248.845
>
> *For moral and character training, see 649.7*

.62 Toilet training

.63 Training in grooming and self-reliance

> Including bathing, dressing, feeding self

.64 Behavior modification, discipline, obedience

> Class a specific application with the application, e.g., behavior modification in dressing habits 649.63

.65 Sex education

.68 Home preschool education

> Development of learning ability, of readiness for school by parents in the home
>
> Home schools and schooling relocated to 371.042; techniques of study for parents relocated to 371.30281

.7 Moral and character training

> Class religious training of children in the home in 291.44; class Christian religious training of children in the home in 248.845

.8 Home care of persons with illnesses and disabilities

> Class services to persons with illnesses and disabilities in 362.1–362.4; class nursing aspects in 610.73

650 Management and auxiliary services

This division is concerned with the art and science of conducting organized enterprises and with auxiliary skills and operations. The auxiliary skills and operations consist chiefly of communication and record keeping fundamental to management

Class here business

See Manual at 330 vs. 650

SUMMARY

650.01–.09	**Standard subdivisions**
.1	**Personal success in business**
651	**Office services**
652	**Processes of written communication**
653	**Shorthand**
657	**Accounting**
658	**General management**
659	**Advertising and public relations**

.01–.09 Standard subdivisions

.1 Personal success in business

Including creative ability; personal efficiency (management of own time and work)

Class here interdisciplinary works on success in business and other public situations

Class interdisciplinary works on success in general, on management of personal and family living in 646.7

> *For success as an executive, see 658.409. For a specific aspect of success in public situations, see the aspect, e.g., techniques of study for success as a student 371.30281*

.12 Financial success

.13 Personal improvement and success in business relationships

Standard subdivisions are added for either or both topics in heading

.14 Success in obtaining jobs and promotions

Standard subdivisions are added for either or both topics in heading

---

> ## 651–657 Auxiliary services

Class comprehensive works in 650

For advertising and public relations, see 659

651 Office services

Including problems of security and confidentiality

Class a specific aspect of security and confidentiality in office services with the aspect, e.g., security and confidentiality in records management 651.5

For processes of written communication, see 652; for accounting, see 657

SUMMARY

651.028	**Auxiliary techniques and procedures**
.2	**Equipment and supplies**
.3	**Office management**
.5	**Records management**
.7	**Communication Creation and transmission of records**
.8	**Data processing Computer applications**
.9	**Office services in specific kinds of enterprises**

.028   Auxiliary techniques and procedures

Materials relocated to 651.29

[.028 4]   Apparatus, equipment, materials

Do not use for apparatus and equipment; class in 651.2. Do not use for materials; class in 651.29

[.028 5]   Data processing   Computer applications

Do not use; class in 651.8

.2   **Equipment and supplies**

Standard subdivisions are added for equipment and supplies together, for equipment alone

Class procurement of office equipment and supplies in 658.72

[.200 1–.200 9]   Standard subdivisions

Relocated to 651.201–651.209

.201–.209   Standard subdivisions [*formerly* 651.2001–651.2009]

.23   Furniture

.26   Processing equipment

For a specific type of equipment, see the use of the equipment, e.g., typewriters 652.3

.29   Forms and supplies

Standard subdivisions are added for forms and supplies together, for forms alone

Including materials [*formerly* 651.028]

.3   **Office management**

.37 Clerical services

For written communication, see 652

See also 657 for accounting

.374 Secretarial and related services

.374 1 Secretarial services

Work of secretaries, stenographers, typists

.374 3 Related services

Including work of filers, messengers, receptionists, switchboard operators

Class work of stenographers, typists in 651.3741

.5 Records management

Class clerical services associated with records management in 651.37

For creation and transmission of records, see 651.7

.504 Special topics

.504 2 Records management in specific types of enterprises

[.504 201–.504 209] Standard subdivisions

Do not use; class in 651.501–651.509

.504 26 Records management in technical enterprises

.504 261 Medical records management

.51 Retention, maintenance, final disposition of records

Standard subdivisions are added for any or all topics in heading

Class filing systems and storage in 651.53

.53 Filing systems

Including comprehensive works on storage of records

Class here filing procedures

For specific aspects of storage, see 651.54–651.59

> 651.54–651.59 Specific aspects of storage

Including space, equipment, control, protection, preservation

Class comprehensive works in 651.53

.54 Storage of original documents

Including storage in filing cabinets, visible and rotary files

For storage of inactive files, see 651.56

.56 Storage of inactive files

Original documents in permanent (dead) storage

.58 Microreproduction of files

Active and inactive

.59 Computerization of files

Active and inactive

.7 Communication   Creation and transmission of records

Class communication as a technique of management in 658.45; class interdisciplinary works on communication in 302.2

See Manual at 658.45 vs. 651.7, 808.06665

.73 Oral communication

Including use of telephone, telephone answering machines, voice mail

.74 Written communication

Including dictating and use of dictating equipment

For specific types of written communication, see 651.75–651.78; for processes of written communication, see 652

See also 653.14 for recording in shorthand and transcribing shorthand notes

[.740 01–.740 09]   Standard subdivisions

Relocated to 651.7401–651.7409

.740 1–.740 9   Standard subdivisions [*formerly* 651.74001–651.74009]

> 651.75–651.78 Specific types of written communication

Class comprehensive works in 651.74

.75 Correspondence

Including layout of letters

.752 Form letters

.755 Memorandums

.759 Mail handling

Including equipment, e.g., mail openers and sealers, postage meters, addressing machines

.77 Minutes

.78 Reports

.79   Internal communication

Including electronic mail, intercom systems, messenger services, paging systems, pneumatic and mechanical conveyor systems

For oral internal communication, see 651.73; for written internal communication, see 651.74

.8   **Data processing**   **Computer applications**

Use in carrying out office functions

Unless it is redundant, add to base number 651.8 the numbers following 00 in 004–006, e.g., use of digital microcomputers 651.8416, but use of digital computers 651.8 (*not* 651.84)

Class interdisciplinary works on data processing in 004

For computer applications for a specific office activity, see the activity, e.g., computerization of files 651.59, word processing 652.5

.9   **Office services in specific kinds of enterprises**

Class specific elements of office services in specific kinds of enterprises in 651.2–651.8

[.900 01–.900 09]   Standard subdivisions

Do not use; class in 651.01–651.09

.900 1–.999 9   Subdivisions for office services in specific kinds of enterprises

Add to base number 651.9 notation 001–999, e.g., office services in libraries 651.902

652   Processes of written communication

For shorthand, see 653

.1   **Penmanship**

See also 745.61 for calligraphy

.3   **Typing**

Including description of typewriters

Class here keyboarding

.300 1–.300 6   Standard subdivisions

.300 7   Education, research, related topics

.300 76   Review and exercise

Do not use for speed and accuracy tests and drills; class in 652.307

.300 8–.300 9   Standard subdivisions

.302   Specific levels of skill

Class speed and accuracy tests and drills in 652.307

| [.302 01–.302 09] | Standard subdivisions |
| | Do not use; class in 652.3001–652.3009 |

.302 4   Basic (Beginning) level

.302 5   Intermediate level

.302 6   Advanced level

.307   Speed and accuracy

Standard subdivisions are added for either or both topics in heading

Class here tests, drills

[.307 076]   Review and exercise

Do not use; class in 651.307

.32   Typing for specific purposes

Other than general commercial and professional typing

[.320 1–.320 9]   Standard subdivisions

Do not use; class in 652.3001–652.3009

.325   Typing for personal use

.326   Typing for specific kinds of enterprises

Including legal, medical, technical typing

[.326 01–.326 09]   Standard subdivisions

Do not use; class in 652.3001–652.3009

.4   **Duplication of records and duplicating methods**

Standard subdivisions are added for either or both topics in heading

Office use of stencil, xerography, other methods

Class interdisciplinary works on photoduplication in 686.4

.5   **Word processing**

Class here text editors

Unless it is redundant, add to base number 652.5 the numbers following 00 in 004–006, e.g., a specific word processing program for microcomputers 652.55369

See also 652.3 for keyboarding

See Manual at 652.5: Text editors

.8   **Cryptography**

Class here interdisciplinary works on cryptography

For cryptographic techniques used for a specific purpose, see the purpose, e.g., cryptographic techniques used for security in computer systems 005.82

653 Shorthand

.076	Review and exercise

Do not use for speed and accuracy tests and drills; class in 653.15

.1 Basic shorthand practice

Class basic practice in a specific system with the system, e.g., Gregg shorthand transcription 653.4270424

.14 Taking dictation, and transcription

See also 651.74 for dictating and use of dictating equipment

.15 Speed and accuracy

Standard subdivisions are added for either or both topics in heading

Class here tests, drills

Class speed and accuracy in transcription in 653.14

[.150 76] Review and exercise

Do not use; class in 653.15

.18 Specific uses

Including court reporting; medical, personal uses

[.180 1–.180 9] Standard subdivisions

Do not use; class in 653.101–653.109

> ## 653.2–653.4 Systems

Class comprehensive works in 653

.2 Abbreviated longhand systems

Systems using conventional letters

.3 Machine systems

Add to base number 653.3 the numbers following 653.1 in 653.14–653.18, e.g., specific uses 653.38

.4 Handwritten systems

For abbreviated longhand systems, see 653.2

.41 Multilingual systems

.42 English-language systems

.421 Early forms

Systems devised before 1837

.422   **Essentially nonphonetic systems**

Class early nonphonetic systems in 653.421

>   **653.423–653.428 Essentially phonetic systems**

Class early phonetic systems in 653.421; class comprehensive works in 653.42

.423   **Geometric disjoined vowel systems**

For Pitman systems, see 653.424

.424   **Pitman systems**

.424 04   Special topics

.424 042   Basic shorthand practice

Add to base number 653.424042 the numbers following 653.1 in 653.14–653.18, e.g., speed and accuracy 653.4240425

.424 07   Education, research, related topics

.424 076   Review and exercise

Do not use for speed and accuracy tests and drills; class in 653.4240425

.424 2   Isaac Pitman system

.424 3   Benn Pitman system

.424 4   Graham system

.424 5   Munson system

.425   **Geometric joined vowel systems**

Including Dewey (1922), Lindsley, Pernin, Sloan systems

.426   **Semigeometric, script-geometric, semiscript systems**

Including Malone system

For Gregg systems, see 653.427

.427   **Gregg systems**

.427 04   Special topics

.427 042   Basic shorthand practice

Add to base number 653.427042 the numbers following 653.1 in 653.14–653.18, e.g., transcription 653.4270424

.427 07   Education, research, related topics

.427 076   Review and exercise

Do not use for speed and accuracy tests and drills; class in 653.4270425

.427 2		Conventional systems
.427 3		Simplified systems
.428		Script systems

        Including Dewey system (1936)

.43–.49   Systems used in other languages

        Add to base number 653.4 notation 3–9 from Table 6, e.g., French-language systems 653.441

[654]   [Unassigned]

        Most recently used in Edition 14

[655]   [Unassigned]

        Most recently used in Edition 17

[656]   [Unassigned]

        Most recently used in Edition 14

657   Accounting

        See Manual at 657 vs. 658.1511, 658.1512

SUMMARY

657.04	**Levels of accounting**
.1	**Constructive accounting**
.2	**Bookkeeping (Record keeping)**
.3	**Financial reporting (Financial statements)**
.4	**Specific fields of accounting**
.6	**Specific kinds of accounting**
.7	**Accounting for specific phases of business activity**
.8	**Accounting for enterprises engaged in specific kinds of activities**
.9	**Accounting for specific kinds of organizations**

.04   Levels of accounting

.042   Elementary level

.044   Intermediate level

        Including college-level accounting

.046   Advanced level

> **657.1–657.9 Elements of accounting**

Unless other instructions are given, observe the following table of preference, e.g., accounting for cost of inventory in a corporation engaged in manufacturing 657.867072 (*not* 657.42, 657.72, 657.95):

Accounting for enterprises engaged in specific kinds of activities	657.8
Financial reporting (Financial statements)	657.3
Accounting for specific phases of business activity	657.7
Constructive accounting	657.1
Bookkeeping (Record keeping)	657.2
Specific fields of accounting	657.4
Accounting for specific kinds of organizations	657.9
Specific kinds of accounting	657.6

Class comprehensive works in 657

.1 Constructive accounting

Development of accounting systems to fit the needs of individual organizations

.2 Bookkeeping (Record keeping)

Including secretarial bookkeeping and accounting

Class elementary accounting in 657.042

.3 Financial reporting (Financial statements)

Class here consolidated financial statements

.32 Preparing financial statements

.4 Specific fields of accounting

For constructive accounting, see 657.1; for bookkeeping, see 657.2

See also 658.1511 for managerial accounting

[.401–.409] Standard subdivisions

Do not use; class in 657.01–657.09

.42 Cost accounting

.45 Auditing

See also 658.4013 for management audits (assessments of management effectiveness)

.450 285 Data processing   Computer applications

Use in auditing

Class auditing of computer-processed accounts in 657.453

.452	Audit reports

Class here audit reporting

.453	Auditing of computer-processed accounts

Including program auditing

.458	Internal auditing

See also 657.48 for analytical accounting

.46	Tax accounting

Including accounting for social security taxes

.47	Fiduciary accounting

Accounting for receiverships, estates, trusts

.48	Analytical (Financial) accounting

Including measurement of profitability, of financial strength, of income, of liquidity, of flow of funds; accounting for inflation

See also 657.458 for internal auditing, 658.1511 for managerial accounting

.6 Specific kinds of accounting

[.601–.609] Standard subdivisions

Do not use; class in 657.01–657.09

.61	Public accounting
.63	Private accounting

.7 Accounting for specific phases of business activity

[.701–.709] Standard subdivisions

Do not use; class in 657.01–657.09

.72	Current assets

Including accounts receivable, cash, inventory

.73	Fixed assets

Including depreciation, valuation and revaluation of land, buildings, equipment; insurance

.74	Current liabilities

Including accounts payable, notes payable, payroll

For tax accounting, see 657.46

.75	Fixed liabilities

Including bonds payable, leases, mortgages, pension plans, purchase contracts

.76   Capital accounting

     Accounting for ownership equity

     Including accounting for stock and dividends

     For measurement of profitability, of income, see 657.48

.8   **Accounting for enterprises engaged in specific kinds of activities**

     Except for modifications shown under specific entries, add to each subdivision identified by * as follows:
001–009   Standard subdivisions
01–07   Specific aspects of accounting
     Add to 0 the numbers following 657 in 657.1–657.7, e.g., cost accounting 042

[.801–.809]   Standard subdivisions

     Do not use; class in 657.01–657.09

.83   Service and professional activities

.832   Social services

     Including libraries, prisons, religious institutions

.832 2   *Hospitals

.832 7   *Educational institutions

.833   Finance and real estate

.833 3   *Finance

     For insurance, see 657.836

.833 5   *Real estate

.834   Professions

.835   *Government

     Central and local governments and authorities

     Class accounting for government corporations (except municipalities) in 657.95. Class accounting for specific government services other than military with the service in a subdivision of 657.83, e.g., educational institutions 657.8327

.835 045   Government auditing

     Number built according to instructions under 657.8

     Class here manuals of government audit procedure

.836   *Insurance

.837   *Hotels and restaurants

*Add as instructed under 657.8

.838	*Public utilities
.839	*Wholesale and retail trade
.84	Communications and entertainment media

> Including motion-picture producers and theaters, publishing houses, television and radio networks and stations, theaters

.86	Other activities
.861	*Labor unions
.862	*Mining
.863	*Agriculture
.867	*Manufacturing

> Including printing

.869	*Construction

.9 **Accounting for specific kinds of organizations**

> Limited to organizations of a specific size or a specific kind of legal or ownership form

> Class organizations engaged in specific kinds of activities in 657.8

[.901–.903]	Standard subdivisions

> Do not use; class in 657.01–657.03

.904	Special topics
.904 2	Small business
[.905–.909]	Standard subdivisions

> Do not use; class in 657.05–657.09

.91	Individual proprietorships
.92	Partnerships

> *For international partnerships, see 657.96*

.95	Corporations

> *For multinational corporations, see 657.96*

.96	Combinations

> Class here mergers, multinational organizations

.97	Cooperatives
.98	Nonprofit organizations

*Add as instructed under 657.8

.99 Branches

658 General management

The science and art of conducting organized enterprises, projects, activities

Class here management of technology; management of services rendered by nonpublic organizations, whether or not for profit; management of public corporations; management of public agencies that themselves provide direct services (in contrast to public agencies that regulate, support, or control services provided by other organizations)

Class sociology of management in 302.35; class specific principles of management in 658.401–658.403; class comprehensive works on management and economics in 330

> *For public administration, see 351. For management of enterprises engaged in a specific field of activity, see the field, plus notation 068 from Table 1, e.g., management of commercial banks 332.12068*

> *See also 306.36 for industrial sociology*

> *See Manual at 658 and T1—068; also at T1—068 vs. 353–354; also at 302.35 vs. 658, T1—068*

SUMMARY

658.001–.009	**Standard subdivisions**
.02–.05	**[Management of enterprises of specific sizes, scopes, forms; data processing]**
.1	**Organization and finance**
.2	**Plant management**
.3	**Personnel management (Human resource management)**
.4	**Executive management**
.5	**Management of production**
.7	**Management of materials**
.8	**Management of distribution (Marketing)**

.001 Philosophy and theory

Including theory of organizations, principles derived from economics and other social and behavioral sciences

[.001 1] Systems

Do not use for systems theory and analysis; class in 658.4032. Do not use for operations research; class in 658.4034. Do not use for models and simulation; class in 658.40352

.002 Miscellany

[.002 85] Data processing   Computer applications

Do not use; class in 658.05

.003–.009 Standard subdivisions

.02   Management of enterprises of specific sizes and scopes

> Class management of enterprises of specific forms regardless of size or scope in 658.04
>
> *See Manual at 658 and T1—068*

[.020 1–.020 9]   Standard subdivisions

> Do not use; class in 658.001–658.009

.022   Small enterprises

.022 08   History and description with respect to kinds of persons

> Class here minority enterprises

.023   Big enterprises

.04   Management of enterprises of specific forms

> *For initiation of specific forms of ownership organization, see 658.114*
>
> *See Manual at 658.04 vs. 658.114, 658.402; also at 658 and T1—068*

>   658.041–658.046   Profit organizations

> Class international profit organizations in 658.049; class comprehensive works in 658

.041   Individual proprietorships

> Including home-based, part-time, retirement enterprises
>
> Class executive management by entrepreneurs in 658.421

.042   Partnerships

> General and limited
>
> Class partnership associations in 658.044

.044   Unincorporated business enterprises

> Including joint stock companies, joint ventures, partnership associations
>
> *For individual proprietorships, see 658.041; for partnerships, see 658.042*

.045   Corporations

> Class combinations in 658.046

.046   Combinations

> Including conglomerates, holding companies, interlocking directorates, subsidiaries, trusts
>
> Class mergers in 658.16

.047 Cooperatives

.048 Nonprofit organizations

Class international nonprofit organizations in 658.049

See also 658.047 for cooperative organizations

.049 International enterprises

Class organization of international enterprises and activities in 658.18

.05 Data processing   Computer applications

Class here use of data processing in managerial operations

Unless it is redundant, add to base number 658.05 the numbers following 00 in 004–006, e.g., use of digital microcomputers 658.05416, but use of digital computers 658.05 (*not* 658.054); however, for data security, see 658.478

See also 651.8 for use of data processing in clerical operations, 658.4032 for systems analysis in decision making

.1 **Organization and finance**

Standard subdivisions are added for organization and finance together, for organization alone

For internal organization, see 658.402

SUMMARY

658.11	**Initiation of business enterprises**
.12	**Legal administration**
.15	**Financial management**
.16	**Reorganization of enterprises**
.18	**Organization of international enterprises**

.11 Initiation of business enterprises

Including location

Class capitalization in 658.152; class acquisitions, consolidations, mergers, take-overs, reorganization of ownership structure in 658.16

See Manual at 338.09 vs. 332.67309, 338.6042, 346.07, 658.11, T1—0681, 658.21, T1—0682

.114 Initiation of business enterprises by form of ownership organization

Class comprehensive works on management of specific forms of ownership organization in 658.04

Add to base number 658.114 the numbers following 658.04 in 658.041–658.049, e.g., initiation of international enterprises 658.1149

See Manual at 658.04 vs. 658.114, 658.402

.12 **Legal administration**

Management of business to insure compliance with law

Including use of legal counsel

.15 **Financial management**

Procurement and use of funds to establish and operate enterprises

Including valuation of businesses

Class here financial decision making, financial planning

Class a specific aspect of valuation of businesses with the aspect, e.g., valuation of capital 658.1522

See Manual at 658.15 and T1—0681; also at 332 vs. 338, 658.15

.151 **Financial control**

Procurement and use of financial information to evaluate performance of organizations and their specific activities and to suggest remedial measures

For budgeting, see 658.154; for management of income and expense, see 658.155

.151 1 **Managerial accounting**

Design and use of accounting procedures to provide internal reports needed for day-to-day management

Class accounting in 657; class internal auditing in 657.458; class budgeting in 658.154

See also 658.4013 for management audits (evaluations of organizational effectiveness)

See Manual at 657 vs. 658.1511, 658.1512

.151 2 **Use of reports**

Including balance sheets, income and expense statements, profit and loss statements

Class here financial reports made to directors, stockholders, top management

See Manual at 657 vs. 658.1511, 658.1512

.152 **Management of financial operations**

Class here management of investment, comprehensive works on capital and its management

For budgeting (including capital budgets), see 658.154; for management of income and expense, see 658.155; for wage and salary administration, see 658.32; for customer credit management, see 658.88

> 658.152 2–658.152 4 Capital and its management

Class comprehensive works in 658.152

.152 2   Procurement of capital

Class here costs and valuation of capital

For procurement of specific kinds of capital, see 658.1524

.152 24   External sources

Including conversion of closely held corporations to corporations whose stocks are publicly traded ("going public"); endowments, grants; issue and sale of stocks and bonds; loans

Class here fund raising

Class debt management in 658.1526

For fund raising for enterprises engaged in a specific field of activity, see the field, plus notation 0681 from Table 1, e.g., private charitable and philanthropic fund raising for social welfare 361.70681

.152 26   Internal sources

Including reserves, savings, proceeds of current operations

.152 4   Procurement and management of specific kinds of capital

[.152 401–.152 409]   Standard subdivisions

Do not use; class in 658.152201–658.152209

.152 42   Long-term (Fixed) capital

Including land, buildings, heavy equipment; stocks and bonds of other companies, long-term loans receivable; leasing

See also 658.72 for procurement of office equipment

.152 44   Short-term (Working) capital

Including accounts receivable, cash, inventory, 30–90 day loans receivable

.152 6   Debt management

Including accounts payable, bonds outstanding, notes payable

.153   Taxes, insurance, charitable donations

Including ways that management can deal with taxes, what insurance is needed for the organization

Class legal aspects of business taxes in 343.068; class interdisciplinary works on and economic aspects of business taxes in 336.207; class interdisciplinary works on charitable donations in 361.765; class interdisciplinary works on insurance in 368

.154   Budgeting

Including capital budgets, budgeting for specific objectives

.155   Management of income and expense

Including distribution of profit, dividend policy

Class here management of profit and loss, comprehensive business works on risk management

Class interdisciplinary works on risk management in 368

For use of income and expense statements, see 658.1512; for taxes, insurance, charitable donations, see 658.153; for health and safety programs, see 658.382; for business security, see 658.47; for determination of prices, see 658.816

See Manual at 368 vs. 658.155: Risk management

.155 2   Cost analysis and control

Standard subdivisions are added for cost analysis and control together, for cost control alone

Class managerial accounting in 658.1511

For cost accounting, see 657.42; for analysis and control of specific kinds of costs, see 658.1553; for cost-benefit analysis, cost-volume-profit analysis, see 658.1554

.155 3   Kinds of costs

Including fixed and overhead costs; variable costs; labor, material costs

For costs of capital, see 658.1522

.155 4   Income (Revenue)

Return on investment, income from operations

Including break-even analysis, cost-benefit analysis, cost-volume-profit analysis, profit and its promotion

.159   Financial administration in enterprises of specific scopes and types

For specific aspects of financial administration in enterprises of specific scopes and types, see the aspect in 658.151–658.155, e.g., budgeting management in small business 658.154

[.159 01–.159 09]   Standard subdivisions

Do not use; class in 658.1501–658.1509

.159 2   Small business

.159 208   History and description with respect to kinds of persons

Class here minority enterprises

.159 9	Foreign (International) enterprises
.16	Reorganization of enterprises

Including acquisitions, consolidations, divestment, mergers, sale, take-overs

Class here comprehensive works on reorganization

For internal reorganization, see 658.402

.18	Organization of international enterprises

Including foreign licensing

Class here organization of international business activities

Class initiation of international enterprises and activities in 658.1149

.2	**Plant management**

Management of buildings, equipment, facilities, grounds

Class here comprehensive business works on energy management

Class procurement of plants (land, buildings, equipment) in 658.15242

For a specific aspect of energy management, see the aspect, e.g., energy management to promote efficiency in production 658.515

See Manual at 658.2 and T1—0682; also at 647 vs. 647.068, 658.2, T1—0682

.200 1–.200 9	Standard subdivisions
.202	Maintenance management

Including total protective maintenance

.21	Location

Class location of businesses in 658.11

See Manual at 338.09 vs. 332.67309, 338.6042, 346.07, 658.11, T1—0681, 658.21, T1—0682

.23	Layout
.24	Lighting
.25	Heating, ventilating, air conditioning
.26	Utilities

Including electricity, gas, power and power distribution, water

For lighting, see 658.24; for heating, ventilating, air conditioning, see 658.25

.27 Equipment

Class procurement of equipment in 658.72

For office equipment, see 651.2; for utilities, see 658.26; for equipment for safety and comfort, see 658.28

.28 Equipment for safety and comfort

Including equipment for noise control, for sanitation

.3 Personnel management (Human resource management)

Class industrial relations, interdisciplinary works on labor in 331

For management of executive personnel, see 658.407

See Manual at 658.3 and T1—0683; also at 331 vs. 658.3

SUMMARY

658.300 1–.300 9	**Standard subdivisions**
.301–.306	**[General topics of personnel management]**
.31	**Elements of personnel management**
.32	**Wage and salary administration**
.38	**Employee health, safety, welfare**

.300 1–.300 7 Standard subdivisions

.300 8 History and description with respect to kinds of persons

Class here affirmative action, discrimination in employment, equal employment opportunity

.300 81 Men

Class here management of men [*formerly also* 658.3042]

.300 82 Women

Class here management of women [*formerly also* 658.3042]

.300 83 Young people

Class here management of young people [*formerly also* 658.3042]

.300 84 Persons in specific stages of adulthood

Class here management of personnel in specific stages of adulthood [*formerly also* 658.3042]

.300 87 Persons with disabilities and illnesses, gifted persons

Class here management of personnel with disabilities and illnesses, gifted persons [*formerly also* 658.3045]

.300 89 Racial, ethnic, national groups

Class here management of personnel belonging to nondominant racial, ethnic, national groups [*formerly also* 658.3041]

.300 9 Historical, geographic, persons treatment

.301   Personnel planning and policy

            Standard subdivisions are added for either or both topics in heading

            Including information and decision making

.302   Supervision

            By immediate supervisors

            Class employee development in 658.3124; class personnel management of supervisors in 658.4071245

.303   Personnel management in enterprises of specific sizes

[.303 01–.303 09]   Standard subdivisions

            Do not use; class in 658.3001–658.3009

.304   Management of personnel occupying specific types of positions and management of problem employees

[.304 1]   Management of personnel belonging to nondominant racial, ethnic, national groups

            Relocated to 658.30089

[.304 2]   Management of personnel of specific ages and sexes

            Management of men relocated to 658.30081, management of women relocated to 658.30082, management of young people relocated to 658.30083, management of persons in specific stages of adulthood relocated to 658.30084

.304 4   Management of personnel occupying specific types of positions

            Including blue collar and professional employees

            For management of office personnel, see 651.30683; for management of supervisors, executive personnel, see 658.407

[.304 401–.304 409]   Standard subdivisions

            Do not use; class in 658.3001–658.3009

.304 5   Management of problem employees

             Management of personnel with disabilities and illnesses, gifted persons relocated to 658.30087

            Class management of problem employees occupying specific types of positions in 658.3044. Class management of a specific type of problem employee provided for elsewhere with the specific type, e.g., alcoholic employees 658.300874

.306   Job analysis

            Including specifications of qualifications required of personnel in each position

            Class here job description, job evaluation, position classification

.31   Elements of personnel management

SUMMARY

658.311	**Recruitment and selection of personnel**
.312	**Conditions of work, performance rating, promotion, demotion, utilization of personnel**
.313	**Separation from service**
.314	**Motivation, morale, discipline**
.315	**Employer-employee relationships**

.311   Recruitment and selection of personnel

.311 1   Recruitment

.311 2   Selection

      Including computerized matching, drug testing, handwriting analysis, security clearance, background investigation, use of lie detector

      Class here comprehensive works on selection and placement

       For placement, see 658.3128

       See also 658.383 for payment of moving expenses

.311 24   Interviewing

.311 25   Testing

      Class here aptitude testing

.312   Conditions of work, performance rating, promotion, demotion, utilization of personnel

      Including telecommuting

>   658.312 1–658.312 4 Conditions of work

      Class comprehensive works in 658.312

      For wage and salary administration, see 658.32; for personnel health, safety, welfare, see 658.38

.312 1   Days and hours of work

      Including lunch periods and breaks

.312 2   Leaves of absence

      Including educational, parental, sabbatical, sick leave; paid vacations

      Class absenteeism in 658.314

.312 4   Education and training

      Standard subdivisions are added for either or both topics in heading

      Class here employee development

.312 404	Development and administration of training programs
	Standard subdivisions are added for either or both topics in heading
	Including programmed instruction, teaching methods, training devices, evaluation of training programs, selection and training of training personnel
.312 408	History and description with respect to kinds of persons
	Class here training of specific kinds of employees other than those occupying specific types of positions [*formerly also* 658.31245]
.312 42	Orientation
	Class here induction
.312 43	In-house work training
	Training needed to enable an employee to do his or her job
	Including retraining, adjustment to automation
.312 44	Other kinds of training
	Including attitude training, rehabilitation training, safety training, training in human relations
.312 45	Training of personnel occupying specific types of positions
	Including blue collar and professional employees
	Training of specific kinds of employees other than those occupying specific types of positions relocated to 658.312408
	Class induction and orientation of personnel occupying specific types of positions in 658.31242; class in-house work training of personnel occupying specific types of positions in 658.31243; class other kinds of training regardless of type of position occupied by employee in 658.31244
	For training of supervisors, see 658.4071245
[.312 450 1–.312 450 9]	Standard subdivisions
	Do not use; class in 658.312401–658.312409
.312 5	Performance rating (Evaluation)
	Class promotion in 658.3126; class demotion in 658.3127
.312 6	Promotion
	Class promotion as an incentive in 658.3142
.312 7	Demotion
	Class demotion as a penalty in 658.3144

.312 8   Utilization of personnel

Including allocation of staff to specific responsibilities, staffing patterns, work teams; placement, transfer of employees from one position to another

Class training in 658.3124; class performance rating in 658.3125; class promotion in 658.3126; class demotion in 658.3127; class motivation in 658.314

.313   Separation from service

Including dismissal for cause

.313 2   Retirement

.313 4   Layoff for retrenchment (Reduction in force)

.314   Motivation, morale, discipline

Standard subdivisions are added for any or all topics in heading

Including absenteeism, misconduct, turnover

Class here promotion of creativity, productivity

Class performance rating in 658.3125

.314 2   Incentives

Including promotion

For incentive payments, see 658.3225

.314 22   Job satisfaction

Class job enrichment in 658.31423

.314 23   Job enrichment

.314 4   Penalties

Including demotion, fines, reprimands

For dismissal for cause, see 658.313

See also 658.3127 for demotion when not a penalty

.314 5   Interpersonal relations

Promotion of effective working relationships between individuals and groups

Including informal, day-to-day relations between superiors and subordinates

Class comprehensive works on employer-employee relationships from a management perspective in 658.315

.315   Employer-employee relationships

For informal relations, see 658.3145

.315 1	Industrial relations counseling
	See also 658.385 for counseling of employees
.315 2	Employee representation in management (Participatory management)
	Including worker self-management
	Class industrial democracy in 331.0112; class worker control of industry in 338.6
.315 3	Labor unions and other employee organizations
	Standard subdivisions are added for labor unions and other employee organizations together, for labor unions alone
	For collective bargaining, see 658.3154; for role of employee organizations in grievances and appeals, see 658.3155
.315 4	Collective bargaining
	Including arbitration, mediation, negotiation of contracts, strikes
.315 5	Grievances
	Class here appeals
.32	Wage and salary administration
	Standard subdivisions are added for either or both topics in heading
	Class management of labor costs in 658.1553
.321	Payroll administration
	Class clerical techniques involved in maintaining payroll records in 651.37; class payroll accounting procedures in 657.74
.322	Compensation plans
.322 2	Wage and salary scales
	Standard subdivisions are added for either or both topics in heading
	Hourly or other periodic scales
	Including longevity, overtime, severance pay
.322 5	Incentive payments
	Including bonuses, piecework rates, profit sharing, stock ownership plans
	Class comprehensive works on incentives in 658.3142
	For merit awards, see 658.3226
.322 6	Merit awards
.325	Employee benefits
	For personnel health, safety, welfare programs and services, see 658.38

.325 3	Pensions
.325 4	Insurance and workers' (workmens') compensation

Use of this number for other benefits not provided for elsewhere discontinued; class in 658.325

.38   Employee health, safety, welfare

Class comprehensive management works on employee benefits in 658.325

.382   Health and safety programs

Programs by management to enhance the well-being and safety of employees, to provide emergency and other forms of medical care

Including mental health programs

Class here employee assistance programs

Class safety of plant and equipment in 658.200289; class safety training in 658.31244; class provision of health and accident insurance in 658.3254; class comprehensive works on safety management in 658.408; class interdisciplinary works on industrial safety in 363.11

.382 2   Programs for substance abuse

Including alcohol abuse and drug abuse programs; drug testing

Class drug testing in employee selection in 658.3112

.383   Economic services

Including discounts, food services, housing, moving expenses, transportation

.385   Counseling services

Including retirement counseling services, vocational guidance services

Class mental health programs and services in 658.382

.4   Executive management

Limited to those activities named below

Class here role, function, powers, position of top and middle management

Class supervision in 658.302. Class a specific executive managerial activity not provided for here with the activity in management, e.g., personnel management 658.3; class application of a specific activity named below in another branch of management with the branch, e.g., production planning 658.503

See Manual at 658.4 and T1—0684; also at 658.4 vs. 658.42, 658.43

SUMMARY

.400 1–.400 9   Standard subdivisions

> 658.401–658.409 Specific executive management activities

Unless other instructions are given, observe the following table of preference, e.g., planning for change 658.406 (*not* 658.4012):

Personal aspects of executive management	658.409
Management of executive personnel	658.407
Internal organization	658.402
Managing change	658.406
Negotiation, conflict management, crisis management	658.405
Planning, policy making, control, quality management	658.401
Decision making and information management	658.403
Social responsibility of executive management	658.408
Project management	658.404

Class comprehensive works in 658.4

For communication, see 658.45; for use of consultants, see 658.46; for business intelligence and security, see 658.47

SUMMARY

.401   Planning, policy making, control, quality management

.401 2   Planning and policy making

Formulation of objectives, goals, courses of action

Standard subdivisions are added for either or both topics in heading

Class here management by objectives, strategic management

Class decision making in 658.403; class forecasting in 658.40355

.401 3   Control and quality management

Control: formulation of standards, evaluation of conformity of performance to standards, formulation of remedial measures

Standard subdivisions are added for either or both topics in heading

Class here management audits (assessments of management effectiveness), total quality management

Class management audits applied to a specific function with the function, e.g., management audits applied to production management 658.5; class total quality management applied to a specific function with the function, e.g., total quality management in marketing 658.8

> *See also 657.45 for financial audits, 658.562 for quality control of products*

.402   Internal organization

Including line and staff, functional, departmental organization; work teams; decentralization, distribution and delegation of authority and responsibility; internal reorganization

Class sociology of economic institutions in 306.3; class comprehensive management works on organization in 658.1; class comprehensive management works on reorganization in 658.16

> *For allocation of personnel to specific responsibilities, see 658.3128*

> *See also 302.3 for social interaction within groups*

> *See Manual at 658.04 vs. 658.114, 658.402*

.403   Decision making and information management

Class here problem solving

.403 001–.403 009   Standard subdivisions

.403 01   Philosophy and theory of decision making

[.403 011]   Systems in decision making

Do not use; class in 658.4032

.403 015   Scientific principles

[.403 015 1]   Mathematical techniques of decision making

Do not use; class in 658.4033

.403 02–.403 09   Standard subdivisions of decision making

.403 2	Systems theory and analysis

Standard subdivisions are added for either or both topics in heading

Including critical path method (CPM), network analysis, program evaluation review technique (PERT)

For decision theory, see 658.40301; for operations research, see 658.4034; for simulation, see 658.40352; for decision analysis, see 658.40354; for forecasting and forecasts, see 658.40355

.403 3	Mathematical techniques of decision making

Including mathematical programming

Class here econometrics as an aid in decision making

For simulation, see 658.40352

.403 4	Operations research

Including probability theory, queuing theory

Class mathematical methods in 658.4033; class simulation in 658.40352; class games in 658.40353

.403 5	Other techniques of decision making
.403 52	Simulation

Class here models

.403 53	Games
.403 54	Decision analysis
.403 55	Forecasting
.403 6	Group decision making

Class specific techniques of group decision making in 658.4032–658.4035

See also 658.4052 for negotiation

.403 8	Information management

Collection, processing, storage, retrieval of information

Class communication in 658.45

See Manual at 658.4038 vs. 658.455

.403 801 1	Systems

Class here information systems

.404	Project management
.405	Negotiation, conflict management, crisis management
.405 2	Negotiation

See also 658.4036 for group decision making

.405 3	Conflict management
.405 6	Crisis management
.406	Managing change

Class here expansion, modernization

For comprehensive works on reorganization of enterprises, see 658.16; for internal reorganization, see 658.402. For managing change in a specific branch of management, see the branch, e.g., changes in production 658.5

.406 2	Externally induced change

Including changes induced by social factors, conversion to metric system, technological changes

.406 3	Innovation by management
.407	Management of executive personnel

Add to base number 658.407 the numbers following 658.3 in 658.31–658.38, e.g., training of supervisors 658.4071245

.408	Social responsibility of executive management

Including protection of environment

Class here comprehensive works on safety management

Class managing welfare services for employees in 658.38; class managing welfare services for persons other than employees in 361.7; class interdisciplinary works on safety in 363.1; class interdisciplinary works on protection of environment in 363.7

For a specific aspect of safety management, see the aspect, e.g., product safety 658.56

See Manual at 363.1

.409	Personal aspects of executive management

Class here success as an executive

Class general success in business in 650.1

.409 2	Executive leadership
.409 3	Personal efficiency

Management by executives of their own time and work

.409 4	Personal characteristics of executives

Including attitudes, life-styles, values

.409 5	The management environment

Including social pressures, work pressures, relations between executives in and out of the organization

.42 **Top management**

Class initiation of business enterprises in 658.11; class comprehensive works on top and middle management in 658.4

For specific activities of top management, see the aspect, e.g., decision making by top management 658.403

See Manual at 658.4 vs. 658.42, 658.43

.421 **Entrepreneurial management**

Class management of small business in 658.022

.422 **Boards of directors**

Class here boards of trustees

.43 **Middle management**

See Manual at 658.4 vs. 658.42, 658.43

.45 **Communication**

As a technique of management

Class mechanics of communication in 651.7

See Manual at 658.45 vs. 651.7, 808.06665

.452 **Oral communication**

See also 808.51 for techniques of public speaking

.453 **Written communication**

.455 **Informational programs**

Including bulletin boards, house organs

See Manual at 658.4038 vs. 658.455

.456 **Conduct of meetings**

Class rules of order in 060.42

.46 **Use of consultants**

Class here techniques of management consulting

Class use of consultants in a specific branch of management with the branch, e.g., use of consultants in market research 658.83

.47 **Business intelligence and security**

Class insurance in 658.153

.472   Security of information and ideas

Standard subdivisions are added for either or both topics in heading

Including industrial espionage, security of trade secrets

For security of information stored in computers, see 658.478

.473   Physical security

Protection from theft by employees and others, from fraud, from terrorism, from other forms of crime

For protection against fires and other disasters, see 658.477; for physical security of computers, see 658.478

.477   Protection against fires and other disasters

.478   Computer security

.5   **Management of production**

Class here production management in manufacturing enterprises, production management in service industries, comprehensive works on logistics

Class marketing in 658.8; class comprehensive works on energy management in 658.2

For internal transportation (materials handling), see 658.781; for physical distribution, see 658.788; for factory operations engineering, see 670.42. For production management in enterprises engaged in a specific kind of activity other than manufacturing, see the activity, plus notation 0685 from Table 1, e.g., management of agricultural production 630.685

See Manual at 658.5 and T1—0685

.500 1–.500 9   Standard subdivisions

.503   General production planning

.503 6   Decision making and use of information

Standard subdivisions are added for either or both topics in heading

.503 8   Product planning

Determination of line of products or services, quantity to be produced

Including diversification

Class marketing in 658.8

For development of new products, see 658.575

.51   Organization of production

For sequencing, see 658.53; for work studies, see 658.54

.514   Use of technology

Including automation, man-machine ratios, modernization

See also 658.577 for development of technology

.515 Promotion of efficiency

For use of technology, see 658.514

.53 Sequencing

Including dispatching, routing, scheduling

.533 Kinds of sequences

Including assembly-line, continuous, single-piece sequences

.54 Work studies

Including work load

.542 Time and motion studies

Use of this number for comprehensive works on work studies discontinued; class in 658.54

.542 1 Time studies

.542 3 Motion studies

.544 Fatigue and monotony studies

Standard subdivisions are added for either or both topics in heading

.56 Product control, packaging, analysis; waste control and utilization

Including product liability, recall, safety

Class product planning in 658.5038; class product design in 658.5752; class comprehensive works on safety management in 658.408

.562 Quality control

Control of products to ensure conformity to standards and specifications

For inspection, see 658.568

.564 Packaging

Including labeling

Class here interdisciplinary works on packaging

For storage containers, see 658.785; for packing for shipment, see 658.7884; for use of packaging in sales promotion, see 658.823; for packaging technology, see 688.8

.566 Product analysis

Determination of materials, parts, subassemblies needed; how much of each to make or buy

.567 Waste control and utilization

.568 Inspection

Class comprehensive works on quality control in 658.562

.57	Research and development (R and D)

Standard subdivisions are added for research and development together, for research alone

.571	Fundamental research
.575	New product development

Class here comprehensive works on product development

> *For decisions to develop new products, see 658.5038; for product improvement research, see 658.576; for market research on new products, see 658.83*

.575 2	Product design

Including generation of product ideas

.576	Product improvement research
.577	Equipment and process research
.7	**Management of materials**

Class here management of supplies

Class comprehensive works on energy management in 658.2; class comprehensive works on logistics in 658.5

> *For management of office supplies, see 651.29*

> *See Manual at 658.7 and T1—0687*

.72	Procurement

Acquisition of equipment, materials, parts, subassemblies, supplies, tools

Class here procurement of office equipment and supplies, comprehensive works on procurement

Class management of costs of materials in 658.1553

> *For procurement of land, buildings, heavy equipment, see 658.15242*

.722	Vendor selection
.723	Contracts

Class here negotiation of contracts

.728	Receiving

Documenting, handling, inspecting incoming items

Including expediting, tracing

.78	Internal control of materials and physical distribution
.781	Internal transportation (Materials handling)

Transportation of materials and parts within plant from one work station to another

.785	Storage (Warehouse management)

Including storage containers

Class location of warehouses in 658.21

.787	Inventory control (Stock control)

Class financial control of inventories in 658.15244

For receiving, see 658.728; for storage, see 658.785

.788	Physical distribution

Class here shipment

Class internal movement of materials in 658.781

.788 2	Traffic management

Selection of carrier and routing

.788 4	Packing for shipment

Class interdisciplinary works on packaging in 658.564

.788 5	Loading and unloading

Standard subdivisions are added for either or both topics in heading

.788 6	Expediting and tracing

Standard subdivisions are added for either or both topics in heading

.8 **Management of distribution (Marketing)**

Of goods and services

Class product design in 658.5752; class comprehensive works on logistics in 658.5

For physical distribution, see 658.788; for advertising, see 659.1

See Manual at 658.8 and T1—0688; also at 658.8, T1—0688 vs. 659; also at 380.1 vs. 658.8

SUMMARY

658.800 1–.800 9	**Standard subdivisions**
.802–.804	**[General topics of marketing management; marketing to specific kinds of buyers]**
.81	**Sales management**
.82	**Sales promotion**
.83	**Market research**
.84	**Marketing channels (Distribution channels)**
.85	**Personal selling (Salesmanship)**
.86	**Marketing through wholesale channels**
.87	**Marketing through retail channels**
.88	**Credit management**

.800 1	Philosophy and theory

[.800 11]	Systems
	Do not use; class in 658.802
.800 19	Psychological principles
	For consumer psychology, see 658.8342
.800 2–.800 6	Standard subdivisions
.800 7	Education, research, related topics
.800 72	Research; statistical methods
	For market research, see 658.83
.800 8–.800 9	Standard subdivisions

.802   General topics of marketing management

Including control, decision making, information, organizing, planning, systems analysis; market segmentation

Class application of general topics to marketing to specific kinds of buyers in 658.804

.804   Marketing to specific kinds of buyers

Including governments and their agencies, hospitals

Class here industrial marketing

Class consumer research in 658.834

For marketing to foreign buyers, see 658.848

.804 01–.804 09   Standard subdivisions of industrial marketing

Do not use for marketing to specific kinds of buyers; class in 658.804

.81   Sales management

Class management of sales personnel in 658.3044

For sales promotion, see 658.82

.810 01   Philosophy and theory

.810 011 2   Forecasting and forecasts

Do not use for sales forecasting; class in 658.818

.810 02–.810 09   Standard subdivisions

.810 1   Sales planning

Class here formulation of goals, objectives, standards for evaluation of sales performance

For market research, see 658.83

.810 2	Organization of sales force

For organization by area, see 658.8103; for organization by product, see 658.8104; for organization by type of customer, see 658.8105

.810 3	Organization of sales force by area
.810 4	Organization of sales force by product
.810 5	Organization of sales force by type of customer

Class here organization of sales force by class of customer

.810 6	Organization and conduct of sales meetings

Standard subdivisions are added for either or both topics in heading

.812	Customer relations

Including claims, complaints, returns, servicing of products

.816	Price determination
.818	Sales forecasting
.82	Sales promotion

Auxiliary operations designed to reinforce and supplement advertising, direct sales efforts

Including use of gifts, prizes, samples, trading stamps

For servicing of products, see 658.812; for use of credit to promote sales, see 658.88

.823	Use of packaging

Class interdisciplinary works on packaging in 658.564

.827	Use of brands and trademarks

Standard subdivisions are added for either or both topics in heading

Including producer and distributor brands

.83	Market research

Class here market analysis; interviewing, use of consultants and research agencies, techniques of consulting in market research

Unless other instructions are given, class a subject with aspects in two or more subdivisions of 658.83 in the number coming first, e.g., research in Germany on consumer preferences 658.83430943 (*not* 658.83943)

Class results of market research in 380–382

For sales forecasting, see 658.818

[.830 9]	Historical, geographic, persons treatment

Do not use; class in 658.839

| .834 | Consumer research |
| [.834 019] | Consumer psychology |

> Do not use; class in 658.8342

| .834 08 | Consumer research with respect to kinds of persons |

> Class here specific types of consumers [*formerly* 658.8348]

| .834 2 | Consumer behavior (Consumer psychology) |

> Including motivation research
>
> *For consumer attitudes, preferences, reactions, see 658.8343*

| .834 3 | Consumer attitudes, preferences, reactions |

> Standard subdivisions are added for any or all topics in heading
>
> Including brand preferences

| [.834 8] | Specific types of consumers |

> Relocated to 658.83408

| .835 | Market study |

> Determination of extent of demand; location, nature, identification of market; extent and nature of competition; types of sales effort needed

| .839 | Historical, geographic, persons treatment |

> Add to base number 658.839 notation 01–9 from Table 2, e.g., market research in Germany 658.83943

| .84 | Marketing channels (Distribution channels) |

> Including auctions, direct-mail marketing, direct marketing, direct selling, fairs, markets, multilevel marketing, pyramid marketing, telemarketing (telephone selling), television selling
>
> Class personal selling through specific channels, e.g., personal selling by telephone, in 658.85; class direct-mail advertising in 659.133
>
> *For marketing through wholesale channels, see 658.86; for marketing through retail channels, see 658.87; for mail-order, telephone-order houses, television selling organizations, see 658.872*

| .848 | Export marketing (International trade) |

> Including marketing to foreign buyers

| .85 | Personal selling (Salesmanship) |

> Techniques for the individual, regardless of channel
>
> Including retail salesmanship
>
> Class comprehensive works on management of telephone selling in 658.84

.86   **Marketing through wholesale channels**

           Including jobbers, manufacturers' outlets

           Class personal selling through wholesale channels in 658.85

              See also 658.8705 for manufacturers' outlets as retail channels

.87   **Marketing through retail channels**

           Including apartment, garage, yard sales; shopping centers

           Class personal selling through retail channels in 658.85

              See Manual at 381.1 vs. 381.4, 658.87

.870 01–.870 09   Standard subdivisions

>   **658.870 1–658.870 8 Retail channels by type of ownership and control**

        Class comprehensive works in 658.87

.870 1   Independent retail stores

             Class independent consumer cooperatives in 658.8707

.870 2   Corporate retail chains

             Class here comprehensive works on retail chain stores

                For voluntary retail chains, see 658.8703; for chain-store consumer cooperatives, see 658.8707

.870 3   Voluntary retail chains

.870 4   Sideline stores

             Class here sideline markets

.870 5   Manufacturers' outlets

                See also 658.86 for manufacturers' outlets as wholesale channels

.870 6   Branch stores

.870 7   Consumer cooperatives

.870 8   Franchise businesses

>   **658.871–658.879 Retail channels by merchandising pattern**

        Class comprehensive works in 658.87

.871   Department stores

.872   Mail-order houses and telephone-order houses

> Standard subdivisions are added for mail-order and telephone-order houses together, for mail-order houses alone
>
> Including television selling organizations
>
> *See also 659.143 for television advertising*

.873   Variety stores

.874   General stores

.875   Specialty shops

.876   Single-line outlets

.878   Supermarkets

.879   Discount stores

.88   Credit management

> Including account security, collections, credit investigations

.882   Mercantile credit

.883   Consumer (Retail) credit

(.9)   **Management of enterprises engaged in specific fields of activity**

> (Optional number; prefer specific subject with use of notation 068 from Table 1)

(.91)   Enterprises other than those engaged in extraction, manufacturing, construction

> (Optional number; prefer specific subject with use of notation 068 from Table 1)
>
> Add to base number 658.91 notation 001–999, e.g., management of banks 658.913321; however, for management of political campaigns, see 324.7

(.92–.99)   Enterprises engaged in extraction, manufacturing, construction

> (Optional number; prefer specific subject with use of notation 068 from Table 1)
>
> Add to base number 658.9 the numbers following 6 in 620–690, e.g., management of mines 658.922

659   Advertising and public relations

> Class here publicity
>
> *See Manual at 658.8, T1—0688 vs. 659*

.1   **Advertising**

> *See also 658.81 for sales management, 658.85 for personal selling*

.104	Special topics
.104 2	Social aspects of advertising
.11	General topics of advertising

Class application of general topics to specific kinds of advertising in 659.13–659.17; class application of general topics to advertising specific kinds of organizations, products, services in 659.19

.111	Planning and control

Including decision making, goals, information

.112	Organization

Managerial organization only

See also 338.7616591 for economics and history of advertising organizations

.112 2	Advertising departments
.112 5	Advertising agencies
.113	Advertising campaigns
.13	Kinds of advertising

Including specialty and entertainment advertising

.131	General kinds of advertising

Class general kinds of advertising in specific media in 659.132–659.136

.131 2	National (General) advertising
.131 4	Retail advertising
.131 5	Advertising directed to vocational uses

Including farm, industrial, professional, trade

See also 659.19 for advertising specific kinds of organizations, products, services

---

> 659.132–659.136 Advertising in specific media

Class comprehensive works in 659.13

For broadcast media, see 659.14; for display advertising, see 659.15; for contests and lotteries, see 659.17

.132	Advertising in printed media

Including directory advertising

For direct advertising, see 659.133

.133   Direct advertising

> Printed advertising delivered or handed directly to consumer
>
> Including broadsides, circulars, letters, mail-order catalogs; direct-mail advertising
>
> Class direct-mail marketing in 658.84

.134   Advertising by location of media

> *For point-of-sale advertising, see 659.157*

.134 2   Outdoor advertising

> Including billboards, on-premise signs, painted displays, roadside signs
>
> Class outdoor transportation advertising in 659.1344
>
> *For advertising by electric signs, see 659.136*

.134 4   Transportation advertising

> Including airplane banners, car cards, traveling displays on exteriors of vehicles, station posters

.136   Advertising by electric signs

.14   Advertising by broadcast media

.142   Radio

.143   Television

> Class television selling as a channel of distribution in 658.84; class television selling organizations in 658.872

.15   Display advertising

> Including demonstrations

.152   Exhibitions and shows

> Standard subdivisions are added for either or both topics in heading
>
> Including fashion modeling, films
>
> Class interdisciplinary works on fashion modeling in 746.92

.157   Point-of-sale advertising

> Including counter, showcase, wall, window displays

.17   Advertising by contests and lotteries

> Standard subdivisions are added for either or both topics in heading
>
> *See also 790.134 for contests as recreation, 795.38 for lotteries as recreation*

.19 Advertising specific kinds of organizations, products, services

Class specific kinds of advertising regardless of kind of organization, product, service in 659.13–659.17

[.190 001–.190 009] Standard subdivisions

Do not use; class in 659.101–659.109

.190 01–.199 99 Subdivisions for specific kinds of organizations, products, services

Add to base number 659.19 notation 001–999, e.g., library advertising 659.1902

.2 Public relations

Planned and sustained effort to establish and maintain mutual understanding between an organization and its public

.28 Public relations in specific kinds of organizations

Class public relations in organizations producing specific kinds of products and services regardless of kind of organization in 659.29

[.280 1–.280 9] Standard subdivisions

Do not use; class in 659.201–659.209

.281–.289 Subdivisions for specific kinds of organizations

Add to base number 659.28 the numbers following 658.04 in 658.041–658.049, e.g., corporations 659.285

.29 Public relations in organizations producing specific kinds of products and services

[.290 001–.290 009] Standard subdivisions

Do not use; class in 659.201–659.209

.290 01–.299 99 Subdivisions for organizations producing specific kinds of products and services

Add to base number 659.29 notation 001–999, e.g., public welfare agencies 659.293616; however, public relations for religion relocated from 659.292 to 200; public relations for government relocated from 659.2935 to 352.748; public relations for armed forces relocated from 659.29355 to 355.342; for public relations in libraries, see 021.7

660 Chemical engineering and related technologies

Class military applications in 623

For pharmaceutical chemistry, see 615.19; for pulp and paper technology, see 676; for elastomers and elastomer products, see 678

SUMMARY

660.01–.09	**Standard subdivisions**
.2–.7	**[General topics in chemical engineering, biotechnology, industrial stoichiometry]**
661	**Technology of industrial chemicals**
662	**Technology of explosives, fuels, related products**
663	**Beverage technology**
664	**Food technology**
665	**Technology of industrial oils, fats, waxes, gases**
666	**Ceramic and allied technologies**
667	**Cleaning, color, coating, related technologies**
668	**Technology of other organic products**
669	**Metallurgy**

>   **660.01–660.09 Standard subdivisions of chemical engineering and related technologies**

> Standard subdivisions are added for chemical engineering and related technologies together, for chemical engineering alone

> Class comprehensive works in 660

.01   **Philosophy and theory**

.011 5   Theory of communication and control

> Do not use for process control; class in 660.2815

.02   **Miscellany**

[.028 4]   Apparatus, equipment, materials

> Do not use for materials; class in 660.282. Do not use for apparatus and equipment; class in 660.283

[.028 9]   Safety measures

> Do not use; class in 660.2804

.03   **Dictionaries, encyclopedias, concordances**

.04   **Chemical technologies of specific states of matter**

> Add to base number 660.04 the numbers following 530.4 in 530.41–530.44, e.g., plasma technology 660.044

> Class industrial gases in 665.7

.05–.09   **Standard subdivisions**

.2   **General topics in chemical engineering**

> *For biochemical engineering, see 660.63; for industrial stoichiometry, see 660.7*

.28 Specific types of chemical plant and specific activities in chemical plants

.280 01–.280 09 Standard subdivisions

.280 4 Safety measures

> *See also 363.179 for interdisciplinary works on hazardous chemicals*

> *See Manual at 604.7 vs. 660.2804*

.280 7 Specific types of chemical plant

.280 71 Bench-scale plants

.280 72 Pilot plants

.280 73 Full-scale plants

> 660.281–660.283 Process and materials

Class specific applications in unit operations in 660.2842; class specific applications in unit processes in 660.2844; class comprehensive works in 660.28

.281 Process design, assembly, control

.281 2 Process design

.281 5 Process control   Computerized process control

Unless it is redundant, add to base number 660.2815 the numbers following 00 in 004–006, e.g., use of digital microcomputers 660.2815416, but use of digital computers 660.2815 (*not* 660.28154)

Class interdisciplinary works on computerized process control in 629.895

.282 Materials

.283 Process equipment

Including piping

Class computer equipment in process control in 660.2815; class interdisciplinary works on piping in 621.8672; class interdisciplinary works on pressure vessels in 681.76041

.283 04 Control of corrosion

Class interdisciplinary works on corrosion in 620.11223

.283 2 Chemical reactors

.284 Unit operations and unit processes

.284 2	Unit operations Transport phenomena engineering

Unit operations: operations basically physical

Class here separation processes

.284 22	Crushing, grinding, screening
.284 23	Mass transfer

Including absorption, gas chromatography

> *For precipitation, filtration, solvent extraction, see 660.28424; for fractional distillation, see 660.28425*

.284 235	Adsorption
.284 24	Precipitation, filtration, solvent extraction
.284 245	Filtration
.284 248	Solvent extraction
.284 25	Fractional distillation
.284 26	Evaporative and drying processes

> *For dehumidification of air and gas, see 660.28429*

.284 27	Heat transfer

Class a specific heat transfer process with the process, e.g., melting 660.284296

.284 29	Other unit operations

Including dehumidification of air and gas

.284 292	Momentum transfer and fluidization

Including mixing

.284 293	Humidification
.284 296	Melting
.284 298	Crystallization
.284 4	Unit processes

Operations basically chemical

Add to base number 660.2844 the numbers following 547.2 in 547.21–547.29, e.g., fermentation 660.28449; however, polymerization relocated from 660.28448 to 668.92

.29	Applied physical chemistry

Add to base number 660.29 the numbers following 541.3 in 541.33–541.39, e.g., catalytic reactions 660.2995; however, for absorption, see 660.28423; for adsorption, see 660.284235; for synthesis (e.g., addition, condensation, hydrolysis, oxidation, reduction) and name reactions, see 660.2844; for polymerization, see 668.92

.6   **Biotechnology**

Application of living organisms or their biological systems or processes to the manufacture of useful products

See also 620.82 for human factors engineering

.62   Industrial microbiology

Class a specific aspect of industrial microbiology with the aspect, e.g., fermentation 660.28449, use of microorganisms in biochemical engineering 660.63

.63   Biochemical engineering

.634   Enzyme technology

.65   Genetic engineering [*formerly also* 575.10724]

.7   **Industrial stoichiometry**

661   Technology of industrial chemicals

Production of chemicals used as raw materials or reagents in manufacture of other products

For industrial gases, see 665.7

SUMMARY

661.001–.009	**Standard subdivisions**
.03–.08	**Inorganic compounds**
.1	**Nonmetallic elements**
.2	**Acids**
.3	**Bases**
.4	**Salts**
.5	**Ammonium salts**
.6	**Sulfur and nitrogen salts**
.8	**Organic chemicals**

.001–.009   Standard subdivisions

>   661.03–661.08   Inorganic compounds

Class acids, bases, salts in 661.2–661.6; class comprehensive works in 661

.03   Metallic compounds

Class here alkali and alkaline-earth compounds

Add to base number 661.03 the numbers following 546.3 in 546.38–546.39, e.g., sodium compounds 661.0382

For metallic compounds other than those of alkali and alkaline-earth metals, see 661.04–661.07

.04–.07	Other inorganic compounds

Add to base number 661.0 the numbers following 546 in 546.4–546.7, e.g., sulfur compounds 661.0723

For hydrogen compounds, see 661.08

.08	Hydrogen compounds

Including heavy water (deuterium oxide), hydrides

.1	**Nonmetallic elements**

For carbon, see 662.9; for gaseous elements, see 665.8

>   **661.2–661.6   Acids, bases, salts**

Class organic acids, bases, salts in 661.8; class comprehensive works in 661

.2	**Acids**
.22	Sulfuric acid
.23	Hydrochloric acid
.24	Nitric acid
.25	Phosphoric acid
.3	**Bases**

Class here alkalis

.32	Sodas
.322	Caustic soda (Sodium hydroxide)
.323	Sodium bicarbonate
.324	Sodium carbonate
.33	Potassium alkalis
.332	Caustic potash (Potassium hydroxide)
.333	Potassium bicarbonate
.334	Potassium carbonate

Class here comprehensive works on potash

For another compound called potash, see the compound, e.g., caustic potash 661.332

.34	Ammonia and ammonium hydroxide

Standard subdivisions are added for ammonia and ammonium hydroxide together, for ammonia alone

.35   Other alkalis

      Including hydroxides and carbonates of cesium, francium, lithium, rubidium, alkaline-earth metals

.4   **Salts**

      For ammonium salts, see 661.5; for sulfur and nitrogen salts, see 661.6

.42   Halogen salts

      Including chlorides, chlorites, chlorates, corresponding salts of other halogens

.43   Phosphorus and silicon salts

      Including phosphides, phosphites, phosphates, corresponding salts of silicon

.5   **Ammonium salts**

.6   **Sulfur and nitrogen salts**

      For ammonium salts, see 661.5

.63   Sulfur salts

      Including sulfides, sulfites, sulfates

      For plaster of paris, see 666.92

.65   Nitrogen salts

      Including nitrides, nitrites, nitrates

.8   **Organic chemicals**

.800 1–.800 9   Standard subdivisions

>   661.802–661.804 Derived chemicals

      Class derived special-purpose chemicals in 661.806–661.808; class comprehensive works in 661.8

.802   Cellulose derivatives

.803   Coal tar chemicals

.804   Petrochemicals

      Industrial chemicals produced from petroleum or natural gas

        For a specific petrochemical, see the chemical, e.g., alcohols 661.82, carbon black 662.93

.805   Synthetic chemicals

>   661.806–661.808   Special-purpose chemicals

         Class comprehensive works in 661.8

.806   Essential oils

         Class essential oils used for manufacture of perfumes in 668.54

.807   Solvents, diluents, extenders

.808   Photographic chemicals and photosensitive surfaces

         Including sensitometry

         Class here comprehensive works on chemical engineering of organic and inorganic photographic chemicals

         For inorganic photographic chemicals, see 661.1–661.6

.81   Hydrocarbons

.814   Aliphatic hydrocarbons

.815   Alicyclic hydrocarbons

.816   Aromatic hydrocarbons

>   661.82–661.89   Compounds based on specific elements other than carbon

         Add to each subdivision identified by * the numbers following 661.81 in 661.814–661.816, e.g., aliphatic esters 661.834

         Unless other instructions are given, observe the following table of preference, e.g., phosphoric acids 661.87 (*not* 661.86):

Sulfur compounds	661.896
Phosphorus compounds	661.87
Silicon compounds	661.88
Organometallic compounds	661.895
Nitrogen compounds	661.894
Oxy and hydroxy compounds	661.82–.86
Halogenated compounds	661.891

         Class comprehensive works in 661.8

>   661.82–661.86   Oxy and hydroxy compounds

         Class comprehensive works in 661.8

.82   *Alcohols and phenols

         For glycerin, see 668.2

*Add as instructed under 661.82–661.89

.83   *Esters

.84   *Ethers

.85   *Aldehydes and ketones

         Subdivisions are added for either or both topics in heading

.86   *Acids

.87   *Phosphorus compounds

.88   *Silicon compounds

.89   Other compounds

.891   *Halogenated compounds

.894   *Nitrogen compounds

.895   *Organometallic compounds

.896   *Sulfur compounds

662   Technology of explosives, fuels, related products

.1   **Fireworks (Pyrotechnics)**

.2   **Explosives**

         Class nuclear explosives in 621.48

         For fireworks, see 662.1

.26   Propellants

         Including black powder (gunpowder), cordite, flashless and coated powders, nitrocellulose (guncotton), smokeless powder

         Class here low (deflagrating) explosives

         For rocket propellants, see 662.666

.27   High explosives

         Including dynamite, PETN (pentaerythritol tetranitrate); primary explosives, e.g., mercury fulminate

.4   **Detonators**

         Including boosters, firing mechanisms, fuses, percussion caps, primers

         Class explosives used in detonators in 662.27

.5   **Matches**

*Add as instructed under 661.82–661.89

.6　　　Fuels

> Class industrial oils, fats, waxes, gases as fuels in 665
>
> *For fuels not provided for here or in 665, see 662.8*
>
> *See also 621.4023 for combustion of fuels*
>
> *See Manual at 622.22, 622.7 vs. 662.6, 669*

.602 86　　　　　　Waste technology

> Class wastes as fuels, comprehensive works on chemical technology of energy from waste materials in 662.87

.62　　　Coal

> *For coke, see 662.72*

[.620 287]　　　　　Testing and measurement

> Do not use; class in 662.622

.622　　　　　　Properties, tests, analysis

.622 09　　　　　　Historical and persons treatment

> Do not use for properties, tests, analysis of coal from specific places; class in 662.6229

.622 1–.622 5　　　Properties, tests, analysis of specific types of coal

> Add to base number 662.622 the numbers following 553.2 in 553.21–553.25, e.g., analysis of bituminous coal 662.6224

.622 9　　　　　　Properties, tests, analysis of coal from specific places

> Add to base number 662.6229 notation 1–9 from Table 2, e.g., properties of Virginia coal 662.6229755
>
> Class specific types of coal regardless of place in 662.6221–662.6225

.623　　　　　　Treatment of coal

> Including desulfurization, sizing, washing; conversion to slurry, slurry dewatering

.624　　　　　　Storage, transportation, distribution of coal

.625　　　　　　Uses of coal

> Including as a fuel, as a raw material
>
> Class a specific use with the use, e.g., metallurgical use 669.81

.65　　　Wood and wood derivatives

> Standard subdivisions are added for wood and wood derivatives together, for wood alone
>
> Including sawdust, wood briquettes
>
> *For charcoal, see 662.74*

.66   Synthetic fuels

         Class synthetic fuel gases in 665.77

.662   Synthetic petroleum

.662 2   Production of synthetic petroleum through hydrogenation and liquefaction of coal

         Including Bergius process

         Class production from coal gas in 662.6623

.662 3   Production of synthetic petroleum through hydrogenation of carbonaceous gases

         Including Fischer-Tropsch processes

.666   Rocket fuels (Rocket propellants)

         Liquid and solid

.669   Other liquid fuels

         Including benzene from waste products

.669 2   Alcohol as fuel

         Including gasohol, methanol

.7   **Coke and charcoal**

.72   Coke

.74   Charcoal

.8   **Other fuels**

.82   Colloidal and mud fuels

.86   Boron fuels

.87   Wastes as fuels

         Class here comprehensive works on the chemical technology of energy from waste materials

         Class waste biomass as fuel in 662.88; class interdisciplinary works on energy from waste materials in 333.7938

         For a specific form of energy from waste materials, see the form, e.g., benzene made from waste products 662.669

.88 Biomass as fuel

Including bagasse

Class here plant biomass as fuel, comprehensive works on the chemical technology of biomass as fuel

Class interdisciplinary works on biomass as fuel in 333.9539

For wood and wood derivatives as fuels, see 662.65

See also 665.776 for gases manufactured from biological wastes

.9 Nonfuel carbons

.92 Graphite and graphite products

Standard subdivisions are added for graphite and graphite products together, for graphite alone

.93 Adsorbent carbons

Including activated carbons, adsorbent charcoals, animal black, bone char, carbon black, decolorizing carbons, lampblack

663 Beverage technology

Commercial preparation, preservation, packaging

Class household preparation of beverages in 641.87; class interdisciplinary works on beverages in 641.2

.1 Alcoholic beverages

For wine, see 663.2; for brewed and malted beverages, see 663.3; for distilled liquors, see 663.5

.102 84 Apparatus and equipment

Do not use for materials; class in 663.11

.11 Materials

.12 Preliminary preparations

.13 Fermentation

.14 Packing

.15 Refrigeration and pasteurization

.16 Distillation

.17 Aging

.19 Bottling

.2   Wine

Including fermented cider

Class here grape wine

Class mead (honey wine) in 663.4; class sake (rice wine) in 663.49

.200 1   Philosophy and theory

.200 2   Miscellany

.200 284   Apparatus and equipment

Do not use for materials; class in 663.201

.200 3–.200 9   Standard subdivisions

.201–.209   Materials, processes, operations

Add to base number 663.20 the numbers following 663.1 in 663.11–663.19, e.g., fermentation 663.203

.22   Specific kinds of grape wine

.222   White wine

Class sparkling white wine in 663.224

.223   Red wine

Including rosé

Class sparkling red wine in 663.224

.224   Sparkling wine

White and red

.3   Brewed and malted beverages

Standard subdivisions are added for either or both topics in heading

For specific kinds of brewed and malted beverages, see 663.4

.302 84   Apparatus and equipment

Do not use for materials; class in 663.31

.31–.39   Materials, processes, operations

Add to base number 663.3 the numbers following 663.1 in 663.11–663.19, e.g., fermentation 663.33

.4   Specific kinds of brewed and malted beverages

Class malt whiskey in 663.52

.42   Beer and ale

.49   Sake and pulque

.5   Distilled liquors

> Including mescal, potato whiskey, tequila, vodka

.500 1   Philosophy and theory

.500 2   Miscellany

.500 284   Apparatus and equipment

> Do not use for materials; class in 663.501

.500 3–.500 9   Standard subdivisions

.501–.509   Materials, processes, operations

> Add to base number 663.50 the numbers following 663.1 in
> 663.11–663.19, e.g., distillation 663.506

.52   Grain whiskey

> Including bourbon

.53   Brandy

.55   Compound liquors

> Distilled spirits flavored with various seeds, roots, leaves, flowers, fruits
>
> Including cordials (liqueurs), gin

.59   Rum

.6   Nonalcoholic beverages

> *For nonalcoholic brewed beverages, see 663.9; for milk, see 637.1*

.61   Bottled drinking water

> Including carbonated water
>
> Class here potable mineral water

.62   Carbonated and mineralized beverages

> Standard subdivisions are added for carbonated and mineralized beverages
> together, for carbonated beverages alone
>
> Class carbonated and mineralized water in 663.61

.63   Fruit and vegetable juices

> Standard subdivisions are added for fruit and vegetable juices together, for
> fruit juices alone
>
> Class fermented cider in 663.2; class carbonated juices in 663.62

.64   Milk substitutes

> Including coconut milk, nondairy coffee whiteners, soybean milk

.9   **Nonalcoholic brewed beverages**

Add to each subdivision identified by * as follows:

0284	Apparatus and equipment
	Do not use for materials; class in 1
1	Materials
2	Preliminary preparations
3	Fermentation and oxidation
4	Firing, roasting, curing
5	Blending
7	Specific varieties
8	Concentrates
9	Packaging

.92   *Cocoa and chocolate

Subdivisions are added for either or both topics in heading

.93   *Coffee

.94   *Tea

.96   Herb teas

Including catnip, maté, sassafras

.97   Coffee substitutes

Including acorns, cereal preparations, chicory

664   Food technology

Commercial preparation, preservation, packaging

Class here comprehensive works on commercial food and beverage technology

Class household preservation, storage, cooking in 641.4–641.8; class interdisciplinary works on food in 641.3

For commercial processing of dairy and related products, see 637; for commercial beverage technology, see 663

SUMMARY

664.001–.009	**Standard subdivisions**
.01–.09	**[Materials, processes, operations, by-products]**
.1	**Sugars, syrups, their derived products**
.2	**Starches and jellying agents**
.3	**Fats and oils**
.4	**Food salts**
.5	**Flavoring aids**
.6	**Special-purpose food and aids**
.7	**Grains, other seeds, their derived products**
.8	**Fruits and vegetables**
.9	**Meats and allied foods**

.001   Philosophy and theory

---

*Add as instructed under 663.9

.001 15	Theory of communication and control
	Do not use for process control; class in 664.02
.001 5	Scientific principles
.001 579	Microorganisms, fungi, algae
	Class here food microbiology
.002	Miscellany
.002 84	Apparatus and equipment
	Do not use for materials; class in 664.01
.002 86	Waste technology [*formerly* 664.096]
[.002 87]	Testing and measurement
	Do not use; class in 664.07
.003–.009	Standard subdivisions
.01	Materials
	For additives, see 664.06
.02	Processes
	Class here process design, control, equipment
.022	Extraction
.023	Refining
.024	Manufacturing processes
	Not provided for elsewhere
	Including fermentation, food biotechnology, food processing with microorganisms
.028	Preservation techniques
	Class here interdisciplinary works on food preservation
	For home preservation of foods, see 641.4
.028 1	Preliminary treatment
	Including peeling
.028 2	Canning
.028 4	Drying and dehydrating
	Standard subdivisions are added for either or both topics in heading
.028 42	Drying and dehydrating by slow, thermal processes
.028 43	Drying and dehydrating through pulverizing and flaking

.028 45	Drying and dehydrating by freeze-drying
.028 5	Low-temperature preservation techniques
	For freeze-drying, see 664.02845
.028 52	Cold storage
.028 53	Deep freezing
.028 6	Chemical preservation
	Including brining, pickling, smoking
	For chemical preservation by use of additives, see 664.0287
.028 7	Chemical preservation by use of additives
.028 8	Irradiation
.06	Additives
	Production, properties, use
	Class flavoring aids in 664.5
	For chemical preservation by use of additives, see 664.0287
.062	Food colors
.07	Tests, analyses, quality controls
	For color, contaminants, flavor, odor, texture
	Including grading
	Class tests, analyses, quality controls of additives in 664.06
.072	Sensory evaluation of food
.08	By-products
.09	Packaging
[.092]	Packaging
	Number discontinued; class in 664.09
[.096]	Waste technology
	Relocated to 664.00286
.1	**Sugars, syrups, their derived products**
	Standard subdivisions are added for sugars, syrups, their derived products together; for sugars and syrups together; for sugars alone
	See also 664.5 for sugar substitutes
.102 8	Auxiliary techniques and procedures [*formerly* 664.11]; apparatus, equipment

.102 84		Apparatus and equipment [*formerly* 664.11]
		Do not use for materials; class in 664.111
.102 86		Waste technology [*formerly* 664.119]
[.102 87]		Testing and measurement
		Do not use; class in 664.117

> **664.11–664.13 Sugars and syrups**

Class comprehensive works in 664.1

.11 **Materials, techniques, processes, operations, by-products of sugars and syrups**

Auxiliary techniques and procedures relocated to 664.1028; apparatus and equipment relocated to 664.10284

Class materials, techniques, processes, operations, by-products of specific sugars and syrups in 664.12–664.13

.111 **Materials**

.112 **Preliminary preparations**

.113 **Extraction and purification**

.114 **Concentration**

Production of syrup

.115 **Crystallization**

Production of sugar

.116 **Additives**

.117 **Tests, analyses, quality controls**

For color, contaminants, flavor, texture

Class tests, analyses, quality controls of additives in 664.116

.118 **By-products**

Including molasses

Class utilization in 664.19

.119 **Packaging**

Waste technology relocated to 664.10286

> **664.12–664.13 Specific sugars and syrups**

Class comprehensive works in 664.1

.12   Cane and beet sugar and syrup

Standard subdivisions are added for cane and beet sugar and syrup together, for cane and beet sugar alone

.122   Cane sugar and syrup

Standard subdivisions are added for cane sugar and syrup, for cane sugar alone

.122 028 4   Apparatus and equipment

Do not use for materials; class in 664.1221

[.122 028 7]   Testing and measurement

Do not use; class in 664.1227

.122 1–.122 9   Materials, processes, operations, by-products

Add to base number 664.122 the numbers following 664.11 in 664.111–664.119, e.g., cane molasses 664.1228

.123   Beet sugar and syrup

Standard subdivisions are added for beet sugar and syrup together, for beet sugar alone

.13   Other sugars and syrups

For honey, see 638.16

.132   Maple sugar and syrup

Standard subdivisions are added for maple sugar and syrup, for maple syrup alone

.133   Corn and sorghum sugars and syrups

.139   Jerusalem artichoke sugar and syrup

.15   Sugar products

.152   Jam, jelly, marmalade

.153   Candy (Sweets)

See also 664.6 for chewing gum

.19   By-product utilization

Class a specific use with the use, e.g., molasses for rum 663.59

.2   Starches and jellying agents

Standard subdivisions are added for starches and jellying agents together, for starches alone

> 664.22–664.23 Starches

Class comprehensive works in 664.2

.22 Cornstarch and potato starch

.23 Cassava and arrowroot starches

.25 Jellying agents

Class here pectin

For gelatin, see 664.26

.26 Gelatin

.3 Fats and oils

Class interdisciplinary works on animal fats and oils in 665.2; class interdisciplinary works on vegetable fats and oils in 665.3

For butter, see 637.2; for peanut butter, see 664.8056596

.32 Margarine

.34 Lard

.36 Salad and cooking oils

.362 Olive oil

.363 Cottonseed oil

.368 Soy oil [*formerly* 664.369]

[.369] Other salad and cooking oils

Number discontinued; class in 664.36

Soy oil relocated to 664.368

.37 Salad dressings

Including mayonnaise

.4 Food salts

Including monosodium glutamate, table salt, tenderizers, sodium-free and other dietetic salts

Class comprehensive works on commercial technology of food flavoring aids in 664.5

.5 **Flavoring aids**

> Including chocolate, sugar substitutes
>
> Class here condiments
>
> Class flavoring aids in a specific kind of food with the kind of food, e.g., chocolate candies 664.153
>
> > *For food salts, see 664.4. For a specific flavoring aid not provided for here, see the aid, e.g., sugar 664.1*

.52–.54 **Essences and spices**

> Add to base number 664.5 the numbers following 633.8 in 633.82–633.84, e.g., vanilla extract 664.52

.55 **Vinegar**

.58 **Composites**

> Including catsup, chutney, sauces
>
> Class salad dressings in 664.37

.6 **Special-purpose food and aids**

> Including chewing gum, snack food
>
> Class special-purpose flavoring aids in 664.5

> 664.62–664.66 **Special-purpose food**

> Class comprehensive works in 664.6. Class a specific food with the food, e.g., vegetables 664.8

.62 **Baby food**

.63 **Low-calorie food**

.64 **Meatless high-protein food**

> Including synthetic meat

.65 **Composites**

> Including complete meals, packaged ingredients for complete recipes
>
> Class packaged ingredients for recipes based on a specific kind of food with the kind, e.g., mixes and prepared doughs for bakery goods 664.753

.66 **Food for animals**

> Class here pet food
>
> > *For animal feed made from grains and other seeds, see 664.76*

.68 **Leavening agents and baking aids**

> Including baking powder, baking soda, cream of tartar, yeast

.7   Grains, other seeds, their derived products

Class sugars and syrups from grain and other seeds in 664.13; class starches and jellying agents from grain and other seeds in 664.2; class fats and oils from grains and other seeds in 664.3

.72   Milling and milling products

Standard subdivisions are added for for milling and milling products together, for milling alone

For animal feeds, see 664.76

.720 01   Philosophy and theory

.720 02   Miscellany

.720 028 6   Waste technology [*formerly* 664.7209]

[.720 028 7]   Testing and measurement

Do not use; class in 664.7204

.720 03–.720 09   Standard subdivisions

.720 1   Preliminary treatment

.720 3   Grinding and deflaking

.720 4   Sifting, grading, quality controls

.720 7   Products

Including flour, meal, refined grain

See also 664.7208 for by-products

.720 8   By-products

Including bran, siftings

.720 9   Packaging

Waste technology relocated to 664.7200286

.722   Wheat

.722 7   Products

See also 664.7228 for by-products

.722 72   Flour

.722 73   Meal

.722 8   By-products

Including bran, siftings

.724   Corn [*formerly* 664.725]

Variant names: Indian corn, maize

.725   Rice

Use of this number for other cereal grains discontinued; class in 664.72

Corn relocated to 664.724

.726   Nuts, legumes, other non-cereal seeds and their flours, meals, by-products

Including cottonseeds, sunflower seeds

Class comprehensive works on commercial processing of nuts in 664.8045; class comprehensive works on commercial processing of legumes in 664.80565

.75   Secondary products

.752   Bakery goods

Including biscuits (United States), crackers

Class mixes and prepared doughs for bakery goods in 664.753

.752 3   Breads

.752 5   Pastries

Including cakes, cookies (biscuits [United Kingdom]), pies

.753   Mixes and prepared doughs

Including biscuit, cake, pancake mixes

.755   Pastas

Including macaroni, noodles, spaghetti, vermicelli

.756   Ready-to-eat cereals

.76   Animal feeds

Class comprehensive works on commercial processing of foods for animals in 664.66

.762   Cereal grains

Individual grains and mixtures

Class formula feeds in 664.768

.763   Other seeds

Individual seeds and mixtures

Class formula feeds in 664.768

.764   Cereal grain and seed mixtures

.768   Formula feeds

Cakes, flakes, granules, pellets, powders basically of cereal grains and other seeds and fortified with vitamins and minerals

.8   **Fruits and vegetables**

Class a specific product derived from fruits and vegetables with the product, e.g., jams 664.152, fats and oils 664.3

.800 1   Philosophy and theory

.800 2   Miscellany

[.800 287]   Testing and measurement

         Do not use; class in 664.807

.800 3–.800 9   Standard subdivisions

.804   Specific fruits and groups of fruits

     Add to base number 664.804 the numbers following 634 in 634.1–634.8, e.g., citrus fruits 664.804304, nuts 664.8045

.805   Specific vegetables and groups of vegetables

     Add to base number 664.805 the numbers following 635 in 635.1–635.8, e.g., salad greens 664.8055

.806–.809   Additives, tests, analyses, quality controls, by-products, packaging

     Add to base number 664.80 the numbers following 664.0 in 664.06–664.09, e.g., packaging vegetables 664.809

     Class additives, tests, analyses, quality controls, by-products, packaging applied to specific fruits and groups of fruits in 664.804; class additives, tests, analyses, quality controls, by-products, packaging applied to specific vegetables and groups of vegetables in 664.805

     See also 664.81–664.88 for preservation techniques

.81–.88   Preservation techniques

     Add to base number 664.8 the numbers following 664.028 in 664.0281–664.0288, e.g., deep freezing fruits 664.853

     Class preservation techniques applied to specific fruits and groups of fruits in 664.804; class preservation techniques applied to specific vegetables and groups of vegetables in 664.805

.9   **Meats and allied foods**

Standard subdivisions are added for meats and allied foods together, for meats alone

.900 1   Philosophy and theory

.900 2   Miscellany

[.900 287]   Testing and measurement

         Do not use; class in 664.907

.900 3–.900 9   Standard subdivisions

.902 Preservation techniques, slaughtering, meat cutting

.902 8 Preservation techniques

Add to base number 664.9028 the numbers following 664.028 in 664.0281–664.0288, e.g., canning 664.90282

.902 9 Slaughtering and meat cutting

Standard subdivisions are added for either or both topics named in the heading

.906–.909 Additives, tests, analyses, quality controls, by-products, packaging

Add to base number 664.90 the numbers following 664.0 in 664.06–664.09, e.g., packaging meats and allied foods 664.909

Class additives, tests, analyses, quality controls, by-products, packaging applied to specific meats or allied foods with the meat or food, e.g., packaging red meats 664.9299

See also 664.9028 for preservation techniques

.92 Red meat

[.920 287] Testing and measurement

Do not use; class in 664.9297

.921–.928 Preservation techniques

Add to base number 664.92 the numbers following 664.028 in 664.0281–664.0288, e.g., canning red meat 664.922
Subdivisions are added for specific red meats, e.g., canning beef 664.922

.929 Additives, tests, analyses, quality controls, by-products, packaging

Add to base number 664.929 the numbers following 664.0 in 664.06–664.09, e.g., packaging red meat 664.9299
Subdivisions are added for specific red meats, e.g., packaging beef 664.9299

See also 664.921–664.928 for preservation techniques

.93 Poultry

[.930 287] Testing and measurement

Do not use; class in 664.9397

.931–.938 Preservation techniques

Add to base number 664.93 the numbers following 664.028 in 664.0281–664.0288, e.g., deep freezing 664.9353
Subdivisions are added for specific kinds of poultry, e.g., deep freezing turkeys 664.9353

.939   Additives, tests, analyses, quality controls, by-products, packaging

> Add to base number 664.939 the numbers following 664.0 in 664.06–664.09, e.g., poultry by-products 664.9398
> Subdivisions are added for specific kinds of poultry, e.g., turkey by-products 664.9398
>
> *See also 664.931–664.938 for preservation techniques*

.94   Fish and shellfish

> Standard subdivisions are added for fish and shellfish together, for fish alone
>
> Class here seafood

[.940 287]   Testing and measurement

> Do not use; class in 664.9497

.941–.948   Preservation techniques

> Add to base number 664.94 the numbers following 664.028 in 664.0281–664.0288, e.g., canning seafood 664.942
> Subdivisions are not added for specific kinds of fish and shellfish, e.g., canning oysters 664.94 (*not* 664.942)

.949   Additives, tests, analyses, quality controls, by-products, packaging

> Add to base number 664.949 the numbers following 664.0 in 664.06–664.09, e.g., quality controls for seafood 664.9497
> Subdivisions are not added for specific kinds of fish and shellfish, e.g., quality controls for catfish 664.94 (*not* 664.9497)
>
> *See also 664.941–664.948 for preservation techniques*

.95   Other meats and allied foods

> Including frogs, turtles, snails, insects

665   Technology of industrial oils, fats, waxes, gases

Class here nonvolatile, lubricating, saponifying oils, fats, waxes

SUMMARY

665.028	Techniques, procedures, apparatus, equipment, materials
.1	Waxes
.2	Animal fats and oils
.3	Vegetable fats and oils
.4	Mineral oils and waxes
.5	Petroleum
.7	Natural gas and manufactured gases
.8	Other industrial gases

.028   Techniques, procedures, apparatus, equipment, materials

.028 2   Extraction

> Including pressurizing, rendering, steam distilling

.028 3	Refining
	Including bleaching, blending, coloring, fractionating, purifying
.028 7	Maintenance and repair
	Do not use for testing and measurement; class in 665.0288
.028 8	Tests, analyses, quality controls
	Do not use for maintenance and repair; class in 665.0287

.1   Waxes

Class polishing waxes in 667.72

For mineral waxes, see 665.4

.12   Vegetable waxes

Including bayberry, candleberry, carnauba, laurel, myrtle waxes

.13   Animal waxes

Including lanolin (wool wax), spermaceti

For beeswax, see 638.17

.19   Blended waxes

.2   Animal fats and oils

Including fish, neat's-foot, whale oils; tallow

Class here interdisciplinary works on animal fats and oils

For animal fats and oils used in food or food preparation, see 664.3

See also 665.13 for spermaceti

.3   Vegetable fats and oils

Class here interdisciplinary works on vegetable fats and oils

For vegetable fats and oils used in food and food preparation, see 664.3

.33   Wood oil

.332   Crude turpentine

Class turpentine oils in 661.806

.333   Tung oil (Chinese wood oil)

.35   Seed oils

For tung oil, see 665.333

.352   Linseed oil (Flaxseed oil)

.353   Castor oil

.354   Cocoa butter (Cacao butter)

.355	Coconut oil

.4 Mineral oils and waxes

Including natural asphalt, shale oil, tar sand

For petroleum, see 665.5

.5 Petroleum

Class here comprehensive works on technology of petroleum and natural gas

Class synthetic petroleum in 662.662

For technology of extraction of petroleum and natural gas, see 622.338; for comprehensive works on technology of natural gas, see 665.7

.53	Refinery treatment and products

Standard subdivisions are added for refinery treatment and products together, for refinery treatment alone

Class preliminary refining of oil sands and oil shale to obtain distillable fluids in 665.4

[.530 286]	Waste technology

Do not use; class in 665.538

.532	Fractional distillation
.533	Cracking processes

Including thermal and catalytic cracking, hydrogenation of residual petroleum distillates

.534	Purification and blending of distillates
.538	Refinery products and by-products

Including waste products

For petrochemicals other than fuels, lubricants, refinery residues (bottoms), see 661.804

.538 2	Highly volatile products
.538 24	Naphthas
.538 25	Aviation fuel

Including high-octane-rating gasoline, jet and turbojet fuel

Class interdisciplinary works on gasoline in 665.53827

.538 27	Gasoline

For high-octane-rating gasoline, see 665.53825

.538 3	Kerosene

For jet and turbojet fuel, see 665.53825

.538 4	Heavy fuel oil

Including absorber oil, diesel fuel, gas oil, heating oil

.538 5	Lubricating oil and grease

Including paraffin wax and petrolatum

.538 8	Residues (Bottoms)

Including asphalt, bunker and road oils, petroleum coke, pitch

Class unusable residues (wastes) in 665.538; class asphalt concrete in 666.893

.538 9	Waste control

Class here pollution control

.54	Storage, transportation, distribution
.542	Storage
.543	Transportation

Including transportation by tankers

For pipeline transportation, see 665.544

.544	Pipeline transportation
.55	Uses

Class a specific use with the use, e.g., automobile engine lubricants 629.255

.7	**Natural gas and manufactured gases**

Standard subdivisions are added for natural gas and manufactured gases together, for natural gas alone

Class here comprehensive works on technology of industrial gases

For technology of extracting natural gas, see 622.3385; for technology of industrial gases not provided for here, see 665.8

.702 86	Waste technology [*formerly* 665.78]

Class production of manufactured gases from biological wastes in 665.776

.73	Processing natural gas

Including extraction of helium

.74	Storage, transportation, distribution of natural gas and manufactured gases

Standard subdivisions are added for natural gas, manufactured gases, or both

.742   Storage

    Standard subdivisions are added for natural gas, manufactured gases, or both

.743   Transportation

    Standard subdivisions are added for natural gas, manufactured gases, or both

    For pipeline transportation, see 665.744

.744   Pipeline transportation

    Standard subdivisions are added for natural gas, manufactured gases, or both

.75   Uses of natural gas and manufactured gases

    Standard subdivisions are added for either or both topics in heading

    Class a specific use with the use, e.g., heating buildings 697.043

.77   Production of manufactured gases

    Class here comprehensive works on technology of manufactured gases

    For storage, transportation, distribution, see 665.74; for uses, see 665.75

.772   Production of manufactured gases from coal and coke

    Including blast-furnace, carbureted-blue, city, coke-oven, producer, water gases

    Class here coal gasification

.773   Production of manufactured gases from petroleum and natural gas

    Including oil, refinery, reformed natural, reformed refinery, liquefied petroleum gases, e.g., butane, butene, pentane, propane, and their mixtures

.776   Production of manufactured gases from biological wastes

    Class here biogas

.779   Production of manufactured gases by mixing fuel gases from several sources

[.78]   Waste technology

    Relocated to 665.70286

.8   **Other industrial gases**

    For ammonia, see 661.34

.81   Hydrogen

.82   Gases derived from liquefaction and fractionation of air

.822	Noble gases

Variant names: inert gases, rare gases

Including argon, helium, krypton, neon, radon, xenon

Class extraction of helium from natural gases in 665.73

.823	Oxygen
.824	Nitrogen
.83	Halogen gases
.84	Sulfur dioxide
.85	Acetylene
.89	Carbon dioxide, ozone, hydrogen sulfide

666　　Ceramic and allied technologies

Standard subdivisions are added for ceramic and allied technologies together, for ceramic technologies alone

SUMMARY

666.04		Special topics
	.1	Glass
	.2	Enamels
	.3	Pottery
	.4	Pottery materials, equipment, processes
	.5	Porcelain
	.6	Earthenware and stoneware
	.7	Refractories and structural clay products
	.8	Synthetic and artificial minerals and building materials
	.9	Masonry adhesives

.04	Special topics
.042	Ceramic-to-metal bonding

.1　　Glass

[.102 8]	Auxiliary techniques and procedures

Do not use; class in 666.13

[.102 84]	Apparatus, equipment, materials

Do not use; class in 666.12

[.102 86]	Waste technology

Do not use; class in 666.14

.104	Special topics
.104 2	Physicochemical phenomena occurring during glassmaking processes

Including phase and structural transformations

> 666.12–666.14 General topics

Class general topics of specific types of glass in 666.15; class general topics of products in 666.19; class comprehensive works in 666.1

.12   Techniques, procedures, apparatus, equipment, materials

For auxiliary techniques and procedures, see 666.13

.121   Materials

> 666.122–666.129 Specific operations in glassmaking

Class tests, analyses, quality controls in 666.137; class comprehensive works in 666.12

.122   Blowing

.123   Pressing

.124   Drawing

.125   Molding and casting

Standard subdivisions are added for either or both topics in heading

.126   Multiform processes

Cold-molding glass powder under pressure, and firing at high temperatures

.129   Annealing and tempering

.13   Auxiliary techniques and procedures

Add to base number 666.13 the numbers following —028 in notation 0285–0289 from Table 1, e.g., quality control in glassmaking 666.137; however, for waste technology, see 666.14

.14   Waste technology

Including recycling

Class here pollution control

Class recycling a specific type of glass or glass product with the type of glass or product, e.g., recycling bottles 666.192

.15   Specific types of glass

See also 669.94 for metallic glass

.152   Window glass

Sheet glass that differs from plate glass primarily in being annealed more quickly and in not being ground and polished

.153   Plate glass

> Class laminated plate glass in 666.154

.154   Laminated glass

.155   Heat-resistant glass

.156   Optical glass

.157   Fiber glass and foam glass

.19   Products

.192   Bottles and jars

> Standard subdivisions are added for either or both topics in heading

.2   **Enamels**

.3   **Pottery**

> Class here comprehensive works on clay technology

> Class pottery in the narrow sense of earthenware in 666.6

> *For specific types of pottery, see 666.5–666.6; for structural clay products, see 666.73*

[.301–.309]   Standard subdivisions

> Do not use; class in 666.31–666.39

.31–.39   Standard subdivisions

> Add to base number 666.3 the numbers following —0 in notation 01–09 from Table 1, e.g., pottery dictionaries 666.33; however, for auxiliary techniques and procedures; apparatus, equipment, materials, see 664.4

.4   **Pottery materials, equipment, processes**

> Add to base number 666.4 the numbers following 738.1 in 738.12–738.15, e.g., kilns 666.43

>   **666.5–666.6   Specific types of pottery**

> Class comprehensive works in 666.3

.5   **Porcelain**

.58   Specific products

> Including figurines, tableware, vases

.6   **Earthenware and stoneware**

> Standard subdivisions are added for either or both topics in heading

.68   Specific products

> Including containers, figurines, industrial products, tableware

.7   Refractories and structural clay products

.72   Refractory materials

> Including alumina, asbestos, chrome, fireclays, mica, talc, zirconia

.73   Structural clay products

.732   Roofing tiles

.733   Tile drains and piping

.737   Bricks

> *For hollow and perforated bricks, see 666.738*

.738   Hollow and perforated bricks

.8   Synthetic and artificial minerals and building materials

.86   Synthetic and artificial minerals

> Standard subdivisions are added for either or both topics in heading
>
> Including cryolite, feldspar, graphite, mica
>
> *For synthetic and artificial gems, see 666.88*

.88   Synthetic and artificial gems

> Standard subdivisions are added for either or both topics in heading
>
> Including diamonds, garnets, rubies, sapphires

.89   Synthetic building materials

> *For structural clay products, see 666.73*

.893   Concrete

> Including asphalt concrete, ready-mix concrete
>
> Class concrete blocks in 666.894

.894   Hollow concrete and cinder blocks

> Class here interdisciplinary works on concrete blocks
>
> *For solid concrete blocks, see 666.895*

.895   Solid concrete blocks

.9   Masonry adhesives

> Class concrete in 666.893

.92   Gypsum plasters

> Including Keene's cement, plaster of paris

.93   Lime mortars

.94   Portland cement

> Class here comprehensive works on cement
>
> *For Keene's cement, see 666.92; for other cements, see 666.95*

.95   Other cements

> Including high-alumina cement, magnesia

667   Cleaning, color, coating, related technologies

.1   Cleaning and bleaching

> Of textiles, leathers, furs, feathers

.12   Dry cleaning

> Including manufacture of dry-cleaning materials

.13   Laundering and finishing operations

> *For soaps, see 668.12; for detergents, see 668.14*

.14   Bleaching

> Including manufacture of bleaching materials

.2   Dyes and pigments

> Standard subdivisions are added for dyes and pigments together, for dyes alone

---

>   667.25–667.26   Dyes
>
> Class comprehensive works in 667.2

.25   Synthetic dyes

.252   Nitro and nitroso dyes

.253   Azo-oxy and azo-tetrazo dyes

.254   Diphenylmethane and triphenylmethane dyes

.256   Hydroxyketone dyes

> Including alizarines, quinoidals

.257   Indigoid dyes

> *See also 667.26 for indigo*

.26   Natural dyes

> Including indigo

.29   Pigments

.3   **Dyeing and printing**

Standard subdivisions are added for dyeing and printing together, for dyeing alone

Class here dyeing and printing of textiles, of textile fibers

Class dyeing and printing of a specific material not provided for here with the material, e.g., dyeing leather 675.25

> *For dyes, see 667.25–667.26*

> *See also 686.2 for printing of books and related products*

.302 86   Waste technology [*formerly* 667.36]

.31–.35   Dyeing specific textiles

Add to base number 667.3 the numbers following 677 in 677.1–677.5, e.g., dyeing nylon 667.3473

[.36]   Waste technology

Relocated to 667.30286

.38   Textile printing

.4   **Inks**

> *For printing ink, see 667.5*

.5   **Printing ink**

.6   **Paints and painting**

Standard subdivisions are added for either or both topics in heading

Including paint removers, sign painting

.62   Oil-soluble paint

.622   Oils, driers, plasticizers

.623   Pigments and extenders

> *For carbon black, see 662.93*

.624   Diluents (Thinners)

.63   Water-soluble paint

Including latex paint, whitewash

.69   Special-purpose paints

Including fire-resistant, luminous, rust-resistant paints

.7   **Polishes, lacquers, varnishes**

Class here methods of applying polishes, lacquers, varnishes

.72   Polishes and polishing

> Standard subdivisions are added for either or both topics in heading

.75   Lacquers and lacquering

> Standard subdivisions are added for either or both topics in heading

.79   Varnishes and varnishing

> Standard subdivisions are added for either or both topics in heading

> Including shellac, spar varnish

> Class here spirit varnishes

> *For japanning and japans, see 667.8*

.8   Japans and japanning

> Standard subdivisions are added for either or both topics in heading

.9   Coatings and coating

> Standard subdivisions are added for either or both topics in heading

> Comprehensive works on methods and materials for producing protective and decorative coatings

> Methods of applying a specific kind of coating relocated to the kind of coating, e.g., painting 667.6

> Class coatings applied to a specific thing and methods of applying the coatings with the thing to which the coating is applied, e.g., coatings for metal 671.73, metal coatings for polymers 668.9, painting a building 698.1, varnishing a violin 787.21923; class a coating made of a specific material with the material, e.g., enamel coatings 666.2, thermoset plastic coatings 668.422

668   Technology of other organic products

SUMMARY

668.1	Surface-active agents (Surfactants)	
.2	Glycerin	
.3	Adhesives and related products	
.4	Plastics	
.5	Perfumes and cosmetics	
.6	Agricultural chemicals	
.9	Polymers and polymerization	

.1   Surface-active agents (Surfactants)

.12   Soaps

.124   Soluble soaps

> Including liquid concentrates, powders

.125   Insoluble soaps (Metallic soaps)

> Including oleates and stearates of aluminum

.127	Scouring compounds
.14	Detergents and wetting agents

Nonsoap materials that manifest surface activity

Standard subdivisions are added for detergents and wetting agents together, for detergents alone

Including fatty-alcohol sulfates, sulfated oils and hydrocarbons

.2   **Glycerin**

.3   **Adhesives and related products**

Standard subdivisions are added for adhesives and related products together, for adhesives alone

For masonry adhesives, see 666.9

>   668.31–668.37   Specific kinds of adhesives

Class products made from specific kinds of adhesives in 668.38; class comprehensive works in 668.3

.31	Synthetic glue
.32	Animal glue

Including casein glue

.33	Vegetable glue

Including mucilage

See also 668.37 for gum

.34	Crude gelatin
.37	Gum and resin

Standard subdivisions are added for either or both topics in heading

.372	Natural gum and resin

Standard subdivisions are added for either or both topics in heading

See also 668.33 for mucilage

.374	Synthetic gum and resin

Standard subdivisions are added for either or both topics in heading

Including epoxy resin

.38	Products made from adhesives

Including tape

Class here sealants

.4   Plastics

[.402 8]   Auxiliary techniques and procedures; apparatus, equipment, materials

                           Do not use; class in 668.41

.404   Special topics

.404 2   Physicochemical phenomena of plastics manufacture

.41   Techniques, procedures, apparatus, equipment, materials

             Class application to specific kinds of plastics in 668.42–668.45; class
             application to forms and products in 668.49

.411   Materials

             Including fillers, plasticizers

> 668.412–668.419 Specific operations

             Class comprehensive works in 668.41

.412   Molding and casting

             Standard subdivisions are added for either or both topics in heading

.413   Extrusion

.414   Laminating

.415   Welding

.416   Reinforcing

.419   Auxiliary techniques and procedures

.419 2   Waste technology

                           Class here pollution control

.419 5–.419 9   Miscellaneous auxiliary techniques and procedures

                           Add to base number 668.419 the numbers following —028 in
                           notation 0285–0289 from Table 1, e.g., quality control in plastics
                           manufacture 668.4197; however, for waste technology, see 668.4192

> 668.42–668.45 Specific kinds of plastics

             Class forms and products of specific kinds of plastics in 668.49; class
             comprehensive works in 668.4

.42   Polymerization plastics

.422   Thermosetting plastics

.422 2   Phenolics

.422 3	Ureas
.422 4	Melamines
.422 5	Polyesters

        Including polyurethanes

        Class interdisciplinary works on polyurethanes in 668.4239

.422 6	Epoxies
.422 7	Silicones
.423	Thermoplastic plastics

        Including acetals, acetates, butyrates, polycarbonates, polyethers

.423 2	Acrylics (Polyacrylics)
.423 3	Styrenes (Polystyrenes)
.423 4	Polyolefins

        Including polyethylenes, polyisobutylenes, polypropylenes

.423 5	Polyamides (Nylons)
.423 6	Vinyls (Polyvinyls)
.423 7	Vinylidene chlorides
.423 8	Polyfluoro hydrocarbons
.423 9	Polyurethanes

        Class here interdisciplinary works on polyurethanes

           For thermosetting polyurethanes, see 668.4225; for polyurethane rubber, see 678.72

.43	Protein plastics

        Including plastics derived from casein

.44	Cellulosics

        Including celluloid

.45	Plastics from natural resins

        Including lignin-derived plastics

        For protein plastics, see 668.43

.49	Forms and products

        Class plastic fibers and fabrics in 677.4

>   668.492–668.495 Specific forms

        Class comprehensive works in 668.49

.492 Laminated plastic

.493 Plastic foams

Including structural foam

.494 Reinforced plastic

.495 Plastic films

.497 Containers

.5 Perfumes and cosmetics

.54 Perfumes

.542 Natural perfumes

Including floral oils and waters

.544 Synthetic perfumes

.55 Cosmetics

.6 Agricultural chemicals

.62 Fertilizers

Add to base number 668.62 the numbers following 631.8 in 631.83–631.85, e.g., superphosphates 668.625

For organic fertilizers, see 668.63

.63 Organic fertilizers

Add to base number 668.63 the numbers following 631.8 in 631.86–631.87, e.g., manufacture of fertilizers from animal wastes 668.636, converting household garbage 668.6375

.64 Soil conditioners

Manufactured and organic

.65 Pesticides

.651 Insecticides, rodenticides, vermicides

.652 Fungicides and algicides

.653 Bactericides

.654 Herbicides (Weed killers)

.9 Polymers and polymerization

Standard subdivisions are added for polymers and polymerization together, for polymers alone

Class here synthetic polymers

Class a specific application with the application, e.g., manufacture of nylon hosiery 687.3; class a specific polymer with the polymer, e.g., plastics 668.4

.92   Polymerization [*formerly* 660.28448]

669   Metallurgy

Class here alloys, extractive metallurgy, process metallurgy, interdisciplinary works on metals

For a specific aspect of metals, see the aspect, e.g., chemistry 546.3, metalworking and primary metal products 671

See Manual at 669: Alloys; also at 622.22, 622.7 vs. 662.6, 669

SUMMARY

669.01–.09	**Standard subdivisions**
.1	**Ferrous metals**
.2	**Precious, rare-earth, actinide-series metals**
.3	**Copper**
.4	**Lead**
.5	**Zinc and cadmium**
.6	**Tin**
.7	**Other nonferrous metals**
.8	**Metallurgical furnace technology**
.9	**Physical and chemical metallurgy**

.01   Philosophy and theory

.02   Miscellany

.028   Specific kinds of techniques and procedures; apparatus, equipment

.028 2   Pyrometallurgy

Extraction by furnace methods, e.g., smelting, roasting

Class electrical zone melting in 669.0284

.028 3   Hydrometallurgy

Extraction by leaching methods

.028 4   Electrometallurgy

Do not use for apparatus and equipment; class in 669.028. Do not use for materials; class in 669.042

Including electrical zone melting, vacuum metallurgy

Class here electrorefining, electrowinning

.03   Dictionaries, encyclopedias, concordances

.04   Special topics

.042   Materials

Class here prepared ores and scrap metals

Class furnace materials in 669.8

.05–.09   Standard subdivisions

>   **669.1–669.7   Metallurgy of specific metals and their alloys**

Class comprehensive works in 669

For physical and chemical metallurgy of specific metals and their alloys, see 669.96

.1   **Ferrous metals**

.14   Reduction and refining of ferrous ores

Class comprehensive works on production of iron and steel in 669.1

[.140 1–.140 9]   Standard subdivisions

Do not use; class in 669.101–669.109

.141   Production of iron

For production of ingot iron, see 669.1423

.141 3   Blast-furnace practice

Class here casting as a part of the refining process, production of pig iron and crude cast iron

Class iron casting as a metalworking process in 672.25; class cast iron products in 672.8

.141 4   Puddling furnace practice

Class here production of wrought iron

[.141 9]   Other iron alloy practices

Number discontinued; class in 669.141

.142   Production of steel

.142 2   Open-hearth furnace practice (Siemens process)

.142 3   Bessemer converter practice

Including production of duplex-process steel, ingot iron

.142 4   Electric furnace practice

Including arc furnace practice

.142 9   Production of crucible steel

>   **669.2–669.7   Nonferrous metals**

Class comprehensive works in 669

.2 **Precious and group 3B metals**

Standard subdivisions are added for precious and group 3B metals together, for precious metals alone

---

> 669.22–669.24 Precious metals

Class comprehensive works in 669.2

.22 Gold

.23 Silver

.24 Platinum

.29 Group 3B metals

Add to base number 669.29 the numbers following 546.4 in 546.4001–546.44, e.g., rare earth elements 669.291, actinide series metals 669.292, uranium 669.2931

.3 **Copper**

Class here brass, Muntz metal; bronze, gunmetal; copper-aluminum alloys; copper-beryllium alloys

.4 **Lead**

.5 **Zinc and cadmium**

.52 Zinc

For brass, Muntz metal, see 669.3

.56 Cadmium

.6 **Tin**

For bronze, gunmetal, see 669.3

.7 **Other nonferrous metals**

Including iridium, osmium, palladium, rhodium, ruthenium; rhenium

See also 669.24 for platinum

.71 Mercury

.72 Light, alkali, alkaline-earth metals

Standard subdivisions are added for light, alkali, alkaline-earth metals together; for light metals alone

For titanium, see 669.7322; for zirconium, see 669.735

.722 Aluminum

For copper-aluminum alloys, see 669.3

.723 Magnesium

.724 Beryllium

For copper-beryllium alloys, see 669.3

.725 Alkali and alkaline-earth metals

Including barium, calcium, cesium, francium, lithium, potassium, radium, rubidium, sodium, strontium

For magnesium, see 669.723; for beryllium, see 669.724

.73 Metals used in ferroalloys

.732 Titanium, vanadium, manganese

.732 2 Titanium

.733 Nickel and cobalt

.733 2 Nickel

.734 Chromium, molybdenum, tungsten

.735 Zirconium and tantalum

.75 Antimony, arsenic, bismuth

.79 Miscellaneous rare metals and metalloids

Limited to gallium, hafnium, indium, niobium, polonium, thallium; germanium, selenium, tellurium

.8 **Metallurgical furnace technology**

Class metallurgical furnace technology used for a specific metal with the metal, e.g., nickel 669.7332

.802 8 Auxiliary techniques and procedures; apparatus, equipment, materials

Do not use for refractory material; class in 669.82

.81 Fuel

.82 Refractory material

Class comprehensive works on technology of refractory materials in 666.72

.83 Firing and heat control

.84 Fluxes and slag

.85 Physical processes

Including heat exchange

.9   Physical and chemical metallurgy

> Standard subdivisions are added for either or both topics in heading

> Physical and chemical phenomena occurring during metallurgical processes; physical and chemical analyses of metals; formation of alloys

> Class metalworking and manufacture of primary metal products in 671–673

.92   Chemical analysis

> Including assaying

> Class chemical analysis of specific metals and their alloys in 669.96

.94   Physicochemical metallurgical phenomena

> Including alloy binary systems, intermetallic compounds, metallic glass, solid solutions, solidification; phase diagrams

> Class physicochemical metallurgical phenomena of specific metals and their alloys in 669.96

.95   Metallography

.950 28   Specific kinds of techniques and procedures; apparatus, equipment, materials

.950 282   Microscopical metallography

                     Optical and electron metallography

.950 283   X-ray metallography

.951–.957   Metallography of specific metals and their alloys

> Add to base number 669.95 the numbers following 669 in 669.1–669.7, e.g., aluminum 669.95722

.96   Physical and chemical metallurgy of specific metals and their alloys

> Add to base number 669.96 the numbers following 669 in 669.1–669.7, e.g., titanium 669.967322

> *For metallography of specific metals and their alloys, see 669.951–669.957*

670 Manufacturing

Including planning and design for manufactured products

Class here manufactured products

Class military applications in 623; class planning and design for specific kinds of products in 671–679; class the arts in 700. Class comprehensive works on products made by a specific process with the process, e.g., seasoned wood 674.38; however, if a specific provision is made for the product, class with the product, e.g., coated papers 676.283 (*not* 676.235)

> *For manufacture of products based on specific branches of engineering, see 620; for manufacture of products based on chemical technologies, see 660; for manufacture of final products for specific uses not provided for elsewhere, see 680*

> *See Manual at 338 vs. 060, 381, 382, 670.294, 910, T1—025, T1—0294, T1—0296*

SUMMARY

670.1–.9	Standard subdivisions and special topics
671	Metalworking processes and primary metal products
672	Iron, steel, other iron alloys
673	Nonferrous metals
674	Lumber processing, wood products, cork
675	Leather and fur processing
676	Pulp and paper technology
677	Textiles
678	Elastomers and elastomer products
679	Other products of specific kinds of materials

.285 Data processing   Computer applications

Class here computer-aided design/computer-aided manufacture (CAD/CAM), computer integrated manufacturing systems (CIM), comprehensive works on computer use in the management of manufacturing and computer-aided design or computer-aided manufacture

Class computer-aided design (CAD) in 620.00420285; class computer use in the management of manufacturing in 658.05

> *For computer-aided manufacture (CAM), see 670.427*

> *See Manual at 670.427 vs. 670.285: Flexible manufacturing systems*

.4 **Special topics**

.42 Factory operations engineering

Class here shop and assembly-line technology

> *For tools and fabricating equipment, see 621.9; for packaging technology, see 688.8*

[.420 685]	Management of factory operations
	Do not use; class in 658.5
.423	Machine-shop practice
.425	Inspection technology
.427	Mechanization and automation of factory operations

Standard subdivisions are added for either or both topics in heading

Class here assembling machines, computer-aided manufacture (CAM), computer control of factory operations

Class computer-aided design (CAD) in 620.00420285; class computer-aided design/computer-aided manufacture (CAD/CAM), computer integrated manufacturing systems (CIM) in 670.285; class automated machine-shop practice in 670.423; class automated inspection technology in 670.425; class comprehensive works on computer control in 629.89

See Manual at 670.427 vs. 670.285: Flexible manufacturing systems

.427 2	Robots

Unless it is redundant, add to base number 670.4272 the numbers following 00 in 004–006, e.g., use of digital microcomputers 670.4272416, but use of digital computers 670.4272 (*not* 670.42724)

.427 5	Computerized process control

Unless it is redundant, add to base number 670.4275 the numbers following 00 in 004–006, e.g., use of digital microcomputers 670.4275416, but use of digital computers 670.4275 (*not* 670.42754)

Class comprehensive works on computerized process control in 629.895

[.685]	Management of production

Do not use; class in 658.5

> ### 671–679 Manufacture of products from specific materials

Class here manufacture of primary products

Class comprehensive works in 670

For manufacture of ceramic products, see 666; for manufacture of plastic products, see 668.49

See Manual at 671–679 vs. 680

671 Metalworking processes and primary metal products

Standard subdivisions are added for metalworking processes and primary metal products together, for metalworking processes alone

Class metallurgy and interdisciplinary works on metals in 669

> *For metalworking processes and primary metal products with iron, steel, other iron alloys as the main metal, see 672; for metalworking processes and primary metal products with nonferrous metals as the main metal, see 673*

> ## 671.2–671.7 Specific metalworking processes

Class specific processes applied to specific primary products in 671.8; class comprehensive works in 671

.2 Founding (Casting)

> *See also 671.32–671.34 for hot-working operations*

.202 84   Materials

Do not use for apparatus and equipment; class in 671.22

.22   Foundry equipment

.23   Patternmaking and moldmaking

.24   Melting

.25   Specific methods of casting

.252   Sand casting

.253   Permanent-mold casting

Including die casting

.254   Centrifugal casting

.255   Investment casting

Variant names: cire perdue, lost-wax, precision casting

.256   Continuous casting

.3 Mechanical working and related processes

Standard subdivisions are added for mechanical working and related processes together, for mechanical working alone

>   671.32–671.34   Mechanical working

      Class here hot-working operations, cold-working operations, high-energy forming

      Class comprehensive works in 671.3

      For shot peening, see 671.36

.32   Rolling

.33   Forging, pressing, stamping

.332   Forging

.334   Stamping

.34   Extruding and drawing

.35   Machining

      Including grinding

      Class here cutting as a machining process, milling

      Class comprehensive works on cutting metal in 671.53

.36   Heat treatment and hardening

      Including age-hardening, annealing, quenching, shot peening, tempering

.37   Powder metallurgical processes (Powder metallurgy)

.373   Sintering

.4   **Electroforming of metals**

.5   **Joining and cutting of metals**

      Standard subdivisions are added for joining and cutting together, for joining alone

      Class ceramic-to-metal bonding in 666.042

.52   Welding

      Including laser welding, underwater welding

      Class underwater welding of a specific type with the type, e.g., underwater arc welding 671.5212

[.520 287]   Testing and measurement

      Do not use; class in 671.520423

.520 4   Special topics

.520 42   Welds (Welded joints)

.520 422   Weldability, weld stability, weld defects

.520 423	Inspection and testing
.521	Electric welding
.521 2	Arc welding
.521 3	Resistance welding
	Including flash, projection, seam, spot welding
.521 4	Electron beam welding
.521 5	Induction welding
.522	Gas welding
.529	Pressure and thermit welding

Including diffusion welding, forge welding, ultrasonic welding

Use of this number for flow welding discontinued; class in 671.52

.53	Cutting

Class cutting as a machining process in 671.35

.56	Soldering and brazing

Standard subdivisions are added for either or both topics in heading

.58	Bonding
.59	Riveting
.7	**Finishing and surface treatment of metals; metal coating of nonmetals**

Including cleaning, deburring

.72	Polishing and buffing

Standard subdivisions are added for polishing and buffing together, for polishing alone

.73	Coating

Including cladding; coating of various metals with a specific metal and metal coating of nonmetals

Class enameling in 666.2; class coating various metals with a specific metal and metal coating of nonmetals using a specific type or method of coating in 671.732–671.736; class comprehensive works on coating in 667.9. Class metal coating of a specific material with the material, e.g., metal coating of plastics 668.4, metal coating of ferrous metals 672.73

.732	Electroplating

Add to base number 671.732 the numbers following 669 in 669.1–669.7, e.g., nickel plating 671.7327332

.733	Hot-metal dipping

.734	Metal spraying

Class here metallizing

For vacuum metallizing, see 671.735

.735	Vapor plating (Vacuum deposition)

Including vacuum metalizing, vapor-phase deposition

.736	Diffusion coating

.8   Primary products

Class here comprehensive works on technology of metal products

For a specific metal product not provided for here, see the product, e.g., metal furniture 684.105

.82	Rolled products
.821	Patternmaking
.823	Strips and sheets
.83	Forged, pressed, stamped products
.832	Pipes
.84	Extruded and drawn products

Including cables

.842	Wires
.87	Powder metal products

672   Iron, steel, other iron alloys

Metalworking processes and primary products

Add to base number 672 the numbers following 671 in 671.2–671.8, e.g., heat treatment 672.36, galvanizing 672.732
Subdivisions are added for any or all topics in heading

For small forge work, see 682

673   Nonferrous metals

Metalworking processes and primary products

Class here alloys of nonferrous metals

Add to each subdivision identified by * the numbers following 671 in 671.2–671.8, e.g., welding aluminum 673.72252

Class metalworking processes and primary products in which nonferrous metals are not the main metal of the final product with the process or the main metal, e.g., nickel plating of various metals 671.7327332, zinc coating of steel 672.73252

.2   **Precious metals**

.22   *Gold

.23   *Silver

.24   *Platinum

[.29]   Rare-earth and actinide-series metals

> Number discontinued; class in 673

.3   ***Copper**

> Class here brass, Muntz metal; bronze, gunmetal; copper-aluminum alloys; copper-beryllium alloys

.4   ***Lead**

.5   **Zinc and cadmium**

.52   *Zinc

> *For brass, Muntz metal, see 673.3*

.56   *Cadmium

.6   ***Tin**

> *For bronze, gunmetal, see 673.3*

.7   **Other nonferrous metals**

[.71]   Mercury

> Number discontinued; class in 673.7

.72   Light, alkali, alkaline-earth metals

> Standard subdivisions are added for light, alkali, alkaline-earth metals together; for light metals alone

> *For titanium, see 673.7322; for zirconium, see 673.735*

.722   *Aluminum

> *For copper-aluminum alloys, see 673.3*

.723   *Magnesium

.724   *Beryllium

> *For copper-beryllium alloys, see 673.3*

[.725]   Alkali and alkaline-earth metals

> Number discontinued; class in 673.72

.73   Metals used in ferroalloys

---

*Add as instructed under 673

.732	Titanium, vanadium, manganese
.732 2	*Titanium
.733	Nickel and cobalt
.733 2	*Nickel
.734	Chromium, molybdenum, tungsten
.735	Zirconium and tantalum
[.75]	Antimony, arsenic, bismuth
	Number discontinued; class in 673.7
[.79]	Miscellaneous rare metals and metalloids
	Number discontinued; class in 673.7

674 Lumber processing, wood products, cork

.001–.009	Standard subdivisions
.01	Philosophy and theory of lumber technology
.02	Miscellany of lumber technology
.021 2	Tables and formulas
	Do not use for specifications; class in 674.5
[.028 6]	Waste technology
	Do not use; class in 674.84
.028 7	Testing and measurement
	Do not use for grading lumber; class in 674.5
.03–.09	Standard subdivisions of lumber technology

> **674.1–674.5 Lumber technology**

Class physical properties of lumber in 620.12; class comprehensive works in 674

.1	**Structure, chemical properties, types of lumber**
.12	Structure
	Gross and microscopic
.13	Chemical properties
	Including chemical properties of wood extracts

*Add as instructed under 673

.14 Specific types of lumber

> Class structure of specific types of lumber in 674.12; class chemical properties of specific types of lumber in 674.13

.142 Hardwoods

> Including basswood, beech, chestnut, elm, maple, oak, poplar

.144 Softwoods

> Including cedar, cypress, fir, hemlock, larch, pine, redwood, spruce

.2 Sawmill operations

> Class wood waste and residues in 674.84

.28 Rough lumber

> Class here dimension stock (cut stock)

.3 Storage, seasoning, preservation of lumber

.32 Storage in lumberyards

.38 Seasoning and preservation

> Standard subdivisions are added for seasoning and preservation together, for seasoning alone

> Class here drying

.382 Use of air

.384 Use of kilns

.386 Use of chemicals

> Class here preservation

.4 Production of finished lumber

.42 Production of surfaced lumber

.43 Production of pattern lumber

> Including shiplap, sidings, tongue-and-groove products

.5 Grading lumber

> Including inspection and specifications

.8 Wood products

Class here comprehensive works on wood-using technologies

> *For a specific product or wood-using technology not provided for here, see the product or technology, e.g., wood as a fuel 662.65, finished lumber 674.4, pulp and paper technology 676, wooden furniture 684.104, carpentry 694*

.82		Containers and pallets

Including barrels, boxes, casks, crates

.83 Veneers and composite woods

Standard subdivisions are added for veneers and composite woods together, for composite woods alone

.833 Veneers

> 674.834–674.836 Composite woods

Class comprehensive works in 674.83

.834 Plywood

See also 674.835 for specialty plywoods

.835 Laminated wood (Sandwich panels, Specialty plywoods)

.836 Particle board

.84 Wood waste and residues

Standard subdivisions are added for either or both topics in heading

Including excelsior, sawdust, wood flour and shavings

Class here pollution control

Class utilization of wood waste and residues in making a specific product with the product, e.g., particle board 674.836

.88 Other products

Including picture frames, signs, spools, toothpicks, wood-cased pencils, woodenware

.9 Cork

675 Leather and fur processing

For leather and fur goods, see 685

.2 Processing of natural leather

[.202 87] Testing and measurement

Do not use; class in 675.29

.22 Preliminary operations

Including fleshing, unhairing (liming), bating hides and skins

.23 Tanning

.24 Dressing

.25   Finishing

             Including dyeing, embossing, glazing, production of patent leather

.29   Properties, tests, quality controls

.3   Fur processing

             Including manufacture of imitation furs

.4   Manufacture of imitation leathers

676   Pulp and paper technology

Standard subdivisions are added for pulp and paper technology together, for paper technology alone

Class here comprehensive works on paper and paper products, on the total process of making paper out of logs or other sources of pulp

Class the process of making pulp, through bleaching, in 676.1; class conversion of pulp into paper or paper products, starting with beating and refining the pulp, in 676.2

SUMMARY

676.04	**Special topics**	
.1	**Pulp**	
.2	**Conversion of pulp into paper, and specific types of paper and paper products**	
.3	**Paper and paperboard containers**	
.4	**Purified pulp**	
.5	**Pulp by-products**	
.7	**Paper from man-made and noncellulosic fibers**	

[.028 6]   Waste technology

                  Do not use; class in 676.042

.04   Special topics

.042   Waste technology

              Class here pollution control

              Class paper recycling in 676.142

.1   Pulp

              Class here the process of making pulp, through bleaching

              Class conversion of pulp into paper, starting with beating and refining the pulp, in 676.2; class pulp by-products in 676.5

[.102 87]   Testing and measurement

                      Do not use; class in 676.17

>   676.12–676.14   Specific pulps

Class comprehensive works in 676.1

For purified pulp, see 676.4

.12   Wood pulp

[.120 287]   Testing and measurement

Do not use; class in 676.121

.121   Properties, tests, quality controls

>   676.122–676.127   Specific processes

Class comprehensive works in 676.12

.122   Mechanical (Ground wood) process

.124   Soda process

.125   Sulfite process

.126   Sulfate (Kraft) process

.127   Semichemical process

.13   Rag pulp

.14   Other pulps

Including bagasse, bamboo, cornstalks, hemp, jute, straw

.142   Wastepaper

Class here paper recycling

.17   Properties, tests, quality controls

Class properties, tests, quality controls of specific pulps in 676.12–676.14

.18   Molded products and pulpboards

.182   Molded products

.183   Pulpboards

Including chip boards, fiberboards, wallboards

>   **676.2–676.5   Pulp products**

Class comprehensive works in 676

For molded products and pulpboards, see 676.18

.2	**Conversion of pulp into paper, and specific types of paper and paper products**

Class paper recycling in 676.142

[.202 87]		Testing and measurement
		Do not use; class in 676.27

> 676.22–676.27   General topics

Class general topics of specific types of paper and paper products in 676.28; class comprehensive works in 676.2

.22	Production by hand
.23	Specific processes of machine production
.232	Basic processes
.234	Finishing

Including calendering, coloring, creping, sizing

For coating, see 676.235

.235	Coating
.27	Properties, tests, quality controls
.28	Specific types of paper and paper products
.280 27	Patents and identification marks

Including watermarks

.282	Graphic arts paper
.282 3	Stationery

Including onionskin paper

.282 4	Book paper

Class coated book paper in 676.283

.282 5	Drawing and art paper

Standard subdivisions are added for either or both topics in heading

.282 6	Currency paper

Papers for printing money, bonds, securities

.283	Coated paper
.284	Specialty paper

.284 2	Tissue paper
	Including cleansing tissues, toilet paper
	Class onionskin paper in 676.2823
.284 4	Blotting and saturating paper
	Standard subdivisions are added for either or both topics in heading
.284 5	Vulcanized and parchment papers
	See also 685 for parchment prepared from the skin of an animal
.284 8	Wallpaper
.286	Unsized paper
	Including newsprint
.287	Wrapping and bag papers
	Including bogus wrapping, butcher, kraft wrapping, Manila paper
.288	Paperboard
	Including bristol board, cardboard, food board, pasteboard
.289	Roofing and building papers
.3	**Paper and paperboard containers**
.32	Boxes and cartons
	Standard subdivisions are added for either or both topics in heading
	Including corrugated and solid paperboard boxes, folding boxes
	For food board containers, see 676.34
.33	Bags
.34	Food board containers
	Including food cartons, paper plates and cups
.4	**Purified pulp**
	Production of alpha cellulose from wood pulp and cotton linters
.5	**Pulp by-products**
	Including fatty acids, lignin, resins, tall oil, turpentine
.7	**Paper from man-made and noncellulosic fibers**

677   Textiles

Production of fibers, fabrics, cordage

Class here comprehensive works on manufacture of textiles and clothing

For manufacture of clothing, see 687

SUMMARY

.001   Philosophy and theory

.002   Miscellany

.002 8   Auxiliary techniques and procedures [*formerly* 677.028]

[.002 84]   Apparatus, equipment, materials

           Do not use; class in 677.028

.002 86   Waste technology [*formerly* 677.029]

           Class waste and reused wool and hair in 677.36; class waste and reused silk in 677.394

[.002 87]   Testing and measurement

           Do not use; class in 677.0287

.003–.009   Standard subdivisions

.02   General topics

.022   Designs (Working patterns)

.028   Techniques, procedures, apparatus, equipment, materials, products

           Auxiliary techniques and procedures relocated to 677.0028

.028 2   Operations

.028 21   Preliminary operations

           Including carding, combing

.028 22   Spinning, twisting, reeling

           Standard subdivisions are added for spinning, twisting, reeling together; for spinning alone

.028 24   Weaving, knitting, felting

.028 242   Weaving

.028 245   Knitting

.028 25	Basic finishing

                 Physical and chemical processes

                 Including beetling, calendering, creping, mercerizing, pressing, shearing, singeing, tentering

                 For dyeing and printing, see 667.3

.028 3	Materials
.028 32	Fibers
.028 35	Textile chemicals
.028 5	Power equipment
.028 52	Spinning machines
.028 54	Looms and loom equipment

                 Standard subdivisions are added for looms and loom equipment together, for looms alone

.028 55	Basic finishing machines
.028 6	Products

                 For tests and quality controls of products, see 677.0287

.028 62	Yarns and threads

                 Standard subdivisions are added for either or both topics in heading

.028 64	Fabrics
.028 7	Testing and measurement

                 Including tests and quality controls of products

[.029]	Waste technology

                 Relocated to 677.00286

>   **677.1–677.5   Textiles of specific composition**

           Class here specific kinds of textile fibers

           Class special-process fabrics regardless of composition in 677.6; class comprehensive works in 677

.1	**Textiles of bast fibers**
.11	Flax
.110 28	Auxiliary techniques and procedures [*formerly* 677.112–677.117]
[.110 284]	Apparatus, equipment, materials

                 Do not use; class in 677.112–677.117

.112–.117	Techniques, procedures, apparatus, equipment, materials, products

Add to base number 677.11 the numbers following 677.028 in 677.0282–677.0287, e.g., linen fabrics 677.1164

Auxiliary techniques and procedures relocated to 677.11028

.12	Hemp
.13	Jute
.15	Ramie
.18	Coir

.2 Textiles of seed-hair fibers

.21	Cotton

.210 28   Auxiliary techniques and procedures [*formerly* 677.212–677.217]

[.210 284]   Apparatus, equipment, materials

Do not use; class in 677.212–677.217

.212–.217	Techniques, procedures, apparatus, equipment, materials, products

Add to base number 677.21 the numbers following 677.028 in 677.0282–677.0287, e.g., cotton ginning, carding, combing 677.2121

Auxiliary techniques and procedures relocated to 677.21028

.23	Kapok

.3 Textiles of animal fibers

.31	Sheep wool

Class here comprehensive works on technology of wool textiles

For llama, alpaca, vicuña, guanaco wool textiles, see 677.32

.310 28   Auxiliary techniques and procedures [*formerly* 677.312–677.317]

[.310 284]   Apparatus, equipment, materials

Do not use; class in 677.312–677.317

.312–.317	Techniques, procedures, apparatus, equipment, materials, products

Add to base number 677.31 the numbers following 677.028 in 677.0282–677.0287, e.g., sheep wool fibers 677.3132

Auxiliary techniques and procedures relocated to 677.31028

.32	Llama, alpaca, vicuña, guanaco wools
.33	Goat hair
.34	Camel's hair

.35	Rabbit hair

.36   Waste and reused wool and hair

> Standard subdivisions are added for any or all topics in heading

.39   Silk

.391   Cultivated silk

.391 028   Auxiliary techniques and procedures [*formerly* 677.3912–677.3917]

[.391 028 4]   Apparatus, equipment, materials

> Do not use; class in 677.3912–677.3917

.391 2–.391 7   Techniques, procedures, apparatus, equipment, materials, products

> Add to base number 677.391 the numbers following 677.028 in 677.0282–677.0287, e.g., beetling cultivated silk 677.39125
>
> Auxiliary techniques and procedures relocated to 677.391028

.392   Wild silk (Tussah silk)

.394   Waste and reused silk

> Standard subdivisions are added for either or both topics in heading

.4   Textiles of man-made fibers

.46   Cellulosics (Rayon and acetates)

> *For textiles of paper fibers, see 677.5*

.460 01–.460 09   Standard subdivisions

.460 1–.460 9   Standard subdivisions of rayon

>   677.461–677.463 Rayon

> Class comprehensive works in 677.46

.461   Nitrocellulose

.462   Cuprammonium rayon

.463   Viscose rayon

.464   Cellulose acetate

.47   Noncellulosics

> *For fiber glass, see 677.52*

.472   Azlon

.473   Polyamides (Nylons)

.474	Other polymerization textiles
.474 2	Acrylics
	Class here polyacrylics
.474 3	Polyesters
.474 4	Vinyls
	Including nytrils, sarans, vinyons
	Class here polyvinyls
.474 5	Olefins
	Including polyethylene, polypropylene
.474 8	Polyfluoro hydrocarbons
.5	**Other textiles of specific fibers**
.51	Textiles of asbestos fibers
.52	Textiles of fiber glass
.53	Textiles of metal fibers
.54	Textiles of unaltered vegetable fibers
	Including bamboo, cane, raffia, rattan, rush
.55	Textiles of elastic fibers
.6	**Special-process fabrics regardless of composition**
	Class here nonwoven fabrics
.61	Fancy-weave fabrics
	For tapestries, carpets, rugs, see 677.64; for openwork fabrics, see 677.65
.615	Fabrics in dobby weave
	Including bird's-eye, figured madras, huckaback, sharkskin
.616	Fabrics in Jacquard weave
	Including brocade, brocatelle, damask, lamé, upholstery fabrics
.617	Fabrics in pile weave
	Including chenille, corduroy, frieze, plush, terry cloth, velour, velvet, velveteen
.62	Woven felt
	Class comprehensive works on felt in 677.63
.624	Flannel and swanskin yard goods

.626	Blankets, lap robes, coverlets
.63	Felt

> *For woven felt, see 677.62*

.632	Yard goods and carpets
.64	Tapestries, carpets, rugs
.642	Tapestry yard goods
.643	Carpets and rugs

> Standard subdivisions are added for either or both topics in heading
>
> *For nonwoven felt carpets, see 677.632*

.65	Openwork fabrics

> *For chain-stitch and knotted fabrics, see 677.66*

.652	Fabrics in leno weave

> Including grenadines, marquisettes

.653	Laces

> Including bobbin, machine, needlepoint laces

.654	Tulles
.66	Chain-stitch and knotted fabrics
.661	Knitted fabrics
.662	Crocheted fabrics
.663	Tatted fabrics
.664	Netted fabrics
.68	Fabrics with functional finishes

> Including drip-dry, durable press fabrics
>
> Class specific types of special-process fabrics regardless of finish in 677.61–677.66

.681	Crease-resistant and wrinkle-resistant fabrics

> Standard subdivisions are added for either or both topics in heading

.682	Waterproof and water-repellent fabrics

> Standard subdivisions are added for either or both topics in heading

.688	Shrinkage-controlled fabrics
.689	Flameproof and flame-resistant fabrics

> Standard subdivisions are added for either or both topics in heading

.69   Bonded and laminated fabrics

> Standard subdivisions are added for either or both topics in heading

.7   Cordage, trimmings and allied products

.71   Ropes, twines, strings

> Class here cordage

> *For passementerie, see 677.76*

.76   Passementerie

> Including decorative bias bindings, braids, cords, gimps, lacings, ribbons, tapes, tinsel; upholstery trimmings

.77   Machine embroidery

> Including clip spot, lappet, Schiffli, swivel (dotted swiss) embroidery

> Class laces in 677.653

.8   Surgical gauze and cotton

> Including bandages, sanitary napkins

678   Elastomers and elastomer products

> Standard subdivisions are added for elastomers and elastomer products together, for elastomers alone

.2   Rubber

> *For rubber products, see 678.3; for properties of rubber, see 678.4; for natural rubber, see 678.62; for synthetic rubber, see 678.72*

.202 84   Apparatus and equipment

> Do not use for materials; class in 678.21

[.202 86]   Waste technology

> Do not use; class in 678.29

.21   Materials

> *For reclaimed rubber, see 678.29*

.22   Mastication

.23   Compounding

> Including use of accelerators, antioxidants, pigments, solvents

.24   Vulcanization

.27   Molding, extruding, calendering

.29   Reclaimed rubber and waste control

Including devulcanizing

Class here pollution control

.3   **Rubber products**

Class elastic fiber textiles in 677.55

> *For natural rubber products, see 678.63; for synthetic rubber products, see 678.723*

.32   Tires

.33   Overshoes

.34   Articles molded and vulcanized in presses

Including doorstops, hollow ware, hot-water bottles, tiles

.35   Extruded articles

Including inner tubes, rubber bands, weather stripping, windshield wipers

.36   Articles made by dipping, spreading, electrodeposition

Including conveyor and driving belts, hose, sheeting

.4   **Properties of rubber**

.5   **Latexes**

> *For natural latexes, see 678.61; for synthetic latexes, see 678.71*

[.502 84]   Apparatus, equipment, materials

Do not use; class in 678.52

.52   Techniques, procedures, apparatus, equipment, materials

.521   Materials

.522   Preliminary treatment

Including preservation, concentration, creaming, centrifuging, preparation of latex biscuits

.524   Vulcanization

.527   Other operations

Including casting, coating, dipping, electrodepositing, molding, spreading

.53   Products

.532   Foam articles

.533   Articles made by dipping and casting

Including feeding-bottle nipples

.538   Articles made by extruding, spreading, spraying, electrodeposition

.54   Properties

.6   **Natural elastomers**

.61   Natural latexes

.62   Natural rubber

> *For natural rubber products, see 678.63; for properties of natural rubber, see 678.64*

.63   Natural rubber products

.64   Properties of natural rubber

.68   Chemical derivatives of natural rubber

> Including cyclo and halogenated rubber, rubber hydrochloride

.7   **Synthetic elastomers**

.71   Synthetic latexes

.72   Synthetic rubber and derivatives

> Standard subdivisions are added for synthetic rubber and derivatives together, for synthetic rubber alone

> Including acrylonitrile rubber (GR-A), butadiene-styrene rubber (GR-S), chloroprene rubber (GR-M), isobutylene rubber (GR-I), polybutadiene rubber, polyurethane rubber

> Class comprehensive works on polyurethanes in 668.4239

.720 28   Auxiliary techniques and procedures; apparatus, equipment, materials

> Do not use for auxiliary techniques and procedures, apparatus, equipment, materials for synthetic rubber; class in 678.722

.722   Techniques, procedures, apparatus, equipment, materials for synthetic rubber

.723   Synthetic rubber products

.724   Properties of synthetic rubber

.728   Chemical derivatives of synthetic rubber

.73   High-styrene resins (Elastoplastics)

679   Other products of specific kinds of materials

.4   **Products of keratinous and dentinal materials**

.43   Ivory products

.47   Feather products

.6   **Products of fibers and bristles**

Including brooms, brushes, mops

.7   **Products of tobacco**

See also 688.4 for tobacco substitutes

.72   Cigars

.73   Cigarettes

680   Manufacture of products for specific uses

Not provided for elsewhere

Class here interdisciplinary works on handicrafts

Class repairs of household equipment by members of household in 643.7. Class manufacture of products based on specific branches of engineering with engineering in 620, e.g., military engineering 623, manufacture of motor vehicles 629.2; except for products provided for in 681–688, class manufacture of products of a specific material with the material in 671–679, e.g., manufacture of steel pipes 672.832, but manufacture of steel toys 688.72

For artistic handicraft work, see 745.5

See Manual at 671–679 vs. 680; also at 680 vs. 745.5

SUMMARY

681   **Precision instruments and other devices**
682   **Small forge work (Blacksmithing)**
683   **Hardware and household appliances**
684   **Furnishings and home workshops**
685   **Leather and fur goods, and related products**
686   **Printing and related activities**
687   **Clothing and accessories**
688   **Other final products, and packaging technology**

681   Precision instruments and other devices

Standard subdivisions are added for precision instruments and other devices together, for precision instruments alone

SUMMARY

681.1   **Instruments for measuring time, counting and calculating machines and instruments**
.2   **Testing, measuring, sensing instruments**
.4   **Optical instruments**
.6   **Printing, writing, duplicating machines and equipment**
.7   **Other scientific and technological instruments, machinery, equipment**
.8   **Musical instruments**

.1   **Instruments for measuring time, counting and calculating machines and instruments**

For testing, measuring, sensing instruments, see 681.2

.11   Instruments for measuring time

.111   Ancient and primitive instruments

        Including hourglasses, water clocks

.111 2   Sundials

.112   Constituent parts (Clockwork)

        Including gears, escapements, bearings, regulating devices

.113   Clocks

        Class here interdisciplinary works on clocks

        For constituent parts, see 681.112; for pneumatic clocks, see 681.115; for electric clocks, see 681.116; for chronographs, chronoscopes, chronometers, see 681.118; for clocks considered as works of art, see 739.3

.114   Watches

        Class here interdisciplinary works on watches

        For constituent parts, see 681.112; for chronographs, chronoscopes, chronometers, see 681.118; for watches considered as works of art, see 739.3

.115   Pneumatic clocks

.116   Electric clocks

.118   Chronographs, chronoscopes, chronometers

        Including metronomes, stopwatches, tachometers, time clocks, time and date recorders

.14   Counting and calculating machines and instruments

        Including cash registers, slide rules, sorting machines, voting machines

        For computers, see 621.39

.145   Calculators

.2	**Testing, measuring, sensing instruments**

Standard subdivisions are added for any or all topics in heading

Including calorimeters, measuring tools

Class here testing, measuring, sensing instruments of general application in science or technology; testing, measuring, sensing instruments for nontechnological application; instruments for measuring physical quantities; electrical and electronic instruments for measuring nonelectrical and nonelectronic quantities

Class testing, measuring, sensing instruments for a specific branch of science (other than instruments for measuring physical quantities) in 681.75. Class testing, measuring, sensing instruments for a specific technological application with the manufacturing number, e.g., aircraft instrumentation 629.135, medical diagnostic equipment 681.761

> *For instruments for measuring electrical quantities, see 621.37; for instruments for testing and measuring electronic signals, see 621.381548; for instruments for measuring time, see 681.11*

.25	Optical testing, measuring, sensing instruments [*formerly also* 681.4]

Including polarimeters [*formerly* 681.416]

Class here fiber optic sensors

Class optical testing, measuring, sensing instruments applied to a specific property with the property, e.g., fiber optic sensors to measure flow 681.28

> *For spectroscopes, see 681.414; for photometers, see 681.415*

.28	Flowmeters
.4	**Optical instruments**

Optical testing, measuring, sensing instruments not provided for below relocated to 681.25

.41	Specific instruments

Including contact lenses

> *For component parts of specific instruments, see 681.42–681.43*

.411	Eyeglasses
.412	Telescopes and binoculars
.412 3	Telescopes
.412 5	Binoculars

Including opera glasses

Class here field glasses

.413	Microscopes

.414	Spectroscopes
.414 2–.414 6	Optical and paraphotic spectroscopes

Add to base number 681.414 the numbers following 535.84 in 535.842–535.846, e.g., infrared spectroscopes 681.4142

.414 8   Other spectroscopes

Including magnetic resonance, microwave, radio-frequency, X-ray and gamma-ray spectroscopes

.415   Photometers

[.416]   Polarimeters

Relocated to 681.25

.418   Photographic equipment

Including cameras, projectors, accessories

Class film and other chemical photographic supplies in 661.808

For photometers, see 681.415; for photocopying equipment, see 681.65

>   681.42–681.43   Component parts

Class comprehensive works in 681.4

.42   Lenses, prisms, mirrors

.423   Lenses

.428   Mirrors

.43   Frames and other housings

.6   **Printing, writing, duplicating machines and equipment**

Including computer output microform (COM) devices, pens, mechanical pencils, rubber stamps

Class here comprehensive works on manufacturing of office equipment

Class facsimile recorders in 621.38235; class wood-cased pencils in 674.88; class interdisciplinary works on office equipment in 651.2

For manufacturing a specific kind of office equipment, see the kind, e.g., calculators 681.145

.61   Stenographic and composing machines, typewriters

.62   Printers and printing presses

Class here computer output printers

.65   Photocopying equipment

.7 **Other scientific and technological instruments, machinery, equipment**

> Not provided for elsewhere

.75 Scientific instruments and equipment

> Standard subdivisions are added for either or both topics in heading
>
> Class here testing, measuring, sensing equipment for specific branches of science
>
> Class comprehensive works on scientific testing, measuring, sensing instruments in 681.2

.753 Physical instruments and equipment

> Standard subdivisions are added for either or both topics in heading
>
> Including instruments with multiple applications based on physical principles, e.g., gyroscopes
>
> Class instruments for measuring physical quantities in 681.2

.754 Chemical instruments and equipment

> Standard subdivisions are added for either or both topics in heading

.755 Geological instruments and equipment

> Standard subdivisions are added for either or both topics in heading

.757 Biological instruments and equipment

> Standard subdivisions are added for either or both topics in heading

.76 Technological equipment

> Including construction, pollution control, mining, surveying equipment
>
> Class here instruments, machinery; testing, measuring, sensing instruments in specific branches of technology not provided for elsewhere
>
> Class comprehensive works on technological testing, measuring, sensing instruments in 681.2

.760 4 Special topics

.760 41 Pressure vessels

> Class a specific use of pressure vessels with the use, e.g., nuclear pressure vessels 621.483

.761 Medical equipment

> Including artificial legs, crutches [*both formerly* 685.38], condoms, diagnostic equipment, prosthetic devices

.763 Agricultural equipment

.763 1 Equipment for plant culture

.763 6 Equipment for animal culture

.766	Equipment for chemical and related technologies
.766 4	Equipment for food and beverage technology
.766 5	Equipment for petroleum and industrial gas technologies
.766 6	Equipment for ceramic technology
.766 8	Equipment for plastic and elastomer technologies
.766 9	Equipment for metallurgy
.767	Equipment for nonchemical manufactures
.767 1	Equipment for metal manufactures
.767 6	Equipment for wood and paper technologies
.767 7	Equipment for textile and clothing technologies

.8 **Musical instruments**

Add to base number 681.8 the numbers following 78 in 786–788, e.g., manufacture of pianos 681.862

Class hand construction of specific instruments or groups of instruments in 786–788; class comprehensive works on hand construction in 784.1923

682 Small forge work (Blacksmithing)

.1 **Horseshoeing**

.4 **Ironwork and hand-forged tools**

Standard subdivisions are added for ironwork and hand-forged tools together, for ironwork alone

683 Hardware and household appliances

Standard subdivisions are added for hardware and household appliances together, for hardware alone

Class here comprehensive works on manufacture of hardware and building supplies

For a specific hardware or building supply product not provided for here, see the product, e.g., tools 621.9, paints 667.6

.3 **Locksmithing**

.31 Bolts and latches

Standard subdivisions are added for either or both topics in heading

.32 Locks and keys

Standard subdivisions are added for either or both topics in heading

.34 Safes and strongboxes

Standard subdivisions are added for either or both topics in heading

.4 **Small firearms**

Class here interdisciplinary works on small firearms, on gunsmithing

For military small firearms, see 623.442

.400 1 Philosophy and theory

.400 2 Miscellany

[.400 288] Maintenance and repair

Do not use; class in 683.403

.400 3–.400 9 Standard subdivisions

> 683.401–683.406 General topics

Class comprehensive works in 683.4

.401 Design

.403 Maintenance and repair

Standard subdivisions are added for either or both topics in heading

.406 Ammunition

.42 Rifles and shotguns

.422 Rifles

.426 Shotguns

.43 Handguns

.432 Pistols

Class here single-shot pistols

.432 5 Automatic pistols

.436 Revolvers

.8 **Household utensils and appliances**

For nonmetallic household utensils and appliances, see the material from which they are made, e.g., woodenware 674.88

.802 88 Maintenance and repair

For maintenance and repair by members of household, see 643.6

.82 Kitchen utensils

Including cutlery, pots, pans, pails

.83   Electrical appliances

    Class comprehensive works on electrical equipment in 621.31042

    For electrical equipment requiring special installation, see 683.88

.88   Heavy equipment

    Electrical, gas, other equipment requiring special installation

    Including dishwashers, dryers, garbage-disposal units, ranges, stoves, washing machines, water heaters

    For refrigerators and freezers, see 621.57; for heating, ventilating, air-conditioning equipment, see 697

684   Furnishings and home workshops

.001–.009   Standard subdivisions for furnishings and home workshops together, for furnishings alone

.08   Woodworking

    Class here comprehensive works on home (amateur) workshops

    For metalworking in home workshops, see 684.09

.082   Woodworking with hand tools

.083   Woodworking with power tools

.084   Surface finishing

.09   Metalworking

.1   Furniture

.100 1–.100 9   Standard subdivisions

>   684.104–684.106   General topics of furniture

    Class comprehensive works in 684.1

.104   Wooden furniture

[.104 028 8]   Maintenance and repair

    Do not use; class in 684.1044

.104 2   Basic construction

.104 3   Surface finishing

.104 4   Maintenance and repair

    Standard subdivisions are added for either or both topics in heading

.104 42   Body restoration

.104 43   Surface refinishing

.105	Metal furniture	
.106	Furniture in other materials	

Including composite materials, plastics, rattan, tiles

>   684.12–684.16   Specific kinds of furniture

Class outdoor furniture in 684.18; class comprehensive works in 684.1

.12   Upholstered furniture

Including couches, sofas, upholstered chairs

.13   Chairs and tables

For upholstered chairs, see 684.12

.14   Desks

.15   Beds

Including frames, springs, mattresses

.16   Cabinets and built-in furniture

Standard subdivisions are added for cabinets and built-in furniture together, for cabinets alone

Including bookcases, chests, china cabinets, dressers, file cabinets, shelving

For built-in wooden shelves, see 694.6

.18   Outdoor furniture

Including garden, patio, porch furniture

Class camping furniture in 685.53

.3   **Fabric furnishings**

Including curtains, draperies, hangings, slipcovers

For carpets and rugs, see 677.643

685   Leather and fur goods, and related products

Standard subdivisions are added for leather and fur goods and related products together, for leather goods alone

Including parchment prepared from the skin of an animal

See also 676.2845 for parchment paper made from pulp

.1   **Saddlery and harness making**

.2   **Leather and fur clothing and accessories**

Class leather and fur footwear in 685.3; class leather and fur gloves and mittens in 685.4

.22	Leather clothing and accessories

Including aprons, belts, jackets, skirts, trousers

.24	Fur clothing and accessories

Standard subdivisions are added for fur clothing and accessories together, for fur clothing alone

Including coats, hats, jackets, muffs, neckpieces, stoles

.3   **Footwear and related products**

For overshoes, see 678.33; for hosiery, see 687.3

.31	Boots and shoes

Standard subdivisions are added for either or both topics in heading

Class shoes for specific activities in 685.36; class shoes for persons with disabilities in 685.38

For wooden shoes and clogs, see 685.32

.310 01	Philosophy and theory
.310 02	Miscellany
[.310 028 8]	Maintenance and repair

Do not use; class in 685.3104

.310 03–.310 09	Standard subdivisions
.310 2	Design
.310 3	Construction
.310 4	Maintenance and repair

Standard subdivisions are added for either or both topics in heading

.32	Wooden shoes and clogs
.36	Footwear and related products for specific activities
.361	Ice skates
.362	Roller skates and skateboards
.363	Snowshoes
.364	Skis

Class manufacture of equipment connected with snow skiing in 688.7693

.367	Stilts

.38	Footwear and related products for persons with disabilities

Standard subdivisions are added for footwear and related products together, for footwear alone

Including orthopedic shoes

Artificial legs, crutches relocated to 681.761

.4   Gloves and mittens

Standard subdivisions are added for either or both topics in heading

Regardless of material

.41   Conventional gloves

.43   Specialized gloves and mittens, gauntlets

Including athletic gloves and mitts, protective gloves for industry

.47   Conventional mittens

.5   Luggage, handbags, camping equipment

.51   Luggage and handbags

Including briefcases, attaché cases

.53   Camping equipment

Including sleeping bags, tents

686   Printing and related activities

Class here design and manufacture of publications, book arts

Class interdisciplinary works on the book in 002

For book illustration, see 741.64

See also 681.6 for manufacture of printing equipment

SUMMARY

686.1	Invention of printing
.2	Printing
.3	Bookbinding
.4	Photocopying (Photoduplication)

.1   Invention of printing

.2   Printing

Class here printing in the Latin alphabet

Class works on desktop publishing that emphasize typography in 686.22, e.g., microcomputer software for typesetting 686.22544536; class comprehensive works on printing and publishing in 070.5; class interdisciplinary works on print media in 302.232

See also 070.593 for self publishing

.209   Historical, geographic, persons treatment

Class invention of printing in 686.1

.21   Printing in non-Latin alphabets and characters

Standard subdivisions are added for either or both topics in heading

Class here typefounding, typecasting, typefaces for non-Latin alphabets and characters

For other specific aspects of printing in non-Latin alphabets and characters, see the aspect, e.g., letterpress printing 686.2312

.218   Greek alphabet

.219   Other non-Latin alphabets and characters

Add to base number 686.219 the numbers following —9 in notation 91–99 from Table 6, e.g., Cyrillic alphabet 686.21918

.22   Typography

.221   Typefounding and typecasting

Standard subdivisions are added for either or both topics in heading

.224   Typefaces

Design, style, specimens of letters, ornaments, other characters and devices

Class here typefaces for the Latin alphabet

Class typefaces for non-Latin alphabets and characters in 686.21; class typefaces for braille and other raised characters in 686.282

.224 7   Specific typefaces and kinds of typefaces for the Latin alphabet

Including Gothic, italic, roman type; Bodoni, Garamond, Times Roman type

.225   Composition (Typesetting)

[.225 028 5]   Data processing   Computer applications

Do not use; class in 686.22544

.225 2   Page design

Including layout, paste-up

.225 3   Hand composition

.225 4   Machine composition

.225 42   Composition by use of human-operated equipment

Including linotype composition

.225 44	Composition by use of automatic equipment

Including phototypesetting (photocomposition)

Class here computerized typesetting

Unless it is redundant, add to base number 686.22544 the numbers following 00 in 004–006, e.g., microcomputer programs for typesetting 686.22544536, the use of digital microcomputers 686.22544416, but the use of digital computers 686.22544 (*not* 686.225444*)

.225 5	Proofreading
.225 6	Imposition and lockup
.23	Presswork (Impression)

Class interdisciplinary works on use of computer printers as low-volume output devices in 004.77. Class a specific use with the use, e.g., use in typesetting 686.22544477

For printing special graphic materials, see 686.28

See also 621.38235 for facsimile transmission, 681.6 for manufacture of printing equipment

.230 4	Special topics
.230 42	Color printing
.231	Mechanical techniques

For photomechanical techniques, see 686.232

.231 2	Printing from type

Class here comprehensive works on letterpress techniques

For printing from plates, see 686.2314

.231 4	Printing from plates

Printing from stereotypes, electrotypes, autotypes, engraved plates, paper mats

See also 686.2315 for printing from planographic plates

.231 5	Planographic (Flat-surface)

Class here lithography and offset (offset lithography)

For photolithography, photo-offset, collotype, see 686.2325

.231 6	Stencil techniques

Including silk-screen printing

.232	Photomechanical techniques

.232 5   Photolithography, photo-offset, collotype (gelatin process)

> *See also 621.381531 for photolithography in manufacture of printed circuits (microlithography)*

.232 7   Photoengraving (Photointaglio)

> Including line and halftone cuts, photogravure

.233   Nonimpact techniques

> Including electrographic, electrophotographic, laser processes

> *See also 686.44 for electrophotographic processes in photocopying*

.28   Printing special graphic materials

.282   Braille and other raised characters

> Standard subdivisions are added for braille and other raised characters together, for braille alone

> Class comprehensive works on braille and other raised-character alphabets in 411

.283   Maps

.284   Music

.288   Materials of direct monetary value

> Including postage stamps, securities

.3   Bookbinding

> Processes and materials

.300 1–.300 9   Standard subdivisions

.302   Hand and fine binding

> Standard subdivisions are added for either or both topics in heading

.303   Specific kinds of commercial binding

.303 2   Library binding

.303 4   Edition binding

.34   Types of covers

.342   Leather

.343   Cloth and imitation leather

.344   Paper

.35   Methods of fastening

> Including hand sewing, oversewing, side-sewing, wire-stitching; perfect binding and other kinds of gluing

.36   Ornamentation

Including gilding, lettering, marbling, tooling

.4   Photocopying (Photoduplication)

Class here interdisciplinary works on photocopying

Class telefax in 621.38235

See also 681.65 for manufacture of photocopying equipment

.42   Blueprinting

.43   Microphotography

Production of microfilm and other microreproductions

.44   Electrostatic and electrophotographic processes

.442   Xerography

.45   Production of photostats

687   Clothing and accessories

Standard subdivisions are added for clothing and accessories together, for clothing alone

Class here casual clothes, sports clothes

Unless other instructions are given, class a subject with aspects in two or more subdivisions of 687 in the number coming last, e.g., military headgear 687.4 (*not* 687.15)

Class interdisciplinary works on clothing in 391; class interdisciplinary works on clothing construction in 646.4

For leather and fur clothing, see 685.2

SUMMARY

687.04	**General topics of clothing**
.1	**Specific kinds of garments**
.2	**Underwear**
.3	**Hosiery**
.4	**Headgear**
.8	**Items auxiliary to clothing construction (Notions)**

.04   General topics of clothing

.042   Patternmaking and grading

Standard subdivisions are added for patternmaking and grading together, for patternmaking alone

.043   Cutting

.044   Tailoring

.1 **Specific kinds of garments**

For footwear, see 685.3; for gloves and mittens, see 685.4; for underwear, see 687.2; for hosiery, see 687.3; for headgear, see 687.4

.11 Miscellaneous kinds of garments

Limited to those provided for below

.112 Dresses

Class here dressmaking

.113 Suits, trousers, jackets

.115 Shirts, blouses, tops

.117 Skirts

.14 Outer coats and related garments

Standard subdivisions are added for outer coats and related garments together, for outer coats alone

Class here comprehensive works on coats

For suit coats, suit jackets, see 687.113

[.140 81] Outer coats and related garments for men

Do not use; class in 687.141

[.140 82] Outer coats and related garments for women

Do not use; class in 687.142

.140 83 Outer coats and related garments for young adults

Do not use for outer coats and related garments for children; class in 687.143

For outer coats and related garments for young adult men aged twenty-one and over, see 687.141; for outer coats and related garments for young adult women twenty-one and over, see 687.142

.140 84 Outer coats and related garments for persons in specific stages of adulthood

Class outer coats and related garments for adult men regardless of age in 687.141; class outer coats and related garments for adult women regardless of age in 687.142

.141 Outer coats and related garments for men

Class outer coats and related garments for young adult men in 687.1408351

.142 Outer coats and related garments for women

Class outer coats and related garments for young adult women in 687.1408352

.143   Outer coats and related garments for children

>   687.144–687.147   Sweaters, wraps, specific types of outer coats

                   Class comprehensive works in 687.14

.144   Overcoats

                           Including topcoats

.145   Raincoats

.146   Sweaters

                           Including pullovers and cardigans

.147   Stoles, cloaks, jackets

.15   Uniforms and symbolic garments

                           Including civil and military uniforms, ceremonial and academic robes,
                           ecclesiastical vestments

.16   Garments for special purposes

                           Including athletic garments, costumes, evening and formal dress,
                           fire-resistant and other protective clothing, maternity garments, wedding
                           clothes

                           Class casual and sports clothes in 687

                           For uniforms and symbolic garments, see 687.15

.165   Nightclothes

.19   Accessories

                           Including aprons, belts, cuffs, handkerchiefs, muffs, neckwear, scarves

                           Class interdisciplinary works on accessories in 391.44; class
                           interdisciplinary works on making costume jewelry in 688.2; class
                           interdisciplinary works on making jewelry in 739.27

                           For gloves and mittens, see 685.4; for headgear, see 687.4

.2   **Underwear**

                           For hosiery, see 687.3

[.208 1]   Underwear for men

                           Do not use; class in 687.21

[.208 2]   Underwear for women

                           Do not use; class in 687.22

[.208 3]   Underwear for young people

                           Do not use; class in 687.23

.208 4	Underwear for persons in specific stages of adulthood

Class underwear for adult men regardless of age in 687.21; class underwear for adult women regardless of age in 687.22

.208 7	Underwear for handicapped and ill persons

Class supporting undergarments worn for medical or health reasons in 687.25

.21	Men's underwear

.22	Women's underwear

Class here comprehensive works on lingerie

For women's nightclothes, see 687.165082

.23	Children's underwear

Class young men's underwear in 687.21; class young women's underwear in 687.22

.25	Supporting undergarments worn for medical or health reasons

Including surgical corsets and belts

.3	**Hosiery**

.4	**Headgear**

Class here hats

Class headscarves in 687.19

[.408 1]	Men's headgear

Do not use; class in 687.41

[.408 2]	Women's headgear

Do not use; class in 687.42

[.408 3]	Young people's headgear

Do not use; class in 687.43

.408 4	Headgear for persons in specific stages of adulthood

Class headgear for adult men regardless of age in 687.41; class headgear for adult women regardless of age in 687.42

.41	Men's headgear

.42	Women's headgear

.43	Children's headgear

Class headgear for young men in 687.41; class headgear for young women in 687.42

.8 **Items auxiliary to clothing construction (Notions)**

Including buttons

Class here comprehensive works on manufacture of sewing equipment and supplies

Class interdisciplinary works on sewing equipment and supplies in 646.1

> *For manufacture of sewing machinery and equipment, see 681.7677. For manufacture of a specific kind of sewing supply, see the kind, e.g., thread 677.02862*

688 Other final products, and packaging technology

.1 **Models and miniatures**

Standard subdivisions are added for either or both topics in heading

Class here interdisciplinary works on models and miniatures

Class interdisciplinary works on handcrafted models and miniatures in 745.5928

> *For models and miniatures of a specific object, see the object, plus notation 0228 from Table 1, e.g., scale models of space stations 629.4420228*

> *See Manual at 745.5928*

.2 **Costume jewelry**

Class here interdisciplinary works on making costume jewelry

Class handcrafted costume jewelry in 745.5942; class interdisciplinary works on costume jewelry in 391.7; class interdisciplinary works on making jewelry in 739.27

.4 **Smokers' supplies**

Including ash trays, cigarette holders and cases, hookahs, lighters, tobacco pouches, tobacco substitutes

.42 Pipes

.5 **Accessories for personal grooming**

Including combs, electric shavers, nail-care tools, razors, razor blades, tweezers

> *For cosmetics, see 668.55; for brushes, see 679.6*

.6 **Nonmotor land vehicles**

Including carriages, carts, wagons, wheelbarrows

> *For cycles, see 629.227*

> *See also 685.362 for skateboards*

> *See Manual at 629.046 vs. 388*

.7 **Recreational equipment**

.72   Toys

Class here interdisciplinary works on mass-produced and handcrafted toys

For handcrafted toys, see 745.592

.722   Dolls, puppets, marionettes

.722 1   Dolls

.722 4   Puppets and marionettes

.723   Dollhouses and furniture

Standard subdivisions are added for either or both topics in heading

.724   Soft toys

Class stuffed dolls in 688.7221

.724 3   Teddy bears

.725   Educational toys

Including construction toys, science sets

.726   Novelties, ornaments, puzzles, tricks

Not provided for elsewhere

.728   Action toys

Mechanical, electrical, electronic, others

Class scale-model action toys in 688.1

> 688.74–688.79 Equipment for sports and games

Not provided for elsewhere

Class comprehensive works in 688.7

.74   Equipment for indoor games of skill

Add to base number 688.74 the numbers following 794 in 794.1–794.8, e.g., chessmen 688.741

.75   Equipment for games of chance

Add to base number 688.75 the numbers following 795 in 795.1–795.4, e.g., playing cards 688.754

.76   Equipment for outdoor sports and games

Add to base number 688.76 the numbers following 796 in 796.1–796.9, e.g., tennis rackets 688.76342; however, for skates, skateboards, skis, see 685.36; for camping equipment, see 685.53

For equipment for equestrian sports and animal racing, see 688.78; for equipment for fishing, hunting, shooting, see 688.79

.78   Equipment for equestrian sports and animal racing

               Including hurdles

.79   Equipment for fishing, hunting, shooting

               Add to base number 688.79 the numbers following 799 in 799.1–799.3, e.g.,
               artificial flies 688.79124

               For small firearms, see 683.4

.8   Packaging technology

               Materials, equipment, techniques

               Class artistic aspects of containers in 700, e.g., earthenware vases 738.38; class
               interdisciplinary works on packaging in 658.564. Class manufacture and use of
               containers made of a specific material with the material, e.g., paper containers
               676.3

[689]   [Unassigned]

               Most recently used in Edition 14

690   Buildings

Planning, analysis, engineering design, construction, destruction of habitable
structures and their utilities

Class interdisciplinary works on design and construction of buildings in 721

See Manual at 624 vs. 690; also at 690 vs. 643.7

SUMMARY

690.01–.09	**Standard subdivisions**
.1–.8	**[Structural elements, general activities, specific types of buildings]**
691	**Building materials**
692	**Auxiliary construction practices**
693	**Construction in specific types of materials and for specific purposes**
694	**Wood construction Carpentry**
695	**Roof covering**
696	**Utilities**
697	**Heating, ventilation, air-conditioning engineering**
698	**Detail finishing**

.01   Philosophy and theory

.02   Miscellany

.021 2   Formulas

                   Do not use for specifications; class in 692.3

[.022 3]   Maps, plans, diagrams

                   Do not use; class in 692.1

.028   Auxiliary techniques and procedures; apparatus, equipment

.028 4	Apparatus and equipment	
	Do not use for materials; class in 691	
[.028 8]	Maintenance and repair	
	Do not use; class in 690.24	
[.028 9]	Safety measures	
	Do not use; class in 690.22	
.029	Commercial miscellany	
[.029 9]	Estimates of labor, time, materials	
	Do not use; class in 692.5	
.03–.09	Standard subdivisions	

.1 Structural elements

Add to base number 690.1 the numbers following 721 in 721.1–721.8, e.g., auxiliary roof structures 690.15; however, for fireplaces, see 697.1; for chimneys, see 697.8

Class structural elements of specific types of buildings in 690.5–690.8; class construction of structural elements in wood in 694

See Manual at 721 vs. 690.1

.2 General activities

Including architectural acoustics

Class application to specific structural elements in 690.1; class application to specific types of buildings in 690.5–690.8; class interdisciplinary works on architectural acoustics in 729.29

.21 Structural analysis

Including statics, dynamics, stability, strength of buildings

.22 Provision for safety

Engineering for safe buildings, safety during construction

.24 Maintenance and repair

Including remodeling

For home repairs by members of household, see 643.7

See Manual at 690 vs. 643.7

.26 Wrecking and razing

.5–.8 Specific types of buildings

Add to base number 690 the numbers following 72 in 725–728, e.g., airport terminal buildings 690.539; however, for construction of buildings for defense against military action, see 623.1; for naval facilities, see 623.64; for military air facilities, see 623.66; for docks and port buildings, see 627.3

.879 Mobile homes

Number built according to instructions under 690.5–690.8

See Manual at 643.2, 690.879, 728.79 vs. 629.226

691 Building materials

Class here construction properties, selection

Class construction in a specific type of material in 693

.1 Timber

.12 Prevention of decay

Including impregnation, painting, spraying with fungicides

.14 Prevention of termite damage

.15 Treatment for fire resistance

.2 Natural stones

Including granite, limestone, marble, sandstone, serpentine, slate, soapstone

.3 Concrete and artificial stones

Including concrete blocks, cinder blocks

.4 Ceramic and clay materials

Including brick, terra-cotta, tile, sun-dried blocks

.5 Masonry adhesives

.6 Glass

.7 Iron and steel (Ferrous metals)

Standard subdivisions are added for either or both topics in heading

.8 Metals

Add to base number 691.8 the numbers following 669 in 669.2–669.7, e.g., aluminum 691.8722

For iron and steel, see 691.7

.9 Other building materials

.92 Plastics and their laminates

Standard subdivisions are added for either or both topics in heading

.95 Insulating materials

Including asbestos, corkboard, diatomaceous earth, kapok, rock wool

.96 Bituminous materials

Including asphalts, tar

.97   Prefabricated materials

.99   Adhesives and sealants

> *For masonry adhesives, see 691.5; for plastics and their laminates, see 691.92*

692   Auxiliary construction practices

Class application of a specific auxiliary practice to a specific subject with the subject, e.g., construction specifications for air conditioning 697.93

.1   Plans and drawings

Interpretation and use of rough sketches, working drawings, blueprints

For detail drawings, see 692.2

.2   Detail drawings

Interpretation and use of large-scale drawings of trims, moldings, other details

.3   Construction specifications

.5   Estimates of labor, time, materials

Class here interdisciplinary works on quantity surveying

Class estimates for a specific subject in building with the subject, plus notation 0299 from Table 1, e.g., estimates for air conditioning 697.930299

.8   Contracting

Provision of construction materials and services in accordance with specifications

693   Construction in specific types of materials and for specific purposes

Class comprehensive works on construction in all types of materials in 690

> *For selection, preservation, construction properties of building materials, see 691; for wood construction, see 694; for roofing materials, see 695*

[.01–.09]   Standard subdivisions

Do not use; class in 690.01–690.09

> ### 693.1–693.7   Construction in specific materials

Class construction in specific materials for specific purposes in 693.8; class comprehensive works in 690

> *For construction in other materials, see 693.9*

.1   **Masonry**

Including construction in natural stone

For masonry using materials other than natural stone, see 693.2–693.5

\>   **693.2–693.5 Masonry using materials other than natural stone**

Class comprehensive works in 693.1

.2   **Stabilized earth materials**

.21   Bricks

For hollow bricks, see 693.4

.22   Sun-dried blocks

Including adobe, cob, pisé, tabby, tapia

.3   **Tiles and terra-cotta**

For hollow tiles, see 693.4

.4   **Artificial stones and hollow bricks**

Including cinder blocks, concrete blocks, hollow tiles

.5   **Concrete**

For concrete blocks, see 693.4

.52   Concrete without reinforcement

.521   Poured concrete

.522   Precast concrete

.54   Concrete with reinforcement (Ferroconcrete)

.541   Poured concrete

.542   Prestressed concrete

.544   Precast concrete

.6   **Lathing, plastering, stuccowork**

.7   **Metals**

.71   Iron and steel (Ferrous metals)

Standard subdivisions are added for either or both topics in heading

.72–.77   Nonferrous metals

Add to base number 693.7 the numbers following 669 in 669.2–669.7, e.g., tin 693.76

.8 **Construction for specific purposes**

.82 Fireproof construction

.83 Insulated construction

.832 Thermal insulation

.834 Acoustical insulation (Soundproofing)

.84 Pest-resistant construction

.842 Termite-resistant construction

.844 Rodent-resistant construction

.85 Shock-resistant construction

.852 Earthquake-resistant construction

.854 Blast-resistant construction

.89 Waterproof, moistureproof, lightning-resistant construction

.892 Waterproof construction

Class moistureproof construction in 693.893

.893 Moistureproof construction

.898 Lightning-resistant construction

.9 **Construction in other materials**

.91 Ice and snow

.92 Sandwich panels

Class sandwich panels in a specific substance with the substance, e.g., wood 694

.96 Glass

.97 Prefabricated materials

Class materials prefabricated in a specific substance with the substance, e.g., precast concrete 693.522

.98 Nonrigid materials

Including pneumatic construction

.99 Miscellaneous materials

Add to base number 693.99 the numbers following 620.19 in 620.191–620.199, e.g., plastics 693.9923; however, for nonrigid materials, see 693.98

694 Wood construction Carpentry

.1 **Planning, analysis, engineering design**

> **694.2–694.6 Carpentry**

Class comprehensive works in 694

.2 **Rough carpentry (Framing)**

Construction of ceilings, floors, foundations, frames, openings, partition frames, posts, roofs, sidings, walls

.6 **Finish carpentry (Joinery)**

On-site construction of doors, doorways; blinds, shutters, windows; balconies, porches, verandas; balustrades, rails, ramps, stairs; trims, e.g., inlays, moldings, paneling; built-in cases and shelves

Class off-site manufacture of finishing items in 680

695 Roof covering

Class wooden roofs in 694.2; class comprehensive works on roofs as structural elements in 690.15

696 Utilities

Class here comprehensive works on energy and environmental engineering of buildings

Class interior electric wiring in 621.31924; class interdisciplinary works on energy for use in buildings in 333.7962

For heating, ventilating, air-conditioning engineering, see 697. For a specific aspect of energy and environmental engineering, see the aspect, e.g., thermal insulation 693.832

.1 **Plumbing**

Design and installation of water fixtures and pipes

.12 Water supply

Including intake pipes, water receiving fixtures, water-softening equipment

For water supply in specific parts of buildings, see 696.18; for hot-water supply, see 696.6

.13 Water drainage

For water drainage in specific parts of buildings, see 696.18

.18 Water supply and drainage in specific parts of buildings

[.180 1–.180 9] Standard subdivisions

Do not use; class in 696.101–696.109

.182 Bathrooms and lavatories

| .183 | Laundries |
| .184 | Kitchens |

> Including installation of dishwashers and garbage-disposal units

.2   Pipe fitting

> Including gas pipes (gas fitting)
>
> *For water pipes, see 696.1; for steam fitting, see 696.3*

.3   Steam pipes (Steam fitting)

.6   Hot-water supply

> Including pipes, water heaters, water-softening equipment

697   Heating, ventilating, air-conditioning engineering

SUMMARY

697.000 1–.000 9	Standard subdivisions
.001–.009	Standard subdivisions of heating
.02–.07	[Local and central heating, heating with specific sources of energy, heating equipment]
.1	Heating with open fires (Radiative heating)
.2	Heating with space heaters (Convective heating)
.3	Hot-air heating
.4	Hot-water heating
.5	Steam heating
.7	Other heating methods
.8	Chimneys and flues
.9	Ventilation and air conditioning

| .000 1–.000 9 | Standard subdivisions |

| .001 | Philosophy and theory of heating |

| .002 | Miscellany of heating |

| .002 8 | Auxiliary techniques and procedures; materials |

> Heating apparatus relocated to 697.07

| .002 84 | Materials of heating |

> Do not use for heating apparatus and equipment; class in 697.07

| .003–.009 | Standard subdivisions of heating |

| .02 | Local heating |

> Class local heating by source of heat in 697.1–697.2

.03   **Central heating**

Class here comprehensive works on district heating

For district heating by hot water, see 697.4; for district heating by steam, see 697.54. For a specific type of central heating, see the type in 697.3–697.7, e.g., solar heating 697.78

.04   **Heating with specific sources of energy**

Class here fuels

Class a specific fuel used in local heating in 697.02; class a specific fuel used in central heating in 697.03

For solar heating, see 697.78; for nuclear heating, see 697.79

.042   Coal and coke heating

.043   Gas heating

.044   Oil heating

.045   Electric heating

.07   **Heating equipment**

Including boilers, furnaces, radiators, thermostats

Class here heating apparatus [*formerly also* 697.0028]

>   **697.1–697.8   Heating**

Class comprehensive works in 697

>   **697.1–697.2   Local heating**

Class chimneys and flues for local heating in 697.8; class comprehensive works in 697.02

.1   **Heating with open fires (Radiative heating)**

Including braziers, fireplaces

Class fireplace-like stoves that have visible fires but which are convective heaters in 697.2

.2   **Heating with space heaters (Convective heating)**

Class comprehensive works on local heating in 697.02

.22   Stationary stoves

Class cooking stoves in 683.88

.24   Portable heaters

> **697.3–697.7 Central heating**

Class chimneys and flues for central heating in 697.8; class comprehensive works in 697.03

.3   **Hot-air heating**

Class radiant panel hot-air heating in 697.72

.4   **Hot-water heating**

Class hot-water supply in 696.6; class radiant panel hot-water heating in 697.72; class comprehensive works on district heating in 697.03

.5   **Steam heating**

Class steam fitting in 696.3; class radiant panel steam heating in 697.72

.500 1   Philosophy and theory

.500 2   Miscellany

.500 28   Auxiliary techniques and procedures; materials

Apparatus relocated to 697.507

.500 284   Materials

Do not use for apparatus and equipment; class in 697.507

.500 3–.500 9   Standard subdivisions

.507   Equipment

Including boilers, furnaces, radiators

Class here apparatus [*formerly also* 697.50028]

.54   District heating

Heating a group of buildings from a central station

Class comprehensive works on steam and hot-water district heating in 697.03

See also 697.4 for hot-water district heating

.7   **Other heating methods**

.72   Radiant panel heating

.78   Solar heating

Class building of solar houses in 690.8370472

.79   Nuclear heating

.8   **Chimneys and flues**

.9   **Ventilation and air conditioning**

.92   Ventilation

.93   Air conditioning

> Class heating in 697.1–697.8

.931   General topics of air conditioning

> Class general topics applied to specific components in 697.932; class general topics applied to specific systems in 697.933; class general topics applied to specific types of buildings in 697.935–697.938

.931 2   Design principles

.931 5   Psychrometrics

> Determination and control of enclosed atmospheric environments for optimum comfort

.931 6   Industrial and commercial applications

> Determination and control of enclosed atmospheric environment for effective operations

.932   Components

> Class here manufacturing

.932 2   Cooling and heating components·

> Including cooling and heating coils, thermostats

.932 3   Humidifying and dehumidifying components

> Including humidistats

.932 4   Air quality components

> Devices for removing particulates, e.g., dust, pollen

> Class here filters

.932 5   Air circulation components

> Including blowers

.933   Systems

> Class here unitary and combination systems [*formerly* 697.934]

> Class system components in 697.932; class systems in specific types of buildings in 697.935–697.938

.933 2   Winter systems

.933 3   Summer systems

.933 4   Year-round systems

[.934]   Unitary and combination systems

> Relocated to 697.933

.935–.938 Air conditioning in specific types of buildings

> Add to base number 697.93 the numbers following 72 in 725–728, e.g., air conditioning in hotels 697.9385

> Class components of systems for specific types of buildings in 697.932

698 Detail finishing

Including cladding, siding, suspended ceilings

Class roof covering in 695

For lathing, plastering, stuccowork, see 693.6; for wooden moldings, paneling, inlays, see 694.6

.1 Painting

.102 Miscellany

.102 8 Auxiliary techniques and procedures; apparatus, equipment, materials

[.102 82] Apparatus, equipment, materials

> Relocated to 698.10284

.102 83 Paint mixing

.102 84 Apparatus, equipment, materials [*formerly* 698.10282]

> Including brushes, rollers, paints, diluents

[.102 88] Application methods

> Do not use for maintenance and repair; class in 698.1028

> Number discontinued; class in 698.1

.12 Exteriors

.14 Interiors

> Class painting woodwork in 698.35

.142 Walls

.146 Floors

.147 Ceilings

.2 Calcimining and whitewashing

Standard subdivisions are added for either or both topics in heading

.3 Finishing woodwork

.32 Staining

> Including graining and marbling

.33 Polishing with wax and oil

.34	Lacquering and varnishing
.35	Painting
.5	**Glazing and leading windows**
.6	**Paperhanging**
.9	**Floor coverings**

Including carpets, rugs; linoleum, tiles

Class comprehensive works on floors in 690.16

[699] [Unassigned]

Most recently used in Edition 14

700

700   The arts   Fine and decorative arts

Description, critical appraisal, techniques, procedures, apparatus, equipment, materials of the fine, decorative, literary, performing, recreational arts

Class here conceptual art

Use 700 and standard subdivisions 700.1–700.9 for artists' books, performance and video art covering the arts in general; use 702.81 and 709 for artists' books, performance and video art limited to fine and decorative arts

For book arts, see 686; for literature, see 800

See Manual at 700

SUMMARY

730	Plastic arts Sculpture
.01–.09	Standard subdivisions of plastic arts
.1–.9	Standard subdivisions of sculpture
731	Processes, forms, subjects of sculpture
732	Sculpture from earliest times to ca. 500, sculpture of nonliterate peoples
733	Greek, Etruscan, Roman sculpture
734	Sculpture from ca. 500 to 1399
735	Sculpture from 1400
736	Carving and carvings
737	Numismatics and sigillography
738	Ceramic arts
739	Art metalwork
740	Drawing and decorative arts
741	Drawing and drawings
742	Perspective in drawing
743	Drawing and drawings by subject
745	Decorative arts
746	Textile arts
747	Interior decoration
748	Glass
749	Furniture and accessories
750	Painting and paintings
.1–.8	Standard subdivisions
751	Techniques, procedures, apparatus, equipment, materials, forms
752	Color
753	Symbolism, allegory, mythology, legend
754	Genre paintings
755	Religion
757	Human figures
758	Other subjects
759	Historical, geographic, persons treatment
760	Graphic arts Printmaking and prints
.01–.09	Standard subdivisions and special topics of graphic arts
.1–.8	Standard subdivisions of printmaking and prints
761	Relief processes (Block printing)
763	Lithographic (Planographic) processes
764	Chromolithography and serigraphy
765	Metal engraving
766	Mezzotinting, aquatinting, related processes
767	Etching and drypoint
769	Prints
770	Photography and photographs
.1–.9	Standard subdivisions of photography and photographs, of photography alone
771	Techniques, procedures, apparatus, equipment, materials
772	Metallic salt processes
773	Pigment processes of printing
774	Holography
778	Specific fields and special kinds of photography; cinematography and video production; related activities
779	Photographs

780	**Music**	
.000 1–.099 9	Relation of music to other subjects	
.1–.9	Standard subdivisions and treatises on music scores, recordings, texts	
781	General principles and musical forms	
782	Vocal music	
783	Music for single voices The voice	
784	Instruments and instrumental ensembles and their music	
785	Ensembles with only one instrument per part	
786	Keyboard, mechanical, electrophonic, percussion instruments	
787	Stringed instruments (Chordophones) Bowed stringed instruments	
788	Wind instruments (Aerophones)	
790	**Recreational and performing arts**	
.01–.09	Recreation centers and standard subdivisions of recreation	
.1–.2	[Recreational activities and the performing arts in general]	
791	Public performances	
792	Stage presentations	
793	Indoor games and amusements	
794	Indoor games of skill	
795	Games of chance	
796	Athletic and outdoor sports and games	
797	Aquatic and air sports	
798	Equestrian sports and animal racing	
799	Fishing, hunting, shooting	

> ### 700.1–700.9   Standard subdivisions of the arts

Use this standard subdivision span for material that includes two or more of the fine and decorative arts and one or more of the other arts, e.g., a work about a painter who is also a sculptor and a poet 700.92. If only one fine or decorative art and one of the other arts is involved, class in the number coming first in the schedule, e.g., a United States painter and poet 759.13

Class comprehensive works in 700

See Manual at 700

.1   **Philosophy and theory of the arts**

.103   Effects of social conditions and factors on the arts

.104   Effects of humanities on the arts

.105   Effects of science and technology on the arts

.108   Effects of other concepts on the arts

       Including humor, mythology, nature, parapsychology

.2–.3   **Standard subdivisions of the arts**

.4   **Special topics in the arts**

.41   Arts displaying specific qualities of style, mood, viewpoint

> Add to base number 700.41 the numbers following — 1 in notation 11–18
> from Table 3–C, e.g., horror in the arts 700.4164

> Class arts dealing with specific themes and subjects regardless of quality
> displayed in 700.42–700.48

.42–.48   Arts dealing with specific themes and subjects

> Add to base number 700.4 the numbers following — 3 in notation 32–38
> from Table 3–C, e.g., historical themes in the arts 700.458

.5–.8   Standard subdivisions of the arts

.9   Historical, geographic, persons treatment of the arts

.92   Persons

> Class here the works themselves and critical appraisal and description of
> works of an artist or artists

> *See Manual at 700.92*

> # 701–770   Fine and decorative arts

> Class comprehensive works in 700

> # 701–708   Standard subdivisions of fine and decorative arts

> Other than historical, geographic, persons treatment

> Class standard subdivisions of specific schools, styles, periods of development
> in 709.012–709.05; class comprehensive works in 700

701   Philosophy and theory of fine and decorative arts

.03–.08   Special topics

> Add to base number 701.0 the numbers following 700.10 in
> 700.103–700.108, e.g., effects of social conditions and factors on fine and
> decorative arts 701.03

.1   Appreciative aspects

> Do not use for systems; class in 701

> Including use of audiovisual aids

> Class here works on art appreciation, including theory, history, and techniques

> *See also 709 for history of the fine arts*

.15   Psychological principles

> Fine arts as products of creative imagination

.17   Aesthetics

Class interdisciplinary works in 111.85

.18   Criticism and appreciation

Class here theory, technique, history

Class works of critical appraisal in 709

.8   Inherent features

Including composition, decorative values, form, light, movement, space, style, symmetry, time, vision

.82   Perspective

See also 742 for drawing aspects of perspective

.85   Color

See also 752 for painting aspects of color

.9   Methodology

Do not use for psychological principles; class in 701.15

702   Miscellany of fine and decorative arts

.8   Techniques, procedures, apparatus, equipment, materials

Including testing and measurement, use of artists' models

.81   Mixed-media and composites

Including artists' books; performance, video art

Class finished works of mixed-media and composite art in 709; class two-dimensional mixed-media art or composites in 760

See Manual at 700

.812   Collage

Class decoupage in 745.546

.813   Montage

.814   Assemblage

.87   Techniques of reproduction, execution, identification

Do not use for testing and measurement; class in 702.8

.872   Reproductions and copies

.874   Forgeries and alterations

.88   Maintenance and repair

Including expertizing

Class here routine maintenance and repair [*formerly* 702.89], conservation, preservation, restoration

Class identification of reproductions, copies, forgeries, alterations in 702.87

.89   Safety measures

Routine maintenance and repair relocated to 702.88

.9   **Commercial miscellany**

Class auction and sales catalogs in which an exhibition is involved in 707.4

703   **Dictionaries, encyclopedias, concordances of fine and decorative arts**

704   **Special topics in fine and decorative arts**   **History and description with respect to kinds of persons**

>   704.03–704.87   History and description with respect to kinds of persons

Class comprehensive works in 704

.03   History and description with respect to racial, ethnic, national groups

Add to base number 704.03 notation 03–99 from Table 5, e.g., art of North American native races 704.0397

Class history and description with respect to groups of miscellaneous specific kinds of persons of a specific racial, ethnic, national group in 704.04–704.87; class the fine and decorative arts of nonliterate peoples in 709.011; class history and description with respect to racial, ethnic, national groups in places where they predominate in 709.1–709.9

.04–.87   History and description with respect to miscellaneous specific kinds of persons

Add to base number 704 notation 04–87 from Table 7, e.g., women as artists 704.042; however, for art dealers, see 380.1457; for the fine and decorative arts of nonliterate peoples, see 709.011

Class description, critical appraisal, works, biography of individual artists in 709.2

See Manual at 709.2 vs. 380.1457092

.9   **Iconography**

See Manual at 704.9

.94   Specific subjects

SUMMARY

704.942	**Human figures**
.943	**Nature and still life**
.944	**Architectural subjects and cityscapes**
.946	**Symbolism and allegory**
.947	**Mythology and legend**
.948	**Religion**
.949	**Other specific subjects**

[.940 1–.940 9]   Standard subdivision

Do not use; class in 704.901–704.909

.942   Human figures

Not provided for in 704.946–704.948

Class here portraits

Unless other instructions are given, observe the following table of preference, e.g., groups of children 704.9425 (*not* 704.9426):

Erotica	704.9428
Specific kinds of persons	704.9423–.9425
Groups of figures	704.9426
Human figures according to attire	704.9421–.9422

Class a work in which the human figure is not the center of interest with the type of work, e.g., cityscapes 704.944

.942 092   Persons

Artists and critics

Class works about the person portrayed in 704.942

> 704.942 1–704.942 2 Human figures according to attire

Class comprehensive works in 704.942

.942 1   Nudes

.942 2   Draped figures

> 704.942 3–704.942 5 Specific kinds of persons

Class comprehensive works in 704.942

.942 3   Men

.942 4   Women

.942 5   Children

.942 6   Groups of figures

.942 8	Erotica

Including pornography

.943	Nature and still life

Standard subdivisions are added for nature and still life together, for nature alone

Not provided for in 704.946–704.948

.943 2	Animals

Hunting scenes are classed in 704.9432, without use of 704.943201–704.943209; hunting scenes in which a specific animal is the center of interest are classed with the animal in 704.94322–704.94329

Add to base number 704.9432 the numbers following 59 in 592–599, e.g., eagles 704.94328942

Class symbolism of animals in 704.946. Class a specific type of a hunting scene in which animals are not the center of interest with the type of scene, e.g., hunters 704.9426

.943 4	Plants

Class symbolism of plants in 704.946

See Manual at 704.9

.943 5	Still life
.943 6	Landscapes

Add to base number 704.9436 notation 1–9 from Table 2, e.g., landscapes of Utah 704.9436792

.943 7	Marine scenes and seascapes

Standard subdivisions are added for either or both topics in heading

.944	Architectural subjects and cityscapes

Standard subdivisions are added for either or both topics in heading

Add to base number 704.944 notation 1–9 from Table 2, e.g., cityscapes of England 704.94442

.946	Symbolism and allegory

Standard subdivisions are added for either or both topics in heading

For religious symbolism, see 704.948

.947	Mythology and legend

Class religious mythology in 704.948

.948	Religion

Class here religious mythology, religious symbolism

Class significance and purpose of art in religion in 291.37; class significance and purpose of art in Christianity in 246; class significance and purpose of art in non-Christian religions in 292–299

(.948 1)	(Permanently unassigned)

(Optional number used to provide local emphasis and a shorter number for a specific religion other than Christianity; prefer the number for the specific religion in 704.9489)

.948 2	Christianity

Class here icons, santos, votive offerings

For specific Christian subjects, see 704.9484–704.9487

> 704.948 4–704.948 7 Specific Christian subjects

Class here icons, santos, votive offerings

Class comprehensive works in 704.9482

.948 4	Biblical characters and events

For Trinity and Holy Family and its members, see 704.9485; for apostles, saints, angels, see 704.9486; for devils, see 704.9487

.948 5	Trinity and Holy Family and its members
.948 52	Trinity
.948 53	Jesus Christ
.948 55	Madonna and Child

Class here Mary without Child

.948 56	Holy Family

Presented as a group

Class Jesus Christ in 704.94853; class Mary with or without Child in 704.94855; class Saint Joseph in 704.94863

.948 6	Apostles, saints, angels
.948 62	Apostles
.948 63	Saints

For Apostles, see 704.94862

.948 64	Angels
.948 7	Devils

.948 9   Other religions

> Add to base number 704.9489 the numbers following 29 in 292–299, e.g., Buddhism in art 704.948943; however, for Old Testament characters and events, see 704.9484

> (Option: To give local emphasis and a shorter number to iconography of a specific religion, class in 291, which is permanently unassigned)

.949   Other specific subjects

> Add to base number 704.949 notation 001–999, e.g., industrial subjects 704.9496

705–706 Standard subdivisions of fine and decorative arts

707 Education, research, related topics of fine and decorative arts

.4   Temporary and traveling collections and exhibits

> Do not use for museums and permanent collections and exhibits; class in 708

> Class here permanent collections on tour, temporary exhibits of a private collection, auction and sales catalogs in which an exhibition is involved

> *For temporary in-house exhibits selected from a museum's or gallery's permanent collection, see 708*

708 Galleries, museums, private collections of fine and decorative arts

> Do not use for history and description of fine and decorative arts with respect to kinds of persons; class in 704.03–704.87

> General art collections

> Class here annual reports dealing with acquisitions, activities, programs, projects

> *For temporary and traveling collections and exhibits, see 707.4*

.001–.008   Standard subdivisions

.009   Historical and persons treatment

> Do not use for geographic treatment; class in 708.1–708.9

> ### 708.1–708.9 Geographic treatment

Class here guidebooks and catalogs of specific galleries, museums, private collections

Class comprehensive works in 708

(Option: To give local emphasis and a shorter number to galleries, museums, private collections of a specific country, use one of the following:

(Option A: Place them first by use of a letter or other symbol, e.g., galleries, museums, private collections in Japan 708.J [preceding 708.1]

(Option B: Class them in 708.1; in that case class galleries, museums, private collections in North America in 708.97)

.1 North America

For galleries, museums, private collections in Middle America, see 708.972

(Option: To give local emphasis and a shorter number to galleries, museums, private collections of a specific country other than United States and Canada, class them in this number; in that case class galleries, museums, private collections in North America in 708.97)

.11 Canada

Add to base number 708.11 the numbers following —71 in notation 711–719 from Table 2, e.g., galleries, museums, private collections in British Columbia 708.111

.13–.19 United States

Add to base number 708.1 the numbers following —7 in notation 73–79 from Table 2, e.g., galleries, museums, private collections in Pennsylvania 708.148

For galleries, museums, private collections in Hawaii, see 708.9969

> ### 708.2–708.8 Europe

Class comprehensive works in 708.94

For galleries, museums, private collections not provided for here, see 708.949, e.g., galleries, museums, private collections in Belgium 708.9493

.2 British Isles   England

.21–.28 England

Add to base number 708.2 the numbers following —42 in notation 421–428 from Table 2, e.g., galleries, museums, private collections in Manchester 708.2733

.29 Scotland, Ireland, Wales

> Add to base number 708.29 the numbers following —4 in notation 41–42 from Table 2, e.g., galleries, museums, private collections in Wales 708.2929

.3–.8 Miscellaneous parts of Europe

> Add to base number 708 the numbers following —4 in notation 43–48 from Table 2, e.g., galleries, museums, private collections in France 708.4

.9 Other geographic areas

> Add to base number 708.9 notation 1–9 from Table 2, e.g., comprehensive works on galleries, museums, private collections in Islamic areas 708.917671, in European countries 708.94

> Class parts of Europe in notation 41–48 from Table 2 in 708.2–708.8

709 Historical, geographic, persons treatment of fine and decorative arts

> Development, description, critical appraisal, works

> Class here finished works of experimental and mixed-media art that do not fit easily into a recognized medium

> Class two-dimensional experimental and mixed-media art in 760

> _See also 364.162 for looting, plundering, theft, destruction of art as a crime_

SUMMARY

709.01	**Arts of nonliterate peoples, and earliest times to 499**
.02	**6th–15th centuries, 500–1499**
.03	**Modern period, 1500–**
.04	**20th century, 1900–1999**
.05	**21th century, 2000–2099**

.01 Arts of nonliterate peoples, and earliest times to 499

.011 Nonliterate peoples

> Regardless of time or place, but limited to nonliterate peoples of the past and nonliterate peoples clearly not a part of contemporary society

.011 2 Paleolithic art

.011 3 Rock art

>   709.012–709.05 Periods of development

        Class here schools and styles not limited by country or locality, comprehensive works on European art limited by period, school, or style

        Add to each subdivision identified by * notation 01–08 from Table 1, e.g., exhibits of cubism 709.04032074

        Class comprehensive works in 709

           For European art limited to a specific location, see the location in 709.4, e.g., art of Germany 709.43

           See Manual at 709.012–709.05 vs. 709.3–709.9

.012   *To 4000 B.C.

.013   *3999–1000 B.C.

.014   *999–1 B.C.

.015   *1st–5th centuries, 1–499 A.D.

.02   *6th–15th centuries, 500–1499

        Class here medieval art

           See Manual at 704.9

.021   *6th–12th centuries, 500–1199

.021 2   *Early Christian art

           For early Christian art before 500, see 709.015

.021 4   *Byzantine art

           For Byzantine art before 500, see 709.015

.021 6   *Romanesque art

.022   *13th century, 1200–1299

        Class here Gothic art

           For Gothic art of an earlier or later period, see the specific period, e.g., 500–1199 709.021

.023   *14th century, 1300–1399

.024   *15th century, 1400–1499

        Class here Renaissance art

           For Renaissance art of an earlier or later period, see the specific period, e.g., 16th century 709.031

*Add as instructed under 709.012–709.05

.03	*Modern period, 1500–

For 20th century, 1900–1999, see 709.04; for 21st century, 2000–2099, see 709.05

.031	*16th century, 1500–1599

.032	*17th century, 1600–1699

Class here baroque art

For baroque art of 18th century, see 709.033

.033	*18th century, 1700–1799

.033 2	*Rococo art

.034	*19th century, 1800–1899

.034 1	*Classical revival (Neoclassicism)

For classical revival of 18th century, see 709.033

.034 2	*Romanticism

For romanticism of 18th century, see 709.033

.034 3	*Naturalism and realism

For naturalism and realism of an earlier or later period, see the specific period, e.g., 18th century 709.033

.034 4	*Impressionism

Including luminism, pleinairism

.034 5	*Neo-impressionism

Including divisionism, pointillism

.034 6	*Postimpressionism

.034 7	*Symbolism and synthetism

.034 8	*Kitsch (Trash)

For kitsch of 20th century, see 709.04013

.034 9	*Art nouveau

For art nouveau of 20th century, see 709.04014

.04	20th century, 1900–1999

Including artists' books; computer, mail, performance, video art

Class here modern art

For 19th century, 1800–1899, see 709.034; for 21st century, 2000–2099, see 709.05

.040 01–.040 08	Standard subdivisions

*Add as instructed under 709.012–709.05

.040 1	*Art deco, kitsch, art nouveau
.040 12	*Art deco
.040 13	*Kitsch (Trash)
	Class comprehensive works on kitsch in 709.0348
.040 14	*Art nouveau
	Class comprehensive works on art nouveau in 709.0349
.040 2	*Functionalism
.040 3	*Cubism and futurism
	Including geometric design
.040 32	*Cubism
.040 33	*Futurism
.040 4	*Expressionism and fauvism
.040 42	*Expressionism
	Class abstract expressionism in 709.04052
.040 43	*Fauvism
.040 5	*Abstractionism, nonobjectivity, constructivism
.040 52	*Abstractionism
	Including abstract expressionism, geometric abstractionism, neoplasticism
.040 56	*Nonobjectivity
.040 57	*Constructivism
.040 6	*Dadaism and surrealism
.040 62	*Dadaism
.040 63	*Surrealism
.040 7	*Composite media and sensations
.040 71	*Pop art
.040 72	*Optical art (Op art)
.040 73	*Kinetic art
.040 74	*Happenings, environments, events
.040 75	*Conceptual art
.040 76	*Land art (Earthworks)
.040 77	*Structuralism

*Add as instructed under 709.012–709.05

.040 78	*Multiple art
.040 79	*Space art
.041–.049	Periods

Add to base number 709.04 the numbers following —0904 in notation 09041–09049 from Table 1, e.g., arts of 1960–1969 709.046

Class a specific school or style in a specific period in 709.0401–709.0407

.05	*21st century, 2000–2099

.1　Treatment by areas, regions, places in general

Class history and description of fine and decorative arts with respect to kinds of persons in 704.03–704.87; class art of nonliterate peoples regardless of place in 709.011

.2　Persons

Class here description, critical appraisal, biography, works of artists not limited to or chiefly identified with a specific form, e.g., painting, or group of forms, e.g., graphic arts

See Manual at 709.2 vs. 380.1457092

.22	Collected persons treatment

Class works of more than one artist in the same geographic area not limited by continent, country, locality in 709.1; class works of more than one artist in the same continent, country, locality in 709.3–709.9

.3–.9　Treatment by specific continents, countries, localities

Class here art of specific periods, e.g., art of 1800–1899 in Germany 709.4309034

Class history and description of fine and decorative arts with respect to kinds of persons in 704.03–704.87; class art of nonliterate peoples regardless of place in 709.011. Class comprehensive works on European art of specific periods with the period in 709.01–709.05 (*not* 709.4), e.g., art of 1800–1899 in Europe 709.034 (*not* 709.409034)

See Manual at 709.012–709.05 vs. 709.3–709.9

710　Civic and landscape art

*Add as instructed under 709.012–709.05

711   Area planning (Civic art)

Design of physical environment for public welfare, convenience, pleasure

Class here plans

Unless other instructions are given, observe the following table of preference, e.g., planning of pedestrian malls in business districts 711.5522 (*not* 711.74):

Specific kinds of areas	711.5
Specific elements	711.6–711.8
Specific levels	711.2–711.4
Procedural and social aspects	711.1

Class comprehensive works on area planning and architecture in 720; class interdisciplinary works on area planning in 307.12

For landscape architecture, see 712

See Manual at 307.12 vs. 711

SUMMARY

.028   Auxiliary techniques and procedures [*formerly* 711.1]; apparatus, equipment, materials

.1   **Procedural and social aspects**

Auxiliary techniques and procedures relocated to 711.028

.12   Professional practice and technical procedures

Including collection of data, preparation and presentation of plans and models

.13   Social factors affecting planning

.14   Economic factors affecting planning

\>   **711.2–711.4 Specific levels**

Class comprehensive works in 711

.2   **International and national planning**

.3   **Interstate, state, provincial, county planning**

For urban counties, see 711.4; for metropolitan areas, see 711.43 ·

.4   **Local community (City) planning**

Class here urban renewal (conservation, rehabilitation, redevelopment)

Class interdisciplinary works on city planning in 307.1216; class interdisciplinary works on urban renewal in 307.3416

For urban renewal of specific kinds of areas, see 711.5

.409 3–.409 9   Treatment by specific continents, countries, localities

Class here specific types of plans for specific cities

\>   711.41–711.45 Specific types of plans

Unless other instructions are given, class a subject with aspects in two or more subdivisions of 711.4 in the number coming last, e.g., plans for small cities in cold climates 711.43 (*not* 711.42)

Class comprehensive works in 711.4

.41   *Plans based on street patterns

Including gridiron, radial, studied irregularity plans

.42   *Plans based on environment

Including plans based on topography and climate

.43   *Plans based on size

Including plans for villages, small and large cities, metropolitan areas

.45   *Plans based on function

Including new towns; plans for cities serving primarily as governmental, industrial, residential centers

---

*Do not use notation 093–099 from Table 1 for specific cities; class in 711.4093–711.4099

.5   **Specific kinds of areas**

Class here planning for urban renewal (conservation, rehabilitation, redevelopment) of specific kinds of areas

Class interdisciplinary works on urban renewal in 307.3416

.55   Functional areas

Class here plazas, squares

For religious centers, see 711.56; for cultural and educational areas, see 711.57; for residential areas, see 711.58; for parking areas, see 711.73

.551   Civic, administrative, governmental areas

Standard subdivisions are added for any or all topics in heading

.552   Commercial and industrial areas

Class planning of transportation facilities in 711.7

.552 2   Commercial areas

Class here business districts, shopping centers

.552 4   Industrial areas

Class here industrial parks

.554   Agricultural areas

.555   Medical centers

.556   Prison and reformatory areas

.557   Hotel and restaurant areas

Including trailer camps for transients

.558   Recreational areas

Including parks, playgrounds, theatrical and performing arts centers

.56   Religious centers

.57   Cultural and educational areas

Including areas for libraries, museums, colleges and universities

Class theatrical and performing arts centers in 711.558

.58   Residential areas

Urban, suburban, rural areas

Including apartment-house districts, trailer parks for long-term residents

For hotel areas, trailer camps for transients, see 711.557; for housing renewal, see 711.59

.59   Housing renewal

Class interdisciplinary works on housing renewal in 307.34

>   **711.6–711.8   Specific elements**

Class comprehensive works in 711.6

.6   **Structural elements**

Adaptation to site and use

Class here comprehensive works on specific elements

For utilities, see 711.7

.7   **Transportation facilities**

Class here comprehensive works on utilities

For nontransportation utilities, see 711.8

.72   Bicycle transportation facilities

.73   Motor vehicle transportation facilities

Including motorcycle transportation facilities, parking areas

.74   Pedestrian transportation facilities

Including pedestrian malls

.75   Railroad transportation facilities

Including rapid transit facilities

.76   Marine transportation facilities

.78   Air transportation facilities

.8   **Nontransportation utilities**

Including water, gas, electricity transmission and supply; communication lines; sanitation and flood control facilities

712   Landscape architecture (Landscape design)

Comprehensive works on plants in landscape architecture relocated to 715

Class engineering aspects of landscape architecture in 624

For specific elements in landscape architecture, see 714–717

.01   Philosophy and theory

Class aesthetics, composition, style in 712.2

.02   Miscellany

.028	Auxiliary techniques and procedures [*formerly* 712.3]; apparatus, equipment, materials

---

> **712.2–712.3 General considerations**

Class general considerations of design of specific kinds of land tracts in 712.5–712.7; class comprehensive works in 712

.2 **Principles**

Including aesthetics, composition, effect, style

.3 **Professional practice and technical procedures**

Including collection of data, preparation and presentation of plans and models, supervision of operations

Auxiliary techniques and procedures relocated to 712.028

> **712.5–712.7 Specific kinds of land tracts**

Class comprehensive works in 712

For trafficways, see 713; for cemeteries, see 718; for natural landscapes, see 719

.5 **Public parks and grounds**

Class here amusement parks, commons, fairgrounds, zoological and botanical gardens; comprehensive works on parks

For private parks, see 712.6; for parks of public reserved lands, see 719.3

.6 **Private parks and grounds**

Class here estates, home gardens, penthouse gardens, yards

.7 **Semiprivate and institutional grounds**

Class here grounds of churches, country clubs, hospitals, hotels, industrial plants, schools

713 **Landscape architecture of trafficways**

See also 625.77 for planting and cultivation of roadside vegetation

---

> **714–717 Specific elements in landscape architecture**

Class comprehensive works in 712

714 **Water features in landscape architecture**

Including cascades, fountains, natural and artificial pools

Class comprehensive works on fountains in 731.72

715   Woody plants in landscape architecture

Cultivated for flowers or for other attributes

Class here comprehensive works on plants in landscape architecture [*formerly* 712]

Class comprehensive works on plants cultivated for their flowers in landscape architecture in 716

See also 635.97 for planting and cultivation of woody plants

.1   **Topiary work**

>   **715.2–715.4   Specific kinds of plants**

Class topiary work on specific kinds of plants in 715.1; class comprehensive works in 715

.2   **Trees**

.3   **Shrubs**

.4   **Vines**

716   Herbaceous plants in landscape architecture

Cultivated for flowers or for other attributes

Including ground cover

Class here comprehensive works on plants cultivated for their flowers in landscape architecture

For woody plants cultivated for their flowers, see 715

See also 635.9 for planting and cultivation of herbaceous plants

717   Structures in landscape architecture

Relationship of buildings, terraces, fences, gates, steps, ornamental accessories to other elements of landscape architecture

Including pedestrian facilities, street furniture

718   Landscape design of cemeteries

.8   **National cemeteries**

719   Natural landscapes

Class natural water features in 714

.3   **Reserved lands**

.32   Public parks and natural monuments

Standard subdivisions are added for either or both topics in heading

.33   Forest and water-supply reserves

.36   Wildlife reserves

720 Architecture

Class here comprehensive works on architecture and civic and landscape art

For civic and landscape art, see 710

SUMMARY

720.1–.9	Standard subdivisions and special topics
721	Architectural structure
722	Architecture from earliest times to ca. 300
723	Architecture from ca. 300 to 1399
724	Architecture from 1400
725	Public structures
726	Buildings for religious and related purposes
727	Buildings for educational and research purposes
728	Residential and related buildings
729	Design and decoration of structures and accessories

.1   **Philosophy and theory**

.103–.108   Special topics

Add to base number 720.10 the numbers following 700.10 in 700.103–700.108, e.g., effects of social conditions and factors on architecture 720.103

.2   **Miscellany**

.22   Illustrations, models, miniatures

[.221]   Drafting illustrations

Do not use; class in 720.284

.222   Pictures and related illustrations

Class here architectural drawings

Add to base number 720.222 notation 1–9 from Table 2, e.g., architectural drawings from England 720.22242

Class architectural drawings for one structure or a specific type of structure with the structure in 725–728, plus notation 0222 from table under 721–729, e.g., architectural drawings of palaces 728.820222

.28   Auxiliary techniques and procedures; apparatus, equipment, materials

Including site planning

.284   Architectural drawing

Do not use for apparatus, equipment, materials; class in 720.28

Class drawings, illustrations, models in 720.22

.286   Remodeling

> Do not use for waste technology; class in 720.28

.288   Maintenance and repair

> Class here routine maintenance and repair [*formerly* 720.289], conservation, preservation, restoration

> Class interdisciplinary works on conservation, preservation, restoration in 363.69

> *See Manual at 930–990: Historic preservation*

.289   Safety measures

> Routine maintenance and repair relocated to 720.288

.4   **Special topics**

[.42]   Architecture for persons with disabilities

> Relocated to 720.87

[.43]   Architecture for persons in late adulthood and with illnesses

> Architecture for persons in late adulthood relocated to 720.846; architecture for persons with illnesses relocated to 720.877

.47   Architecture and the environment

.472   Energy resources

> Including use of solar energy

> Class here energy conservation

.473   Earth-sheltered buildings

> Class here underground architecture

.48   Buildings by shape, buildings with atriums

> Including circular, single-story buildings

> Class environmental aspects of buildings by shape and of buildings with atriums in 720.47

.483   Tall buildings

> Class here skyscrapers

.49   Multiple-purpose buildings

> Class environmental aspects of multiple-purpose buildings in 720.47; class multiple-purpose buildings by shape and multiple-purpose buildings with atriums in 720.48. Class a multiple-purpose building with one primary purpose with the single-purpose buildings of that type, e.g., an apartment building with a floor of commercial space 728.314

.8   **Architecture with respect to kinds of persons**

.846 Persons in late adulthood [*formerly* 720.43]

.87 Architecture for persons with disabilities [*formerly* 720.42], persons with illnesses, gifted persons

.877 Shut-in (Housebound) persons

> Class here architecture for persons with illnesses [*formerly* 720.43]

> *For persons with mental illness, see 720.874*

.9 **Historical, geographic, persons treatment**

> Class here architectural aspects of historic buildings, schools and styles limited to a specific country or locality

> Class architectural drawings in 720.222; class comprehensive works on specific schools and styles not limited to a specific country or locality in 722–724

> *See Manual at 913–919: Historic sites and buildings; also at 930–990: Historic preservation*

[.901–.905] Historical periods

> Do not use; class in 722–724

[.93] Ancient world

> Do not use; class in 722

.94 Europe   Western Europe

.946 090 2 Iberian architecture of 6th–15th centuries

> Class here Mudéjar architecture [*formerly also* 723.3]

.95 Asia

> Class here Buddhist, Oriental architecture

> Class Buddhist architecture of a national style with the style, e.g., Japanese Buddhist architecture 720.952

.954 South Asia   India

> Class here Hindu, Jain architecture

> ## 721–729   Specific aspects of architecture

Add to each subdivision identified by * as follows:

01	Philosophy and theory
0103–0108	Special topics
	Add to 010 the numbers following 700.10 in 700.103–700.108, e.g., effects of social conditions and factors on architecture 0103
02	Miscellany
0222	Pictures and related illustrations
	Class here architectural drawings
	Add to 0222 notation 1–9 from Table 2, e.g., architectural drawings from England 022242
028	Auxiliary techniques and procedures; apparatus, equipment, materials
0286	Remodeling
	Do not use for waste technology; class in 028
0288	Maintenance and repair
	Class here routine maintenance and repair [*formerly* 0289], conservation, preservation, restoration
0289	Safety measures
	Routine maintenance and repair relocated to 0288
04	Special topics
[042]	Architecture for persons with disabilities
	Relocated to 087
[043]	Architecture for persons in late adulthood and with illnesses
	Architecture for persons in late adulthood relocated to 0846; architecture for persons with illnesses relocated to 0877
047–049	Architecture and the environment, buildings by shape, buildings with atriums, multiple-purpose buildings
	Add to 04 the numbers following 720.4 in 720.47–720.49, e.g., energy conservation 0472
08	Architecture with respect to kinds of persons
0846	Persons in late adulthood [*formerly also* 043]
087	Persons with disabilities [*formerly also* 042], persons with illnesses, gifted persons
0877	Shut-in (Housebound) persons
	Class here architecture for persons with illnesses [*formerly also* 043]
	For persons with mental illness, see 0874
09	Historical, geographic, persons treatment
	Class architectural drawings in 0222
	See Manual at 913–919: Historic sites and buildings; also at 930–990: Historic preservation

Class comprehensive works in 720

721   Architectural structure

Class here interdisciplinary works on design and construction

Class architectural structure of specific types of structures in 725–728

For structural engineering, see 624.1; for engineering design and construction, see 690; for design and decoration, see 729

See Manual at 721; also at 721 vs. 690.1

.01–.02   Standard subdivisions

Notation from Table 1 as modified under 720.1–720.2, e.g., remodeling 721.0286; however, for materials, see 721.044

.04   Special topics

.042   Buildings by shape, buildings with atriums

Including circular, single-story buildings

Class architectural construction of buildings of specific materials regardless of shape in 721.044

.044   Specific materials

.044 1–.044 6   Masonry

Add to base number 721.044 the numbers following 693 in 693.1–693.6, e.g., architectural construction in reinforced concrete 721.04454

.044 7   Metals

Add to base number 721.0447 the numbers following 669 in 669.1–669.7, e.g., architectural construction in aluminum 721.0447722

.044 8   Wood

.044 9   Other materials

Add to base number 721.0449 the numbers following 693.9 in 693.91–693.99, e.g., architectural construction in glass 721.04496

.046   Architecture and the environment, multiple-purpose buildings

Add to base number 721.046 the numbers following 720.4 in 720.47–720.49, e.g., energy conservation 721.04672; however, for buildings by shape, buildings with atriums, see 721.042

> **721.1–721.8   Structural elements**

Class here decoration, design

Class decoration of structural elements in specific mediums in 729.4–729.8; class comprehensive works in 721

.1	**Foundations**
.2	**Walls**

Including footings, entablatures; colonnades, partitions; bearing and retaining walls

See also 725.96 for free-standing walls

.3	**Columnar constructions**

Including abutments, colonnettes, columns, pedestals, piers, pilasters, posts

For colonnades, entablatures, see 721.2

.36	Architectural orders
.4	**Curved constructions and details**
.41	Arcades and arches

For groined arches, see 721.44

See also 725.96 for free-standing arches

.43	Vaults

For specific types of vaults, see 721.44–721.45

>   721.44–721.45 Specific types of vaults

Class comprehensive works in 721.43

.44	Groined vaults

Including groined arches

.45	Other types of vaults

Including expanding, fan, rib, tunnel vaults

.46	Domes

Class cupolated roofs in 721.5

.48	Niches
.5	**Roofs and roof structures**

Standard subdivisions are added for roofs and roof structures together, for roofs alone

Including dormers, gables; cornices, pediments; cupolas, pinnacles, spires, towers; chimneys, skylights

.6	**Floors**
.7	**Ceilings**

.8		**Other elements**

Including balustrades, fastenings, fireplaces

.82 Openings

Class here blinds

.822 Doors and doorways

Standard subdivisions are added for either or both topics in heading

.823 Windows

Class windows as parts of roof structures in 721.5

.83 Means of vertical access

Including ramps

.832 Stairs

Including escalators

.833 Elevators

.84 Extensions

Including balconies, decks, patios, porches

> ## 722–724 Architectural schools and styles

Class architects of specific schools and styles not limited to a specific type of structure in 720.92; class details of construction of specific schools and styles in 721; class specific types of structures regardless of school or style in 725–728; class design and decoration of structures of specific schools and styles in 729; class comprehensive works, schools and styles from ca. 300 limited to a specific country or locality in 720.9

722 Architecture from earliest times to ca. 300

.1 *Ancient Chinese, Japanese, Korean architecture

Class here ancient Oriental architecture

For ancient south and southeast Asian architecture, see 722.4; for ancient Middle Eastern architecture, see 722.5

.11 *Ancient Chinese architecture

Class ancient Tibetan architecture in 722.4

.12 *Ancient Japanese architecture

.13 *Ancient Korean architecture

.2 *Ancient Egyptian architecture

*Add as instructed under 721–729

.3   ***Ancient Semitic architecture**

        Class comprehensive works on Semitic architecture in 720.8992

.31   *Phoenician architecture

        Class here architecture of Tyre, ancient Sidon

          For colonial Phoenician, see 722.32

.32   *Colonial Phoenician architecture

        Including architecture of Carthage, Utica, ancient Cyprus

.33   *Ancient Palestinian architecture

        Including ancient Israelite, Judean, Jewish architecture

.4   ***Ancient south and southeast Asian architecture**

.44   *Ancient Indian architecture

.5   ***Ancient Middle Eastern architecture**

        For ancient Egyptian architecture, see 722.2; for ancient Semitic architecture, see 722.3; for ancient Aegean architecture, see 722.61

.51   *Mesopotamian architecture

.52   *Ancient Persian architecture

.6   ***Ancient western architecture**

        For Roman architecture, see 722.7; for Greek (Hellenic) architecture, see 722.8; for other ancient western architecture, see 722.9

.61   *Aegean, Minoan, Mycenaean architecture

        Subdivisions are added for any or all topics in heading

.62   *Etruscan architecture

.7   ***Roman architecture**

.709 37   Architecture of Italian Peninsula and adjacent territories

        Class architecture of Roman empire in 722.7

.8   ***Greek (Hellenic) architecture**

        Class here comprehensive works on Greek and Roman architecture

        For Roman architecture, see 722.7

.809 38   Architecture of Greece

        Class architecture of Hellenistic world in 722.8

.9   ***Other ancient western architecture**

*Add as instructed under 721–729

723 †Architecture from ca. 300 to 1399

Class here medieval architecture

.1 †**Early Christian architecture**

.2 †**Byzantine architecture**

.3 †**Saracenic architecture**

Class here Moorish architecture

Mudéjar architecture relocated to 720.9460902

.4 †**Romanesque and Norman architecture**

.5 †**Gothic architecture**

724 †Architecture from 1400

Class here modern architecture

.1 †**1400–1800**

Class here colonial styles

For colonial styles of a later period, see the period, e.g., 1800–1899 724.5

.12 †1400–1499

Class here Renaissance architecture

For Renaissance architecture of an earlier or later period, see the period, e.g., 1500–1599 724.14

.14 †1500–1599

.16 †1600–1699

Class here comprehensive works on baroque architecture

For baroque architecture of 1700–1799, see 724.19

.19 †1700–1799

Class here Georgian, rococo architecture

.2 †**Classical revival architecture**

Class here neoclassical architecture

.22 †Roman revival architecture

.23 †Greek revival architecture

.3 †**Gothic revival architecture**

---

†Do not use notation 09 from Table 1; class architecture limited to a specific country or locality in 720.9, persons treatment in 720.92

.5   **†1800–1899**

Class here eclecticism, revivals, Victorian architecture

For classical revival architecture, see 724.2; for gothic revival architecture, see 724.3. For eclecticism and revivals of another specific period, see the period, e.g., 1700–1799 724.19

.52   †Italianate revivals

Including Renaissance revival, Romanesque revival architecture

.6   **†1900–1999**

Including art nouveau, expressionism, functionalism, international style

.7   **†2000–**

> ## 725–728   Specific types of structures

Class here development of architectural schools and styles, comprehensive works on specific structures and their interior design and decorations, interdisciplinary works on design and construction

Class comprehensive works in 720. Class structures rehabilitated to a single new use with the new use, e.g., warehouses converted into apartments 728.314; class structures rehabilitated to multiple new uses with the old use, e.g., warehouses converted into retail stores and apartments 725.35

For structural engineering, see 624.1; for engineering design and construction of specific types of habitable structures, see 690.5–690.8; for interior decoration, see 747

725   *Public structures

Not used primarily for religious, educational, research, residential purposes

SUMMARY

725.1	**Government buildings**
.2	**Commercial and communications buildings**
.3	**Transportation and storage buildings**
.4	**Industrial buildings**
.5	**Welfare and health buildings**
.6	**Correctional institutions**
.7	**Refreshment facilities and park structures**
.8	**Recreation buildings**
.9	**Other public structures**

.1   *Government buildings

Class here international government, civic center buildings

---

*Add as instructed under 721–729

†Do not use notation 09 from Table 1; class architecture limited to a specific country or locality in 720.9, persons treatment in 720.92

.11	*Legislative buildings
	Class here capitols
.12	*Executive buildings
	Class here buildings containing branches of executive department
.13	*County and city government buildings
	Subdivisions are added for either or both topics in heading
.14	*Customs buildings
.15	*Court, record, archive buildings
	Subdivisions are added for any or all topics in heading
.16	*Post offices
.17	*Official residences
	Including embassy, legation, consulate buildings
	Class here executive mansions, palaces of rulers
.18	*Military and police buildings
	Including armories, arsenals, barracks, castles, fortresses, forts
	Subdivisions are added for either or both topics in heading
	Class engineering of forts and fortresses in 623.1; class comprehensive works on castles in 728.81
.19	*Fire stations
.2	***Commercial and communications buildings**
	Subdivisions are added for commercial and communications buildings together, for commercial buildings alone
	For refreshment facilities, see 725.7
.21	*Retail trade buildings
	Class here bazaars, shopping malls, shops, stores
.23	*Office and communications buildings
	Including medical office buildings and clinics, radio and television buildings and towers
	Subdivisions are added for either or both topics in heading
.24	*Financial institutions
	For exchanges, see 725.25

*Add as instructed under 721–729

.25   *Exchanges

         Including board of trade, chamber of commerce buildings, stock and commodity exchange

.3   *Transportation and storage buildings

         Subdivisions are added for transportation and storage buildings together, for transportation buildings alone

.31   *Railroad and rapid transit stations

         Class here passenger stations

         Subdivisions are added for either or both topics in heading

           For railroad freight stations, see 725.32

.32   *Railroad freight stations

.33   *Railroad and rapid transit buildings

         Including roundhouses

         Subdivisions are added for either or both topics in heading

           For railroad and rapid transit stations, see 725.31

.34   *Marine transportation facilities

         Including docks, piers

         Class engineering of naval facilities in 623.64; class engineering of harbors, ports, roadsteads in 627.2

           See also 725.4 for shipyards

.35   *Warehouses

         Class here comprehensive works on storage buildings

           For a specific kind of storage building other than warehouse, see the kind, e.g., storage elevators 725.36

.36   *Storage elevators

.38   *Motor vehicle transportation buildings

         Including bus terminals, filling stations, garages, parking facilities

.39   *Air transportation buildings

         Including air terminals, hangars

         Class engineering of military air facilities in 623.66

.4   *Industrial buildings

         Including factories, mills, plants, shipyards

*Add as instructed under 721–729

.5 ***Welfare and health buildings**

> Subdivisions are added for welfare and health buildings together, for welfare buildings alone

.51 *General hospital and sanatorium buildings

> Class here comprehensive works on health buildings

>> *For a specific kind of health building not provided for here, see the kind, e.g., medical office buildings and clinics 725.23, children's hospital buildings 725.57*

.52 *Psychiatric hospital buildings

.53 *Buildings of institutions for persons with mental disabilities

.54 *Buildings of institutions for persons with physical disabilities

.55 *Buildings of institutions for the poor

> Class buildings of institutions for indigent persons in late adulthood in 725.56

.56 *Buildings of institutions for persons in late adulthood

.57 *Child welfare institutions and children's hospital buildings

> Subdivisions are added for either or both topics in heading

.59 Other types of welfare buildings

.592 *Veterinary hospitals and shelters

> Subdivisions are added for either or both topics in heading

.594 *Veterans' homes

.597 *Morgues and crematories

> Subdivisions are added for either or both topics in heading

.6 ***Correctional institutions**

> Class here prison and reformatory buildings

.7 ***Refreshment facilities and park structures**

.71 *Restaurant buildings

.72 *Bars (Pubs)

.73 *Bathhouses and saunas

> Class here comprehensive works on public and domestic bathhouses and saunas

> Subdivisions are added for either or both topics in heading

>> *For domestic bathhouses and saunas, see 728.96*

*Add as instructed under 721–729

.74   *Swimming pools

Class here comprehensive works on public and domestic swimming pools

For domestic swimming pools, see 728.962

.76   *Amusement park buildings and casinos

Subdivisions are added for either or both topics in heading

.8   **Recreation buildings**

For refreshment facilities and park structures, see 725.7

.804   General categories of recreation buildings

.804 2   *Multiple-purpose complexes

Class here cultural centers

Class community centers for adult education in 727.9

.804 3   *Sports complexes (Sports centers, Sports pavilions)

.81   *Concert and music halls

Subdivisions are added for either or both topics in heading

For opera houses, see 725.822

.82   *Buildings for shows and spectacles

.822   *Theaters and opera houses

Subdivisions are added for either or both topics in heading

.823   *Motion picture theaters (Cinemas)

Subdivisions are added for either or both topics in heading

.827   *Buildings for outdoor performances and for outdoor sports

Including grandstands

Class here amphitheaters, astrodomes, stadiums

Subdivisions are added for either or both topics in heading

For racetrack buildings, see 725.89

.83   *Auditoriums

Class here performing arts centers

For concert and music halls, see 725.81; for theaters and opera houses, see 725.822

.84   *Buildings for indoor games

Including bowling alleys; pool halls; halls for card games, checkers, chess

For gymnasiums, see 725.85

*Add as instructed under 721–729

.85   *Athletic club buildings and gymnasiums

> Subdivisions are added for either or both topics in heading

.86   *Dance halls and rinks

> Subdivisions are added for either or both topics in heading

.87   *Boathouses and recreation pier buildings

> Class here canoe club, yacht club buildings

> Subdivisions are added for either or both topics in heading

.88   *Riding-club buildings

.89   *Racetrack buildings

.9   **Other public structures**

.91   *Convention centers

> Class here exhibition buildings

.94   *Memorial buildings

> Class memorial buildings for a specific purpose with the purpose, e.g., memorial library buildings 727.8

.96   Arches, gateways, walls

> Standard subdivisions are added for any or all topics in heading

> *See also 721.2 for walls as structural elements, 721.41 for arches as structural elements*

.97   *Towers

> Including bell, clock towers

> *See also 726.2 for minarets, 726.597 for church towers*

.98   Bridges, tunnels, moats

> Class engineering of moats in 623.31; class engineering of tunnels in 624.193; class engineering of bridges in 624.2

726   *Buildings for religious and related purposes

SUMMARY

*Add as instructed under 721–729

> ### 726.1–726.3 Buildings associated with non-Christian religions

Class comprehensive works in 726. Class a specific kind of building for religious purposes associated with a specific religion with the building, e.g., Buddhist monasteries 726.7843

See also 726.5 for buildings associated with Christianity

.1   *Temples and shrines

Standard subdivisions are added for either or both topics in heading

See Manual at 726.1

.12–.19   Temples and shrines of a specific non-Christian religion

Add to base number 726.1 the numbers following 29 in 292–299, e.g., Buddhist temples and shrines 726.143; however, for mosques and minarets, see 726.2; for synagogues and Judaic temples, see 726.4

.2   *Mosques and minarets

Standard subdivisions are added for either or both topics in heading

.3   *Synagogues and Jewish temples

Standard subdivisions are added for either or both topics in heading

.4   *Accessory houses of worship

For all religions

Including chapels, parish houses, Sunday school buildings; comprehensive works on baptistries

For baptistries as a part of church buildings, see 726.596; for mortuary chapels, see 726.8

See also 726.595 for side chapels, 726.9 for residential parish houses

.5   *Buildings associated with Christianity

Class here church buildings

For a specific kind of building not provided for here, see the building, e.g., cathedrals 726.6, Franciscan monasteries 726.773

.51   Design, decoration, construction of structural elements

Add to base number 726.51 the numbers following 721 in 721.1–721.8, e.g., design, decoration, construction of church vaulting 726.5143

Class decoration of structural elements in specific mediums in 726.524–726.528

.52   Decoration in specific mediums, built-in church furniture, design and decoration of parts

---

*Add as instructed under 721–729

.524–.528	Decoration in specific mediums

Add to base number 726.52 the numbers following 729 in 729.4–729.8, e.g., decoration in relief 726.525

Class decorations of built-in church furniture in 726.529. Class decoration in a specific medium not in an architectural context with the medium, e.g., sculpture 730

.529	Built-in church furniture

Class built-in church furniture in a specific medium not in an architectural context with the medium, e.g., carved pew ends 731.54

.529 1	Sacramental furniture

Including altars, baptismal fonts, confessionals, tabernacles

.529 2	Rostral furniture

Including lecterns, prayer desks, pulpits

.529 3	Seats and canopies

Including baldachins, bishops' thrones, choir stalls, pews

.529 6	Screens and railings

Including altar and rood screens, altar and chancel railings, reredoses

.529 7	Organ cases
.529 8	Lighting fixtures
.58	Buildings of specific denominations

Add to base number 726.58 the numbers following 28 in 281–289, e.g., Anglican church buildings 726.583; however, for geographic treatment of buildings of specific denominations, see 726.509

Class specific parts of church buildings of specific denominations in 726.59

.59	Parts

Class design and construction of parts in 726.51; class design and decoration of parts in 726.52

.591	Entrances and approaches
.592	Naves and transepts
.593	Chancels, sanctuaries, choir lofts, pulpit platforms
.594	Clerestories
.595	Side chapels

See also 726.4 for chapels as separate buildings

.596	Sacristies and baptistries

Class comprehensive works on baptistries in 726.4

.597	Towers and steeples
.6	***Cathedrals**

> *For details and parts of cathedrals, see 726.51–726.59*

.62	Cathedrals of Eastern churches

> *For Eastern Orthodox cathedrals, see 726.63*

.620 9	Historical and persons treatment

> Do not use for geographic treatment; class in 726.609

.63	Eastern Orthodox cathedrals
.630 9	Historical and persons treatment

> Do not use for geographic treatment; class in 726.609

.64	Roman Catholic cathedrals
.640 9	Historical and persons treatment

> Do not use for geographic treatment; class in 726.609

.65	Anglican cathedrals
.650 9	Historical and persons treatment

> Do not use for geographic treatment; class in 726.609

.69	*Accessory structures

> Including cathedral cloisters, chapter houses
>
> Class here comprehensive works on cloisters
>
> *For monastic cloisters, see 726.79*

.7	***Monastic buildings**

> Class here abbeys, convents, friaries, monasteries, priories
>
> Class monastic churches either as a place of public worship or as a separate church building in 726.5

.77	Monastic buildings of specific Christian orders
[.770 1–.770 9]	Standard subdivisions

> Do not use; class in 726.701–726.709

.771–.779	Subdivisions of monastic buildings of specific Christian orders

> Add to base number 726.77 the numbers following 271 in 271.1–271.9, e.g., Franciscan monasteries 726.773; however, for geographic treatment of buildings of specific orders, see 726.709

.78	Monastic buildings of orders of other religions

> Add to base number 726.78 the numbers following 29 in 292–299, e.g., Buddhist monasteries 726.7843

*Add as instructed under 721–729

.79　　　　Parts and accessory structures

Including cells, cloisters, refectories

Class monastic libraries in 727.8

.8　　　*Mortuary chapels and tombs

Subdivisions are added for either or both topics in heading

.9　　　Other buildings for religious and related purposes

Including episcopal palaces, missions, parsonages, buildings of religious associations, buildings housing roadside shrines

727　　*Buildings for educational and research purposes

Class here school buildings

Subdivisions are added for buildings for educational and research purposes, for buildings for educational purposes alone

---

\>　　**727.1–727.3　Buildings for education at specific levels**

Class professional and technical school buildings at a specific level in 727.4; class comprehensive works in 727

For buildings for adult education, see 727.9

.1　　*Elementary school buildings

.2　　*Secondary school buildings

.3　　*College and university buildings

Subdivisions are added for either or both topics in heading

Class specialized buildings of colleges and universities in 727.4–727.8

.38　　Accessory structures

Including dining halls, dormitories, student unions

.4　　Professional and technical school buildings

.400 01–.400 09　　Standard subdivisions

.400 1–.499 9　　Specific types of professional and technical school buildings

Add to base number 727.4 notation 001–999, e.g., law school buildings 727.434

.5　　Research buildings

Class here laboratory, observatory buildings

.500 01–.500 09　　Standard subdivisions

*Add as instructed under 721–729

.500 1–.599 9   Specific types of research buildings

> Add to base number 727.5 notation 001–999, e.g., physics laboratories 727.553

.6   Museum buildings

.600 01–.600 09   Standard subdivisions

.600 1–.699 9   Specific types of museum buildings

> Add to base number 727.6 notation 001–999, e.g., science museum buildings 727.65; however, for art museum buildings, see 727.7

.7   *Art museum and gallery buildings

> Subdivisions are added for either or both topics in heading

.8   *Library buildings

.82   *General libraries

.820 9   Historical and persons treatment

> Do not use for geographic treatment; class in 727.809

.821–.828   Specific kinds of general libraries

> Add to base number 727.82 the numbers following 027 in 027.1–027.8, e.g., public library buildings 727.824; then add further as instructed under 721–729, e.g., energy conservation in public library buildings 727.8240472; however, for geographic treatment, see 727.809; for branch libraries, see 727.84

.83   *Libraries devoted to specific subjects

.830 9   Historical and persons treatment

> Do not use for geographic treatment; class in 727.809

.84   *Branch libraries

.840 9   Historical and persons treatment

> Do not use for geographic treatment; class in 727.809

.9   Other buildings for educational and research purposes

> Including community centers for adult education, learned society buildings

728   *Residential and related buildings

> Class here domestic architecture, conventional housing
>
> Subdivisions are added for residential and related buildings, for residential buildings alone
>
> *For official residences, see 725.17; for episcopal palaces, parsonages, see 726.9; for residential educational buildings, see 727.1–727.3*

---

*Add as instructed under 721–729

.1 ***Low-cost housing**

Dwellings designed along simple lines to reduce construction costs

Class specific types of low-cost housing in 728.3–728.7

.3 **Specific kinds of conventional housing**

[.301–.309] Standard subdivisions

Do not use; class in 728.01–728.09

.31 *Multiple dwellings

.312 *Row houses and townhouses

Including duplex houses

Subdivisions are added for either or both topics in heading

.314 *Apartments (Flats)

Including apartment hotels, tenements

.37 *Separate houses

Class here cottages

For farmhouses, see 728.6; for vacation houses, see 728.72; for large and elaborate private dwellings, see 728.8

.372 *Multistory houses

.373 *Single-story houses

Class here bungalows, ranch and split-level houses

> **728.4–728.7 Special-purpose housing**

Class comprehensive works in 728

.4 ***Club houses**

Country, city, fraternal clubs

Class a type of club house not provided for here with the type, e.g., racetrack club houses 725.89

.5 ***Hotels and motels**

Subdivisions are added for either or both topics in heading

For apartment hotels, see 728.314

.6 ***Farmhouses**

Class here farm cottages

Class comprehensive works on farm buildings in 728.92

---

*Add as instructed under 721–729

.7	***Vacation houses, cabins, hunting lodges, houseboats, mobile homes**
.72	*Vacation houses
.73	*Cabins

Class vacation cabins in 728.72

.78	*Houseboats
.79	*Mobile homes

Including campers, trailers

For houseboats, see 728.78

See Manual at 643.2, 690.879, 728.79 vs. 629.226

.8	***Large and elaborate private dwellings**

Class here chateaux, manor houses, mansions, plantation houses, villas

.81	*Castles

Fortified residences

Class here comprehensive works on architecture of castles

For castles as military structures, see 725.18

.82	*Palaces

Residences of nobility

Class fortified palaces in 728.81

See also 725.17 for palaces of rulers, 726.9 for episcopal palaces

.9	***Accessory domestic structures**

Including gatehouses

.92	*Agricultural structures

Class here farm buildings

For farmhouses, see 728.6

.922	*Barns
.924	*Greenhouses

Class here conservatories

.927	*Birdhouses

Class here aviaries

.93	*Decks and patios

Subdivisions are added for either or both topics in heading

*Add as instructed under 721–729

.96   Swimming pools and related structures

>> Including bathhouses, saunas

>> Class comprehensive works on bathhouses and saunas in 725.73

.962   *Swimming pools

>> Class comprehensive works on swimming pools in 725.74

.98   *Garages

729 Design and decoration of structures and accessories

Class here interior design (the art or practice of planning and supervising the design and execution of architectural interiors and their furnishings)

Class design and decoration of structures and accessories of specific types of buildings in 725–728

For interior decoration, see 747

See Manual at 729

> ### 729.1–729.2 Design in specific planes

Class design of structural elements in specific planes in 721.1–721.8; class comprehensive works in 729

.1 Design in vertical plane

Including elevations, facades, sections

.11   Composition

.13   Proportion

.19   Inscriptions and lettering

>> Standard subdivisions are added for either or both topics in heading

.2 Design in horizontal plane (Plans and planning)

Class here modular design

.23   Proportion

.24   *Interior arrangement

.25   *Lines of interior communication

.28   Lighting

.29   Acoustics

*Add as instructed under 721–729

>   **729.4–729.8   Decoration in specific mediums**

Class comprehensive works in 729. Class decoration in a specific medium not in an architectural context with the medium, e.g., sculpture 730

.4   Decoration in paint

As an adjunct to architecture

.5   Decoration in relief

Including carved and sculptured decoration and ornament, Gothic tracery

.6   Decoration in veneer and incrustation

Use of wood, stone, metal, enamel in architectural decoration

.7   Decoration in mosaic

Class comprehensive works on mosaics in 738.5

.8   Decoration in ornamental glass

730   Plastic arts   Sculpture

Class assemblages, constructions; kinetic, sound sculpture; land art; mixed media and composites in 709.04

SUMMARY

730.01–.09	**Standard subdivisions of plastic arts**
.1–.9	**Standard subdivisions of sculpture**
731	**Processes, forms, subjects of sculpture**
732	**Sculpture from earliest times to ca. 500, sculpture of nonliterate peoples**
733	**Greek, Etruscan, Roman sculpture**
734	**Sculpture from ca. 500 to 1399**
735	**Sculpture from 1400**
736	**Carving and carvings**
737	**Numismatics and sigillography**
738	**Ceramic arts**
739	**Art metalwork**

.01   Philosophy and theory of plastic arts

.02   Miscellany of plastic arts

.028   Techniques, procedures, apparatus, equipment, materials of plastic arts

Class here techniques of two or more of the plastic arts, e.g., firing of clays in sculpture and ceramics

.03–.09   Standard subdivisions of plastic arts

>   **730.1–730.9 Standard subdivisions of sculpture**

    Class comprehensive works in 730

.1   **Philosophy and theory of sculpture**

.11   Appreciative aspects

    Do not use for systems; class in 730.1

    Class psychological principles in 730.19

.117   Aesthetics

.118   Criticism and appreciation

    Theory, technique, history

    Class works of critical appraisal in 730.9

.18   Inherent features

    Including color, composition, decorative values, form, movement, space, style, symmetry, vision

.2   **Miscellany of sculpture**

[.28]   Auxiliary techniques and procedures

    Do not use; class in 731.028

[.284]   Apparatus, equipment, materials

    Do not use for materials; class in 731.2. Do not use for apparatus and equipment; class in 731.3

.3–.8   **Standard subdivisions of sculpture**

.9   **Historical, geographic, persons treatment of sculpture**

    Class here schools and styles limited to a specific country or locality

    Class comprehensive works on specific schools and styles not limited to country or locality in 732–735; class sculpture of nonliterate peoples regardless of time or place in 732.2

[.901–.905]   Historical periods

    Do not use; class in 732–735

.92   Persons treatment

    Class here description, critical appraisal, biography of sculptors and their works regardless of process, representation, style or school, period, place

    Class sculptors who also work in the other plastic arts in 730.092

.922	Collected persons treatment

Including works of sculptors from several geographic areas

Class works of more than one sculptor in the same geographic area, region, place in general (*not* limited by continent, country, locality) in 730.91

.922 3	Ancient world

Class works of more than one sculptor in 732–733

.922 4–.922 9	Modern world

Class works of more than one sculptor in 730.94–730.99

[.93]	Ancient world

Do not use; class in 732–733

.95	Asia

Class here Buddhist, Oriental sculpture

For Buddhist sculpture in an area not provided for here, see the area, e.g., Buddhist sculpture in Hawaii 730.9969

.954	South Asia India

Class here Hindu, Jain sculpture

For Hindu sculpture in an area not provided for here, see the area, e.g., Hindu sculpture in Indonesia 730.9598

> ## 731–735 Sculpture

Class comprehensive works in 730

See Manual at 731–735 vs. 736–739

731   Processes, forms, subjects of sculpture

Class processes, forms, subjects of specific periods and by specific schools in 732–735

.028	Auxiliary techniques and procedures [*formerly* 731.4]

Comprehensive works on techniques, procedures, apparatus, equipment, materials together relocated to 731.4

Class comprehensive works on basic and auxiliary techniques and procedures in 731.4

[.028 4]	Apparatus, equipment, materials

Do not use for materials; class in 731.2. Do not use for apparatus and equipment; class in 731.3

[.028 8]	Maintenance and repair
	Do not use; class in 731.48
.028 9	Safety measures [*formerly* 731.48]
.092	Persons treatment
	Do not use for individual sculptors; class in 730.92

> **731.2–731.4   Techniques, procedures, apparatus, equipment, materials**

Class forms employing techniques, procedures, apparatus, equipment, materials in 731.5; class subjects employing techniques, procedures, apparatus, equipment, materials in 731.8; class comprehensive works in 731.4

.2   ***Materials**

Including ceramic materials, found objects, metals, paper, papier-mâché, plastics, rope, stone, textiles, wax, wire, wood

Class use of materials in specific techniques in 731.4

.3   ***Apparatus and equipment**

Including tools, machines, accessories

Class use of apparatus and equipment in specific techniques in 731.4

.4   ***Techniques and procedures**

Class here comprehensive works on techniques, procedures, apparatus, equipment, materials together [*formerly* 731.028]

Auxiliary techniques and procedures relocated to 731.028, e.g., data processing 731.0285

For materials, see 731.2; for apparatus and equipment, see 731.3

.41   *Direct-metal sculpture

Including beating, bending, cutting, hammering, shaping, soldering, welding metals (including pipe and wire)

Class art metalwork in 739

.42   *Modeling

In clay, wax, other plastic materials with and without armatures

.43   *Molding

Preparation of molds and models

Class use of molds in 731.45

.45   *Casting

Including sand casting

*Do not use notation 092 from Table 1 for individual sculptors; class in 730.92

.452	*Cement and plaster casting

.453   *Plastics casting

.456   *Casting in bronze

> Including lost-wax casting
>
> Class here casting in metals
>
> *For casting in metals other than bronze, see 731.457*

.457   *Casting in metals other than bronze

> Class comprehensive works on casting in metals in 731.456

.46   *Carving and chiseling techniques in sculpture

> Standard subdivisions are added for either or both topics in heading

.462   *Sculpturing in wood

.463   *Sculpturing in stone

.47   *Firing and baking

> Standard subdivisions are added for either or both topics in heading
>
> Including firing and baking clay models for molding
>
> Class techniques of firing and baking in ceramics in 738.143

.48   *Maintenance and repair

> Class here conservation, preservation, restoration
>
> Safety measures relocated to 731.0289

.5   *Forms

> Development, description, critical appraisal, collections of works not limited by time or place
>
> *For sculpture in the round, see 731.7*

.54   *Sculpture in relief

> Class iconography of sculpture in relief in 731.8

.542   *Portals and doors

> Standard subdivisions are added for either or both topics in heading

.549   *Monumental reliefs

> *For monumental brasses, see 739.522*

.55   *Mobiles and stabiles

---

*Do not use notation 092 from Table 1 for individual sculptors; class in 730.92

.7	***Sculpture in the round**

Development, description, critical appraisal, collections of works

Including totem poles

Class iconography of sculpture in the round in 731.8

.72 *Decorative sculpture

Including garden sculpture, fountains, sculptured vases and urns

.74 *Busts

.75 *Masks

.76 *Monuments

For monumental brasses, see 739.522

.8 *Iconography

Development, description, critical appraisal, works not limited by time or place

.81 *Equestrian sculpture

.82–.89 Other specific subjects

Add to base number 731.8 the numbers following 704.94 in 704.942–704.949, e.g., mythology and legend 731.87; however, for individual sculptors, see 730.92; for busts, see 731.74; for masks, see 731.75

>   **732–735 Schools and styles of sculpture**

Class comprehensive works in 730.9

732 Sculpture from earliest times to ca. 500, sculpture of nonliterate peoples

[.09] Historical, geographic, persons treatment

Do not use for persons treatment; class in 730.92. Do not use for historical and geographic treatment; class in 732

.2 †Sculpture of nonliterate peoples

Regardless of time or place

.22 †Paleolithic sculpture

.23 †Rock art (sculpture)

*Do not use notation 092 from Table 1 for individual sculptors; class in 730.92
†Do not use notation 092 from Table 1; class persons treatment in 730.92

> **732.3–732.9 Ancient sculpture**

Class comprehensive works in 732

.3   †**Ancient Palestinian sculpture**

Including Israelite, Judean, Jewish sculpture

.4   †**Ancient south and southeast Asian sculpture**

.44   †Ancient Indian sculpture

.5   †**Mesopotamian and ancient Persian sculpture**

.6   †**Ancient British, Celtic, Germanic, Iberian, Slavic sculpture**

.7   †**Ancient Oriental sculpture**

> *For ancient Oriental sculpture of a specific place not provided for here, see the place, e.g., ancient Indian sculpture 732.44*

.71   †Ancient Chinese sculpture

.72   †Ancient Japanese sculpture

.73   †Ancient Korean sculpture

.8   †**Ancient Egyptian sculpture**

.9   **Sculpture of other ancient areas**

> Add to base number 732.9 the numbers following — 39 in notation 392–398 from Table 2, e.g., Phoenician sculpture 732.944; however, for persons treatment, see 730.92; for ancient sculpture of Greek Archipelago, see 733.309391

> *For Greek, Etruscan, Roman sculpture, see 733*

733   †Greek, Etruscan, Roman sculpture

.3   †**Greek (Hellenic) sculpture**

Class comprehensive works on Greek and Roman sculpture in 733

.309 38   Sculpture of Greece

Class sculpture of Hellenistic world in 733.3

.4   †**Etruscan sculpture**

.5   †**Roman sculpture**

.509 37   Sculpture of Italian Peninsula and adjacent territories

Class sculpture of Roman Empire in 733.5

734   †*Sculpture from ca. 500 to 1399

Class here medieval sculpture

*Do not use notation 09 from Table 1; class geographic treatment in 730.9, persons treatment in 730.92

†Do not use notation 092 from table 1; class persons treatment in 730.92

.2   ***Styles**

.22   *Early Christian and Byzantine sculpture

.222   *Early Christian sculpture

.224   *Byzantine sculpture

.24   *Romanesque sculpture

.25   *Gothic sculpture

735 *Sculpture from 1400

Class here modern sculpture

.2   **Specific periods**

.21   *1400–1799

Including baroque, Renaissance sculpture

.22   *1800–1899

Including classical revival sculpture, romanticism, realism

.23   *1900–1999

.230 4   Schools and styles

Add to base number 735.2304 the numbers following 709.040 in 709.0401–709.0407, e.g., abstractionism in sculpture 735.230452; however, for geographic treatment, see 730.9; for persons treatment, see 730.92

.231–.239   Periods

Add to base number 735.23 the numbers following —0904 in notation 09041–09049 from Table 1, e.g., sculpture of 1960–1969 735.236; however, for geographic treatment, see 730.9; for persons treatment, see 730.92

.24   *2000–2099

\>   **736–739 Other plastic arts**

Processes and products

Class comprehensive works in 730. Class a plastic art not provided for here with the art in 745–749, e.g., textile arts 746

See also 731–735 for sculpture

See Manual at 731–735 vs. 736–739

*Do not use notation 09 from Table 1; class geographic treatment in 730.9, persons treatment in 730.92

736   Carving and carvings

Standard subdivisions are added for either or both topics in heading

.2   **Precious and semiprecious stones (Glyptics)**

Standard subdivisions are added for either or both topics in heading

Class engraved seals, stamps, signets in 737.6; class setting of precious and semiprecious stones in 739.27

.202 8   Lapidary work

Do not use for auxiliary techniques and procedures; apparatus, equipment, materials; class in 736.202

Including cutting, polishing, engraving gems

.22   Specific forms

Class carving in specific materials regardless of form in 736.23–736.28

For scarabs, see 736.20932

.222   Cameos

.223   Intaglios

.224   Figurines

>   736.23–736.28   Specific stones

Class comprehensive works in 736.2

.23   Diamonds

.24   Jade

See also 731–735 for jade sculpture

.25   Sapphires

.28   Obsidian

.4   **Wood**

Including butter prints and molds, whittling

See also 731–735 for wood sculpture, 745.51 for wood handicrafts

.5   **Stone**

Including lettering, inscriptions, designs

Class here effigial and sepulchral slabs

See also 731–735 for stone sculpture

.6   **Ivory, bone, horn, shell, amber**

.62	Ivory

> Class netsukes of ivory in 736.68
>
> *See also 731–735 for ivory sculpture*

.68	Netsukes
.7	**Ornamental fans**

> Class fans of a specific material with the material, e.g., ivory fans 736.62

.9	**Other materials**
.93	Wax
.94	Ice and snow
.95	Soap
.98	Paper cutting and folding
.982	Origami
.984	Silhouettes

> Class comprehensive works on drawing and cutting silhouettes in 741.7

737 Numismatics and sigillography

> Standard subdivisions are added for numismatics and sigillography, for numismatics alone
>
> *For paper money, see 769.55*

.2	**Medals and related objects**
.22	Medals

> Class here medallions

.222	Commemorative medals
.223	Civilian and military medals

> Including decorations, orders

.224	Religious medals
.23	Amulets and talismans
.24	Buttons and pins

> Standard subdivisions are added for either or both topics in heading

.242	Political (Campaign) buttons and pins

> Standard subdivisions are added for either or both topics in heading

.243	Sports buttons and pins

> Standard subdivisions are added for either or both topics in heading

.3   **Counters and tokens**

> Standard subdivisions are added for either or both topics in heading

.4   **Coins**

> Class here counterfeit coins

.409 3–.409 9   Specific continents and localities

> > Do not use for specific countries; class in 737.49

.43   Gold coins

.430 93–.430 99   Specific continents and localities

> > Do not use for specific countries; class in 737.49

.49   Coins of specific countries

> By place of origin

> Add to base number 737.49 notation 3–9 from Table 2, e.g., Roman coins minted in Egypt 737.4932

.6   **Engraved seals, signets, stamps**

> Standard subdivisions are added for any or all topics in heading

> Class here sigillography

> Class interdisciplinary works on sigillography in 929.9

738   Ceramic arts

> Class here pottery

> Works about "pottery" in the sense of porcelain and earthenware or stoneware are classed here, in the sense of only porcelain are classed in 738.2

> Class ceramic sculpture in 731–735

> *For glass, see 748*

SUMMARY

738.01–.09	Standard subdivisions
.1	Techniques, procedures, apparatus, equipment, materials
.2	Porcelain
.3	Earthenware and stoneware
.4	Enamels
.5	Mosaics
.6	Ornamental bricks and tiles
.8	Other products

.028   Auxiliary techniques and procedures [*formerly* 738.14]

> Class comprehensive works on techniques and procedures in 738.14

[.028 4]   Apparatus, equipment, materials

> Do not use for materials; class in 738.12. Do not use for apparatus and equipment; class in 738.13

[.028 8]   Maintenance and repair

> Do not use; class in 738.18

.028 9   Safety measures [*formerly* 738.18]

.09   Historical, geographic, persons treatment

> Class here brands of pottery

.092   Persons treatment

> Class here ceramic artists; description, critical appraisal, biography of potters regardless of material or product

> *For enamelers, see 738.4092; for mosaicists, see 738.5092*

.1   **Techniques, procedures, apparatus, equipment, materials**

.12   Materials

> Including clays, e.g., kaolin; color materials

> Class use of materials in specific techniques in 738.14

.127   Glazes

.13   Apparatus and equipment

> Including potter's wheels

> Class use of apparatus and equipment in specific techniques in 738.14

.136   Kilns

.14   Techniques and procedures

> Auxiliary techniques and procedures relocated to 738.028, e.g., data processing 738.0285

> Class techniques of making specialized products in 738.4–738.8

> *For decorative treatment, see 738.15; for conservation, preservation, restoration, see 738.18*

.142   Modeling and casting

.143   Firing

> Before and after glazing

.144   Glazing

.15   Decorative treatment

Including sgrafitto decoration, slip tracing, transfer painting, underglaze and overglaze painting

For glazing, see 738.144

.18   Maintenance and repair

Including expertizing

Class here conservation, preservation, restoration

Safety measures relocated to 738.0289

>   **738.2–738.8 Products**

Development, description, critical appraisal, collections of works

Class comprehensive works in 738

.2   Porcelain

Class comprehensive works on porcelain, earthenware, stoneware in 738

[.202 8]   Auxiliary techniques and procedures; apparatus, equipment, materials

Do not use for auxiliary techniques and procedures; class in 738.028

[.202 84]   Apparatus, equipment, materials

Do not use for materials; class in 738.12. Do not use for apparatus and equipment; class in 738.13

.209   Historical and geographic treatment of porcelain

Class here brands

[.209 2]   Persons treatment

Do not use; class in 738.092

.27   Specific types and varieties of porcelain

Including blue and white transfer ware

.270 9   Historical treatment

Do not use for geographic treatment; class in 738.209

[.270 92]   Persons treatment

Do not use; class in 738.092

.28   Specific porcelain products

Class specific products of specific types or varieties in 738.27; class specialized products in 738.4–738.8

.280 9   Historical treatment

Do not use for geographic treatment; class in 738.209

[.280 92]	Persons treatment
	Do not use; class in 738.092

.3   **Earthenware and stoneware**

      Standard subdivisions are added for either or both topics in heading

[.302 8]	Auxiliary techniques and procedures; apparatus, equipment, materials
	Do not use for auxiliary techniques and procedures; class in 738.028
[.302 84]	Apparatus, equipment, materials
	Do not use for materials; class in 738.12. Do not use for apparatus and equipment; class in 738.13

.309   Historical and geographic treatment

      Class here brands

[.309 2]	Persons treatment
	Do not use; class in 738.092

.37   Specific types and varieties of earthenware and stoneware

      Including delftware, faience

.370 9   Historical treatment

      Do not use for geographic treatment; class in 738.309

[.370 92]	Persons treatment
	Do not use; class in 738.092

.372   Majolica

.372 09   Historical treatment

      Do not use for geographic treatment; class in 738.309

[.372 092]	Persons treatment
	Do not use; class in 738.092

.38   Specific earthenware and stoneware products

      Class specific products of specific types and varieties in 738.37; class specialized products in 738.4–738.8

.380 9   Historical treatment

      Do not use for geographic treatment; class in 738.309

[.380 92]	Persons treatment
	Do not use; class in 738.092

.382 Middle Eastern and western vessels

Standard subdivisions are added for a specific type of vessel, e.g., ancient Egyptian vases 738.3820932

Ancient and classical

[.382 092] Persons treatment

Do not use; class in 738.092

> **738.4–738.8 Specialized products and techniques of making them**

Class comprehensive works in 738

.4 **Enamels**

Including basse-taille, champlevé, ronde bosse

For nielloing, see 739.15; for jewelry, see 739.27; for enameling glass, see 748.6

.42 Cloisonné

.46 Surface-painted enamels

.5 **Mosaics**

Class here mosaic painting, comprehensive works on mosaics in all materials

Class mosaics of a specific material not provided for here with the material, e.g., mosaic glass 748.5

.52 Mosaics used with architecture

Including floors, pavements, walls; fixed screens and panels

.56 Mosaics applied to portable objects

Including mosaic jewelry, ornaments, ornamental objects, movable panels

.6 **Ornamental bricks and tiles**

Standard subdivisions are added for either or both topics in heading

.8 **Other products**

Including braziers, candlesticks, lamps, lighting fixtures, stoves

.82 Figurines

Including figure groups, animals, plants

See also 738.83 for dolls

.83 Dolls

Class comprehensive works on handicrafting dolls in 745.59221

739   Art metalwork

For numismatics, see 737

SUMMARY

.028   Auxiliary techniques and procedures [*formerly* 739.14]

> Class comprehensive works on techniques and procedures in 739.14

[.028 4]   Apparatus, equipment, materials

> Do not use for materials; class in 739.12. Do not use for apparatus and equipment; class in 739.13

.028 8   Maintenance and repair [*formerly* 739.16]

> Class here conservation, preservation, restoration

.028 9   Safety measures [*formerly* 739.16]

.1   Techniques, procedures, apparatus, equipment, materials

> Class techniques, procedures, apparatus, equipment, materials for a specific kind of metalwork with the kind, e.g., goldsmithing 739.22028

.12   Materials

> Class use of materials in specific techniques in 739.14

.13   Apparatus and equipment

> Including tools, machines, accessories

> Class use of apparatus and equipment in specific techniques in 739.14

.14   Techniques and procedures

> Including bending, casting, drawing, forging, rolling, shaping metals by hammering and beating (repoussé work), stamping, welding

> Auxiliary techniques and procedures relocated to 739.028, e.g., data processing 739.0285

> *For decorative treatment, see 739.15*

.15   Decorative treatment

> Including chasing, damascening, nielloing, painting, patinating

[.16]   Maintenance and repair and safety measures

        Maintenance and repair relocated to 739.0288

        Safety measures relocated to 739.0289

.2   **Work in precious metals**

        Class clocks and watches in precious metals in 739.3

>   739.22–739.24 Work in specific metals

        Class jewelry in specific metals in 739.27; class comprehensive works in 739.2

.22   Goldsmithing

        Class comprehensive works on goldsmithing and silversmithing in 739.2

.220 28   Auxiliary techniques and procedures [*formerly* 739.224]

        Class here comprehensive works on techniques, procedures, apparatus, equipment, materials together

        Class comprehensive works on basic and auxiliary techniques and procedures in 739.224

[.220 284]   Apparatus, equipment, materials

        Do not use for materials; class in 739.222. Do not use for apparatus and equipment; class in 739.223

.220 288   Maintenance and repair [*formerly* 739.226]

        Class here conservation, preservation, restoration

.220 289   Safety measures [*formerly* 739.226]

[.220 9]   Historical, geographic, persons treatment

        Do not use; class in 739.227

(.220 92)   Persons treatment

        (Optional number; prefer 739.2272)

.222–.225   Techniques, procedures, apparatus, equipment, materials

        Add to base number 739.22 the numbers following 739.1 in 739.12–739.15, e.g., decorative treatment 739.225; however, auxiliary techniques and procedures relocated from 739.224 to 739.22028, e.g., data processing 739.220285; for historical, geographic, persons treatment, see 739.227

        Class techniques, apparatus, equipment, materials for specific products in 739.228; class comprehensive works in 739.22028

[.226]   Maintenance and repair and safety measures

        Maintenance and repair relocated to 739.220288; safety measures relocated to 739.220289

.227   Historical, geographic, persons treatment

> Add to base number 739.227 notation 001–9 from Table 2, e.g., goldsmiths 739.2272
> (Option: Class goldsmiths in 739.22092)

> Class "goldsmiths" in the sense of both goldsmiths and silversmiths in 739.2092

.228   *Products

> Gold and gold-plate

.228 2   *Religious articles

.228 3   *Tableware

> Utensils used for setting a table or serving food and drink

> Including flatware, hollow ware

> Class tableware for religious use in 739.2282

.228 4   *Receptacles

> Including boxes, loving cups, vases

> Class religious receptacles in 739.2282

.23   Silversmithing

> Add to base number 739.23 the numbers following 739.22 in 739.22028–739.228, e.g., silversmiths 739.2372, silver tableware 739.2383

.24   Platinumwork

.27   Jewelry

> Design of settings, mounting gems, repair work

> Class here interdisciplinary works on making fine and costume jewelry

> Class interdisciplinary works on jewelry in 391.7; class interdisciplinary works on making costume jewelry in 688.2

> > *For carving precious and semiprecious stones, see 736.2; for making handcrafted costume jewelry, see 745.5942. For jewelry made in a material other than precious metal, see the material in 700–770, e.g., mosaic jewelry 738.56*

.270 28   Auxiliary techniques and procedures [*formerly* 739.274]

> > Class here comprehensive works on techniques, procedures, apparatus, equipment, materials together

> > Class comprehensive works on basic and auxiliary techniques and procedures in 739.274

[.270 284]   Apparatus, equipment, materials

> > Do not use for materials; class in 739.272. Do not use for apparatus and equipment; class in 739.273

*Do not use notation 09 from Table 1; class in 739.227

.270 288	Maintenance and repair [*formerly* 739.276]

Class here conservation, preservation, restoration

.270 289	Safety measures [*formerly* 739.276]
.272–.275	Techniques, procedures, apparatus, equipment, materials

Add to base number 739.27 the numbers following 739.1 in 739.12–739.15, e.g., decorative treatment 739.275; however, auxiliary techniques and procedures relocated from 739.274 to 739.27028, e.g., data processing 739.270285

Class techniques, apparatus, equipment, materials for specific products in 739.278; class comprehensive works in 739.27028

[.276]	Maintenance and repair and safety measures

Maintenance and repair relocated to 739.270288; safety measures relocated to 739.270289

.278	Products

Including belt buckles, shoe buckles, watch fobs

.278 2	Finger rings
.3	**Clocks and watches**

Standard subdivisions are added for either or both topics in heading

Class here clockcases regardless of material

Add to base number 739.3 the numbers following 739.22 in 739.22028–739.227, e.g., decorative treatment 739.35
Subdivisions are added for either clocks or watches

Class clocks as furniture in 749.3; class interdisciplinary works on clocks in 681.113; class interdisciplinary works on watches in 681.114

> **739.4–739.5 Work in base metals**

Class watches and clocks in base metals in 739.3; class comprehensive works in 739

For arms and armor, see 739.7

.4	**Ironwork**

Class here wrought iron, cast iron, stainless steel

.402 8–.47	Techniques, procedures, apparatus, equipment, materials; historical, geographic, persons treatment

Add to base number 739.4 the numbers following 739.22 in 739.22028–739.227, e.g., decorative treatment 739.45

.48	Products

Including balcony motifs, balustrades, grills, knockers, ornamental nails

[.480 9]	Historical, geographic, persons treatment

Do not use; class in 739.47

.5   Work in metals other than iron

.51   Copper and its alloys

For brass, see 739.52

.511   Copper

.512   Bronze

See also 731–735 for bronze sculpture

.52   Brass

.522   Monumental brasses

Class here rubbing and rubbings for study and research of brasses

Class rubbings as art form in 760

.53   Tin and its alloys

For bronze, see 739.512

.532   Tin

.533   Pewter

.54   Lead

.55   Zinc and its alloys

Subdivisions are added for zinc and its alloys together, for zinc alone

For brass, see 739.52

.56   Nickel

.57   Aluminum

.58   Chromium

.7   Arms and armor

Standard subdivisions are added for arms and armor together, for arms alone

Class here decorative treatment of shapes, handles, grips, metalwork

Class comprehensive works on technology and art of arms and armor in 623.44; class interdisciplinary works on arms and armor in 623.44

See also 623.441 for stone weapons

>   739.72–739.74 Arms

Class comprehensive works in 739.7

.72	Edged weapons

Including axes, daggers, dirks, knives, spears

Class edged arrows in 739.73; class interdisciplinary works on knives in 621.932

.722	Swords and sabers

Standard subdivisions are added for either or both topics in heading

.723	Bayonets

.73	Missile-hurling weapons

Including air guns, bows and arrows, spring guns

For firearms, see 739.74

.74	Firearms

Add to base number 739.74 the numbers following 623.4 in 623.42–623.44, e.g., pistols 739.74432

Class interdisciplinary works on small firearms in 683.4

.75	Armor

.752	Shields

740   Drawing and decorative arts

SUMMARY

741	Drawing and drawings
742	Perspective in drawing
743	Drawing and drawings by subject
745	Decorative arts
746	Textile arts
747	Interior decoration
748	Glass
749	Furniture and accessories

741   Drawing and drawings

Class comprehensive works on drawing and painting in 750; class comprehensive works on two-dimensional art in 760

For drawing and drawings by subject, see 743

SUMMARY

741.01–.09	Standard subdivisions
.2	Techniques, procedures, apparatus, equipment, materials
.5	Cartoons, caricatures, comics
.6	Graphic design, illustration, commercial art
.7	Silhouettes
.9	Collections of drawings

.01	Philosophy and theory
.011	Appreciative aspects
	Do not use for systems; class in 741.01
	Class psychological principles in 741.019
.011 7	Aesthetics
.011 8	Criticism and appreciation
	Including theory, technique, history
	Class works of critical appraisal in 741.09
.018	Inherent features
	Including color, composition, decorative values, form, light, movement, space, style, symmetry, time
	Class perspective in 742
.028	Auxiliary techniques and procedures [*formerly* 741.2]
	Class comprehensive works on basic and auxiliary techniques and procedures in 741.2
[.028 4]	Apparatus, equipment, materials
	Do not use; class in 741.2
.028 8	Maintenance and repair
	Including expertizing
	Class here conservation, preservation, restoration [*formerly* 741.218]; routine maintenance and repair [*formerly* 741.219]
	Class identification of reproductions, copies, forgeries, alterations in 741.217
.028 9	Safety measures [*formerly* 741.219]
.074	Museums and exhibits
	For collections of drawings, see 741.9
.09	Historical, geographic, persons treatment
	For collections of drawings from specific periods and places, see 741.92–741.99
.092	Persons treatment
	Class here description, critical appraisal, biography of artists regardless of medium, process, subject, period, place
	Class artists working in special applications in 741.5–741.7; class collections of drawings in 741.9

.2   *Techniques, procedures, apparatus, equipment, materials

Including one-color washes highlighting drawings

Class here comprehensive works on basic and auxiliary techniques and procedures

Auxiliary techniques and procedures relocated to 741.028, e.g., data processing 741.0285

Class techniques, procedures, apparatus, equipment, materials used in special applications in 741.5–741.7; class techniques, procedures, apparatus, equipment, materials used in drawing specific subjects in 743.4–743.8; class collections of drawings regardless of medium or process in 741.9

> *For perspective, see 742*
>
> *See also 751.422 for watercolor*

.21   *Techniques of reproduction and conservation

.217   *Reproduction

Execution and identification

.217 2   *Reproductions and copies

Standard subdivisions are added for either or both topics in heading

.217 4   *Forgeries and alterations

[.218]   Conservation, preservation, restoration

Relocated to 741.0288

[.219]   Routine maintenance and repair and safety measures

Routine maintenance and repair relocated to 741.0288; safety measures relocated to 741.0289

>   741.22–741.29 Specific mediums

Class comprehensive works in 741.2

.22   *Charcoal

.23   *Chalk and crayon

.235   *Pastel

.24   *Pencil

.25   *Silverpoint

.26   *Ink

Class here brush, marker, pen drawing

---

*Do not use notation 092 from Table 1 for individual artists; class in 741.092

.29 *Scratchboard and airbrush drawing

> **741.5–741.7 Special applications**

Class here works that began with drawing but use other techniques such as painting, printing, photography to create the final product ꞌ

Class comprehensive works in 741.6

.5 Cartoons, caricatures, comics

Including fotonovelas

Class here cartoon fiction, graphic novels (visual novels)

Class cartoons or caricatures whose purpose is to inform or persuade with the subject of the cartoon or caricature, e.g., political cartoons 320.0207

.507 4 Museums and exhibits

Do not use for collections; class in 741.59

.509 2 Persons treatment

Class collections by individual artists in 741.593–741.599

.58 Animated cartoons

Class photographic techniques in 778.5347; class comprehensive works on cartoon films in 791.433

.59 Collections

Class here cartoons with subordinate text

[.590 93–.590 99] Specific continents, countries, localities

Do not use; class in 741.593–741.599

.593–.599 Treatment by specific continents, countries, localities

Add to base number 741.59 notation 3–9 from Table 2, e.g., collections of cartoons from London 741.59421
Collections by individual artists are classed at country level only. Notation 074 from Table 1 for collections is not added. For example, a collection of an individual artist from London is classed in 741.5942 (*not* 741.95421, 741.9542074421)

.6 Graphic design, illustration, commercial art

Class here comprehensive works on special applications of drawing

Class graphic arts, comprehensive works on two-dimensional art in 760. Class a specific type of illustration, a specific form of graphic design, a specific form of commercial art, not provided for here with the type or form, e.g., original oil paintings for book jackets 759

See Manual at 741.6 vs. 800

---

*Do not use notation 092 from Table 1 for individual artists; class in 741.092

.64	Books and book jackets
	Standard subdivisions are added for either or both topics in heading
	Class illumination of manuscripts and books in 745.67
.642	Children's books
.65	Magazines and newspapers
.652	Magazines and magazine covers
	Standard subdivisions are added for either or both topics in heading
.66	Covers for sheet music and recordings
.67	Advertisements and posters
	Standard subdivisions are added for advertisements and posters together, for advertisements alone
.672	Fashion drawing
	Class fashion design in 746.92
.674	Commercial posters
	Class here comprehensive works on posters
	For art posters (posters as a specific form of prints), see 769.5
.68	Calendars, postcards, greeting and business cards
.682	Calendars
.683	Postcards
	Class government-issued postcards without illustration in 769.566
.684	Greeting cards
.685	Business cards (Trade cards)
.69	Labels and match covers
.692	Labels
.694	Match covers
.7	**Silhouettes**
	Class cut-out silhouettes in 736.984

.9 **Collections of drawings**

Regardless of medium or process

Class here exhibition catalogs

Preliminary drawings are classed with the finished work unless they are treated as works of art in their own right

Class collections by artists devoted to special applications in 741.5–741.7; class collections of drawings by subject not from a specific period or place in 743.9

.92 Specific periods

Not limited geographically

.921 Earliest times to 499

.922 500–1399

.923 1400–1799

.924 1800–

.924 1 1800–1899

.924 2 1900–1999

.93–.99 Specific continents, countries, localities

Add to base number 741.9 notation 3–9 from Table 2, e.g., collections of drawings from London 741.9421
Collections by individual artists are classed at country level only. Notation 074 from Table 1 for collections is not added. For example, a collection of an individual artist from London is classed in 741.942 (*not* 741.9421, 741.942074421)

742 **Perspective in drawing**

Theory, principles, methods

Class perspective in special applications in 741.5–741.7; class perspective in drawing specific subjects in 743.4–743.8; class comprehensive works on perspective in the arts in 701.82

743 ***Drawing and drawings by subject**

Standard subdivisions are added for drawing and drawings by subject, for drawing alone

.4 ***Drawing human figures**

Class here nudes

For drawing draped figures, see 743.5

.42 *Portraiture

Class portraiture of specific kinds of persons in 743.43–743.45

*Do not use notation 092 from Table 1 for artists; class in 741.092

> 743.43–743.45 Specific kinds of persons

Class anatomy of specific kinds of persons in 743.49; class comprehensive works in 743.4

.43 *Men

.44 *Women

.45 *Children

.46 *Bones (Skeletal system)

.47 *Muscles (Muscular system)

.49 *Anatomy for artists

Including parts and regions of body, e.g., head, abdomen, hands

For bones, see 743.46; for muscles, see 743.47

.5 ***Drawing draperies and draped figures**

For fashion drawing, see 741.672

.6 ***Drawing animals**

Add to base number 743.6 the numbers following 59 in 592–599, e.g., drawing birds 743.68; however, for artists, see 741.092

.7 ***Drawing plants**

Including flowers, fruits

.8 **Drawing other subjects**

Add to base number 743.8 the numbers following 704.94 in 704.943–704.949, e.g., landscapes 743.836; however, for artists, see 741.092

.9 **Collections of drawings by subject (Iconography)**

Not limited by period or by place of production

Add to base number 743.9 the numbers following 704.94 in 704.942–704.949, e.g., collections of drawings of buildings 743.94

Class collections of drawings by subject from a specific period or place in 741.92–741.99

[744] **[Unassigned]**

Most recently used in Edition 17

745 **Decorative arts**

Class here folk art

For a decorative art not provided for here, see the art in 736–739, 746–749, e.g., interior decoration 747

*Do not use notation 092 from Table 1 for artists; class in 741.092

.1   **Antiques**

> *For a specific kind of antique, see the kind, e.g., brasses 739.52, passenger automobiles 629.222*
>
> *See Manual at 745.1*

.102 8   Techniques, procedures, apparatus, equipment, materials

.102 87   Techniques of reproduction, execution, identification

> Do not use for testing and measurement; class in 745.1028

.102 872   Reproductions and copies

.102 874   Forgeries and alterations

.102 88   Maintenance and repair

> Including expertizing
>
> Class here routine maintenance and repair [*formerly* 745.10289]; conservation, preservation, restoration
>
> Class identification of reproductions, copies, forgeries, alterations in 745.10287

.102 89   Safety measures

> Routine maintenance and repair relocated to 745.10288

.2   **Industrial art and design**

> Creative design of mass-produced commodities
>
> Standard subdivisions are added for either or both topics in heading
>
> *For design of a specific commodity, see the commodity, e.g., automobiles 629.231*

.4   **Pure and applied design and decoration**

> Standard subdivisions are added for any or all topics in heading
>
> Class here design source books
>
> *For industrial design, see 745.2. For design in a specific art form, see the form, e.g., design in architecture 729*

[.409]	Historical, geographic, persons treatment
	Do not use; class in 745.44
(.409 2)	Persons treatment
	(Optional number; prefer 745.4492)
.44	Historical, geographic, persons treatment

>   745.441–745.445   Periods of development

Class here schools and styles not limited by country or locality

Class comprehensive works in 745.44

.441	Nonliterate peoples, and earliest times to 499

Including paleolithic art

Class here design and decoration by nonliterate peoples regardless of time or place

.442	500–1399

Including Byzantine, early Christian, Gothic, Romanesque styles

.443	1400–1799

Including baroque, Renaissance, rococo styles

.444	1800–1999
.444 1	1800–1899

Including art nouveau, classical revival, romantic styles

.444 2	1900–1999
.445	2000–2099
.449	Geographic and persons treatment

Add to base number 745.449 notation 1–9 from Table 2, e.g., artists 745.4492
   (Option: Class persons treatment in 745.4092)

Class design and decoration by nonliterate peoples regardless of place in 745.441

.5 **Handicrafts**

Creative work done by hand with aid of simple tools or machines

Including work in bread dough

Class home (amateur) workshops in 684.08; class interdisciplinary works on handicrafts in 680

For decorative coloring, see 745.7; for floral arts, see 745.92

See Manual at 680 vs. 745.5

> 745.51–745.58 Specific materials

Class specific objects made from specific materials in 745.59; class comprehensive works in 745.5

For textile handicrafts, see 746; for glass handicrafts, see 748

.51 Woods

Including bamboo; ornamental woodwork

Class treen (woodenware) in 674.88; class woodworking in 684.08; class cabinetmaking (wooden furniture making) in 684.104; class artistic aspects of furniture in 749

For ornamental woodwork in furniture, see 749.5

.512 Marquetry

Class here inlaying

.513 Scrollwork

.53 Leathers and furs

Class construction of clothing in 646.4

.531 Leathers

.537 Furs

.54 Papers

Including endpapers, paper boxes, tissue papers, wallpapers; gift wrapping, quilling

Class paper cutting and folding in 736.98

.542 Papier-mâché

Class papier-mâché used in sculpture in 731.2

.546 Decoupage

Including potichomania

.55	Shells
.56	Metals

         Class art metalwork in 739

.57	Rubber and plastics
.572	Plastics
.58	Beads, found and other objects

         Class specific objects made from other objects in 745.59

.582	Beads

         For bead embroidery, see 746.5

.584	Found objects

         Including cattails, hosiery, scrap, stones

.59	Making specific objects

         Class here handicrafts in composite materials

.592	Toys, models, miniatures, related objects

         Standard subdivisions are added for toys, models, miniatures, related objects together; for toys alone

         Including paper airplanes

         Class interdisciplinary works on mass-produced and handcrafted toys in 688.72

>   745.592 2–745.592 4   Toys and related objects

         Class comprehensive works in 745.592

         For toy soldiers, see 745.59282

.592 2	Dolls, puppets, marionettes

         Class here clothing

.592 21	Dolls

         Class porcelain dolls in 738.83

.592 24	Puppets and marionettes
.592 3	Dollhouses and furniture

         Standard subdivisions are added for either or both topics in heading

         See also 749.0228 for miniature furniture

.592 4	Soft toys

         Class stuffed dolls in 745.59221

.592 43	Teddy bears
.592 8	Models and miniatures

Standard subdivisions are added for either or both topics in heading

Including ships in bottles

Class here interdisciplinary works on handcrafted models and miniatures

Class models and miniatures produced by assembly-line or mechanized manufacturing, interdisciplinary works on models and miniatures in 688.1. Class miniature and model educational exhibits, models for technical and professional use with the subject illustrated, e.g., handcrafted miniature anthropological exhibits 599.9074

See Manual at 745.5928

.592 82	Military models and miniatures

Standard subdivisions are added for either or both topics in heading

Including toy soldiers

.593	Useful objects

For toys, models, miniatures, related objects, see 745.592

.593 2	Lampshades
.593 3	Candles and candlesticks
.593 32	Candles
.593 4	Snuffboxes
.593 6	Decoys

Class carved birds not used for hunting in 730

.594	Decorative objects
.594 1	Objects for special occasions

Including holidays, weddings

Class here greeting cards

For Easter eggs, see 745.5944

.594 12	Christmas
.594 2	Costume jewelry

Class interdisciplinary works on costume jewelry in 391.7; class interdisciplinary works on making costume jewelry in 688.2; class interdisciplinary works on making jewelry in 739.27

.594 3	Artificial flowers

Class arrangement of artificial flowers in 745.92

.594 4	Egg decorating
	Including Easter eggs

.6 Calligraphy, heraldic design, illumination

.61 Calligraphy

Class here artistic, decorative lettering

Class penmanship in 652.1; class typography in 686.22

.619 Styles

.619 7 Latin (Western) styles

.619 74 Carolingian calligraphy

.619 75 Black-letter and Gothic calligraphy

.619 77 Italic calligraphy

.619 78 Roman calligraphy

.619 8 Greek calligraphy

.619 9 Other styles

Add to base number 745.6199 the numbers following —9 in notation 91–99 from Table 6, e.g., Chinese calligraphy 745.619951

.66 Heraldic design

.67 Illumination of manuscripts and books

Standard subdivisions are added for either or both topics in heading

Class here facsimiles of manuscripts reproduced for their illuminations

Class development, description, critical appraisal of manuscripts in 091; class development, description, critical appraisal of illustrated books in 096.1

See also 741.64 for book illustration

.674 Illuminated manuscripts and books by language

Add to base number 745.674 notation 1–9 from Table 6, e.g., illuminated manuscripts in Byzantine Greek 745.67487; however, for illuminated manuscripts in Latin, see 745.67094

Class illuminated manuscripts and books in specific languages produced in specific countries and localities in 745.67093–745.67099

.7 Decorative coloring

Class printing, painting, dyeing textiles in 746.6

.72 Painting and lacquering

.723 Painting

Including rosemaling, tolecraft

.726   Lacquering

Class here japanning

.73   Stenciling

.74   Decalcomania

.75   Gilding

Class gilding as an aspect of bookbinding in 686.36; class gilding as an aspect of illumination of manuscripts and books in 745.67

.8   **Cycloramas, dioramas, panoramas**

.9   **Other decorative arts**

.92   Floral arts

Flower arrangement: selection and arrangement of plant materials and appropriate accessories

Class here arrangement of artificial flowers, three-dimensional arrangements

Class making artificial flowers in 745.5943; class potted plants as interior decorations in 747.98

>   745.922–745.925   Three-dimensional arrangements with specific materials

Class arrangements with specific materials for special occasions in 745.926; class comprehensive works in 745.92

.922   Flower arrangements in containers

.922 4   Occidental compositions

.922 5   Oriental compositions

.922 51   Chinese flower arrangements

.922 52   Japanese flower arrangements

.923   Flower arrangements without containers

Including boutonnieres, corsages, set floral pieces

.924   Fruit and vegetable arrangements

Including carving of vegetables to produce artificial flowers

.925   Arrangements with other plant materials

Including driftwood, pods and cones, dried and gilded grasses and leaves

.926   Three-dimensional arrangements for special occasions

Including arrangements for church services, funerals, holidays, weddings

.928 Two-dimensional arrangements

Use of seeds and other dried plant materials in pictures, hangings, trays, for other decorative purposes

746 Textile arts

Class here textile handicrafts

Add to each subdivision identified by * as follows:

028 Auxiliary techniques and procedures; apparatus, equipment, materials

0288 Maintenance and repair
Including expertizing
Class here conservation, preservation, restoration [*formerly* 0488]
Class identification of reproductions, copies, forgeries, alterations in 048

04 Special topics
041 Patterns
Class patterns for specific products in 043
042 Stitches
Class stitches for specific products in 043
043 Products
Use only with base numbers for techniques
For laces and related fabrics, see 746.2; for rugs and carpets, see 746.7
0432 Costume [*formerly* 746.92]
Including sweaters
0433 Pictures, hangings, tapestries [*formerly* 746.3]
Standard subdivisions are added for any or all topics in heading
0434–0438 Interior furnishings [*formerly* 746.94–746.98]
Add to base number 043 the numbers following 746.9 in 746.94–746.98, e.g., bedclothing 0437
048 Reproductions, copies, forgeries, alterations
Execution and identification
[0487] Reproductions, copies, forgeries, alterations
Notation discontinued; class in 048
[0488] Conservation, preservation, restoration
Relocated to 0288

Class domestic sewing and related operations in 646.2. Class a specific textile product not provided for here with the product, e.g., stuffed animals 745.5924

SUMMARY

746.04	**Specific materials**
.1	**Yarn preparation and weaving**
.2	**Laces and related fabrics**
.3	**Pictures, hangings, tapestries**
.4	**Needlework and handwork**
.5	**Bead embroidery**
.6	**Printing, painting, dyeing**
.7	**Rugs**
.9	**Other textile products**

.04   Specific materials

Add to base number 746.04 the numbers following 677 in 677.1–677.7, e.g., silk 746.0439, string art 746.0471

Class products in a specific material with the product, e.g., string pictures 746.3

> **746.1–746.9 Products and processes**

Unless other instructions are given, observe the following table of preference, e.g., embroidered rugs 746.74 (*not* 746.44):

Laces and related fabrics	746.2
Rugs	746.7
Yarn preparation and weaving	746.1
Needlework and handwork	746.4
Bead embroidery	746.5
Printing, painting, dyeing	746.6
Pictures, hangings, tapestries	746.3
Other textile products	746.9

Class home sewing and clothing in 646; class textile manufacturing in 677; class comprehensive works in 746

.1   Yarn preparation and weaving

.11   Carding and combing

.12   Spinning, twisting, reeling

Standard subdivisions are added for spinning, twisting, reeling together; for spinning alone

.13   Dyeing

.14   *Weaving

Including card weaving

For weaving unaltered vegetable fibers, see 746.41; for nonloom weaving, see 746.42

---

*Add as instructed under 746

.2	**Laces and related fabrics**
.22	*Laces

> Including crocheted, darned laces
>
> *For tatting, see 746.436*

.222	*Bobbin laces
.224	*Needlepoint laces
.226	*Knitted laces
.27	Passementerie

> Including braids, cords, fringes

.3	***Pictures, hangings, tapestries**

> Subdivisions are added for any or all topics in heading
>
> Pictures, hangings, tapestries made by a specific process relocated to the process, plus notation 0433 from table under 746, e.g., needlepoint pictures 746.4420433

[.309]	Historical, geographic, persons treatment

> Do not use; class in 746.39

(.309 2)	Persons treatment

> (Optional number; prefer 746.392)

.39	Historical, geographic, persons treatment

> Add to base number 746.39 notation 001–9 from Table 2, e.g., artists 746.392
> (Option: Class persons treatment in 746.3092)

.4	**Needlework and handwork**

> Standard subdivisions are added for either or both topics in heading

.41	Weaving, braiding, matting unaltered vegetable fibers

> Including raffia work, rushwork

.412	Basketry
.42	Nonloom weaving and related techniques

> Including braiding, plaiting, twining
>
> Class nonloom weaving of unaltered vegetable fibers in 746.41
>
> *For card weaving, see 746.14*

.422	*Knotting
.422 2	*Macramé

---

*Add as instructed under 746

.422 4	*Netting

Including knotless netting, sprang

.43	*Knitting, crocheting, tatting
.432	*Knitting

Class comprehensive works on knitting and crocheting in 746.43

.434	*Crocheting
.436	*Tatting
.44	*Embroidery

Including couching, cutwork, drawn work, hardanger, smocking

.440 28	Auxiliary techniques and procedures; apparatus, equipment, materials

Including machine embroidery

.442	*Canvas embroidery and needlepoint

Including bargello

Subdivisions are added for either or both topics in heading

Class cross-stitch and counted thread embroidery in 746.443

.443	*Cross-stitch

Class here counted thread embroidery

.445	*Appliqué
.446	*Crewelwork
.46	*Patchwork and quilting

Class here quilts

Subdivisions are added for either or both topics in heading

.460 437	Bedclothing

Number built according to instructions under 746

Class quilts in 746.46

.5	***Bead embroidery**
.6	***Printing, painting, dyeing**

Including hand decoration, stenciling

.62	*Printing

Block and silk-screen

.66	*Resist-dyeing

*Add as instructed under 746

.662	*Batik	
.664	*Tie-dyeing	

.7　　　*Rugs

　　　　　Class here carpets

[.709]　　　　　Historical, geographic, persons treatment

　　　　　Do not use; class in 746.79

(.709 2)　　　　　Persons treatment

　　　　　(Optional number; prefer 746.792)

.72　　　*Woven rugs

　　　　　Class here Navaho rugs; Jacquard, plain, tapestry, twill weaves

　　　　　For pile rugs, see 746.75

.73　　　*Crocheted, knitted, braided rugs

.74　　　*Hooked and embroidered rugs

.75　　　Pile rugs

.750 95　　　　　Asian pile rugs

　　　　　Class here Oriental-style rugs

　　　　　For styles from Caucasus region, see 746.759

[.750 951–.750 958]　　　　　Asian countries and localities other than southeast Asia

　　　　　Do not use; class in 746.751–746.758

>　　　746.751–746.759　Oriental-style rugs

　　　Class comprehensive works in 746.75095

.751–.758　　　Styles from specific Asian countries and localities other than southeast Asia

　　　　　Add to base number 746.75 the numbers following —5 in notation 51–58 from Table 2, e.g., Chinese rugs 746.751

　　　　　See also 746.750959 for styles from southeast Asia

.759　　　Styles from Caucasus region

.79　　　Historical, geographic, persons treatment

　　　　　Add to base number 746.79 notation 001–9 from Table 2, e.g., artists 746.792
　　　　　(Option: Class persons treatment in 746.7092)

.9　　　Other textile products

---

*Add as instructed under 746

.92   Costume

Class here fashion design

Costume made by a specific process relocated to the process, plus notation 0432 from table under 746, e.g., crocheted sweaters 746.4340432

Class interdisciplinary works on clothing in 391; class interdisciplinary works on clothing construction in 646.4

See Manual at 391 vs. 646.3, 746.92

>   746.94–746.98   Other interior furnishings

Other interior furnishings made by a specific process relocated to the process, plus notation 0434–0438 from table under 746, e.g., crocheted afghans 746.4340437

Class comprehensive works in 746.9

.94   *Draperies

Class here curtains

.95   *Furniture covers

Class here antimacassars, kneelers, slipcovers, upholstery

.96   *Table linens

Class here doilies, mats, napkins (serviettes), scarves, tablecloths; fair linens

.97   *Bedclothing

Class here bedspreads, blankets; sheets, pillowcases

For afghans, see 746.430437; for quilts, see 746.46

.98   *Towels

Class here toweling

747   Interior decoration

Design and decorative treatment of interior furnishings

Class here interior decoration of residential buildings

Class interior design in 729; class textile arts and handicrafts in 746; class interior decoration of specific types of residential buildings in 747.88

For furniture and accessories, see 749

[.09]   Historical, geographic, persons treatment

Do not use; class in 747.2

(.092)   Persons treatment

(Optional number; prefer 747.2)

---

*Add as instructed under 746

.1   **Decoration under specific limitations**

Including decorating on a budget

Class a specific aspect of decoration under limitations with the aspect, e.g., decorating dining rooms on a budget 747.76

.2   **Historical, geographic, persons treatment**

Class here artists
(Option: Class persons treatment in 747.092)

>   747.201–747.205   Periods of development

Class here schools and styles not limited by country or locality

Class comprehensive works in 747.2

.201   Earliest times to 499

.202   500–1399

.203   1400–1799

.203 4   1400–1499

Class here Renaissance period

For Renaissance decoration of an earlier or later period, see the specific period, e.g., interior decoration in the 1500s 747.2035

.203 5   1500–1599

.203 6   1600–1699

.203 7   1700–1799

.204   1800–1999

.204 8   1800–1899

.204 9   1900–1999

Add to base number 747.2049 the numbers following —0904 in notation 09041–09049 from Table 1, e.g., interior decoration in the 1970s 747.20497

.205   2000–2099

.21–.29   Geographic treatment

Add to base number 747.2 the numbers following 708 in 708.1–708.9, e.g., interior decoration and artists in Islamic areas 747.2917671

Individual artists are classed in notation at country level only. Standard subdivisions —074, —075, and —092 from Table 1 are not added for individual artists, e.g., an exhibition of the work of a Canadian, collecting the person's works, and a biography of the artist 747.211 (*not* 747.211074, 747.211075, or 747.211092, respectively)

>   **747.3–747.4   Decoration of specific elements**

Class decoration of specific elements in specific rooms of residential buildings in 747.7; class decoration of specific elements in specific types of buildings in 747.8; class specific decorations of specific elements in 747.9; class comprehensive works in 747

.3   **Ceilings, walls, doors, windows**

Including decorative hangings, painting, paneling, woodwork

Class here textile wall coverings, wallpapers

For draperies, see 747.5

.4   **Floors**

For rugs and carpets, see 747.5

.5   **Draperies, upholstery, rugs and carpets**

.7   **Decoration of specific rooms of residential buildings**

Class specific decorations regardless of room in 747.9

.73   Studies

Class here home libraries

.75   Living rooms, drawing rooms, parlors

Standard subdivisions are added for any or all topics in heading

.76   Dining rooms

.77   Bedrooms

Class here nurseries

.78   Bathrooms

Including powder rooms

.79   Other rooms

.791   Recreation rooms

Class here family rooms

.797   Kitchens

.8   **Decoration of specific types of buildings**

Class specific decorations regardless of type of building in 747.9

.85–.87   Decoration of public, religious, educational, research buildings

Add to base number 747.8 the numbers following 72 in 725–727, e.g., decoration of theaters 747.85822

.88   Decoration of specific types of residential buildings

> Add to base number 747.88 the numbers following 728 in 728.1–728.9, e.g., decoration of hotels 747.885

> Class decoration of residential buildings of institutions in 747.85–747.87; class comprehensive works on decoration of residential buildings in 747

> *For decoration of specific rooms of residential buildings, see 747.7*

.9   Specific decorations

> Unless other instructions are given, observe the following table of preference, e.g., decorative lighting for Christmas 747.92 (*not* 747.93):

Decorating with houseplants	747.98
Decorative lighting	747.92
Decorating with color	747.94
Decorations for specific occasions	747.93

> *See also 747.5 for draperies, upholstery, rugs and carpets*

.92   Decorative lighting

.93   Decorations for specific occasions

> Including holidays, parties, weddings

.94   Decorating with color

.98   Decorating with houseplants

748   Glass

.092   Persons treatment

> Class here glassmakers

> Class works about "glassmakers" when referring only to makers of glassware in 748.29

.2   Glassware

> Class here blown, cast, decorated, fashioned, molded, pressed glassware

> Class stained glass in 748.5

> *For methods of decoration, see 748.6; for specific articles, see 748.8*

.202 8   Techniques, procedures, apparatus, equipment, materials

.202 82   Glassblowing

.202 86   Bottle and jar cutting

> Do not use for waste technology; class in 748.2028

> Standard subdivisions are added for either or both topics in heading

.202 87   Reproductions, copies, forgeries, alterations

> Do not use for testing and measurement; class in 748.2028

> Execution and identification

.202 88   Maintenance and repair

> Including expertizing

> Class here conservation, preservation, restoration

> Class identification of reproductions, copies, forgeries, alterations in 748.20287

[.209]   Historical, geographic, persons treatment

> Do not use; class in 748.29

(.209 2)   Persons treatment

> (Optional number; prefer 748.29)

.29   Historical, geographic, persons treatment

> Class here glassware makers
> (Option: Class persons treatment in 748.2092)

.290 1–.290 5   Periods of development

> Class here schools and styles not limited by country or locality

> Add to base number 748.290 the numbers following 747.20 in 747.201–747.205, e.g., glassware of 1700–1799 748.29037

.291–.299   Geographic treatment

> Add to base number 748.29 the numbers following 708 in 708.1–708.9, e.g., glassware and glassmakers of Pennsylvania 748.29148

> Individual glassmakers are classed in notation at country level only. Standard subdivisions —074, —075, and —092 from Table 1 are not added for individual glassmakers, e.g., an exhibition of the work of a Canadian glassmaker, collecting the person's works, and a biography of the glassmaker 748.2911 (*not* 748.2911074, 748.2911075, or 748.2911092, respectively)

.5   Stained, painted, leaded, mosaic glass

> Standard subdivisions are added for stained, painted, leaded, mosaic glass together; for stained glass alone; for painted glass alone; for leaded glass alone

> Class comprehensive works on mosaics in 738.5

> *For specific articles, see 748.8*

.502 8   Techniques, procedures, apparatus, equipment, materials

.502 82   Glass painting and staining

.502 84	Leaded glass craft
	Do not use for apparatus, equipment, materials of stained, painted, leaded, mosaic glass together; class in 748.5028
.502 85	Mosaic glass craft
	Do not use for data processing; class in 748.5028
.502 88	Maintenance and repair
	Class here routine maintenance and repair [*formerly* 748.50289]; conservation, preservation, restoration
.502 89	Safety measures
	Routine maintenance and repair relocated to 748.50288
[.509]	Historical, geographic, persons treatment
	Do not use; class in 748.59
(.509 2)	Persons treatment
	(Optional number; prefer 748.59)
.59	Historical, geographic, persons treatment
	Class here artists (Option: Class persons treatment in 748.5092)
.590 1–.590 5	Periods of development
	Class here schools and styles not limited by country or locality
	Add to base number 748.590 the numbers following 747.20 in 747.201–747.205, e.g., 500–1399 748.5902
.591–.599	Geographic treatment
	Add to base number 748.59 the numbers following 708 in 708.1–708.9, e.g., stained glass of Chartres 748.59451
	Individual artists are classed in notation at country level only. Standard subdivisions —074, —075, and —092 from Table 1 are not added for individual artists, e.g., an exhibition of the work of a Canadian, collecting the person's works, and a biography of the artist 748.5911, *not* 748.5911074, 748.5911075, or 748.5911092, respectively
.6	**Methods of decoration**
	Including cutting, enameling, sandblasting
	Class methods of decoration of specific articles in 748.8
	For painted glass, see 748.5
[.609 2]	Persons treatment
	Do not use; class in 748.29

.62	Engraving	
.63	Etching	
.8	**Specific articles**	

> Including mirrors, ornaments

> Class mirrors as furniture in 749.3; class glass lamps and lighting fixtures in 749.63

.82   Bottles

> Bottles of artistic interest regardless of use

> Class manufacture of glass bottles in 666.192

.83   Tableware

> Class here drinking glasses

.84   Paperweights

.85   Glass beads

749   Furniture and accessories

> Standard subdivisions are added for furniture and accessories together, for furniture alone

> *For upholstery, see 747.5*

[.09]   Historical, geographic, persons treatment

> Do not use; class in 749.2

(.092)   Persons treatment

> (Optional number; prefer 749.2)

.1   **Antique furniture**

> Class specific kinds of antique furniture in 749.3

.102 8   Auxiliary techniques and procedures; apparatus, equipment, materials

.102 87   Reproductions, copies, forgeries, alterations

> Do not use for testing and measurement; class in 749.1028

> Execution and identification

.102 88   Maintenance and repair

> Including expertizing

> Class here routine maintenance and repair [*formerly* 749.10289], conservation, preservation, restoration

> Class identification of reproductions, copies, forgeries, alterations in 749.10287

.102 89	Safety measures

Routine maintenance and repair relocated to 749.10288

[.109]	Historical, geographic, persons treatment

Do not use; class in 749.2

.2 Historical, geographic, persons treatment

Class here antiques and reproductions, furniture makers (Option: Class persons treatment in 749.092)

.201–.205 Periods of development

Class here schools and styles not limited by country or locality

Add to base number 749.20 the numbers following 747.20 in 747.201–747.205, e.g., Renaissance period 749.2034

.21–.29 Geographic treatment

Add to base number 749.2 the numbers following 708 in 708.1–708.9, e.g., English furniture and furniture makers 749.22

Individual furniture makers are classed in notation at country level only. Standard subdivisions —074, —075, and —092 from Table 1 are not added for individual furniture makers, e.g., an exhibition of the work of a Canadian furniture maker, collecting the person's works, and a biography of the furniture maker 749.211 (*not* 749.211074, 749.211075, or 749.211092, respectively)

.3 Specific kinds of furniture

Including beds, cabinets, chests, clockcases, desks, mirrors, screens, tables

Class outdoor furniture in 749.8

For built-in furniture, see 749.4; for heating and lighting fixtures and furniture, see 749.6; for picture frames, see 749.7

[.301–.308]	Standard subdivisions

Do not use; class in 749.01–749.08

[.309]	Historic, geographic, persons treatment

Do not use; class in 749.2

.32 Chairs

.4 Built-in furniture

Class built-in church furniture in architectural design in 726.529

For heating and lighting fixtures and furniture, see 749.6

.5   **Ornamental woodwork in furniture**

> Including inlay trim, lacquer work, marquetry, scrollwork

> Class ornamental woodwork in a specific kind of furniture with the kind, e.g., picture frames 749.7

.6   **Heating and lighting fixtures and furniture**

.62   Heating

> Including mantels, fireplace and inglenook fixtures and furniture

.63   Lighting

> Including chandeliers, lamps, sconces

> Class built-in church lighting fixtures in architectural design in 726.5298

.7   **Picture frames**

> Including shadow boxes

> Class here picture framing

.8   **Outdoor furniture**

> Class furniture used both indoors and outdoors in 749.3

750   Painting and paintings

> Class here comprehensive works on painting and drawing

> Unless other instructions are given, observe the following table of preference, e.g., an individual Canadian painter of landscapes 759.11 (*not* 758.10971), landscape painting in Canada 758.10971 (*not* 759.11):

Individual painters and their work	759.1–759.9
Techniques, procedures, apparatus, equipment, materials	751.2–751.6
Iconography	753–758
Specific forms	751.7
Geographic treatment	759.1–759.9
Periods of development	759.01–759.07
Color	752

> Class comprehensive works on graphic arts, two-dimensional art in 760. Class painting in a specific decorative art with the art, e.g., illumination of manuscripts and books 745.67

> *For drawing and drawings, see 741*

SUMMARY

750.1–.8	Standard subdivisions
751	Techniques, procedures, apparatus, equipment, materials, forms
752	Color
753	Symbolism, allegory, mythology, legend
754	Genre paintings
755	Religion
757	Human figures
758	Other subjects
759	Historical, geographic, persons treatment

.1   **Philosophy and theory**

.11   Appreciative aspects

> Do not use for systems; class in 750.1

> Class psychological principles in 750.19

.117   Aesthetics

.118   Criticism and appreciation

> Including theory, technique, history

> Class works of critical appraisal in 759

.18   Inherent features

> Including composition, decorative values, form, light, movement, perspective, space, style, symmetry, vision

> *For color, see 752*

.28   Auxiliary techniques and procedures [*formerly* 751.4]

> *For comprehensive works on basic and auxiliary techniques and procedures, see 751.4*

[.284]   Apparatus, equipment, materials

> Do not use for materials; class in 751.2. Do not use for apparatus and equipment; class in 751.3

[.288]   Maintenance and repair

> Do not use; class in 751.6

.289   Safety measures [*formerly* 751.67]

[.9]   **Historical, geographic, persons treatment**

> Do not use; class in 759

(.92)   Persons treatment

> (Optional number; prefer 759)

751 *Techniques, procedures, apparatus, equipment, materials, forms

.2 *Materials

Including coatings, fixatives, mediums, pigments, surfaces

Class use of materials in specific techniques in 751.4

.3 *Apparatus, equipment, artists' models

Class use of apparatus and equipment in specific techniques in 751.4

.4 *Techniques and procedures

Class here comprehensive works on basic and auxiliary techniques and procedures

Auxiliary techniques and procedures relocated to 750.28, e.g., data processing 750.285

For techniques of reproduction, see 751.5; for maintenance and repair, see 751.6

.42 *Use of water-soluble mediums

For tempera painting, see 751.43

.422 *Watercolor painting

Including casein painting, gouache

Class ink painting in color in 751.425

.422 4 Watercolor painting techniques by subject

Add to base number 751.4224 the numbers following 704.94 in 704.942–704.949, e.g., techniques of landscape painting in watercolor 751.422436; however, for individual painters, see 759.1–759.9

.425 *Ink painting

.425 1 *Chinese ink painting

.425 14 Chinese ink painting techniques by subject

Add to base number 751.42514 the numbers following 704.94 in 704.942–704.949, e.g., techniques of landscape painting in Chinese ink painting 751.4251436; however, for individual painters, see 759.1–759.9

.425 2 *Japanese ink painting

.426 *Acrylic painting

.43 *Tempera painting

.44 *Fresco painting

*Do not use notation 092 from Table 1 for individual painters; class in 759.1–759.9

.45 *Oil painting

.454 Oil painting techniques by subject

> Add to base number 751.454 the numbers following 704.94 in 704.942–704.949, e.g., techniques of landscape painting in oils 751.45436; however, for individual painters, see 759.1–759.9

.46 *Encaustic (Wax) painting

.49 *Other methods

> Including finger, polymer, roller (brayer), sand painting

> *For mosaic painting, see 738.5*

.493 *Collage

> With painting as the basic technique

.494 *Airbrush

.5 *Techniques of reproduction

> Execution, identification, determination of authenticity of reproductions, copies, forgeries, alterations

> *For printmaking and prints, see 760*

.58 *Forgeries and alterations

.6 *Maintenance and repair

.62 *Conservation, preservation, restoration

> Standard subdivisions are added for any or all topics in heading

> Including expertizing

> Class identification of reproductions, copies, forgeries, alterations in 751.5

[.67] Routine maintenance and repair and safety measures

> Use of this number for routine maintenance and repair discontinued; class in 751.6

> Safety measures relocated to 750.289

.7 *Specific forms

.73 *Murals and frescoes

> Class here painted graffiti, street art

.74 *Panoramas, cycloramas, dioramas

> Standard subdivisions are added for any or all topics in heading

.75 *Scene paintings

> Including theatrical scenery

---

*Do not use notation 092 from Table 1 for individual painters; class in 759.1–759.9

.76   *Glass underpainting

            Class glass underpainting as a technique of glass decoration in 748.6

.77   *Miniatures

            Class miniatures done as illuminations in manuscripts and books in 745.67

752   *Color

            Class technology of color in 667; class comprehensive works on color in the fine
            and decorative arts in 701.85

> ### 753–758 Iconography

            Class here development, description, critical appraisal, works regardless of
            form

            Class comprehensive works in 750

            See Manual at 753–758

753   *Symbolism, allegory, mythology, legend

.6   *Symbolism and allegory

            Standard subdivisions are added for either or both topics in heading

            For religious symbolism, see 755

.7   *Mythology and legend

            Class religious mythology in 755

754   *Genre paintings

755   *Religion

            Class here religious symbolism

            Add to base number 755 the numbers following 704.948 in 704.9482–704.9489,
            e.g., paintings of Holy Family 755.56; however, for individual painters, see
            759.1–759.9

[756]   [Unassigned]

            Most recently used in Edition 19

---

*Do not use notation 092 from Table 1 for individual painters; class in 759.1–759.9

757   *Human figures

Not provided for in 753–755, 758

Class here portraits

Unless other instructions are given, observe the following table of preference, e.g., groups of nude women 757.4 (*not* 757.22 or 757.6):

Erotica	757.8
Miniature portraits	757.7
Specific kinds of persons	757.3–757.5
Groups of figures	757.6
Human figures according to attire	757.2

.2   ***Human figures according to attire**

.22   *Nudes

.23   *Draped figures

> ## 757.3–757.5 Specific kinds of persons

Class here portraits of individuals

Class comprehensive works in 757

.3   ***Men**

.4   ***Women**

.5   ***Children**

.6   ***Groups of figures**

.7   ***Miniature portraits**

.8   ***Erotica**

Including pornography

758   Other subjects

.1   ***Landscapes**

Add to base number 758.1 notation 1–9 from Table 2, e.g., landscapes of Utah 758.1792; however, for individual painters, see 759.1–759.9

.2   ***Marine scenes and seascapes**

Standard subdivisions are added for either or both topics in heading

---

*Do not use notation 092 from Table 1 for individual painters; class in 759.1–759.9

.3 ***Animals**

Including hunting scenes

Class hunting scenes in which animals are not the center of interest with the subject, e.g., hunters 757.6

See Manual at 753–758

.4 ***Still life**

.42 *Flowers

.5 ***Plants**

For flowers, see 758.42

See Manual at 753–758

[.6] **Industrial and technical subjects**

Relocated to 758.96

.7 ***Architectural subjects and cityscapes**

Standard subdivisions are added for either or both topics in heading

Add to base number 758.7 notation 1–9 from Table 2, e.g., cityscapes of England 758.742; however, for individual painters, see 759.1–759.9

.9 **Other subjects**

Not provided for elsewhere

Add to base number 758.9 notation 001–999, e.g., paintings of industrial and technical subjects 758.96 [*formerly also* 758.6], of historical events 758.99; however, for individual painters, see 759.1–759.9

759 Historical, geographic, persons treatment

Class here development, description, critical appraisal, works

Class exhibitions of paintings not limited by place, period, or subject in 750.74

(Option: Class person treatment in 750.92)

---

*Do not use notation 092 from Table 1 for individual painters; class in 759.1–759.9

>   759.01–759.07   Periods of development

Class here schools and styles not limited by country or locality, works on one or two periods of European painting

Class works on three or more periods of European painting in 759.94; class comprehensive works in 759. Class schools associated with a specific locality with the locality in 759.1–759.9, e.g., Florentine school of Italian painting 759.551

When classifying works of more than one painter, notation 074 and —075 from Table 1 for Museums, collections, exhibits and Museum activities, respectively, take preference over notation 0922 for Collected persons treatment

.01   *Nonliterate peoples, and earliest times to 499

.011   *Nonliterate peoples

Regardless of time or place

Class paintings of both nonliterate and literate cultures in 759.1–759.9

.011 2   *Paleolithic painting and paintings

Standard subdivisions are added for either or both topics in heading

.011 3   *Rock art (painting and paintings)

.02   *500–1399

Class here medieval painting and paintings

See Manual at 753–758

.021   *500–1199

.021 2   *Early Christian painting and paintings

Standard subdivisions are added for either or both topics in heading

For early Christian painting and paintings before 500, see 759.01

.021 4   *Byzantine painting and paintings

Standard subdivisions are added for either or both topics in heading

For Byzantine painting and paintings before 500, see 759.01

.021 6   *Romanesque painting and paintings

Standard subdivisions are added for either or both topics in heading

.022   *1200–1399

Class here Gothic painting and paintings

For Gothic painting and paintings of an earlier or later period, see the specific period, e.g., 500–1199 759.021

---

*Do not use notation 092 from Table 1 for individual painters; class in 759.1–759.9

.03   *1400–1599

Class here Renaissance painting and paintings

For Renaissance painting and paintings before 1400, see 759.022

.04   *1600–1799

.046   *1600–1699

Class here baroque painting and paintings

For baroque painting and paintings of 1700–1799, see 759.047

.047   *1700–1799

Including rococo painting and paintings

.05   *1800–1899

Add to base number 759.05 the numbers following 709.034 in 709.0341–709.0349, e.g., romanticism in painting 759.052; however, for individual painters, see 759.1–759.9

.06   *1900–1999

Class here modern painting

Add to base number 759.06 the numbers following 709.040 in 709.0401–709.0407, e.g., surrealist painting 759.0663; however, for individual painters, see 759.1–759.9

For 1800–1899, see 759.05; for 2000–2099, see 759.07

.07   *2000–2099

> **759.1–759.9 Geographic treatment**

Individual painters are classed in notation at country level only. Standard subdivisions —074, —075, and —092 from Table 1 are not added for individual painters, e.g., an exhibition of the work of a Canadian painter, collecting the person's works, and a biography of the painter 759.11 (*not* 759.11074, 759.11075, or 759.11092, respectively)

Class painting and paintings of nonliterate peoples in 759.011; class western painting of one or two specific periods in 759.02–759.07; class comprehensive works in 759

(Option: To give local emphasis and a shorter number to painting and paintings of a specific country, use one of the following:

(Option A: Place them first by use of a letter or other symbol for the country, e.g., Burmese painting and paintings 759.B [preceding 759.1]

(Option B: Class them in 759.1; in that case class painting and paintings of North America in 759.97)

---

*Do not use notation 092 from Table 1 for individual painters; class in 759.1–759.9

.1   **North America**

> *For painting and paintings of Middle America, see 759.972*

> (Option: To give local emphasis and a shorter number to painting and paintings of a specific country other than United States and Canada, class them in this number; in that case class painting and paintings of North America in 759.97)

.11   Canada

> Add to base number 759.11 the numbers following —71 in notation 711–719 from Table 2, e.g., painting and paintings of Toronto 759.113541

.13   United States

> Class painting and paintings of specific states in 759.14–759.19

> *See also 759.97295 for painting and paintings of Puerto Rico*

.14–.19   Specific states of United States

> Add to base number 759.1 the numbers following —7 in notation 74–79 from Table 2, e.g., painting and paintings of San Francisco 759.19461

> Class individual painters in 759.13

> *For painting and paintings of Hawaii, see 759.9969*

>   **759.2–759.8   Europe**

> Class comprehensive works in 759.94

> *For countries and localities not provided for here, see the country or locality in 759.949, e.g., painting and paintings of Belgium 759.9493*

.2   **British Isles   England**

> When classifying individual painters, England, Scotland, Wales, and Northern Ireland are considered to be separate countries. Therefore, an English painter is classed in 759.2, a Scottish painter in 759.2911, a Welsh painter in 759.2929, and a Northern Ireland painter in 759.2916

.21–.28   England

> Add to base number 759.2 the numbers following —42 in notation 421–428 from Table 2, e.g., painting and paintings of Manchester 759.2733

.29   Scotland, Ireland, Wales

> Add to base number 759.29 the numbers following —4 in notation 41–42 from Table 2, e.g., painting and paintings of Scotland 759.2911

.3–.8   **Miscellaneous parts of Europe**

> Add to base number 759 the numbers following —4 in notation 43–48 from Table 2, e.g., painting and paintings of France 759.4; however, individual painters from countries of former Soviet Central Asia relocated from 759.7 to 759.9584–759.9587

.9   **Other geographic areas**

.91   Areas, regions, places in general

Add to base number 759.91 the numbers following — 1 in notation 11–19 from Table 2, e.g., Western Hemisphere 759.91812

Individual painters are classed in the notation for their respective countries, e.g., painters from Canada 759.11

.93–.99   Continents, countries, localities

Class here painting and paintings of specific periods, e.g., painting and paintings of 1800–1899 in South America 759.9809034

Add to base number 759.9 notation 3–9 from Table 2, e.g., individual painters from countries of former Soviet Central Asia 759.9584–759.9587 [*formerly* 759.7], comprehensive works on painting and paintings of Europe 759.94, Etruscan painting and paintings 759.9375; however, for individual Hawaiian painters, see 759.13; for individual Siberian painters, see 759.7

Class works on one or two periods of European painting in 759.02–759.07, e.g., painting and paintings of 1800–1899 in Europe 759.05 (*not* 759.9409034); class painting and paintings from parts of Europe in notation 41–48 from Table 2 in 759.2–759.8

760   Graphic arts   Printmaking and prints

Graphic arts: any and all nonplastic representations on flat surfaces, including painting, drawing, prints, and photographs

Including copy art made with photoduplication equipment, rubbings, typewriter art, typographical designs; two-dimensional mixed-media art and composites

Class here two-dimensional art; prints and at least one other of the graphic arts

Class comprehensive works on graphic and plastic arts in 701–709. Class rubbings used for study and research in a specific field with the field, e.g., monumental brasses 739.522

For printing, see 686.2; for drawing and drawings, see 741; for painting and paintings, see 750; for photography and photographs, see 770

See Manual at 700

SUMMARY

760.01–.09	**Standard subdivisions and special topics of graphic arts**
.1–.8	**Standard subdivisions of printmaking and prints**
761	**Relief processes (Block printing)**
763	**Lithographic (Planographic) processes**
764	**Chromolithography and serigraphy**
765	**Metal engraving**
766	**Mezzotinting, aquatinting, related processes**
767	**Etching and drypoint**
769	**Prints**

.01–.03   Standard subdivisions of graphic arts

.04	Special topics of graphic arts
.044	Iconography

> Add to base number 760.044 the numbers following 704.94 in 704.942–704.949, e.g., landscapes in graphic arts 760.04436

.05–.08	Standard subdivisions of graphic arts
.09	Historical, geographic, persons treatment of graphic arts
.090 1–.090 5	Periods of development

> Not limited by country or locality

> Add to base number 760.090 the numbers following 709.0 in 709.01–709.05, e.g., graphic arts of the Renaissance 760.09024

.1   Philosophy and theory of printmaking and prints

.11   Appreciative aspects

> Do not use for systems; class in 760.1

> Class psychological principles in 760.19

.117   Aesthetics

.118   Criticism and appreciation

> Including theory, technique, history

> Class works of critical appraisal in 769.9

.18   Inherent features

> Including color, composition, decorative values, form, light, movement, perspective, space, style, symmetry, vision

.2   Miscellany of printmaking and prints

.28   Techniques, procedures, apparatus, equipment, materials of printmaking and prints

> Class techniques, procedures, apparatus, equipment, materials for making specific kinds of prints in 761–767

.3–.6   Standard subdivisions of printmaking and prints

.7   Education, research, related topics of printmaking and prints

.75   Museum activities and services

> Do not use for collecting; class in 769.12

.8   History and description of printmaking and prints with respect to kinds of persons

[.9]   Historical, geographic, persons treatment of printmaking and prints

> Do not use; class in 769.9

(.92)   Persons treatment

(Optional number; prefer 769.92)

> ### 761–769 Printmaking and prints

Class comprehensive works in 760

> ### 761–767 Printmaking

Fine art of executing a printing block or plate representing a picture or design conceived by the printmaker or copied from another artist's painting or drawing or from a photograph

Techniques, procedures, equipment, materials

Class maintenance and repair in 769.0288; class techniques, procedures, apparatus, equipment, materials of reproduction in 769.1; class techniques, procedures, apparatus, equipment, materials employed by individual printmakers in 769.92; class comprehensive works in 760.28

761   Relief processes (Block printing)

Including raw potato printing, rubber-stamp printing

.2   **Wood engraving**

.3   **Linoleum-block printing**

.8   **Metal engraving**

[762]   [Unassigned]

Most recently used in Edition 14

763   Lithographic (Planographic) processes

For chromolithography, see 764.2

.2   **Surfaces**

.22   Stone lithography

.23   Aluminum lithography

.24   Zinc lithography

764   Chromolithography and serigraphy

.2   **Chromolithography**

.8   **Serigraphy**

Class here silk-screen printing

> ### 765–767 Intaglio processes

Class comprehensive works in 765

765   Metal engraving

Class here comprehensive works on metal relief and metal intaglio processes, on intaglio processes

For metal relief engraving, see 761.8; for mezzotinting and aquatinting, see 766; for etching and drypoint, see 767

.2   **Line engraving**

.5   **Stipple engraving**

.6   **Criblé engraving**

766   Mezzotinting, aquatinting, related processes

.2   **Mezzotinting**

.3   **Aquatinting**

.7   **Composite processes**

Use of two or more processes in a single print

767   Etching and drypoint

.2   **Etching**

.3   **Drypoint**

[768]   [Unassigned]

Most recently used in Edition 14

769   Prints

Works produced using a printing block, screen, or plate

Class here description, critical appraisal, collections regardless of process

.028 8   Maintenance and repair

Class here conservation, preservation, restoration [*formerly* 769.18]

.075   Museum activities and services

Do not use for collecting; class in 769.12

[.09]   Historical, geographic, persons treatment

Do not use; class in 769.9

.1   **Collecting and reproduction of prints**

Class collecting and reproduction of specific forms of prints in 769.5

.12	Collecting prints
.17	Techniques of reproduction
.172	Reproductions and copies
.174	Forgeries and alterations
[.18]	Conservation, preservation, restoration

> Relocated to 769.0288

.4   ***Iconography**

> Add to base number 769.4 the numbers following 704.94 in 704.942–704.949, e.g., portrait prints 769.42; however, for individual printmakers, see 769.92

> Class postage stamps by subject in 769.564; class printmakers regardless of subject in 769.92

.5   ***Forms of prints**

> Including lettering, inscriptions, designs on name cards, diplomas, decorative prints, art posters

> Class prints other than postage stamps on a specific subject regardless of form in 769 4; class comprehensive works on posters in 741.674

.52	*Bookplates
.53	*Paper dolls
.55	Paper money

> Class here counterfeit paper money

[.550 9]	Historical, geographic, persons treatment

> Do not use; class in 769.559

.559	Historical, geographic, persons treatment

> Add to base number 769.559 notation 001–9 from Table 2, e.g., paper money of France 769.55944; however, for individual printmakers, see 769.92

.56	Postage stamps and related devices

> Standard subdivisions are added for postage stamps and related devices together, for postage stamps alone

> Class here philately (study and collecting of stamps)

> Unless other instructions are given, class a subject with aspects in two or more subdivisions of 769.56 in the number coming first, e.g., counterfeit stamps depicting plants 769.562 (*not* 769.56434)

> Class stamps other than for prepayment of postage in 769.57

---

*Do not use notation 092 from Table 1 for individual printmakers; class in 769.92

[.560 9]	Historical, geographic, persons treatment
	Do not use; class in 769.569

.561   *United Nations postage stamps, postal stationery, covers

.562   *Counterfeit postage stamps, covers, cancellations

.563   *Postage stamps commemorating persons and events

.564   Postage stamps depicting various specific subjects (Iconography)

> Add to base number 769.564 the numbers following 704.94 in 704.943–704.949, e.g., postage stamps of plants of the world 769.56434; however, for individual printmakers, see 769.92

> *For stamps commemorating persons and events, see 769.563*

.565   *Covers

.566   *Postal stationery

> Postal-service-issued stationery (e.g., letter sheets, envelopes, postcards) bearing imprinted stamps

> Class illustrated postcards in 741.683

.567   *Postmarks, cancellations, cachets

> Standard subdivisions are added for any or all topics in heading

> *See also 769.562 for counterfeit cancellations*

.569   Historical, geographic, persons treatment

> Add to base number 769.569 notation 001–9 from Table 2, e.g., postage stamps from San Marino 769.5694549; however, for individual printmakers, see 769.92

.57   *Stamps other than for prepayment of postage

> Including Christmas seals, officially sealed labels, ration coupons; postage-due, postal savings, and savings stamps

.572   *Revenue stamps

.9   Historical, geographic, persons treatment of printmaking and prints

> Add to base number 769.9 notation 001–9 from Table 2, e.g., printmaking in England 769.942

> Class the history of a specific process with the process, e.g., history of lithography 763.09

.92   Persons

> Class here engravers, printmakers

> *See Manual at 769.92*

> (Option: Class in 760.92)

---

*Do not use notation 092 from Table 1 for individual printmakers; class in 769.92

770   Photography and photographs

Standard subdivisions are added for photography and photographs together, for photography alone

Class technological photography in 621.367

SUMMARY

770.1–.9	**Standard subdivisions**
771	**Techniques, procedures, apparatus, equipment, materials**
772	**Metallic salt processes**
773	**Pigment processes of printing**
774	**Holography**
778	**Specific fields and special kinds of photography; cinematography and video production; related activities**
779	**Photographs**

.1   Philosophy and theory

.11   Inherent features

Do not use for systems; class in 770.1

Including color, composition, decorative values, form, light, movement, perspective, space, style, symmetry, vision

.2   Miscellany

.23   Photography as a profession, occupation, hobby

.232   Photography as a profession and occupation

.233   Photography as a hobby

.28   Auxiliary techniques and procedures [*formerly* 771]

For comprehensive works on basic and auxiliary techniques and procedures, see 771

[.284]   Apparatus, equipment, materials

Do not use; class in 771

[.286]   Waste technology

Do not use; class in 771.47

.9   Historical, geographic, persons treatment

.92   Persons treatment

Class here photographers regardless of type of photography

Class photographs in 779

For motion picture photographers, see 778.53092; for television and video photographers, see 778.59092

771 *Techniques, procedures, apparatus, equipment, materials

Including techniques of pinhole photography, of photography without camera; comprehensive works on basic and auxiliary techniques and procedures

Class here interdisciplinary works on description, use, manufacture of apparatus, equipment, materials

Auxiliary techniques and procedures relocated to 770.28, e.g., data processing 770.285

Class techniques, procedures, apparatus, equipment, materials used in special processes in 772–774; class techniques, procedures, apparatus, equipment, materials used in specific fields and special kinds of photography in 778

For manufacture of a specific kind of apparatus, equipment, material, see the apparatus, equipment, or material, e.g., cameras 681.418

.1 **Studios, laboratories, darkrooms**

Class laboratory and darkroom practice in 771.4

.2 **Furniture and fittings**

.3 **Cameras and accessories**

Standard subdivisions are added for cameras and accessories, for cameras alone

.31 Specific makes (brands) of cameras

Arrange alphabetically by trade name

.32 Specific types of cameras

Including 35mm single-lens reflex, automatic, instant, large format, miniature

Class specific makes of specific types of cameras in 771.31

.35 Optical parts of cameras

Class optical parts of specific makes of cameras in 771.31

For shutters, see 771.36; for focusing and exposure apparatus, see 771.37

.352 Lenses

.356 Filters

.36 Camera shutters

Class shutters of specific makes of cameras in 771.31

.37 Focusing and exposure apparatus

Including exposure meters, range finders, viewfinders

Class focusing and exposure apparatus of specific makes of cameras in 771.31

*Do not use notation 092 from Table 1 for photographers; class in 770.92

.38   Accessories

                 Including carrying cases, tripods

.4   Darkroom and laboratory practice

                 Standard subdivisions are added for either or both topics in heading

                 For chemical materials, see 771.5

.43   Preparation of negatives

.44   Preparation of positives

                 Including contact printing, enlarging, developing, mounting

.45   Preservation and storage of negatives and transparencies

.46   Preservation and storage of positives

                 For mounting, see 771.44

.47   Waste technology

.49   Developing and printing apparatus

                 Including enlargers, frames, trays, utensils

.5   Chemical materials

.52   Support materials

                 Including backings of cellulose compounds, ceramics, glass, metal, paper

.53   Photosensitive surfaces

.532   Specific photosensitive surfaces

.532 2   Plates

.532 3   Papers

.532 4   Films

.54   Developing and printing supplies

                 Including developing, fixing, intensifying, reducing, toning solutions

---

> **772–774   Special processes**

                 Techniques, procedures, apparatus, equipment, materials

                 Class processing techniques in specific fields and special kinds of photography in 778; class comprehensive works in 771

                 For photomechanical printing techniques, see 686.232

772   *Metallic salt processes

---

*Do not use notation 092 from Table 1 for photographers; class in 770.92

.1 ***Direct positive and printing-out processes**

Early photographic processes

For platinum printing-out process, see 772.3

.12 *Daguerreotype process

.14 *Ferrotype, tintype, wet-collodion processes

.16 *Kallitype processes

.3 ***Platinotype processes**

Including platinum printing-out process

.4 ***Silver processes**

Use of silver halides in principal light-sensitive photographic emulsions

773 *Pigment processes of printing

Early photographic printing processes

.1 ***Carbon and carbro processes**

Including Mariotype, ozotype, ozobrome

.2 ***Powder (Dusting-on) processes**

Including peppertype processes

Class xerography in 686.44

.3 ***Imbibition processes**

.5 ***Gum-bichromate processes**

.6 ***Photoceramic and photoenamel processes**

.7 ***Diazotype processes**

.8 ***Oil processes**

Including bromoil process

774 *Holography

.015 3 Physical principles [*formerly also* 535.4]

[775–777][Unassigned]

Most recently used in Edition 14

---

*Do not use notation 092 from Table 1 for photographers; class in 770.92

778 Specific fields and special kinds of photography; cinematography and video production; related activities

Class here interdisciplinary works on use and manufacture of apparatus, equipment, materials of specific fields and specific kinds of photography

> *For manufacture of a specific kind of apparatus, equipment, materials, see the apparatus, equipment, or material, e.g., cameras 681.418*

SUMMARY

778.2	Photographic projection
.3	Special kinds of photography
.4	Stereoscopic photography and projection
.5	Cinematography, video production, related activities
.6	Color photography
.7	Photography under specific conditions
.8	Special effects and trick photography
.9	Photography of specific subjects

.2 *Photographic projection

Including filmstrips, slides

> *For stereoscopic projection, see 778.4; for motion picture projection, see 778.55*

.3 *Special kinds of photography

Not provided for elsewhere

Including Kirlian photography (high-voltage, high-frequency photopsychography)

Class a special kind of photography in relation to cinematography and video production in 778.5. Class a specific application of photography with the application, e.g., use of photography in astronomy 522.63

> *For technological photography and photo-optics, see 621.367*
>
> *See also 133.892 for parapsychological aspects of Kirlian photography*
>
> *See Manual at 778.3 vs. 621.367*

.31 *Photomicrography

.32 *Photography in terms of focus

.322 *Telephotography

> *For aerial and space photography, see 778.35; for panoramic photography, see 778.36*

.324 *Close-up photography

Including photomacrography

---

*Do not use notation 092 from Table 1 for photographers; class in 770.92

.34   *Infrared photography

   Interdisciplinary works

    For technological infrared photography, see 621.3672

.35   *Aerial and space photography

   Including interpretation

    For photogrammetry, see 526.982

.36   *Panoramic photography

.37   *High-speed photography

   Including use of short-duration electronic flash

   Class use of normal photographic electronic flash (flashbulb photography) in 778.72

.4   ***Stereoscopic photography and projection**

    For stereoscopic motion picture photography, see 778.5341; for stereoscopic motion picture projection, see 778.55

.5   **Cinematography, video production, related activities**

    See Manual at 791.43, 791.45 vs. 778.5

.52   General topics of cinematography and video production

   Add to base number 778.52 the numbers following 778.5 in 778.53–778.58, e.g., lighting for cinematography and video production 778.52343

>   778.53–778.58   Cinematography, motion picture projection, preservation and storage of motion picture films

   Class comprehensive works in 778.53

.53   Cinematography (Motion picture photography)

   Class here comprehensive works on cinematography, motion picture projection, preservation and storage of motion picture films

   Class comprehensive works on motion picture production and cinematography in 791.43

    For motion picture projection, see 778.55; for storage of motion picture films, see 778.58

    See Manual at 791.43, 791.45 vs. 778.5

.530 288   Maintenance and repair

    Do not use for preservation; class in 778.58

.532   Darkroom and laboratory practice

---

*Do not use notation 092 from Table 1 for photographers; class in 770.92

.534	Specific types and elements of cinematography

See also 778.56 for specific kinds of cinematography

.534 1	Stereoscopic cinematography
.534 2	Color cinematography
.534 3	Lighting
.534 4	Sound

Including sound synchronization and scoring, postsynchronization

.534 5	Special effects

Including double-image, trick photography

.534 6	Time-lapse cinematography
.534 7	Animated cartoons
.534 9	Amateur cinematography

Class darkroom and laboratory practice for amateurs in 778.532; class specific types and elements of amateur cinematography in 778.5341–778.5347

.534 91	Specific types of cameras

Class specific types of cameras for professional in 778.53

.535	Editing films

Including titling

Class editing in a specific type or element of cinematography in 778.534

.538	Cinematography of specific subjects

Add to base number 778.538 notation 001–999, e.g., cinematography of birds 778.538598

Class specific types and elements of cinematography regardless of subject in 778.534

.55	Motion picture projection
[.554]	Projection of specific kinds of motion pictures

Number and its subdivisions discontinued; class in 778.55

.56	Special kinds of cinematography

Not provided for elsewhere

Including cinematography using photomacrography or photomicrography techniques; high-speed cinematography

Class a specific application with the application, e.g., use of cinematography in diagnosis of diseases 616.075028

See also 778.534 for specific types and elements of cinematography

.58   Preservation and storage of motion picture films

Standard subdivisions are added for either or both topics in heading

See also 025.1773 for archiving of motion picture films

.59   Video production (Television photography)

Class here home video systems

Unless other instructions are given, class a subject with aspects in two or more subdivisions of 778.59 in the number coming first, e.g., lighting for studio production 778.592 (*not* 778.594)

Class comprehensive works on television production in 791.45; class interdisciplinary works on television in 384.55. Class a specific application of video production with the application, e.g., use of video production in diagnosis of diseases 616.075028

See also 006.7 for interactive video

See Manual at 791.43, 791.45 vs. 778.5

.590 288   Maintenance and repair

Do not use for preservation; class in 778.597

.592   Specific elements of video production

Including lighting, sound

.593   Editing and post-production

Standard subdivisions are added for either or both topics in heading

Including animation, titling, visual effects

.594   Specific modes of video production

Including electronic field production (EFP), studio production

See also 070.195 for electronic news gathering

.596   Special kinds of video production

Not provided for elsewhere

Including video production using photomacrography or photomicrography techniques; underwater video production

Class video recording formats and recorders used for special kinds of video production in 778.599

.597   Preservation and storage of videotapes and discs

Standard subdivisions are added for either or both topics in heading

See also 025.1773 for archiving of videotapes and discs

.598	Video production of specific subjects

> Add to base number 778.598 notation 001–999, e.g., video production of birds 778.598598
>
> Class video recording formats and recorders used in recording specific subjects in 778.599

.599	Video recording formats and recorders

> Class here interdisciplinary works on description, use, manufacture
>
> *For manufacture, see 621.38833*

.599 2	Recordings

> Tape, film, disc

.599 3	Recorders

> Class here camcorders, video cameras

> ### 778.6–778.8 Specific topics in photography

> Class specific topics in relation to cinematography and video production in 778.5; class comprehensive works in 770

.6	***Color photography**

> Class here photography of colors
>
> Class color photomicrography in 778.31

.602 8	Auxiliary techniques and procedures; apparatus, equipment, materials

> *For processing auxiliary techniques and procedures, apparatus, equipment, materials in color photography, see 778.66*

.62	***Photography of colors in monochrome**

> Orthochromatic and panchromatic

.63	***Direct process reproduction in color photography**

> Including Lippmann process

.65	***Additive processes in color photography**

.66	***Processing techniques, procedures, apparatus, equipment, materials in color photography**

> Class here subtractive processes, production of color films and prints by subtractive analysis and subtractive synthesis, respectively
>
> Class direct process reproduction in color photography in 778.63; class additive processes in color photography in 778.65

.7	***Photography under specific conditions**

*Do not use notation 092 from Table 1 for photographers; class in 770.92

.71   *Outdoor photography

.712   *Photography in sunlight

.719   *Night photography

> *For infrared photography, see 778.34*

.72   *Indoor photography and photography by artificial light

> Class here use of normal photographic electronic flash (flashbulb photography)
>
> Class short-duration flash in high-speed photography in 778.37
>
> *For infrared photography, see 778.34*

.73   *Underwater photography

.75   *Photography under extreme climatic conditions

.76   *Available light photography

> Class outdoor available light photography in 778.71; class indoor available light photography in 778.72

.8   *Special effects and trick photography

> Standard subdivisions are added for either or both topics in heading
>
> Including composite, high-contrast, tabletop photography; photomontage; photography of specters, distortions, multiple images, silhouettes

.9   Photography of specific subjects

> Class here comprehensive works on techniques of photographing, photographs of, and photographers of a specific subject
>
> Add to base number 778.9 the numbers following 704.94 in 704.942–704.949, e.g., portrait photography 778.92; however, for photographers, see 770.92
>
> Class photography by specific methods regardless of subject in 778.3–778.8

779   Photographs

> Add to base number 779 the numbers following 704.94 in 704.942–704.949, e.g., photographs of children 779.25
>
> *See Manual at 779*

---

*Do not use notation 092 from Table 1 for photographers; class in 770.92

780   Music

After general topics (780 and 781) the basic arrangement of the schedule is based on the voice, instrument, or ensemble making the music. Vocal music is classed in 782–783; instrumental music in 784–788

Unless other instructions are given, class a subject with aspects in two or more subdivisions of 780 in the number coming last, e.g., sacred vocal music 782.22 (*not* 781.7)

When instructed, add the indicator 0 or 1 and the notation from the subdivisions coming earlier in the schedule, e.g., rock songs 782.42166 (*not* 781.66). In building numbers, do not add by use of 0 or 1 (alone or in combination) more than twice, e.g., history of rock protest songs 782.421661592 (*not* 782.42166159209)
(Option: Add as many times as desired)

This schedule does not distinguish scores, texts, or recordings
(Option: To distinguish scores, texts, recordings, use one of the following:
(Option A: Prefix a letter or other symbol to the number for treatises, e.g., scores for violin M787.2 or 787.2, violin recordings R787.2 or MR787.2; use a special prefix to distinguish miniature scores from other scores, MM787.2
(Option B: Add to the number for treatises the numbers following 78 in 780.26–780.269, e.g., miniature scores of music for violin 787.20265
(Option C: Class recordings in 789, e.g., recordings of folk music 789.2, recordings of violin folk music 789.2072)

See Manual at 780

SUMMARY

780.000 1–.099 9		Relation of music to other subjects
.1–.9		Standard subdivisions and treatises on music scores, recordings, texts
781		General principles and musical forms
.01–.09		Standard subdivisions
.1		Basic principles
.2		Elements of music
.3		Composition
.4		Techniques of music
.5		Kinds of music
.6		Traditions of music
.7		Sacred music
.8		Musical forms

782	**Vocal music**	
.001–.009	Standard subdivisions	
.01–.08	[General principles and musical forms]	
.1	Dramatic vocal forms	Operas
.2	Nondramatic vocal forms	
.3	Services (Liturgy and ritual)	
.4	Secular forms	
.5	Mixed voices	
.6	Women's voices	
.7	Children's voices	
.8	Men's voices	
.9	Other types of voices	
783	**Music for single voices**	**The voice**
.001–.009	Standard subdivisions	
.01–.09	[General principles and musical forms]	
.1	Single voices in combination	
.2	Solo voice	
.3	High voice	
.4	Middle voice	
.5	Low voice	
.6–.8	Woman's, child's, man's voice	
.9	Other types of voice	
784	**Instruments and instrumental ensembles and their music**	
.01–.09	Standard subdivisions	
.1	General principles, musical forms, instruments	
.2	Full (Symphony) orchestra	
.3	Chamber orchestra	
.4	Light orchestra	
.6	Keyboard, mechanical, electronic, percussion bands	
.7	String orchestra	
.8	Wind band	
.9	Brass band	
785	**Ensembles with only one instrument per part**	
.001–.009	Standard subdivisions	
.01–.09	[General principles, musical forms, instruments]	
.1	Ensembles by size	
.2	Ensembles with keyboard	
.3	Ensembles without electrophones and with percussion and keyboard	
.4	Ensembles without keyboard	
.5	Ensembles without keyboard and with percussion	
.6	Keyboard, mechanical, aeolian, electrophone, percussion ensembles	
.7	String ensembles	Bowed string ensembles
.8	Woodwind ensembles	
.9	Brass ensembles	
786	**Keyboard, mechanical, electrophonic, percussion instruments**	
.2	Pianos	
.3	Clavichords	
.4	Harpsichords	
.5	Keyboard wind instruments	Organs
.6	Mechanical and aeolian instruments	
.7	Electrophones	Electronic instruments
.8	Percussion instruments	
.9	Drums and devices used for percussive effects	

787	**Stringed instruments (Chordophones)**		**Bowed stringed instruments**
.2	Violins		
.3	Violas		
.4	Cellos (Violoncellos)		
.5	Double basses		
.6	Other bowed stringed instruments		Viols
.7	Plectral instruments		
.8	Plectral lute family		
.9	Harps and musical bows		
788	**Wind instruments (Aerophones)**		
.2	Woodwind instruments and free aerophones		
.3	Flute family		
.4	Reed instruments		
.5	Double-reed instruments		
.6	Single-reed instruments		
.7	Saxophones		
.8	Free reeds		
.9	Brass instruments (Lip-reed instruments)		

.000 1–.099 9   Relation of music to other subjects

Works in which the focus is music

Add to base number 780.0 three-digit notation 001–999, e.g., music and literature 780.08, music and Welsh literature 780.0891 (*not* 780.089166), music and the performing arts 780.079 (*not* 780.07902)

See Manual at 780.079 vs. 790.2

.1   Philosophy and theory

For general principles, theory of music, see 781

.14   Languages and communication

.148   Musical notation, abbreviations, symbols

Including staff notation, neumes, tablature, tonic sol-fa; braille musical notation

Class transcription from one form of notation to another in 780.149

.149   Editing

.15   Analytical guides and program notes

Do not use for scientific principles; class in 781.2

(.16)   Bibliographies, catalogs, indexes

(Optional number; prefer 016.78)

(.162)   †Bibliographies and catalogs of music literature

(.164)   †Bibliographies and catalogs of scores and parts

Including bibliographies and catalogs of manuscript scores and parts

†(Optional number; prefer 016.78)

(.166)	†Discographies

Bibliographies and catalogs of music recorded on phonorecords (cylinders, discs, wires, tapes, films)

Including biodiscographies

[.19]   Psychological principles

Do not use; class in 781.11

.2   Miscellany

.202   Synopses and outlines

For synopses of stories and plots, see 782.00269

.216   Lists, inventories, catalogs of music

Class here thematic catalogs

Class bibliographic catalogs of music in 016.78

For thematic catalogs of individual composers, see 780.92

.26   Treatises on music scores, recordings, texts

Standard subdivisions are added for a combination of two or more topics in heading, for scores alone

In schedules other than 780, indicate scores, recordings, texts, and treatises about them by adding the numbers following 78 in 780.262–780.269, e.g., bibliography of music manuscripts 016.780262, bibliography of manuscripts of violin music 016.78720262, discography of violin music 016.78720266

See Manual at 780.26; also at 780.92

(Option: To distinguish scores and recordings within 780, add to the number for treatises the numbers following 78 in 780.26–780.269, e.g., miniature scores of music for violin 787.20265. Other options are described at 780)

(Option: Class here law of music; prefer appropriate subdivisions of 340)

\>   780.262–780.265 Scores

Class comprehensive works in 780.26

For words and other vocal sounds to be sung or recited with music, see 780.268

.262   *Manuscripts

Including autograph scores, sketch books

---

*(Option: Use this standard subdivision to distinguish scores and recordings; see details in note under 780.26)

†(Optional number; prefer 016.78)

.263   *Printed music

> *For performance scores, see 780.264; for study scores, see 780.265*
>
> *See also 070.5794 for music publishing, 686.284 for music printing*

.264   *Performance scores and parts

Standard subdivisions are added for either or both topics in heading

Including full scores, conducting scores, piano-vocal scores

.265   *Study scores (Miniature scores, Pocket scores)

.266   *Sound recordings of music

Class here comprehensive works on music recordings

> *For video recordings, see 780.267*
>
> *See also 781.49 for recording of music*

.267   *Video recordings of music

.268   Words and other vocal sounds to be sung or recited with music

Including librettos, lyrics, poems, screenplays

Class here texts

The words must be discussed in a musical context. If the words are presented as literature, folklore, or religious text, class the work in 800, 398, or 200, respectively

Use this number only for building other numbers, e.g., lyrics of songs 782.420268, texts of choral symphonies 784.221840268; never use it by itself

Class comprehensive works in 782.00268

> *For stories, plots, synopses, see 780.269*

.269   Stories, plots, synopses

Standard subdivisions are added for any or all topics in heading

Including scenarios

Use this number only for building other numbers, e.g., plots of operas 782.10269, synopses of choral symphonies 784.221840269; never use it by itself

Class comprehensive works in 782.00269

.28   Auxiliary techniques and procedures; apparatus, equipment, materials

> *For instruments, see 784*
>
> *See also 780.26 for scores, 780.266 for recordings, 781.4 for techniques of music*

---

*(Option: Use this standard subdivision to distinguish scores and recordings; see details in note under 780.26)

.285	Data processing Computer applications

> *For computer composition, see 781.34; for the computer as a musical instrument, see 786.76*

.7   **Education, research, performances, related topics**

> Including use of apparatus and equipment in study and teaching

.72   Research; statistical methods

> Class here musicology

.76   Review, exercises, examinations, works for self-instruction

.77   Special teaching and learning methods

> Including programmed teaching
>
> > *For techniques for acquiring musical skills and learning a repertoire, see 781.42*

.78   Performances (Concerts and recitals)

> Do not use for use of apparatus and equipment in study and teaching; class in 780.7
>
> Add to base number 780.78 notation 3–9 from Table 2, e.g., concerts in London 780.78421
>
> > *See also 781.43 for performance techniques*

.79   Competitions, festivals, awards, financial support

> Add to base number 780.79 notation 3–9 from Table 2, e.g., festivals in France 780.7944
>
> Class performances at festivals and competitions in 780.78

.8   **History and description of music with respect to kinds of persons**

.89   Music with respect to specific racial, ethnic, national groups

> > *For folk music, see 781.62*
> >
> > *See Manual at 781.62 vs. 780.89*

.9   **Historical, geographic, persons treatment**

> No distinction is made between the music of a place and music in a place, e.g., Viennese music and music played in Vienna are both classed in 780.943613
>
> Class critical appraisal in analytical guides and program notes in 780.15

> 780.901–780.905 Periods of stylistic development of music

Even though the periods are those of western music, this does not limit the use of these numbers to western or European music only

Class here schools, styles, time periods not limited ethnically or by country or locality

Class comprehensive works in 780.9

.901   Ancient times through 499

.902   500–1449

Including Gothic style, ars antiqua, ars nova, medieval music

For 1450–1499, see 780.9031

.903   1450–

Class here modern music

For 1900–1999, see 780.904; for 2000–2099, see 780.905

.903 1   Ca. 1450–ca. 1600

Including Renaissance music

.903 2   Ca. 1600–ca. 1750

Including baroque music, nuove musiche

.903 3   Ca. 1750–ca. 1825

Including preclassicism, classicism, rococo style

Class here 18th century music

For rococo style of earlier period, music of 1700–1750, see 780.9032

.903 4   Ca. 1825–ca. 1900

Including nationalism, romanticism

Class here 19th century music

For music of earlier part of 19th century, see 780.9033; for 20th century nationalism, see 780.904

.904   1900–1999

Including avant-garde music, impressionism, neoclassicism

For early impressionism, see 780.9034

[.904 1–.904 9]   Individual decades

Do not use; class in 780.904

.905	2000–2099
.92	Persons associated with music

Class here composers, performers, critics; thematic catalogs of individual composers

Class general thematic catalogs in 780.216

See Manual at 780.92; also at 791.092

(Option: Class individual composers in 789)

.94	Europe Western Europe

Use only for works that stress that they are discussing the European origin and character of music in contrast to music from other sources

---

> ### 781–788   Principles, forms, ensembles, voices, instruments

Class here music of all traditions
(Option: 781–788 may be used for only one tradition of music; in that case, class all other traditions in 789. For example, if it is desired to emphasize western art music, class it here, and class all other traditions of music in 789, e.g., jazz 789.5; or, if it is desired to emphasize jazz, class it here, and class all other traditions of music in 789, e.g., western art music 789.8)

Unless other instructions are given, class a subject with aspects in two or more subdivisions of 781–788 in the number coming last, e.g., jazz mass 782.323165 (*not* 781.65), Johann Sebastian Bach's cello sonatas 787.4183 (*not* 784.183)

Class comprehensive works in 780

781   General principles and musical forms

Class here music theory

Use the subdivisions of 781 only when the subject is not limited to voice, instrument, or ensemble. If voice, instrument, or ensemble is specified, class with voice, instrument, or ensemble; and then add as instructed. For example, rehearsal of music 781.44, rehearsal of opera (a form for the voice) 782.1144

See Manual at 780.92

SUMMARY

781.01–.09	**Standard subdivisions**
.1	**Basic principles of music**
.2	**Elements of music**
.3	**Composition**
.4	**Techniques of music**
.5	**Kinds of music**
.6	**Traditions of music**
.7	**Sacred music**
.8	**Musical forms**

.01–.09	Standard subdivisions

Notation from Table 1 as modified under 780.1–780.9, e.g., music theory during the Renaissance 781.09031

.1	**Basic principles of music**

.11	Psychological principles

For aesthetics, appreciation, taste, see 781.17

.12	Religious principles

.17	Artistic principles

Class here aesthetics, appreciation, taste

> **781.2–781.8 Other principles and musical forms**

Add to each subdivision identified by * as follows:
01–09   Standard subdivisions
                    Notation from Table 1 as modified under 780.1–780.9, e.g.,
                    performances 078
1   General principles
                    Add to 1 the numbers following 781 in 781.1–781.7, e.g., rock
                    music 166, rehearsing rock music 166144

In building numbers, do not add by use of 0 or 1 (alone or in combination) more than twice, e.g., history of rock protest songs 782.421661592 (*not* 782.42166159209)
          (Option: Add as many times as desired)

Class comprehensive works in 781

.2	***Elements of music**

Class here scientific principles

.22	*Time

For playing time, see 781.432

.222	*Pulse

.224	*Rhythm

.226	*Meter

.23	*Musical sound

.232	*Pitch

.233	*Volume

.234	*Timbre (Tone color)

*Add as instructed under 781.2–781.8

.235   *Attack and decay

> Subdivisions are added for either or both topics in heading

.236   *Silence

> Including rests

.237   *Intervals

> *For consonance, see 781.238; for dissonance, see 781.239*

.238   *Consonance

.239   *Dissonance

.24   *Melody

.246   *Scales and scalic formations

> Subdivisions are added for either or both topics in heading
>
> Class comprehensive works on modes in 781.263

.247   *Ornaments

> Including embellishments, trills

.248   *Themes

> Including subject, countersubject, idée fixe, leitmotif
>
> *See also 780.216 for thematic catalogs*

.25   *Harmony

> Class here harmonic organization, comprehensive works on harmony and counterpoint
>
> Class intervals in 781.237; class figured bass in 781.47
>
> *For homophony, see 781.285; for counterpoint, see 781.286*

.252   *Chords

> Including arpeggios

.254   *Cadences

.256   *Harmonic rhythm

.258   *Tonality

> Key relationships
>
> *For tonal systems, see 781.26*

.26   *Tonal systems

.262   *Diatonicism

---

*Add as instructed under 781.2–781.8

.263		*Medieval church modes

Class here comprehensive works on modes, modes of western folk music

For other modes, see 781.264

.264   Other modes

Including ancient Greek modes, Byzantine echoi, Indian rāgas

Class modes of western folk music in 781.263

.265   *Macrotonality

Tonality based on units larger than the diatonic whole tone

Including pentatonicism

.266   *Whole tonality

Tonality based on scales of diatonic whole tones

.267   *Atonality

Music with no fixed tonic or key center

For dodecaphony, see 781.268

.268   *Dodecaphony (Twelve-tone system, Note rows)

Class comprehensive works on serialism in 781.33

.269   *Microtonality

Tonality based on melodic units smaller than the diatonic semitone

.28   *Texture

.282   *Monody

Music with a single melodic line

.283   *Heterophony

Music with a single melodic line simultaneously varied by two or more performers

.284   *Polyphony

Two or more melodic lines

For homophony, see 781.285; for counterpoint, see 781.286

.285   *Homophony

Two or more mutually dependent melodic lines

.286   *Counterpoint

Two or more independent melodic lines

Class comprehensive works on harmony and counterpoint in 781.25

*Add as instructed under 781.2–781.8

.3 ***Composition**

.302 85   Data processing   Computer applications

Do not use for computer composition; class in 781.34

.32   *Indeterminacy and aleatory composition

Forms of composition based on chance

.33   Serialism

.330 1–.330 9   Standard subdivisions

Notation from Table 1 as modified under 780.1–780.9, e.g., performances of serial music 781.33078

.331   Basic principles of serialism

.331 1   Psychological principles

For aesthetics, appreciation, taste, see 781.3317

.331 2   Religious principles

.331 7   Artistic principles

Class here aesthetics, appreciation, taste

.332–.338   Specific elements of serialism

Add to base number 781.33 the numbers following 781.2 in 781.22–781.28, e.g., serialized rhythm 781.3324; however, for atonality, see 781.267

.34   *Computer composition

See also 786.76 for computers as a musical instrument

.344–.346   Computer science aspects

Unless it is redundant, add to base number 781.34 the numbers following 00 in 004–006, e.g., use of digital microcomputers 781.34416, but use of digital computers 781.34 (*not* 781.344)

.36   *Extemporization (Improvisation)

.37   *Arrangement

Including transcription

For arrangements, see 781.38

.374   *Orchestration

.377   *Paraphrase and parody

.38   *Arrangements

*Add as instructed under 781.2–781.8

.382–.388   Original voice, instrument, ensemble of the arrangements

> Add to base number 781.38 the numbers following 78 in 782–788, e.g., arrangements of violin music 781.3872
>
> Use these numbers only for building other numbers; never use them by themselves
>
> *See Manual at 781.382–781.388*

.4   ***Techniques of music**

> *For techniques of composition, see 781.3*

.42   *Techniques for acquiring musical skills and learning a repertoire

.423   *Sight and score reading

> Subdivisions are added for either or both topics in heading

.424   *Listening and ear training

> Subdivisions are added for either or both topics in heading

.426   *Memorizing

.43   *Performance techniques

> *For extemporization, see 781.36; for specific performance techniques, see 781.44–781.48*
>
> *See also 784.193 for techniques for playing instruments*

.432   *Playing time

.434   *Harmonization

.436   *Transposition

.438   *Ensemble technique

>   781.44–781.48   Specific performance techniques

> Class comprehensive works in 781.43

.44   *Rehearsal and practice

> Subdivisions are added for either or both topics in heading

.45   *Conducting

.46   *Interpretation

> Including rubato

.47   *Accompaniment

> Including continuo (figured bass, thorough bass)
>
> *See Manual at 781.47*

*Add as instructed under 781.2–781.8

.48   *Breathing and resonance

> Subdivisions are added for either or both topics in heading
>
> Class breathing and resonance associated with instrumental performance in 784.1932

.49   *Recording of music

> *See also 621.3893 for sound recording and reproducing equipment, 780.266 for treatises on music recordings*

.5   ***Kinds of music**

.52   *Music for specific times

.522   *Music for days of week

.522 2   *Sunday

.522 8   *Saturday

.523   *Music for times of day

.524   *Music for the seasons

.524 2   *Spring

.524 4   *Summer

.524 6   *Fall (Autumn)

> Including harvest

.524 8   *Winter

.53   *Music in specific settings

.532   *Outdoor music

> Including street music

.534   *Indoor music

> *For specific indoor settings, see 781.535–781.539*

>   781.535–781.539   Specific indoor settings
>
> Class music in religious settings in 781.7; class comprehensive works in 781.534

.535   *Domestic setting

.536   *Court setting

.538   *Theater setting

.539   *Concert hall setting

*Add as instructed under 781.2–781.8

.54	*Music for specific media

Background or mood music

.542	*Film music

See also 778.5344 for sound synchronization of motion pictures

.544	*Radio music
.546	*Television music

See also 778.592 for sound synchronization of television programs

.55	*Music accompanying public entertainments
.552	*Dramatic music

Class here incidental music

Class incidental music for specific media in 781.54; class dramatic vocal music in 782.1

.554	*Dance music

For ballet music, see 781.556

.556	*Ballet music
.56	*Program music

Music depicting nonmusical concepts, e.g., music depicting the sea

Class musical forms depicting nonmusical concepts in 784.18, e.g., nocturnes 784.18966

.57	*Music accompanying activities

Including inaugurations, initiations

Class music accompanying stages of the life cycle in 781.58; class music reflecting other themes and subjects regardless of activity in 781.59

See also 781.55 for music accompanying public entertainments

.58	*Music accompanying stages of the life cycle
.582	*Birth and infancy

Including music for infant baptism and circumcision

Class here music for confinement

.583	*Attainment of puberty

Including music for bar or bat mitzvahs

.584	*Attainment of majority

Including music for debuts

*Add as instructed under 781.2–781.8

.586	*Courtship and engagement
.587	*Weddings and marriage

        Subdivisions are added for either or both topics in heading

.588	*Dying and death

        Including music for burials, cremations, funerals, mourning

.59	*Music reflecting other themes and subjects
.592	*Protest
.593	*Work
.594	*Sports and recreation
.595	*Sea life
.599	*Patriotic, political, military music

        Class here music commemorating historical events

        Subdivisions are added for any or all topics in heading

.6   ***Traditions of music**

        Works emphasizing a specific tradition

        (Option: If 781–788 is used for only one tradition of music, class all other traditions in 789)

        See Manual at 781.6

.62   Folk music

        Music indigenous to the cultural group in which it occurs, usually evolved through aural transmission

        See also 780.9 for music of and performed in a specific location

        See Manual at 781.62 vs. 780.62

.620 01–.620 07   Standard subdivisions

        Notation from Table 1 as modified under 780.1–780.9, e.g., performances of folk music 781.620078

.620 08   History and description of folk music with respect to kinds of persons

[.620 089]   Treatment with respect to specific racial, ethnic, national groups

        Do not use; class in 781.621–781.629

.620 09   Historical, geographic, persons treatment

.620 090 1–.620 090 5   Historical periods

        Add to base number 781.620090 the numbers following 780.90 in 780.901–780.905, e.g., folk music of the Renaissance 781.62009031

*Add as instructed under 781.2–781.8

.620 091–.620 099	Geographic and persons treatment

For geographic treatment of folk music of specific racial, ethnic, national groups, see 781.621–781.629

.620 1–.620 5	General principles of folk music

Add to base number 781.620 the numbers following 781 in 781.1–781.5, e.g., folk music for springtime 781.6205242, rehearsing folk music for springtime 781.6205242144

.620 6	Stylistic influences of other traditions of music

Add to base number 781.6206 the numbers following 781.6 in 781.63–781.69, e.g., influence of jazz on folk music 781.62065, performances of folk music influenced by jazz 781.62065078

.621–.629	Folk music of specific racial, ethnic, national groups

Add to base number 781.62 notation 1–9 from Table 5, e.g., Spanish folk music 781.6261; then add further as follows:

001–008	Standard subdivisions
	Notation from Table 1 as modified under 780.1–780.9, e.g., performances of Spanish folk music 781.62610078
009	Historical, geographic, persons treatment
00901–00905	Historical periods
	Add to base number 0090 the numbers following 780.90 in 780.901–780.905, e.g., Spanish folk music of the Renaissance 781.6261009031
[0093–0099]	Treatment by specific continents, countries, localities
	Do not use; class in 03–09
01	General principles
	Add to 01 the numbers following 781 in 781.1–781.5, e.g., Spanish folk music for springtime 781.6261015242, rhythm in Spanish folk music for springtime 781.62610152421224
02	Stylistic influence of other traditions of music
	Add to 02 the numbers following 781.6 in 781.63–781.69, e.g., influence of jazz on Spanish folk music 781.6261025, performances of Spanish folk music influenced by jazz 781.6261025078
03–09	Specific continents, countries, localities
	Add to 0 notation 3–9 from Table 2, e.g., Spanish folk music in New York City 781.626107471

In building numbers, do not add by use of 0 or 1 (alone or in combination) more than twice, e.g., history of Spanish protest folk-songs 782.421626101592 (*not* 782.42162610159209)
(Option: Add as many times as desired)

>   781.63–781.69   Other traditions of music

         Add to each subdivision identified by † as follows:
            01–09   Standard subdivisions
                    Notation from Table 1 as modified under 780.1–780.9, e.g., performances 078
            1   General principles and stylistic influences of other traditions of music
            11–15   General principles
                    Add to 1 the numbers following 781 in 781.1–781.5, e.g., springtime music 15242, melody in springtime music 15242124
            16   Stylistic influences of other traditions of music
                    Add to 16 the numbers following 781.6 in 781.62–781.69, e.g., influence of folk music 162, performances of influence of folk music 162078

         In building numbers, do not add by use of 0 or 1 (alone or in combination) more than twice, e.g., history of rock protest songs 782.421661592 (*not* 782.42166159209)
            (Option: Add as many times as desired)

         Class comprehensive works in 781.6

.63   †Popular music

         For western popular music, see 781.64

.64   †Western popular music

         Class country and western music in 781.642

         Most works on western popular music are predominantly about popular songs and are classed in 782.42164

         For jazz, see 781.65; for rock, see 781.66

.642   †Country music

         Class here bluegrass music

.643   †Blues

         Class here rhythm and blues

.644   †Soul

.645   †Ragtime

.646   †Reggae

.649   †Rap

         Use this number only for building numbers in 782–783, e.g., comprehensive works on rap 782.421649; never use it by itself

.65   †Jazz

---

†Add as instructed under 781.63–781.69

.652	†Early jazz

Class here origins of jazz

.653	†Traditional jazz

Including New Orleans, Dixieland, Southwest and Kansas City, Harlem, white New York styles; Chicago breakdown

.654	†Mainstream jazz

Including swing

.655	†Modern jazz

Including bop (bebop), hard bop, cool jazz, progressive jazz

For avant-garde jazz, see 781.656

.656	†Avant-garde jazz

.657	†Hybrid styles

Including Afro-Cuban, third stream, Indo-jazz

.66	†Rock (Rock 'n' roll)

Including acid, folk, hard, punk, soft rock

.68	†Western art (Classical) music

Classical music as only one of many traditions

Class here comprehensive works on art music

Class general works on art (classical) music in 780

For nonwestern art music, see 781.69

.69	†Nonwestern art music

.7 Sacred music

Class sacred music accompanying stages of life cycle in 781.58; class works about "church music" in the sense of Christian church music in 781.71; class sacred vocal music in 782.22

.700 1–.700 9	Standard subdivisions

Notation from Table 1 as modified under 780.1–780.9, e.g., performances of sacred music 781.70078

.701–.706	General principles of sacred music

Add to base number 781.70 the numbers following 781 in 781.1–781.6, e.g., harmonic rhythm in sacred music 781.70256, appreciation of harmonic rhythm in sacred music 781.70256117

.71	Christian sacred music

For music of Christian church year, see 781.72

---

†Add as instructed under 781.63–781.69

.710 01–.710 09   Standard subdivisions

> Notation from Table 1 as modified under 780.1–780.9, e.g., performances of Christian sacred music 781.70078

.710 1–.710 6   General principles of Christian sacred music

> Add to base number 781.710 the numbers following 781 in 781.1–781.6, e.g., harmonic rhythm in Christian sacred music 781.710256, appreciation of harmonic rhythm in Christian sacred music 781.710256117

.711–.718   Christian sacred music of specific denominations

> Add to base number 781.71 the numbers following —2 in notation 21–28 from Table 7, e.g., Baptist sacred music 781.7161; then add further as follows:
> 001–009   Standard subdivisions
> > Notation from Table 1 as modified under 780.1–780.9, e.g., performances of Baptist sacred music 781.71610078
> 01–06   General principles
> > Add to 0 the numbers following 781 in 781.1–781.6, e.g., harmonic rhythm in Baptist sacred music 781.71610256, appreciation of harmonic rhythm in Baptist sacred music 781.71610256117

.72   *Music of Christian church year

.722   *Advent

.723   *Christmas day

> Class here Christmas season
>
> *For Epiphany, see 781.724*

.724   *Epiphany

.725   *Lent

.725 5   *Passiontide

> *For Holy Week, see 781.726*

.726   *Holy Week

> Including Palm Sunday, Maundy Thursday, Good Friday

.727   *Easter Sunday

> Class here Eastertide (Easter season)
>
> *For Ascensiontide, see 781.728*

.728   *Ascensiontide

.729   *Pentecost and Trinity Sunday

*Add as instructed under 781.2–781.8

.729 3	*Pentecost (Whitsunday)
.729 4	*Trinity Sunday
.73	*Sacred music of classical (Greek and Roman) and Germanic religions
.74–.79	Sacred music of other religions

> Add to base number 781.7 the numbers following —29 in notation 294–299 from Table 7, e.g., Judaic sacred music 781.76; then add further as follows:
>
> 001–009   Standard subdivisions
> > Notation from Table 1 as modified under 780.1–780.9, e.g., performances of Judaic sacred music 781.760078
>
> 01–06   General principles
> > Add to base number 0 the numbers following 781 in 781.1–781.6, e.g., harmonic rhythm in Judaic sacred music 781.760256, appreciation of harmonic rhythm in Judaic sacred music 781.760256117

.8   ***Musical forms**

Class here formal analysis; works that do not specify voice, instrument, or ensemble

Class works for specific voice, instrument, or ensemble with the voice, instrument, or ensemble, e.g., Brahms' Variations on a theme by Schumann 786.21825 (*not* 781.825)

> *For vocal forms, see 782.1–782.4; for instrumental forms, see 784.183–784.189*

| .82 | Specific musical forms |
| [.820 1–.820 9] | Standard subdivisions |

> Do not use; class in 781.801–781.809

| .822 | *Binary, ternary, da capo forms |

> Subdivisions are added for a combination of two or more forms

.822 2	*Binary form
.822 3	*Ternary form
.822 5	*Da capo form
.823	*Strophic form
.824	*Rondos

> Including sonata-rondos

| .825 | *Variations |

> Including theme and variations

| .826 | *Paraphrase forms |

> Including musical parody

*Add as instructed under 781.2–781.8

.827   *Ground bass (Ostinato)

                Including chaconnes, passacaglias

.828   *Cantus firmus

>   **782–788   Ensembles, voices, instruments**

             Class comprehensive works in 780

             See Manual at 780: Citation order

782   Vocal music

             Class orchestral music with vocal parts in 784.22

             For music for single voices, see 783

             See Manual at 782; also at 782: Flow chart

SUMMARY

782.001–.009	**Standard subdivisions**
.01–.08	**[General principles and musical forms]**
.1	**Dramatic vocal forms Operas**
.2	**Nondramatic vocal forms**
.3	**Services (Liturgy and ritual)**
.4	**Secular forms**
.5	**Mixed voices**
.6	**Women's voices**
.7	**Children's voices**
.8	**Men's voices**
.9	**Other types of voices**

.001–.009   Standard subdivisions

               Notation from Table 1 as modified under 780.1–780.9, e.g.,
               performances of vocal music 782.0078

.01–.07   General principles of vocal music

               Add to base number 782.0 the numbers following 781 in 781.1–781.7, e.g.,
               patriotic vocal music 782.0599, rhythm in patriotic vocal music
               782.05991224

.08   Musical forms

               Add to base number 782.08 the numbers following 784.18 in
               784.182–784.189, e.g., vocal music in waltz form 782.08846

               For vocal forms, see 782.1–782.4

---

*Add as instructed under 781.2–781.8

> **782.1–782.4 Vocal forms**

Class here treatises about and recordings of vocal forms for specific voices and ensembles

Add to each subdivision identified by * as follows:
01–09   Standard subdivisions
        Notation from Table 1 as modified under 780.1–780.9, e.g., performances 078
1   General principles and musical forms
11–17   General principles
        Add to 1 the numbers following 781 in 781.1–781.7, e.g., rock music 166, rehearsing rock music 166144
18   Musical forms
        Add to 18 the numbers following 784.18 in 784.182–784.189, e.g., da capo form 1822, composition in da capo form 182213

In building numbers, do not add by use of 0 or 1 (alone or in combination) more than twice, e.g., history of rock protest songs 782.421661592 (*not* 782.42166159209)
(Option: Add as many times as desired)

Class comprehensive works in 782

.1   ***Dramatic vocal forms   Operas**

Regardless of type of voice or vocal group

Class here concert versions

See Manual at 782.1 vs. 792.5

.109 2   Persons associated with dramatic vocal forms, with operas

Class here biographies of singers known equally well as opera and recital singers, of conductors known primarily as opera conductors

Class biographies of singers known primarily as recital singers in 782.42168092; class biographies of conductors known equally well for conducting operas and orchestral music in 784.2092

.109 4   European opera

Use only for works that stress that they are discussing European opera in contrast to operas from all other sources

.12   *Operettas

.13   *Singspiels

---

*Add as instructed under 782.1–782.4

.14   *Musical plays

Musical plays differ from other dramatic musical forms by the fact that in them the action is predominantly outside the music, while in the other dramatic forms the action is predominantly in the music

Class here ballad operas, musicals, revues

For masques, see 782.15

See Manual at 782.1 vs. 792.5

.15   *Masques

.2   *Nondramatic vocal forms

For secular forms, see 782.4

.22   *Sacred vocal forms

For specific sacred vocal forms, see 782.23–782.29

> 782.23–782.29   Specific sacred vocal forms

Class comprehensive works in 782.22

For services, see 782.3

.23   *Oratorios

Including passions

.24   *Large-scale vocal works   Cantatas

Class here comprehensive works on cantatas

For oratorios, see 782.23; for secular cantatas, see 782.48

.25   *Sacred songs

Class here small-scale sacred vocal forms

If the songs are called hymns, class them in 782.27; if called carols, class them in 782.28; otherwise, class them here

Class comprehensive works on songs in 782.42

For motets, see 782.26

.253   *Spirituals

.254   *Gospel music

.26   *Motets

.265   *Anthems

.27   *Hymns

For hymns without music, see 264.23; for carols, see 782.28

*Add as instructed under 782.1–782.4

.28	*Carols	
.29	*Liturgical forms	
.292	*Chant	

Including responses, e.g., litanies, suffrages

Class here plainsong

Class Gregorian chant in 782.3222; class Anglican chant in 782.3223

> 782.294–782.298 Specific texts

Class comprehensive works in 782.29

.294	*Psalms
.295	*Biblical texts

Including amens, canticles

For psalms, see 782.294

.296   *Non-Biblical texts

Class parts of the mass in 782.323

.297   *Tropes

Accretions to the liturgy

For liturgical drama, see 782.298

.298   *Liturgical drama

.3   ***Services (Liturgy and ritual)**

Musical settings of prescribed texts of specific religions

Class texts used by a specific religion with the religion, e.g., liturgy and ritual of a Christian church 264

.32   *Christian services

.322   Services of specific denominations

[.322 01–.322 09]   Standard subdivisions

Do not use; class in 782.3201–782.3209

---

*Add as instructed under 782.1–782.4

.322 1–.322 8   Subdivisions for services of specific denominations

Add to base number 782.322 the numbers following —2 in notation 21–28 from Table 7, e.g., music for Methodist services 782.3227; then add further as follows:

    001–009   Standard subdivisions

          Notation from Table 1 as modified under 780.1–780.9, e.g., performances of music for Methodist services 782.32270078

    01–07   General principles

        Add to 0 the numbers following 781 in 781.1–781.7, e.g., music for Methodist Easter Sunday services 782.32270727, composition of music for Methodist Easter Sunday services 782.3227072713

    08   Musical forms

        Add to 08 the numbers following 784.18 in 784.182–784.189, e.g., preludes for Methodist services 782.322708928, composition of preludes for Methodist services 782.32270892813

Class specific liturgies of specific denominations in 782.323–782.326

>   **782.323–782.326   Specific liturgies**

    Class comprehensive works in 782.32

.323   *Mass (Communion service)

This number is used for music including both the common and the proper of the mass. Masses written from 1350 to today are usually limited to the common and are thus classed in 782.3232. The major exception is the requiem mass, which is classed in 782.3238. Music for an individual part of the mass is classed with that part, e.g., gradual 782.3235

.323 2   *Common (Ordinary) of the mass

Including Kyrie, Gloria, Credo, Sanctus, Benedictus, Agnus Dei

For common of requiem mass, see 782.3238

.323 5   *Proper of the mass

Including introit, gradual, tract, sequence, offertory, communion

For proper of requiem mass, see 782.3238

.323 8   *Requiem mass

.324   *Divine office

Including matins, lauds, prime, terce, sext, none, vespers, compline

See also 782.325 for morning prayer, 782.326 for evening prayer

*Add as instructed under 782.1–782.4

.325   *Morning prayer

        Including matins of the Anglican church

.326   *Evening prayer

        Including evensong of the Anglican church

.33   *Services of classical (Greek and Roman) and Germanic religions

.34–.39   Services of other specific religions

        Add to base number 782.3 the numbers following —29 in notation 294–299
        from Table 7, e.g., music for Judaic services 782.36; then add further as
        follows:
        001–009   Standard subdivisions
                    Notation from Table 1 as modified under 780.1–780.9,
                    e.g., performances of music for Judaic services
                    782.360078
        01–07   General principles
                    Add to 0 the numbers following 781 in 781.1–781.7, e.g.,
                    music for Judaic spring services 782.3605242, composition
                    of music for Judaic spring services 782.360524213
        08   Musical form
                    Add to 08 the numbers following 784.18 in
                    784.182–784.189, e.g., preludes for Judaic services
                    782.3608928, composition of preludes for Judaic services
                    782.360892813

.4   *Secular forms

.42   *Songs

        Class here comprehensive works on songs

        For sacred songs, see 782.25

.421 680 92   Persons associated with art songs

                    Number built according to instructions under
                    782.1–782.4

                    Class here biographies of singers known primarily as
                    recital singers

                    Class biographies of singers known equally well as
                    opera and recital singers in 782.1092

.43   *Forms derived from poetry   Madrigals

        Including ballads, balletts, chansons, frottole

.47   *Song cycles

.48   *Secular cantatas

---

*Add as instructed under 782.1–782.4

> ## 782.5–782.9 Vocal executants

Add to each subdivision identified by † as follows:

01–09   Standard subdivisions
         Notation from Table 1 as modified under 780.1–780.9, e.g.,
         performances 078

1   General principles and musical forms

11–17   General principles
         Add to 1 the numbers following 781 in 781.1–781.7, e.g., rock
         music 166, rehearsing rock music 166144

18   Musical forms
         Add to 18 the numbers following 784.18 in 784.182–784.189,
         e.g., da capo form 1822, composition in da capo form 182213
         Class dramatic vocal forms in 782.1
         For nondramatic vocal forms, see 2–4

2–4   Nondramatic vocal forms
         Add the numbers following 782 in 782.2–782.4, e.g., secular
         cantatas 48

In building numbers, do not add by use of 0 or 1 (alone or in combination) more than twice, e.g., texts of rock protest songs for mixed voices 782.5421661592 (*not* 782.54216615920268)
    (Option: Add as many times as desired)

Use 782.5–782.9 for scores and parts of vocal forms for specific kinds of vocal ensembles, e.g., mixed-voice choirs 782.5, children's choirs 782.7. Use 782.1–782.4 for treatises about and recordings of vocal forms for specific kinds of vocal ensembles. Class performance techniques for a specific ensemble or form with the ensemble or form, e.g., breathing techniques for choral music 782.5148, for opera 782.1148

Class comprehensive works in 782

    See Manual at 782

.5   **†Mixed voices**

Class here choral music, music intended equally for choral or part-song performance, choral music with solo parts, unison voices

    For part songs, see 783.1

> ## 782.6–782.9 Types of voices

Class comprehensive works in 782

.6   **†Women's voices**

Class here music intended equally for women's or children's voices

Class music for children's voices in 782.7

.66   †Soprano (Treble) voices

†Add as instructed under 782.5–782.9

.67	†Mezzo-soprano voices
.68	†Contralto (Alto) voices

.7　†Children's voices

        Class music intended equally for women's or children's voices in 782.6

.76	†Soprano (Treble) voices
.77	†Mezzo-soprano voices
.78	†Contralto (Alto) voices
.79	†Changing voices

.8　†Men's voices

.86	†Treble and alto voices

        Class here countertenor, falsetto, castrato voices

        Subdivisions are added for either or both topics in heading

.87	†Tenor voices
.88	†Baritone voices
.89	†Bass voices

.9　†Other types of voices

.96	†Speaking voices (Choral speech)
.97	†Sprechgesang
.98	†Whistle

783　Music for single voices　　The voice

Use 783 for scores and parts of vocal forms for specific kinds or ensembles of single voice. Use 782.1–782.4 for treatises about and recordings of vocal forms for specific kinds or ensembles of single voice. Class performance techniques for a specific kind or ensemble of single voice or for a specific form with the kind, ensemble, or form, e.g., breathing techniques for part songs 783.1148, for opera 782.1148

    See Manual at 782

.001–.009　　Standard subdivisions

        Notation from Table 1 as modified under 780.1–780.9, e.g., performances of music for single voice 783.0078

.01–.07　　General principles of music for single voices

        Add to base number 783.0 the numbers following 781 in 781.1–781.7, e.g., patriotic music for single voices 783.0599, rhythm in patriotic music for single voices 783.05991224

---

†Add as instructed under 782.5–782.9

.08   Musical forms

Add to base number 783.08 the numbers following 784.18 in
784.182–784.189, e.g., vocal music in waltz form for the single voice
783.08846

> *For dramatic vocal forms, see 782.1; for nondramatic vocal forms, see
> 783.09*

.09   Nondramatic vocal forms

Add to base number 783.09 the numbers following 782 in 782.2–782.4, e.g.,
carols for single voices 783.0928

.1   Single voices in combination

Class here part songs

Class music intended equally for choral or part-song performance in 782.5

.101–.109   Standard subdivisions

Notation from Table 1 as modified under 780.1–780.9, e.g.,
performances of part songs 783.1078

.11   General principles and musical forms

.111–.117   General principles of single voices in combination

Add to base number 783.11 the numbers following 781 in 781.1–781.7,
e.g., patriotic part songs 783.11599, rehearsing patriotic part songs
783.11599144

.118   Musical forms

Add to base number 783.118 the numbers following 784.18 in
784.182–784.189, e.g., part songs in waltz form 783.118846, rehearsing
part songs in waltz form 783.118846144

> *For dramatic vocal forms, see 782.1; for nondramatic vocal forms,
> see 783.119*

.119   Nondramatic vocal forms

Add to base number 783.119 the numbers following 782 in 782.2–782.4,
e.g., carols for single voices in combination 783.11928

>   783.12–783.19 Ensembles by size

Add to each subdivision identified by † as follows:
01–09   Standard subdivisions
           Notation from Table 1 as modified under 780.1–780.9, e.g.,
           performances 078
1   General principles and musical forms
11–17   General principles
           Add to 1 the numbers following 781 in 781.1–781.7, e.g., rock
           music 166, rehearsing rock music 166144
18   Musical forms
           Add to 18 the numbers following 784.18 in 784.182–784.189,
           e.g., da capo form 1822, composition in da capo form 182213
           Class dramatic vocal forms in 782.1
           For nondramatic vocal forms, see 2–4
2–4   Nondramatic vocal forms
           Add the numbers following 782 in 782.2–782.4, e.g., secular
           cantatas 48
6–9   Types of voices
           Add the numbers following 782 in 782.6–782.9, e.g., female
           voices 6; then add notation 01–4 from this table, e.g., secular
           cantatas for female voice 648

In building numbers, do not add by use of 0 or 1 (alone or in combination)
more than twice, e.g., texts of rock protest songs for two singers
783.12421661592 (*not* 783.124216615920268)
    (Option: Add as many times as desired)

Class comprehensive works in 783.1

.12   †Duets

.13   †Trios

.14   †Quartets

.15   †Quintets

.16   †Sextets

.17   †Septets

.18   †Octets

.19   †Nonets and larger combinations

>   **783.2–783.9 Solo voices**

Add to each subdivision identified by ‡ notation 01–4 from table under
783.12–783.19, e.g., secular cantatas 48

Class comprehensive works in 783.2

†Add as instructed under 783.12–783.19

.2   ‡**Solo voice**

Class here comprehensive works on types of single voices

For specific types of single voices, see 783.3–783.9

> 　　　　**783.3–783.9　Specific types of single voices**

Class single voices in ensembles in 783.12–783.19; class comprehensive works in 783.2

.3   ‡**High voice**

Class woman's soprano voice in 783.66; class child's soprano voice in 783.76; class man's treble voice and alto voice in 783.86; class tenor voice in 783.87

.4   ‡**Middle voice**

Class woman's mezzo-soprano voice in 783.67; class child's mezzo-soprano voice in 783.77; class baritone voice in 783.88

.5   ‡**Low voice**

Class woman's contralto voice in 783.68; class child's contralto voice in 783.78; class bass voice in 783.89

.6–.8   **Women's, children's, men's voices**

Add to base number 783 the numbers following 782 in 782.6–782.8, e.g., bass voice 783.89

.9   ‡**Other types of voice**

.96   ‡Speaking voice

.97   ‡Sprechgesang

.98   ‡Whistle

.99   ‡Voice instruments

Including didjeridu, mirliton (kazoo), roarers, voice disguisers (sympathetic instruments relying on the human voice for their sound production)

---

‡Add as instructed under 783.2–783.9

> ## 784–788 Instruments and their music

Add to each subdivision identified by * as follows:
01–09 Standard subdivisions
Notation from Table 1 as modified under 780.1–780.9, e.g., performances 078
See Manual at 784–788: Add table: 092
1 General principles, musical forms, instruments
11–17 General principles
Add to 1 the numbers following 781 in 781.1–781.7, e.g., performance techniques 143
For techniques for playing instruments, see 193
18–19 Musical forms and instruments
Add to 1 the numbers following 784.1 in 784.18–784.19, e.g., sonata form 183, techniques for playing instruments 193

In building numbers, do not add by use of 0 or 1 (alone or in combination) more than twice, e.g., history of atonality in piano sonatas 786.21831267 (*not* 786.2183126709)
(Option: Add as many times as desired)

Class comprehensive works in 784

See Manual at 784–788

784   Instruments and instrumental ensembles and their music

For ensembles with only one instrument per part, see 785; for specific instruments and their music, see 786–788

See also 787 for music for unspecified melody instrument

See Manual at 784–788

SUMMARY

784.01–.09	**Standard subdivisions**
.1	**General principles, musical forms, instruments**
.2	**Full (Symphony) orchestra**
.3	**Chamber orchestra**
.4	**Light orchestra**
.6	**Keyboard, mechanical, electronic, percussion bands**
.7	**String orchestra**
.8	**Wind band**
.9	**Brass band**

.01–.09 Standard subdivisions

Notation from Table 1 as modified under 780.1–780.9, e.g., performances 784.078

.1   General principles, musical forms, instruments

SUMMARY

784.11–.17	General principles of instruments and instrumental ensembles and their music
.18	Musical forms
.19	Instruments

.11–.17   General principles of instruments and instrumental ensembles and their music

> Add to base number 784.1 the numbers following 781 in 781.1–781.7, e.g., performance techniques 784.143

> *For techniques for playing instruments, see 784.193*

.18   Musical forms

SUMMARY

784.180 1–.181	Standard subdivisions and general principles of musical forms
.182	General musical forms
.183	Sonata form and sonatas
.184	Symphonies
.185	Suites and related forms
.186	Concerto form
.187	Contrapuntal forms
.188	Dance forms
.189	Other instrumental forms

.180 1–.181   Standard subdivisions and general principles of musical forms

> Add to 784.18 as instructed under 781.2–781.8, e.g., rhythm in musical forms 784.181224

>   784.182–784.189   Specific musical forms

> Add to each subdivision identified by † as instructed under 781.2–781.8, e.g., composing waltzes 784.1884613

> Class comprehensive works in 784.18

.182   †General musical forms

.182 2   †Binary, ternary, da capo forms

> Subdivisions are added for a combination of two or more forms

.182 3   †Strophic form

.182 4   †Rondos

> Including sonata-rondos

.182 5   †Variations

> Including theme and variations

†Add as instructed under 781.2–781.8

.182 6	†Paraphrase forms
	Including musical parody
.182 7	†Ground bass (Ostinato)
	Including chaconnes, passacaglias

> 784.183–784.189 Instrumental forms

Except for concerto form, comprehensive works on an instrumental form regardless of the executant are classed here, e.g., symphony form 784.184. Individual works and works for a specific executant are classed with the executant, e.g., Camille Saint-Saëns' Symphony No. 3 (for full orchestra including an organ) 784.2184, Charles Marie Widor's Symphony No. 5 (for solo organ) 786.5184

Class comprehensive works in 784.18

.183	†Sonata form and sonatas
	Subdivisions are added for either or both topics in heading
	Class sonata-rondos in 784.1824
.183 2	†Sonatinas
.184	†Symphonies
	Including sinfoniettas
	Class symphonies, sinfoniettas for full orchestras in 784.2184
.184 3	†Symphonic poems
	Class symphonic poems for full orchestras in 784.21843
.184 5	†Sinfonia concertantes
.185	†Suites and related forms
	Including cassations
	Subdivisions are added for a combination of two or more forms
.185 2	†Divertimentos
.185 4	†Partitas
.185 6	†Serenades
.185 8	†Suites

†Add as instructed under 781.2–781.8

.186	†Concerto form

Use this subdivision only for concerto as a form other than solo instruments with full orchestra, e.g., concerto forms for wind bands 784.8186, Bartok's Concerto for orchestra 784.2186

Including cadenzas, concertantes

Class comprehensive works on concertos in 784.23

.186 2	†Concertinos
.187	†Contrapuntal forms
.187 2	†Fugues
.187 4	†Inventions
.187 5	†Canzonas
.187 6	†Fancies and ricercares

Including innomines, tientos

Subdivisions are added for either or both topics in heading

See also 784.1894 for fantasias (an improvisatory form)

.187 8	†Canons
.188	†Dance forms
.188 2	†European dance forms

Including galliards, saltarellos

For dances of the classical suite, see 784.1883; for European dance forms of the nineteenth and later centuries, see 784.1884

.188 23	†Pavans
.188 3	†Dances of the classical suite

Including gavottes, sicilianas

.188 35	†Minuets
.188 4	†European dance forms of the nineteenth and later centuries

Including galops, mazurkas, polonaises

.188 44	†Polkas
.188 46	†Waltzes
.188 5	†Asian dance forms
.188 6	†African dance forms
.188 7	†North American dance forms

Including cakewalks, hoedowns, square dances

For Latin-American dance forms, see 784.1888

†Add as instructed under 781.2–781.8

.188 8	†Latin-American dance forms
	Including rumbas, sambas
.188 85	†Tangos
.188 9	†Dance forms of the Pacific Ocean islands and other parts of the world
.189	†Other instrumental forms
	Class here small-scale and character instrumental forms
.189 2	†Introductory forms
	Music preceding other music or other activities
.189 24	†Fanfares
.189 26	†Overtures
	Class here concert overtures
	Class overtures for full orchestras in 784.218926
.189 28	†Preludes
.189 3	†Intermediate forms
	Music for between or after other activities
	Including interludes, intermezzos, postludes, voluntaries
	Class voluntaries for organs in 786.51893
	For incidental music, see 781.552
.189 4	†Forms of music of an improvisatory or virtuoso nature
	Including arabesques, fantasias, impromptus
	See also 784.1876 for fancies (a contrapuntal form)
.189 45	†Rhapsodies
.189 47	†Toccatas
.189 49	†Artistic études
.189 6	†Romantic and descriptive forms
	Including ballades, meditations, songs without words
.189 64	†Elegies
.189 66	†Nocturnes
.189 68	†Romances
.189 7	†Marches
.189 9	†Forms derived from vocal music

†Add as instructed under 781.2–781.8

.189 92	†Forms derived from sacred music
	Including chorale preludes
	Class chorale preludes for organs in 786.518992
	For instrumental forms derived from liturgical forms, see 784.18993
.189 925	†Chorales
.189 93	†Instrumental forms derived from liturgical forms
.19	Instruments
	For specific instruments, see 786–788
.190 28	Auxiliary techniques and procedures
[.190 284]	Apparatus, equipment, materials
	Do not use; class in 784.19
[.190 287]	Testing and measurement
	Do not use; class in 784.1927
[.190 288]	Maintenance and repair
	Do not use; class in 784.1928
[.190 94–.190 99]	Treatment by specific continents, countries, localities in modern world
	Do not use; class in 784.194–784.199
.192	**Techniques and procedures for instruments themselves**
	See also 784.193 for techniques for playing instruments
.192 2	Description and design
.192 3	Construction
	For construction by machine, see 681.8
.192 7	Testing, measurement, verification
.192 8	Maintenance, tuning, repair
	Including temperament
.193	†Techniques for playing instruments
	Class comprehensive works on performance techniques in 784.143
.193 2	†Breathing and resonance
.193 4	†Embouchure
	Including lipping, tonguing
.193 6	†Arm techniques

†Add as instructed under 781.2–781.8

.193 62	†Forearm techniques
.193 64	†Wrist techniques
.193 65	†Hand techniques

> *For left-hand techniques, see 784.19366; for right-hand techniques, see 784.19367*

.193 66	†Left-hand techniques
.193 67	†Right-hand techniques
.193 68	†Finger techniques

Including fingering, touch, vibrato

.193 69	†Bowing techniques
.193 8	†Leg techniques

Including pedaling

.194–.199	Treatment by specific continents, countries, localities in modern world

Add to base number 784.19 notation 4–9 from Table 2, e.g., instruments of Germany 784.1943

.2   *Full (Symphony) orchestra

Class here comprehensive works on orchestral combinations, music intended equally for orchestral or chamber performance

> *For other orchestral combinations, see 784.3–784.9; for chamber music, see 785*

.209 2	Persons associated with full (symphony) orchestras

Class here biographies of conductors known equally well for conducting operas and orchestral music

Class biographies of conductors known primarily as opera conductors in 782.1092

.22	*Orchestra with vocal parts
.23	*Orchestra with one or more solo instruments

Class here comprehensive works on concertos

> *For concerto form, see 784.186; for orchestra with more than one solo instrument, see 784.24; for orchestra with one solo instrument, see 784.25*

.24	*Orchestra with more than one solo instrument

Including concerti grossi

---

*Add as instructed under 784–788

†Add as instructed under 781.2–781.8

.25   *Orchestra with one solo instrument

             Class here comprehensive works on solo concertos

             For specific solo instruments, see 784.26–784.28

.26–.28   Specific solo instruments with orchestra

             Add to base number 784.2 the numbers following 78 in 786–788, e.g.,
             orchestra with solo piano 784.262, rehearsing orchestra with solo piano
             784.262144

> ## 784.3–784.9 Other orchestral combinations and band

Add to each subdivision identified by † as follows:
01–09   Standard subdivisions
                    Notation from Table 1 as modified under 780.1–780.9, e.g.,
                    performances 078
1   General principles, musical forms, instruments
11–17   General principles
                    Add to 1 the numbers following 781 in 781.1–781.7, e.g.,
                    sacred music 17, rehearsing sacred music 17044
18–19   Musical forms and instruments
                    Add to 1 the numbers following 784.1 in 784.18–784.19, e.g.,
                    waltz form 18846, bowing techniques 19369
2   Featured voices, instruments, ensembles
                    Add to 2 the numbers following 78 in 782–788, e.g., flutes 2832

Class comprehensive works on orchestral combinations and band, on band in
784; class comprehensive works on orchestral combinations in 784.2

.3   **†Chamber orchestra**

             For chamber music, see 785

.4   **†Light orchestra**

             Class here salon orchestra

.44   †School orchestra

.46   †Orchestra with toy instruments

.48   †Dance orchestra (Dance band)

             Class here big bands

.6   **†Keyboard, mechanical, electronic, percussion bands**

.68   †Percussion band

             Class here rhythm band

.7   **†String orchestra**

---

*Add as instructed under 784–788
†Add as instructed under 784.3–784.9

.8 †**Wind band**

Band consisting of woodwind instruments, brass instruments, or both

For brass band, see 784.9

.83 †Marching band

.84 †Military band

.89 †Woodwind band

.9 †**Brass band**

785 **Ensembles with only one instrument per part**

Class here chamber music

Class works for solo melody instrument with keyboard or other accompaniment in 786–788

See Manual at 784–788

SUMMARY

785.001–.009	**Standard subdivisions**
.01–.09	**General principles, musical forms, instruments**
.1	**Ensembles by size**
.2	**Ensembles with keyboard**
.3	**Ensembles without electrophones and with percussion and keyboard**
.4	**Ensembles without keyboard**
.5	**Ensembles without keyboard and with percussion**
.6	**Keyboard, mechanical, aeolian, electrophone, percussion ensembles**
.7	**String ensembles Bowed string ensembles**
.8	**Woodwind ensembles**
.9	**Brass ensembles**

.001–.009 Standard subdivisions

Notation from Table 1 as modified under 780.1–780.9, e.g., performances of chamber music 785.0078

.01–.07 General principles of ensembles with only one instrument per part

Add to base number 785.0 the numbers following 781 in 781.1–781.7, e.g., performance techniques 785.043, jazz ensembles 785.065

For techniques for playing instruments, see 785.093

.08–.09 Musical forms and instruments

Add to base number 785.0 the numbers following 784.1 in 784.18–784.19, e.g., waltz form 785.08846, techniques for playing instruments 785.093

.1 **Ensembles by size**

These provisions, when applied throughout 785, refer to the number of instruments, except when percussion instruments are involved; in that case they refer to the number of performers

†Add as instructed under 784.3–784.9

.12 *Duets

.13 *Trios

.14 *Quartets

.15 *Quintets

.16 *Sextets

.17 *Septets

.18 *Octets

.19 *Nonets and larger ensembles

> ### 785.2–785.9 Specific kinds of ensembles

Add to each subdivision identified by † as follows:
```
01–09   Standard subdivisions
            Notation from Table 1 as modified under 780.1–780.9, e.g.,
            performances 078
1       General principles, musical forms, size of ensemble
11–17   General principles
            Add to 1 the numbers following 781 in 781.1–781.7, e.g.,
            sacred music 17, conducting sacred music 17045
            Class instrumental techniques for mixed ensembles in
            784.193; class instrumental techniques for specific instruments
            in 786–788, e.g., bowing techniques for violins 787.219369
18      Musical forms
            Add to 18 the numbers following 784.18 in 784.182–784.189,
            e.g., waltz form 18846
19      Size of ensemble
            Add to 19 the numbers following 785.1 in 785.12–785.19, e.g.,
            octets 198
```

In building numbers, do not add by use of 0 or 1 (alone or in combination) more than twice, e.g., history of atonality in piano duets 785.621921267 (*not* 785.62192126709)
(Option: Add as many times as desired)

Class comprehensive works in 785

> ### 785.2–785.5 Ensembles consisting of two or more instrumental groups

Class comprehensive works in 785

.2 †Ensembles with keyboard

> *For ensembles without electrophones and with percussion and keyboard, see 785.3*

---

*Add as instructed under 784–788
†Add as instructed under 785.2–785.9

.22 †Ensembles of woodwind, brass, strings, keyboard

.23 †Ensembles of woodwind, brass, keyboard

.24 †Ensembles of woodwind, strings, keyboard

.25 †Ensembles of brass, strings, keyboard

.26 †Ensembles of woodwind and keyboard

Three or more instruments

See also 788.2 for ensembles of one woodwind instrument and keyboard

.27 †Ensembles of brass and keyboard

Three or more instruments

See also 788.9 for ensembles of one brass instrument and keyboard

.28 †Ensembles of strings and keyboard

Three or more instruments

See also 787 for ensembles of one stringed instrument and keyboard

.29 †Ensembles with electrophones, percussion, keyboard

.292 †Ensembles of woodwind, brass, strings, electrophones, percussion, keyboard

.293 †Ensembles of woodwind, brass, electrophones, percussion, keyboard

.294 †Ensembles of woodwind, strings, electrophones, percussion, keyboard

.295 †Ensembles of brass, strings, electrophones, percussion, keyboard

.296 †Ensembles of woodwind, electrophones, percussion, keyboard

.297 †Ensembles of brass, electrophones, percussion, keyboard

.298 †Ensembles of strings, electrophones, percussion, keyboard

.299 †Ensembles with electrophones and keyboard

.299 2 †Ensembles of woodwind, brass, strings, electrophones, keyboard

.299 3 †Ensembles of woodwind, brass, electrophones, keyboard

.299 4 †Ensembles of woodwind, strings, electrophones, keyboard

.299 5 †Ensembles of brass, strings, electrophones, keyboard

.299 6 †Ensembles of woodwind, electrophones, keyboard

.299 7 †Ensembles of brass, electrophones, keyboard

.299 8 †Ensembles of strings, electrophones, keyboard

†Add as instructed under 785.2–785.9

.299 9	†Ensembles of electrophones and keyboard
	Two or more electrophones
	See also 786.7 for ensembles of one electrophone and keyboard

.3   **†Ensembles without electrophones and with percussion and keyboard**

.32	†Ensembles of woodwind, brass, strings, percussion, keyboard
.33	†Ensembles of woodwind, brass, percussion, keyboard
.34	†Ensembles of woodwind, strings, percussion, keyboard
.35	†Ensembles of brass, strings, percussion, keyboard
.36	†Ensembles of woodwind, percussion, keyboard
.37	†Ensembles of brass, percussion, keyboard
.38	†Ensembles of strings, percussion, keyboard
.39	†Ensembles of keyboard and percussion

.4   **†Ensembles without keyboard**

For ensembles without keyboard and with percussion, see 785.5

.42	†Ensembles of woodwind, brass, strings
.43	†Ensembles of woodwind and brass (Wind ensembles)
.44	†Ensembles of woodwind and strings
.45	†Ensembles of brass and strings
.46	†Ensembles with electrophones
.462	†Ensembles of woodwind, brass, strings, electrophones
.463	†Ensembles of woodwind, brass, electrophones
.464	†Ensembles of woodwind, strings, electrophones
.465	†Ensembles of brass, strings, electrophones
.466	†Ensembles of woodwinds and electrophones
.467	†Ensembles of brass and electrophones
.468	†Ensembles of strings and electrophones

.5   **†Ensembles without keyboard and with percussion**

.52	†Ensembles of woodwind, brass, strings, percussion
.53	†Ensembles of woodwind, brass, percussion
.54	†Ensembles of woodwind, strings, percussion

†Add as instructed under 785.2–785.9

.55	†Ensembles of brass, strings, percussion
.56	†Ensembles of woodwind and percussion
.57	†Ensembles of brass and percussion
.58	†Ensembles of strings and percussion
.59	†Ensembles with electrophones and percussion
.592	†Ensembles of woodwind, brass, strings, electrophones, percussion
.593	†Ensembles of woodwind, brass, electrophones, percussion
.594	†Ensembles of woodwind, strings, electrophones, percussion
.595	†Ensembles of brass, strings, electrophones, percussion
.596	†Ensembles of woodwind, electrophones, percussion
.597	†Ensembles of brass, electrophones, percussion
.598	†Ensembles of strings, electrophones, percussion
.599	†Ensembles of electrophones and percussion

> ### 785.6–785.9 Ensembles consisting of only one instrumental group

The inclusion of "only one kind" in the 785.6–785.9 headings limits the subdivisions to individual kind of instruments, not to family of instruments. For example, a string quartet, which usually consists of two violins, a viola, and a cello is classed in 785.7194 string quartets, *not* 785.72194 violin quartets

When adding from 786–788 to indicate the instrument, add *only* the notation for the instrument; do not follow the footnote leading to add instructions. After indicating the instrument, add as instructed under 785.2–785.9, where notation 19 is used to indicate size of ensemble. For example, 785.7194 means string quartets, *not* string instruments of Europe (the meaning that would result from following the footnote instruction). The correct number for string quartets of Europe is 785.7194094

Class comprehensive works in 785

.6   †Keyboard, mechanical, aeolian, electrophone, percussion ensembles

.62–.65   Keyboard ensembles

Add to base number 785.6 the numbers following 786 in 786.2–786.5 for the instrument only, e.g., music for piano ensembles 785.62; then add further as instructed under 785.2–785.9, e.g., music for three pianos 785.62193

Notation 19 from table under 785.2–785.9 for size of ensemble can mean either number of instruments or, when only one instrument is used, number of performers. For example, 785.62192 can mean either music for two pianos or music for piano (four hands)

†Add as instructed under 785.2–785.9

.66   †Ensembles of mechanical and aeolian instruments   Ensembles of
                   mechanical instruments

.664–.668   Ensembles with only one kind of mechanical instrument

> Add to base number 785.66 the numbers following 786.6 in
> 786.64–786.68 for the instrument only, e.g., music for carillons 785.664

.669   †Aeolian ensembles

.67   †Electrophone ensembles

> *For ensembles of a specific kind or group of electrically amplified or
> modified standard instruments, see the instrument or group of
> instruments, e.g., electric guitar ensembles 785.787*
>
> *See also 786.7 for electronic music for one performer*

.673–.676   Ensembles with only one type of electrophone instrument

> Add to base number 785.67 the numbers following 786.7 in
> 786.73–786.76 for the instrument only, e.g., music for synthesizers
> 785.674; then add further as instructed under 785.2–785.9, e.g., sextets
> for synthesizers 785.674196

.68   †Percussion ensembles

> Class here ensembles for more than one performer; see note under 785.1
>
> *See also 786.8 for percussion music for one performer*

.7   †String ensembles   Bowed string ensembles

.72–.79   Ensembles of only one kind of stringed instrument

> Add to base number 785.7 the numbers following 787 in 787.2–787.9 for
> the instrument only, e.g., music for guitar 785.787; then add further as
> instructed under 785.2–785.9, e.g., quartet for guitars 785.787194

.8   †Woodwind ensembles

.83–.88   Ensembles of only one kind of woodwind instrument

> Add to base number 785.8 the numbers following 788 in 788.3–788.8 for
> the instrument only, e.g., music for saxophones 785.87; then add further as
> instructed under 785.2–785.9, e.g., quartet for saxophones 785.87194

.9   †Brass ensembles

.92–.99   Ensembles of only one kind of brass instrument

> Add to base number 785.9 the numbers following 788.9 in 788.92–788.99
> for the instrument only, e.g., music for trombones 785.93; then add further
> as instructed under 785.2–785.9, e.g., quartet for trombones 785.93194

†Add as instructed under 785.2–785.9

> ## 786–788 Specific instruments and their music

Class here music for solo instrument, music for solo instruments accompanied by one other instrument when the accompanying instrument clearly has a subsidiary role

Unless the forerunner of a modern instrument has its own notation, class it with the modern instrument. For example, the shawm, a forerunner of the oboe and an instrument without its own number, is classed with the oboe in 788.52; however, the vihuela, the forerunner of the guitar, is classed in 787.86 (its own number), *not* with the guitar in 787.87

Class chamber music in 785; class comprehensive works in 784

For voice instruments, see 783.99

786   *Keyboard, mechanical, electrophonic, percussion instruments

Class here comprehensive works on keyboard instruments, on keyboard stringed instruments; music for unspecified keyboard instrument

See Manual at 784–788

SUMMARY

786.2	**Pianos**
.3	**Clavichords**
.4	**Harpsichords**
.5	**Keyboard wind instruments Organs**
.6	**Mechanical and aeolian instruments**
.7	**Electrophones Electronic instruments**
.8	**Percussion instruments**
.9	**Drums and devices used for percussive effects**

> ### 786.2–786.5 Keyboard instruments

Class mechanical keyboard instruments in 786.66; class keyboard idiophones in 786.83; class comprehensive works in 786. Class music for more than one performer on one keyboard instrument as an ensemble with the ensemble in 785.62–785.65, e.g., piano (four hands) 785.62192

> ### 786.2–786.4 Keyboard stringed instruments

Class comprehensive works in 786

.2   ***Pianos**

.28   *Prepared pianos

.3   ***Clavichords**

**Add as instructed under 784–788

.4 ***Harpsichords**

Class here spinets, virginals

.5 ***Keyboard wind instruments   Organs**

Class concertinas in 788.84; class accordions in 788.86

.55 *Reed organs and regals

Variant names for reed organs: American organs, cabinet organs, harmoniums

Subdivisions are added for either or both topics in heading

.59 *Electronic organs

Class here comprehensive works on keyboard electrophones

Class a keyboard instrument whose sound is generated by conventional means, even though amplified or modified electronically, with the instrument, e.g., electric piano 786.2

See also 786.74 for synthesizers

.6 ***Mechanical and aeolian instruments**

Subdivisions are added for mechanical and aeolian instruments together, for mechanical instruments alone

---

> 786.64–786.68   Mechanical instruments

Class comprehensive works in 786.6

.64 *Mechanical struck idiophones

Including carillons, mechanized bells

Class here comprehensive works on mechanical idiophones

For mechanical plucked idiophones, see 786.65

.65 *Mechanical plucked idiophones

Including music boxes, symphonions

.66 *Mechanical keyboard instruments

Mechanical instruments with attached functional keyboard

Including player pianos (pianolas)

Class mechanical wind keyboard instruments in 786.68

.67 *Mechanical stringed instruments

Class mechanical stringed keyboard instruments in 786.66

*Add as instructed under 784–788

.68   *Mechanical wind instruments

    Including fair organs

.69   *Aeolian instruments

    Instruments activated by the blowing of the wind

.7   *Electrophones   Electronic instruments

    Class here music made from electrically produced or manipulated sounds

    Class keyboard electrophones in 786.59. Class a specific electrically amplified or modified standard instrument other than keyboard instruments with the instrument, e.g., electric guitar 787.87

.73   *Monophonic electrophones

    Electronic sound producers capable of producing only one pitch at a time

    Including ondes martenot, theremins

.74   *Synthesizers

    Class here electronic music

    For tapes, see 786.75; for computers, see 786.76

.75   Tapes

    Class here musique concrète (concrete music)

.76   Computers

    See also 781.34 for using computers to compose music

.8   *Percussion instruments

    For drums, see 786.92–786.98; for struck stringed instruments, see 787.7

.82   *Idiophones (Vibrating sonorous solids)

    Class here comprehensive works on percussion instruments of definite pitch

    Class percussion instruments of indefinite pitch in 786.88

    For mechanical idiophones, see 786.64; for keyboard idiophones, see 786.83; for set idiophones, see 786.84–786.87; for single idiophones, see 786.88

.83   *Keyboard idiophones

    Class here celestas

\>   786.84–786.87 Set idiophones

    Class comprehensive works in 786.84

*Add as instructed under 784–788

.84   *Percussed idiophones

             Sonorous solids struck by or against nonsonorous objects, e.g., sticks struck
             on ground

             Class here comprehensive works on set idiophones (similar sonorous solids
             combined to form one instrument)

                   *For plucked idiophones, see 786.85; for friction idiophones, see 786.86;
                   for concussion idiophones, see 786.87*

.842–.848   Sonorous solids of specific shapes

             Add to base number 786.84 the numbers following 786.884 in
             786.8842–786.8848, e.g., bar idiophones 786.843, performances on bar
             idiophones 786.843078

.85   *Plucked idiophones

             Elastic bars or rods, usually of metal, fixed at one end and vibrated by
             plucking the free end

             Including sanzas (thumb pianos)

.86   *Friction idiophones

             Objects rubbed to produce sounds of definite pitch

.862–.868   Sonorous solids of specific shapes

             Add to base number 786.86 the numbers following 786.884 in
             786.8842–786.8848, e.g., vessels 786.866, rehearsing on vessels
             786.866144

.87   *Concussion idiophones

             Two or more similar sonorous objects struck together to make both vibrate

.872–.878   Sonorous objects of specific shapes

             Add to base number 786.87 the numbers following 786.884 in
             786.8842–786.8848, e.g., blocks 786.873, rehearsing playing of blocks
             786.873144

.88   *Single idiophones

             Idiophones consisting of a single sonorous object

             Class here comprehensive works on percussion instruments of indefinite
             pitch

                   *For a specific percussion instrument of indefinite pitch not provided for
                   here, see the instrument, e.g., cymbals 786.873*

.884   *Percussed idiophones

.884 2   *Sticks and rods

                Including triangles

                Subdivisions are added for either or both topics in heading

*Add as instructed under 784–788

.884 3	*Bars, plates, blocks

Including anvils, gongs

Subdivisions are added for any or all topics in heading

.884 4	*Troughs
.884 5	*Tubes
.884 6	*Vessels

For bells, see 786.8848

.884 8	*Bells
.884 85	*Hand bells
.885	*Rattled idiophones

Including maracas, sistrums

.886	*Scraped idiophones

Idiophones consisting of two objects, a notched one being scraped by the other to create vibrations in one or the other

Including football rattles, washboards

.887	*Plucked idiophones

Including jew's harps

.888	*Friction idiophones

Including musical saws

.9   *Drums and devices used for percussive effects

Subdivisions are added for drums and devices used for percussive effects together, for drums alone

---

> 786.92–786.98 Drums (Membranophones, Vibrating stretched membranes)

Class comprehensive works in 786.9

.92	*Struck drums

For kettle-shaped drums, see 786.93; for tubular drums, see 786.94; for frame-shaped drums, see 786.95

.93	*Kettle-shaped drums

Including timpani (kettledrums), nakers (naqara), tabla

.94	*Tubular drums

Including snare drums (side drums)

*Add as instructed under 784–788

.95	*Frame-shaped drums

Drums with depth of body not exceeding radius of membrane

Including bass drums, tambourines

.96	*Rattle drums

Drums whose membrane or membranes are struck by pellets or pendants

.97	*Plucked drums

Drums each with a string that when plucked transmits a vibration to the membrane through which the string passes

.98	*Friction drums

Drums whose membrane is made to vibrate by being rubbed either directly or by an attached stick or cord

Including quicas, rommelpots

.99	*Devices used for percussion effects

Including motor horns, popguns, sirens, whips

787 *Stringed instruments (Chordophones)   Bowed stringed instruments

Class here music for unspecified melody instrument, comprehensive works on the lute family (instruments whose strings run from the resonating belly to the neck)

Class keyboard stringed instruments in 786; class mechanical stringed instruments in 786.67

See Manual at 784–788

.2	***Violins**

Class here comprehensive works on violin family

For violas, see 787.3; for cellos, see 787.4; for double basses, see 787.5

.3	***Violas**
.4	***Cellos (Violoncellos)**
.5	***Double basses**
.6	***Other bowed stringed instruments Viols**

For double basses, see 787.5

.62	*Descant viols
.63	*Treble viols
.64	*Tenor viols
.65	*Bass viols (Viola da gambas)

*Add as instructed under 784–788

.66   *Viola d'amores

.69   *Hurdy-gurdies (Vielles)

.7   ***Plectral instruments**

> Class here zithers, comprehensive works on struck stringed instruments
>
> *For plectral lute family, see 787.8; for harps and musical bows, see 787.9*

> 787.72–787.75   Zithers

> Class comprehensive works in 787.7

.72   *Stick, tube, trough zithers

> Subdivisions are added for any or all topics in heading

.73   *Frame, ground, harp, raft zithers

> Subdivisions are added for any or all topics in heading

.74   *Board zithers

> Including cimbaloms, dulcimers, santirs, yang ch'ins
>
> Class here struck board zithers
>
> *For plucked board zithers, see 787.75*

.75   *Plucked board zithers

> Including Appalachian dulcimers, autoharps, concert zithers, psalteries, Tyrolean zithers

.78   *Lyres

.8   ***Plectral lute family**

> Class here long-necked, short-necked lutes

.82   *Round-backed lute family

> Including sitars, tamburas
>
> *For lutes, see 787.83; for mandolins, see 787.84*

.83   *Lutes

.84   *Mandolins

.85   *Flat-backed lute family

> Including biwas, citterns, shamisens
>
> *For vihuelas, see 787.86; for guitars, see 787.87; for banjos, see 787.88; for ukuleles, see 787.89*

.86   *Vihuelas

*Add as instructed under 784–788

.87	*Guitars
.875	*Balalaikas
.88	*Banjos
.89	*Ukuleles

.9   *Harps and musical bows

Subdivisions are added for harps and musical bows together, for harps alone

.92   *Musical bows

Stringed instruments each with one or more strings stretched across a single flexible string bearer

Class pluriarcs in 787.93

.93   *Pluriarcs (Compound musical bows)

Stringed instruments with strings stretched across several string bearers

---

> 787.94–787.98 Harps

Class comprehensive works in 787.9

.94   *Bow (Arched) harps and angle harps

Harps with neck forming an arch with the resonator

Subdivisions are added for either or both topics in heading

.95   *Frame harps

Harps with pillar joining end of neck to resonator

Including Celtic harps, orchestral harps

.98   *Bridge harps (Harp-lutes)

Lute-bodied harps with strings that are perpendicular to body of the harp and that pass through a bridge

Including koras

788   *Wind instruments (Aerophones)

Class keyboard wind instruments in 786.5; class mechanical wind instruments in 786.68

See Manual at 784–788

.2   *Woodwind instruments and free aerophones

Subdivisions are added for woodwind instruments and free aerophones together, for woodwind instruments alone

For specific woodwind instruments, see 788.3–788.8

*Add as instructed under 784–788

.29   *Free aerophones

> Aerophones in which the airstream is not directed into or through a cavity or tube but directly into the outer air, or the air remains static and the instrument when moved vibrates through friction with the air

> Including bull-roarers

> Class free aerophones used for percussion effects in 786.99

> **788.3–788.8 Specific woodwind instruments**

> Class comprehensive works in 788.2

.3   ***Flute family**

> Class here nose flutes

.32   *Transverse (Side-blown) flutes

> Variant name: flutes

> *For piccolos and fifes, see 788.33; for bass flutes, see 788.34*

.33   *Piccolos and fifes

> Subdivisions are added for either or both topics in heading

.34   *Bass flutes

.35   *Duct, end-blown, notched flutes

> Including flageolets, penny whistles, shakuhanchis

> Subdivisions are added for any or all topics in heading

> *For recorders, see 788.36*

.36   *Recorders

.363   *Sopranino recorders

.364   *Descant (Soprano) recorders

.365   *Treble (Alto) recorders

.366   *Tenor recorders

.367   *Bass recorders

.37   *Multiple flutes   Pan pipes

> Several flutes formed into one instrument

.38   *Vessel flutes

> Including ocarinas

---

*Add as instructed under 784–788

.4 ***Reed instruments**

> *For double-reed instruments, see 788.5; for single-reed instruments, see 788.6; for free reeds, see 788.8*

.49   *Bagpipes

> Including cornemuses; Northumbrian, uillean (union) pipes
>
> Class here single-reed and double-reed bagpipes

.5 ***Double-reed instruments**

> Including crumhorns, racketts
>
> *For bagpipes, see 788.49*

.52   *Oboes

.53   *Cors anglais (English horns)

.58   *Bassoons

> *For double bassoons, see 788.59*

.59   *Double bassoons (Contrabassoons)

.6 ***Single-reed instruments**

> *For bagpipes, see 788.49; for saxophones, see 788.7*

.62   *Clarinets

> *For bass clarinets, see 788.65*

.65   *Bass clarinets

.7 ***Saxophones**

.72   *Soprano saxophones

.73   *Alto saxophones

.74   *Tenor saxophones

.75   *Bass saxophones

.8 ***Free reeds**

> Instruments consisting of sets of individual free reeds

.82   *Mouth organs   Harmonicas

> Including shengs

.84   *Concertinas

> Including bandoneons

.86   *Accordions

*Add as instructed under 784–788

.863	*Button accordions Melodeons
.865	*Piano accordions

.9   *Brass instruments (Lip-reed instruments)

.92	*Trumpets
.93	*Trombones
.94	*French horns (Horns)

> *See also 788.53 for English horns*

.95	*Bugles
.96	*Cornets
.97	*Flugelhorns (Saxhorns)
.974	*Tenor horns

> Including B-flat horns (also called baritones in United Kingdom and Germany), E-flat horns (also called alto horns in North America and France)

.975	*Euphoniums and baritones (American)

> Subdivisions are added for either or both topics in heading

.98	*Tubas
.99	*Other brass instruments

> Including cornetts, ophicleides, serpents

(789)   Composers and traditions of music

(Optional number and subdivisions; prefer 780–788)

(Option A: Arrange treatises about all composers at 789 plus an alphabeting mark; then to the result add notation following 78 in 780–788

(Option B: Use 789 and its subdivisions for traditions of music

(Option C: Use 789 and its subdivisions for recordings of music

(If Option A is used with either option B or C, class comprehensive works on traditions of music in 789.1)

Unless other instructions are given, class a subject with aspects in two or more subdivisions of 789 in the number coming last, e.g., Spanish folk music for springtime 789.261015242 (*not* 789.2015242)

(.1)   †General principles of traditions of music

Add to base number 789.1 the numbers following 781 in 781.1–781.5, e.g., treatment of springtime music in various traditions 789.15242

(If Option A is used with either Option B or C, class here comprehensive works on traditions of music)

---

*Add as instructed under 784–788

†(Optional number; prefer 781–788)

(.2)   **†Folk music**

> Music indigenous to the cultural group in which it occurs, usually evolved through aural transmission

(.200 1–.200 7)   †Standard subdivisions

> Notation from Table 1 as modified under 780.1–780.9, e.g., performances of folk music 789.20078

(.200 8)   †History and description of folk music with respect to kinds of persons

[.200 89]   Treatment with respect to specific racial, ethnic, national groups

> Do not use; class in 789.21–789.29

(.200 9)   †Historical, geographic, persons treatment

(.200 901–.200 905)   †Historical periods

> Add to base number 789.20090 the numbers following 780.90 in 780.901–780.905, e.g., Renaissance folk music 789.2009031

(.200 91–.200 99)   †Geographic and persons treatment

> *For geographic treatment of folk music of specific racial, ethnic, national groups, see 789.21–789.29*

(.201)   †General principles, stylistic influences of other traditions, musical forms

(.201 1–.201 5)   †General principles

> Add to base number 789.201 the numbers following 781 in 781.1–781.5, e.g., folk music for springtime 789.2015242, rhythm in folk music for springtime 789.20152421224

(.201 6)   †Stylistic influences of other traditions of music

> Add to base number 789.2016 the numbers following 789 in 789.3–789.9, e.g., influence of jazz on folk music 789.20165, performances of folk music influenced by jazz 789.20165078

(.201 8)   †Musical forms

> Add to base number 789.2018 the numbers following 784.18 in 784.182–784.189, e.g., march form in folk music 789.201897

(.202–.208)   †Voices, instruments, ensembles

> Add to base number 789.20 the numbers following 78 in 782–788, e.g., folk songs for women singers 789.202642

†(Optional number; prefer 781–788)

(.21–.29)   †Folk music of specific racial, ethnic, national groups

Add to base number 789.2 notation 1–9 from Table 5, e.g., Spanish folk
music 789.261; then add further as follows:

001–008   Standard subdivisions
            Notation from Table 1 as modified under 780.1–780.9,
            e.g., performances of Spanish folk music 789.2610078
009   Historical, geographic, persons treatment
00901–00905   Historical periods
            Add to 0090 the numbers following 780.90 in
            780.091–780.095, e.g., Spanish folk music of the
            Renaissance 789.261009031
[0093–0099]   Treatment by specific continents, countries, localities
            Do not use; class in 03–09
01   General principles, stylistic influences of other traditions of
            music, musical forms
011–015   General principles
            Add to 01 the numbers following 781 in 781.1–781.5,
            e.g., Spanish folk music for springtime 789.261015242,
            rhythm in Spanish folk music for springtime
            789.2610152421224
016   Stylistic influences of other traditions of music
            Add to 016 the numbers following 789 in 789.3–789.9,
            e.g., influence of jazz on Spanish folk music
            789.2610165, performances of Spanish folk music
            influenced by jazz 789.2610165078
018   Musical forms
            Add to 018 the numbers following 784.18 in
            784.182–784.189, e.g., march form in Spanish folk
            music 789.26101897
02   Voices, instruments, ensembles
            Add to 02 the numbers following 78 in 782–788, e.g.,
            Spanish folk music for the guitar 789.26102787
03–09   Specific continents, countries, localities
            Add to 0 notation 3–9 from Table 2, e.g., Spanish folk
            music in New York City 789.26107471

†(Optional number; prefer 781–788)

> ## (789.3–789.9) Other traditions of music

Add to each subdivision identified by * as follows:

001–009   Standard subdivisions
    Notation from Table 1 as modified under 780.1–780.9, e.g., performance 0078

01   General principles, stylistic influences of other traditions of music, musical forms

011–015   General principles
    Add to 01 the numbers following 781 in 781.1–781.5, e.g., springtime music 015242, melody in springtime music 015242124

016   Stylistic influences of other traditions of music
    Add to 016 the numbers following 789 in 789.2–789.9, e.g., influence of folk music 0162, performances of music influenced by folk music 0162078

018   Musical forms
    Add to 018 the numbers following 784.18 in 784.182–784.189, e.g., march form 01897

1   Voices, instruments, ensembles
    Add to 1 the numbers following 78 in 782–788, e.g., guitar music 1787

Class comprehensive works in 789

(.3)   †*Popular music

For western popular music, see 789.4

(.4)   †*Western popular music

Including skiffle

Class country and western music in 789.42

For jazz, see 789.5; for rock, see 789.6

(.42)   †*Country music

Class here bluegrass music

(.43)   †*Blues

Class here rhythm and blues

(.44)   †*Soul

(.45)   †*Ragtime

(.46)   †*Reggae

(.5)   †*Jazz

*Add as instructed under 789.3–789.9
†(Optional number; prefer 781–788)

(.52)   †*Early jazz

> Class here origins of jazz

(.53)   †*Traditional jazz

> Including New Orleans, Dixieland, Southwest and Kansas City, Harlem, white New York styles; Chicago breakdown

(.54)   †*Mainstream jazz

> Including swing

(.55)   †*Modern jazz

> Including bop (bebop), hard bop, cool jazz, progressive jazz
>
> *For avant-garde jazz, see 789.56*

(.56)   †*Avant-garde jazz

(.57)   †*Hybrid styles

> Including Afro-Cuban, third stream, Indo-jazz

(.6)   †*Rock (Rock 'n' roll)

> Including acid, folk, hard, punk, soft rock

(.7)   †Sacred music

(.700 1–.700 9)   †Standard subdivisions

> Notation from Table 1 as modified under 780.1–780.9, e.g., performances of sacred music 789.70078

(.701)   †General principles, stylistic influences of other traditions of music, musical forms

> Add to base number 789.701 the numbers following 01 in notation 011–018 from table under 789.3–789.9, e.g., influence of folk music 789.70162

(.702)   †Voices, instruments, ensembles

> Add to base number 789.702 the numbers following 78 in 782–788, e.g., sacred music for the guitar 789.702787

(.71)   †*Christian sacred music

> *For music of Christian church year, see 789.72*

(.72)   †*Music of Christian church year

(.722–.729)   †Sacred music of specific parts of Christian church year

> Add to base number 789.72 the numbers following 781.72 in 781.722–781.729, e.g., Christmas music 789.723; then add further as instructed under 789.3–789.9, e.g., Christmas music for the guitar 789.7231787

*Add as instructed under 789.3–789.9

†(Optional number; prefer 781–788)

(.73)   †*Sacred music of classical (Greek and Roman) and Germanic religions

(.74–.79)   †Sacred music of other specific religions

> Add to base number 789.7 the numbers following —29 in notation 294–299 from Table 7, e.g., Judaic sacred music 789.76; then add further as instructed under 789.3–789.9, e.g., Judaic sacred music for the guitar 789.761787

(.8)   †*Western art (Classical) music

> Class here comprehensive works on art music

> *For nonwestern art music, see 789.9*

(.9)   †*Nonwestern art music

790   Recreational and performing arts

> Class here interdisciplinary works on recreation

> *For sociology of recreation, see 306.48; for music, see 780*

> *See Manual at 790*

SUMMARY

790.01–.09	**Recreation centers and standard subdivisions of recreation**
.1	**Recreational activities**
.2	**The performing arts in general**
791	**Public performances**
.01–.09	**Standard subdivisions and amusement parks**
.1	**Traveling shows**
.3	**Circuses**
.4	**Motion pictures, radio, television**
.5	**Puppetry and toy theaters**
.6	**Pageantry**
.8	**Animal performances**
792	**Stage presentations**
.01–.09	**Standard subdivisions and types of stage presentation**
.1	**Tragedy and serious drama**
.2	**Comedy and melodrama**
.3	**Pantomime**
.5	**Dramatic vocal forms Opera**
.6	**Musical plays**
.7	**Variety shows and theatrical dancing**
.8	**Ballet and modern dance**
.9	**Stage productions**

*Add as instructed under 789.3–789.9
†(Optional number; prefer 781–788)

793	**Indoor games and amusements**	
.01–.08	**Standard subdivisions**	
.2	**Parties and entertainments**	
.3	**Social, folk, national dancing**	
.4	**Games of action**	
.5	**Forfeit and trick games**	
.7	**Games not characterized by action**	
.8	**Magic and related activities**	
.9	**Other indoor diversions**	
794	**Indoor games of skill**	
.1	**Chess**	
.2	**Checkers (Draughts)**	
.3	**Darts**	
.4	**Go**	
.6	**Bowling**	
.7	**Ball games**	
.8	**Electronic games** **Computer games**	
795	**Games of chance**	
.01	**Philosophy and theory**	
.1	**Games with dice**	
.2	**Wheel and top games**	
.3	**Games dependent on drawing numbers or counters**	
.4	**Card games**	
796	**Athletic and outdoor sports and games**	
.01–.09	**Standard subdivisions and general kinds of sports and games**	
.1	**Miscellaneous games**	
.2	**Activities and games requiring equipment**	
.3	**Ball games**	
.4	**Weight lifting, track and field, gymnastics**	
.5	**Outdoor life**	
.6	**Cycling and related activities**	
.7	**Driving motor vehicles**	
.8	**Combat sports**	
.9	**Ice and snow sports**	
797	**Aquatic and air sports**	
.028 9	**Safety measures**	
.1	**Boating**	
.2	**Swimming and diving**	
.3	**Other aquatic sports**	
.5	**Air sports**	
798	**Equestrian sports and animal racing**	
.2	**Horsemanship**	
.4	**Horse racing** **Flat racing**	
.6	**Driving and coaching**	
.8	**Dog racing**	
799	**Fishing, hunting, shooting**	
.1	**Fishing**	
.2	**Hunting**	
.3	**Shooting other than game**	

.01	Philosophy and theory of recreation
.013	Value, influence, effect

.013 2	Psychological principles
.013 5	Effective use of leisure
[.019]	Psychological principles

Do not use; class in 790.0132

.02–.05	Standard subdivisions of recreation
.06	Organizations dealing with and management of recreation
.068	Recreation centers

Do not use for management of recreation; class in 790.069

Indoor and outdoor

Including parks and community centers as recreation centers

Add to base number 790.068 notation 1–9 from Table 2, e.g., recreation centers of California 790.068794

.069	Management of recreation

Add to base number 790.069 the numbers following —068 in notation 0681–0688 from Table 1, e.g., personnel management 790.0693

.07	Education, research, related topics of recreation
.08	History and description of recreation with respect to groups of persons

For activities and programs for specific classes of people, see 790.19

.09	Historical, geographic, persons treatment of recreation
.1	**Recreational activities**

For a specific activity, see the activity, e.g., paper cutting and folding 736.98, piano playing 786.2143, outdoor sports 796

[.101–.109]	Standard subdivisions

Do not use; class in 790.01–790.09

.13	Activities generally engaged in by individuals

Class here hobbies

.132	Collecting

Class collecting a specific kind of object with the object, plus notation 075 from Table 1, e.g., coin collecting 737.4075, sports cards 796.075

.133	Play with toys

Including electric trains

Model racing cars relocated to 796.156

For play with a specific toy not provided for here, see the toy, e.g., flying model airplanes 796.154

.134 Participation in contests

See also 659.17 for advertising by means of contests

.138 Passive (Spectator) activities

Including listening, reading, watching

.15 Activities generally engaged in by groups

.19 Activities and programs for specific classes of people

Class activities generally engaged in by individuals in 790.13; class activities generally engaged in by groups other than families in 790.15

.191 Activities and programs for families

.192 Activities and programs by age level

Class activities for specific sexes regardless of age in 790.194; class activities for invalids, convalescents, persons with disabilities regardless of age in 790.196

.192 2 Children

.192 6 Adults aged 65 and over

.194 Activities and programs for groups by sex

Class activities for invalids, convalescents, persons with disabilities regardless of sex in 790.196

.196 Activities and programs for invalids, convalescents, persons with disabilities

See also 615.85153 for recreational therapy

.2 The performing arts in general

Works that treat only public performances, e.g., stage, radio, television, music, are classed in 791. Works that also include athletic and outdoor sports and games are classed here

For a specific art, see the art, e.g., symphony orchestra performances 784.2078, motion pictures 791.43

See Manual at 780.079 vs. 790.2

.208 837 5 Students

Class here public entertainment activities of students [formerly also 371.89]

791   Public performances

Other than musical, sport, game performances

Class here performances at fairs

For stage presentations, see 792; for magic, see 793.8

See also 780 for musical performances, 793–796 for sport and game performances

SUMMARY

791.01–.09	**Standard subdivisions and amusement parks**
.1	**Traveling shows**
.3	**Circuses**
.4	**Motion pictures, radio, television**
.5	**Puppetry and toy theaters**
.6	**Pageantry**
.8	**Animal performances**

.06   Organizations and management

.068   Amusement parks

Do not use for management; class in 791.069

Add to base number 791.068 notation 1–9 from Table 2, e.g., amusement parks of United States 791.06873

.069   Management

Add to base number 791.069 the numbers following —068 in notation 0681–0688 from Table 1, e.g., marketing 791.0698

.092   Persons

See Manual at 791.092

.1   Traveling shows

Including medicine shows

For circuses, see 791.3; for showboats, see 792.022

.12   Minstrel shows and skits

See also 792.7 for vaudeville

.3   Circuses

Class here amateur circuses

.32   Animal performances

.33   Clowns

.34   Acrobatics and trapeze work

.35   Freaks and sideshows

.38 Parades

.4 Motion pictures, radio, television

Unless other instructions are given, class a subject with aspects in two or more subdivisions of 791.4 in the number coming last, e.g., critical appraisal of a specific film 791.4372 (*not* 791.433)

See also 302.234 for social aspects of motion pictures, radio, and television as mass media

See Manual at 363.31 vs. 303.376, 791.4; also at 384.54, 384.55, 384.8 vs. 791.4

.43 Motion pictures

Class here dramatic films

Class photographic aspects of motion pictures in 778.53; class made-for-TV movies, videotapes of motion pictures in 791.45

See also 384.8 for communication aspects of motion pictures

See Manual at 791.092; also at 791.43, 791.45 vs. 778.5

.430 1–.430 8 Standard subdivisions

Notation from Table 1 as modified under 792.01–792.02, e.g., makeup for motion pictures 791.43027; however, for programming (scheduling), see 384.84; for types of presentation, see 791.433

.430 9 Historical, geographic, persons treatment

Class here description, critical appraisal of specific companies and studios

For description, critical appraisal of specific films, see 791.437

.433 Types of presentation

Including home and amateur films, cartoon films, puppet films

Class animation of films in 741.58

.436 Special aspects of films

Class here film genres

.436 1 Films displaying specific qualities

Add to base number 791.4361 the numbers following —1 in notation 12–17 from Table 3–C, e.g., comedies 791.43617

.436 2–.436 8 Films dealing with specific themes and subjects

Add to base number 791.436 the numbers following —3 in notation 32–38 from Table 3–C, e.g., films of the West and westerns 791.436278

.437   **Films**

Class here screenplays

Class texts of plays in 800. Class subject-oriented films themselves with the subject, e.g., films on flower gardening 635.9

See Manual at 791.437 and 791.447, 791.457, 792.9

.437 2   Single films

Arrange alphabetically by title of film

.437 5   Two or more films

Class here collections of film reviews

Class works which focus on a specific aspect of films with the aspect in 791.436, e.g., westerns 791.436278; class critical appraisal of films associated with a specific person with the person, e.g., films of a motion-picture photographer 778.5092, of a director 791.430233092

.44   **Radio**

Class here dramatic programs

See also 384.54 for communication aspects of radio

See Manual at 791.092

.440 1–.440 8   Standard subdivisions

Notation from Table 1 as modified under 792.01–792.02, e.g., value of radio 791.44013; however, for programming (scheduling), see 384.5442; for types of presentation, see 791.443

.440 9   Historical, geographic, persons treatment

Class here description, critical appraisal of specific companies and stations

For description, critical appraisal of specific programs, see 791.447

.443   **Types of presentation**

Including commercials, live or recorded programs, network programs

Class a specific genre or type of program with a specific type of presentation in 791.446

.446   **Special aspects of radio programs**

Class here radio genres, types of programs

.446 1   Programs displaying specific qualities

Add to base number 791.4461 the numbers following —1 in notation 12–17 from Table 3–C, e.g., comedies 791.44617

.446 2–.446 8	Programs dealing with specific themes and subjects

> Add to base number 791.446 the numbers following —3 in notation 32–38 from Table 3–C, e.g., programs of the West and westerns 791.446278

.447	Radio programs

> Class here radio plays
>
> Class texts of plays in 800. Class subject-oriented programs themselves with the subject, e.g., programs on flower gardening 635.9
>
> *See Manual at 791.437 and 791.447, 791.457, 792.9*

.447 2	Single programs

> Arrange alphabetically by name of program

.447 5	Two or more programs

> Class here collections of program reviews
>
> Class works which focus on a specific aspect of programs with the aspect in 791.446, e.g., westerns 791.446278; class critical appraisal of programs associated with a specific person with the person, e.g., programs of a director 791.440233092

.45	Television

> Class here dramatic and audience programs, use of videotapes
>
> Class use of videotapes not provided for here with the use, e.g., video recordings of rock music 781.66
>
> *See also 384.55 for communication aspects of television*
>
> *See Manual at 791.092; also at 791.43, 791.45 vs. 778.5*

.450 1–.450 8	Standard subdivisions

> Notation from Table 1 as modified under 792.01–792.02, e.g., scenery and lighting for television 791.45025; however, for programming (scheduling), see 384.5531; for types of presentation, see 791.453

.450 9	Historical, geographic, persons treatment

> Class here description, critical appraisal of specific companies, stations, networks
>
> *For description, critical appraisal of specific programs, see 791.457*

.453	Types of presentation

> Including commercials, live or recorded programs, network programs
>
> Class a specific genre or type of program with a specific type of presentation in 791.456

.456	Special aspects of television programs

Class here television genres, types of programs

.456 1	Programs displaying specific qualities

Add to base number 791.4561 the numbers following —1 in notation 12–17 from Table 3–C, e.g., comedies 791.45617

.456 2–.456 8	Programs dealing with specific themes and subjects

Add to base number 791.456 the numbers following —3 in notation 32–38 from Table 3–C, e.g., programs of the West and westerns 791.456278

.457	Programs

Class here television plays

Class texts of plays in 800. Class subject-oriented programs themselves with the subject, e.g., programs on flower gardening 635.9

See Manual at 791.437 and 791.447, 791.457, 792.9

.457 2	Single programs

Arrange alphabetically by name of program

.457 5	Two or more programs

Class here collections of program reviews

Class works which focus on a specific aspect of programs with the aspect in 791.456, e.g., westerns 791.456278; class critical appraisal of programs associated with a specific person with the person, e.g., programs of a television photographer 778.59092, of a director 791.450233092

.5	**Puppetry and toy theaters**
.53	Puppetry

Class here marionettes, shadow puppets

Class puppet films in 791.433

.538	Production scripts of puppet plays

Class texts of plays in 800

.6	**Pageantry**

Including parades, floats for parades

For circus parades, see 791.38; for water pageantry, see 797.203

See also 794.17 for living chess

See Manual at 394.5 vs. 791.6

.62	Pageants

.622	Religious pageants
.624	Historical and patriotic pageants
.64	Cheerleading

> Add to base number 791.64 the numbers following 796.3 in 796.31–796.35, e.g., cheerleading at American football games 791.6432

.8   **Animal performances**

> Including cockfighting

> *For circus animal performances, see 791.32; for equestrian sports and animal racing, see 798*

.82	Bullfighting
.84	Rodeos

> Class here Wild West shows

792   Stage presentations

> Class here dramatic presentation, theater

> Class texts of plays in 800

> *For motion pictures, radio, television, see 791.4; for puppetry and toy theaters, see 791.5*

> *See Manual at 791.092*

SUMMARY

792.01–.09	Standard subdivisions and types of stage presentation
.1	Tragedy and serious drama
.2	Comedy and melodrama
.3	Pantomime
.5	Dramatic vocal forms Opera
.6	Musical plays
.7	Variety shows and theatrical dancing
.8	Ballet and modern dance
.9	Stage productions

.01	Philosophy, theory, aesthetics
.013	Value, influence, effect

> Class influence and effect on a specific subject with the subject, e.g., influence and effect on crime 364.254

.015	Criticism and appreciation

> Do not use for scientific principles; class in 792.01

.02	Techniques, procedures, apparatus, equipment, materials, miscellany
[.021]	Tabulated and related materials

> Do not use; class in 792.0291

>   792.022–792.028 Techniques, procedures, apparatus, equipment, materials

      Do not use for miscellany; class in 792.029

      Use notation 01–09 (except —028 for apparatus, equipment, materials) from Table 1 under each subdivision identified by *, e.g., periodicals on amateur theater 792.022205, data processing for special effects 792.0240285

      Class comprehensive works in 792.02

.022	*Types of stage presentation
	Including showboats, street theater
.022 2	*Amateur theater
.022 3	*Little theater
.022 4	*Summer theater
.022 6	*Children's theater
.022 8	*Arena theater (Theater-in-the-round)
.023	*Supervision
.023 2	*Production
.023 3	*Direction
.023 6	*Programming
.024	*Special effects
	Including sound effects, visual effects
.025	*Setting
	Including lighting, scenery
.026	*Costuming
.027	*Makeup
.028	*Acting and performance
	Including impersonation, improvisation, use of expression and gestures
.029	Miscellany
	Do not use for commercial miscellany; class in 792.0299
.029 07	Humorous treatment
.029 08	Audiovisual treatment

*Add as instructed under 792.022–792.028

.029 1–.029 8   Miscellaneous works

> Add to base number 792.029 the numbers following —02 in notation 021–028 from Table 1, e.g., stage as a profession 792.0293; however, for apparatus, equipment, materials, see 792.022–792.028

.029 9   Commercial miscellany

> Including price lists, prospectuses, trade catalogs

.09   Historical, geographic, persons treatment

> Class here description, critical appraisal of specific theaters and companies

> *For specific productions in specific theaters or by specific companies, see 792.9*

> ## 792.1–792.8   Specific kinds of performances

> Add to each subdivision identified by † the numbers following 792 in 792.01–792.09, e.g., costuming for ballet 792.8026

> Class comprehensive works in 792

.1   **†Tragedy and serious drama**

.12   †Tragedy

.14   †Historical drama

.16   †Religious and morality plays

> Including miracle, mystery, passion plays

> *See also 792.09 for treatment of religious concepts in the theater, 792.27 for modern mystery plays*

.2   **†Comedy and melodrama**

.23   †Comedy

.27   †Melodrama

> Including modern mystery (suspense) drama

> *See also 792.16 for religious mystery-plays*

.3   **†Pantomime**

> Class here mime

.5   **†Dramatic vocal forms   Opera**

> Class interdisciplinary works on dramatic vocal forms, on opera in 782.1

> *For musical plays, see 792.6; for variety shows, see 792.7*

> *See Manual at 782.1 vs. 792.5*

†Add as instructed under 792.1–792.8

.509   Historical, geographic, persons treatment

Class here description, critical appraisal of specific theaters and companies

For specific productions in specific theaters or by specific companies, see 792.54

.54   Opera productions

Class here production and stage guides

.542   Single operas

Arrange alphabetically by title

.545   Two or more operas

Class here collections of reviews

Class critical appraisal of operas associated with a specific person other than the composer or librettist with the person, e.g., operas associated with a singer 782.1092, with a director 792.50233092

.6   **†Musical plays**

Class interdisciplinary works on musical plays in 782.14

See Manual at 782.1 vs. 792.5

.609   Historical, geographic, persons treatment

Class here description, critical appraisal of specific theaters and companies

For specific productions in specific theaters or by specific companies, see 792.64

.62   Dancing

Including choreography

Class comprehensive works on theatrical dancing in 792.78; class comprehensive works on choreography in 792.82

.64   Musical play productions

Class here production and stage guides

.642   Single musical plays

Arrange alphabetically by name

.645   Two or more musical plays

Class here collections of reviews

Class critical appraisal of musical plays associated with a specific person other than the composer or librettist with the person, e.g., musical plays associated with a singer 782.14092, with a director 792.60233092

†Add as instructed under 792.1–792.8

.7	**†Variety shows and theatrical dancing**

Class here burlesque, cabaret, vaudeville, music hall and night club presentations

Subdivisions are added for variety shows and theatrical dancing together, for variety shows alone

Class stage productions in 792.9

See also 791.12 for minstrel shows and skits

.78	**†Theatrical dancing [*formerly* 792.8]**

Including tap dancing

Class stage productions in 792.9

For dancing in musical plays, see 792.62

See Manual at 792.78 vs. 792.8, 793.3

.8	**†Ballet and modern dance**

Class here comprehensive works on dancing

Subdivisions are added for either or both topics in heading

Theatrical dancing relocated to 792.78

For dancing in musical plays, see 792.62; for tap dancing, see 792.78; for social, folk, national dancing, see 793.3

See Manual at 791.092; also at 792.78 vs. 792.8, 793.3

.809	Historical, geographic, persons treatment

Class here description, critical appraisal of specific theaters and companies

For specific productions in specific theaters or by specific companies, see 792.84

.82	Choreography

Class here choreology, e.g., Labanotation, Benesh

.84	Ballet productions

Class here stories, plots, analyses, librettos, production scripts, stage guides

.842	Single ballets

Arrange alphabetically by title

.845	Two or more ballets

Class here collections of reviews

Class critical appraisal of ballets associated with a specific person with the person, e.g., ballets associated with a director 792.80233092

†Add as instructed under 792.1–792.8

.9 **Stage productions**

Class here production scripts, stage guides; description, critical appraisal of specific productions in specific theaters and companies

Class description, critical appraisal, production scripts of operas in 792.54; class description, critical appraisal, production scripts of musical plays in 792.64; class description, critical appraisal, production scripts of ballets in 792.84

See Manual at 791.437 and 791.447, 791.457, 792.9

.92 Single productions

Arrange alphabetically by title

.95 Two or more productions

Class here collections of reviews

Class critical appraisal of productions associated with a specific person other than the playwright with the person, e.g., productions associated with a director 792.0233092

793 Indoor games and amusements

For indoor games of skill, see 794; for games of chance, see 795

.01 Philosophy and theory

.019 Activities and programs for specific classes of people

Do not use for psychological principles; class in 793.01

Add to base number 793.019 the numbers following 790.19 in 790.191–790.196, e.g., indoor games and amusements for children 793.01922

.08 History and description with respect to kinds of persons

For activities and programs for specific classes of people, see 793.019

.2 **Parties and entertainments**

.21 Children's parties

.22 Seasonal parties

Class children's seasonal parties in 793.21

.24 Charades and tableaux

.3 **Social, folk, national dancing**

Including belly, jazz dancing

See Manual at 792.78 vs. 792.8, 793.3

.31 Folk and national dancing

[.310 9]	Historical, geographic, persons treatment
	Do not use; class in 793.319

.319   Historical, geographic, persons treatment

> Add to base number 793.319 notation 001–9 from Table 2, e.g., folk dances of Germany 793.31943

.32   Clog dancing

.33   Ballroom dancing (Round dances)

> Including disco dancing, fox trot, jitterbug, waltz

.34   Square dancing

.35   Dances with accessory features

> Including cotillions, germans, sword dances

.38   Balls

> Class ballroom dancing in 793.33

.4   **Games of action**

.5   **Forfeit and trick games**

.7   **Games not characterized by action**

> *For charades and tableaux, see 793.24*

.73   Puzzles and puzzle games

> Including acrostics, quizzes, rebuses; jigsaw puzzles
>
> Class puzzles as formal instructional devices for the teaching of a specific subject with the subject, plus notation 07 from Table 1, e.g., puzzles teaching the use of the Bible 220.07
>
> *For mathematical games and recreations, see 793.74*

.732   Crossword puzzles

.734   Word games

> Including anagrams, palindromes, Scrabble®

.735   Riddles

> Class riddles as folk literature, interdisciplinary works on riddles in 398.6

.738   Maze puzzles

.74   Mathematical games and recreations

.8   **Magic and related activities**

> Including scientific recreations
>
> Class here conjuring

.85	Card tricks [*formerly* 795.438]
.87	Juggling
.89	Ventriloquism

.9 Other indoor diversions

.92 War games (Battle games)

> See also 355.48 for military use of war games, 796.1 for outdoor war games

.93 Adventure games   Fantasy games

Including Dungeons and Dragons®, RuneQuest®

Class here mystery games, role-playing games

> See also 793.92 for war games (battle games)

[.930 285]   Data processing   Computer applications

Do not use; class in 793.932

.932 Computer adventure games   Computer fantasy games

Class here video adventure, video fantasy games

Unless it is redundant, add to base number 793.932 the numbers following 00 in 004–006, e.g., programs for digital microcomputers 793.932536, but use of digital computers 793.932 (*not* 793.9324)

Class comprehensive works on computer games in 794.8

> See Manual at 793.932 vs. 794.822

.96 String games

Including making cat's cradles

794 Indoor games of skill

Class here board games

Class war games in 793.92; class adventure, fantasy, mystery games in 793.93; class games combining skill and chance in 795

> For backgammon, see 795.15

.1 Chess

[.102 85]   Data processing   Computer applications

Do not use; class in 794.172

.12   **Strategy and tactics**

> Including specific strategies and tactics, e.g., combinations, sacrifices, traps, pitfalls, attack, counterattack, defense
>
> Class specific strategies and tactics applied during a specific portion of a game in 794.122–794.124; class strategy and tactics with individual chessmen in 794.14

.122   Openings

.123   Middle games

.124   End games

.14   **Individual chessmen**

> Including specific attributes, e.g., position, moves, power, value
>
> Class specific attributes of a specific piece in 794.142–794.147

.142   Pawns

.143   Rooks (Castles)

.144   Knights

.145   Bishops

.146   Queen

.147   King

.15   **Collections of games**

.152   Master matches

> Class master matches by individual players in 794.159

.157   Tournaments and championships

> Class tournaments and championships of individual players in 794.159

.159   Games, matches, tournaments, championships of individual players

.17   **Special forms of chess**

> Including living chess, simultaneous play

.172   Electronic chess   Computer chess

> Unless it is redundant, add to base number 794.172 the numbers following 00 in 004–006, e.g., use of digital microcomputers 794.172416, but use of digital computers 794.172 (*not* 794.1724)

.18   **Variants of chess**

> Including fairy chess, shogi

.2   **Checkers (Draughts)**

.3	**Darts**
.4	**Go**
.6	**Bowling**

> See also 796.315 for lawn bowling

| .7 | **Ball games** |

Class athletic ball games in 796.3

> For bowling, see 794.6

| .72 | Billiards |

> For pool, see 794.73

.73	Pool (Pocket billiards)
.735	Snooker
.75	Pinball games
.8	**Electronic games Computer games**

Class here video games

Class computerized forms of a specific indoor game or amusement with the game or amusement in 793–795, plus notation 0285 from Table 1, e.g., computerized checkers 794.20285

| [.802 85] | Data processing   Computer applications |

> Do not use; class in 794.81

| .81 | Data processing   Computer applications |

Unless it is redundant, add to base number 794.81 the numbers following 00 in 004–006, e.g., programs for digital microcomputers 794.81536, but use of digital computers 794.81 (*not* 794.814)

Class data processing for specific genres of computer games in 794.82; class data processing for computerized athletic and outdoor sports and games in 794.86–794.89

| .82 | Specific genres of computer games |

Class computerized war games (battle games) in 793.920285; class computerized adventure, fantasy, mystery games in 793.932; class computerized athletic and outdoor sports and games in 794.86–794.89

| .822 | Arcade games |

Unless it is redundant, add to base number 794.822 the numbers following 00 in 004–006, e.g., programs for digital microcomputers 794.822536, but use of digital computers 794.822 (*not* 794.8224)

> See Manual at 793.932 vs. 794.822

.86–.89	Computerized athletic and outdoor sports and games

Add to base number 794.8 the numbers following 79 in 796–799, e.g., computerized baseball 794.86357

795 Games of chance

Class here gambling

Class gambling on a specific activity with the activity, e.g., on horse racing 798.401

See also 364.172 for gambling as a crime, 616.85841 for compulsive gambling

.01	Philosophy and theory

Including betting systems

.015 192	Probabilities

Class here probabilities of winning

See Manual at 795.015192 vs. 519.2

.1	**Games with dice**
.12	Craps
.15	Backgammon
.2	**Wheel and top games**
.23	Roulette
.27	Slot machines
.3	**Games dependent on drawing numbers or counters**

Including bingo

.32	Dominoes
.34	Mah jong
.38	Lotteries

Including lotto

.4	**Card games**
.41	Games in which skill is a major element
.411	Cribbage
.412	Poker
.413	Whist and bridge whist
.414	Auction bridge

.415	Contract bridge

Class here comprehensive works on bridge

> *For bridge whist, see 795.413; for auction bridge, see 795.414*

.415 2	Bidding
.415 3	Play of the hand
.415 4	Scoring systems
.415 8	Collections of games and matches
.416	Pinochle
.418	Rummy and its variants

Including canasta

.42	Games based chiefly on chance

Including baccarat, faro

.423	Blackjack (Twenty-one)
.43	Games in which card position is a major element

Including solitaire, patience

[.438]	Card tricks

Relocated to 793.85

796   Athletic and outdoor sports and games

Class computerized athletic and outdoor sports and games in 794.86

> *For aquatic and air sports, see 797; for equestrian sports and animal racing, see 798; for fishing, hunting, shooting, see 799*

> *See also 617.1027 for sports medicine*

> *See Manual at 796; also at 613.71 vs. 646.75, 796*

SUMMARY

796.01–.09	**Standard subdivisions and general kinds of sports and games**
.1	**Miscellaneous games**
.2	**Activities and games requiring equipment**
.3	**Ball games**
.4	**Weight lifting, track and field, gymnastics**
.5	**Outdoor life**
.6	**Cycling and related activities**
.7	**Driving motor vehicles**
.8	**Combat sports**
.9	**Ice and snow sports**

.01	Philosophy and theory

[.019]   Activities and programs for specific classes of persons

> Do not use for psychological principles; class in 796.01
>
> Relocated to 796.08

[.019 1]   Activities and programs for families

> Number discontinued; class in 796

.04   General kinds of sports and games

> *See Manual at 796.08 vs. 796.04*

>   796.042–796.044   Specific types

> Class specific types of variant sports and games in 796.045; class comprehensive works in 796.04

.042   Amateur sports

> Class here intramural sports [*formerly* 371.89]
>
> *For college sports, see 796.043*

.043   College sports

.044   Professional sports

.045   Variant sports and games

> Versions of sports and games developed by modifying the basic version of the original sports and games

.045 6   Wheelchair sports

> Class here sports and games modified for participation of persons with physical disabilities

.06   Organizations, facilities, management

.068   Facilities

> Do not use for management; class in 796.069
>
> Class here physical education facilities [*formerly* 371.624]; field houses, playgrounds, stadiums
>
> Add to base number 796.068 notation 1–9 from Table 2, e.g., playgrounds of London 796.068421
>
> *See also 725.8 for architecture of recreational buildings*

.069   Management

> Add to base number 796.069 the numbers following —068 in notation 0681–0688 from Table 1, e.g., financial management 796.0691

.07   Education, research, related topics

.071   Education

> Do not use for teaching; class in 796.077

.077   Coaching

> Do not use for programmed texts; class in 796.07

> Class here teaching

.08   History and description of sports and games with respect to kinds of persons

> Class here activities and programs for specific classes of persons [*formerly* 796.019]

> Class general kinds of sports and games for specific kinds of persons in 796.04

> *See Manual at 796.08 vs. 796.04*

.087   Persons with disabilities and illnesses, gifted persons

> Class sports and games modified for participation of persons with physical disabilities in 796.0456

.1   Miscellaneous games

> Not provided for elsewhere

.13   Singing and dancing games

.14   Active games

> *For activities and games requiring equipment, see 796.2*

.15   Play with remote-control models, kites, similar devices

> Standard subdivisions are added for play with remote-control models, kites, similar devices together; for play with remote-control models alone

> Class here play with control line models

> Class comprehensive works on play with mechanical and scientific toys in 790.133

> *See Manual at 796.15 vs. 629.0460228*

.152   Model ships

.154   Model aircraft

> Class here model airplanes

.156   Model land vehicles

> Including model racing cars [*formerly* 790.133]

> Class here model automobiles

> *For play with remote-control trains, see 790.133*

.158	Kites

.2 **Activities and games requiring equipment**

Not provided for elsewhere

Including flying discs (Frisbees®), marbles, Yo-Yos®

.21	Roller skating

Class here in-line skating (rollerblading)

Skateboarding relocated to 796.22

.22	Skateboarding [*formerly* 796.21]
.24	Pitching games

Including horseshoes, quoits

.3 **Ball games**

SUMMARY

796.31	Ball thrown or hit by hand
.32	Inflated ball thrown or hit by hand
.33	Inflated ball driven by foot
.34	Racket games
.35	Ball driven by club, mallet, bat

.31	Ball thrown or hit by hand
.312	Handball
.315	Lawn bowling

See also 794.6 for indoor bowling

.32	Inflated ball thrown or hit by hand
.323	Basketball
.323 01–.323 09	Standard subdivisions

Notation from Table 1 as modified under 796.3320202–796.332077, e.g., basketball courts 796.323068

.323 2	Strategy and tactics
.323 3	Refereeing
.323 6	Specific types of basketball

Class strategy and tactics regardless of type in 796.3232; class refereeing of specific types of basketball in 796.3233

See Manual at 796.08 vs. 796.04

[.323 601–.323 609]	Standard subdivisions

Do not use; class in 796.32301–796.32309

.323 62		Precollege basketball
.323 63		College basketball
.323 64		Professional and semiprofessional basketball
.323 8		Variants of basketball

> Including wheelchair basketball, women's rules
>
> > *See also 796.323082 for women playing by standard rules*
> >
> > *See Manual at 796.08 vs. 796.04*

.324		Netball
.325		Volleyball
.33		Inflated ball driven by foot

> Including Gaelic football

SUMMARY

796.332	**American football**
.333	**Rugby** **Union rugby**
.334	**Soccer (Association football)**
.335	**Canadian football**
.336	**Australian-rules football**

.332	American football
.332 02	Miscellany
.332 020 2	Handbooks and guides

> Do not use for synopses and outlines; class in 796.33202

.332 020 22	Official rules
.332 020 24	Spectators' guides
.332 028	Auxiliary techniques and procedures [*formerly* 796.3322]; apparatus, equipment, materials
.332 06	Organizations, facilities, management

> Including clubs, leagues

.332 068	Grounds and their layout

> Do not use for management; class in 796.332069
>
> Add to base number 796.332068 notation 1–9 from Table 2, e.g., football fields of Washington, D.C. 796.332068753

.332 069	Management

> Add to base number 796.332069 the numbers following —068 in notation 0681–0688 from Table 1, e.g., financial management 796.3320691

.332 07	Education, research, related topics
.332 071	Education
	Do not use for teaching; class in 796.332077
.332 075	Museum activities and services Collecting
	Class here collectibles, e.g., football cards
.332 077	Coaching
	Do not use for programmed texts; class in 796.33207
	Class here teaching
.332 08	History and description of American football with respect to kinds of persons
	See Manual at 796.08 vs. 796.04
.332 2	Strategy and tactics
	Auxiliary techniques and procedures relocated to 796.332028, e.g., safety measures 796.3320289
.332 22	Formations
.332 23	Line play
.332 24	Backfield play
.332 25	Passing
.332 26	Blocking and tackling
.332 27	Kicking
.332 3	Refereeing and umpiring
.332 6	Specific types of American football
	Class strategy and tactics regardless of type in 796.3322; class refereeing and umpiring of specific types of American football in 796.3323
	See Manual at 796.08 vs. 796.04
[.332 601–.332 609]	Standard subdivisions
	Do not use; class in 796.33201–796.33209
.332 62	Precollege football
.332 63	College football
	Including bowl games
	See also 796.332648 for Super Bowl
.332 64	Professional and semiprofessional football
.332 648	Super Bowl

.332 8	Variants of football
	Including six-man football, touch football
	See Manual at 798.08 vs. 798.04
.333	**Rugby Rugby Union**
.333 01–.333 09	Standard subdivisions
	Notation from Table 1 as modified under 796.3320202–796.332077, e.g., official rules 796.33302022
.333 2	Strategy and tactics
.333 23	Forward play
.333 24	Halfback play
.333 25	Three-quarter play
.333 26	Back play
.333 3	Refereeing and umpiring
.333 6	Specific types of rugby
	Class strategy and tactics regardless of type in 796.3332; class refereeing and umpiring of specific types of rugby in 796.3333
	See Manual at 796.08 vs. 796.04
[.333 601–.333 609]	Standard subdivisions
	Do not use; class in 796.33301–796.33309
.333 62	Clubs
	Including college and university
.333 63	County cup competition
.333 64	Tours
.333 65	International rugby
.333 8	Rugby League
	Former heading: Variants of rugby
.334	**Soccer (Association football)**
	See also 796.33 for Gaelic football
.334 01–.334 09	Standard subdivisions
	Notation from Table 1 as modified under 796.3320202–796.332077, e.g., coaching 796.334077
.334 2	Strategy and tactics
.334 22	Formations

.334 23	Forward play
.334 24	Halfback play
.334 25	Back play
.334 26	Goalkeeping
.334 3	Refereeing and umpiring
.334 6	Specific types of soccer

> Class strategy and tactics regardless of type in 796.3342; class refereeing and umpiring of specific types of soccer in 796.3343
>
> *See Manual at 796.08 vs. 796.04*

[.334 601–.334 609]	Standard subdivisions

> Do not use; class in 796.33401–796.33409

.334 62	Amateur soccer
.334 63	League soccer
.334 64	Cup competition

> *For World Cup competition, see 796.334668*

.334 66	International soccer
.334 668	World Cup competition
.334 8	Variants of soccer

> *See Manual at 796.08 vs. 796.04*

.335	**Canadian football**
.335 01–.335 09	Standard subdivisions

> Notation from Table 1 as modified under 796.3320202–796.332077, e.g., coaching 796.335077

.335 2	Strategy and tactics
.335 3	Refereeing and umpiring
.335 6	Specific types of Canadian football

> Class strategy and tactics regardless of type in 796.3352; class refereeing and umpiring of specific types of Canadian football in 796.3353
>
> *See Manual at 796.08 vs. 796.04*

[.335 601–.335 609]	Standard subdivisions

> Do not use; class in 796.33501–796.33509

.335 62	Precollege Canadian football
.335 63	College Canadian football

.335 64		Professional and semiprofessional Canadian football
.335 648		Grey Cup
.335 8		Variants of Canadian football

Including touch football

See Manual at 796.08 vs. 796.04

.336		Australian-rules football
.34	Racket games	

Including court tennis (royal tennis), paddle tennis

.342	Tennis (Lawn tennis)	
.342 01–.342 09		Standard subdivisions

Notation from Table 1 as modified under 796.3320202–796.332077, e.g., layout of tennis courts 796.342068

.342 2		Strategy and tactics
.342 21		Service
.342 22		Forehand
.342 23		Backhand
.342 27		Singles
.342 28		Doubles
.342 3		Refereeing
.343	Squash	

Class here rackets, racquetball

.345	Badminton	
.346	Table tennis	
.347	Lacrosse	
.35	Ball driven by club, mallet, bat	

Including hurling

.352	Golf	
.352 01–.352 09		Standard subdivisions

Notation from Table 1 as modified under 796.3320202–796.332077, e.g., official rules 796.35202022

See also 712.5 for design and construction of golf courses

.352 2	Variants of golf
	Including miniature golf
	See Manual at 796.08 vs. 796.04
.352 3	Tactics of play
	Class here grip, swing, adapting to specific golf courses
.352 32	Play with woods
.352 33	Play with distance irons
	Class here comprehensive works on play with irons
	For play with chipping or pitching irons, see 796.35234
.352 34	Play with chipping or pitching irons
.352 35	Putting
.352 4	Refereeing
.352 6	Specific types of golf
	Class tactics of play regardless of type in 796.3523; class refereeing of specific types of golf in 796.3524
	See Manual at 796.08 vs. 796.04
[.352 601–.352 609]	Standard subdivisions
	Do not use; class in 796.35201–796.35209
.352 62	Amateur golf
	Class open games and matches in 796.35266
.352 64	Professional golf
	Class open games and matches in 796.35266
.352 66	Open games and matches
	Including British Open, Masters Tournament
.353	Polo
.354	Croquet
.355	Field hockey
	Including indoor hockey
	See also 796.962 for ice hockey
.357	Baseball
.357 01–.357 09	Standard subdivisions
	Notation from Table 1 as modified under 796.3320202–796.332077, e.g., coaching 796.357077

.357 2	Strategy and tactics
.357 22	Pitching
.357 23	Catching
.357 24	Infield play

Class here comprehensive works on fielding

For outfield play, see 796.35725

.357 25	Outfield play
.357 26	Batting
.357 27	Base running
.357 3	Umpiring
.357 6	Specific types of baseball

Class strategy and tactics regardless of type in 796.3572; class umpiring of specific types of baseball in 796.3573

See Manual at 796.08 vs. 796.04

[.357 601–.357 609]	Standard subdivisions

Do not use; class in 796.35701–796.35709

.357 62	Precollege baseball

Class here Little league

.357 63	College baseball
.357 64	Professional and semiprofessional baseball
.357 646	World series games
.357 648	All-star games
.357 8	Variants of baseball

Including softball

See Manual at 796.08 vs. 796.04

.358	Cricket
.358 01–.358 09	Standard subdivisions

Notation from Table 1 as modified under 796.3320202–796.332077, e.g., coaching 796.358077

.358 2	Strategy and tactics
.358 22	Bowling
.358 23	Fielding
.358 24	Wicketkeeping

.358 26	Batting
.358 3	Umpiring
.358 6	Specific types of cricket

> Class strategy and tactics regardless of type in 796.3582; class umpiring of specific types of cricket in 796.3583

> *See Manual at 796.08 vs. 796.04*

| [.358 601–.358 609] | Standard subdivisions |

> Do not use; class in 796.35801–796.35809

| .358 62 | Amateur cricket |

> Including school, college and university

.358 63	County cricket
.358 65	International cricket
.358 8	Variants of cricket

> Including single-wicket cricket

> *See Manual at 796.08 vs. 796.04*

.4	**Weight lifting, track and field, gymnastics**
.406	Organizations, facilities, management
.406 8	Gymnasiums and stadiums

> Do not use for management; class in 769.4069

> Add to base number 796.4068 notation 1–9 from Table 2, e.g., gymnasiums of Japan 796.406852

| .406 9 | Management |

> Add to base number 796.4069 the numbers following —068 in notation 0681–0688 from Table 1, e.g., financial management 796.40691

| .407 | Education, research, related topics |
| .407 1 | Education |

> Do not use for teaching; class in 796.4077

| .407 7 | Coaching |

> Do not use for programmed texts; class in 796.407

> Class here teaching

| .41 | Weight lifting |

> *See also 613.71 for weight training for fitness*

> *See Manual at 613.71 vs. 646.75, 796*

.42	Track and field

Class here running

For field events, see 796.43; for orienteering, see 796.58

See also 613.7172 for running as an exercise

.420 6	Organizations, facilities, management
.420 68	Athletic fields

Do not use for management; class in 796.42069

Add to base number 796.42068 notation 1–9 from Table 2, e.g., athletic fields of Russia 796.4206847

.420 69	Management

Add to base number 796.42069 the numbers following —068 in notation 0681–0688 from Table 1, e.g., personnel management 796.420693

.422	Sprints

Class sprint relays in 796.427

.423	Middle-distance races

Class middle-distance relay races in 796.427

.424	Distance races

Class distance relay races in 796.427

For marathon, see 796.4252; for triathlon, see 796.4257; for cross country races, see 796.428

.425	Non-track races

Class here road running

For cross country races, see 796.428; for race walking, see 796.429

.425 2	Marathon
.425 7	Triathlon
.426	Hurdles and steeplechase

Class hurdle and steeplechase relay races in 796.427

.427	Relay races
.428	Cross-country races
.429	Race walking (Heel-and-toe races)
.43	Jumping, vaulting, throwing

Class here field events

.432   Jumping

Including long jump (broad jump), triple jump (hop, step, and jump), high jump

.434   Pole vaulting

See also 796.44 for gymnastic vaulting

.435   Throwing

Including boomerang and discus throwing, javelin hurling, shot-putting

See also 796.24 for throwing games

.44   Sports gymnastics

Including rhythmic gymnastics, use of horizontal and parallel bars, vaulting

For trapeze work, rope climbing, tightrope walking, see 796.46; for acrobatics, tumbling, trampolining, contortion, see 796.47

See also 613.714 for gymnastic exercises

.46   Trapeze work, rope climbing, tightrope walking

See also 791.34 for trapeze work and tightrope walking as circus acts

.47   Acrobatics, tumbling, trampolining, contortion

Including floor exercise

See also 791.34 for acrobatics as circus acts

.48   Olympic games

Arrange specific games chronologically

Class Paralympics in 796.0456; class Special Olympics in 796.0874. Class a specific activity with the activity, e.g., basketball 796.323, swimming 797.21

For winter Olympic games, see 796.98

.480 93–.480 99   Geographic treatment

Do not use for specific games; class in 796.48

.5   Outdoor life

Class a specific activity of outdoor life not provided for here with the activity, e.g., fishing 799.1

.51   Walking

Class here backpacking, hiking

Orienteering relocated to 796.58

For walking by kind of terrain, see 796.52

See Manual at 913–919 vs. 796.51

.52	Walking and exploring by kind of terrain
.522	Mountains, hills, rocks

        Class here mountaineering

.522 3	Rock climbing
.525	Caves

        Class here spelunking

        See also 797.2 for cave swimming

.53	Beach activities

        For aquatic sports, see 797.1–797.3

.54	Camping

        Including snow camping

.542	Kinds of camps

        Class here camps operated for profit

        Class activities in specific kinds of camps in 796.545

.542 2	Institutional camps

        Including church, school, scouts, YMCA camps

        Class institutional day camps in 796.5423

.542 3	Day camps
.545	Activities

        Including campfires, games, woodcraft

        For beach activities, see 796.53

.56	Dude ranching and farming
.58	Orienteering [*formerly* 796.51]

        Class orientation in 912.014

.6   **Cycling and related activities**

        Use of wheeled vehicles not driven by motor or animal power

        Including soapbox racing

        For roller skating, see 796.21; for skateboarding, see 796.22

>   796.62–796.64 Cycling

        Class comprehensive works in 796.6

.62	Bicycle racing

    Class triathlon in 796.4257; class racing on mountain bikes in 796.63

    See also 796.75 for motorcycle racing

.63	Mountain biking (All-terrain cycling)
.64	Bicycle touring for pleasure

    See also 796.62 for touring as a form of racing

.68	Landsailing (Sand yachting)
.7	**Driving motor vehicles**

    For snowmobiling, see 796.94

>   796.72–796.76 Driving for competition

    Class comprehensive works in 796.7

.72	Automobile racing

    See also 796.156 for toy car racing

.720 6	Organizations, facilities, management
.720 68	Racetracks and speedways

    Do not use for management; class in 796.72069

    Add to base number 796.72068 notation 1–9 from Table 2, e.g., Indianapolis Motor Speedway 796.7206877252

.720 69	Management

    Add to base number 796.72069 the numbers following —068 in notation 0681–0688 from Table 1, e.g., financial management 796.720691

.73	Automobile rallies
.75	Motorcycle and motor scooter racing
.756	Motocross
.76	Midget car racing (Karting)

>   796.77–796.79 Driving for pleasure

    Class comprehensive works in 796.7

.77	Driving sports cars for pleasure
.78	Driving family cars for pleasure

.79	Travel for pleasure by mobile home

Including travel by camper, trailer

See also 647.94 for trailer camps

.8	**Combat sports**

Class here martial arts

Class combat with animals in 791.8

.81	Unarmed combat

For boxing, see 796.83

.812	Wrestling

Including arm wrestling

.812 2	Greco-Roman wrestling
.812 3	Freestyle (Catch-as-catch-can) wrestling
.812 5	Sumo
.815	Jujitsu and related martial arts forms

See also 613.7148 for related therapeutic exercises

.815 2	Judo

Class here jujitsu

.815 3	Karate
.815 4	Aikido
.815 5	Chinese forms

T'ai chi ch'üan relocated to 613.7148

For kempo and kung fu, see 796.8159

.815 9	Kempo and kung fu
.83	Boxing
.86	Fencing

Including bojutsu, kendo

Class here sword fighting

.9	**Ice and snow sports**

Including snowboarding

For sled dog racing, see 798.83; for ice fishing, see 799.122

See also 796.54 for snow camping, 798.6 for horse-drawn sleighing

.91	Ice skating

.912	Figure skating
	Including ice dancing, pair skating
.914	Speed skating
.92	Snowshoeing
.93	Skiing
.932	Cross-country skiing
	Including biathlon
	Class here Nordic combination, Nordic skiing
	For jumping, see 796.933
.933	Jumping
.935	Alpine (Downhill) skiing
	Including downhill, giant slalom, slalom, supergiant slalom racing
.937	Freestyle skiing
	Including ballet, mogul, trick skiing
.94	Snowmobiling
.95	Sledding and coasting
	Including bobsledding, lugeing, tobogganing
.96	Ice games
.962	Ice hockey
	See also 796.355 for field hockey
.962 01–.962 09	Standard subdivisions
	Notation from Table 1 as modified under 796.3320202–796.332077, e.g., coaching 796.962077
.962 2	Strategy and tactics
	Including skating
.962 27	Goalkeeping
.962 3	Refereeing
.962 6	Specific types of ice hockey
	Class strategy and tactics regardless of type in 796.9622
	See Manual at 796.08 vs. 796.04
[.962 601–.962 609]	Standard subdivisions
	Do not use; class in 796.96201–796.96209

.962 62		Junior hockey
.962 63		College hockey
.962 64		Professional hockey
.962 648		Stanley Cup
.962 66		International hockey

Class here specific tournaments

.964	Curling	
.97	Iceboating	
.98	Winter Olympic games	

Arrange specific games chronologically

Class a specific activity with the activity, e.g., skating 796.91

.980 93–.980 99		Geographic treatment

Do not use for specific games; class in 796.98

797   Aquatic and air sports

Class computerized aquatic and air sports in 794.87

.028 9	Safety measures

Class comprehensive works on water safety in aquatic sports in 797.200289

> **797.1–797.3 Aquatic sports**

Class comprehensive works in 797

For fishing, see 799.1

.1	**Boating**
.12	Types of vessels

Class seamanship for specific types of vessels in 623.882; class boat racing with specific types of vessels in 797.14

.121	Rafting
.122	Canoeing
.122 4	Kayaking
.123	Rowboating
.124	Sailboating

See also 796.68 for landsailing, 797.33 for sailboarding

.124 6   Yachting

                          Class here comprehensive works on yachting

                          Class motor yachting in 796.1256

                          See also 643.2 for yachts permanently docked as dwellings

.125   Motorboating

.125 6   Yachting

.129   Houseboating

                          See also 643.2 for houseboats permanently docked as dwellings

.14   Boat racing and regattas

                        Standard subdivisions are added for any type of racing, e.g., yacht racing in Britain 797.140941

.2   **Swimming and diving**

                        Standard subdivisions are added for swimming and diving together, for diving alone

                        Class here water parks

.200 1–.200 9   Standard subdivisions

.203   Water pageantry

                        See also 797.21 for synchronized swimming

.21   Swimming

                        Class triathlon in 796.4257

                        For underwater swimming, see 797.23

.217   Synchronized swimming

.23   Underwater swimming

                        Including scuba, skin diving, snorkeling

.24   Springboard and platform diving

                        Standard subdivisions are added for either or both topics in heading

.25   Water games

                        Including water polo

.3   **Other aquatic sports**

.32   Surfing (Surf riding)

.33   Windsurfing (Boardsailing, Sailboarding)

.35   Water skiing

.37		Jet skiing
.5		**Air sports**

Including bungee jumping

.51	Balloon flying

> 797.52–797.54 Flying motor-driven aircraft

Class comprehensive works in 797.5

.52	Racing
.53	Flying for pleasure
.54	Stunt flying

Class here display aerobatics

.55	Gliding and soaring

Including hang gliding

.56	Parachuting (Skydiving)

798   Equestrian sports and animal racing

Class computerized equestrian sports and animal racing in 794.88

> **798.2–798.6 Equestrian sports**

Class rodeos in 791.84; class hunting with aid of horses in 799.23; class comprehensive works in 798

For polo, see 796.353

See also 636.108971027 for equine sports medicine

.2   Horsemanship

For horse racing, see 798.4

See Manual at 798.2

.23   Riding

Class here training of both horse and rider, dressage

Class training of only the horse in 636.1088

For jumping, see 798.25

.230 74	Museums, collections, exhibits

Do not use for riding exhibitions; class in 798.24

[.230 79]	Competitions and awards

Do not use; class in 798.24

.24 Riding exhibitions and competitions

Including three-day events

Class jumping in 798.25

.25 Jumping

.4 Horse racing   Flat racing

.400 1–.400 5 Standard subdivisions

.400 6 Organizations, facilities, management

.400 68 Racetracks

Do not use for management; class in 798.40069

Add to base number 798.40068 notation 1–9 from Table 2, e.g., racetracks of England 798.4006842

.400 69 Management

Add to base number 798.40069 the numbers following —068 in notation 0681–0688 from Table 1, e.g., management of marketing 798.400698

.400 7–.400 8 Standard subdivisions

.400 9 Historical, geographic, persons treatment

Class here specific races

.401 Betting

Including pari-mutuel

.45 Steeplechasing and hurdling

.46 Harness racing

.6 Driving and coaching

Including horse-drawn sleighing

For harness racing, see 798.46

.8 Dog racing

.83 Sled dog racing

.85 Greyhound racing

799 **Fishing, hunting, shooting**

Class computerized fishing, hunting, shooting games in 794.89

See also 688.79 for the manufacture of both mass-produced and handcrafted equipment

SUMMARY

799.1	Fishing
.2	Hunting
.3	Shooting other than game

.1   **Fishing**

> Class shellfishing in 799.254; class interdisciplinary works on fishing in 639.2

.11   Freshwater fishing

> Class here coarse fishing

> Class fishing for specific kinds of freshwater fish in 799.17

>   **799.12–799.14   Specific methods of fishing**

> Class specific methods of freshwater fishing in 799.11; class specific methods of saltwater fishing in 799.16; class specific methods of fishing for specific kinds of fish in 799.17; class comprehensive works in 799.1

.12   Angling

> Class here game, pan fishing

> Class game fishing is the sense of fishing for salmon, trout, graylings in 799.1755

.122   Bait (Bottom, Still) fishing

> Including ice fishing

.124   Fly fishing

> Class here casting

> *For bait-casting, see 799.126*

> *See also 688.79124 for making artificial flies*

.126   Bait-casting (Spin-fishing)

.128   Trolling

.13   Net fishing

.14   Other methods of fishing

> Including spearfishing

.16   Saltwater fishing

> Class fishing for specific kinds of saltwater fish in 799.17

[.160 916 3–.160 916 7]   Saltwater fishing in specific bodies of water

> Do not use; class in 799.166

.166   Saltwater fishing in specific bodies of water

[.166 01–.166 09]   Standard subdivisions

Do not use; class in 799.1601–796.1609

.166 1–.166 9   Subdivisions for saltwater fishing in specific bodies of water

Add to base number 799.166 the numbers following 551.46 in 551.461–551.469, e.g., fishing in Mediterranean Sea 799.1662, in Black Sea 799.16629

.17   Specific kinds of fishes

Class comprehensive works on fishing for freshwater fish in 799.11; class comprehensive works on fishing for saltwater fish in 799.16

[.170 1–.170 9]   Standard subdivisions

Do not use; class in 799.101–799.109

.172–.177   Subdivisions for specific kinds of fishes

Add to base number 799.17 the numbers following 597 in 597.2–597.7, e.g., trout fishing 799.1757

Class coarse fishing, game fishing in sense of sports fishing in 799.12; class game fishing in sense of fishing for salmon, trout, graylings in 799.1755

.2   Hunting

Class here comprehensive works on commercial and sports hunting [*formerly* 639.1], sports trapping, comprehensive works on hunting and shooting sports

For commercial, subsistence hunting, see 639.1; for shooting other than game, see 799.3

.202   Miscellany

.202 8   Techniques, procedures, apparatus, equipment, materials

.202 82   Blowpipes, bolas, boomerangs, lassos, nets, slings, spears

.202 83   Guns

.202 832   Rifles

.202 833   Pistols

.202 834   Shotguns

.202 85   Bows and arrows

Do not use for data processing or computers; class in 799.2028

[.209]   Historical, geographic, persons treatment

Do not use; class in 799.29

> 799.21–799.23 Methods

Class methods of hunting specific kinds of animals in 799.24–799.27; class comprehensive works in 799.2

.21 Shooting game

.213 Shooting game with guns

.215 Shooting game with bows and arrows

.23 Hunting with aid of animals

.232 Hunting with falcons

.234 Hunting with dogs

> 799.24–799.27 Hunting specific kinds of animals

Class comprehensive works in 799.2

.24 Birds

Class here fowling, game birds, wildfowling

Class waterfowling in 799.244

[.242] Upland game birds

Relocated to 799.246

[.243] Shore and bay birds

Relocated to 799.24833

.244 Waterfowl

Including specific kinds of waterfowl [*formerly* 799.24841]

Class here ducks, lowland game birds

Add to base number 799.244 the numbers following 598.41 in 598.412–598.418, e.g., geese 799.2447

.246 Upland game birds [*formerly* 799.242]

Class here Galliformes [*formerly* 799.24861]

Add to base number 799.246 the numbers following 598.6 in 598.62–598.65, e.g., Columbiformes 799.2465 [*formerly* 799.24865], turkeys 799.24645

.248 Specific kinds of birds other than waterfowl and upland game birds

[.248 01–.248 09] Standard subdivisions

Do not use; class in 799.2401–799.2409

.248 3–.248 9   Subdivisions for specific kinds of birds other than waterfowl and upland game birds

> Add to base number 799.248 the numbers following 598 in 598.3–598.9, e.g., comprehensive works on shore and bay birds 799.24833 [*formerly* 799.243]; however, specific kinds of waterfowl relocated from 799.24841 to 799.244; Galliformes relocated from 799.24861 to 799.246; Columbiformes relocated from 799.24865 to 799.2465

> Class comprehensive works in 799.24

.25   Small game hunting

> *For birds, see 799.24*

.252–.259   Specific kinds of small game

> Add to base number 799.25 the numbers following 59 in 592–599, e.g., shellfishing 799.254, fox hunting 799.259775

.26   Big game hunting

> Class here comprehensive works on hunting big game mammals

> *For specific kinds, see 799.27*

.27   Specific kinds of big game

> *For birds, see 799.24*

[.270 1–.270 9]   Standard subdivisions

> Do not use; class in 799.2601–799.2609

.271–.278   Specific kinds of big game mammals

> Add to base number 799.27 the numbers following 599 in 599.1–599.8, e.g., white-tailed deer 799.27652; however, for comprehensive works on big game, on big game mammals, see 799.26

.279   Reptiles

> Add to base number 799.279 the numbers following 597.9 in 597.92–597.98, e.g., crocodiles 799.2798

.29   Historical, geographic, persons treatment

> Add to base number 799.29 notation 001–9 from Table 2, e.g., hunting in Germany 799.2943

.3   **Shooting other than game**

> *For ballistic devices, see 799.20282–799.20285*

.31   Shooting with guns

.312   Shooting at stationary targets

> *For biathlon, see 796.932*

.313	Shooting at moving targets
.313 2	Trapshooting
	Class here skeet shooting
.32	Shooting with bow and arrow (Archery)

800 Literature (Belles-lettres) and rhetoric

Class here works of literature, works about literature

After general topics (800–809) the basic arrangement is literature by language, then literature of each language by form, then each form by historical period; however, miscellaneous writings are arranged first by historical period, then by form. More detailed instructions are given at the beginning of Table 3

Unless other instructions are given, observe the following table of preference, e.g., collections of drama written in poetry from more than two literatures 808.82 (*not* 808.81):

> Drama
> Poetry
> > Class epigrams in verse with miscellaneous writings
> Fiction
> Essays
> Speeches
> Letters
> Miscellaneous writings
> Humor and satire

Class folk literature in 398.2; class librettos, poems, words written to be sung or recited with music in 780.268; class interdisciplinary works on language and literature in 400; class interdisciplinary works on the arts in 700

> *See Manual at 800; also at 080 vs. 800; also at 741.6 vs. 800; also at 800 vs. 398.2; also at 800 vs. 398.245, 590, 636*

SUMMARY

801–807	**Standard subdivisions**
808	**Rhetoric and collections of literary texts from more than two literatures**
809	**History, description, critical appraisal of more than two literatures**
810	**American literature in English**
.1–.9	Standard subdivisions; collections; history, description, critical appraisal of American literature in English
811–818	Specific forms of American literature in English
820	**English and Old English (Anglo-Saxon) literatures**
.1–.9	Standard subdivisions; collections; history, description, critical appraisal of English literature
821–828	Specific forms of English literature
829	Old English (Anglo-Saxon) literature

830	Literatures of Germanic (Teutonic) languages German literature	
.01–.09	Standard subdivisions of literatures of Germanic (Teutonic) languages	
.1–.9	Standard subdivisions; collections; history, description, critical appraisal of German literature	
831–838	Specific forms of German literature	
839	Other Germanic (Teutonic) literatures	

840	Literatures of Romance languages French literature
.01–.09	Standard subdivisions of literatures of Romance languages
.1–.9	Standard subdivisions; collections; history, description, critical appraisal of French literature
841–848	Specific forms of French literature
849	Provençal (Langue d'oc), Franco-Provençal, Catalan literatures

850	Literatures of Italian, Sardinian, Dalmatian, Romanian, Rhaeto-Romanic languages Italian literature
.1–.9	Standard subdivisions; collections; history, description, critical appraisal of Italian literature
851–858	Specific forms of Italian literature
859	Romanian and Rhaeto-Romanic literatures

860	Literatures of Spanish and Portuguese languages Spanish literature
.01–.09	Standard subdivisions of literatures of Spanish and Portuguese languages
.1–.9	Standard subdivisions; collections; history, description, critical appraisal of Spanish literature
861–868	Specific forms of Spanish literature
869	Portuguese literature

870	Literatures of Italic languages Latin literature
.01–.09	Standard subdivisions of literatures of Italic languages
.1–.9	Standard subdivisions; collections; history, description, critical appraisal of Latin literature
871–878	Specific forms of Latin literature
879	Literatures of other Italic languages

880	Literatures of Hellenic languages Classical Greek literature
.01–.09	Standard subdivisions of classical (Greek and Latin) literatures
.1–.9	Standard subdivisions; collections; history, description, critical appraisal of classical Greek literature
881–888	Specific forms of classical Greek literature
889	Modern Greek literature

890	Literatures of other specific languages and language families
891	East Indo-European and Celtic literatures
892	Afro-Asiatic (Hamito-Semitic) literatures Semitic literatures
893	Non-Semitic Afro-Asiatic literatures
894	Altaic, Uralic, Hyperborean, Dravidian literatures
895	Literatures of East and Southeast Asia Sino-Tibetan literatures
896	African literatures
897	Literatures of North American native languages
898	Literatures of South American native languages
899	Literatures of non-Austronesian languages of Oceania, of Austronesian languages, of miscellaneous languages

801   Philosophy and theory

   .3   Value, influence, effect

.9	**Nature and character**
.92	Psychology

Including literature as a product of imagination

.93	Aesthetics
.95	Criticism

Class here theory, technique, history of literary criticism

Class textual criticism of specific literary forms in 801.959; class works of critical appraisal in 809

See Manual at 800: Literary criticism

[.951]	Poetry

Relocated to 808.1

[.952]	Drama

Relocated to 808.2

[.953]	Fiction

Relocated to 808.3

[.954]	Essays

Relocated to 808.4

[.955]	Speeches

Relocated to 808.5

[.956]	Letters

Relocated to 808.6

[.957]	Humor and satire

Relocated to 808.7

.959	Textual criticism

802–803 Standard subdivisions

[804]   [Unassigned]

Most recently used in Edition 16

805   Serial publications

Class collections of literary texts in serial form in 808.80005; class history, description, critical appraisal in serial form in 809.005

806–807 Standard subdivisions

808   Rhetoric and collections of literary texts from more than two literatures

Do not use for history and description of rhetoric with respect to kinds of persons; class in 808.008. Do not use for collections of literary texts from more than two literatures with respect to kinds of persons; class in 808.89

Including literary plagiarism

Class a specific aspect of literary plagiarism with the aspect, e.g., plagiarism in the work of an American fiction writer of the late 20th century 813.54

SUMMARY

808.001–.009	**Standard subdivisions of rhetoric**
.02–.06	**General topics in rhetoric**
.1	**Rhetoric of poetry**
.2	**Rhetoric of drama**
.3	**Rhetoric of fiction**
.4	**Rhetoric of essays**
.5	**Rhetoric of speech**
.6	**Rhetoric of letters**
.7	**Rhetoric of humor and satire**
.8	**Collections of literary texts from more than two literatures**

>   808.001–808.7   Rhetoric

Effective use of language

Class here composition

Class general treatment of standard usage of language (prescriptive linguistics) in 418; class theory, technique, history of literary criticism in 801.95; class comprehensive works in 808. Class treatment of standard usage in a specific language with the specific language, plus notation 8 from Table 4, e.g., English usage 428

See Manual at 808.001–808.7 vs. 070.52

.001–.009   Standard subdivisions of rhetoric

>   808.02–808.06   General topics in rhetoric

Class comprehensive works in 808

.02	Authorship and editorial techniques

Writing in publishable form

Class here comprehensive works on preparation and submission of manuscripts

Class authorship and editorial techniques for specific kinds of composition in 808.06

> *For submission of manuscripts to agents and publishers, see 070.52*
>
> *See also 001.4 for research*
>
> *See Manual at 808.001–808.7 vs. 070.52*

.027	Editorial techniques

Preparation of manuscripts in publishable form

Class here style manuals

.04	Rhetoric in specific languages

Class preparation of manuscripts in specific languages in 808.02; class rhetoric of specific kinds of composition in specific languages in 808.06

.042	Rhetoric in English
.042 01–.042 09	Standard subdivisions
.042 7	Study of rhetoric through critical reading

Including collections and single works for critical reading

> *See Manual at 808.0427*

.043–.049	Rhetoric in other languages

Add to base number 808.04 notation 3–9 from Table 6, e.g., German rhetoric 808.0431; then to the result add the numbers following 808.042 in 808.04201–808.0427, e.g., study of German rhetoric through critical reading 808.04317

.06	Rhetoric of specific kinds of writing

Class rhetoric in specific literary forms in 808.1–808.7

.062	Abstracts and summaries

.066   Professional, technical, expository literature

> Add to base number 808.066 three-digit numbers 001–999 (but no standard subdivisions), e.g., legal writing 808.06634, writing of legal dictionaries 808.06634 (*not* 808.06634003), writing on bridge engineering 808.066624 (*not* 808.0666242); then, for writing in a foreign language, add 0 and to the result add notation 2–9 from Table 6, e.g., legal writing in Spanish for speakers of another language 808.06634061

> *For abstracts and summaries, see 808.062; for expository adult easy literature, see 808.067; for expository writing for children, see 808.0688*

> *See Manual at 005.15 vs. 808.066005; also at 340 vs. 808.06634; also at 658.45 vs. 651.7, 808.06665*

.067   Adult easy literature

> Works for adults learning to read or for adult beginners in foreign languages

.068   Children's literature

.068 1–.068 7   Specific literary forms

> Add to base number 808.068 the numbers following 808 in 808.1–808.7, e.g., drama 808.0682

.068 8   Expository writing

> ## 808.1–808.7 Rhetoric in specific literary forms

> Class here aesthetics, appreciation, character and nature, composition, theory of specific literary forms

> Observe table of preference under 800

> Class theory, technique, history of textual criticism of specific literary forms in 801.959; class specific forms for children in 808.0681–808.0687; class works of critical appraisal of specific literary forms in 809.1–809.7; class comprehensive works on theory, technique, history of literary criticism in 801.95; class comprehensive works on rhetoric in specific literary forms in 808

> *See Manual at 800: Literary criticism*

.1   **Rhetoric of poetry**

> Class here theory, technique, history of criticism of poetry [*formerly* 801.951]; prosody

> Add to base number 808.1 the numbers following —10 in notation 102–108 from Table 3–B, e.g., lyric poetry 808.14

> *See Manual at 808.1 vs. 414.6*

.2   Rhetoric of drama

Class here theory, technique, history of criticism of drama [*formerly* 801.952]

Add to base number 808.2 the numbers following — 20 in notation 202–205 from Table 3–B, e.g., one-act plays 808.241

.3   Rhetoric of fiction

Class here theory, technique, history of criticism of fiction [*formerly* 801.953]; rhetoric of novelettes and novels

.31–.38   Fiction of specific scopes and kinds

Add to base number 808.3 the numbers following — 30 in notation 301–308 from Table 3–B, e.g., science fiction 808.38762

.39   Fiction displaying specific elements

Add to base number 808.39 the numbers following — 2 in notation 22–27 from Table 3–C, e.g., characters in fiction 808.397

Class fiction of specific scopes and kinds displaying specific elements in 808.31–808.38

.4   Rhetoric of essays

Class here theory, technique, history of criticism of essays [*formerly* 801.954]

.5   Rhetoric of speech

Art or technique of oral expression

Class here theory, technique, history of criticism of speeches [*formerly* 801.955]; voice, expression gesture

.51   Public speaking (Oratory)

Including after-dinner, platform, television speaking; making speeches and toasts for special occasions

For preaching, see 251; for debating and public discussion, see 808.53

.53   Debating and public discussion

.54   Recitation

Class here oral interpretation

Class choral speaking in 808.55

.543   Storytelling

.545   Reading aloud

.55   Choral speaking

.56   Conversation

.6   Rhetoric of letters

Class here theory, technique, history of criticism of letters [*formerly* 801.956]

.7   **Rhetoric of humor and satire**

Class here theory, technique, history of criticism of humor and satire [*formerly* 801.957]; rhetoric of parody

.8   **Collections of literary texts from more than two literatures**

Texts by more than one author in more than two languages not from the same language family

Collections of texts from literatures of two languages relocated to 810–890

Class works that are limited to a specific topic found in subdivisions of 808.8 and consist equally of literary texts and history, description, critical appraisal of literature with the topic in 808.8, e.g., texts and criticism of literature of the 18th century 808.80033, texts and criticism of drama 808.82; class collections of texts from more than two literatures in the same language with the literature of that language, e.g., collections of works from English, American, and Australian literatures in English (more than one literary form) 820.8; class collections of texts from literatures in more than two languages from the same family with the literature of that family, e.g., French, Italian, and Spanish literatures 840

See Manual at 808.8; also at 080 vs. 800

.800 01–.800 07   Standard subdivisions

[.800 08]   History and description with respect to kinds of persons

Do not use; class in 808.89

[.800 09]   Historical, geographic, persons treatment

Do not use; class in 809

.800 1–.800 5   Collections from specific periods

Add to base number 808.800 the numbers following —090 in notation 0901–0905 from Table 1, e.g., collections of 18th century literature 808.80033

.801–.803   Collections displaying specific features

Add to base number 808.80 notation 1–3 from Table 3–C, e.g., collections of literature featuring classicism 808.80142, on death 808.803548

>   808.81–808.88   Collections in specific forms

Except for modifications shown under specific entries, add to each subdivision identified by * as follows:

001–008   Standard subdivisions
009   Historical and geographic treatment
[00901–00905]   Historical periods
                Do not use; class in 01–05
[0092]   Persons treatment
                Do not use; class with the specific form, without adding notation from Table 1
01–05   Historical periods
                Add to 0 the numbers following —090 in notation 0901–0905 from Table 1, e.g., 18th century 033

Observe table of preference under 800

Class comprehensive works in 808.8

.81   *Collections of poetry

.812–.818   Specific kinds of poetry

Add to base number 808.81 the numbers following — 10 in notation 102–108 from Table 3–B, e.g., collections of narrative poetry 808.813

.819   Poetry displaying specific features

Add to base number 808.819 notation 1–3 from Table 3–C, e.g., collections of poetry about animals 808.819362

Class poetry of specific kinds displaying specific features in 808.812–808.818

.82   *Collections of drama

.822–.825   Specific media, scopes, kinds of drama

Add to base number 808.82 the numbers following — 20 in notation 202–205 from Table 3–B, e.g., collections of tragedies 808.82512

.829   Drama displaying specific features

Add to base number 808.829 notation 1–3 from Table 3–C, e.g., collections of plays about Faust 808.829351

Class drama of specific media, scopes, kinds displaying specific features in 808.822–808.825

.83   *Collections of fiction

.831–.838   Specific scopes and types of fiction

Add to base number 808.83 the numbers following — 30 in notation 301–308 from Table 3–B, e.g., collections of love stories 808.8385

---

*Add as instructed under 808.81–808.88

.839   Fiction displaying specific features

> Add to base number 808.839 notation 1–3 from Table 3–C, e.g., collections of fiction about animals 808.839362
>
> Class fiction of specific scopes and types displaying specific features in 808.831–808.838

.84   *Collections of essays

.849   Essays displaying specific features

> Add to base number 808.849 notation 1–3 from Table 3–C, e.g., collections of descriptive essays 808.84922

.85   *Collections of speeches

.851–.856   Specific kinds of speeches

> Add to base number 808.85 the numbers following —50 in notation 501–506 from Table 3–B, e.g., debates 808.853

.859   Speeches displaying specific features

> Add to base number 808.859 notation 1–3 from Table 3–C, e.g., collections of descriptive speeches 808.85922
>
> Class speeches of specific kinds displaying specific features in 808.851–808.856

.86   *Collections of letters

.869   Letters displaying specific features

> Add to base number 808.869 notation 1–3 from Table 3–C, e.g., collections of letters displaying classicism 808.869142

.87   *Collections of humor and satire

> Limited to collections (or texts and criticism) of works in two or more literary forms including both verse and prose
>
> Class here parody
>
> *See also 808.888 for humor and satire in two or more prose forms*
>
> (Option: Give preference to humor and satire over all other literary forms)

.879   Humor and satire displaying specific features

> Add to base number 808.879 notation 1–3 from Table 3–C, e.g., collections of literary humor about holidays 808.879334

.88   *Collections of miscellaneous writings

*Add as instructed under 808.81–808.88

.882   Anecdotes, epigrams, graffiti, jokes, quotations

Including riddles that are jokes

Class humor and satire in two or more literary forms, including both verse and prose, in 808.87; class riddles as folk literature, interdisciplinary works on riddles in 398.6

.883   Diaries, journals, notebooks, reminiscences

Class interdisciplinary collections of diaries in 900. Class diaries, journals, notebooks, reminiscences of nonliterary authors with the appropriate subject, e.g., diaries of astronomers 520.922

.887   Works without identifiable form

Class here experimental and nonformalized works

Class experimental works with an identifiable literary form with the form, e.g., experimental novels 808.83

.888   Prose literature

Class prose without identifiable form in 808.887. Class a specific form of prose literature with the form, e.g., essays 808.84

.89   Collections for and by specific kinds of persons

Add to base number 808.89 notation 8–9 from Table 3–C, e.g., collections of literature in more than one language by persons of African descent 808.89896

Class literature displaying specific features for and by specific kinds of persons in 808.801–808.803; class literature in specific forms for and by specific kinds of persons in 808.81–808.88; class literatures of specific languages for and by specific kinds of persons in 810–890

809   History, description, critical appraisal of more than two literatures

History, description, critical appraisal of works by more than one author in more than two languages not from the same language family

Class here collected biography

History, description, critical appraisal of literatures of two languages relocated to 810–890

Class theory, technique, history of literary criticism in 801.95. Class history, description, critical appraisal of more than two literatures in the same language with the literature of that language, e.g., history of English, American, and Australian literatures in English (more than one literary form) 820.9; class history, description, critical appraisal of literatures in more than two languages from the same family with the literature of that family, e.g., French, Italian, and Spanish literatures 840

See Manual at 808.8

.001–.007	Standard subdivisions

[.008]   History and description with respect to kinds of persons

> Do not use; class in 809.8

[.009]   Historical, geographic, persons treatment

> Do not use for persons; class in 809. Do not use for historical periods; class in 809.01–809.05. Do not use for geographic treatment; class in 809.89

.01–.05   Literature from specific periods

> Add to base number 809.0 the numbers following —090 in notation 0901–0905 from Table 1, e.g., history, description, critical appraisal of 18th century literature 809.033

.1–.7   **Literature in specific forms**

> Add to base number 809 the numbers following 808.8 in 808.81–808.87, e.g., history, description, critical appraisal of narrative poetry 809.13, of poetry about animals 809.19362

> Class theory, technique, history of literary criticism of specific literary forms in 808.1–808.7

> *See Manual at 800: Literary criticism*

.8   **Literature for and by specific kinds of persons**

> Class here history and description of literature with respect to kinds of persons

> Unless other instructions are given, observe the following table of preference, e.g., history, description, critical appraisal of literature for or by American Roman Catholic girls 809.892827 (*not* 809.813, 809.89222, or 809.8973):

Persons of specific age groups	809.89282–.89285
Persons of specific sexes	809.89286–.89287
Persons occupied with geography, history, related disciplines	809.8929
Persons of other specific occupational and miscellaneous characteristics	809.89204–.89279
Persons of specific racial, ethnic, national groups	809.803–.889
Persons resident in specific continents, countries, localities	809.893–.899
Persons resident in specific regions	809.891

> Class literature in specific forms for and by specific kinds of persons in 809.1–809.7; class literature displaying specific features for and by specific kinds of persons in 809.9; class literatures of specific languages for and by specific kinds of persons in 810–890

>   **809.803–809.889 Literature for and by persons of specific racial, ethnic, national groups**

> Class comprehensive works in 809.8

.803–.879	Literature for and by persons of general and larger western racial, ethnic, national groups

> Add to base number 809.8 notation 03–79 from Table 5, e.g., North Americans 809.81

.88	Literature for and by persons of other racial, ethnic, national groups
.881	Ancient Greeks
.888	Modern Greeks and Cypriots
.889	Persons of other racial, ethnic, national groups

> Add to base number 809.889 the numbers following —9 in notation 91–99 from Table 5, e.g., Jewish literature 809.88924

.89	Literature for and by other specific kinds of persons

> Add to base number 809.89 the numbers following —9 in notation 91–99 from Table 3–C, e.g., literature in more than one language by painters 809.89275, by residents of Canada 809.8971

.9	**Literature displaying specific features**

> Class literature in specific forms displaying specific features in 809.1–809.7

.91–.92	Literature displaying specific qualities and elements

> Add to base number 809.9 notation 1–2 from Table 3–C, e.g., history, description, critical appraisal of literature displaying tragedy and horror 809.916
>
> Class literature dealing with specific themes and subjects and displaying specific qualities and elements in 809.933

.93	Literature displaying other aspects
.933	Literature dealing with specific themes and subjects

> Add to base number 809.933 the numbers following —3 in notation 32–38 from Table 3–C, e.g., history, description, critical appraisal of literature dealing with marriage 809.933543

.935	Literature emphasizing subjects

> Works not basically belletristic discussed as literature, in which the real interest is in the literary quality of the text rather than the subject of the text
>
> Add to base number 809.935 notation 001–999, e.g., religious works as literature 809.9352, biography and autobiography as literature 809.93592
>
> Class literary examination of texts in which the real interest is in the subject of the texts with the texts, e.g., literary examination of sacred books in order to reach conclusions about meaning, structure, authorship, date 291.82

> ## 810–890   Literatures of specific languages and language families

Literature is classed by the language in which originally written
(Option: Class translations into a language requiring local emphasis with the literature of that language)

Class here collections of texts from literatures of two languages [*formerly also* 808.8]; history, description, critical appraisal of literatures of two languages [*all formerly also* 809]

Unless there is a specific provision for a dialect, literature in a dialect is classed with the literature of the basic language

Literature in a pidgin or creole is classed with the source language from which more of its vocabulary comes than from its other source language(s)

Under each literature identified by *, add to designated base number notation 1–8 from Table 3–A for works by or about individual authors, notation 01–89 from Table 3–B for works by or about more than one author. If the base number is not identified in a note, it is the number given for the literature, e.g., for Dutch 839.31. Full instructions for building numbers are given at the start of Table 3

The numbers used in this schedule for literatures of individual languages do not necessarily correspond exactly with those in 420–490 or with the notation in Table 6. Use notation from Table 6 only when so instructed, e.g., at 899

Unless other instructions are given, class a work containing or discussing literatures of two languages in 810–890 in the number coming first, e.g., a collection of English and French texts 820.8 (*not* 840.8), but a collection of classical Greek and Latin texts 880

Class texts by more than one author in more than two languages not from the same language family in 808.8; class history, description, critical appraisal of works by more than one author in more than two languages not from the same language family in 809; class comprehensive works in 800

(Option: For any group of literatures, add notation 04 from Table 1 and then add notation 01–89 from Table 3–B, e.g., collections of lyric poetry written in African languages 896.0410408)

(Option: To give preferred treatment to, or make available more and shorter numbers for the classification of, literature of any specific language that it is desired to emphasize, use one of the following options:

(Option A: Class in 810, where full instructions appear

(Option B: Give preferred treatment by placing before 810 through use of a letter or other symbol, e.g., literature of Arabic language 8A0, for which the base number is 8A

(continued)

> ## 810–890 Literatures of specific languages and language families (continued)

(Option C: Where two or more countries share the same language, either [1] use initial letters to distinguish the separate countries, or [2] use the special number designated for literatures of those countries that are *not* preferred. Full instructions appear under 810.1–818, 819, 820.1–828, 828.99, 840.1–848, 848.99, 860.1–868, 868.99, 869, 869.899)

810 American literature in English

English-language literature of North America, South America, Hawaii, and associated islands

Class comprehensive works on American literature in English and English literature in 820

(Option: To give local emphasis and a shorter number to a specific literature other than American literature in English, e.g., Afrikaans literature, class it here; in that case class American literature in English in 820. Other options are described under 810–890)

> **810.1–818 Subdivisions of American literature in English**

Except for modifications shown below, add to base number 81 as instructed at beginning of Table 3, e.g., a collection of American poetry in English 811.008

Special interpretations of and exceptions to notation from Table 3 for use with American literature in English:

810.8099	Collections for and by persons resident in Hawaii
810.999	History, description, critical appraisal of literature for and by persons resident in Hawaii

Assign period numbers for the United States (including Puerto Rico), for Canada, for comprehensive works on American literature in English

PERIOD TABLES FOR AMERICAN LITERATURE IN ENGLISH

For Canada

3	Colonial period to 1867
4	1867–1899
5	1900–1999
52	1900–1945
54	1945–1999
6	2000–

For United States

1	Colonial period, 1607–1776
2	1776–1829
3	1830–1861
	Class here 19th century
	For 1800–1829, see 2; for 1861–1899, see 4
4	1861–1899
5	1900–1999
52	1900–1945
54	1945–1999
6	2000–

Class comprehensive works in 810

(Option: Distinguish literatures of specific countries by initial letters, e.g., literature of Canada C810, of Jamaica J810, of United States U810; or class literatures not requiring local emphasis in 819. If literatures are identified by one of these methods, assign period numbers for Middle and South American literature as well as for United States and Canadian literature. Other options are described under 810–890)

.1–.9   Standard subdivisions; collections; history, description, critical appraisal of American literature in English

Numbers built according to instructions under 810.1–818 and at beginning of Table 3

811–818 Specific forms of American literature in English

Numbers built according to instructions under 810.1–818 and at beginning of Table 3

(819)   American literatures in English not requiring local emphasis

(Optional number and subdivisions; prefer 810–818 for all American literatures in English. Other options are described under 810–890)

Class here English-language literatures of specific American countries other than the country requiring local emphasis, e.g., libraries emphasizing United States literature may class here Canadian literature, and libraries emphasizing Canadian literature may class here United States literature

(.1)   *†Canada

(.3)   *†United States

(.5)   *†Mexico

(.7)   †Central America

(.700 1–.708)   †Subdivisions of Central American literature in English

Add to base number 819.70 as instructed at beginning of Table 3, e.g., collections of Central American dramatic poetry in English 819.7010208

(.71–.77)   †Specific countries

Add to 819.7 the numbers following —728 in notation 7281–7287 from Table 2, e.g., English-language literature of Costa Rica 819.76; then to the base number thus derived add further as instructed at beginning of Table 3, e.g., collections of English-language literature of Costa Rica displaying naturalism 819.7608012

(.8)   †West Indies (Antilles) and Bermuda

(.800 1–.808)   †Subdivisions of English-language literatures of West Indies (Antilles) and Bermuda

Add to base number 819.80 as instructed at beginning of Table 3, e.g., collections of English-language literature of West Indies for children 819.800809282

(.81)   *†Cuba

(.82)   *†Jamaica

(.83)   *†Dominican Republic

(.84)   *†Haiti

(.85)   *†Puerto Rico

(.86)   *†Bahama Islands

(.87)   *†Leeward Islands

(.88)   *†Windward and other southern islands

---

*Add to base number as instructed at beginning of Table 3
†(Optional number; prefer 810–818)

(.89)   *†Bermuda

(.9)   †South America

(.900 1–.908)   †Subdivisions of English-language literatures of South America

> Add to base number 819.90 as instructed at beginning of Table 3, e.g., collections of English-language one-act plays from South America 819.90204108

(.91–.99)   †Specific countries

> Add to 819.9 the numbers following —8 in notation 81–89 from Table 2, e.g., English-language literature of Brazil 819.91; then add further as instructed at beginning of Table 3, e.g., history and critical appraisal of English-language literature of Brazil 819.9109

*Add to base number as instructed at beginning of Table 3
†(Optional number; prefer 810–818)

820   English and Old English (Anglo-Saxon) literatures

For American literature in English, see 810

> ### 820.1–828 Subdivisions of English literature

Except for modifications shown under specific entries, add to base number 82 as instructed at beginning of Table 3, e.g., a collection of English poetry 821.008

Assign period numbers for Great Britain and Ireland, for comprehensive works on literature in English language

PERIOD TABLE FOR ENGLISH

For Great Britain and Ireland, for comprehensive works on literature in English language

1	Early English period, 1066–1400
	Class here medieval period
2	1400–1558
3	Elizabethan period, 1558–1625
	Including Jacobean period
	Class here 16th century, Renaissance period
	For 1500–1558, the pre-Elizabethan part of the Renaissance, see 2
4	1625–1702
	Including Caroline and Restoration periods
5	Queen Anne period, 1702–1745
	Class here 18th century
	For 1700–1702, see 4; for 1745–1799, see 6
6	1745–1799
7	1800–1837
	Class here romantic period
8	Victorian period, 1837–1899
	Class here 19th century
	For 1800–1837, see 7
9	1900–
91	1900–1999
912	1900–1945
914	1945–1999
92	2000–

Class comprehensive works in 820

(Option: Distinguish English-language literatures of specific countries by initial letters, e.g., literature of England E820, of Ireland Ir820, of Scotland S820, of Wales W820, or of all British Isles B820, of Australia A820, of India In820; or class literatures not requiring local emphasis in 828.99. If literatures are identified by one of these methods, assign optional period numbers for literature of Ireland, Africa, Asia, Australia, and New Zealand. Other options are described under 810–890

(continued)

>   **820.1–828 Subdivisions of English literature (continued)**

(OPTIONAL PERIOD TABLES FOR ENGLISH
     (For Ireland
         (1   Medieval and early modern to 1659
         (2   1660–1799
         (3   1800–1899
         (4   1900–1945
             Class here Irish literary revival, 20th century
                For Irish literary revival in 19th century, see 3; for
                1945–1999, see 5
         (5   1945–1999
         (6   2000–

     (For African countries other than South Africa
         (1   Early period to 1959
         (2   1960–1999
             Class here 20th century
                For 1900–1959, see 1
         (3   2000–

     (For Asian countries
         (1   Early period to 1858
         (2   1858–1947
         (3   1947–1999
             Class here 20th century
                For 1900–1947, see 2
         (4   2000–

     (For Australia
         (1   Early period to 1889
         (2   1890–1945
         (3   1945–1999
             Class here 20th century
                For 1900–1945, see 2
         (4   2000–

     (For New Zealand
         (1   Early period to 1907
         (2   1907–1999
         (3   2000–

     (For South Africa
         (1   Early period to 1909
         (2   1909–1961
             Class here 20th century
                For 1900–1909, see 1; for 1961–1994, see 3; for
                1994–1999, see 4
         (3   1961–1994
         (4   1994–   )

.1–.9　　**Standard subdivisions; collections; history, description, critical appraisal of English literature**

> Numbers built according to instructions under 820.1–828 and at beginning of Table 3

821　　English poetry

> Number built according to instructions under 820.1–828 and at beginning of Table 3

822　　English drama

> Number built according to instructions under 820.1–828 and at beginning of Table 3

.3　　　**Drama of Elizabethan period, 1558–1625**

> Number built according to instructions under 820.1–828 and at beginning of Table 3

.33　　　William Shakespeare

> (Option: Subarrange works about and by Shakespeare according to the following table, which may be adapted for use with any specific author:
>
> A　　Authorship controversies
> 　　　　(Option: Class here bibliography; prefer 016.82233)
> B　　Biography
> D　　Critical appraisal
> 　　　　Class critical appraisal of individual works in O-Z
> E　　Textual criticism
> 　　　　Class textual criticism of individual works in O-Z
> F　　Sources, allusions, learning
> G　　Societies, concordances, miscellany
> H　　Quotations, condensations, adaptations
> I　　Complete works in English without notes
> J　　Complete works in English with notes
> K　　Complete works in translation
> L　　Partial collections in English without notes
> M　　Partial collections in English with notes
> N　　Partial collections in translation
> >O-Z　Individual works
> 　　　　Use the first number of each pair for texts, the second for
> 　　　　description and critical appraisal
> 　　　　Class poems in 821.3
> >O-R　Comedies
> O1–2　　All's well that ends well
> O3–4　　As you like it
> O5–6　　The comedy of errors
> O7–8　　Love's labour's lost
> P1–2　　Measure for measure
> P3–4　　The merchant of Venice
> P5–6　　The merry wives of Windsor

(continued)

.33   William Shakespeare (continued)

P7–8	A midsummer night's dream
Q1–2	Much ado about nothing
Q3–4	The taming of the shrew
Q5–6	The tempest
Q7–8	Twelfth night
R1–2	The two gentlemen of Verona
R3–4	The winter's tale
>S-V	Tragedies
S1–2	Antony and Cleopatra
S3–4	Coriolanus
S5–6	Cymbeline
S7–8	Hamlet
T1–2	Julius Caesar
T3–4	King Lear
T5–6	Macbeth
T7–8	Othello
U1–2	Pericles
U3–4	Romeo and Juliet
U5–6	Timon of Athens
U7–8	Titus Andronicus
V1–2	Troilus and Cressida
>W-X	Histories
W1–2	Henry IV, parts 1–2
W3–4	Henry V
W5–6	Henry VI, parts 1–3
W7–8	Henry VIII
X1–2	King John
X3–4	Richard II
X5–6	Richard III
Y	Poems
	(Optional numbers; prefer 821.3)
Y1–2	General works
Y3–4	Venus and Adonis
Y5–6	The rape of Lucrece
Y7–8	Sonnets
Z	Spurious and doubtful works)

823–827 Other specific forms of English literature

Numbers built according to instructions under 820.1–828 and at beginning of Table 3

828   English miscellaneous writings

Number built according to instructions under 820.1–828 and at beginning of Table 3

(.99)	English-language literatures not requiring local emphasis

(Optional number and subdivisions; prefer 820–828 for all non-American English-language literatures. Other options are described under 810–890)

Class here English-language literatures of specific non-American countries other than the country requiring local emphasis, e.g., libraries emphasizing British literature may class here Australian, Indian, other literatures, and libraries emphasizing Indian literature may class here British literature

(.991)	†Scotland and Ireland

(Option: Class here all English-language literature of United Kingdom, of Great Britain, of British Isles. Add to 828.991 as instructed at beginning of Table 3 for United Kingdom, for Great Britain, for British Isles)

(.991 1)	*†Scotland
(.991 5)	*†Ireland
(.992)	*†England and Wales
(.992 9)	*†Wales
(.993)	†New Zealand, Australia, India, South Africa
(.993 3)	*†New Zealand
(.993 4)	*†Australia
(.993 5)	*†India
(.993 6)	*†South Africa
(.994–.999)	†Other parts of the world

English-language literature except of British Isles, North America, South America, Hawaii, New Zealand, Australia, India, South Africa, and associated islands

Add to 828.99 notation 4–9 from Table 2, e.g., English-language literature of Israel 828.995694; then add 0 and to the base number thus derived add further as instructed at beginning of Table 3, e.g., English-language poetry of Israel 828.99569401

829   *Old English (Anglo-Saxon) literature

Special interpretations of and exceptions to notation from Table 3 for use with Old English appear below under 829.2–829.8

.1   Poetry

For Caedmon, see 829.2; for Beowulf, see 829.3; for Cynewulf, see 829.4

.2   Caedmon

.3   Beowulf

---

*Add to base number as instructed at beginning of Table 3

†(Optional number; prefer 820–828)

.4 **Cynewulf**

.8 **Prose literature**

830 Literatures of Germanic (Teutonic) languages German literature

For English and Old English (Anglo-Saxon) literatures, see 820

.01–.09 Standard subdivisions of literatures of Germanic (Teutonic) languages

---

> **830.1–838 Subdivisions of German literature**

Class here literature in Alsatian, Franconian, Pennsylvania Dutch (Pennsylvania German), Swabian, Swiss-German dialects

Add to base number 83 as instructed at beginning of Table 3, e.g., a collection of German poetry 831.008

PERIOD TABLE

1	Early period to 1099
	Class here Old High German literature
2	1100–1349
	Class here medieval period, 750–1349; Middle High German literature
	For 750–1099, see 1
21	1100–1249
	Class here Blütezeit
22	1250–1349
3	1350–1517
4	Reformation period, 1517–1625
5	1625–1749
	Class here baroque period
6	1750–1832
	Class here 18th century, classical period, romantic period
	For 1700–1749, see 5; for later romantic period, see 7
7	1832–1856
	Class here 19th century
	For 1800–1829, see 6; for 1856–1899, see 8
8	1856–1899
9	1900–
91	1900–1990
912	1900–1945
914	1945–1990
92	1990–

Class comprehensive works in 830

See also 839.1 for Yiddish (Judeo-German) literature, 839.4 for low German (Plattdeutsch) literature

.1–.9   **Standard subdivisions; collections; history, description, critical appraisal of German literature**

> Numbers built according to instructions under 830.1–838 and at beginning of Table 3

831–838 Specific forms of German literature

> Numbers built according to instructions under 830.1–838 and at beginning of Table 3

839   Other Germanic (Teutonic) literatures

SUMMARY

839.1	**Yiddish literature**
.2	**Frisian Literature**
.3	**Netherlandish literatures**
.4	**Low German (Plattdeutsch) literature**
.5	**Scandinavian (North Germanic) literatures**
.6	**West Scandinavian literatures Old Norse (Old Icelandic) literature**
.7	**Swedish literature**
.8	**Danish and Norwegian literatures**
.9	**East Germanic literatures**

[.09]   Yiddish literature

> Relocated to 839.1

.1   ***Yiddish literature [*formerly* 839.09]**

> PERIOD TABLE
> 1   Early period to 1699
> 2   Period of enlightenment, 1700–1859
>   Including 19th century
>   *For 1860–1899, see 3*
> 3   1860–1945
>   Class here 20th century
>   *For 1945–1999, see 4*
> 4   1945–
>
> Use of this number for comprehensive works on Old Low Germanic literatures discontinued; class in 839
>
> Old Frisian literature relocated to 839.2; Old Low Franconian literature relocated to 839.31; Old Low German literature, Old Saxon literature relocated to 839.4

>   **839.2–839.4 Modern Low Germanic literatures**

> Class comprehensive works in 839

*Add to base number as instructed at beginning of Table 3

.2 ***Frisian literature**

Including Old Frisian literature [*formerly* 839.1]

PERIOD TABLE
1 Early period to 1609
2 1609–1799
3 1800–1899
4 1900–1999
5 2000–

.3 **Netherlandish literatures**

.31 *Dutch literature

Including Old Low Franconian literature [*formerly* 839.1]

Class here Flemish literature

PERIOD TABLE
1 Medieval period to 1449
2 Renaissance period, 1450–1599
3 1600–1699
4 1700–1799
5 1800–1899
6 1900–1999
62 1900–1945
64 1945–1999
7 2000–

.36 *Afrikaans literature

PERIOD TABLE
1 Early period to 1875
2 1875–1904
3 1904–1924
4 1924–1961
Class here 20th century
*For 1900–1904, see 2; for 1904–1924, see 3; for
1961–1994, see 5; for 1994–1999, see 6*
5 1961–1994
6 1994–

.4 ***Low German (Plattdeutsch) literature**

Including Old Low German literature, Old Saxon literature [*both formerly*
839.1]

PERIOD TABLE
1 Early period to 1599
2 1600–1899
3 1900–1999
4 2000–

.5 **Scandinavian (North Germanic) literatures**

For specific Scandinavian literatures, see 839.6–839.8

*Add to base number as instructed at beginning of Table 3

> ### 839.6–839.8 Specific Scandinavian literatures

    Class comprehensive works in 839.5

.6   **West Scandinavian literatures**   **Old Norse (Old Icelandic) literature**

.600 1–.600 9   Standard subdivisions of West Scandinavian literatures

.601–.68   Subdivisions of Old Norse (Old Icelandic) literature

    Add to base number 839.6 as instructed at beginning of Table 3, e.g., history and criticism of Old Norse poetry 839.61009

.69   Modern West Scandinavian literatures   Modern Icelandic literature

.690 01–.690 09   Standard subdivisions of modern West Scandinavian literatures

.690 1–.698   Subdivisions of Modern Icelandic literature

    Add to base number 839.69 as instructed at beginning of Table 3, e.g., a collection of modern Icelandic poetry 839.691008

    PERIOD TABLE

1	Early period, 1500–1719
2	Age of enlightenment, 1720–1835
3	1835–1899
	Class here 19th century
	For 1800–1835, see 2
4	1900–1999
5	2000–

    See also 839.699 for Faeroese literature

.699   *Faeroese literature

> ### 839.7–839.8 East Scandinavian literatures

    Class comprehensive works in 839.5

*Add to base number as instructed at beginning of Table 3

.7   ***Swedish literature**

PERIOD TABLE
1   Medieval period to 1519
2   Reformation period, 1520–1639
3   Age of Stjernhjelm, 1640–1739
         Class here 17th century
         For 1600–1639, see 2
4   Age of Dalin, 1740–1779
         Class here 18th century
         For 1700–1739, see 3; for 1780–1799, see 5
5   Age of Gustavus, 1780–1799
6   1800–1899
7   1900–1999
72   1900–1945
74   1945–1999
8   2000–

.8   **Danish and Norwegian literatures**

.81   *Danish literature

PERIOD TABLE
1   Medieval period to 1499
2   Reformation period, 1500–1559
3   Learned period, 1560–1699
4   Age of Holberg, 1700–1749
5   Period of enlightenment, 1750–1799
6   1800–1899
7   1900–1999
72   1900–1945
74   1945–1999
8   2000–

Class Dano-Norwegian literature in 839.82

.82   *Norwegian (Bokmål, Riksmål) literature

Class here Dano-Norwegian literature, comprehensive works on Norwegian literature

PERIOD TABLE
1   Medieval period to 1499
2   Reformation period, 1500–1559
3   Learned period, 1560–1699
4   1700–1749
5   Period of enlightenment, 1750–1799
6   1800–1899
7   1900–1999
72   1900–1945
74   1945–1999
8   2000–

For New Norwegian literature, see 839.83

*Add to base number as instructed at beginning of Table 3

.83   *Norwegian (New Norwegian, Landsmål) literature

PERIOD TABLE
6	1800–1899
7	1900–1999
72	1900–1945
74	1945–1999
8	2000–

Class comprehensive works on Norwegian literature in 839.82

.9   **East Germanic literatures**

840   Literatures of Romance languages   French literature

Class comprehensive works on Italic languages in 870

For literatures of Italian, Sardinian, Dalmatian, Romanian, Rhaeto-Romanic languages, see 850; for literatures of Spanish and Portuguese languages, see 860

.01–.09   Standard subdivisions of literatures of Romance languages

*Add to base number as instructed at beginning of Table 3

> **840.1–848   Subdivisions of French literature**

Except for modifications shown under specific entries, add to base number 84 as instructed at beginning of Table 3, e.g., a collection of French poetry 841.008

Assign period numbers for European countries, for comprehensive works on literature in French language

PERIOD TABLE FOR FRENCH

For European countries, for comprehensive works on literature in French language

1	Early period to 1399
	Class here medieval period
2	1400–1499
3	Renaissance period, 1500–1599
4	Classical period, 1600–1715
5	1715–1789
	Class here 18th century, Enlightment, Age of Reason
	For 1700–1715, see 4; for 1789–1799, see 6
6	Revolution and Empire, 1789–1815
7	Constitutional monarchy, 1815–1848
	Class here 19th century
	For 1800–1815, see 6; for 1848–1899, see 8
8	1848–1899
9	1900–
91	1900–1999
912	1900–1945
914	1945–1999
92	2000–

Class comprehensive works in 840

See also 849 for Provençal literature

(Option: Distinguish French-language literatures of specific countries by initial letters, e.g., literature of Canada C840, of France F840; or class literatures not requiring local emphasis in 848.99. If literatures are identified by one of these methods, assign the following optional period numbers for Belgium and non-European countries. Other options are described under 810–890

(OPTIONAL PERIOD TABLES FOR FRENCH

(For Asian and African countries

(1	Early period to 1959
(2	1960–1999
	Class here 20th century
	For 1900–1959, see 1
(3	2000–

(continued)

> **840.1–848 Subdivisions of French literature (continued)**

    (For Belgium
        (1   Early period to 1829
        (2   1830–1899
              Class here 19th century
                For 1800–1829, see 2
        (3   1900–1999
        (32   1900–1945
        (34   1945–1999
        (4   2000–

    (For Canada
        (3   Colonial period to 1867
        (4   1867–1899
        (5   1900–
        (52   1900–1945
        (54   1945–1999
        (6   2000–)

.1–.9   Standard subdivisions; collections; history, description, critical appraisal of French literature

    Numbers built according to instructions under 840.1–848 and at beginning of Table 3

841–847 Specific forms of French literature

    Numbers built according to instructions under 840.1–848 and at beginning of Table 3

848   French miscellaneous writings

    Number built according to instructions under 840.1–848 and at beginning of Table 3

(.99)   French-language literatures not requiring local emphasis

    (Optional number and subdivisions; prefer 840–848 for all French-language literatures. Other options are described under 810–890)

    Class here literatures of specific countries, e.g., libraries emphasizing literature of France may class here Belgian and Canadian literatures, libraries emphasizing Canadian literature may class here literature of France

(.991)   *†France

(.992)   *†Canada

(.993)   *†Belgium

*Add to base number as instructed at beginning of Table 3
†(Optional number; prefer 840–848)

(.994–.999)   †Other parts of the world

> French-language literature except of France, Belgium, Canada
>
> Add to 848.99 notation 4–9 from Table 2, e.g., French-language literature of Tahiti 848.9996211; then add 0 and to the base number thus derived add further as instructed at beginning of Table 3, e.g., French-language drama of Tahiti 848.999621102

849   Provençal (Langue d'oc), Franco-Provençal, Catalan literatures

.01–.8   Subdivisions of Provençal (Langue d'oc) literature

> Add to base number 849 as instructed at beginning of Table 3, e.g., a collection of Provençal poetry 849.1008

PERIOD TABLE FOR PROVENÇAL (LANGUE D'OC)

1	Early period to 1099
2	Golden age, 1100–1299
3	1300–1499
4	1500–1899
5	1900–1999
52	1900–1945
54	1945–1999
6	2000–

.9   *Catalan literature

PERIOD TABLE

1	First period to 1349
2	Second period, 1350–1449
3	Golden age, 1450–1499
	Class here 15th century
	For 1400–1449, see 3
4	1500–1899
5	1900–1999
52	1900–1945
54	1945–1999
6	2000–

850   Literatures of Italian, Sardinian, Dalmatian, Romanian, Rhaeto-Romanic languages   Italian literature

> Class comprehensive works on literatures of Romance languages in 840; class comprehensive works on literatures of Italic languages in 870

---

*Add to base number as instructed at beginning of Table 3
†(Optional number; prefer 840–848)

> **850.1–858   Subdivisions of Italian literature**

Add to base number 85 as instructed at beginning of Table 3, e.g., a collection of Italian poetry 851.008

PERIOD TABLE FOR ITALIAN

1	Early period to 1375
2	Period of classical learning, 1375–1492
	Class here Renaissance period
	For later Renaissance period, see 3
3	1492–1542
4	1542–1585
	Class here 16th century
	For 1500–1542, see 3; for 1585–1599, see 5
5	1585–1748
6	1748–1814
	Class here 18th century
	For 1700–1748, see 5
7	1814–1859
	Class here 19th century, romantic period
	For 1800–1814, see 6; for 1859–1899, see 8
8	1859–1899
9	1900–
91	1900–1999
912	1900–1945
914	1945–1999
92	2000–

Class comprehensive works in 850

.1–.9   Standard subdivisions; collections; history, description, critical appraisal of Italian literature

Numbers built according to instructions under 850.1–858 and at beginning of Table 3

851–858 Specific forms of Italian literature

Numbers built according to instructions under 850.1–858 and at beginning of Table 3

859   Romanian and Rhaeto-Romanic literatures

.01–.8   Subdivisions of Romanian literature

> Add to base number 859 as instructed at beginning of Table 3, e.g., a collection of Romanian poetry 859.1008

PERIOD TABLE

1	Early period to 1799
2	1800–1899
3	1900–1989
32	1900–1945
34	1945–1989
35	1989–

.9   **Rhaeto-Romanic literatures**

Including Friulian, Ladin, Romansh literatures

860   Literatures of Spanish and Portuguese languages   Spanish literature

Class comprehensive works on literatures of Romance languages in 840

.01–.09   Standard subdivisions of literatures of Spanish and Portuguese languages

> **860.1–868 Subdivisions of Spanish literature**

Class here Judeo-Spanish (Ladino), Papiamento literature

Except for modifications shown under specific entries, add to base number 86 as instructed at beginning of Table 3, e.g., a collection of Spanish poetry 861.008

Assign period numbers for Spain, for comprehensive works on literature in Spanish language

PERIOD TABLE FOR SPANISH
For Spain, for comprehensive works on literature in Spanish language
1   Early period to 1369
2   1369–1516
3   Golden Age, 1516–1699
4   1700–1799
5   1800–1899
6   1900–1999
62   1900–1945
64   1945–1999
7   2000–

Class comprehensive works in 860

See also 849.9 for Catalan literature

(Option: Distinguish Spanish-language literatures of specific countries by initial letters, e.g., literature of Chile Ch860, of Colombia Co860, of Mexico M860 [or, of all American countries A860], of Spain S860; or class literatures not requiring local emphasis in 868.99. If literatures are identified by one of these methods, assign the following optional period numbers for literature of American countries. Other options are described under 810–890

(OPTIONAL PERIOD TABLE FOR SPANISH
  (For American countries
    (1   Colonial and revolutionary period, 1519–1826
    (2   1826–1888
            Class here 19th century
              For 1800–1826, see 1; for 1888–1899, see 3
    (3   1888–1909
    (4   1910–1999
    (42   1910–1945
    (44   1945–1999
    (5   2000–   )

.1–.9   Standard subdivisions; collections; history, description, critical appraisal of Spanish literature

Numbers built according to instructions under 860.1–868 and at beginning of Table 3

861–867 Specific forms of Spanish literature

> Numbers built according to instructions under 860.1–868 and at beginning of Table 3

868   Spanish miscellaneous writings

> Number built according to instructions under 860.1–868 and at beginning of Table 3

(.99)   Spanish-language literatures not requiring local emphasis

> (Optional number and subdivisions; prefer 860–868 for all Spanish-language literatures. Other options are described under 810–890)
>
> Class here literatures of specific countries other than the country requiring local emphasis, e.g., libraries emphasizing literature of Spain may class here Hispanic-American literatures, and libraries emphasizing literature of Mexico may class here literatures of other Hispanic-American countries and of Spain

(.991)   *†Spain

(.992)   †Hispanic North America

> Class here comprehensive works on Spanish-language literature of Hispanic America
>
> *For Hispanic South America, see 868.993*

(.992 001–.992 08)   †Subdivisions of Spanish-language literatures of Hispanic North America

> Add to base number 868.9920 as instructed at beginning of Table 3, e.g., collections of Spanish-language one-act plays of Hispanic North America 868.99202041

(.992 1)   *†Mexico

(.992 2)   †Central America

(.992 200 1–.992 208)   †Subdivisions of Spanish-language literatures of Central America

> Add to base number 868.99220 as instructed at beginning of Table 3, e.g., collections of Spanish-language one-act plays of Central America 868.992202041

(.992 21–.992 27)   †Specific countries

> Add to 868.9922 the numbers following —728 in notation 7281–7287 from Table 2, e.g., Spanish-language literature of Costa Rica 868.99226; then to the base number thus derived add further as instructed at beginning of Table 3, e.g., collections of Spanish-language literature of Costa Rica displaying naturalism 868.9922608012

---

*Add to base number as instructed at beginning of Table 3
†(Optional number; prefer 860–868)

(.992 3)　　　　　　　†West Indies (Antilles)

(.992 300 1–.992 308)　　　†Spanish-language literatures of West Indies (Antilles)

> Add to base number 868.99230 as instructed at beginning of Table 3, e.g., collections of Spanish-language one-act plays of West Indies 868.99230204108

(.992 31)　　　　　　*†Cuba

(.992 33)　　　　　　*†Dominican Republic

(.992 35)　　　　　　*†Puerto Rico

(.993)　　　　　†Hispanic South America

(.993 001–.993 08)　　　†Subdivisions of Spanish-language literatures of Hispanic South America

> Add to base number 868.9930 as instructed at beginning of Table 3, e.g., collections of Spanish-language dramatic poetry of Hispanic South America 868.993010208

(.993 2–.993 7)　　　†Argentina, Chile, Bolivia, Peru, Colombia, Ecuador, Venezuela

> Add to 868.993 the numbers following —8 in notation 82–87 from Table 2, e.g., Spanish-language literature of Chile 868.9933; then to the base number thus derived add further as instructed at beginning of Table 3, e.g., history and critical appraisal of Spanish-language literature of Chile 868.993309

(.993 9)　　　　　　†Paraguay and Uruguay

> Add to 868.993 the numbers following —8 in notation 89 from Table 2, e.g., Spanish-language literature of Uruguay 868.99395; then to the base number thus derived add further as instructed at beginning of Table 3, e.g., history and critical appraisal of Spanish-language literature of Uruguay 868.9939509

(.994–.999)　　　†Other parts of the world

> Spanish-language literature except of Spain, Hispanic America

> Add to 868.99 notation 4–9 from Table 2, e.g., Spanish-language literature of the United States 868.9973; then add 0 and to the base number thus derived add further as instructed at beginning of Table 3, e.g., Spanish-language poetry of the United States 868.997301

---

*Add to base number as instructed at beginning of Table 3
†(Optional number; prefer 860–868)

869 *Portuguese literature

Class here Galician (Gallegan) literature

Assign period numbers for Portugal, for comprehensive works on literature in Portuguese language

PERIOD TABLE FOR PORTUGUESE
For Portugal, for comprehensive works on literature in Portuguese language
1   Early period to 1499
2   1500–1799
        Including classical period
3   1800–1899
4   1900–1999
41   1900–1945
42   1945–1999
5   2000–

See also 860 for Papiamento literature

(Option: Distinguish Portuguese-language literatures of specific countries by initial letters, e.g., literature of Brazil B869, of Portugal P869; or class literatures not requiring local emphasis in 869.899. If literatures are identified by one of these methods, assign the following optional period numbers for literature of Brazil. Other options are described under 810–890

(OPTIONAL PERIOD TABLE FOR PORTUGUESE
(For Brazil
(1   Period of formation, 1500–1749
(2   Period of transformation, 1750–1829
(3   1830–1921
        Class here 19th century
        For 1800–1829, see 2
(4   1921–1999
(5   2000–   )

(.899)   Portuguese-language literatures not requiring local emphasis

(Optional number and subdivisions; prefer 869.01–869.8 for all Portuguese-language literatures. Other options are described under 810–890)

Class here literatures of specific countries other than the country requiring local emphasis, e.g., libraries emphasizing literature of Portugal may class here Brazilian literature, and libraries emphasizing Brazilian literature may class here literature of Portugal

(.899 1)   *‡Portugal

(.899 2)   *‡Brazil

*Add to base number as instructed at beginning of Table 3

‡(Optional number; prefer 869.01–869.8)

(.899 4–.899 9)   ‡Other parts of world

> Portuguese-language literature except of Portugal, Brazil

> Add to 869.899 notation 4–9 from Table 2, e.g., Portuguese-language literature of India 869.89954; then add 0 and to the base number thus derived add further as instructed at beginning of Table 3, e.g., Portuguese-language drama of India 869.8995402

870   Literatures of Italic languages   Latin literature

> Class comprehensive works of or on literatures of classical (Greek and Latin) languages in 880

> *For literatures of Romance languages, see 840*

.01–.09   Standard subdivisions of literatures of Italic languages

---

> ### 870.1 878 Subdivisions of Latin literature

> Add to base number 87 as instructed at beginning of Table 3, e.g., a collection of Latin poetry 871.008; however, observe the special interpretations of and exceptions to notation from Table 3 that appear below, e.g., collections of Latin poetry of the medieval period 871.0308, critical appraisal of Latin epic poetry and fiction of the Roman period 873.0109

> PERIOD TABLE FOR LATIN
> 1   Roman period to ca. 499
> 2   Pre-Carolingian period, ca. 500–ca. 749
> 3   Medieval period, ca. 750–1349
> 4   Modern period, 1350–

> Class comprehensive works in 870

.1–.9   **Standard subdivisions; collections; history, description, critical appraisal of Latin literature**

> Numbers built according to instructions under 870.1–878 and at beginning of Table 3

871   †Latin poetry

> *For dramatic poetry, see 872; for epic poetry, see 873; for lyric poetry, see 874*

.01–.04   Specific periods

> Use period table under 870.1–878

> Do not use 871.02–871.08 for specific kinds

872   †Latin dramatic poetry and drama

---

†Add as instructed under 870.1–878 and at beginning of Table 3
‡(Optional number; prefer 869.01–869.8)

.01–.04	Specific periods

Use period table under 870.1–878

Do not use 872.02–872.05 for specific media, scopes, kinds

873 †Latin epic poetry and fiction

.01–.04	Specific periods

Use period table under 870.1–878

Do not use 873.01–873.08 for specific scopes and kinds

874 †Latin lyric poetry

.01–.04	Specific periods

Use period table under 870.1–878

875 †Latin speeches

.01–.04	Specific periods

Use period table under 870.1–878

Do not use 875.01–875.06 for specific kinds

876 †Latin letters

.01–.04	Specific periods

Use period table under 870.1–878

877 †Latin humor and satire

.01–.04	Specific periods

Use period table under 870.1–878

878 †Latin miscellaneous writings

.000 1–.000 9	Standard subdivisions
.002–.008	Specific kinds of miscellaneous writings

Numbers built according to instructions under 870.1–878 and at beginning of Table 3

.01–.04	Specific periods

Use period table under 870.1–878

879 Literatures of other Italic languages

.4	Latinian literatures other than Latin
.7	Literatures of Sabellian languages
.9	Osco-Umbrian literatures

†Add as instructed under 870.1–878 and at beginning of Table 3

880   Literatures of Hellenic languages   Classical Greek literature

Class here comprehensive works of or on literatures of classical (Greek and Latin) languages

For Latin literature, see 870

.01–.09   Standard subdivisions of classical (Greek and Latin) literatures

---

> **880.1–888 Subdivisions of classical Greek literature**

Add to base number 88 as instructed at beginning of Table 3, e.g., a collection of classical Greek poetry 881.008; however, observe the special interpretations of and exceptions to notation from Table 3 that appear below, e.g., collections of classical Greek poetry of the medieval and Byzantine periods 881.0208, critical appraisal of classical Greek epic poetry and fiction of the ancient period 883.0109

PERIOD TABLE FOR CLASSICAL GREEK
1   Ancient period to ca. 499
2   Medieval and Byzantine periods, ca. 500–1599
3   Modern period, 1600–

Class comprehensive works in 880

.1–.9   **Standard subdivisions; collections; history, description, critical appraisal of classical Greek literature**

Numbers built according to instructions under 880.1–888 and at beginning of Table 3

881   ‡Classical Greek poetry

For dramatic poetry, see 882; for epic poetry, see 883; for lyric poetry, see 884

.01–.03   Specific periods

Use period table under 880.1–888

Do not use 881.02–881.08 for specific kinds

882   ‡Classical Greek dramatic poetry and drama

.01–.03   Specific periods

Use period table under 880.1–888

Do not use 882.02–882.05 for specific media, scopes, kinds

883   ‡Classical Greek epic poetry and fiction

.01–.03   Specific periods

Use period table under 880.1–888

Do not use 883.01–883.08 for specific scopes and kinds

‡Add as instructed under 880.1–888 and at beginning of Table 3

884 ‡Classical Greek lyric poetry

.01–.03 Specific periods

> Use period table under 880.1–888

885 ‡Classical Greek speeches

.01–.03 Specific periods

> Use period table under 880.1–888

> Do not use 885.01–885.06 for specific kinds

886 ‡Classical Greek letters

.01–.03 Specific periods

> Use period table under 880.1–888

887 ‡Classical Greek humor and satire

.01–.03 Specific periods

> Use period table under 880.1–888

888 ‡Classical Greek miscellaneous writings

.000 1–.000 9 Standard subdivisions

.002–.008 Specific kinds of miscellaneous writings

> Numbers built according to instructions under 880.1–888 and at beginning of Table 3

.01–.03 Specific periods

> Use period table under 880.1–888

889 *Modern Greek literature

> Class here Katharevusa and Demotic literature

PERIOD TABLE

1	Early period to 1821
2	1821–1899
3	1900–1999
32	1900–1945
34	1945–1999
4	2000–

---

*Add to base number as instructed at beginning of Table 3

‡Add as instructed under 880.1–888 and at beginning of Table 3

890   Literatures of other specific languages and language families

Class texts by more than one author in more than two languages not from the same language family in 808.8; class history, description, critical appraisal of works by more than one author in more than two languages not from the same language family in 809

SUMMARY

891   East Indo-European and Celtic literatures

SUMMARY

.1   Indo-Iranian literatures

For Indo-Aryan (Indic) literatures, see 891.2–891.4; for Iranian literatures, see 891.5

>   891.2–891.4 Indo-Aryan (Indic) literatures

Class comprehensive works in 891.1

.2   *Sanskrit literature

Class here classical Sanskrit literature

.29   Vedic (Old Indic) literature

.3   Middle Indic literatures

Class here comprehensive works on Prakrit literatures

For modern Prakrit literatures, see 891.4

---

*Add to base number as instructed at beginning of Table 3

.37   *Pali literature

.4   **Modern Indic literatures**

Class here modern Prakrit literatures

PERIOD TABLE FOR SPECIFIC MODERN INDIC LITERATURES
1   Early period to 1345
2   1345–1645
3   1645–1845
4   1845–1895
            Class here 19th century
              For 1800–1845, see 3; for 1895–1899, see 5
5   1895–1919
6   1920–1939
7   1940–
71   1940–1999
            Class here 20th century
              For 1900–1919, see 5; for 1920–1939, see 6
72   2000–

Class comprehensive works on Prakrit literatures in 891.3

(Option: Treat literatures of all modern Indic languages as literature of one language, with base number 891.4. Add to 891.4 as instructed at beginning of Table 3, e.g., a collection of poetry in modern Indic languages 891.41008)

.41   Sindhi and Lahnda literatures

.410 1–.418   Subdivisions of Sindhi literature

Add to base number 891.41 as instructed at beginning of Table 3, e.g., a collection of Sindhi poetry 891.411008

Use period table under 891.4

.419   *Lahnda literature

Use period table under 891.4

.42   *Panjabi literature

Use period table under 891.4

.43   Western Hindi literatures   Hindi literature

.430 01–.430 09   Standard subdivisions of Western Hindi literatures

.430 1–.438   Subdivisions of Hindi literature

Add to base number 891.43 as instructed at beginning of Table 3, e.g., a collection of Hindi poetry 891.431008

Use period table under 891.4

.439   *Urdu literature

Use period table under 891.4

*Add to base number as instructed at beginning of Table 3

.44	*Bengali literature

Use period table under 891.4

.45	Assamese, Bihari, Oriya literatures

.451	*Assamese literature

Use period table under 891.4

.454	*Bihari literature

Class here literatures in Bhojpuri, Magahi, Maithili

Use period table under 891.4

.456	*Oriya literature

Use period table under 891.4

.46	*Marathi literature

Class here Konkani literature

Use period table under 891.4

.47	Gujarati, Bhili, Rajasthani literatures

.470 1–.478	Subdivisions of Gujarati literature

Add to base number 891.47 as instructed at beginning of Table 3, e.g., a collection of Gujarati poetry 891.471008

Use period table under 891.4

.479	*Rajasthani literature

Class here Jaipuri, Marwari literatures

Use period table under 891.4

.48	*Sinhalese literature

Class here Divehi (Maldivian), Sinhalese-Maldivian literatures

Use period table under 891.4

.49	Other Indo-Aryan (Indic) literatures

Including Awadhi, Bagheli, Chattisgarhi, Eastern Hindi, Nuristani (Kafiri), Pahari literatures

See also 894.8 for Dravidian literatures, 895.4 for Tibeto-Burman literatures, 895.95 for Munda literatures

.495	*Nepali literature

.497	*Romany literature [*formerly* 891.499]

*Add as instructed at beginning of Table 3

.499   Dardic (Pisacha) literatures

           Including Kashmiri, Khowar, Kohistani, Shina literatures

           Use of this number for Nuristani (Kafiri) literature discontinued; class in 891.49

           Romany literature relocated to 891.497

.5   **Iranian literatures**

.51   *Old Persian literature

           Class here ancient West Iranian literatures

           See also 891.52 for Avestan literature

.52   *Avestan literature

           Class here ancient East Iranian literatures

.53   Middle Iranian literatures

           Including Khotanese (Saka), Pahlavi (Middle Persian), Sogdian literatures

.55   *Modern Persian (Farsi) literature

           PERIOD TABLE

           1   Period of formal development, ca. 1000–1389
           2   1389–1899
           3   1900–1999
           4   2000–

           Dari literature relocated to 891.56

           Class Tajik literature in 891.57

.56   *Dari literature [*formerly* 891.55]

.57   *Tajik literature [*formerly* 891.59]

.59   Other modern Iranian literatures

           Including Pamir literatures, Ossetic literature

           Tajik literature relocated to 891.57

.593   *Pashto (Afghan) literature

           Use of this number for Pamir literatures discontinued; class in 891.59

.597   Kurdish literatures   Kurdish (Kurmanji) literature

.597 01–.597 8   Subdivisions of Kurdish (Kurmanji) literature

           Add to base number 891.597 as instructed at beginning of Table 3, e.g., a collection of Kurdish poetry 891.5971008

.598   *Baluchi literature

*Add as instructed at beginning of Table 3

.6 **Celtic literatures**

Including Gaulish

.62 *Irish Gaelic literature

PERIOD TABLE
1   Early period to 1171
2   1171–1599
       1600–1699 relocated to 3
3   1600–1875
       Including 1600–1699 [*formerly* 2], 1850–1875 [*formerly* 4]
4   1875–1999
       1850–1875 relocated to 3
42   1875–1922
         Class here Irish literary revival
43   1922–1999
5   2000–

.63 *Scottish Gaelic literature

PERIOD TABLE
1   Early period to 1599
2   1600–1829
3   1830–1999
32   1830–1899
         Class here 19th century
         For 1800–1829, see 2
34   1900–1999
4   2000–

.64 *Manx literature

.66 *Welsh (Cymric) literature

PERIOD TABLE
1   Early period to 1599
12   Early period to 1299
14   1300–1599
2   1600–1999
22   1600–1799
24   1800–1899
26   1900–1945
         Class here 20th century
         For 1945–1999, see 28
28   1945–1999
3   2000–

.67 *Cornish literature

*Add to base number as instructed at beginning of Table 3

.68   *Breton literature

PERIOD TABLE
1	Early period to 1799
2	1800–1899
3	1900–1999
4	2000–

.7   East Slavic literatures   Russian literature

Class comprehensive works on Slavic (Slavonic) literatures in 891.8

.700 1–.700 9   Standard subdivisions of East Slavic literatures

.701–.78   Subdivisions of Russian literature

Add to base number 891.7 as instructed at beginning of Table 3, e.g., a collection of Russian poetry 891.71008

PERIOD TABLE
1	Early period to 1699
2	1700–1799
3	1800–1917
4	1917–1991
	Class here 20th century
	For 1900–1917, see 3; for 1991–1999, see 5
42	1917–1945
44	1945–1991
5	1991–

.79   Ukrainian and Belarusian literatures

.790 1–.798   Subdivisions of Ukrainian literature

Add to base number 891.79 as instructed at beginning of Table 3, e.g., a collection of Ukrainian poetry 891.791008

PERIOD TABLE
1	Early period to 1798
2	1798–1917
3	1917–1991
	Class here 20th century
	For 1900–1917, see 2; for 1991–1999, see 4
32	1917–1945
34	1945–1991
4	1991–

.799   *Belarusian literature

PERIOD TABLE
1	Early period to 1798
2	1798–1917
3	1917–1991
	Class here 20th century
	For 1900–1917, see 2; for 1991–1999, see 4
4	1991–

*Add to base number as instructed at beginning of Table 3

.8   **Slavic (Slavonic) literatures**

Class here comprehensive works on literatures of Balto-Slavic languages

For East Slavic literatures, see 891.7; for Baltic literatures, see 891.91–891.93

.81   South Slavic literatures   Bulgarian literature

For Serbo-Croatian literature, see 891.82; for Slovenian literature, see 891.84

.810 01–.810 09   Standard subdivisions of South Slavic literatures

.810 1–.818   Subdivisions of Bulgarian literature

Add to base number 891.81 as instructed at beginning of Table 3, e.g., a collection of Bulgarian poetry 891.811008

PERIOD TABLE

1	Early period to 1849
2	1850–1899
3	1900–1991
4	1991–

.819   *Macedonian literature

.82   *Serbo-Croatian literature

Class here Croatian, Dalmatian (Slavic), Serbian literatures

PERIOD TABLE

1	Early period to ca. 1549
2	Period of renaissance, ca. 1550–1699
3	1700–1799
4	1800–1899
5	1900–1991
52	1900–1945
54	1945–1991
6	1991–

(Option: Distinguish literatures written in different scripts by initial letters, e.g., Croatian literature C891.82, Serbian literature S891.82. Other options are described under 810–890)

.84   *Slovenian literature

PERIOD TABLE

1	Early period to ca. 1549
2	Period of renaissance, ca. 1550–1699
3	1700–1799
4	1800–1899
5	1900–1991
6	1991–

*Add to base number as instructed at beginning of Table 3

.85	West Slavic literatures	Polish literature

Including Kashubian literature

> *For Czech literature, see 891.86; for Slovak literature, see 891.87; for Wendish literature, see 891.88; for Polabian literature, see 891.89*

.850 01–.850 09   Standard subdivisions of West Slavic literatures

.850 1–.858   Subdivisions of Polish literature

Add to base number 891.85 as instructed at beginning of Table 3, e.g., a collection of Polish poetry 891.851008

PERIOD TABLE

1	Early period to 1399
2	1400–1499
3	Golden age, 1500–1599
4	1600–1699
5	1700–1795
6	1795–1919
7	1919–1989

Class here 20th century
> *For 1900–1919, see 6; for 1989–1999, see 8*

72	1919–1945
73	1945–1989
8	1989–

.86   *Czech literature

Class here literature in Moravian dialects [*formerly* 891.87]

PERIOD TABLE

1	Early period to 1399
2	1400–1449
3	Humanist period, 1450–1620
4	1620–1899
5	1900–1989
52	1900–1945
54	1945–1989
6	1989–

.87   *Slovak literature

Literature in Moravian dialects relocated to 891.86

.88   *Wendish (Lusatian, Sorbian) literature

.89   *Polabian literature

.9   Baltic and other Indo-European literatures

>   891.91–891.93   Baltic literatures
>
> Class comprehensive works in 891.9

---

*Add to base number as instructed at beginning of Table 3

.91   Old Prussian literature

.92   *Lithuanian literature

       PERIOD TABLE
          1   Early period to 1799
          2   1800–1899
          3   1900–1991
          4   1991–

.93   *Latvian (Lettish) literature

       PERIOD TABLE
          1   Early period to 1799
          2   1800–1899
          3   1900–1991
          4   1991–

.99   Other Indo-European literatures

Add to 891.99 the numbers following —9199 in notation 91991–91998 from Table 6, e.g., Armenian literature 891.992, Hittite literature 891.998; then to the number given for each literature listed below add further as instructed at beginning of Table 3, e.g., a collection of Armenian poetry 891.9921008

    891.991 Albanian

    891.992 Armenian

    PERIOD TABLE FOR ARMENIAN
          1   Early period to 599
          2   600–999
          3   1000–1399
          4   1400–1849
          5   1850–1991
               Including 19th century
               For 1800–1849, see 4
          6   1991–

892   Afro-Asiatic (Hamito-Semitic) literatures   Semitic literatures

For non-Semitic Afro-Asiatic literatures, see 893

.1   East Semitic literatures   Akkadian (Assyro-Babylonian) literature

Class here literatures in Assyrian, Babylonian dialects of Akkadian

For Eblaite literature, see 892.6

See also 899.95 for Sumerian literature

\>   **892.2–892.9 West Semitic literatures**

Class comprehensive works in 892

---

*Add to base number as instructed at beginning of Table 3

.2   Aramaic literatures

For Eastern Aramaic literatures, see 892.3

.29   Western Aramaic literatures

Including Samaritan literature

.3   Eastern Aramaic literatures   Syriac literature

.4   *Hebrew literature

PERIOD TABLE
1	Early period to 699
2	700–1699
	Class here medieval period
3	1700–1819
4	1820–1885
	Class here 19th century
	For 1800–1819, see 3; for 1885–1899, see 5
5	1885–1947
6	1947–1999
	Class here 20th century
	For 1900–1947, see 5
7	2000–

.6   Canaanite literatures

Including Eblaite literature

Class here comprehensive works on Canaanitic literatures

For Hebrew, see 892.4

.67   Ugaritic literature

.7   Literatures of Arabic and Maltese languages   Arabic literature

Class here classical Arabic literature, Judeo-Arabic literature

See also 892.9 for South Arabian literatures

*Add to base number as instructed at beginning of Table 3

.701–.78   Subdivisions of Arabic literatures

> Add to base number 892.7 as instructed at beginning of Table 3, e.g., a
> collection of Arabic poetry 892.71008

> Assign period numbers for Asian countries, for African countries, for
> comprehensive works on literature in Arabic language

PERIOD TABLE

1	Pre-Islamic period to 622
2	Early Islamic and Mukhadrami period, 622–661
	Class here 7th century
	For 600–622, see 1; for 661–699, see 32
3	661–1258
32	Umayyad period, 661–749
34	Abbasid period, 750–1258
4	1258–1799
5	1800–1945
6	1945–1999
	Class here 20th century
	For 1900–1945, see 5
7	2000–

> *See also 892.9 for South Arabian literatures*

.79   *Maltese literature

.8   Ethiopian literatures

> Including Gurage, Harari literatures

> Class here comprehensive works on South Semitic literatures

> *For South Arabian literatures, see 892.9*

.81   Ge'ez literature

.82   *Tigré literature

.83   *Tigrinya literature

.87   *Amharic literature

.9   South Arabian literatures

> Including Mahri, Sokotri literatures

> Class comprehensive works on South Semitic literatures in 892.8

> *See also 892.7 for North Arabic literatures*

*Add to base number as instructed at beginning of Table 3

893   Non-Semitic Afro-Asiatic literatures

Add to 893 the numbers following —93 in notation 931–937 from Table 6, e.g., Berber literatures 893.3, Somali literature 893.54; then to the number given for each literature listed below add further as instructed at beginning of Table 3, e.g., a collection of Somali poetry 893.541008

893.1 Egyptian

893.2 Coptic

893.33 Tamazight

893.34 Kabyle

893.38 Tamashek

893.54 Somali

893.55 Oromo

893.72 Hausa

894   Altaic, Uralic, Hyperborean, Dravidian literatures

SUMMARY

894.1–.3	**Altaic literatures**
.4	**Samoyedic literatures**
.5	**Finno-Ugric literatures**
.6	**Hyperborean (Paleosiberian) literatures**
.8	**Dravidian literatures**

.1–.3   Altaic literatures

Add to 894 the numbers following —94 in notation 941–943 from Table 6, e.g., Mongolian literature 894.23, Altai literature 894.33; then to the number given for each literature listed below add further as instructed at beginning of Table 3, e.g., a collection of Mongolian poetry 894.231008

894.23 Mongolian, Khalkha Mongolian

894.315 Chuvash

894.323 Uighur

894.325 Uzbek

894.332 Yakut

894.345 Kazakh

894.347 Kirghiz

894.35 Turkish (Osmanli), Ottoman Turkish

PERIOD TABLE FOR TURKISH, OSMANLI, OTTOMAN TURKISH
1	Early period to 1499
2	1500–1849
3	1850–1999
	Including 19th century
	For 1800–1849, see 2
4	2000–

894.361 Azerbaijani

894.364 Turkmen

894.387 Tatar

894.388 Crimean Tatar

Class comprehensive works in 894

For Ainu, see 894.6; for Japanese, see 895.6; for Korean, see 895.7

> **894.4–894.5   Uralic literatures**

Class comprehensive works in 894.5

.4   Samoyedic literatures

.5   Finno-Ugric literatures

Class here comprehensive works on Uralic literatures, on Uralic and Yukaghir literatures

For Samoyedic literatures, see 894.4; for Yukaghir literatures, see 894.6

.51   Ugric literatures

Including Ostyak (Khanty), Vogul literatures

.511   *Hungarian (Magyar) literature

PERIOD TABLE

1	Early period to 1799
2	1800–1899
3	1900–1989
32	1900–1945
34	1945–1989
4	1989–

.53   Permic literatures

Including Votyak (Udmurt), Zyrian (Komi) literatures

.54   Finnic literatures

Including Karelian, Livonian, Veps literatures

For Permic literatures, see 894.53; for Sami literature, see 894.55; for Middle Volga literatures, see 894.56

.541   *Finnish (Suomi) literature

PERIOD TABLE

1	Early period to 1799
2	1800–1899
3	1900–1999
4	2000–

.545   *Estonian literature

PERIOD TABLE

1	Early period to 1861
	Including 19th century
	For 1861–1899, see 2
2	1861–1991
3	1991–

.55   *Sami literature

.56   Middle Volga literatures

Including Mari, Mordvin literatures

.6   Hyperborean (Paleosiberian) literatures

Class comprehensive works on Uralic and Yukaghir literatures in 894.5

---

*Add to base number as instructed at beginning of Table 3

.8   **Dravidian literatures**

PERIOD TABLE FOR SPECIFIC DRAVIDIAN LITERATURES

1	Early period to 1345
2	1345–1645
3	1645–1845
4	1845–1895

       Class here 19th century
       For 1800–1845, see 3; for 1895–1899, see 5

5	1895–1919
6	1920–1939
7	1940–
71	1940–1999

       Class here 20th century
       For 1900–1919, see 5; for 1920–1939, see 6

72	2000–

(Option: Treat literatures of all Dravidian languages as literature of one language, with base number 894.8. Add to 894.8 as instructed at beginning of Table 3, e.g., a collection of poetry in Dravidian languages 894.81008)

.81   South Dravidian literatures

     Including Kota, Toda literatures

     Class here literatures of the Dravida group

.811   *Tamil literature

     Use period table under 894.8

.812   *Malayalam literature

     Use period table under 894.8

.814   *Kannada (Kanarese) literature

     Use period table under 894.8

.82   Central Dravidian literatures

.823   *Gondi literature

     Use period table under 894.8

.824   *Khond (Kandh) literature

     Use period table under 894.8

.827   *Telugu literature

     Use period table under 894.8

.83   North Dravidian literatures   Brahui literature

.830 01–.830 09   Standard subdivisions of North Dravidian literatures

---

*Add to base number as instructed at beginning of Table 3

.830 1–.838   Subdivisions of Brahui literature

Add to base number 894.83 as instructed at beginning of Table 3, e.g., a collection of Brahui poetry 894.831008

Use period table under 894.8

895   Literatures of East and Southeast Asia   Sino-Tibetan literatures

Here are classed literatures of South Asian languages closely related to the languages of East and Southeast Asia

For literature of Austronesian languages of East and Southeast Asia, see 899.2

.1   *Chinese literature

PERIOD TABLE

1	Origins, 15th century to 221 B.C.
	Class here classical age
2	221 B.C.–618 A.D.
	Class here middle epoch
22	Period of Ch'in (Qin) anC Han dynasties, 221 B.C.–220 A.D.
24	Period of Six Dynasties and Sui dynasty, 220–618 A.D.
3	Period of T'ang and Five dynasties and Ten kingdoms, 618–960
	Class here renaissance and neoclassicism
4	960–1912
42	Period of Sung dynasty, 960–1279
44	Period of Yüan (Mongol) dynasty, 1271–1368
	For period of Yüan dynasty during 1271–1279, see 42
46	Period of Ming dynasty, 1368–1644
48	Period of Ch'ing (Manchu) dynasty, 1644–1912
5	1912–
51	1912–1949
52	1949–

.4   **Tibeto-Burman literatures   Tibetan literature**

For Burmese literature, see 895.8

.400 1–.400 9   Standard subdivisions of Tibeto-Burman literatures

.401–.48   Subdivisions of Tibetan literature

Add to base number 895.4 as instructed at beginning of Table 3, e.g., a collection of Tibetan poetry 895.41008

.49   Literatures of Eastern Himalayan languages

Including Chepang, Limbu, Magari, Sunwar, Newari literatures

Class here literatures of Kiranti languages

Use of this number for literatures of Himalayan languages other than Kiranti languages and Newari discontinued; class in 895.4

See also 891.495 for Nepali literature

---

*Add to base number as instructed at beginning of Table 3

.6 ***Japanese literature**

PERIOD TABLE
1	Early period to 1185
14	Heian period, 794–1185
2	Medieval period, 1185–1603
22	Kamakura period, 1185–1334
24	1334–1603
	Class here Muromachi period
3	Tokugawa (Edo) period, 1603–1868
32	1603–1769
	Including Genroku period
34	1770–1868
4	1868–1945
	Including Bunka-Bunsei period (1804–1830)
42	Meiji period, 1868–1912
44	1912–1945
	Class here 20th century
	For 1900–1912, see 42; for 1945–1999, see 5
5	1945–1999
6	2000–

.7 ***Korean literature**

PERIOD TABLE
1	Early period to 1392
2	Yi period, 1392–1910
28	1894–1910
3	1910–1945
4	1945–1999
	Class here 20th century
	For 1900–1910, see 28; for 1910–1945, see 3
5	2000–

.8 ***Burmese literature**

PERIOD TABLE
1	Early period to 1799
2	1800–1899
3	1900–1999
4	2000–

.9 **Literatures of miscellaneous languages of Southeast Asia; Munda literatures**

Limited to the literatures provided for below

Class literatures in Austroasiatic languages in 895.93

For literatures in Austronesian languages, see 899.2

.91 Tai literatures Thai (Siamese) literature

.910 01–.910 09 Standard subdivisions of literatures of Tai languages

---

*Add to base number as instructed at beginning of Table 3

.910 1–.918   Subdivisions of Thai (Siamese) literature

                  Add to base number 895.91 as instructed at beginning of Table 3, e.g., a collection of Thai poetry 895.911008

                  PERIOD TABLE

1	Early period to 1799
2	1800–1899
3	1900–1999
4	2000–

.919   Other Tai literatures

                  Including Shan literature

                  For Viet-Muong literatures, see 895.92

.919 1   *Lao literature

.92–.97   Viet-Muong, Mon-Khmer, Munda, Hmong-Mien literatures

                  Add to 895.9 the numbers following —959 in notation 9592–9597 from Table 6, e.g., Vietnamese literature 895.922, Mundari literature 895.95; then to the number given for each literature listed below add further as instructed at beginning of Table 3, e.g., a collection of Vietnamese poetry 895.9221008

                  895.922 Vietnamese

                  PERIOD TABLE FOR VIETNAMESE

1	Early period to 1799	
2	1800–1899	
3	1900–1999	
32	1900–1945	
	Class here 20th century	
	For 1945–1999, see 34	
34	1945–1999	
4	2000–	

                  895.932 Khmer (Cambodian)

                  895.972 Hmong (Miao)

*Add as instructed at beginning of Table 3

896   African literatures

Add to 896 the numbers following —96 in notation 961–965 from Table 6, e.g., Songhai literature 896.5, Swahili literature 896.392; then to the number given for each literature listed below add further as instructed at beginning of Table 3, e.g., a collection of Swahili poetry 896.3921008

896.3214 Wolof

896.322 Fulani (Fulah)

896.332 Ibo (Igbo)

896.333 Yoruba

896.3374 Ewe

896.3378 Gã

896.3385 Akan, Fante, Twi

896.3452 Bambara

896.348 Mende

896.3616 Sango

896.3642 Efik

896.3915 Bemba

896.3918 Nyanja, Chichewa (Chewa)

896.392 Swahili

896.3931 Kongo

896.3932 Kimbundu (Mbundu)

896.39461 Rwanda (Kinyarwanda)

896.39465 Rundi

896.3954 Kikuyu

896.3957 Ganda (Luganda)

896.3962 Duala

896.39686 Lingala

896.3975 Shona

896.39771 Northern Sotho

896.39772 Southern Sotho

896.39775 Tswana

896.3978 Tsonga

896.3985 Xhosa

(continued)

896   African literatures (continued)

896.3986 Zulu

896.3987 Swazi (siSwati)

PERIOD TABLE FOR SPECIFIC AFRICAN LITERATURES
1   Early period to 1959
2   1960–1999
                Class here 20th century
                For 1900–1959, see 1
3   2000–

Class Afrikaans literature in 839.96; class Malagasy literature in 899.3. Class literature in an African creole having a non-African primary source language with the source language, e.g., Krio literature 820

> *For Ethiopian literatures, see 892.8; for non-Semitic Afro-Asiatic literatures, see 893*

(Option: Treat literatures of all African languages as literature of one language, with base number 896. Add to 896 as instructed at beginning of Table 3, e.g., a collection of poetry in African languages 896.1008)

897   Literatures of North American native languages

Class here comprehensive works on literatures of North and South American native languages

Add to 897 the numbers following —97 in notation 971–979 from Table 6, e.g., Navajo literature 897.2, Nahuatl literature 897.452; then to the number given for each literature listed below add further as instructed at beginning of Table 3, e.g., a collection of Nahuatl literature 897.4521008

897.124 Eastern Canadian Inuktitut

897.19 Aleut

897.4152 Maya, Yucatec Maya

897.452 Nahuatl (Aztec)

> *For literatures of South American native languages, see 898*

(Option: Treat literatures of all North American native languages as literature of one language, with base number 897. Add to 897 as instructed at beginning of Table 3, e.g., a collection of poetry in North American native languages 897.1008)

898   Literatures of South American native languages

Add to 898 the numbers following —98 in notation 982–984 from Table 6, e.g., Quechua literature 898.323, Tucano literature 898.35; then to the number given for each literature listed below add further as instructed at beginning of Table 3, e.g., a collection of Quechua poetry 898.3231008

898.323 Quechua (Kechua)

898.324 Aymara

898.372 Jivaroa proper

898.382 Guaraní

898.3829 Tupí (Nhengatu)

Class comprehensive works on literatures of North and South American native languages in 897

(Option: Treat literatures of all South American native languages as literature of one language, with base number 898. Add to 898 as instructed at beginning of Table 3, e.g., a collection of poetry in South American Native languages 898.1008)

899   Literatures of non-Austronesian languages of Oceania, of Austronesian languages, of miscellaneous languages

Add to 899 the numbers following —99 in notation 991–999 from Table 6, e.g., Polynesian literatures 899.4, Maori literature 899.442; then to the number for each literature listed below add further as instructed at beginning of Table 3, e.g., a collection of Maori poetry 899.4421008

899.211 Tagalog (Filipino)

PERIOD TABLE FOR TAGALOG (FILIPINO)
1	Early period to 1799
2	1800–1899
3	1900–1999
4	2000–

899.221 Indonesian (Bahasa Indonesia)

PERIOD TABLE FOR INDONESIAN (BAHASA INDONESIA)
1	Early period to 1899
2	1900–1999
3	2000–

899.222 Javanese

899.28 Malay (Bahasa Malaysia)

899.3 Malagasy

899.42 Hawaiian

899.442 Maori

899.444 Tahitian

899.462 Samoan

899.92 Basque

899.95 Sumerian

899.9623 Abkhaz

899.9625 Adyghe

899.969 Georgian

899.992 Esperanto

.993   Interlingua literature

> Number built according to instructions under 899

[.993 01–.993 8]   Subdivisions of Interlingua literature

> Numbers discontinued; class in 899.993

900 Geography, history, and auxiliary disciplines

Class here social situations and conditions; general political history; military, diplomatic, political, economic, social, welfare aspects of specific wars

Class interdisciplinary works on ancient world, on specific continents, countries, localities in 930–990. Class historical and geographic treatment of a specific discipline or subject with the discipline or subject, plus notation 09 from Table 1, e.g., historical and geographic treatment of natural sciences 509, of economic situations and conditions 330.9, of purely political situations and conditions 320.9, history of military science 355.009

See also 303.49 for projected events (future history)

See Manual at 900

SUMMARY

930	History of ancient world to ca. 499	
.01–.09	Standard subdivisions	
.1–.5	[Archaeology and historical periods]	
931	China to 420	
932	Egypt to 640	
933	Palestine to 70	
934	India to 647	
935	Mesopotamia and Iranian Plateau to 637	
936	Europe north and west of Italian peninsula to ca. 499	
937	Italian peninsula and adjacent territories to 476	
938	Greece to 323	
939	Other parts of ancient world to ca. 640	

940	General history of Europe	Western Europe	
.01–.09	Standard subdivisions		
.1–.5	[Historical periods]		
941	British Isles		
942	England and Wales		
943	Central Europe	Germany	
944	France and Monaco		
945	Italian Peninsula and adjacent islands	Italy	
946	Iberian Peninsula and adjacent islands	Spain	
947	Eastern Europe	Russia	
948	Scandinavia		
949	Other parts of Europe		

950	General history of Asia	Orient	Far East
.01–.09	Standard subdivisions		
.1–.4	[Historical periods]		
951	China and adjacent areas		
952	Japan		
953	Arabian Peninsula and adjacent areas		
954	South Asia	India	
955	Iran		
956	Middle East (Near East)		
957	Siberia (Asiatic Russia)		
958	Central Asia		
959	Southeast Asia		

960	General history of Africa	
.01–.09	Standard subdivisions	
.1–.3	[Historical periods]	
961	Tunisia and Libya	
962	Egypt and Sudan	
963	Ethiopia and Eritrea	
964	Northwest African coast and offshore islands	Morocco
965	Algeria	
966	West Africa and offshore islands	
967	Central Africa and offshore islands	
968	Southern Africa	Republic of South Africa
969	South Indian Ocean islands	

970	General history of North America	
.001–.009	Standard subdivisions	
.01–.05	Historical periods	
971	Canada	
972	Middle America	Mexico
973	United States	
974	Northeastern United States (New England and Middle Atlantic states)	
975	Southeastern United States (South Atlantic states)	
976	South central United States	Gulf Coast states
977	North central United States	
978	Western United States	
979	Great Basin and Pacific Slope region of United States	Pacific Coast states

980	General history of South America	
.001–.009	Standard subdivisions	
.01–.04	Historical periods	
981	Brazil	
982	Argentina	
983	Chile	
984	Bolivia	
985	Peru	
986	Colombia and Ecuador	
987	Venezuela	
988	Guiana	
989	Paraguay and Uruguay	

990	General history of other parts of world, of extraterrestrial worlds	Pacific Ocean islands
.01–.09	Standard subdivisions of Pacific Ocean islands	
993	New Zealand	
994	Australia	
995	Melanesia	New Guinea
996	Other parts of Pacific	Polynesia
997	Atlantic Ocean islands	
998	Arctic islands and Antarctica	
999	Extraterrestrial worlds	

.1–.9   Standard subdivisions of geography and history

901   Philosophy and theory of history

902   Miscellany of history

[.23]   Maps, plans, diagrams

Do not use; class in 911

903   Dictionaries, encyclopedias, concordances of history

904   Collected accounts of events

Class here adventure

Class travel in 910; class collections limited to a specific period in 909; class collections limited to a specific area or region but not limited by continent, country, locality in 909.09; class collections limited to a specific continent, country, locality in 930–990. Class history of a specific kind of event with the event, e.g., geological history of California earthquakes 551.2209794

See Manual at 900: Historic events vs. nonhistoric events

.5   Events of natural origin

.7   Events induced by human activity

905–906 Standard subdivisions of history

907   Education, research, related topics of history

.2   Historical research

Class here historiography

Class writing of history in 808.0669

.201–.209   Geographic and persons treatment

Add to base number 907.20 notation 1–9 from Table 2, e.g., historians and historiographers 907.202

Class historians and historiographers who specialize in a specific area with the area in 930–990, plus notation 007202 from table under 930–990, e.g., the biography of a German who specializes in French history in general 944.007202; class historians and historiographers who specialize in specific historical periods of a specific area with the historical period for the area studied, plus notation 092 from Table 1, e.g., biography of a German historian who specializes in the French Revolutionary period 944.04092

908   History with respect to kinds of persons

[.9]   Racial, ethnic, national groups

Do not use; class in 909.04

909   World history

Civilization and events not limited geographically

Class collected accounts of events not limited by period, area, region, subject in 904; class history of ancient world to ca. 499 in 930; class history of specific continents, countries, localities in modern world in 940–990

See Manual at 305 vs. 306, 909, 930–990; also at 909, 930–990 vs. 320; also at 909, 930–990 vs. 320.4, 321, 321.09; also at 909, 930–990 vs. 400; also at 909, 930–990 vs. 910

(Option: Class elementary textbooks on general history in 372.89045)

[.001–.008]   Standard subdivisions

> Do not use; class in 901–908

[.009]   Historical treatment

> Do not use; class in 907.2

.04   History with respect to racial, ethnic, national groups

> Add to base number 909.04 notation 03–99 from Table 5, e.g., world history of Jews 909.04924; then add 0* and to the result add the numbers following 909 in 909.1–909.8, e.g., world history of Jews in 18th century 909.0492407

> (Option: Class here general history of racial, ethnic, national groups in a specific continent, country, locality; prefer subdivision 004 from table under 930–990. If option is chosen, add notation 03–99 from Table 5 as above; then add 00 instead of 0 as above for world history by period, e.g., world history of Jews in 18th century 909.04924007; for specific areas add 0 and to the result add notation 3–9 from Table 2, e.g., history of Jews in Germany 909.04924043)

> 909.07–909.08 General historical periods

> Class here general histories covering three or more continents (or three or more countries if not on the same continent)

> Class specific historical periods in 909.1–909.8; class comprehensive works in 909

> *For ancient history, see 930*

.07   Ca. 500–1450/1500

> Including Crusades

> Class here Middle Ages

> *See also 940.1 for history of Europe during Middle Ages, 940.18 for history of Europe during the Crusades*

.08   Modern history, 1450/1500–

.09   Areas, regions, places in general

> Not limited by continent, country, locality

> Class here interdisciplinary works on areas, regions, places in general (other than landforms, oceans, seas)

> Class interdisciplinary works on landforms, oceans, seas in 551.4

> *For geography of and travel in areas, regions, places in general, see 910.91*

.090 1–.090 9   Standard subdivisions

---

*Add 00 for standard subdivisions; see instructions at beginning of Table 1

.091–.099   Specific areas, regions, places in general

> Add to base number 909.09 the numbers following —1 in notation 11–19 from Table 2, e.g., history of tropical regions 909.093, of Caribbean Sea 909.096365, of western civilization 909.09821; then add 0* and to the result add the numbers following 909 in 909.1–909.8, e.g., history of tropical regions in 20th century 909.093082

>   **909.1–909.8   Specific historical periods**

Class general historical periods in 909.07–909.08; class comprehensive works in 909

For historical periods through 5th century, see 930.2–930.5

.1   **6th–12th centuries, 500–1199**

Class comprehensive works on Middle Ages in 909.07

.2   **13th century, 1200–1299**

.3   **14th century, 1300–1399**

.4   **15th century, 1400–1499**

.5   **16th century, 1500–1599**

.6   **17th century, 1600–1699**

.7   **18th century, 1700–1799**

.8   **1800–**

.81   19th century, 1800–1899

Class here industrial revolution

.82   20th century, 1900–1999

.821   1900–1919

Class here early 20th century

For World War I, see 940.3. For a part of early 20th century not provided for here, see the part, e.g., 1930–1939 909.823

.822   1920–1929

.823   1930–1939

.824   1940–1949

For World War II, see 940.53

*Add 00 for standard subdivisions; see instructions at beginning of Table 1; however, class historical atlases in 911.1

.825	1950–1959

> Class here late 20th century, post World War II period

> *For a part of late 20th century, post World War II period not provided for here, see the part, e.g., 1980–1989 909.828*

.826	1960–1969
.827	1970–1979
.828	1980–1989
.829	1990–1999
.83	21st century, 2000–2099

> *See also 303.49 for futurology*

910 Geography and travel

Class general works on civilization, other than accounts of travel, in 909; class works on civilization, other than accounts of travel, in ancient world and specific places in modern world in 930–990. Class geographic treatment of specific disciplines or subjects with the discipline or subject, e.g., geographic treatment of religion 200.9, of geomorphology 551.409

> *See Manual at 338 vs. 060, 381, 382, 670.294, 910, T1—025, T1—0294, T1—0296; also at 550 vs. 910; also at 578 vs. 304.2, 508, 910; also at 909, 930–990 vs. 910*

(Option: Class elementary textbooks on general geography in 372.891045)

SUMMARY

910.01–.02	**[The earth (Physical geography) and philosophy and theory of geography and travel]**
.2–.9	**Standard subdivisions and accounts of travel**
911	**Historical geography**
912	**Graphic representations of surface of earth and of extraterrestrial worlds**
913–919	**Geography of and travel in ancient world and specific continents, countries, localities in modern world; extraterrestrial worlds**

.01	Philosophy and theory of geography and travel
.014	Language and communication

> Class here discourses on place names and their origin, history, meaning

> Class dictionaries and gazetteers of place names in 910.3

.02	The earth (Physical geography)

> Class physical geography of a specific geological feature with the feature in 550, e.g., glaciers 551.312

> *See also 551.4 for geomorphology*

> *See Manual at 550 vs. 910*

.020 9	Historical and persons treatment
[.020 91]	Areas, regions, places in general
	Do not use; class in 910.021
[.020 93–.020 99]	Specific continents, countries, localities; extraterrestrial worlds
	Do not use; class in 913–919, plus notation 02 from table under 913–919

.021   **Physical geography of areas, regions, places in general**

Add to base number 910.021 the numbers following — 1 in notation 11–18 from Table 2, e.g., physical geography of forests 910.02152

(.1)   **Topical geography**

(Optional number; prefer specific subject, e.g., economic geography 330.91–330.99)

Do not use for philosophy and theory of geography and travel; class in 910.01

Add to base number 910.1 notation 001–899, e.g., economic geography 910.133; then add 0* and to the result add notation 1–9 from Table 2, e.g., economic geography of British Isles 910.133041

.2   **Miscellany**

.202   **World travel guides**

Do not use for synopses and outlines; class in 910.2

Class here guidebooks and tour books providing tourists updated information about places in many areas of the globe: how to travel, what to see, where to stay, how to plan a vacation

Class guides to areas, regions, places in general in 910.91; class guides to specific continents, countries, localities in 913–919, plus notation 04 from table under 913–919

.22   **Illustrations, models, miniatures**

.222   **Pictures and related illustrations**

Including aerial photographs not limited to one specific area or region

.223   **Diagrams**

Do not use for maps and plans; class in 912

.25   **Directories of persons and organizations**

Class here city directories, telephone books

Class city directories, telephone books of a specific place in 913–919, plus notation 0025 from table under 913–919

*Add 00 for standard subdivisions; see instructions at beginning of Table 1

.3 **Dictionaries, encyclopedias, concordances, gazetteers**

Class here works on place names systematically arranged for ready reference

Class discourses on place names in 910.014; class historical material associated with place names in general in 909; class historical material associated with place names of specific places in 930–990

.4 **Accounts of travel**

Not geographically limited

For travel accounts that emphasize civilization of places visited, see 909; for discovery and exploration, see 910.9

See also 508 for scientific exploration and travel, 910.202 for world travel guides

.41 Trips around the world

.45 Ocean travel and seafaring adventures

Including pirates' expeditions

Class how to plan a cruise vacation in 910.202; class ocean trips around the world in 910.41; class travel in specific oceans in 910.9163–910.9167

.452 Shipwrecks

Class water transportation safety in 363.123

For a specific shipwreck, see the location of the wreck in 910.9163–910.9167, e.g., sinking of Titanic 910.91634, wreck of Exxon Valdez 910.916434

See Manual at 900: Historic events vs. nonhistoric events

.5–.8 **Standard subdivisions**

.9 **Historical, geographic, persons treatment**

Class here discovery, exploration, growth of geographic knowledge

.91 Geography of and travel in areas, regions, places in general

Class physical geography of areas, regions, places in general in 910.02; class interdisciplinary works on landforms, oceans, seas in 551.4

(Option: Class elementary geography textbooks on specific areas, regions, places in general in 372.8911)

.92 Geographers, travelers, explorers regardless of country of origin

.93–.99   Discovery and exploration by specific countries

> Do not use for geography of and travel in specific continents, countries, localities; extraterrestrial worlds; class in 913–919
>
> Add to base number 910.9 notation 3–9 from Table 2 for the country responsible, e.g., explorations by Great Britain 910.941
>
> Class discovery and exploration by a specific country in areas, regions, places in general in 910.91; class discovery and exploration by a specific country in specific continents, countries, localities, extraterrestrial worlds in 913–919, plus notation 04 from table under 913–919; class periods of discovery and exploration in history in 930–990

911   Historical geography

> Growth and changes in political divisions
>
> Class here historical atlases

.09   Historical treatment

[.091–.099]   Geographic and persons treatment

> Do not use; class in 911.1–911.9

.1–.9   Geographic and persons treatment

> Add to base number 911 notation 1–9 from Table 2, e.g., historical geography of China 911.51

912   Graphic representations of surface of earth and of extraterrestrial worlds

> Class here atlases, maps, charts, plans
>
> Class map drawing in 526.0221
>
> *For graphic representation of a specific subject other than geography and travel, see the subject, plus notation 0223 from table 1, e.g., railroad atlases 385.0223*
>
> *See Manual at 912 vs. T1—0223*

.01   Philosophy and theory

.014   Map reading

> Do not use for language; class in 912.01
>
> Class here orientation
>
> Class orienteering in 796.58

.014 8   Map scales, symbols, abbreviations

.09   Historical and persons treatment of maps and map making

> Class maps of specific areas, regions, places in general in 912.19; class maps of specific continents, countries, localities, extraterrestrial worlds in 912.3–912.9

.1 Areas, regions, places in general

.19   Specific areas, regions, places in general

> Add to base number 912.19 the numbers following — 1 in notation 11–19 from Table 2, e.g., maps of Western Hemisphere 912.19812

.3–.9 Specific continents, countries, localities, extraterrestrial worlds

> Class here land atlases of countries, tax maps that provide general descriptions of assessed land and structures

> Add to base number 912 notation 3–9 from Table 2, e.g., maps of Du Page County, Illinois 912.77324

913–919 Geography of and travel in ancient world and specific continents, countries, localities in modern world; extraterrestrial worlds

> Class here comprehensive works on ancient and modern geography of and travel in specific continents, countries, localities

> Add to base number 91 notation 3–9 from Table 2, e.g., geography of England 914.2, of Norfolk, England 914.261; then add further as follows:

001	Philosophy and theory
0014	Language and communication
	Class here discursive works on place names and their origin, history, and meaning
	Class dictionaries and gazetteers of place names in 003
002	Miscellany
0022	Illustrations, models, miniatures
00222	Pictures and related illustrations
	Including aerial photographs
	Class photographs reflecting the civilization of places in 930–990
[00223]	Maps, plans, diagrams
	Do not use; class in 912
0025	Directories of persons and organizations
	Class here city directories, telephone books
003	Dictionaries, encyclopedias, concordances, gazetteers
	Class here works on place names systematically arranged for ready reference
	Class discourses on place names in 0014; class historical material associated with place names in 930–990
005–008	Standard subdivisions
01	Prehistoric geography
	Do not add to notation 4–6 from Table 2 if there is a corresponding notation 3 from Table 2, e.g., prehistoric geography of Greece 913.801 (*not* 914.9501), of Russia 914.701
	Class prehistoric physical geography in 02; class prehistoric geography of areas, regions, places in general in 09

> (continued)

913–919 Geography of and travel in ancient world and specific continents, countries, localities in modern world; extraterrestrial worlds (continued)

02   The earth (Physical geography)
Class physical geography of a specific geological feature with the feature in 550, e.g., glaciers of Canada 551.3120971
See also 551.4 for geomorphology
See Manual at 550 vs. 910

04   Travel
Class here discovery, exploration; guidebooks
Class world travel guides in 910.202; class travel accounts that emphasize the civilization of country visited in 930–990
See Manual at 913–919: Add table: 04; also at 913–919 vs. 796.51

040901–040905   Historical periods for regions
Do not use for historical periods of continents, countries, localities; class in 041–049
Use for regions not sharing the same historical period numbers as a country, e.g., travel in central Europe during 19th century 914.30409034
Class historical periods for regions sharing the same historical period numbers as a country with the historical periods of the country in 041–049, e.g., travel in southern Low Countries during 19th century 914.9043

041–049   Historical periods
Add to 04 the historical period numbers following 0 that appear in subdivisions of 930–990, e.g., travel in England during period of House of Tudor 914.2045
However, for United States historical periods, add to 04 the numbers following 973 in 973.1–973.9, e.g., travel in United States during the Nixon administration 917.304924
For historical periods for regions not sharing the same historical period numbers as a country, see 040901–040905

09   Areas, regions, places in general
Add to 09 the numbers following —1 in notation 11–18 from Table 2, e.g., geography of urban regions of England 914.209732
Class physical geography of areas, regions, places in 02; class travel in 04; class civilization in 930–990, plus notation 0091–0098 from Table under 930–990

Class historical geography in 911; class graphic representations in 912; class area studies in 940–990; class comprehensive works, geography of and travel in more than one continent in 910; class interdisciplinary works on geography and history of ancient world, of specific continents, countries, localities in 930–990

See Manual at 913–919; also at 333.7–333.9 vs. 508, 913–919, 930–990; also at 520 vs. 500.5, 523.1, 530.1, 919.9

(Option: Class elementary geography textbooks on ancient world, on specific continents, countries, localities in 372.8913–372.8919)

919 Travel in other parts of world and on extraterrestrial worlds   Travel in Pacific Ocean islands

Number built according to instructions under 913–919

.904   Travel on extraterrestrial worlds

Number built according to instructions under 913–919

Class here projected accounts [*formerly* 629.4501]

See Manual at 629.43, 629.45 vs. 919.904

.920 4   Travel in planets of solar system and their satellites

Number built according to instructions under 913–919

Class here projected accounts of planetary flights [*formerly* 629.455]

Class projected accounts of flights to a specific planet with the planet in 919.921–919.929, plus notation 04 from table under 913–919, e.g., projected accounts of flights to Mars 919.92304

920   Biography, genealogy, insignia

Class here autobiographies, diaries, reminiscences, correspondence

Class biography of persons associated with a specific discipline or subject with the discipline or subject, plus notation 092 from Table 1, e.g., biography of chemists 540.92
(Option: Class individual biography in 92 or B, collected biography in 92 or 920 undivided)

See Manual at T1—092

.001–.007   Standard subdivisions of biography

.008   History and description of biography with respect to kinds of persons

[.008 1–.008 2]   Men and women

Do not use; class in 920.7

[.008 8]   Occupational and religious groups

Do not use; class with the specific group, plus notation 092 from Table 1, e.g., biography of Lutherans 284.1092
(Option: Class in in 920.1–928.9)

[.008 9]	Racial, ethnic, national groups

Do not use; class in 920.0092

.009   General collections of biography by period, region, group

Class collections by specific continents, countries, localities in 920.03–920.09

.009 01–.009 05   Historical periods

Add to base number 920.0090 the numbers following —090 in notation 0901–0905 from Table 1, e.g., general biography of 19th century 920.009034

.009 1   Areas, regions, places in general

Add to base number 920.0091 the numbers following —1 in notation 11–19 from Table 2, e.g., biographies of suburbanites 920.0091733

.009 2   Racial, ethnic, national groups

Add to base number 920.0092 notation 03–99 from Table 5, e.g., biographies of Swedes 920.0092397

.02   General collections of biography

Not limited by period, place, group and not associated with a specific subject

.03–.09   General collections of biography by specific continents, countries, localities

Not associated with a specific subject

Add to base number 920.0 notation 3–9 from Table 2, e.g., collections of biographies of persons resident in England 920.042

Class collections by sex regardless of continent, country, locality in 920.7

>   **920.1–928.9 Biography of specific classes of persons**

Add to notation for each term identified by † notation 3–9 from Table 2, e.g., Baptists from Louisiana 922.6763

Class comprehensive works in 920.02

(Option A: Use subdivisions identified by *

(Option B: Class individual biography in 92 or B; class collected biography in 92 or 920 undivided

(Option C: Class individual biography of men in 920.71; class individual biography of women in 920.72

(Prefer specific discipline or subject, plus notation 092 from Table 1, e.g., collected biography of scientists 509.22)

(.1)	***Bibliographers**
(.2)	***Librarians and book collectors**
(.3)	***Encyclopedists**

Class lexicographers in 924

(.4)	***Publishers and booksellers**
(.5)	***Journalists and news commentators**
.7	**Persons by sex**

Class here individual biography of persons not associated with a specific discipline or subject, collected biography of persons by sex

(Option: Class here all individual biography; prefer specific discipline or subject, plus notation 092 from Table 1)

.71	Men
.72	Women
(.9)	***Persons associated with other subjects**

Not provided for in 920.1–920.5, 921–928

Add to base number 920.9 notation 001–999, e.g., astrologers 920.91335

(921)   ***Philosophers and psychologists**

> **(921.1–921.8) Modern western philosophers and psychologists**

Class comprehensive works in 921

(.1)	***United States and Canadian philosophers and psychologists**
(.2)	***British philosophers and psychologists**

Including English, Scottish, Irish, Welsh philosophers and psychologists

(.3)	***German and Austrian philosophers and psychologists**
(.4)	***French philosophers and psychologists**
(.5)	***Italian philosophers and psychologists**
(.6)	***Spanish and Portuguese philosophers and psychologists**
(.7)	***Russian philosophers and psychologists**
(.8)	***†Other modern western philosophers and psychologists**
(.9)	***Ancient, medieval, Oriental philosophers and psychologists**

Add to base number 921.9 the numbers following 18 in 181–189, e.g., Aristotelian philosophers 921.95

---

*(Optional number; prefer specific subject or discipline, as described under 920.1–928.9)

†Add as instructed under 920.1–928.9

(922)   *Religious leaders, thinkers, workers

> ### (922.1–922.8) Christians

> Class comprehensive works in 922

(.1)   *†Early and Eastern churches

Subdivisions are added for either or both topics in heading

(.2)   *Roman Catholics

(.21)   *Popes

(.22)   *Saints

(.24–.29)   *†Roman Catholics from specific continents, countries, localities of modern world

For popes, see 922.21; for saints, see 922.22

(.3)   *†Anglicans

(.4)   *†Lutherans, Huguenots, continental Protestants

Subdivisions are added for any or all topics in heading

(.5)   *†Presbyterians, Congregationalists, American Reformed

Subdivisions are added for any or all topics in heading

(.6)   *†Baptists, Disciples of Christ, Adventists

Subdivisions are added for any or all topics in heading

(.7)   *†Methodists

(.8)   *Members of other Christian denominations and sects

(.81)   *†Unitarians and Universalists

Subdivisions are added for either or both topics in heading

(.83)   *†Latter-Day Saints

(.84)   *†Swedenborgians

(.85)   *†Christian Scientists

(.86)   *†Friends (Quakers)

(.87)   *†Mennonites

(.88)   *†Shakers

(.89)   *Other Christian denominations and sects

Not provided for elsewhere

---

*(Optional number; prefer specific subject or discipline, as described under 920.1–928.9)
†Add as instructed under 920.1–928.9

(.9)   ***Adherents of other religions**

(.91)   *Atheists and Deists

(.94)   *Adherents of Indic religions

(.943)   *Buddhists

(.944)   *Jains

(.945)   *Hindus

(.946)   *Sikhs

(.95)   *Zoroastrians (Parsees)

(.96)   *Adherents of Judaism

(.97)   *Adherents of Islam

(.99)   *Other religions

> Not provided for elsewhere

(923)   *Persons in social sciences

(.1)   ***†Heads of state**

> Class here kings, queens, presidents

(.2)   ***†Persons in political science and politics**

> Class here legislators, governors, politicians, statesmen, diplomats, nobility; political scientists
>
> *For heads of state, see 923.1*

(.3)   ***Persons in economics**

(.31)   *†Labor leaders

(.33–.39)   *†Persons in economics from specific continents, countries, localities of modern world

> *For labor leaders, see 923.31*

(.4)   ***Criminals and persons in law**

(.41)   *†Criminals

(.43–.49)   *†Persons in law

(.5)   ***†Public administrators and military persons**

> Subdivisions are added for either or both topics in heading
>
> *For heads of state, see 923.1; for governors, politicians, statesmen, see 923.2*

---

*(Optional number; prefer specific subject or discipline, as described under 920.1–928.9)
†Add as instructed under 920.1–928.9

(.6)   *†**Philanthropists, humanitarians, social reformers**

> Subdivisions are added for any or all topics in heading

(.7)   *†**Educators**

(.8)   *†**Persons in commerce, communications, transportation**

> Subdivisions are added for any or all topics in heading

(.9)   ***Explorers, geographers, pioneers**

(924)   *Philologists and lexicographers

> Add to base number 924 notation 1–9 from Table 6, e.g., lexicographers of Chinese 924.951

(925)   *Scientists

> Add to base number 925 the numbers following 5 in 510–590, e.g., botanists 925.8

(926)   *Persons in technology

> Add to base number 926 the numbers following 6 in 610–690, e.g., engineers 926.2
>
> *See also 920.4 for booksellers*

(927)   *Persons in the arts and recreation

> Add to base number 927 the numbers following 7 in 710–790, e.g., baseball players 927.96357
>
> *For persons in literature, see 928*

(928)   *Persons in literature, history, biography, genealogy

> Including historians, writers and critics of belles-lettres
>
> *See also 923.9 for explorers, geographers, pioneers*

(.1)   ***Americans**

(.2–.9)   ***Writers in literature, history, biography, genealogy by language**

> Add to base number 928 notation 2–9 from Table 6 for language in which person has written, e.g., writers in Italian 928.51
>
> Class Americans in 928.1

929   Genealogy, names, insignia

.1   **Genealogy**

> *For family histories, see 929.2; for sources, see 929.3*
>
> *See Manual at 929.1*

---

*(Optional number; prefer specific subject or discipline, as described under 920.1–928.9)

†Add as instructed under 920.1–928.9

.102 8   Auxiliary techniques and procedures [*formerly* 929.1072]

[.102 84]   Apparatus, equipment, materials

                   Do not use; class in 929.3

.107 2   Research

                Class here the specific techniques and procedures involved in doing
                genealogical research in a specific area

                Auxiliary techniques and procedures relocated to 929.1028, e.g., data
                processing 929.10285

                Class comprehensive works on genealogical research in 929.1

[.109 4–.109 9]   Treatment by specific continents, countries, localities in modern world

                   Do not use; class in 929.107204–929.107209

.2   Family histories

Class family histories emphasizing the contributions of the members of the
family to a specific occupation with the occupation, e.g., the Rothschilds as a
family of bankers 332.10922; class family histories of a prominent person that
emphasize the person's life with the biography number for the person, e.g.,
forebears, family, and life of Winston Churchill 941.082092

> *For royal houses, peerage, gentry, see 929.7*

> *See Manual at 929.2; also at 929.2 vs. 929.7*

(Option: Arrange alphabetically by name)

.202 8   Auxiliary techniques and procedures; apparatus, equipment, materials

                Class the techniques of compiling family histories in 929.1

.3   Genealogical sources

Standard subdivisions are added for miscellaneous collections and individual
sources

Class here census records, court records, tax lists, wills

Use only for sources published by a genealogical organization or compiled by a
genealogist. Sources published or compiled by other agencies are normally
classed with the subject of the publication, e.g., United States population
census records 304.60973; however, if the source has been either enhanced or
rearranged to emphasize the genealogical content, the source is classed here,
e.g., United States population census records with name indexes added 929.373

Class how to use sources in 929.1; class cemetery records used as genealogical
sources in 929.5

> *For epitaphs, see 929.5*

[.309 3–.309 9]   Treatment by specific continents, countries, localities

                Do not use; class in 929.33–929.39

.33–.39 Treatment by specific continents, countries, localities

Regardless of form

Add to base number 929.3 notation 3–9 from Table 2, e.g., sources from New York 929.3747

.4 Personal names

See also 929.97 for names of houses, pets, ships

.42 Surnames

.44 Forenames

Class here lists of names for babies

.5 Cemetery records

Regardless of form

Including epitaphs

.6 Heraldry

Including crests

Class here armorial bearings, comprehensive works on coats of arms [*both formerly* 929.82]

For royal houses, peerage, gentry, orders of knighthood, see 929.7

.7 Royal houses, peerage, gentry, orders of knighthood

Class here rank, precedence, titles of honor; genealogies tracing or establishing titles of honor; works emphasizing lineage or descent with respect to royalty, the peerage, or gentry; history and genealogy of royal families

Class histories of a royal family that include general historical events or biographies of members of the royal family in 930–990

See Manual at 929.2 vs. 929.7

[.709 41–.709 49]   Specific countries of Europe

Do not use; class in 929.72–929.79

.71 Orders of knighthood

Class Christian orders of knighthood in 255.791; class Christian orders of knighthood in church history in 271.791

> 929.72–929.79 Treatment of royal houses, peerage, gentry by specific countries of Europe

Class comprehensive works in 929.7094

.72 Great Britain and Ireland

.73–.79   Other countries of Europe

>Add to base number 929.7 the numbers following —4 in notation 43–49 from Table 2, e.g., royal houses of France 929.74

.8   Awards, orders, decorations, autographs

.81   Awards, orders, decorations

>Add to base number 929.81 notation 1–9 from Table 2, e.g., orders of Germany 929.8143

>Subdivisions are added for any or all of topics in heading

>Class awards, orders, decorations associated with a specific subject with the subject, plus notation 079 from Table 1, e.g., American football awards 796.332079

>*For armorial bearings, see 929.6*

[.82]   Armorial bearings

>Armorial bearings, comprehensive works on coats of arms relocated to 929.6; seals relocated to 929.9

.88   Autographs

.9   Forms of insignia and identification

>Including seals [*formerly* 929.82], identification cards, motor vehicle registration plates

>Class seals with armorial bearings in 929.6. Class forms of insignia and identification not provided for here with the form, e.g., coats of arms 929.6; class a specific aspect of identification cards not provided for here with the aspect, e.g., forgery of identification cards 364.163; class identification marks in a specific subject with the subject, plus notation 027 from Table 1, e.g., airline insignia 387.70275

>*See also 737.6 for artistic aspects of seals*

.92   Flags and banners

>Standard subdivisions are added for either or both topics in heading

>Including national, state, provincial, ship, ownership flags and banners

>Class military use in 355.15

.95   Service marks and trademarks

>Standard subdivisions are added for either or both topics in heading

.97   Names

>Including names of houses, ships, pets

>Class here interdisciplinary works on onomastics (study of origin, history, use of proper names)

>*For place names, see 910.014; for personal names, see 929.4*

[.970 142]   Etymology

                              Do not use; class in 412

> ## 930–990   History of ancient world; of specific continents, countries, localities; of extraterrestrial worlds

Civilization and events

Class here interdisciplinary works on geography and history of ancient world, of specific continents, countries, localities

Add to base number 9 notation 3–9 from Table 2, e.g., general history of Europe 940, of England 942, of Norfolk, England 942.61; then add further as follows:

001	Philosophy and theory
002	Miscellany
00223	Maps, plans, diagrams
	Do not use for historical atlases; class in 911.1–911.9
003	Dictionaries, encyclopedias, concordances
004	Racial, ethnic, national groups

Add to 004 notation 03–99 from Table 5, e.g., history and civilization of North American native peoples in New York 974.700497

Class indigenous groups in the prehistoric period with the period, e.g., Inca empire before Spanish conquest 985.019; class relation of racial, ethnic, national groups to a war with the war, plus notation 089 from Table 1, e.g., relation of Arabs to World War II 940.53089927

(Option: Class in 909.04)

005–006	Standard subdivisions
007	Education, research, related topics
0072	Historical research
	Class here historiography
007202	Historians and historiographers

Class historians and historiographers specializing in a specific historical period of a specific area with the historical period for the area studied, plus notation 092 from Table 1, e.g., the biography of a Canadian historian who specializes in United States Revolutionary War 973.3092

See Manual at 930–990: Biography

008	History with respect to kinds of persons
[0089]	Racial, ethnic, national groups
	Do not use; class in 004
009	Areas, regions, places, persons

(continued)

> ## 930–990 History of ancient world; of specific continents, countries, localities; of extraterrestrial worlds (continued)

0091–0098	Areas, regions, places in general
	Add to 009 the numbers following — 1 in notation 11–18 from Table 2, e.g., urban regions 009732
0099	Collected persons treatment
	Description, critical appraisal, biography of persons associated with the history of the continent, country, locality but limited to no specific period
	Class persons of a specific period in 01–09, plus notation 092 from Table 1; class historians and historiographers in 007202
	See Manual at 930–990: Biography
[00992]	Collected treatment
	Notation discontinued; class in 0099
01–09	Historical periods
	Class here indigenous groups in the prehistoric period, e.g., Inca empire before Spanish conquest 985.019 (*not* 985.00498323)
	Add to 0 the period division numbers following 0 from the appropriate continent, country, locality in 930–990, e.g., period of 1760–1820 in British history 073 (from 941.073), period of 1815–1847 in German history 073 (from 943.073), period of 1815–1847 in Austrian history 042 (from 943.6042)
	Unless other period notation is specified, add to each geographic subdivision of an area the period notation for the area as a whole, e.g., period of Ottoman Empire in Saudi Arabia 953.803 (based on period of Ottoman Empire in Arabian Peninsula 953.03)
	Class areas, regions, places in general in a specific period in 0091–0098; class racial, ethnic, national groups in a specific period in 004. Class relation of racial, ethnic, national groups to a war with the war, plus notation 089 from Table 1, e.g., relation of Arabs to World War II 950.53089927
	See Manual at 930–990: Biography; also at 930–990: Add table: 01–09

The schedules that follow do not enumerate all the countries and localities that appear in Table 2; however, the foregoing instructions apply to history of any place in notation 3–9 from Table 2, e.g., period of 1815–1847 in Viennese history 943.613042

(continued)

> **930–990 History of ancient world; of specific continents, countries, localities; of extraterrestrial worlds (continued)**

Class sociology of war in 303.66; class sociology of military institutions in 306.27; class social factors affecting war in 355.02; class social causes of war in 355.0274; class historical geography in 911; class geography of ancient world, of specific continents, countries, localities in 913–919; class comprehensive works in 909

See Manual at 930–990; also at 305 vs. 306, 909, 930–990; also at 320 vs. 909, 930–990; also at 333.7–333.9 vs. 508, 913–919, 930–990; also at 909, 930–990 vs. 320.4, 321, 321.09; also at 909, 930–990 vs. 400; also at 909, 930–990 vs. 910; also at 930–990 vs. 355.009

(Option: Class elementary history textbooks on ancient world, on specific continents, countries, localities in 372.893–372.899)

930   History of ancient world to ca. 499

SUMMARY

930.01–.09	Standard subdivisions
.1–.5	[Archaeology and historical periods]
931	China to 420
932	Egypt to 640
933	Palestine to 70
934	India to 647
935	Mesopotamia and Iranian Plateau to 637
936	Europe north and west of Italian peninsula to ca. 499
937	Italian peninsula and adjacent territories to 476
938	Greece to 323
939	Other parts of ancient world to ca. 640

.01–.09   Standard subdivisions

As modified under 930–990; however, for archaeology, see 930.1

.1   **Archaeology**

Study of past civilizations through discovery, collection, interpretation of material remains

Class here prehistoric archaeology; interdisciplinary works on archaeology

> *For industrial archaeology, see 609; for archaeology of specific oceans and seas, see 909.0963–909.0967; for archaeology of continents, countries, localities provided for in notation 3 from Table 2, see 931–939; for archaeology of modern period, ancient and prehistoric archaeology of continents, countries, localities not provided for in notation 3 from Table 2, see 940–990*

> *See also 700 for artistic aspects of archaeological objects*

.102   Miscellany

.102 8   Techniques, procedures, apparatus, equipment, materials

.102 804   Underwater archaeology

> *For archaeology of specific oceans and seas, see 909.0963–909.0967*

.102 82   Discovery of remains

.102 83   Excavation of remains

.102 85   Interpretation of remains

Including dating techniques

>   930.11–930.16   Specific prehistoric ages

Class comprehensive works in 930.1

.11   Eolithic Age

.12   Paleolithic (Old Stone) Age

Class here comprehensive works on Stone Ages

> *For Mesolithic Age, see 930.13; for Neolithic Age, see 930.14*

.13   Mesolithic (Middle Stone) Age

.14   Neolithic (New Stone) Age

.15   Copper and Bronze Age

.16   Iron Age

.2–.5   **Historical periods**

Add to base number 930 the numbers following —0901 in notation 09012–09015 from Table 1, e.g., world history in 1st century A.D. 930.5; however, for specific prehistoric ages, see 930.11–930.16

> ## 931–939 Specific places

Class archaeology and history of specific oceans and seas in 909.0963–909.0967; class archaeology and history of modern period, ancient and prehistoric archaeology and history of continents, countries, localities not provided for in notation 3 from Table 2 in 940–990; class comprehensive works in 930

931   *China to 420

(Option: Class in 951.011–951.014)

.01   Earliest history to ca. 1523 B.C.

.02   Period of Shang (Yin) dynasty, ca. 1523–ca. 1028 B.C.

.03   Period of Chou dynasty and warring states, ca. 1028–222 B.C.

.04   Period of Ch'in (Qin) to Chin (Tsin) dynasties, 221 B.C.–420 A.D.

         Including Han dynasty, 202 B.C.–220 A.D.

932   *Egypt to 640

(Option: Class in 962.01)

.01   Earliest history to 332 B.C.

.011   Prehistoric period to ca. 3100 B.C.

.012   Protodynastic, Old Kingdom, first intermediate periods, ca. 3100–2052 B.C.

         Including 1st–11th dynasties

.013   Middle Kingdom and second intermediate periods, 2052–1570 B.C.

         Including 12th–17th dynasties

.014   Period of New Kingdom, 1570–1075 B.C.

         Including 18th–20th dynasties

.015   Late and Saite periods, 1075–525 B.C.

         Including 21st–26th dynasties, period of sovereignty of Cush

.016   Persian periods and last Egyptian kingdom, 525–332 B.C.

         Including 27th–31st dynasties

.02   Hellenistic, Roman, Byzantine periods, 332 B.C.–640 A.D.

.021   Hellenistic period, 332–30 B.C.

.022   Roman period, 30 B.C.–324 A.D.

*Add as instructed under 930–990

.023   Byzantine (Coptic) period, 324–640

933   *Palestine to 70

See also 220.93 for Biblical archaeology, 220.95 for history of Biblical events

(Option: Class general works in 956.9401; class Jordan in 956.9501)

.01   Earliest history to return of Jews from bondage in Egypt, ca. 1225 B.C.

.02   Great age of Twelve Tribes, ca. 1225–922 B.C.

Including rule of Judges, Saul, David, Solomon

.03   Periods of partition, conquest, foreign rule, 922–168 B.C.

Including periods of Assyrian, Babylonian, Persian, Hellenistic rule

.04   168–63 B.C.

Including Hasmonean (Maccabean) period

.05   Period of Roman protectorate and rule to destruction of Jerusalem, 63 B.C.–70 A.D.

934   *India to 647

(Option: Class in 954.01)

.01   Pre-Aryan civilizations to ca. 1500 B.C.

.02   Indo-Aryan (Vedic) period, ca. 1500–ca. 600 B.C.

Including Iron Age culture in south India

.03   Ca. 600–ca. 322 B.C.

.04   Period of Maurya dynasty, ca. 322–185 B.C.

.043   Ca. 322–ca. 274 B.C.

.045   Reign of Aśoka, ca. 274–ca. 237 B.C.

.047   Ca. 237–185 B.C.

.05   Period of changing dynasties, 185 B.C.–318 A.D.

.06   Period of Gupta dynasty, 318–500

.07   500–647

Including reign of Harsha, 606–647

935   *Mesopotamia and Iranian Plateau to 637

(Option: Class Mesopotamia in 956.701; class Iranian Plateau in 955.01)

.01   Elamite, Sumerian, Akkadian, Ur periods to ca. 1900 B.C.

*Add as instructed under 930–990

.02   Period of Babylonian Empire and Kingdom of Mitanni, ca. 1900–ca. 900 B.C.

> Including reign of Hammurabi, ca. 1792–ca. 1750 B.C.

.03   Period of Assyrian Empire, ca. 900–625 B.C.

.04   Period of Median and Neo-Babylonian (Chaldean) Empires, 625–539 B.C.

> Including reign of Nebuchadnezzar II, 605–562 B.C.

.05   Period of Persian Empire, 539–332 B.C.

> *For Persian Wars, see 938.03*

.06   Hellenistic, Seleucid, Parthian periods, 332 B.C.–226 A.D.

.07   Period of Neo-Persian (Sassanian) Empire, 226–637

936   *Europe north and west of Italian Peninsula to ca. 499

Class here comprehensive works on ancient Europe

For a specific part of ancient Europe not provided for here, see the part, e.g., Italy 937, Russia 947.01

(Option: Class in 940.11)

.1   *British Isles to 410   Northern Britain and Ireland

For southern Britain, see 936.2

(Option: Class British Isles in 941.012; class northern Britain in 941.1012; class Ireland in 941.5012)

.101–.104   Historical periods

> Add to base number 936.1 the numbers following 936.2 in 936.201–936.204, e.g., Roman period 936.104

.2   *Southern Britain to 410   England

(Option: Class in 942.012)

.201   Earliest period to ca. 600 B.C.

.202   Celtic period, ca. 600–55 B.C.

.203   Period of early Roman contacts, 55 B.C.–43 A.D.

.204   Roman period, 43–410

.3   *Germanic regions to 481

(Option: Class general works in 943.012; class Austria in 943.601; class Liechtenstein in 943.648; class general works on Scandinavia in 948.012; class Norway in 948.1012; class Sweden in 948.5012; class Denmark in 948.9012; class Netherlands in 949.2012)

---

*Add as instructed under 930–990

| .301 | Earliest period to 113 B.C. |

| .302 | Period of contacts with Roman Republic and Empire, 113 B.C.–481 A.D. |

.4 *Celtic regions to 486

For British Isles, see 936.1

(Option: Class general works in 944.012; class Belgium in 949.3012; class Luxembourg in 949.35012; class Switzerland in 949.4012)

| .401 | Earliest period to 125 B.C. |

| .402 | Gallo-Roman period, 125 B.C.–486 A.D. |

.6 *Iberian Peninsula and adjacent islands to 415

(Option: Class general works in 946.012; class Portugal in 946.9012)

| .601 | Earliest period to ca. 1000 B.C. |

| .602 | Period of Greek, Phoenician, and early Celtic and Germanic contacts, ca. 1000–218 B.C. |

| .603 | Roman period, 218 B.C.–415 A.D. |

937 *Italian Peninsula and adjacent territories to 476

(Option: Class in 945.012)

| .01 | Earliest period and Roman Kingdom to ca. 500 B.C. |

| .02 | Period of Roman Republic, ca. 500–31 B.C. |

For specific periods, see 937.03–937.05

> 937.03–937.05 Specific periods under the Republic

Class comprehensive works in 937.02

| .03 | Period of unification of Italy, ca. 500–264 B.C. |

| .04 | Period of Punic Wars, 264–146 B.C. |

| .05 | Period of civil strife, 146–31 B.C. |

| .06 | Period of Roman Empire, 31 B.C.–476 A.D. |

For specific periods, see 937.07–937.09

> 937.07–937.09 Specific periods under the Empire

Class comprehensive works in 937.06

*Add as instructed under 930–990

.07	Early and middle periods, 31 B.C.–284 A.D.
.08	Period of absolutism, 284–395
.09	Final period, 395–476

938   *Greece to 323

(Option: Class in 949.5012)

.01	Earliest times to 775 B.C.
.02	775–500 B.C.
.03	Persian Wars, 500–479 B.C.
.04	Period of Athenian supremacy, 479–431 B.C.
.05	Period of Peloponnesian War, 431–404 B.C.
.06	Period of Spartan and Theban supremacy, 404–362 B.C.
.07	Period of Macedonian supremacy, 362–323 B.C.
.08	Hellenistic period, 323–146 B.C.
.09	Roman era, 146 B.C.–323 A.D.

939   *Other parts of ancient world to ca. 640

.1   *Aegean Islands to 323

(Option: Class in 949.58012)

.101–.109   Historical periods

Add to base number 939.1 the numbers following 938 in 938.01–938.09, e.g., Hellenistic period 939.108

.18   *Crete to 323

(Option: Class in 949.59012)

.2   *Western Asia Minor to ca. 640

Class here comprehensive works on Asia Minor

For eastern Asia Minor, see 939.3

(Option: Class in 956.1012)

.3   *Eastern Asia Minor and Cyprus to ca. 640

(Option: Class eastern Asia Minor in 956.1012)

.37   *Cyprus to ca. 640

(Option: Class in 956.93012)

*Add as instructed under 930–990

.4   *Middle East to ca. 640

Class a specific part of Middle East not provided for here with the part, e.g., Egypt 932, Palestine 933

(Option: Class in 956.012)

.43   *Syria

Including Antioch

(Option: Class Antioch in 956.4, Syria in 956.9101)

.44   *Phoenicia to ca. 640

(Option: Class in 956.9202)

.46   *Edom and Moab to 70

(Option: Class Edom in 956.94901; Moab in 956.95601)

.47   *Arabia Deserta to 637

(Option: Class in 956.701)

.48   *Arabia Petraea to 622

Including Sinai Peninsula; Petra

(Option: Class Arabia Petraea in 953.01; Sinani Peninsula in 953.101; Petra in 956.95701)

.49   *Arabia Felix to 622

Class here comprehensive works on Arabia

For Arabia Deserta, see 939.47; for Arabia Petraea, see 939.48

(Option: Class Arabia Felix, Arabia in 953.01)

.5   *Black Sea and Caucasus regions

Including Albania, Colchis, Iberia, Sarmatia

(Option: Class Caucasus in 947.5; Albania in 947.54; Colchis, Iberia in 947.58; Black Sea region, Sarmatia in 947.7)

.51   *Scythia

(Option: Class in 949.83012)

.55   *Armenia

(Option: Class in 956.62012)

.6   *Central Asia to ca. 640

(Option: Class general works in 958; class Afghanistan in 958.101; class Soviet Central Asia in 958.407)

*Add as instructed under 930–990

.7 ***North Africa to ca. 640**

For Egypt, see 932

(Option: Class in 961.01)

.71 *Mauretania to 647

(Option: Class in 965.01, Morocco in 964.01)

.72 *Numidia to 647

(Option: Class in 965.501)

.73 *Carthage to 647

(Option: Class in 961.101)

.74 *Tripolis to 644

Class here comprehensive works on ancient Libya

For Cyrenaica, see 939.75; for Marmarica, see 939.76

(Option: Class in 961.201)

.75 *Cyrenaica to 644

(Option: Class in 961.201)

.76 *Marmarica to 644

(Option: Class in 961.201)

.77 *Gaetulia to 647

(Option: Class in 965.701)

.78 *Ethiopia to 500

(Option: Class in 962.501)

.8 ***Southeastern Europe to ca. 640**

See also 939.5 for Caucasian Albania

(Option: Class Hungary in 943.9011; class Turkey in Europe in 949.61012; class Albania in 949.65012; class Yugoslavia in 949.7012; class Serbia in 949.71011; class Romania in 949.8012; class Bulgaria in 949.9012)

*Add as instructed under 930–990

> ## 940–990   General history of modern world, of extraterrestrial worlds

Class here area studies; comprehensive works on ancient and modern history of specific continents, countries, localities

Except for modifications shown under specific entries, add to each subdivision identified by ‡ as follows:

08	History and description with respect to kinds of persons
	Class enemy sympathizers, pacifists in 1
089	Racial, ethnic, national groups
	Add to base number 089 notation 03–99 from Table 5, e.g., Arabs with respect to the war 089927
1	Social, political, economic history
	Standard subdivisions are added for any or all topics in heading
	Including causes, results, efforts to preserve or restore peace
	Class general diplomatic history in 2; class prisoner-of-war camps in 7. Class results in and effects on a specific country with the history of the country, e.g., effect of Vietnamese War on United States 973.923, not 959.70431
2	Diplomatic history
	Class diplomatic causes, efforts to preserve or restore peace, diplomatic results in 1
3	Participation of specific groups of countries, of specific countries, localities, groups
	Class military participation of specific groups of countries, of specific countries, localities, groups in 4. Class participation in a specific activity with the activity, e.g., efforts to preserve or restore peace 1
34–39	Participation of specific countries and localities
	Add to 3 notation 4–9 from Table 2, e.g., participation by France 344
4	Military operations and units
	Standard subdivisions are added for either or both topics in heading
	Class here military history
	Class units engaged in a specific type of service with the service, e.g., medical units 7; class an aspect of military history not provided for here with the aspect, e.g., prisoner-of-war camps 7
42	Land operations
45	Naval operations
48	Air operations
6	Celebrations, commemorations, memorials
	Including decorations and awards, rolls of honor, cemeteries, monuments
7	Prisoners of war, medical and social services
	Including prisoner-of-war camps
8	Other military topics
	Including deserters; military life and customs; servicemen missing in action; unconventional warfare, propaganda

(continued)

> ## 940–990 General history of modern world, of extraterrestrial worlds (continued)

Class comprehensive works in 909

For general history of ancient world, see 930

See Manual at 930–990: Wars

940 General history of Europe   Western Europe

SUMMARY

940.01–.09	Standard subdivisions	
.1	Early history to 1453	
.2	1453–	
.3	World War I, 1914–1918	
.4	Military history of World War I	
.5	1918–	
941	British Isles	
.01–.08	[Historical periods of British Isles]	
.1	Scotland	
.2	Northeastern Scotland	
.3	Southeastern Scotland	
.4	Southwestern Scotland	
.5	Ireland	
.6	Ulster Northern Ireland	
.7	Republic of Ireland	
.8	Leinster	
.9	Munster	
942	England and Wales	
.01–.08	Historical periods of England and Wales, of England alone	
943	Central Europe Germany	
.000 1–.000 9	Standard subdivisions of central Europe	
.001–.009	Standard subdivisions of Germany	
.01–.08	Historical periods of Germany	
.1	Northeastern Germany	
.6	Austria and Liechtenstein	
.7	Czech Republic and Slovakia	
.8	Poland	
.9	Hungary	
944	France and Monaco	
.01–.08	Historical periods of France and Monaco, of France alone	
.9	Southeastern France and Monaco Provence region	
945	Italian Peninsula and adjacent islands Italy	
.01–.09	Historical periods of Italian Peninsula and adjacent islands, of Italy	
.4	Emilia-Romagna region and San Marino	
.6	Central Italy and Vatican City	
.8	Sicily and adjacent islands	

946		**Iberian Peninsula and adjacent islands Spain**
	.000 1–.000 9	Standard subdivisions of Iberian Peninsula and adjacent islands
	.001–.009	Standard subdivisions of Spain
	.01–.08	Historical periods of Spain
	.7	Eastern Spain and Andorra
	.8	Andalusia autonomous community and Gibraltar
	.9	Portugal

947		**Eastern Europe Russia**
	.000 1–.000 9	Standard subdivisions of eastern Europe
	.001–.009	Standard subdivisions of Russia
	.01–.08	Historical periods of Russia
	.5	Caucasus
	.6	Moldova
	.7	Ukraine
	.8	Belarus
	.9	Lithuania, Latvia, Estonia

948		**Scandinavia**
	.01–.08	Historical periods of northern Europe, of Scandinavia
	.1	Norway
	.2	Southeastern Norway (Østlandet)
	.3	Southwestern Norway (Sørlandet and Vestlandet)
	.4	Central and northern Norway (Trøndelag and Nord-Norge)
	.5	Sweden
	.6	Southern Sweden (Götland)
	.7	Central Sweden (Svealand)
	.8	Northern Sweden (Norrland)
	.9	Denmark and Finland

949		**Other parts of Europe**
	.1	Northwestern islands
	.2	Netherlands (Holland)
	.3	Southern Low Countries Belgium
	.4	Switzerland
	.5	Greece
	.6	Balkan Peninsula
	.7	Yugoslavia, Croatia, Slovenia, Bosnia and Hercegovina, Macedonia
	.8	Romania
	.9	Bulgaria

.01–.09	Standard subdivisions
	As modified under 930–990

.1   Early history to 1453

Class here Middle Ages, 476–1453

For ancient history to ca. 499, see 936

(.11)	Ancient history to ca. 499
	(Optional number; prefer 936)
.12	Ca. 500–799
	Class here Dark Ages

.14	Age of feudalism, 800–1099
.142	800–899
.144	900–999
.146	1000–1099

> *For period of First Crusade, see 940.18*

.17	1100–1453

> *For period of Crusades, 1100–1299, see 940.18; for 1300–1453, see 940.19*

.18	Period of Crusades, 1100–1299

Including First Crusade, 1096–1099

Class comprehensive works on Crusades in 909.07

.182	1100–1199
.184	1200–1299
.19	1300–1453
.192	1300–1399

Including period of Black Death

.193	1400–1453
.2	**1453–**

> *For World War I, see 940.3; for 1918 to present, see 940.5*

.21	Renaissance period, 1453–1517

Class here 15th century

> *For 1400–1453, see 940.193*

> *See also 945.05 for Renaissance period in Italy*

.22	1517–1789

> *For Reformation period, 1517–1648, see 940.23; for 1648–1789, see 940.25*

.23	Reformation period, 1517–1648

> *For Thirty Years' War, see 940.24*

.232	1517–1618
.24	‡Thirty Years' War, 1618–1648
.25	1648–1789

‡Add as instructed under 940–990

.252	1648–1715

Class here 17th century

For 1600–1648, see 940.23

.252 5	1688–1701

Class here War of the League of Augsburg (War of the Grand Alliance), 1688–1697

For North American aspects of War of the League of Augsburg, see 973.25

.252 6	War of the Spanish Succession, 1701–1714

For North American aspects of War of the Spanish Succession, see 973.25

.253	1715–1789
.253 2	War of the Austrian Succession, 1740–1748

For North American aspects of War of the Austrian Succession, see 973.26

.253 4	Seven Years' War, 1756–1763

For North American aspects of Seven Years' War, see 973.26

.27	‡Period of French Revolution and Napoleon I, 1789–1815

Class here Napoleonic Wars in specific European countries, e.g., war in Spain (Peninsular War), 1807–1814

.28	1815–1914

Class here comprehensive works on 19th-20th centuries

For comprehensive works on 20th century, see 940.5

.282	1815–1829
.283	1830–1848
.284	Revolutions of 1848
.285	1848–1859
.286	1860–1869
.287	1870–1899
.288	1900–1914
.3	**World War I, 1914–1918**

For military history, see 940.4

.308	World War I with respect to kinds of persons [*formerly* 940.315]

Class noncombatants, pacifists, enemy sympathizers in 940.316

‡Add as instructed under 940–990

.31   Social, political, economic history

Add to base number 940.31 the numbers following 940.531 in 940.5311–940.5317, e.g., internment camps 940.317; however, World War I with respect to kinds of persons relocated from 940.315 to 940.308

For diplomatic history, see 940.32

.32   Diplomatic history

For diplomatic causes, see 940.3112; for efforts to preserve or restore peace, see 940.312; for diplomatic results, see 940.314

.322   Allies and associated powers

Add to base number 940.322 notation 4–9 from Table 2, e.g., diplomatic history of Great Britain 940.32241

.324   Central Powers

Add to base number 940.324 notation 4–9 from Table 2, e.g., diplomatic history of Germany 940.32443

.325   Neutrals

Add to base number 940.325 notation 4–9 from Table 2, e.g., diplomatic history of Switzerland 940.325494

.33   Participation of specific groups of countries

Class a specific activity with the activity, e.g., diplomatic history among neutrals 940.325

For participation of specific countries and localities, see 940.34–940.39

.332   Allies and associated powers

.334   Central Powers

.335   Neutrals

.34–.39   Participation of specific countries and localities

Class here mobilization in specific countries and localities

Add to base number 940.3 notation 4–9 from Table 2, e.g., participation of Great Britain 940.341

Class a specific activity with the activity, e.g., efforts by a specific country to preserve or restore peace 940.312

.4   Military history of World War I

SUMMARY

.400 1–.400 8   Standard subdivisions

.400 9   Historical, geographic, persons treatment

> Do not use for military participation of specific countries; class in 940.409

.400 92   Persons

> Do not use for personal narratives; class in 940.481–940.482

.401   Strategy

.401 2   Allies and associated powers

.401 3   Central Powers

.402   Mobilization

> *For mobilization in specific countries and localities, see 940.34–940.39*

.403   Racial minorities as troops

.405   Repressive measures and atrocities

> Class internment camps in 940.317

.409   Military participation of specific countries

> Add to base number 940.409 notation 4–9 from Table 2, e.g., military participation of Germany 940.40943

.41   Operations and units

> Standard subdivisions are added for either or both topics in heading

> Class here land operations

> *For land campaigns and battles of 1914–1916, see 940.42; for land campaigns and battles of 1917–1918, see 940.43; for air operations, see 940.44; for naval operations, see 940.45*

>   940.412–940.413   Military units and their operations

Class here organization, history, rosters, service records

Class comprehensive works in 940.41. Class units engaged in a special service with the service, e.g., ambulance companies 940.4753

For operations in Europe, see 940.414; for operations in Asia, see 940.415; for operations in Asia, see 940.416; for rolls of honor and lists of dead, see 940.467

.412   Military units of Allies and associated powers

Add to base number 940.412 notation 4–9 from Table 2, e.g., French units 940.41244

.413   Military units of Central Powers

Add to base number 940.413 notation 4–9 from Table 2, e.g., Austrian units 940.413436

.414   Operations in Europe

.414 3   German fronts

.414 4   French front

Class here western front

For German western front, see 940.4143

.414 5   Italian front

.414 7   Russian front

Class here eastern front

For German eastern front, see 940.4143

.415   Operations in Asia

.416   Operations in Africa

.42   Land campaigns and battles of 1914–1916

.421   1914, western front

.422   1914, eastern front

.423   1914, other areas

.424   1915, western and Austro-Italian fronts

.425   1915, eastern Europe

.426   1915, other areas

Including Gallipoli Campaign

.427	1916, European fronts
.427 2	Western and Austro-Italian fronts
.427 5	Eastern front
.429	1916, other areas
.429 1	Asia Minor
.43	Land campaigns and battles of 1917–1918
.431	1917, western and Austro-Italian fronts
.432	1917, eastern front
.433	1917, other areas
.434	1918, western and Austro-Italian fronts

Including final German offensives

Class final allied offensives in 940.435–940.436

> **940.435–940.436 Final allied offensives**

Class comprehensive works in 940.434

.435	Allied offensives of July 18–September 24, 1918
.436	Allied offensives of September 25–November 11, 1918
.437	1918, eastern front
.438	1918, other areas
.439	Armistice, November 11, 1918
.44	Air operations

Including antiaircraft defenses

Class here combined air and naval operations

For naval operations, see 940.45

.442	Air raids

Class specific events by year in 940.444–940.448

.443	Air bases

> **940.444–940.448 Events by year**

Class comprehensive works in 940.44

.444	Events of 1914

.445	Events of 1915
.446	Events of 1916
.447	Events of 1917
.448	Events of 1918
.449	Operations of specific countries

> Class here aircraft, fliers, units
>
> Add to base number 940.449 notation 4–9 from Table 2, e.g., air operations of Germany 940.44943
>
> Class events by year regardless of country in 940.444–940.448

.45	Naval operations
.451	Submarine warfare
.451 2	German use

> Class events by year in 940.4514

.451 3	Allied use

> Add to base number 940.4513 notation 4–9 from Table 2, e.g., United States use of submarines 940.451373
>
> Class events by year in 940.4514

.451 4	Specific events
.451 6	Antisubmarine warfare

> Class events by year in 940.4514

.452	Blockades and blockade running

> Class events by year in 940.454–940.458

.453	Naval bases

> 940.454–940.458   Events by year

> Class events in submarine warfare by year in 940.4514; class comprehensive works in 940.45

.454	Events of 1914
.455	Events of 1915
.456	Events of 1916
.457	Events of 1917
.458	Events of 1918

.459   Naval operations of specific countries

> Class here ships, crews, units

> Add to base number 940.459 notation 4–9 from Table 2, e.g., naval operations of Italy 940.45945

> Class events by year regardless of country in 940.454–940.458

.46–.48   Celebrations, commemorations, memorials; prisoners of war; medical and social services; other military topics

> Add to base number 940.4 the numbers following 940.54 in 940.546–940.548, e.g., prisoners of war 940.472

.5   **1918–**

SUMMARY

940.51	**1918–1929**	
.52	**1930–1939**	
.53	**World War II, 1939–1945**	
.54	**Military history of World War II**	
.55	**1945–1999**	
.56	**2000–**	

.51   1918–1929

.52   1930–1939

> Class Holocaust in 940.5318

.53   World War II, 1939–1945

> Class here Sino-Japanese Conflict, 1937–1945

>> *For military history, see 940.54; for Sino-Japanese Conflict during 1937–1941, see 951.042*

.530 8   World War II with respect to kinds of persons [*formerly* 940.5315]

> Class noncombatants, pacifists, enemy sympathizers in 940.5316; class Holocaust in 940.5318

.531   Social, political, economic history

> *For diplomatic history, see 940.532*

.531 1   Causes

.531 12   Political and diplomatic causes

.531 13   Economic causes

.531 14   Social and psychological causes

.531 2   Efforts to preserve or restore peace

.531 4   Political, diplomatic, economic results

> Class results in and effects on a specific country with the history of the country, e.g., on Norway 948.1045

.531 41	Conferences and treaties

> *For consequences of conferences and treaties, see 940.53142*

.531 42	Consequences of conferences and treaties
.531 422	Reparations
.531 424	Territorial questions
.531 425	Establishment of new nations
.531 426	Establishment of mandates
.531 44	Reconstruction
[.531 5]	World War II with respect to kinds of persons

Relocated to 940.5308

.531 6	Noncombatants, pacifists, enemy sympathizers
.531 61	Noncombatants

Including children

.531 62	Pacifists
.531 63	Enemy sympathizers
.531 7	Concentration and related camps

Class here internment camps

Class camps as a part of the Holocaust in 940.5318; class prisoner-of-war camps in 940.5472

.531 709	Historical, geographic, persons treatment

Use area notation to indicate country maintaining the camps, e.g., internment camps maintained by the United States 940.53170973

> *For camps by location, see 940.53174–940.53179*

.531 74–.531 79	Camps by location

Add to base number 940.5317 notation 4–9 from Table 2, e.g., Manzanar internment camp for Japanese-Americans 940.531779487

Class extermination camps in 940.5318

.531 8	Holocaust

Class here Holocaust, 1933–1945

.532	Diplomatic history

> *For diplomatic causes, see 940.53112; for efforts to preserve or restore peace, see 940.5312; for diplomatic results, see 940.5314*

.532 2   United Nations (Allies)

> Add to base number 940.5322 notation 4–9 from Table 2, e.g., diplomatic history of Great Britain 940.532241

.532 4   Axis Powers

> Add to base number 940.5324 notation 4–9 from Table 2, e.g., diplomatic history of Japan 940.532452

.532 5   Neutrals

> Add to base number 940.5325 notation 4–9 from Table 2, e.g., diplomatic history of Switzerland 940.5325494

.533   Participation of specific groups of countries

> Class here national groups, anti-Axis and pro-Axis national groups, mobilization
>
> Class a specific activity with the activity, e.g., diplomatic history among Axis Powers 940.5324
>
> *For participation of specific countries, see 940.534–940.539*

.533 2   United Nations (Allies)

.533 4   Axis Powers

.533 5   Neutrals

.533 6   Occupied countries

> Class here governments-in-exile; resistance, underground movements
>
> *For countries occupied by Axis Powers, see 940.5337; for countries occupied by United Nations (Allies), see 940.5338*

.533 7   Countries occupied by Axis Powers

.533 8   Countries occupied by United Nations (Allies)

.534–.539   Participation of specific countries and localities

> Add to base number 940.53 notation 4–9 from Table 2, e.g., participation of Great Britain 940.5341
>
> Class a specific activity with the activity, e.g., efforts by a specific country to preserve or restore peace 940.5312

.54   Military history of World War II

SUMMARY

940.540 01–.540 09	Standard subdivisions
.540 1–.540 9	[General aspects]
.541	Operations and units
.542	Campaigns and battles by theater
.544	Air operations
.545	Naval operations
.546	Celebrations, commemorations, memorials
.547	Prisoners of war; medical and social services
.548	Other military topics

.540 01–.540 08   Standard subdivisions

.540 09   Historical, geographic, persons treatment

> Do not use for military participation of specific countries; class in 940.5409

.540 092   Persons

> Do not use for personal narratives; class in 940.5481–940.5482

.540 1   Strategy

.540 12   United Nations (Allies)

.540 13   Axis Powers

.540 2   Mobilization

> *For mobilization in specific countries, see 940.534–940.539*

.540 3   African Americans and American native peoples as troops

.540 4   Racial minorities as troops

> *For African Americans and American native peoples as troops, see 940.5403*

.540 5   Repressive measures and atrocities

> Class concentration and related camps in 940.5317; class Holocaust in 940.5318

.540 9   Military participation of specific countries

> Add to base number 940.5409 notation 4–9 from Table 2, e.g., military participation of Germany 940.540943

.541   Operations and units

> *For campaigns and battles by theater, see 940.542; for air operations, see 940.544; for naval operations, see 940.545*

>   940.541 2–940.541 3   Military units and their operations

Class here organization, history, rosters, service records

Class comprehensive works in 940.541. Class units engaged in a special service with the service, e.g., ambulance companies 940.54753

For rolls of honor and lists of dead, see 940.5467

.541 2   Military units of United Nations (Allies)

Add to base number 940.5412 notation 4–9 from Table 2, e.g., French units 940.541244

.541 3   Military units of Axis Powers

Add to base number 940.5413 notation 4–9 from Table 2, e.g., Japanese units 940.541352

.542   Campaigns and battles by theater

.542 1   European theater

Add to base number 940.5421 the numbers following —4 in notation 41–49 from Table 2, e.g., battles in France 940.54214

.542 3   Middle East and African theaters

.542 5   East and southeast Asian and East Indian theaters

Including theaters covering Asian mainland, Japan, Netherlands East Indies, Philippines

Class Sino-Japanese Conflict during 1937–1941 in 951.042

.542 6   Pacific Ocean theater

Including theaters covering Hawaiian Islands, South Pacific Ocean islands

For East Indian theater, see 940.5425

See also 940.5425 for Japan and Philippines

.542 8   American theater

.542 9   Other areas

.544   Air operations

Including antiaircraft defenses

Class here combined air and naval operations

For naval operations, see 940.545

.544 2   Campaigns and battles

For campaigns and battles by theater, see 940.542

.544 3   Air bases

> Add to base number 940.5443 notation 4–9 from Table 2, e.g., air bases in England 940.544342

.544 9   Operations of specific countries

> Class here aircraft, fliers, units

> Add to base number 940.5449 notation 4–9 from Table 2, e.g., operations of Germany 940.544943

> Class campaigns and battles of specific countries in 940.5442

.545   Naval operations

> *For campaigns and battles by theater, see 940.542*

.545 1   Submarine warfare

.545 16   Antisubmarine warfare

.545 2   Blockades and blockade running

> Standard subdivisions are added for either or both topics in heading

.545 3   Naval bases

.545 9   Operations of specific countries

> Class here ships, crews, units

> Add to base number 940.5459 notation 4–9 from Table 2, e.g., Australian naval operations 940.545994

> Class a specific kind of operation with the operation, e.g., blockades 940.5452

.546   Celebrations, commemorations, memorials

> Including commemorative meetings, flag presentations, decorations and awards

> *For celebrations, commemorations, memorials of a specific event, see the event, e.g., Battle of the Coral Sea 940.5426*

.546 5   Monuments and cemeteries

> Add to base number 940.5465 notation 4–9 from Table 2, e.g., monuments and cemeteries in France 940.546544

.546 7   Rolls of honor and lists of dead

> Add to base number 940.5467 notation 4–9 from Table 2, e.g., lists of Japanese dead 940.546752

.547   Prisoners of war; medical and social services

.547 2	Prisoner-of-war camps

Class here prisoners of war

Add to base number 940.5472 notation 4–9 from Table 2, e.g., prisoner-of-war camps maintained by Germany 940.547243

For prisoners exchange, see 940.5473

.547 3	Prisoners exchange
.547 5	Medical services

For hospitals, see 940.5476

.547 509 4–.547 509 9	Services in the modern world

Services of specific countries relocated to 940.54754–940.54759

.547 52	Sanitary affairs
.547 53	Ambulance services
.547 54–.547 59	Services of specific countries [*formerly also* 940.5475094–940.5475099]

Add to base number 940.5475 notation 4–9 from Table 2, e.g., French medical services 940.547544

.547 6	Hospitals
.547 609	Historical and persons treatment

For hospitals in specific places, see 940.54763

.547 63	Hospitals in specific places

Add to base number 940.54763 notation 4–9 from Table 2, e.g., hospitals in Rome 940.5476345632

Class hospitals maintained in specific places by specific countries in 940.54764–940.54769

.547 64–.547 69	Hospitals maintained by specific countries

Add to base number 940.5476 notation 4–9 from Table 2, e.g., hospitals maintained by Italy 940.547645

.547 7	Relief and welfare services

Standard subdivisions are added for either or both topics in heading

.547 709	Historical and persons treatment

For activities in specific places, see 940.54779

.547 71	Activities of Red Cross

.547 78   Activities conducted by specific countries

> Add to base number 940.54778 notation 4–9 from Table 2, e.g., activities conducted by Switzerland 940.54778494
>
> Class Red Cross activities conducted by specific countries in 940.54771

.547 79   Activities in specific places

> Add to base number 940.54779 notation 4–9 from Table 2, e.g., welfare activities in Paris 940.5477944361
>
> Class activities of Red Cross in specific places in 940.54771; class welfare activities conducted in specific places by specific countries in 940.54778

.547 8   Religious life and chaplain services

> Standard subdivisions are added for either or both topics in heading

.548   Other military topics

> Including deserters, servicemen missing in action

>   940.548 1–940.548 2   Personal narratives

> Class comprehensive works in 940.548. Class personal narratives on a specific subject with the subject, plus notation 092 from Table 1, e.g., on blockade running 940.5452092

.548 1   Personal narratives of individuals from United Nations (Allies)

> Add to base number 940.5481 notation 4–9 from Table 2, e.g., personal narratives of Britons 940.548141

.548 2   Personal narratives of individuals from Axis Powers

> Add to base number 940.5482 notation 4–9 from Table 2, e.g., personal narratives of Germans 940.548243

.548 3   Military life and customs of United Nations (Allies)

> Add to base number 940.5483 notation 4–9 from Table 2, e.g., military life in United States Navy 940.548373

.548 4   Military life and customs of Axis Powers

> Add to base number 940.5484 notation 4–9 from Table 2, e.g., military life in Luftwaffe 940.548443

.548 5   Unconventional warfare

> Class here counterintelligence, infiltration, intelligence, psychological warfare, sabotage, subversion
>
> *For unconventional warfare of United Nations, see 940.5486; for unconventional warfare of Axis Powers, see 940.5487; for propaganda, see 940.5488*

.548 6	Unconventional warfare of United Nations (Allies)

Add to base number 940.5486 notation 4–9 from Table 2, e.g., intelligence operation of United States 940.548673

.548 7	Unconventional warfare of Axis Powers

Add to base number 940.5487 notation 4–9 from Table 2, e.g., intelligence operations of Germany 940.548743

.548 8	Propaganda
.548 809	Historical and persons treatment

. *For propaganda in specific places, see 940.54889*

.548 86	Propaganda by United Nations (Allies)

Add to base number 940.54886 notation 4–9 from Table 2, e.g., propaganda by United States 940.5488673

.548 87	Propaganda by Axis Powers

Add to base number 940.54887 notation 4–9 from Table 2, e.g., propaganda by Germany 940.5488743

.548 89	Propaganda in specific places

Add to base number 940.54889 notation 4–9 from Table 2, e.g., propaganda in United States 940.5488973

Class propaganda by one side or one country regardless of location in 940.54886–940.54887

.55	1945–1999
.554	1945–1949
.555	1950–1959
.556	1960–1969
.557	1970–1979
.558	1980–1989
.559	1990–1999
.56	2000–

941   *British Isles

Class here Great Britain, United Kingdom

See Manual at 941

---

*Add as instructed under 930–990

SUMMARY

941.01–.08	**[Historical periods of British Isles]**	
.1	**Scotland**	
.2	**Northeastern Scotland**	
.3	**Southeastern Scotland**	
.4	**Southwestern Scotland**	
.5	**Ireland**	
.6	**Ulster**	**Northern Ireland**
.7	**Republic of Ireland**	
.8	**Leinster**	
.9	**Munster**	

.01   Early history to 1066

> *For ancient history to 410, see 936.1*

(.012)   Ancient history to 410

> (Optional number; prefer 936.1)

> Add to base number 941.012 the numbers following 936.20 in 936.201–936.204, e.g., 4th century 941.0124

.013–.019   Pre-Anglo-Saxon period through reign of Saxon kings, 410–1066

> Add to base number 941.01 the numbers following 942.01 in 942.013–942.019, e.g., period of Danish kings 941.018

.02–.05   Norman period through House of Tudor period, 1066–1603

> Add to base number 941.0 the numbers following 942.0 in 942.02–942.05, e.g., reign of Henry VIII 941.052

.06   House of Stuart and Commonwealth periods, 1603–1714

> (Option: Class here Anglo-Dutch Wars; prefer 949.204)

.061   Reign of James I, 1603–1625

.062   Reign of Charles I, 1625–1649

> Class Civil War in 942.062

.063   Period as Commonwealth, 1649–1660

> *For protectorate of Oliver Cromwell, see 941.064; for protectorate of Richard Cromwell, see 941.065*

.064   Protectorate of Oliver Cromwell, 1653–1658

.065   Protectorate of Richard Cromwell, 1658–1659

.066   Reign of Charles II, 1660–1685 (Restoration)

.067   1685–1689

> Class here reign of James II, 1685–1688

.068   Reigns of William III (of Orange) and Mary II, 1689–1702

.069	Reign of Anne, 1702–1714
.07	Period of House of Hanover, 1714–1837
.071	Reign of George I, 1714–1727
.072	Reign of George II, 1727–1760

(Option: Class here War of Jenkins' Ear; prefer 946.055)

.073	Reign of George III, 1760–1820

Including formation of United Kingdom

.074	Reign of George IV, 1820–1830
.075	Reign of William IV, 1830–1837
.08	Period of Victoria and House of Windsor, 1837–
.081	Reign of Victoria, 1837–1901

Class here 19th century

For 1800–1820, see 941.073; for 1820–1830, see 941.074; for 1830–1837, see 941.075

(Option: Class here Crimean War, South African [Second Anglo-Boer] War; prefer 947.0738 for Crimean War, 968.048 for South African [Second Anglo-Boer] War)

.082	1901–1999

For reign of George V, see 941.083; for 1936–1945, see 941.084; for 1945–1999, see 941.085

.082 3	Reign of Edward VII, 1901–1910
.083	Reign of George V, 1910–1936
.084	1936–1945

Class here reigns of Edward VIII, 1936, and George VI, 1936–1952; period of World War II, 1939–1945

For reign of George VI during 1945–1949, see 941.0854; for reign of George VI during 1950–1952, see 941.0855

.085	1945–1999

Class here reign of Elizabeth II, 1952 to present

For 2000 and beyond, see 941.086

.085 4	1945–1949
.085 5	1950–1959
.085 6	1960–1969
.085 7	1970–1979

.085 8		1980–1989
.085 9		1990–1999
.086		2000–

.1   ***Scotland**

> *For northeastern Scotland, see 941.2; for southeastern Scotland, see 941.3; for southwestern Scotland, see 941.4*

.101   Early history to 1057

> *For ancient history to 410, see 936.1*

(.101 2)   Ancient history of northern Britain to 410

> (Optional number; prefer 936.1)

.102   1057–1314

> Including Battle of Bannockburn, 1314

.103   1314–1424

.104   Reigns of James I through James V, 1424–1542

.105   Reformation period, 1542–1603

> Class here 16th century

> *For 1500–1542, see 941.104*

.106–.108   Personal union with England to present, 1603–

> Add to base number 941.10 the numbers following 941.0 in 941.06–941.08, e.g., reign of Edward VII 941.10823

.2   ***Northeastern Scotland**

.201–.208   Historical periods

> Add to base number 941.2 the numbers following 941.1 in 941.101–941.108, e.g., Reformation period 941.205

.3   ***Southeastern Scotland**

.301–.308   Historical periods

> Add to base number 941.3 the numbers following 941.1 in 941.101–941.108, e.g., Reformation period 941.305

.4   ***Southwestern Scotland**

.401–.408   Historical periods

> Add to base number 941.4 the numbers following 941.1 in 941.101–941.108, e.g., Reformation period 941.405

.5   ***Ireland**

*Add as instructed under 930–990

.501	Early history to 1086
	Including Battle of Clontarf, 1014
	For ancient history to 410, see 936.1
(.501 2)	Ancient history to 410
	(Optional number; prefer 936.1)
.502	1086–1171
.503	Period under House of Plantagenet, 1171–1399
.504	Period under Houses of Lancaster and York, 1399–1485
.505	Period under House of Tudor, 1485–1603
.506	Period under House of Stuart, 1603–1691
.507	1691–1799
.508	1800–
.508 1	1800–1899
.508 2	1900–
.508 21	1900 1921
	Including Sinn Fein Rebellion (Easter Rebellion), 1916; Anglo-Irish War, 1919–1921
.508 22	1921–1949
.508 23	1950–1969
.508 24	1970–
.6	***Ulster Northern Ireland**
.608	1800–
.608 1	1800–1899
.608 2	1900–
.608 21	1900–1920
	Including Government of Ireland Act, 1920
.608 22	1921–1949
.608 23	1949–1968
.608 24	1969–
.7	***Republic of Ireland**
	For Leinster, see 941.8; for Munster, see 941.9
.708	1800–

*Add as instructed under 930–990

.708 1	1800–1899	
.708 2	1900–	
.708 21	1900–1921	
.708 22	1922–1949	

Including period as Irish Free State, 1922–1937; as Eire, 1937–1949

.708 23	1949–1969	
.708 24	1970–	

.8   *Leinster

.808   1800–

Add to base number 941.808 the numbers following 941.708 in 941.7081–941.7082, e.g., 1949–1969 941.80823

.9   *Munster

.908   1800–

Add to base number 941.908 the numbers following 941.708 in 941.7081–941.7082, e.g., 1949–1969 941.90823

942   *England and Wales

Subdivisions are added for England and Wales together, for England alone

See Manual at 941

> 942.01–942.08   Historical periods of England and Wales together, of England alone

Class comprehensive works in 942

.01   Early history to 1066

For ancient history to 410, see 936.2

(.012)   Ancient history of southern Britain to 410

(Optional number; prefer 936.2)

Add to base number 942.012 the numbers following 936.20 in 936.201–936.204, e.g., Celtic period 942.0122

.013   Pre-Anglo-Saxon period, 410–449

.014   449–ca. 600

Including reign of King Arthur

.015   Period of Heptarchy, ca. 600–829

Class supremacy of Wessex in 942.016

*Add as instructed under 930–990

.015 3	Supremacy of Northumbria, 603–685
.015 7	Supremacy of Mercia, 757–796
.016	Supremacy of Wessex, 829–924
	Class here 9th century
	For 800–829, see 942.015
.016 1	Reign of Egbert, 829–839
.016 2	Reign of Ethelwulf, 839–858
.016 3	Reigns of Ethelbald, Ethelbert, Ethelred I, 858–871
.016 4	Reign of Alfred the Great, 871–899
.016 5	Reign of Edward the Elder, 899–924
.017	Reigns of Saxon kings of England, 924–1016
.017 1	Reign of Athelstan, 924–940
.017 2	Reigns of Edmund I, Edred, Edwy, 940–959
.017 3	Reigns of Edgar and Edward the Martyr, 959–978
.017 4	Reigns of Ethelred II and Edmund II, 978–1016
.018	Reigns of Danish kings, 1016–1042
	Class here 11th century
	For 1000–1016, see 942.0174; for 1042–1066, see 942.019; for 1066–1099, see 942.02
.018 1	Reign of Canute, 1016–1035
.018 2	Reign of Harold I, 1035–1040
.018 3	Reign of Hardecanute, 1040–1042
.019	1042–1066
	Including reigns of Edward the Confessor, 1042–1066, and Harold II, 1066
.02	Norman period, 1066–1154
	Class here 12th century
	For 1154–1199, see 942.03
.021	Reign of William I, 1066–1087
	Including Battle of Hastings, 1066
.022	Reign of William II, 1087–1100
.023	Reign of Henry I, 1100–1135
.024	Reign of Stephen, 1135–1154

| .03 | Period of House of Plantagenet, 1154–1399 |
| | Class here medieval period |

        For 1066–1154, see 942.02; for 1399–1485, see 942.04

.031	Reign of Henry II, 1154–1189
.032	Reign of Richard I, 1189–1199
.033	Reign of John, 1199–1216
.034	Reign of Henry III, 1216–1272
	Class here 13th century

        For 1200–1216, see 942.033; for 1272–1299, see 942.035

.035	Reign of Edward I, 1272–1307
.036	Reign of Edward II, 1307–1327
.037	Reign of Edward III, 1327–1377
	Class here 14th century

        For 1300–1307, see 942.035; for 1307–1327, see 942.036; for 1377–1399, see 942.038

        (Option: Class here Hundred Years' War; prefer 944.025)

.038	Reign of Richard II, 1377–1399
.04	Period of Houses of Lancaster and York, 1399–1485
	Class here Wars of the Roses, 1455–1485
.041	Reign of Henry IV, 1399–1413
.042	Reign of Henry V, 1413–1422
.043	Reign of Henry VI, 1422–1461
.044	Reign of Edward IV, 1461–1483
.045	Reign of Edward V, 1483
.046	Reign of Richard III, 1483–1485
.05	Period of House of Tudor, 1485–1603
.051	Reign of Henry VII, 1485–1509
.052	Reign of Henry VIII, 1509–1547
.053	Reign of Edward VI, 1547–1553
.054	Reign of Mary I, 1553–1558
.055	Reign of Elizabeth I, 1558–1603
	Including Spanish Armada, 1588

.06–.08   House of Stuart and Commonwealth periods to present, 1603–

> Add to base number 942.0 the numbers following 941.0 in 941.06–941.08, e.g., reign of Victoria 942.081

.062   ‡Reign of Charles I, 1625–1649

> Number built according to instructions under 942.06–942.08

> Class here Civil War, 1642–1649

943   Central Europe   Germany

Class here Holy Roman Empire

SUMMARY

943.000 1–.000 9	**Standard subdivisions of central Europe**
.001–.009	**Standard subdivisions of Germany**
.01–.08	**Historical periods of Germany**
.1	**Northeastern Germany**
.6	**Austria and Liechtenstein**
.7	**Czech Republic and Slovakia**
.8	**Poland**
.9	**Hungary**

.000 1–.000 8   Standard subdivisions of central Europe

> As modified under 930–990

.000 9   Historical periods; areas, regions, places; persons of central Europe

.000 901–.000 905   Historical periods

> Add to base number 943.0009 the numbers following —090 in notation 0901–0905 from Table 1, e.g., central Europe during the Middle Ages 943.000902

> Class specific periods of Holy Roman Empire in 943.02–943.05; class comprehensive works on Holy Roman Empire in 943

.000 91–.000 99   Areas, regions, places in general; persons

> As modified under 930–990

.001–.009   Standard subdivisions of Germany

> As modified under 930–990

>   943.01–943.08 Historical periods of Germany

> Class comprehensive works in 943

‡Add as instructed under 940–990

SUMMARY

.01   Early history to 843

> For ancient history to 481, see 936.3

(.012)   Ancient history to 481

> (Optional number; prefer 936.3)

(.012 1)   Earliest period to 113 B.C.

> (Optional number; prefer 936.301)

(.012 2)   Period of contacts with Roman Republic and Empire, 113 B.C.–481 A.D.

> (Optional number; prefer 936.302)

.013   Period of Merovingian dynasty in Germany, 481–751

> Class comprehensive works on Merovingian dynasty in France and Germany in 944.013

.014   751–843

> Class here Carolingian dynasty in Germany, 751–911

> Class comprehensive works on Carolingian dynasty in France and Germany in 944.014

> For 843–911, see 943.021

>   943.02–943.05   Specific periods of Holy Roman Empire

> Class comprehensive works in 943

.02   Period of early Holy Roman Empire, 843–1519

> After Treaty of Verdun, 843

> Class here medieval period

.021   843–911

.022   Period of Conrad I and House of Saxony, 911–1024

.023   Period of Salian (Franconian) emperors and Lothair II, 1024–1137

.024   Period of Hohenstaufen dynasty, 1138–1254

           Including reign of Frederick I Barbarossa, 1152–1190

           Class here 12th century

           For 1100–1137, see 943.023; for later period of Hohenstaufen
           dynasty, see 943.025

.025   Later period of Hohenstaufen dynasty and Interregnum, 1198–1273

.026   1273–1378

.027   Period of House of Luxemburg, 1378–1438

           For reign of other Luxemburgian emperors, see 943.026

.028   Reigns of Albert II and Frederick III, 1438–1493

           Class here 15th century

           For 1400–1438, see 943.027; for 1493–1499, see 943.029

.029   Reign of Maximilian I, 1493–1519

.03   Period of Reformation and Counter-Reformation, 1519–1618

.031   Reign of Charles V, 1519–1556

           Including wars with France; Peasants' War, 1524–1525; Schmalkaldic
           War, 1546–1547
           (Option: Class wars with France in 944.028)

.032   Reign of Ferdinand I, 1556–1564

.033   Reign of Maximilian II, 1564–1576

.034   Reign of Rudolf II, 1576–1612

.035   Reign of Matthias, 1612–1619

.04   1618–1705

.041   Period of Thirty Years' War, 1618–1648

           Class reign of Matthias during Thirty Years' War in 943.035; class reign
           of Ferdinand II during Thirty Years' War in 943.042; class reign of
           Ferdinand III during Thirty Years' War in 943.043; class comprehensive
           works on Thiry Years' War in 940.24

.042   Reign of Ferdinand II, 1619–1637

.043   Reign of Ferdinand III, 1637–1657

.044   Reign of Leopold I, 1658–1705

.05   1705–1790

           Class here rise of Prussia

.051	Reign of Joseph I, 1705–1711
.052	Reign of Charles VI, 1711–1740
.053	1740–1786

Class here reign of Frederick the Great, King of Prussia, 1740–1786

For reign of Charles VII, see 943.054; for reign of Francis I, see 943.055; for reign of Joseph II, see 943.057

.054	Reign of Charles VII, 1742–1745
.055	Reign of Francis I, 1745–1765

Including period of Seven Years' War, 1756–1763

Class comprehensive works on Seven Years' War in 940.2534

.057	Reign of Joseph II, 1765–1790
.06	Period of Napoleonic Wars, 1790–1815

Including Confederation of the Rhine

Class comprehensive works on Napoleonic Wars in 940.27

.07	Period of German Confederation, 1815–1866

Class here 19th century

For 1800–1815, see 943.06; for 1866–1899, see 943.08

.073	1815–1847
.076	1848–1866

Including Schleswig-Holstein War, 1864; Austro-Prussian War (Seven Weeks' War), 1866
(Option: Class Schleswig-Holstein War in 948.904)

.08	1866–
.081	1866–1871

Class here period of North German Confederation

For Franco-German War, see 943.082

.082	‡Franco-German War, 1870–1871

(Option: Class in 944.07)

.083	Reign of William I, 1871–1888

Class here German Empire, 1871–1918

For reigns of Frederick III and William II, see 943.084

.084	Reigns of Frederick III and William II, 1888–1918
.085	Period of Weimar Republic, 1918–1933

‡Add as instructed under 940–990

.086	Period of Third Reich, 1933–1945

Class Holocaust in 940.5318

.087	1945–1999

Class here 20th century; Federal Republic, 1949 to present; comprehensive works on Federal and Democratic Republics

> *For 1900–1918, see 943.084; for period of Weimar Republic, see 943.085; for period of Third Reich, 1933–1945, see 943.086; for 2000 and beyond, see 943.088; for German Democratic Republic, see 943.1087*

.087 4	1945–1949
.087 5	1950–1959
.087 6	1960–1969
.087 7	1970–1979
.087 8	1980–1989
.087 9	1990–1999
.088	2000–
.1	***Northeastern Germany**
.108 7	1945–1999

Class here East Germany, 1945–1990; German Democratic Republic, 1949–1990

Add to base number 943.1087 the numbers following 943.087 in 943.0874–943.0879, e.g., 1960–1969 943.10876

.6	***Austria and Liechtenstein**

Subdivisions are added for Austria and Liechtenstein together, for Austria alone

> *For ancient history to 481, see 936.3*

(.601)	Ancient history to 481

(Optional number; prefer 936.3)

>	943.602–943.605 Historical periods of Austria and Liechtenstein together, of Austria alone

Class comprehensive works in 943.6

.602	Medieval period, 481–1500
.602 2	481–976

*Add as instructed under 930–990

.602 3	Period of House of Babenberg, 976–1246
.602 4	1246–1273
.602 5	1273–1500
.603	1500–1815

See also 940.2532 for War of the Austrian Succession

.604	1815–1919

Class here Austrian Empire, 1804–1919

For Austrian Empire during 1804–1815, see 943.603

.604 2	1815–1847
.604 3	1848–1867
.604 4	Period of Austro-Hungarian Monarchy, 1867–1919
.605	1919–
.605 1	Period of Republic, 1919–1938
.605 2	1938–1955
.605 22	Anschluss and war periods, 1938–1945
.605 23	1945–1955
.605 3	1955–
.64	*Western Austria, and Liechtenstein

Subdivisions are added for Western Austria and Liechtenstein together, for Western Austria alone

.648	†Liechtenstein

For ancient history to 481, see 936.3

.7	***Czech Republic and Slovakia**
.702	Early history to 1918

Class here Kingdom of Bohemia

.702 1	Early history to 907

Including Great Moravian Empire

.702 2	907–1526
.702 23	Period of Přemyslid dynasty, 907–1306
.702 24	Period of House of Luxemburg, 1306–1526

Including Hussite Wars, 1419–1436

*Add as instructed under 930–990

†Add as instructed under 930–990; however, do not add historical periods

.702 3	1526–1815
.702 32	1526–1620
.702 33	1620–1800
.702 34	1800–1815
.702 4	1815–1918
.703	1918–1992

Class here Czechoslovakia

For 1945–1992, see 943.704

.703 2	Period of Czechoslovak Republic, 1918–1939
.703 3	1939–1945

Class here Protectorate of Bohemia and Moravia

.704	1945–1992
.704 2	1945–1968

Including reform and repression, 1968

.704 3	1968–1992
.705	1993–

Period of two sovereign nations

.71	*Czech Republic

For Moravia, see 943.72

.710 2–.710 5	Historical periods

Add to base number 943.71 the numbers following 943.7 in 943.702–943.705, e.g., period as a sovereign nation 943.7105

.72	*Moravia
.720 2–.720 5	Historical periods

Add to base number 943.72 the numbers following 943.7 in 943.702–943.705, e.g., period as a part of Czech Republic 943.7205

.73	*Slovakia
.730 2–.730 5	Historical periods

Add to base number 943.73 the numbers following 943.7 in 943.702–943.705, e.g., Slovak Republic 943.73033

.8	***Poland**
.802	Early history to 1795

*Add as instructed under 930–990

.802 2	Early history to 1370
	Including period of Piast dynasty
.802 3	Period of Jagellon dynasty, 1370–1572
.802 4	Period of elective kings, 1572–1697
.802 5	1697–1795
	Including partitions of 1772, 1793, 1795
.803	Period of foreign rule, 1795–1918
.803 2	1795–1862
.803 3	1863–1918
.804	Period of Republic, 1918–1939
.805	1939–
	Class here 20th century
	For 1900–1918, see 943.8033; for 1918–1939, see 943.804
.805 3	1939–1945
.805 4	1945–1956
.805 5	1956–1980
.805 6	1980–1989
.805 7	1989–
.9	***Hungary**
.901	Early history to 894
	For ancient history to ca. 640, see 939.8
(.901 1)	Ancient history to ca. 640
	(Optional number; prefer 939.8)
.902	Period of House of Árpád, 894–1301
.903	Period of elective kings, 1301–1526
.904	Turkish and House of Hapsburg periods, 1526–1918
.904 1	Turkish period, 1526–1686
.904 2	Period of House of Hapsburg, 1686–1918
	For period of Austro-Hungarian Monarchy, see 943.9043
.904 3	Period of Austro-Hungarian Monarchy, 1867–1918
.905	1918–
.905 1	1918–1941

*Add as instructed under 930–990

.905 2	1942–1956
	Including uprising and suppression, 1956
.905 3	1956–1989
.905 4	1989–

944   *France and Monaco

Subdivisions are added for France and Monaco together, for France alone

SUMMARY

944.01	Early history to 987
.02	Medieval period, 987–1589
.03	Period of House of Bourbon, 1589–1789
.04	Revolutionary period, 1789–1804
.05	Period of First Empire, 1804–1815
.06	Period of Restoration, 1815–1848
.07	Period of Second Republic and Second Empire (period of Napoleon III), 1848–1870
.08	1870–

>   944.01–944.08   Historical periods of France and Monaco together, of France alone

Class comprehensive works in 944

.01   Early history to 987

For ancient history to 486, see 936.4

(.012)   Ancient history to 486

(Optional number; prefer 936.4)

(.012 1)   Earliest period to 125 B.C.

(Optional number; prefer 936.401)

(.012 2)   Gallo-Roman period, 125 B.C.–486 A.D.

(Optional number; prefer 936.402)

.013   Period of Merovingian dynasty, 486–751

Class here comprehensive works on Merovingian dynasty in France and Germany

For Merovingian dynasty in Germany, see 943.013

.014   Period of Carolingian dynasty, 751–987

Class here comprehensive works on Carolingian dynasty in France and Germany

For Carolingian dynasty in Germany, see 943.014

---

*Add as instructed under 930–990

.02　　　　　　Medieval period, 987–1589

.021　　　　　　Period of Capetian dynasty, 987–1328

Including reigns of Hugh Capet, Robert II, Henry I, 987–1060

For reigns of other Capetian kings, see 944.022–944.024

.022　　　　　　Reigns of Philip I, Louis VI, Louis VII, 1060–1180

.023　　　　　　Reigns of Philip II, Louis VIII, Louis IX, 1180–1270

.024　　　　　　Reigns of Philip III, Philip IV, Louis X, Jean I, Philip V, Charles IV, 1270–1328

.025　　　　　　‡Period of House of Valois, 1328–1589

Including reigns of Philip VI, Jean II, Charles V, 1328–1380

Class here Hundred Years' War, 1337–1453
(Option: Class Hundred Years' War in 942.037)

For reigns of other Valois kings, see 944.026–944.029

.026　　　　　　Reigns of Charles VI and Charles VII, 1380–1461

.027　　　　　　Reigns of Louis XI, Charles VIII, Louis XII, 1461–1515

Class here comprehensive works on French invasions of Italy, 1494–1559
(Option: Class French invasions of Italy in 945.06)

For invasions during period of House of Angoulême, see 944.028

.028　　　　　　Period of House of Angoulême, 1515–1589

Including reigns of Francis I and Henry II, 1515–1559

Class here 16th century

For 1500–1515, see 944.027; for reigns of Francis II, Charles IX, Henry III, see 944.029; for 1589–1600, see 944.031

(Option: Class here wars with Holy Roman Emperor Charles V; prefer 943.031)

.029　　　　　　Reigns of Francis II, Charles IX, Henry III, 1559–1589

.03　　　　　　Period of House of Bourbon, 1589–1789

.031　　　　　　Reign of Henry IV, 1589–1610

.032　　　　　　Reign of Louis XIII, 1610–1643

.033　　　　　　Reign of Louis XIV, 1643–1715

Including War of Devolution, 1667–1668

Class here 17th century

For 1600–1610, see 944.031; for 1610–1643, see 944.032

‡Add as instructed under 940–990

| .034 | Reign of Louis XV, 1715–1774 |
| | Class here 18th century |

> *For a specific part of 18th century not provided for here, see the part, e.g., Reign of Terror 944.044*

| .035 | 1774–1789 |
| | Class here period of Louis XVI, 1774–1792 |

> *For period of Louis XVI during 1789–1792, see 944.041*

.04	Revolutionary period, 1789–1804
.041	Period of Estates-General, National Assembly, Legislative Assembly, 1789–1792
.042	Period of First Republic, 1792–1799
	Including Vendean War, 1793–1800

> *For period of National Convention, see 944.043; for period of Directory, see 944.045*

| .043 | Period of National Convention, 1792–1795 |

> *For Reign of Terror, see 944.044*

.044	Period of Reign of Terror, 1793–1794
.045	Period of Directory, 1795–1799
.046	Period of Consulate, 1799–1804
.05	Period of First Empire, 1804–1815
	Including reign of Louis XVIII, 1814–1815; Hundred Days, 1815
	Class here reign of Napoleon I, 1804–1814
	Class Napoleonic Wars in 940.27
.06	Period of Restoration, 1815–1848
	Class here 19th century

> *For a specific part of 19th century not provided for here, see the part, e.g., Second Empire 944.07*

.061	Reign of Louis XVIII, 1815–1824
.062	Reign of Charles X, 1824–1830
.063	Period of Louis Philippe, 1830–1848 (July Monarchy)
.07	Period of Second Republic and Second Empire (period of Napoleon III), 1848–1870
	(Option: Class here Franco-German War; prefer 943.082)

.08	1870–
.081	Period of Third Republic, 1870–1945

Class here 20th century

For 1945–1958, see 944.082; for 1958–1999, see 944.083

.081 2	1870–1899

Including Paris Commune, 1871

.081 3	1900–1914
.081 4	Period of World War I, 1914–1918
.081 5	1918–1939
.081 6	Period of World War II, 1939–1945
.082	Period of Fourth Republic, 1945–1958
.083	Period of Fifth Republic, 1958–

For 2000 and beyond, see 944.084

.083 6	1958–1969
.083 7	1970–1979
.083 8	1980–1989
.083 9	1990–1999
.084	2000–
.9	***Southeastern France and Monaco Provence region**

Subdivisions are added for two or more topics in heading, for southeastern France alone, for Provence region alone

.94	*Alpes-Maritimes, Corsica, Monaco
.949	†Monaco

For ancient history to 486, see 936.4

945   *Italian Peninsula and adjacent islands   Italy

>	945.01–945.09 Historical periods of Italian Peninsula and adjacent islands together, of Italy

Class comprehensive works in 945

.01	Early history to 774

Including Gothic and Lombard kingdoms, 476–774

For ancient history to 476, see 937

---

*Add as instructed under 930–990

†Add as instructed under 930–990; however, do not add historical periods

(.012)	Ancient history to 476
	(Optional number; prefer 937)
	Add to base number 945.012 the numbers following 937.0 in 937.01–937.09, e.g., Punic Wars 945.0124
.02	Period of Carolingian (Frankish) dynasty, 774–962
.03	Period of German emperors, 962–1122
	Class here medieval period
	For a part of medieval period not provided for here, see the part, e.g., Carolingian dynasty 945.02
.04	1122–1300
.05	Renaissance period, 1300–1494
	Class here late Middle Ages
	Class a part of late Middle Ages not provided for here with the part, e.g., 1494–1500 945.06
.06	1494–1527
	(Option: Class here French invasions of Italy; prefer 944.027)
.07	Period of Spanish and Austrian domination, 1527–1796
.08	1796–1900
.082	Napoleonic period, 1796–1814
.083	Period of Risorgimento, 1814–1861
.084	Reigns of Victor Emmanuel II and Umberto I, 1861–1900
.09	1900–
.091	Reign of Victor Emmanuel III, 1900–1946
	Class here 20th century, Fascist period
	For 1946–1999, see 945.092
	(Option: Class here Ethiopian War and Italo-Ethiopian War; prefer 963.043 for Ethiopian War, 963.056 for Italo-Ethiopian War)
.092	Period of Republic, 1946–
	For 2000 and beyond, see 945.093
.092 4	1946–1949
.092 5	1950–1959
.092 6	1960–1969
.092 7	1970–1979

.092 8	1980–1989
.092 9	1990–1999
.093	2000–

.4 *Emilia-Romagna region and San Marino

> Subdivisions are added for Emilia-Romagna region and San Marino together, for Emilia-Romagna region alone

.49 †San Marino

> *For ancient history to 476, see 937.4*

.6 *Central Italy and Vatican City

> Subdivisions are added for central Italy and Vatican City together, for central Italy alone

.63 *Rome (Roma) province and Vatican City

> Subdivisions are added for Rome province and Vatican City together, for Rome province alone

.634 *Vatican City

.8 *Sicily and adjacent islands

> Subdivisions are added for Sicily and adjacent islands together, for Sicily alone

.85 †Malta

> *For ancient history to 476, see 937.8*

946 Iberian Peninsula and adjacent islands   Spain

.000 1–.000 8 Standard subdivisions of Iberian Peninsula and adjacent islands

> As modified under 930–990

.000 9 Historical periods; areas, regions, places; persons of Iberian Peninsula and adjacent islands

.000 901–.000 905 Historical periods

> Add to base number 946.0009 the numbers following —090 in notation 0901–0905 from Table 1, e.g., Iberian Peninsula during the Middle Ages 946.000902

.000 91–.000 99 Areas, regions, places in general; persons

> As modified under 930–990

.001–.009 Standard subdivisions of Spain

> As modified under 930–990

---

*Add as instructed under 930–990

†Add as instructed under 930–990; however, do not add historical periods

>   **946.01–946.08 Historical periods of Spain**

Class comprehensive works in 946

.01   **Early history to 711**

Class here period of Visigothic domination, 415–711

For ancient history to 415, see 936.6

(.012)   **Ancient history to 415**

(Optional number; prefer 936.6)

(.012 1)   Earliest period to ca. 1000 B.C.

(Optional number; prefer 936.601)

(.012 2)   Period of Greek, Phoenician, early Celtic and Germanic contacts, ca. 1000–218 B.C.

(Optional number; prefer 936.602)

(.012 3)   Roman period, 218 B.C.-415 A.D.

(Optional number; prefer 936.603)

.02   **Period of Moorish dynasties and reconquest, 711–1479**

.03   **Reign of Ferdinand V and Isabella I, 1479–1516**

Including union of Castile and Aragon

.04   **Period of House of Hapsburg, 1516–1700**

For later period of House of Hapsburg, see 946.051

.042   **Reign of Charles I, 1516–1556**

.043   **Reign of Philip II, 1556–1598**

.05   **Later period of House of Hapsburg and period of House of Bourbon, 1598–1808**

.051   **Later period of House of Hapsburg, 1598–1700**

Including reign of Philip III, 1598–1621

For reign of Philip IV, see 946.052; for reign of Charles II, see 946.053

.052   **Reign of Philip IV, 1621–1665**

.053   **Reign of Charles II, 1665–1700**

.054   **1700–1808**

Class here comprehensive works on House of Bourbon in Spain

For the reign of a specific Bourbon ruler, see the reign, e.g., reign of Isabella II 946.072

.055   Reign of Philip V, 1700–1746

> Including Anglo-Spanish War (War of Jenkins' Ear), 1739–1741
> (Option: Class War of Jenkins' Ear in 941.072)
>
> *See also 940.2526 for War of the Spanish Succession*

.056   Reign of Ferdinand VI, 1746–1759

.057   Reign of Charles III, 1759–1788

.058   Reign of Charles IV, 1788–1808

.06   Period of Peninsular War and rule of Joseph Bonaparte, 1808–1814

> Class comprehensive works on Peninsular War in 940.27

.07   1814–1931

.072   Reigns of Ferdinand VII and Isabella II, 1814–1868

> Including first Bourbon Restoration
>
> (Option: Class here Spanish-Moroccan War; prefer 964.03)

.073   1868–1874

> Including revolution 1868–1871; second Bourbon Restoration,
> 1871–1873; First Republic, 1873–1874

.074   Reigns of Alfonso XII and Alfonso XIII, 1874–1931

> (Option: Class here Spanish-American War; prefer 973.89)

.08   1931–

> Class here 20th century
>
> *For 1900–1931, see 946.074*

.081   ‡Period of Second Republic, 1931–1939

> Class here Civil War, 1936–1939

.082   Period of Francisco Franco, 1939–1975

.082 4   1939–1949

.082 5   1950–1959

.082 6   1960–1969

.082 7   1970–1975

.083   Reign of Juan Carlos I, 1975–

.7   *Eastern Spain and Andorra

> Subdivisions are added for eastern Spain and Andorra together, for eastern
> Spain alone

*Add as instructed under 930–990

‡Add as instructed under 940–990

.79	†Andorra

For ancient history to 415, see 936.6

.8   *Andalusia autonomous community and Gibraltar

Subdivisions are added for Andalusia autonomous community and Gibraltar together, for Andalusia autonomous community alone

.89	†Gibraltar

For ancient history to 415, see 936.6

.9   *Portugal

.901	Early history to 1143

For ancient history to 415, see 936.6

(.901 2)	Ancient history to 415

(Optional number; prefer 936.6)

Add to base number 946.9012 the numbers following 946.012 in 946.0121–946.0123, e.g., period of Greek contacts 946.90122

.902	1143–1640
.903	Period of House of Braganza, 1640–1910
.903 2	1640–1750

Including restoration of Portuguese monarchy

.903 3	1750–1807

Including Pombaline reforms

.903 4	Period of monarchy in exile, 1807–1820

Including period of Peninsular War

Class comprehensive works on Peninsular War in 940.27

.903 5	1820–1847
.903 6	1847–1910
.904	1910–
.904 1	Period of Republic, 1910–1926
.904 2	1926–1968

Including period of Salazar, 1933–1968

Class here Novo Estado, 1933–1974

For Novo Estado during 1968–1974, see 946.9043

.904 3	1968–1974

---

*Add as instructed under 930–990

†Add as instructed under 930–990; however, do not add historical periods

.904 4   1974–

947   Eastern Europe   Russia

SUMMARY

947.000 1–.000 9   **Standard subdivisions of eastern Europe**
.001–.009   **Standard subdivisions of Russia**
.01–.08   **Historical periods of Russia**
.5   **Caucasus**
.6   **Moldova**
.7   **Ukraine**
.8   **Belarus**
.9   **Lithuania, Latvia, Estonia**

.000 1–.000 8   Standard subdivisions of eastern Europe

As modified under 930–990

.000 9   Historical periods; areas, regions, places; persons of eastern Europe

.000 901–.000 905   Historical periods

Add to base number 947.0009 the numbers following —090 in notation 0901–0905 from Table 1, e.g., eastern Europe during the Middle Ages 947.000902

.000 91–.000 99   Areas, regions, places in general; persons

As modified under 930–990

.001–.009   Standard subdivisions of Russia

As modified under 930–990

\>   947.01–947.08 Historical periods of Russia

Class comprehensive works in 947

.01   Early history to 862

.02   Period of Kievan Rus, 862–1240

.03   Period of Tatar suzerainty, 1240–1462

.04   1462–1689

.041   Reign of Ivan III, 1462–1505

.042   Reign of Basil III, 1505–1533

.043   Reign of Ivan IV (the Terrible), 1533–1584

Including Livonian War, 1557–1582
(Option: Class Livonian War in 948.502)

.044   Reigns of Theodore I and Boris Godunov, 1584–1605

.045	Time of Troubles, 1605–1613
	Including reigns of False Dmitri I and False Dmitri II
.046	Period of House of Romanov, 1613–1917
	For reigns of specific Romanovs, see 947.047–947.083
.047	Reign of Michael, 1613–1645
.048	Reign of Alexis, 1645–1676
.049	Reigns of Theodore III and regent Sophia, 1676–1689
.05	Reign of Peter I (the Great), 1689–1725
	Including Great Northern War, 1700–1721
	(Option: Class Great Northern War in 948.05 or 948.503)
.06	1725–1796
.061	Reigns of Catherine I, Peter II, Anna, Ivan VI, 1725–1741
.062	Reigns of Elizabeth and Peter III, 1741–1762
.063	Reign of Catherine II (the Great), 1762–1796
.07	1796–1855
	Class here 19th century
	For 1855–1900, see 947.08
.071	Reign of Paul I, 1796–1801
.072	Reign of Alexander I, 1801–1825
	Including period of invasion by Napoleon, 1812
.073	Reign of Nicholas I, 1825–1855
.073 8	‡Crimean War, 1853–1856
	(Option: Class in 941.081)
.08	1855–
.081	Reign of Alexander II, 1855–1881
	Including Russo-Turkish War, 1877–1878
	(Option: Class Russo-Turkish War in 956.1015)
.082	Reign of Alexander III, 1881–1894
.083	Reign of Nicholas II, 1894–1917
	(Option: Class here Russo-Japanese War; prefer 952.031)

‡Add as instructed under 940–990

.084	1917–1991

Class here 20th century; Communist period; comprehensive works on Union of Soviet Socialist Republics, 1923–1991

For 1900–1917, see 947.083; for 1953–1991, see 947.085. For a specific part of Union of Soviet Socialist Republics, see the part, e.g., Ukraine 947.7085

.084 1	Period of revolutions, Alexander Kerensky, Vladimir Il´ich Lenin, 1917–1924
.084 2	Period of Joseph Stalin, 1924–1953

(Option: Class here Russo-Finnish War; prefer 948.97032)

.085	1953–1991
.085 2	Periods of Georgi Malenkov, Nikolay Aleksandrovich Bulganin, Nikita Sergeevich Khrushchev, 1953–1964
.085 3	Period of Leonid Il´ich Brezhnev and Aleksey Nikolayevich Kosygin, 1964–1982
.085 4	Periods of ĪU. V. Andropov, K. U. Chernenko, and Mikhail Sergeevich Gorbachev, 1982–1991
.086	1991–

Class here comprehensive works on Commonwealth of Independent States, 1991–

For a specific part of Commonwealth of Independent States, see the part, e.g., Ukraine 947.7086

> ### 947.5–947.9   Countries of former Soviet Union other than Russia; Caucasus area of Russia

Except for modifications shown under specific entries, add to each subdivision identified by † as follows:

07	1796–1855
	Class here period as part of Russia
	Add to base number 07 the numbers following 947.07 in 947.071–947.073, e.g., reign of Paul I 071
	For a period as part of Russia not provided for here, see the period, e.g., period during reign of Alexander II 081
08	1855–
081	Reign of Alexander II, 1855–1881
082	Reign of Alexander III, 1881–1894
083	Reign of Nicholas II, 1894–1917
084	1917–1953
	Class here 20th century
	For 1900–1917, see 083; for 1953–1991, see 085; for 1991–1999, see 086
0841	1917–1940
	Class here period of independent countries, ca. 1917–ca. 1920
0842	Period of Joseph Stalin, 1940–1953
085	1953–1991
	Class here period as part of Soviet Union, ca. 1920–1991
	For ca. 1920–1940, see 0841; for period of Joseph Stalin, 1940–1953, see 0842
0852	Periods of Georgi Malenkov, Nikolay Aleksandrovich Bulganin, Nikita Sergeevich Khrushchev, 1953–1964
0853	Period of Leonid Il´ich Brezhnev and Aleksey Nikolayevich Kosygin, 1964–1982
0854	Periods of ĪU. V. Andropov, K. U. Chernenko, and Mikhail Sergeevich Gorbachev, 1982–1991
086	1991–

Class comprehensive works in 947

.5   ***†Caucasus**

(Option: Class here ancient Caucasus; prefer 939.5)

.52   *Caucasus area of Russia

.520 1–.520 8   Historical periods

Add to base number 947.520 the numbers following 947.0 in 947.01–947.08, e.g., later 20th century 947.52085

.54   *†Azerbaijan

(Option: Class here ancient Albania; prefer 939.5)

---

*Add as instructed under 930–990

†Add historical periods as instructed under 947.5–947.9

.56   *†Armenia

.58   *†Georgia

>(Option: Class here ancient Colchis, Iberia; prefer 939.5)

.6   *†Moldova

.7   *†Ukraine

>(Option: Class here ancient Black Sea region, Sarmatia; prefer 939.5)

.8   *†Belarus

.9   *†Lithuania, Latvia, Estonia

>Class here Baltic States

.93   *Lithuania

.930 6   Period of union with Poland, 1569–1795

.930 7–.930 8   †1795–

.96   *Latvia

.960 5–.960 6   1721–1796

>Add to base number 947.960 the numbers following 947.0 in 947.05–947.06, e.g., reign of Peter I 947.9605

.960 7–.960 8   †1796–

.98   *Estonia

.980 5–.980 6   1721–1796

>Add to base number 947.980 the numbers following 947.0 in 947.05–947.06, e.g., reign of Peter I 947.9805

.980 7–.980 8   †1796–

948   *Scandinavia

>Class here northern Europe

SUMMARY

948.01–.08	**Historical periods**
.1	**Norway**
.2	**Southeastern Norway (Østlandet)**
.3	**Southwestern Norway (Sørlandet and Vestlandet)**
.4	**Central and northern Norway (Trødelag and Nord-Norge)**
.5	**Sweden**
.6	**Southern Sweden (Götland)**
.7	**Central Sweden (Svealand)**
.8	**Northern Sweden (Norrland)**
.9	**Denmark and Finland**

*Add as instructed under 930–990

†Add historical periods as instructed under 947.5–947.9

>	948.01–948.08 Historical periods
	Class comprehensive works in 948
.01	Early history to 800
	For ancient history to 481, see 936.3
(.012)	Ancient history to 481
	(Optional number; prefer 936.3)
.02	Period of migration and conquest, 800–1387
	Class here medieval period
	For 1387–1523, see 948.03
.022	Viking period, 800–1066
.023	1066–1387
.03	1387–1523
	Class here period of Union of Kalmar, 1397–1523
.04	Period of reformation and rise of Sweden, 1523–1648
.05	Period of conflict, 1648–1792
	(Option: Class here Great Northern War; prefer 947.05)
.06	1792–1814
.07	1814–1905
.08	1905–1999
.081	1905–1919
.082	1920–1929
.083	1930–1939
.084	1940–1949
.084 2	Period of World War II, 1940–1945
.084 3	1945–1949
.085	1950–1959
.086	1960–1969
.087	1970–1979
.088	1980–1989
.089	1990–1999

.09	2000–

.1 *Norway

> *For southeastern Norway, see 948.2; for southwestern Norway, see 948.3; for central and northern Norway, see 948.4*

.101 Early history to 1387

> Class here medieval period
>
> *For ancient history to 481, see 936.3*

(.101 2) Ancient history to 481

> (Optional number; prefer 936.3)

.101 4 Viking period, ca. 800–ca. 1050

.102 Period of union with Denmark, 1387–1814

> Including period of Union of Kalmar, 1397–1523

.103 Period of union with Sweden, 1814–1905

.103 1 1814–1884

.103 6 1884–1905

.104 1905–1999

.104 1 1905–1945

.104 5 1945–1959

.104 6 1960–1969

.104 7 1970–1979

.104 8 1980–1989

.104 9 1990–1999

.105 2000–

.2 *Southeastern Norway (Østlandet)

.201–.205 Historical periods

> Add to base number 948.2 the numbers following 948.1 in 948.101–948.105, e.g., Viking period 948.2014

.3 *Southwestern Norway (Sørlandet and Vestlandet)

.301–.305 Historical periods

> Add to base number 948.3 the numbers following 948.1 in 948.101–948.105, e.g., Viking period 948.3014

.4 *Central and northern Norway (Trøndelag and Nord-Norge)

*Add as instructed under 930–990

.401–.405	Historical periods	

Add to base number 948.4 the numbers following 948.1 in 948.101–948.105, e.g., Viking period 948.4014

.5   ***Sweden**

For southern Sweden, see 948.6; for central Sweden, see 948.7; for northern Sweden, see 948.8

.501   Early history to 1523

Class here medieval period

For ancient history to 481, see 936.3

(.501 2)   Ancient history to 481

(Optional number; prefer 936.3)

.501 4   Viking period, ca. 800–ca. 1060

.501 8   Period of Union of Kalmar, 1397–1523

.502   Period of House of Vasa, 1523–1654

(Option: Class here Livonian War; prefer 947.043)

.503   1654–1818

(Option: Class here Great Northern War; prefer 947.05)

.504   1818–1905

.505   1905–1999

.505 1   1905–1945

.505 5   1945–1959

.505 6   1960–1969

.505 7   1970–1979

.505 8   1980–1989

.505 9   1990–1999

.506   2000–

.6   ***Southern Sweden (Götland)**

.601–.606   Historical periods

Add to base number 948.6 the numbers following 948.5 in 948.501–948.506, e.g., period of House of Vasa 948.602

.7   ***Central Sweden (Svealand)**

**Add as instructed under 930–990

.701–.706	Historical periods

Add to base number 948.7 the numbers following 948.5 in 948.501–948.506, e.g., period of House of Vasa 948.702

.8 *Northern Sweden (Norrland)

.801–.806	Historical periods

Add to base number 948.8 the numbers following 948.5 in 948.501–948.506, e.g., period of House of Vasa 948.802

.9 Denmark and Finland

.900 1–.900 9	Standard subdivisions of Denmark

As modified under 930–990

> 948.901–948.906 Historical periods of Denmark

Class comprehensive works in 948.9

.901	Early history to 1387

Class here medieval period

For ancient history to 481, see 936.3; for 1387–1523, see 948.902

(.901 2)	Ancient history to 481

(Optional number; prefer 936.3)

.901 3	481–ca. 800
.901 4	Viking period, ca. 800–1047
.901 5	1047–1387

Class here period of Estrith dynasty, 1047–1448

For 1387–1448, see 948.902

.902	Period of union with Norway and Sweden, 1387–1523

Class here period of Union of Kalmar, 1397–1523

.903	Period of union with Norway, 1523–1814

For Great Northern War, see 947.05

.904	1814–1906

(Option: Class here Schleswig-Holstein War; prefer 943.076)

.905	1906–1999
.905 1	1906–1945
.905 5	1945–1959

*Add as instructed under 930–990

.905 6		1960–1969
.905 7		1970–1979
.905 8		1980–1989
.905 9		1990–1999
.906		2000–
.97	*Finland	
.970 1		Early history to end of Swedish rule, 1809

For Great Northern War, see 947.05

.970 2		Period of Russian rule, 1809–1917
.970 3		1917–
.970 31		1917–1939
.970 32		1939–1945

Including Russo-Finnish War, 1939–1940
(Option: Class Russo-Finnish War in 947.0842)

.970 33		1945–1982
.970 34		1982–

949   Other parts of Europe

SUMMARY

.1   *Northwestern islands

.12	*Iceland	
.120 1		Early history to 1262
.120 2		Medieval period, 1262–1550
.120 3		1550–1848
.120 4		Modern period, 1848–1940

Including independence under Danish crown, 1918–1944

For 1940–1944, see 949.1205

*Add as instructed under 930–990

.120 5	1940–
	Class here 20th century; period of Republic, 1944–
	For 1900–1940, see 949.1204
.15	†Faeroes

.2 *Netherlands (Holland)

Class here comprehensive works on Low Countries, on Benelux countries

.201	Early history to 1477
	For ancient history to 481, see 936.3
(.201 2)	Ancient history to 481
	(Optional number; prefer 936.3)
.202	Period of House of Hapsburg, 1477–1568
.203	Period of struggle for independence, 1568–1648
.204	Period of Dutch Republic, 1648–1795
	Including Anglo-Dutch Wars, 1652–1653, 1665–1667; Great Wars against England, France, and allies, 1672–1678; Coalition War, 1690–1697
	(Option: Class Anglo-Dutch Wars in 941.06)
.205	1795–1830
	Including Batavian Republic, 1795–1806; Kingdom of Holland, 1806–1813
	Class here Napoleonic era
.206	1830–1901
	Class here 19th century
	For 1800–1830, see 949.205
.207	1901–
.207 1	Reign of Wilhelmina, 1890–1948
	For reign of Wilhelmina during 1890–1901, see 949.206
.207 2	Reign of Juliana, 1948–1980
.207 3	Reign of Beatrix, 1980–

.3 Southern Low Countries   Belgium

[.300 01–.300 09]	Standard subdivisions of southern Low Countries
	Relocated to 949.3001–949.3009

*Add as instructed under 930–990

†Add as instructed under 930–990; however, do not add historical periods

.300 1–.300 9	Standard subdivisions of southern Low Countries [*formerly* 949.30001–949.30009], of Belgium
	As modified under 930–990
.301	Early history to 1477
	For ancient history to 486, see 936.4
(.301 2)	Ancient history to 486
	(Optional number; prefer 936.4)
.302	Period of foreign rule, 1477–1830
.303	1830–1909
	Class here 19th century
	For 1800–1830, see 949.302
.304	1909–
.304 1	Reign of Albert I, 1909–1934
.304 2	Reign of Léopold III, 1934–1951
.304 3	Reign of Baudouin I, 1951–1993
.304 4	Reign of Albert II, 1993–
.35	*Luxembourg
.350 1	Early history to 1482
	For ancient history to 486, see 936.4
(.350 12)	Ancient history to 486
	(Option: Class here ancient history; prefer 936.4)
.350 2	Period of foreign rule, 1482–1830
.350 3	1830–1890
	Class here 19th century
	For 1800–1830, see 949.3502; for 1890–1899, see 949.35041
.350 4	1890–
.350 41	1890–1918
.350 42	1918–1945
.350 43	1945–1999
	Class here 20th century
	For 1900–1918, see 949.35041; for 1918–1945, see 949.35042
.350 44	2000–

*Add as instructed under 930–990

.4	***Switzerland**
.401	Early history to 1291

For ancient history to 486, see 936.4

(.401 2)	Ancient history to 486

(Optional number; prefer 936.4)

.402	1291–1499
.403	1499–1648
.404	1648–1798
.405	Napoleonic period, 1798–1815

Class here Helvetic Republic, 1798–1803

.406	1815–1900
.406 2	Period of restoration, 1815–1848
.406 3	1848–1900
.407	1900–
.407 1	1900–1918
.407 2	1918–1945
.407 3	1945–1999

Class here 20th century

For 1900–1918, see 949.4071; for 1918–1945, see 949.4072

.407 4	2000–
.5	***Greece**
.501	Early history to 717

For ancient history to 323, see 938

(.501 2)	Ancient history to 323

(Optional number; prefer 938)

Add to base number 949.5012 the numbers following 938.0 in 938.01–938.09, e.g., Persian Wars 949.50123

.501 3	Early Byzantine period, 323–717

Including wars against Avars and Persians

Class here Eastern Roman (Byzantine) Empire, 323–717

*Add as instructed under 930–990

.502   Middle Byzantine period, 717–1081

    Including 1057–1081 [*formerly* 949.503]

    Class here comprehensive works on Byzantine Empire

    For early Byzantine period, see 949.5013; for late Byzantine period, see 949.503. For a specific part of Byzantine Empire, see the part, e.g., Byzantine Empire in Egypt 932.023

.503   Late Byzantine period, 1081–1204

    1057–1081 relocated to 949.502

.504   Period of Latin and Greek states and Turkish conquest, 1204–1453

.505   Period of Turkish domination, 1453–1821

.506   War of Independence, 1821–1830

    1830–1833 relocated to 949.507; period of monarchy, 1833–1924 relocated to 949.5072

.507   1830–

    Including 1830–1833 [*formerly* 949.506]

.507 2   Period of monarchy, 1833–1924 [*formerly* 949.506]

    Including Greco-Turkish War, 1896–1897
    (Option: Class Greco-Turkish War in 956.1015)

    For Balkan Wars, see 949.6

.507 3   Period of Republic, 1924–1935

.507 4   The period of the restoration of the monarchy, 1935–1967

.507 5   Period of military junta, 1967–1974

.507 6   Period of restoration of democratic rule, 1974–

.58   *Former Aegean Islands region (Aigaio Nēsoi periphereia)

    Class here comprehensive works on Aegean Islands [*formerly* 949.9]; Sporades

.580 1   Early history to 717

    For ancient history to 323, see 939.1

(.580 12)   Ancient history to 323

    (Optional number; prefer 939.1)

    Add to base number 949.58012 the numbers following 938.0 in 938.01–938.09, e.g., mythical age to 775 B.C. 949.580121

.59   *Crete region (Krētē periphereia) [*formerly* 949.98]

---

*Add as instructed under 930–990

.590 1	Early history to 827
	For ancient history to 323, see 939.18
(.590 12)	Ancient history to 323
	(Optional number; prefer 939.18)
	Add to base number 949.59012 the numbers following 938.0 in 938.01–938.09, e.g., mythical age to 775 B.C. 949.590121
.590 13	First Byzantine period, 323–827
.590 2	Period of Arab rule, 827–961
.590 3	Second Byzantine period, 961–1206
.590 4	Period of Venetian rule, 1206–1669
.590 5	Period of Turkish domination, 1669–1898
.590 6	Period of autonomy, 1898–1913
.590 7	1913–
.590 72	Period of incorporation into Greece, 1913–1924
.590 73–.590 76	1924–
	Add to base number 949.5907 the numbers following 949.507 in 949.5073–949.5076, e.g., restoration of monarchy 949.59074

.6   *Balkan Peninsula

Including Balkan Wars, 1912–1913

.61   *Turkey in Europe (Turkish Thrace)

.610 1	History to 1918
.610 11–.610 14	Early history to 1453
	Add to base number 949.6101 the numbers following 949.50 in 949.501–949.504, e.g., period of Byzantine prosperity, 717–1081 949.61012
	For ancient history to 323, see 939.8
.610 15	1453–1918
	Class here period of Ottoman empire, 1453–1922
	For 1918–1922, see 949.61023
.610 2–.610 4	1918–
	Add to base number 949.61 the numbers following 956.1 in 956.102–956.104, e.g., 1918–1923 949.61023

.65   *Albania

*Add as instructed under 930–990

.650 1	Early history to 1912
	For ancient history to 323, see 939.8
(.650 12)	Ancient history to 323
	(Optional number; prefer 939.8)
.650 2	1912–1946
.650 3	1946–1992
	Class here period of People's Republic, 1946–1991
.650 4	1992–

.7   *Yugoslavia, Croatia, Slovenia, Bosnia and Hercegovina, Macedonia

.701	Early history to 1918
	For ancient history to ca. 640, see 939.8; for Balkan Wars, see 949.6
(.701 2)	Ancient history to ca. 640
	(Optional number; prefer 939.8)
.702	Yugoslavia, 1918–1991
.702 1	Period of Kingdom, 1918–1939
	Class 1939–1941 in 949.7022
.702 2	Period of World War II, 1939–1945
.702 3	Administration of Josip Broz Tito, 1945–1980
.702 4	1980–1991
.703	Period of five sovereign nations, 1991–
	See also 949.7103 for Yugoslavia (1991–)

.71   *Serbia

.710 1	Early history to 1918
	For ancient history to ca. 640, see 939.8
(.710 11)	Ancient history to ca. 640
	(Optional number; prefer 939.8)
.710 12	Ca. 640–1389
.710 13	Turkish period, 1389–1878
	For 1804–1878, see 949.71014
.710 14	Period of revolt and autonomy, 1804–1878
.710 15	Period of independence, 1878–1918

*Add as instructed under 930–990

.710 2   1918–1991

             Add to base number 949.7102 the numbers following 949.702 in 949.7021–949.7024, e.g., period of World War II 949.71022

.710 3   1991–

             Class here Yugoslavia (1991–   )

             For Montenegro, see 949.745

             See also 949.702 for Yugoslavia (1918–1991)

[.77]   Bulgaria

           Relocated to 949.9

.8   ***Romania**

.801   Early history to 1861

             For ancient history to ca. 640, see 939.8

(.801 2)   Ancient history to ca. 640

             (Optional number; prefer 939.8)

.801 3   Ca. 640–1250

.801 4   Period of Wallachia and Moldavia principalities, 1250–ca. 1500

.801 5   Turkish period, ca. 1500–1821

             Including reign of Michael the Brave, 1593–1601; Phanarist period, 1711–1821

.801 6   1821–1861

.802   Period of monarchy, 1861–1947

             Class here period of Kingdom, 1881–1947; 20th century

             For Balkan Wars, see 949.6; for 1947–1999, see 949.803

.803   1947–

.803 1   Period of People's Republic, 1947–1989

.803 2   1989–

.83   *Black Sea area

             For ancient Scythia, see 939.51

.9   ***Bulgaria [*formerly* 949.77]**

           Aegean Islands relocated to 949.58

.901   Early history to 1878

             For ancient history to ca. 640, see 939.8

---

*Add as instructed under 930–990

(.901 2)	Ancient history to ca. 640
	(Optional number; prefer 939.8)
.901 3	Ca. 640–1018
	Class here First Bulgarian Empire, ca. 680–1014
.901 4	Period of Byzantine rule and Second Bulgarian Empire, 1018–1396
.901 5	Turkish period, 1396–1878
.902	1878–1946
	Class here 20th century
	For 1946–1999, see 949.903
.902 2	1878–1918
	For Balkan Wars, see 949.6
.902 3	1918–1946
.903	1946–
.903 1	Period of People's Republic, 1946–1991
.903 2	1991–
.98	*Sofia region (Sofiĭska oblast)
	Crete region (Krētē periphereia) relocated to 949.59

950   General history of Asia   Orient   Far East

SUMMARY

.01–.09	Standard subdivisions
	As modified under 930–990

.1   Early history to 1162

.2   Period of Mongol and Tatar Empires, 1162–1480

Including reigns of Genghis Khan, ca. 1200–1227; Kublai Khan, ca. 1259–1294; Timur (Tamerlane), ca. 1336–1405

---

*Add as instructed under 930–990

.3	**Period of European exploration and penetration, 1480–1905**
.4	**1905–**
.41	1905–1945
.42	1945–1999
.424	1945–1949
.425	1950–1959
.426	1960–1969
.427	1970–1979
.428	1980–1989
.429	1990–1999
.43	2000–

951 China and adjacent areas

[.000 1–.000 9] Standard subdivisions of China and adjacent areas

Relocated to 951.001–951.009

.001–.009 Standard subdivisions of China and adjacent areas [*formerly* 951.0001–951.0009], of China alone

As modified under 930–990

.01 Early history to 960

For ancient history to 420, see 931

(.011–.014) Ancient history to 420

(Optional numbers; prefer 931)

Add to base number 951.01 the numbers following 931.0 in 931.01–931.04, e.g., Shang dynasty 951.012

.015 Period of Northern and Southern dynasties, 420–581

.016 Period of Sui dynasty, 581–618

.017 Period of T'ang dynasty, 618–907

.018 Period of Five dynasties and Ten kingdoms, 907–960

.02 960–1644

.024 Period of Sung dynasty, 960–1279

.025 Period of Yüan (Mongol) dynasty, 1271–1368

For period of Yüan dynasty during 1271–1279, see 951.024

.026   Period of Ming dynasty, 1368–1644

.03   Period of Ch'ing (Manchu) dynasty, 1644–1912

.032   1644–1795

.033   1796–1850

> Including Opium War, 1840–1842
>
> Class here 19th century
>
> *For 1850–1864, see 951.034; for 1864–1899, see 951.035*

.034   Period of Taiping Rebellion, 1850–1864

.035   1864–1911

> Including Sino-Japanese War, 1894–1895 [*formerly* 952.031]; Boxer
> Rebellion, 1899–1901
>   (Option: Class Sino-Japanese War in 952.031)

.036   Period of Revolution of 1911–1912

.04   Period of Republic, 1912–1949

.041   1912–1927

.042   Period of nationalist government, 1927–1949

> Including Sino-Japanese Conflict during 1937–1941
>   (Option: Class Sino-Japanese Conflict during 1937–1941 in 952.033)
>
> Class comprehensive works on Sino-Japanese Conflict, 1937–1945, in
> 940.53

.05   Period of People's Republic, 1949–

> Class here 20th century
>
> *For 2000 and beyond, see 951.06. For a specific part of 20th century not
> provided for here, see the part, e.g., Revolution of 1911–1912 951.036*

.055   1949–1959

.056   1960–1969

> Including Cultural Revolution

.057   1970–1979

.058   1980–1989

.059   1990–1999

.06   2000–

.2   *Southeastern China and adjacent areas

.24   *East China Sea area

*Add as instructed under 930–990

.249	*Taiwan (Formosa) and adjacent islands
.249 02	Early history to 1683
	For ancient history to 420, see 931
.249 03	Chinese period, 1683–1895
.249 04	Japanese period, 1895–1945
.249 05	Period of Republic of China (Nationalist China), 1945–
.25	*Hong Kong
.250 1–.250 3	Chinese period to 1843
	Add to base number 951.250 the numbers following 951.0 in 951.01–951.03, e.g., period of Ming dynasty 951.25026
.250 4	Period as a British dependency, 1843–
	For 1945 to present, see 951.2505
.250 5	1945–
.26	†Macao
	For ancient history to 420, see 931

.7   *Mongolia

.73   †Outer Mongolia (Mongolian People's Republic)

.9   *Korea

.901	Early history to 1392
.902	Period of Yi dynasty, 1392–1910
.903	Japanese period, 1910–1945
.904	1945–
.904 1	1945–1950
.904 2	‡Korean War, 1950–1953
.904 3	1953–
.93	*North Korea (People's Democratic Republic of Korea)
.930 43	1953–

Class here administration of Kim Il-sŏng, 1948–1994

For administration of Kim Il-sŏng during 1948–1950, see 951.93041; for administration of Kim Il-sŏng during 1950–1953, see 951.93042

---

*Add as instructed under 930–990
†Add as instructed under 930–990; however, do not add historical periods
‡Add as instructed under 940–990

.95	*South Korea (Republic of Korea)

952   *Japan

.01	Early history to 1185
.02	Feudal period, 1185–1868

Class here chūsei period

.021	Kamakura period, 1185–1334
.022	Namboku period, 1334–1392
.023	Muromachi period, 1392–1573
.024	Momoyama period, 1573–1603
.025	Tokugawa (Edo) period, 1603–1868

Class here kinsei period

.03	1868–1945
.031	Meiji period, 1868–1912

Including Russo-Japanese War, 1904–1905
(Option: Class Russo-Japanese War in 947.083)

Sino-Japanese War relocated to 951.035

(Option: Class here Sino-Japanese War, 1894–1895; prefer 951.035)

.032	Taishō period, 1912–1926
.033	Shōwa period, 1926–1989

Class here 20th century

For Shōwa period during 1945–1989, see 952.04. For a specific part of 20th century not provided for here, see the part, e.g., Russo-Japanese War, 1904–1905 952.031

(Option: Class here Sino-Japanese Conflict, 1937–1941; prefer 951.042)

.04	1945–1999
.044	1945–1949
.045	1950–1959
.046	1960–1969
.047	1970–1979
.048	1980–1989

*Add as instructed under 930–990

.049	1990–1999

Class here Heisei period, 1989 to present

For Heisei period in 1989, see 952.048; for 2000 and beyond, see 952.05

.05	2000–

953   *Arabian Peninsula and adjacent areas

For ancient history to 622, see 939.49

(.01)	Ancient history to 622

(Optional number; prefer 939.49)

.02	622–1517
.03	Period of Ottoman Empire, 1517–1740

Class period of struggles to overthrow Turks in 953.04

.04	1740–1926

Class here period of struggles to overthrow Turks, 1740–1918

.05	1926–
.052	1926–1964
.053	1964–

.1   *Sinai Peninsula

.101–.105	Historical periods

Add to base number 953.1 the numbers following 962 in 962.01–962.05, e.g., period of Ottoman Empire 953.103

For ancient history to 622, see 939.48

.3   *Yemen

For ancient history to 622, see 939.49

.305	1918–
.305 3	Period as Republic of Yemen, 1990–
.32	*Northern Yemen

For ancient history to 622, see 939.49

.320 5	1918–

Including Yemen Arab Republic, 1962–1990

.320 53	Period as part of Republic of Yemen, 1990–

*Add as instructed under 930–990

.35	*Southern Yemen

For ancient history to 622, see 939.49

.350 5	1967–

Including People's Democratic Republic of Yemen, 1970–1990

.350 53	Period as part of Republic of Yemen, 1990–

.5   †Oman and United Arab Emirates

For ancient history to 622, see 939.49

.53	†Oman

For ancient history to 622, see 939.49

.57	†United Arab Emirates

For ancient history to 622, see 939.49

.6   †Persian Gulf States

For ancient history to 622, see 939.49; for Oman and United Arab Emirates, see 953.5

.63	†Qatar

For ancient history to 622, see 939.49

.65	†Bahrain

For ancient history to 622, see 939.49

.67	†Kuwait

For ancient history to 622, see 939.49

(Option: Class here Gulf Crisis and War, 1990–1991; prefer 956.70442)

.8   *Saudi Arabia

For ancient history to 622, see 939.49

.805 3	1964–

Class military operations in Saudia Arabia during Gulf Crisis and War, 1990–1991, in 956.704424

954   *South Asia   India

For ancient history of India to 647, see 934

SUMMARY

954.02	647–1785
.03	**Period of British rule, 1785–1947**
.04	1947–1971
.05	1971–

*Add as instructed under 930–990

†Add as instructed under 930–990; however, do not add historical periods

(.01)	Ancient history to 647
	(Optional number; prefer 934)

Add to base number 954.01 the numbers following 934.0 in 934.01–934.07, e.g., reign of Aśoka 954.0145

.02	647–1785
.021	647–997
.022	Period of Muslim conquests, 997–1206
.022 3	Period of Ghazni dynasty, 997–1196
.022 5	Period of Ghor dynasty, 1196–1206
.023	1206–1414
.023 2	Period of slave kings of Delhi, 1206–1290
.023 4	Period of Khalji dynasty, 1290–1320
.023 6	Period of Tughluk dynasty, 1320–1414
.024	1414–1526
.024 2	Period of Sayyid dynasty, 1414–1451
.024 5	Period of Lodi dynasty, 1451–1526
.025	Period of Mogul Empire, 1526–1707
.025 2	Reign of Babur, 1526–1530
.025 3	Reign of Humayun, 1530–1556
.025 4	Reign of Akbar, 1556–1605
.025 6	Reign of Jahangir, 1605–1627
.025 7	Reign of Shahjahan, 1628–1658
.025 8	Reign of Aurangzeb, 1658–1707
.029	Period of European penetration, 1707–1785
.029 2	1707–1744
.029 4	Period of Anglo-French conflict, 1744–1757
	Including Battle of Plassey, 1757
.029 6	1757–1772
	Including governorship of Lord Clive, 1757–1767
.029 8	Governorship of Warren Hastings, 1772–1785
.03	Period of British rule, 1785–1947

For governorship of Lord Clive, see 954.0296; for governorship of Warren Hastings, see 954.0298

.031   Period of East India Company, 1785–1858

.031 1   Governorships of Sir John Macpherson, Marquis Cornwallis (first term), John Shore (Lord Teignmouth), 1785–1798

.031 2   Governorships of Marquess Wellesley, Marquess Cornwallis (second term), Sir George Barlow, 1798–1807

.031 3   Governorships of 1st Earl of Minto, Marquess of Hastings, Earl Amherst, 1807–1828

.031 4   Governorships of Lord Bentinck, Baron Metcalfe, Earl of Auckland, 1828–1842

.031 5   Governorships of Earl of Ellenborough and Viscount Hardinge, 1842–1848

.031 6   Governorship of Marquis of Dalhousie, 1848–1856

.031 7   Governorship of Earl Canning, 1856–1862

         Including Sepoy Mutiny, 1857–1858

         For governorship of Earl Canning during 1858–1862, see 954.0351

.035   Period of control by crown, 1858–1947

         Class here period of Indian national movement, 1885–1947; 20th century

         For 1947–1971, see 954.04; for 1971–1999, see 954.05

.035 1   Governorships of Earl Canning, 8th Earl of Elgin, Baron Lawrence, 1858–1868

.035 2   Governorships of Earl of Mayo and Earl of Northbrook, 1869–1876

.035 3   Governorships of Earl of Lytton and Marquess of Ripon, 1876–1884

.035 4   Governorships of Marquis of Dufferin and Marquess of Lansdowne, 1884–1894

.035 5   Governorships of 9th Earl of Elgin and Marquis of Curzon, 1894–1905

.035 6   Governorships of 4th Earl of Minto and Baron Hardinge, 1905–1916

.035 7   Governorships of Viscount Chelmsford and Marquess of Reading, 1916–1926

.035 8   Governorships of Earl of Halifax and Marquess of Willingdon, 1926–1936

.035 9   Governorships of Marquess of Linlithgow, Earl of Wavell, Earl Mountbatten, 1936–1947

.04   1947–1971

.042   Prime ministership of Jawaharlal Nehru, 1947–1964

| .043 | Prime ministership of Lal Bahadur Shastri, 1964–1966 |

(Option: Class here Indo-Pakistan War, 1965; prefer 954.9045)

| .045 | First prime ministership of Indira Gandhi, 1966–1977 |

For first prime ministership of Indira Gandhi during 1971–1977, see 954.051

| .05 | 1971– |

| .051 | Later half of first prime ministership of Indira Gandhi, 1971–1977 |

(Option: Class here Indo-Pakistan War, 1971; prefer 954.92051)

| .052 | 1977– |

Including prime ministerships of Morarji Desai, 1977–1979; of Charan Singh, 1979; of Rajiv Gandhi, 1984–1989; of Vishwanath Pratap Singh, 1989–1990; of Chandra Shekhar, 1990–1991; of P. V. Narasimha Rao, 1991 to present; second prime ministership of Indira Gandhi, 1980–1984

.9 **Other jurisdictions**

Class here Pakistan (West and East, 1947–1971)

| .900 1–.900 9 | Standard subdivisions of Pakistan (West and East, 1947–1971) |

As modified under 930–990

| (.901) | Ancient history of Pakistan (West and East, 1947–1971) to 647 |

(Optional number; prefer 934)

Add to base number 954.901 the numbers following 934.0 in 934.01–934.07, e.g., reign of Aśoka 954.90145

> 954.902–954.905 Historical periods of Pakistan (West and East, 1947–1971)

Class comprehensive works in 954.9

For ancient history to 647, see 934

(Option: Class early history to 647 in 954.901; prefer 934)

| .902–.903 | 647–1947 |

Add to base number 954.90 the numbers following 954.0 in 954.02–954.03, e.g., period of East India Company 954.9031

| .904 | 1947–1971 |

| .904 2 | Administration of Mahomed Ali Jinnah, 1947–1948 |

| .904 3 | 1948–1958 |

.904 5	Administration of Mohammad Ayub Khan, 1958–1969

      Including Indo-Pakistan War, 1965
       (Option: Class Indo-Pakistan War, 1965, in 954.043)

.904 6	Administration of Aga Muhammad Yahya Khan, 1969–1971
.905	1971–
.91	*Pakistan
.910 5	1971–

      For Indo-Pakistan War, 1971, see 954.9205

.92	*Bangladesh
.920 5	1971–
.920 51	‡Indo-Pakistan War, 1971

      (Option: Class Indo-Pakistan War, 1971, in 954.051)

.93	*Sri Lanka
.930 1	Early history to 1795
.930 2	British period, 1795–1948
.930 3	1948–
.930 31	Period as independent Commonwealth state, 1948–1972
.930 32	Period as republic, 1972–
.95	†Maldives
.96	†Nepal
.98	†Bhutan

955 *Iran

   For ancient history to 637, see 935

(.01)	Early history to 637

    (Optional number; prefer 935)

    Add to base number 955.01 the numbers following 935.0 in 935.01–935.07, e.g., period of Sassanian Empire 955.017

.02	Period of Arab, Turkish, Mongol, Turkoman domination, 637–1499
.03	Period of Persian dynasties, 1499–1794
.04	1794–1906
.05	1906–

*Add as instructed under 930–990

†Add as instructed under 930–990; however, do not add historical periods

‡Add as instructed under 940–990

.051	1906–1925
.052	Reign of Reza Shah Pahlavi, 1925–1941
.053	Reign of Mohammed Reza Pahlavi, 1941–1979
.054	1979–
.054 2	‡Iraqi-Iranian Conflict, 1980–1988

Class here period of Ruhollah Khomeini

(Option: Class in 956.70441)

.054 3	1988–

956 *Middle East (Near East)

SUMMARY

956.01–.05	**[Historical periods]**
.1	**Turkey**
.2	**Western Turkey**
.3	**North central Turkey**
.4	**South central Turkey**
.5	**East central Turkey**
.6	**Eastern Turkey**
.7	**Iraq**
.9	**Syria, Lebanon, Cyprus, Israel, Jordan**

.01	Early history to 1900

For ancient history to ca. 640, see 939.4

(.012)	Ancient history to ca. 640

(Optional number; prefer 939.4)

.013	640–1000
.014	Period of Seljuk supremacy, 1000–1300
.015	1300–1900

Class here Ottoman Empire, ca. 1300–1922

For 1900–1918, see 956.02; for 1918–1922, see 956.03. For a specific part of the Ottoman Empire, see the part, e.g., Ottoman Empire in Turkey 956.1015

.02	1900–1918
.03	1918–1945

*Add as instructed under 930–990

‡Add as instructed under 940–990

.04	1945–1980

         Class here 20th century

         For 1900–1918, see 956.02; for 1918–1945, see 956.03; for 1980–1999, see 956.05

.042	Israel-Arab War, 1948–1949
.044	Sinai Campaign, 1956
.046	Israel-Arab War, 1967 (Six Days' War)
.048	Israel-Arab War, 1973 (Yom Kippur War)
.05	1980–
.052	Israel-Lebanon-Syria Conflict, 1982–1985
.053	1985–1999
.054	2000–
.1	***Turkey**

         For divisions of Turkey, see 956.2–956.6

.101	Early history to 1918

         For ancient history to ca. 640, see 939.2

(.101 2)	Ancient history to ca. 640

         (Optional number; prefer 939.2)

.101 3	640–1100
.101 4	Period of Seljuk dynasty, 1100–1300
.101 5	1300–1918

         Class here period of Ottoman Empire, 1300–1922

         For 1918–1922, see 956.1023

         (Option: Class here Russo-Turkish War of 1877–1878, Greco-Turkish War; prefer 947.081 for Russo-Turkish War of 1877–1878, 949.5072 for Greco-Turkish War)

.102	1918–1950

         Class here 20th century; Republic, 1923 to present

         For 1900–1918, see 956.1015; for 1950–1999, see 956.103

.102 3	1918–1923
.102 4	Administration of Kemal Atatürk, 1923–1938
.102 5	Administration of İsmet İnönü, 1938–1950

*Add as instructed under 930–990

.103	1950–1999
.103 5	1950–1959
.103 6	1960–1969
.103 7	1970–1979
.103 8	1980–1989
.103 9	1990–1999
.104	2000–

> ### 956.2–956.6 Divisions of Turkey

Class comprehensive works in 956.1

For Turkey in Europe, see 949.61

.2   *Western Turkey

.201–.204   Historical periods

> Add to base number 956.2 the numbers following 956.1 in 956.101–956.104, e.g., period of Ottoman Empire 956.2015
>
> *For ancient history to ca. 640, see 939.2*

.3   *North central Turkey

.301–.304   Historical periods

> Add to base number 956.3 the numbers following 956.1 in 956.101–956.104, e.g., period of Ottoman Empire 956.3015
>
> *For ancient Bithynia to ca. 640, see 939.25; for ancient Paphlagonia to ca. 640, see 939.31; for ancient Galatia to ca. 640, see 939.32*

.4   *South central Turkey

.401–.404   Historical periods

> Add to base number 956.4 the numbers following 956.1 in 956.101–956.104, e.g., period of Ottoman Empire 956.4015
>
> *For ancient Pisidia to ca. 640, see 939.27; for ancient Lycia to ca. 640, see 939.28; for ancient Pamphylia to ca. 640, see 939.29; for ancient Cappadocia to ca. 640, see 939.34; for ancient Cilicia to ca. 640, see 939.35; for ancient Commagene to ca. 640, see 939.36; for ancient Antioch to ca. 640, see 939.43*

[.45]   Cyprus

> Relocated to 956.93

.5   *East central Turkey

*Add as instructed under 930–990

.501–.504   Historical periods

> Add to base number 956.5 the numbers following 956.1 in 956.101–956.104, e.g., period of Ottoman Empire 956.5015

> *For ancient history to ca. 640, see 939.33*

.6   *Eastern Turkey

.601–.604   Historical periods

> Add to base number 956.6 the numbers following 956.1 in 956.101–956.104, e.g., period of Ottoman Empire 956.6015

> *For ancient Armenia to ca. 640, see 939.55*

.7   *Iraq

> *For ancient history to 637, see 935*

(.701)   Ancient history to 637

> (Optional number; prefer 935 for Mesopotamia, 939.47 for Arabia Deserta)

> Add to base number 956.701 the numbers following 935.0 in 935.01–935.07, e.g., Hellenistic period 956.7016

.702   637–1553

.703   Period of Ottoman Empire, 1553–1920

.704   1920–

.704 1   Period of mandate, 1920–1932

> Class here reign of Faysal I, 1921–1933

> *For reign of Faysal I during 1932–1933, see 956.7042*

.704 2   Period of independent monarchy, 1932–1958

> Including reigns of Ghazi I, Faisal II

.704 3   Period of Republic, 1958–

> *For administration of Saddam Hussein, see 956.7044*

.704 4   Administration of Saddam Hussein, 1979–

.704 41   1979–1990

> (Option: Class here Iraqi-Iranian Conflict, 1980–1988; prefer 955.0542)

.704 42   ‡Gulf Crisis and War, 1990–1991

> Class here Iraq-Kuwait Crisis, 1990–1991, Persian Gulf War, 1991

> (Option: Class in 953.67)

---

*Add as instructed under 930–990

‡Add as instructed under 940–990

.704 423 1	Participation of specific groups of countries
	Number built according to instructions under 940–990
	For participation of specific countries, see 956.7044234–956.7044239
.704 423 12	Participation of Arab countries
.704 43	1991–

.9   ***Syria, Lebanon, Cyprus, Israel, Jordan**

.91   *Syria

For early history to ca. 640, see 939.43

(.910 1)	Early history to ca. 640
	(Optional number; prefer 939.43)
.910 2	640–1516
.910 3	Period of Ottoman Empire, 1516–1920
.910 4	1920–
.910 41	Period of mandate, 1920–1945
.910 42	Period of Republic, 1945–

Including period as a part of United Arab Republic, 1958–1961

Class Israel-Arab War, 1948–1949, in 956.042; class Israel-Arab War, 1967, in 956.046; class Israel-Arab War, 1973, in 956.048; class Israel-Lebanon-Syria Conflict, 1982–1985, in 956.052; class comprehensive works on United Arab Republic in 962.053

.92   *Lebanon

For early history to ca. 640, see 939.44

(.920 2)	Early history to ca. 640
	(Optional number; prefer 939.44)
.920 3	640–1926
.920 32	640–1517
.920 34	Period of Ottoman Empire, 1517–1920
	Including period of autonomy, 1861–1918
.920 35	Period of mandate, 1920–1941
	For 1926–1941, see 956.92042
.920 4	1926–
.920 42	1926–1941

*Add as instructed under 930–990

.920 43	1941–
	Class Israel-Arab War, 1948–1949, in 956.042
	For 1975 to present, see 956.92044
.920 44	Period of civil war and religious strife, 1975–
	Class Israel-Lebanon-Syria Conflict, 1982–1985, in 956.052
.93	*Cyprus [*formerly* 956.45]
.930 1	Early history to 1571
	For ancient history to ca. 640, see 939.37
(.930 12)	Ancient history to ca. 640
	(Optional number; prefer 939.37)
.930 2	1571–1878
.930 3	British period, 1878–1960
.930 4	1960–
.94	*Palestine Israel
	For early history to 70, see 933
	See also 320.54095694 for Zionism, 909.04924 for world history of Jews
(.940 1)	Early history to 70
	(Optional number; prefer 933)
	Add to base number 956.9401 the numbers following 933.0 in 933.01–933.05, e.g., age of Solomon 956.94012
.940 2	Mishnaic and Talmudic periods, 70–640
.940 3	640–1917
	Including period of Ottoman Empire
.940 4	Period of British control, 1917–1948
.940 5	1948–
	Class here 20th century
	For 1900–1917, see 956.9403; for 1917–1948, see 956.9404
.940 52	1948–1967
	Class Israel-Arab War, 1948–1949, in 956.042; class Sinai Campaign, 1956, in 956.044; class Israel-Arab War, 1967, in 956.046
.940 53	1967–1974
	Class Israel-Arab War, 1973, in 956.048

*Add as instructed under 930–990

.940 54	1974–

> Class Israel-Lebanon-Syria Conflict, 1982–1985, in 956.052

.949	*Darom district

> For ancient Judah, Judea to 70, see 933; for ancient Edom to 70, see 939.46

.95	*West Bank and Jordan

Subdivisions are added for West Bank and Jordan together, for Jordan alone

> For early history to 70, see 933

(.950 1)	Early history to 70

(Optional number; prefer 933)

.950 2	70–640
.950 3	640–1923

Including period of Ottoman Empire

.950 4	1923–
.950 42	Period of mandate, 1923–1946
.950 43	Period of Hashemite Kingdom, 1946–

Class Israel-Arab War, 1948–1949, in 956.042; class Israel-Arab War, 1967, in 956.046

> For 1967 to present, see 956.95044

.950 44	1967–
.953	*Nablus district

Class here comprehensive works on West Bank

> For a part of West Bank not provided for here, see the part, e.g., Hebron district 956.951

.956	*Karak and Ṭafīlah provinces

> For ancient Moab to 70, see 939.46

.957	*Maʻān Province

> For ancient Petra to 70, see 939.48

957   *Siberia (Asiatic Russia)

.03	Pre-Russian period to 1581
.07	1581–1855
.08	1855–

Add to base number 957.08 the numbers following 947.08 in 947.081–947.085, e.g., period of Siberia under Stalin 957.0842

*Add as instructed under 930–990

958   *Central Asia

For early history to ca. 640, see 939.6

(Option: Class here early history to ca. 640; prefer 939.6)

.01–.04   Historical periods

Add to base number 958.0 the numbers following 950 in 950.1–950.4, e.g., period of Mongol and Tartar Empires 958.02

.1   *Afghanistan

.101   Early history to 1221

For earliest history to ca. 640, see 939.6

(Option: Class here earliest history to ca. 640; prefer 939.6)

.102   1221–1709

.103   1709–1919

.104   1919–

.104 2   1919–1933

.104 3   Reign of Muhammad Zahir Shah, 1933–1973

.104 4   Period of Republic, 1973–1978

.104 5   Period of Democratic Republic, 1978–1991

.104 6   1991–

.4   *Turkestan

For Turkmenistan, see 958.5; for Tajikistan, see 958.6; for Uzbekistan, see 958.7

.407   Pre-Russian period to 1855

For early history to ca. 640, see 939.6

(Option: Class here early history to ca. 640; prefer 939.6)

.408   1855–

Add to base number 958.408 the numbers following 947.08 in 947.081–947.086, e.g., later 20th century 958.4085

.5   *Turkmenistan

.507–.508   Historical periods

Add to base number 958.5 the numbers following 958.4 in 958.407–958.408, e.g., pre-Russian period 958.507

.6   *Tajikistan

*Add as instructed under 930–990

.607–.608   Historical periods

> Add to base number 958.6 the numbers following 958.4 in 958.407–958.408, e.g., Russian period 958.608

.7   *Uzbekistan

.707–.708   Historical periods

> Add to base number 958.7 the numbers following 958.4 in 958.407–958.408, e.g., later 20th century 958.7085

959   *Southeast Asia

SUMMARY

959.01–.05	[Historical periods]
.1	Myanmar (Burma)
.3	Thailand
.4	Laos
.5	Commonwealth of Nations territories Malaysia
.6	Cambodia (Khmer Republic, Kampuchea)
.7	Vietnam
.8	Indonesia
.9	Philippines

.01   Early history to 1499

.02   1500–1699

.03   1700–1799

.04   1800–1899

.05   1900–

.051   1900–1941

> Class here 20th century

> *For 1941–1945, see 959.052; for 1945–1999, see 959.053*

.052   Period of Japanese occupation, 1941–1945

.053   1945–1999

.054   2000–

.1   *Myanmar (Burma)

.102   Early history to 1826

.103   Period of British conquest, 1826–1885

.104   Period of British rule, 1886–1948

> Class here 20th century

> *For 1948–1999, see 959.105*

*Add as instructed under 930–990

.105		1948–
.3	***Thailand**	
.302		Early history to 1782
.302 1		Earliest history to 1219
.302 2		Period as Sukhothai, 1219–1350
.302 3		Period as Ayutthaya, 1350–1767
.302 4		Reign of Tāk Sin, 1767–1782
.303		1782–1910
.303 1		Reign of Phutthayǫtfā Čhulālōk (Rama I), 1782–1809
.303 2		Reign of Phutthalœtla Naphālai (Rama II), 1809–1824
.303 3		Reign of Nangklao (Rama III), 1824–1851
.303 4		Reign of Mongkut (Rama IV), 1851–1868
.303 5		Reign of Chulalongkorn (Rama V), 1868–1910
.304		1910–
.304 1		Reign of Vajiravudh (Rama VI), 1910–1925
.304 2		Reign of Prajadhipok (Rama VII), 1925–1935
.304 3		Reign of Ananda Mahidol (Rama VIII), 1935–1946
.304 4		Reign of Bhumibol Adulyadej (Rama IX), 1946–
.4	***Laos**	
.403		Early history to 1949

Including period as a part of French Indochina, 1893–1954

.404	1949–

Class here 20th century

For 1900–1949, see 959.403

.404 1	1949–1975

Class military operations in Laos during Vietnamese War in 959.70434

.404 2	Period as People's Democratic Republic, 1975–
.5	***Commonwealth of Nations territories** **Malaysia**
.503	Early history to 1946
.504	1946–1963

*Add as instructed under 930–990

.505	Period of federation, 1963–

Class here 20th century

For 1900–1946, see 959.503; for 1946–1963, see 959.504

.505 1	Prime ministership of Tunku Abdul Rahman Putra Al-Haj, 1963–1970

Including separation of Singapore, 1965

.505 2	Prime ministership of Tun Haji Abdul Razak bin Dato' Hussein, 1971–1976
.505 3	Prime ministership of Datuk Hussein Onn, 1976–1981
.505 4	Prime ministership of Mahathir bin Mohamad, 1981–
.55	*Brunei
.550 3	Early history to 1888

1888–1946 relocated to 959.5504

.550 4	Period as British protectorate, 1888–1983

Including 1888–1946 [*formerly* 959.5503], 1946–1983 [*formerly* 959.5505]

.550 5	1984–

1946–1983 relocated to 959.5504

.57	*Singapore
.570 3	Early history to 1946
.570 4	1946–1963
.570 5	Periods of federation with Malaysia, 1963–1965, and separate nationhood, 1965–

Class here 20th century

For 1900–1946, see 959.5703; for 1946–1963, see 959.5704

.6	***Cambodia (Khmer Republic, Kampuchea)**
.603	Early history to 1949

Including period as a part of French Indochina, 1863–1949

.604	1949–

Class here 20th century

Class military operations in Cambodia during Vietnamese War in 959.70434

For 1900–1949, see 959.603

.604 1	1949–1970

*Add as instructed under 930–990

.604 2	1970–
.7	***Vietnam**
.703	Early history to 1949

Including period as a part of French Indochina, 1883–1954

Class here comprehensive works on French Indochina

For Laos as a part of French Indochina, see 959.403; for Cambodia as a part of French Indochina, see 959.603; for Indochinese War, 1946–1954, see 959.7041

.704	1949–
.704 1	‡Indochinese War, 1946–1954
.704 2	1954–1961
.704 3	Vietnamese War, 1961–1975
.704 308	Vietnamese War with respect to kinds of persons [*formerly* 959.70431]
.704 309 2	Persons

Class here personal narratives [*formerly* 959.70438]

.704 31	Social, political, economic history

Including causes, results, efforts to preserve or restore peace, internment camps

Vietnamese War with respect to kinds of persons relocated to 959.704308

Class prisoner-of-war camps in 959.70437. Class results in and effects on a specific country with the history of the country, e.g., on United States 973.923

For general diplomatic history, see 959.70432

.704 32	Diplomatic history

Class diplomatic causes, efforts to preserve or restore peace, diplomatic results in 959.70431

.704 33	Participation of specific countries, localities, groups

Class military participation of specific countries, localities, groups in 959.70434

.704 331	North Vietnam
.704 332	South Vietnam
.704 332 2	National Liberation Front

Class here Vietcong

*Add as instructed under 930–990

‡Add as instructed under 940–990

.704 332 5	Government forces
.704 334–.704 339	Foreign participation

Add to base number 959.70433 notation 4–9 from Table 2, e.g., United States participation 959.7043373

Class a specific activity with the activity, e.g., efforts to preserve or restore peace 959.70431

.704 34	Military operations and units

Class here military history

Class units engaged in a specific type of service with the service, e.g., medical units 959.70437; class an aspect of military history not provided for here with the aspect, e.g., prisoner-of-war camps 959.70437

.704 342	Land operations
.704 345	Naval operations
.704 348	Air operations
.704 36	Celebrations, commemorations, memorials

Including decorations and awards, rolls of honor, cemeteries, monuments

.704 37	Prisoners of war, health and social services

Including prisoner-of-war camps

.704 38	Other topics

Including deserters; military life and customs; servicemen missing in action; unconventional warfare, propaganda

Personal narratives relocated to 959.7043092

.704 4	1975–
.8	***Indonesia**
.801	Early history to 1602
.801 2	Earliest history to 1478
.801 5	Period of Muslim rule, 1478–1602
.802	Dutch period, 1602–1945
.802 1	Period of Dutch East India Company, 1602–1798
.802 2	Periods under control of British and Netherlands governments, 1798–1945

Including Java War, 1825–1830

*Add as instructed under 930–990

.803	Period of Republic, 1945–
	Class here 20th century
	For 1900–1945, see 959.8022; for 2000 and beyond, see 959.804
.803 5	1945–1959
	Class here administration of Sukarno, 1945–1967
	For administration of Sukarno during 1960–1967, see 959.8036
.803 6	1960–1969
.803 7	1970–1979
.803 8	1980–1989
.803 9	1990–1999
.804	2000–
.9	***Philippines**
.901	Early history to 1564
.902	Spanish period, 1564–1898
.902 7	Period of insurrection against Spanish, 1896–1898
.903	United States period, 1898–1946
	Class here 20th century
	For 1946–1999, see 959.904
.903 1	Philippine-American War, 1898–1901
.903 2	Period of United States rule, 1901–1935
.903 5	Period of Commonwealth, 1935–1946
.904	Period of Republic, 1946–
.904 1	Administration of Manuel Roxas, 1946–1948
.904 2	Administration of Elpidio Quirino, 1948–1954
.904 3	Administration of Ramon Magsaysay, 1954–1957
.904 4	Administration of Carlos Garcia, 1957–1961
.904 5	Administration of Diosdado Macapagal, 1961–1965
.904 6	Administration of Ferdinand Marcos, 1965–1986
.904 7	Administration of Corazon Cojuangco Aquino, 1986–1992
.904 8	1992–

960   General history of Africa

*Add as instructed under 930–990

SUMMARY

.01–.09   Standard subdivisions

As modified under 930–990

.1   Early history to 640

.2   640–1885

.21   640–1450

.22   1450–1799

.23   1800–1885

.3   1885–

.31   1885–1945

Class here 20th century

For 1945–1999, see 960.32

.312   1885–1914

.314   1914–1918

.316   1918–1945

.32   1945–1999

.324   1945–1949

.325   1950–1959

.326   1960–1969

.327   1970–1979

.328   1980–1989

.329   1990–1999

.33   2000–

961 *Tunisia and Libya

Class here North Africa

For early history to ca. 640, see 939.7

(.01)	Early history to ca. 640
	(Optional number; prefer 939.7)
.02	Periods of Arab rule and Ottoman Empire, ca. 640–1830
.022	Period of Arab rule, ca. 640–ca. 1520
.023	Period of Ottoman Empire, ca. 1520–1830

(Option: Class here Tripolitan War with the United States, United States War with Algiers; prefer 973.47 for Tripolitan War, 973.53 for War with Algiers)

.03	Period of European conquest and hegemony, 1830–1950

Including 20th century

For 1950–1999, see 961.04

.04	1950–1999
.045	1950–1959
.046	1960–1969
.047	1970–1979
.048	1980–1989
.049	1990–1999
.05	2000–
.1	***Tunisia**

For early history to 647, see 939.73

(.101)	Early history to 647
	(Optional number; prefer 939.73)
.102	Period of Arab rule, 647–1516
.103	Period of Ottoman Empire, 1516–1881
.104	1881–1956
.105	1956–
.105 1	Administration of Habib Bourguiba, 1956–1987
.105 2	1987–

*Add as instructed under 930–990

.2	***Libya**

For early history to 644, see 939.74

(.201)	Early history to 644

(Optional number; prefer 939.74)

.202	Periods of Arab rule and Ottoman Empire, 644–1911
.203	Period of Italian rule, 1911–1952
.204	1952–
.204 1	Reign of Idris I, 1952–1969
.204 2	Period of Muammar Qaddafi, 1969–

962 Egypt and Sudan

.000 1–.000 8	Standard subdivisions of Egypt and Sudan

As modified under 930–990

.000 9	Historical periods; areas, regions, places; persons of Egypt and Sudan
.000 901–.000 905	Historical periods

Add to base number 962.0009 the numbers following —090 in notation 0901–0905 from Table 1, e.g., Egypt and Sudan during 20th century 962.000904

.000 91–.000 99	Areas, regions, places in general; persons

As modified under 930–990

.001–.009	Standard subdivisions of Egypt

As modified under 930–990

(.01)	Early history to 640

(Optional number; prefer 932)

Add to base number 962.01 the numbers following 932.0 in 932.01–932.02, e.g., period of New Kingdom 962.0114

>	962.02–962.05 Historical periods of Egypt

Class comprehensive works in 962

For early history to 640, see 932

(Option: Class early history to 640 in 962.01; prefer 932)

.02	Period of Arab rule, 640–1517
.03	Period of Ottoman Empire, 1517–1882

*Add as instructed under 930–990

.04   Period of British occupation and protectorate, 1882–1922

.05   1922–

.051   Reign of Fu'ād I, 1922–1936

.052   Reign of Faruk I, 1936–1952, and regency (Fu'ād II), 1952–1953

                          Class Israel-Arab War, 1948–1949, in 956.042

.053   Administrations of Mohammed Naguib and Gamal Abdel Nasser,
                       1953–1970

                          Including United Arab Republic, 1958–1961

                          Class Sinai Campaign, 1956, in 956.044; class Israel-Arab War, 1967, in
                          956.046

                             For Syrian part of United Arab Republic, see 956.91042

.054   Administration of Anwar Sadat, 1970–1981

                          Class Israel-Arab War, 1973, in 956.048

.055   1981–

                          Including administration of Muḥammad Ḥusnī Mubārak, 1981 to present

.4   *Sudan

                          For parts of Sudan, see 962.5–962.9

.401   Early history to 500

.402   500–1820

.402 2   Period of Christian kingdoms, 500–1504

.402 3   Period of Funj Sultanate, 1504–1820

.403   Period as Anglo-Egyptian Sudan, 1820–1956

                          Including 20th century

                          Class here period of Egyptian and British rule

                             For 1956–1999, see 962.404

.404   1956–

                          Including administration of Ja'far Muḥammad Numayrī, 1969–1985

>   **962.5–962.9 Parts of Sudan**

                 Class comprehensive works in 962.4

.5   *Eastern and Northern regions of Sudan

                 For early history to 500, see 939.78

---

*Add as instructed under 930–990

(.501)   Early history to 500

Class here ancient Ethiopia

(Optional number; prefer 939.78)

.502–.504   500–

Add to base number 962.50 the numbers following 962.40 in 962.402–962.404, e.g., period of Christian kingdoms 962.5022

.6   *Khartoum province and Central region of Sudan

.601–.604   Historical periods

Add to base number 962.6 the numbers following 962.4 in 962.401–962.404, e.g., period as a part of Anglo-Egyptian Sudan 962.603

.7   *Darfur region of Sudan

.701–.704   Historical periods

Add to base number 962.7 the numbers following 962.4 in 962.401–962.404, e.g., period as a part of Anglo-Egyptian Sudan 962.703

.8   *Kordofan region of Sudan

.801–.804   Historical periods

Add to base number 962.8 the numbers following 962.4 in 962.401–962.404, e.g., period as a part of Anglo-Egyptian Sudan 962.803

.9   *Southern regions of Sudan

.901–.904   Historical periods

Add to base number 962.9 the numbers following 962.4 in 962.401–962.404, e.g., period as a part of Anglo-Egyptian Sudan 962.903

963   *Ethiopia and Eritrea

Subdivisions are added for Ethiopia and Eritrea together, for Ethiopia alone

---

>   963.01–963.07 Historical periods for Ethiopia and Eritrea together, for Ethiopia alone

Class comprehensive works in 963

.01   Early history to 640

See also 939.78 for ancient Ethiopia (a part of what is now modern Sudan, not modern Ethiopia)

*Add as instructed under 930–990

.02	640–1543
.03	1543–1855
.04	1855–1913
.041	Reign of Theodore II, 1855–1868
.042	1868–1889

Including reign of John IV, 1872–1889

.043	Reign of Menelik II, 1889–1913

Including Ethiopian War, 1895–1896
(Option: Class Ethiopian War in 945.091)

.05	1913–1941

Class here 20th century

*For 1900–1913, see 963.043; for 1941–1974, see 963.06; for
1974–1999, see 963.07*

.053	Reign of Lij Yasu, 1913–1916
.054	Period of Jah Rastafari (Haile Selassie) as regent and king, 1917–1930
.055	Reign of Haile Selassie (Jah Rastafari) as emperor, 1930–1974

*For reign during 1935–1936, see 963.056; for reign during
1936–1941, see 963.057; for reign during 1941–1974, see 963.06*

.056	Italo-Ethiopian War, 1935–1936

(Option: Class in 945.091)

.057	Period of Italian rule, 1936–1941
.06	1941–1974

Including deposition of Haile Selassie, 1974

.07	1974–
.071	1974–1993

Class here chairmanship of Mengistu Haile-Mariam, 1977–1991;
Somali-Ethiopian conflicts, 1977–1989

.072	1993–
.5	***Eritrea**

964   Northwest African coast and offshore islands   Morocco

[.000 1–.000 9]   Standard subdivisions of northwest African coast and offshore islands

Relocated to 964.001–964.009

*Add as instructed under 930–990

.001–.009   Standard subdivisions of northwest African coast and offshore islands [*formerly* 964.0001–964.0009], of Morocco

         As modified under 930–990

(.01)   Ancient history to 647

         (Optional number; prefer 939.71)

>   964.02–964.05   Historical periods of Morocco

         Class comprehensive works in 964

         For early history to 647, see 939.71

         (Option: Class early history to 647 in 964.01; prefer 939.71)

.02   Periods of Arab and Berber rule, 647–1830

.03   1830–1899

         Including Spanish-Moroccan War, 1859–1860
            (Option: Class Spanish-Moroccan War in 946.072)

         Class here 19th century

         For 1800–1830, see 964.02

.04   1900–1956

         Including reign of Muḥammad V, 1927–1961

         Class here 20th century; period of French and Spanish protectorates, 1912–1956

         For 1956–1999, reign of Muhammad V during 1956–1961, see 964.05

.05   1956–

         Including reigns of Muḥammad V, 1956–1961; Hassan II, 1961 to present

.8   **†Western Sahara**

.9   ***Canary Islands**

.906   Early history to 1402

.907   Periods of French, Portuguese, Spanish rule, 1402–1927

.908   Period as Provinces of Spain, 1927–

.908 1   1927–1939

.908 2–.908 3   Periods of Francisco Franco and Juan Carlos I, 1939–

         Add to base number 964.908 the numbers following 946.08 in 946.082–946.083, e.g., 1960–1969 964.90826

---

*Add as instructed under 930–990

†Add as instructed under 930–990; however, do not add historical periods

965 *Algeria

For early history to 647, see 939.71

(.01) Early history to 647

(Optional number; prefer 939.71)

.02 Periods of Arab and Berber rule and Ottoman Empire, 647–1830

.03 Period of French rule, 1830–1962

For 1900–1962, see 965.04

.04 1900–1962

Class here 20th century

For 1962–1999, see 965.05

.046 ‡Period of Revolution, 1954–1962

.05 1962–

.051 1962–1965

.052 1965–1979

.053 Administration of Chadli Bendjedid, 1979–1992

.054 1992–

.5 *Northeastern provinces

For ancient Numidia to 647, see 939.72

.7 *Sahara provinces

For ancient Gaetulia to 647, see 939.77

966 *West Africa and offshore islands

SUMMARY

.01–.03 Historical periods

Add to base number 966.0 the numbers following 960 in 960.1–960.3, e.g., early history to 640 966.01

*Add as instructed under 930–990

‡Add as instructed under 940–990

.1   *Mauritania

.101   Early history to 1903

.101 6   300–1200

Class here comprehensive works on period of Ghana Empire

For period of Ghana Empire in Mali history, see 966.2301

.101 7   1200–1500

Class here period of Mali Empire

.103   French period, 1903–1960

Class here 20th century

For 1900–1903, see 966.101; for 1960–1999, see 966.105

.105   1960–

.2   *Mali, Burkina Faso, Niger

.201   Early history to ca. 1900

.201 7   1200–1400

Class here period of Mali Empire

For period of Mali Empire in Mauritanian history, see 966.1017

.201 8   1400–1500

Class here period of Songhai Empire

.202   French period, ca. 1900–1960

Class here 20th century

For 1960–1999, see 966.203

.203   1960–

.23   *Mali

.230 1   Early history to 1902

Class comprehensive works on Mali Empire in 966.2017

.230 3   Period as French Sudan, 1902–1960

Class here 20th century, French period

For 1900–1902, see 966.2301; for 1960–1999, see 966.2305

.230 5   1960–

.230 51   1960–1991

Class here administration of Moussa Traoré, 1968–1991

.230 52   1991–

*Add as instructed under 930–990

.25   *Burkina Faso

             Former name: Upper Volta

.250 1   Early history to 1897

                 Including kingdom of Mossi

.250 3   French period, 1897–1960

                 Class here 20th century

                 For 1960–1999, see 966.2505

.250 5   1960–

                 Including administration of Thomas Sankara, 1983–1987

.26   *Niger

.260 1   Early history to 1900

.260 3   French period, 1900–1960

                 Class here 20th century

                 For 1960–1999, see 966.2605

.260 5   1960–

                 Including administration of Seyni Kountché, 1974–1987

.3   *Senegal

.301   Early history to 1895

                 Including kingdom of Tekrur

.303   French period, 1895–1960

                 Class here 20th century

                 For 1960–1999, see 966.305

.305   1960–

                 Including administration of Abdou Diouf, 1981 to present;
                 Confederation of Senegambia, 1982 to present

                 For Gambian part of Senegambia, see 966.51031

.4   *Sierra Leone

.401   Early history to 1787

.402   Period as a British colony, 1787–1896

.403   Period as both colony and protectorate, 1896–1961

                 Class here 20th century

                 For 1961–1999, see 966.404

*Add as instructed under 930–990

.404	1961–

.5   *Gambia, Guinea, Guinea-Bissau, Cape Verde

.51   *Gambia

.510 1   Early history to 1807

.510 2   Period as a British colony, 1807–1965

        Class here 20th century

        For 1965–1999, see 966.5103

.510 3   1965–

.510 31   Administration of Dawda Kairaba Jawara, 1965–

        Including period as a part of Senegambia, 1982 to present

        Class comprehensive works on Senegambia in 966.305

.52   *Guinea

.520 1   Early history to 1882

.520 3   Period as French Guinea, 1882–1958

        Class here 20th century

        For 1958–1999, see 966.5205

.520 5   1958–

.57   *Guinea-Bissau

.570 1   Early history to 1879

.570 2   Period as Portuguese Guinea, 1879–1974

.570 3   1974–

.58   *Cape Verde

.580 1   Early history to 1900

.580 2   1900–1975

.580 3   1975–

.580 31   Administration of Aristides Pereira, 1975–1991

.580 32   1991–

.6   Liberia and Côte d'Ivoire

.62   *Liberia

.620 1   Early history to 1847

.620 2   1847–1945

*Add as instructed under 930–990

.620 3		1945–
		Class here 20th century
		Including administration of Samuel K. Doe, 1980–1990
		For 1900–1945, see 966.6202
.68		*Côte d'Ivoire (Ivory Coast)
.680 1		Early history to 1904
.680 3		French period, 1904–1960
		Class here 20th century
		For 1900–1904, see 966.6801; for 1960–1999, see 966.6805
.680 5		1960–
.680 51		Administration of Félix Houphouët-Boigny, 1960–

.7   ***Ghana**

See also 966.1016 for Ghana Empire

.701		Early history to 1874
.701 6		Period of Akan states, 1295–1740
		Including Akwamu, Bono kingdoms
.701 8		Period of Asante (Ashanti) empire, 1740–1874
.703		Period as Gold Coast, 1874–1957
		Class here 20th century, British period
		For 1957–1999, see 966.705
.705		1957–
		Including administration of Kwame Nkrumah, 1957–1966; of Jerry J. Rawlings, 1981 to present

.8   **Togo and Benin**

.81		*Togo
.810 1		Early history to 1894
.810 2		German period, 1894–1914
.810 3		Anglo-French period, 1914–1960
		Class here 20th century
		For 1900–1914, see 966.8102; for 1960–1999, see 966.8104
.810 4		1960–
.810 41		1960–1967

*Add as instructed under 930–990

.810 42	Administration of Gnassingbé Eyadéma, 1967–
.83	*Benin

See also 966.9301 for kingdom of Benin

.830 1	Early history to 1904
.830 18	Period of kingdom of Dahomey, 1600–1904
.830 3	French period, 1904–1960

Class here 20th century

For 1900–1904, see 966.83018; for 1960–1999, see 966.8305

.830 5	1960–
.830 51	1960–1991
.830 52	1991–

.9   ***Nigeria**

.901	Early history to 1886
.903	Period as a British colony, 1886–1960

Class here 20th century

For 1960–1999, see 966.905

.905	1960–
.905 1	1960–1967
.905 2	Period of Nigerian Civil War, 1967–1970
.905 3	1970–

Including administration of Ibrahim Badamosi Babangida, 1983–1993

967   *Central Africa and offshore islands

Class here Sub-Saharan Africa (Africa south of the Sahara)

For each specific part of Sub-Saharan Africa not provided for here, see the part, e.g., Nigeria 966.9

SUMMARY

967.01–.03	**Historical periods**
.1	**Cameroon, Sao Tome and Principe, Equatorial Guinea**
.2	**Gabon and Republic of the Congo**
.3	**Angola**
.4	**Central African Republic and Chad**
.5	**Zaire, Rwanda, Burundi**
.6	**Uganda and Kenya**
.7	**Djibouti and Somalia**
.8	**Tanzania**
.9	**Mozambique**

*Add as instructed under 930–990

.01–.03	Historical periods

> Add to base number 967.0 the numbers following 960 in 960.1–960.3, e.g., early history to 640 967.01

.1	***Cameroon, Sao Tome and Principe, Equatorial Guinea**

> Class here Islands of Gulf of Guinea, Lower Guinea area

.11	*Cameroon
.110 1	Early history to 1884
.110 2	Period as Kamerun, 1884–1916

> Class here German period

.110 3	Anglo-French period, 1916–1959

> Class here 20th century
>
> *For 1900–1916, see 967.1102; for 1960–1999, see 967.1104*

.110 4	1960–

> Including administration of Paul Biya, 1982 to present

.15	*Sao Tome and Principe
.150 1	Early history to 1975
.150 2	Period of Republic, 1975–
.18	*Equatorial Guinea
.180 1	Early history to 1469
.180 2	Portuguese, British, Spanish periods, 1469–1968

> Including 20th century
>
> *For 1968–1999, see 967.1803*

.180 3	1968–
.180 31	Administration of Francisco Macías Nguema, 1968–1979
.180 32	Administration of Teodoro Obiang Nguema Mbasogo, 1979–
.2	***Gabon and Republic of the Congo**
.201	Early history to 1910
.203	Period as French Equatorial Africa, 1910–1959

> Class here 20th century; comprehensive works on French Equatorial Africa
>
> *For 1900–1910, see 967.201; for 1959–1999, see 967.205; for Ubangi-Shari as part of French Equatorial Africa, see 967.4103; for Chad as part of French Equatorial Africa, see 967.4302*

---

*Add as instructed under 930–990

.205		1959–
.21	*Gabon	
.210 1		Early history to 1839
.210 2		French period, 1839–1960

Including period as a part of French Equatorial Africa; 20th century

Class comprehensive works on French Equatorial Africa in 967.203

For 1960–1999, see 967.2104

.210 4		1960–
.210 41		1960–1967
.210 42		Administration of Omar Bongo, 1967–
.24	*Republic of the Congo	
.240 1		Early history to 1885
.240 3		Period as Middle Congo, 1885–1960

Class here 20th century, French period

Class comprehensive works on French Equatorial Africa in 967.203

For 1960–1999, see 967.2405

.240 5		1960–
.240 51		1960–1979
.240 52		Administration of Denis Sassou Nguesso, 1979–1992
.240 53		1992–
.3	***Angola**	
.301		Early history to 1648
.302		1648–1899

Including 17th century

For 1600–1648, see 967.301

.303		1900–1975
.304		1975–
.304 1		Administration of António Agostinho Neto, 1975–1979
.304 2		Administration of José Eduardo dos Santos, 1979–
.4	***Central African Republic and Chad**	
.41	*Central African Republic	

*Add as instructed under 930–990

.410 1	Early history to 1890

.410 3	Period as Ubangi-Shari, 1890–1960

Class here 20th century, French period, period as part of French Equatorial Africa

Class comprehensive works on French Equatorial Africa in 967.203

For 1960–1999, see 967.4105

.410 5	1960–

.43	*Chad

.430 1	Early history to 1850

Including kingdom of Kanem

Class Kanem-Bornu in 966.9801

.430 2	Colonial period, 1850–1960

Including period as part of French Equatorial Africa; 20th century

Class comprehensive works on French Equatorial Africa in 967.203

For 1960–1999, see 967.4304

.430 4	1960–
.430 41	1960–1975
.430 42	1975–1982
.430 43	Administration of Hissein Habré, 1982–1990
.430 44	1990–

.5	**Zaire, Rwanda, Burundi**

.51	*Zaire

.510 1	Early history to 1885
.510 2	Belgian period, 1885–1960
.510 22	Period as Congo Free State, 1885–1908
.510 24	Period as Belgian Congo, 1908–1960

Class here 20th century

For 1900–1908, see 967.51022; for 1960–1999, see 967.5103

.510 3	1960–
.510 31	1960–1965
.510 33	Administration of Mobutu Sese Seko, 1965–

.57	*Rwanda and Burundi

Class here former Ruanda-Urundi

*Add as instructed under 930–990

.570 1	Early history to 1899
.570 2	German period, 1899–1917
.570 3	Belgian period, 1917–1962

Class here 20th century

For 1900–1917, see 967.5702; for 1962–1999, see 967.5704

.570 4	1962–
.571	*Rwanda
.571 04	1962–

Including administration of Juvénal Habyarimana, 1973–1994

.572	*Burundi
.572 04	1962–

Including administration of Jean-Baptiste Bagaza, 1976–1987

.6　　*Uganda and Kenya

Class here East Africa

.601	Early history to 1894
.603	1894–1961

Class here 20th century

For 1961–1999, see 967.604

.604	1961–
.61	*Uganda
.610 1	Early history to 1894

Including kingdoms of Ankole, Buganda, Bunyoro, Busoga, Karagwe

.610 3	British period, 1894–1962

Class here 20th century

For 1962–1999, see 967.6104

.610 4	1962–
.610 41	First administration of A. Milton Obote, 1962–1971
.610 42	Administration of Idi Amin, 1971–1979
.610 43	Second administration of A. Milton Obote, 1980–1985
.610 44	Administration of Yoweri Museveni, 1986–
.62	*Kenya

*Add as instructed under 930–990

.620 1	Early history to 1895
.620 3	British period, 1895–1963
	Class here 20th century
	For 1963–1999, see 967.6204
.620 4	1963–
.620 41	Administration of Jomo Kenyatta, 1963–1978
.620 42	Administration of Daniel Arap Moi, 1978–

.7 *Djibouti and Somalia

Class here Somaliland

.71 *Djibouti

.710 1	Early history to 1881
.710 3	French period, 1881–1977
.710 32	Period as French Somaliland, 1881–1967
	Class here 20th century
	For 1967–1977, see 967.71034; for 1977–1999, see 967.7104
.710 34	Period as French Territory of the Afars and Issas, 1967–1977
.710 4	1977–

.73 *Somalia

.730 1	Early history to 1884
	Including kingdom of Mogadishu
.730 3	Period of British and Italian control, 1884–1960
	Class here 20th century
	For 1960–1999, see 967.7305
.730 5	1960–
	Including administration of Maxamed Siyaad Barre, 1969–1990
	Class Somali-Ethiopian conflicts, 1977–1989, in 963.071
.730 51	1960–1969
.730 52	Administration of Maxamed Siyaad Barre, 1969–1990
.730 53	1990–

.8 *Tanzania

.804	Period as United Republic, 1964–
.804 1	Administration of Julius K. Nyerere, 1964–1985

*Add as instructed under 930–990

.804 2	1985–
.81	*Zanzibar and Pemba regions
.810 1	Early history to 1700
.810 2	Period of Arab rule, 1700–1890
.810 3	Period as a British protectorate, 1890–1963

Class here 20th century

> For 1963–1999, see 967.8104

.810 4	1963–
.82	*Tanganyika
.820 1	Early history to 1884
.820 2	German period, 1884–1916
.820 3	British period, 1916–1961

Class here 20th century

> For 1900–1916, see 967.8202; for 1961–1999, see 967.8204

.820 4	1961–
.9	***Mozambique**
.901	Early history to 1648
.902	1648–1900

Including 17th century

Class here Portuguese period, 1648–1975

> For 1600–1648, see 967.901; for 1900–1975, see 967.903

.903	1900–1975
.905	1975–
.905 1	Administration of Samora Machel, 1975–1986
.905 2	1986–

968 *Southern Africa Republic of South Africa

See Manual at 968

*Add as instructed under 930–990

SUMMARY

.000 1–.000 8   Standard subdivisions of southern Africa [*formerly* 968.001–968.008]

> As modified under 930–990

.000 9   Areas, regions, places; persons of southern Africa [*formerly* 968.009]; historical periods of southern Africa

.000 901–.000 905   Historical periods

> Add to base number 969.0009 the numbers following —090 in notation 0901–0905 from Table 1, e.g., southern Africa during 20th century 968.000904

.000 91–.000 99   Areas, regions, places in general; persons

> As modified under 930–990

.001–.008   Standard subdivisions of Republic of South Africa

> As modified under 930–990

> Standard subdivisions of southern Africa relocated to 968.0001–968.0008

.009   Areas, regions, places; persons of Republic of South Africa

> As modified under 930–990

> Areas, regions, places; persons of southern Africa relocated to 968.0009

>   **968.02–968.06   Historical periods of Republic of South Africa**

> Class comprehensive works in 968

.02   Early history to 1488

.03   Period of European exploration and settlement, 1488–1814

.04   1814–1910

.041   1814–1835

> Class here Mfecane (Difaqane)

.042   Great Trek, 1835–1838

.044	1838–1854
.045	1854–1899

> See also 968.2046 for First Anglo-Boer War

.048   South African (Second Anglo-Boer) War, 1899–1902

(Option: Class South African (Second Anglo-Boer) War in 941.081)

.048 08   South African War with respect to kinds of persons [*formerly* 968.0481]

.048 092   Persons

Class here personal narratives [*formerly* 968.0488]

.048 1   Social, political, economic history

Including causes, results, efforts to preserve or restore peace, internment camps

South African War with respect to kinds of persons relocated to 968.04808

Class prisoner-of-war camps in 968.0487. Class results in and effects on a specific country with the history of the country, e.g., on Great Britain 941.0823

> For general diplomatic history, see 968.0482

.048 2   Diplomatic history

Class diplomatic causes, efforts to preserve or restore peace, diplomatic results in 968.0481

.048 3   Participation of specific countries, localities, groups

Class military participation of specific countries, localities, groups in 968.0484

.048 31   Great Britain

.048 32   Boer Republics

.048 4   Military operations and units

Class here military history

Class units engaged in a specific type of service with the service, e.g., medical units 968.0487; class an aspect of military history not provided for here with the aspect, e.g., prisoner-of-war camps 968.0487

.048 6   Celebrations, commemorations, memorials

Including decorations and awards, rolls of honor, cemeteries, monuments

.048 7   Prisoners of war, health and social services

Including prisoner-of-war camps

.048 8   Other topics

> Including deserters; military life and customs; servicemen missing in action; unconventional warfare, propaganda

> Personal narratives relocated to 968.048092

.049   1902–1910

.05   Period of Union, 1910–1961

> Class here 20th century

> *For 1900–1902, see 968.048; for 1902–1910, see 968.049; for 1961–1999, see 968.06*

.052   Prime ministership of Louis Botha, 1910–1919

.053   First prime ministership of Jan Christiaan Smuts, 1919–1924

.054   Prime ministership of James Barry Munnik Hertzog, 1924–1939

.055   Second prime ministership of Jan Christiaan Smuts, 1939–1948

.056   Prime ministership of Daniel François Malan, 1948–1954

.057   Prime ministership of Johannes Gerhardus Strijdom, 1954–1958

.058   Prime ministership of Hendrik Frensch Verwoerd, 1958–1966

> Including Sharpeville Massacre, 1960

> *For 1961–1966, see 968.061*

.06   Period as Republic, 1961–

.061   Period of prime ministership of Hendrik Frensch Verwoerd under republic, 1961–1966

.062   Prime ministership of B. J. Vorster, 1966–1978

.062 7   1976–1977

> Class here Soweto and related riots

.063   Administration of P. W. Botha, 1978–1989

.064   Administration of F. W. de Klerk, 1989–1994

.065   Administration of Nelson Mandela, 1994–

.2   ***Transvaal**

.203   Early history to 1835

.204   1835–1910

> Class here 19th century

> *For 1800–1835, see 968.203*

*Add as instructed under 930–990

.204 2	Period of Great Trek and Boer settlement, 1835–1852
.204 5	Period as South African Republic, 1852–1877
.204 6	Period of British control, 1877–1881
	Including First Anglo-Boer War, 1880–1881
.204 7	1881–1899
.204 75	Jameson raid, 1895–1896
.204 8	Period of South African (Second Anglo-Boer) War, 1899–1902
.204 9	Period as Transvaal Colony, 1902–1910
.205–.206	Periods of union and republic, 1910–

Add to base number 968.20 the numbers following 968.0 in 968.05–968.06, e.g., period of World War II 968.2055

.4   *Natal

.403	Early history to 1824
.403 8	Period of early Nguni kingdoms, ca. 1500–1816
	Including kingdoms of Mthethwa, Ndwandwe, Qwabe
.403 9	Reign of Shaka, 1816–1828

> *For reign of Shaka during 1824–1828, see 968.4041*

.404	1824–1910

Class here period of Zululand, 1816–1879

> *For reign of Shaka, see 968.4039*

.404 1	Period of early British settlement, 1824–1835

Class here reign of Dingaan, 1828–1840

> *For reign of Dingaan during 1835–1840, see 968.4042*

.404 2	Period of Great Trek and Boer settlement, 1835–1843
	Including Battle of Blood River, 1838; republic of Natalia
.404 5	Period as a British colony, 1843–1899
	Including reign of Cetewayo, 1872–1879; Zulu War, 1879; annexation of Zululand, 1897
.404 8	Period of South African (Second Anglo-Boer) War, 1899–1902
.404 9	1902–1910
.405–.406	Periods of union and republic, 1910–

Add to base number 968.40 the numbers following 968.0 in 968.05–968.06, e.g., period of World War I 968.4052

*Add as instructed under 930–990

.5	***Orange Free State**
.503	Early history to 1828
.504	1828–1910

    Class here 19th century

    For 1800–1828, see 968.503

.504 2	Periods of Great Trek and as Orange River Sovereignty, 1835–1854
.504 5	Period as Orange Free State, 1854–1899
.504 8	Period of South African (Second Anglo-Boer) War, 1899–1902
.504 9	Period as Orange River Colony, 1902–1910
.505–.506	Periods of union and republic, 1910–

    Add to base number 968.50 the numbers following 968.0 in
968.05–968.06, e.g., prime ministership of James Barry Munnik Hertzog
968.5054

.7	***Cape of Good Hope**
.702	Early history to 1488
.703	Period of exploration and settlement, 1488–1814
.703 1	1488–1652
.703 2	Period of Dutch control, 1652–1795

    Class period of control by Batavian Republic in 968.7033

.703 3	1795–1806

    Including periods of British occupation, 1795–1803, control by
Batavian Republic, 1803–1806

.704	1806–1910
.704 2	Period of British control, 1806–1854

    Including period of Great Trek

    Class period of British occupation, 1795–1803, in 968.7033

.704 5	Period of self-government, 1854–1899
.704 8	Period of South African (Second Anglo-Boer) War, 1899–1902
.704 9	1902–1910
.705–.706	Union and republic, 1910–

    Add to base number 968.70 the numbers following 968.0 in
968.05–968.06, e.g., first prime ministership of Jan Christiaan Smuts
968.7053

---

*Add as instructed under 930–990

.8	***Namibia, Botswana, Lesotho, Swaziland**
.801–.803	Historical periods

Add to base number 968.80 the numbers following 960 in 960.1–960.3, e.g., 20th century 968.8031

.81	*Namibia
.810 1	Early history to 1884
.810 2	German period, 1884–1915
.810 3	South African period, 1915–1990
.810 4	1990–
.83	*Botswana
.830 1	Early history to 1885
.830 2	Period as Bechuanaland, 1885–1966

Class here 20th century, British period

For 1966–1999, see 968.8303

.830 3	1966–
.830 31	1966–1990

Including administration of Seretse Khama, 1966–1980

.830 32	1990–
.85	*Lesotho
.850 1	Early history to 1868
.850 2	Period as Basutoland, 1868–1966

Including 20th century

Class here British period

For 1966–1999, see 968.8503

.850 3	1966–
.850 31	First reign of Moshoeshoe II, 1966–1990

Class here prime ministership of Leabua Jonathan, 1966–1986

.850 32	1990–
.87	*Swaziland
.870 1	Early history to 1840
.870 2	British period, 1840–1968

Including 20th century

For 1968–1999, see 968.8703

*Add as instructed under 930–990

.870 3	1968–
	Including reigns of Sobhuza II, 1968–1982; Mswari III, 1986 to present

.9   ***Zimbabwe, Zambia, Malawi**

.901   Early history to 1888

.902   Period of British control, 1888–1953

      Class here 20th century

       For 1953–1963, see 968.903; for 1964–1999, see 968.904

.903   Period as Federation of Rhodesia and Nyasaland (Central African Federation), 1953–1963

      Class here prime ministership of Roy Welensky, 1956–1963

.904   1964–

.91   *Zimbabwe

.910 1   Early history to 1889

      Including Karanga kingdoms of Changamire, the Monomotapas

.910 2   Period as Southern Rhodesia, 1889–1953

      Class here 20th century, British period

       For 1953–1963, see 968.9103; for 1964–1980, see 968.9104; for 1980–1999, see 968.9105

.910 3   Period of federation, 1953–1963

.910 4   Period as Rhodesia, 1964–1980

      Class here prime ministership of Ian Douglas Smith, 1965–1979

.910 5   Period as Republic of Zimbabwe, 1980–

.910 51   Prime ministership of Robert Gabriel Mugabe, 1980–

.94   *Zambia

.940 1   Early history to 1890

      Including kingdoms of the Barotse, of the Bemba

.940 2   Period of British control, 1890–1953

      Including periods as North-eastern Rhodesia and North-western Rhodesia provinces, 1890–1911; as Northern Rhodesia, 1911–1953

      Class here 20th century

       For 1953–1963, see 968.9403; for 1964–1999, see 968.9404

.940 3   Period of federation, 1953–1963

*Add as instructed under 930–990

.940 4	Period as Republic of Zambia, 1964–
.940 41	Administration of Kenneth D. Kaunda, 1964–1991
.940 42	1991–
.97	*Malawi
.970 1	Early history to 1891
	Including kingdom of Malawi
.970 2	Period as Nyasaland, 1891–1953
	Class here 20th century, British period
	For 1953–1963, see 968.9703; for 1964–1999, see 968.9704
.970 3	Period of federation, 1953–1963
.970 4	1964–
.970 41	Administration of H. Kamuzu Banda, 1964–1994
.970 42	1994–

969 †South Indian Ocean islands

.1	***Madagascar**
.101	Early history to 1895
	Including kingdoms of Betsimisaraka, Boina, Menabe, Merina
.103	French period, 1895–1960
	Class here 20th century
	For 1960–1999, see 969.105
.105	1960–
.105 1	1960–1975
	Class here administration of Philibert Tsiranana, 1960–1972
.105 2	Administration of Didier Ratsiraka, 1975–1993
.105 3	1993–
.4	**†Comoro Islands**
.41	†Comoros (Federal and Islamic Republic of the Comoros)
.45	†Mayotte
.6	**†Seychelles**
.7	**†Chagos Islands**
.8	***Réunion and Mauritius**

*Add as instructed under 930–990

†Add as instructed under 930–990; however, do not add historical periods

.81	*Réunion
.810 2	Early history to 1946
.810 4	Period as a Department of France, 1946–

Class here 20th century

For 1900–1946, see 969.8102

.82	*Mauritius
.820 1	Early history to 1810
.820 2	Period of British rule, 1810–1968

Including 20th century

For 1968–1999, see 969.8203

.820 3	1968–
.9	**†Isolated islands**

Including Amsterdam, Cocos (Keeling), Crozet, Kerguelen, Prince Edward, Saint Paul

970 General history of North America

SUMMARY

970.001–.009	**Standard subdivisions**
.01–.05	**Historical periods**
971	**Canada**
972	**Middle America** **Mexico**
973	**United States**
974	**Northeastern United States (New England and Middle Atlantic states)**
975	**Southeastern United States (South Atlantic states)**
976	**South central United States** **Gulf Coast states**
977	**North central United States** **Lake states**
978	**Western United States**
979	**Great Basin and Pacific Slope region of United States** **Pacific Coast states**

.001–.003	Standard subdivisions
.004	Racial, ethnic, national groups

Add to base number 970.004 notation 03–99 from Table 5, e.g., general history and civilization of North American native peoples in North America 970.00497
    (Option: Class North American native peoples in North America in 970.1; class specific native peoples in 970.3)

Class history and civilization of North American native peoples in a specific place before European discovery and conquest with the place, without using notation 00497, e.g., Aztecs before 1519 972.018

See Manual at 970.004

*Add as instructed under 930–990

†Add as instructed under 930–990; however, do not add historical periods

.005–.009   Standard subdivisions

As modified under 930–990

>   970.01–970.05   Historical periods

Class comprehensive works in 970

.01   Early history to 1599

.011   Earliest history to 1492

Including pre-Columbian claims

For Chinese claims, see 970.012; for Norse claims, see 970.013; for Welsh claims, see 970.014

.012   Chinese claims

.013   Norse claims

.014   Welsh claims

>   970.015–970.019   Period of European discovery and exploration

Class comprehensive works in 970.01

.015   Discoveries by Columbus

.016   Spanish and Portuguese explorations

.017   English explorations

.018   French explorations

.019   Explorations by other nations

.02   1600–1699

.03   1700–1799

.04   1800–1899

.05   1900–

.051   1900–1918

Class here period of World War I, 1914–1918

.052   1918–1945

Class here period of World War II, 1939–1945

.053   1945–1999

Class here 20th century

For 1900–1918, see 970.051; for 1918–1945, see 970.052

.053 4	1945–1949
.053 5	1950–1959
.053 6	1960–1969
.053 7	1970–1979
.053 8	1980–1989
.053 9	1990–1999
.054	2000–

(.1) **North American native peoples**   **Indians of North America**

(Optional number; prefer 970.00497)

Class special topics in 970.3–970.5

(.3) **Specific native peoples**

(Optional number; prefer 971–979 with use of subdivision 00497 from table under 930–990, e.g., the Hopi in Arizona 979.10049745)

Arrange alphabetically by name of people

Class government relations with specific native peoples in 970.5

(.4) **Native peoples in specific places in North America**

(Optional number; prefer 971–979 with use of subdivision 00497 from table under 930–990, e.g., native peoples in United States 973.0497, in Arizona 979.100497)

Add to base number 970.4 the numbers following —7 in notation 71–79 from Table 2, e.g., Indians in Arizona 970.491

Class specific native peoples in specific places in 970.3; class government relations in specific places in 970.5

(.5) **Government relations with North American native peoples**

(Optional number; prefer 323.1197 for comprehensive works; a specific subject with the subject, e.g., Black Hawk War 973.56, relation to the state in Canada 323.1197071)

History and policy

> ## 971–979   Countries and localities

Class comprehensive works in 970. Class specific native peoples in a specific place with the place in 971–979 with use of subdivision 00497 from table under 930–990, e.g., the Hopi in Arizona 979.10049745
    (Option: Class native peoples in specific places in North America in 970.4)

971   *Canada

---

*Add as instructed under 930–990

SUMMARY

971.01–.06	Historical periods	
.1	British Columbia	
.2	Prairie Provinces	
.3	Ontario	
.4	Quebec	
.5	Atlantic Provinces	Maritime Provinces
.6	Nova Scotia	
.7	Prince Edward Island	
.8	Newfoundland and Labrador, Saint Pierre and Miquelon	
.9	Northern territories	

> 971.01–971.06   Historical periods

Class comprehensive works in 971

SUMMARY

971.01	Early history to 1763
.02	Period of early British rule, 1763–1791
.03	Period of Upper and Lower Canada, 1791–1841
.04	Period of Province of Canada, 1841–1867
.05	Period of Dominion of Canada, 1867–1911
.06	1911–

.01   Early history to 1763

.011   Earliest history to 1632

.011 1   Period before European discovery and exploration

.011 2   Norse explorations

.011 3   French explorations

.011 4   English explorations

.016   Period of French and English expansion, 1632–1689

Class here 17th century

For 1600–1632, see 971.011; for 1689–1699, see 971.018

.016 2   Period of Company of New France, 1632–1663

.016 3   1663–1689

.018   Period of struggle of France and England for supremacy, 1689–1763

Including periods of War of the League of Augsburg, 1688–1697; War
of the Spanish Succession, 1701–1714; War of the Austrian Succession,
1740–1748
(Option: Class here North American aspects of War of the League of
Augsburg, War of the Spanish Succession, War of the Austrian
Succession; prefer 973.25 for War of the League of Augsburg, War
of the Spanish Succession, 973.26 for War of the Austrian
Succession)

Class here comprehensive works on period as a French royal province,
1663–1763

Class North American aspects of War of the League of Augsburg, War
of the Spanish Succession in 973.25; class North American aspects of
War of the Austrian Succession in 973.26; class comprehensive works
on War of the League of Augsburg in 940.2525; class comprehensive
works on War of the Spanish Succession in 940.2526; class
comprehensive works on War of the Austrian Succession in 940.2532

For 1663–1689, see 971.0163

.018 7   Expulsion of Acadians, 1755

.018 8   Period of Seven Years' War, 1756–1763

Class North American aspects of Seven Years' War in 973.26; class
comprehensive works on Seven Years' War in 940.2534

(Option: Class here North American aspects of Seven Years' War;
prefer 973.26)

.02   Period of early British rule, 1763–1791

.022   1763–1774

Including Quebec Act, 1774

(Option: Class here Pontiac's conspiracy, 1763–1764; prefer 973.27)

.024   Period of American Revolution, 1774–1783

Including settlement of Loyalists from United States, 1774–1789

For settlement of Loyalists during 1783–1789, see 971.028

.028   1783–1791

Class here Constitutional Act, 1791

.03   Period of Upper and Lower Canada, 1791–1841

Class here 19th century

For 1841–1867, see 971.04; for 1867–1899, see 971.05

.032   1791–1812

.034	Period of War of 1812, 1812–1814
	(Option: Class here War of 1812; prefer 973.52)
.036	1814–1837
.038	Period of rebellions of 1837–1838
	Including Family Compact of Upper Canada, Chateau Clique of Lower Canada
.039	1838–1841
	Class here Durham mission and report, 1838–1839; Act of Union, 1840
.04	Period of Province of Canada, 1841–1867
.042	1841–1864
.048	Period of Fenian activities, 1866–1871
.049	Period of Confederation, 1864–1867
	Including Charlottetown and Quebec Conferences, 1864; British North America Act, 1867
	For period of Fenian activities, see 971.048
.05	Period of Dominion of Canada, 1867–
	For 1911 to present, see 971.06
.051	First prime ministership of Sir John A. Macdonald, 1867–1873
	Including Riel's first (Red River) rebellion, 1869–1870
	For Fenian activities during 1867–1871, see 971.048
.052	Prime ministership of Alexander Mackenzie, 1873–1878
.054	Second prime ministership of Sir John A. Macdonald, 1878–1891
	Including Riel's second (Northwest) rebellion, 1885
.055	1891–1896
	Including prime ministerships of Sir John J. C. Abbott, 1891–1892; of Sir John Sparrow Thompson, 1892–1894; of Sir Mackenzie Bowell, 1894–1896; of Sir Charles Tupper, 1896
.056	Prime ministership of Sir Wilfrid Laurier, 1896–1911
.06	1911–
.061	1911–1921
.061 2	Prime ministership of Sir Robert Laird Borden, 1911–1920
.061 3	First prime ministership of Arthur Meighen, 1920–1921
.062	1921–1935

.062 2	First and second prime ministerships of William Lyon Mackenzie King, 1921–1930
	Including second prime ministership of Arthur Meighen, 1926
.062 3	Prime ministership of Richard Bedford Bennett, 1930–1935
.063	1935–1957
.063 2	Third prime ministership of William Lyon Mackenzie King, 1935–1948
.063 3	Prime ministership of Louis Stephen Saint-Laurent, 1948–1957
.064	1957–
.064 2	Prime ministership of John G. Diefenbaker, 1957–1963
.064 3	Prime ministership of Lester B. Pearson, 1963–1968
.064 4	First prime ministership of Pierre Elliott Trudeau, 1968–1979
.064 5	Prime ministership of Joe (Charles Joseph) Clark, 1979–1980
.064 6	Second prime ministership of Pierre Elliott Trudeau, 1980–1984
	Including prime ministership of John Turner, 1984
.064 7	Prime ministership of Brian Mulroney, 1984–1993
	Including prime ministership of Kim Campbell, 1993
.064 8	Prime ministership of Jean Chrétien, 1993–

>	**971.1–971.9 Specific provinces and territories**
	Class comprehensive works in 971
.1	***British Columbia**
.101	Early history to 1790
.102	Period of settlement and colony, 1790–1871
	Including colony of New Caledonia
.103	Period as a Province of Canada, 1871–
	For 1945 to present, see 971.04
.104	1945–
.2	***Prairie Provinces**
.201	Early history to 1869
	Including Rupert's Land
.202	1869–1945
.203	1945–

*Add as instructed under 930–990

.3	***Ontario**
.301	Early history to 1791
.302	Period of Upper Canada and Act of Union, 1791–1867
.303	Period as a Province of Canada, 1867–
	For 1945 to present, see 971.304
.304	1945–
.4	***Quebec**
.401	Early history to 1763
.401 2	Earliest history to 1608
	Including period of explorations by Jacques Cartier, 1534–1535
.401 4	French period, 1608–1763
.402	British period, 1763–1867
	Including period of Lower Canada, 1791–1841
.403	Period as a Province of Canada, 1867–
	For 1945 to present, see 971.404
.404	1945–
.5	***Atlantic Provinces　　　Maritime Provinces**
	For Nova Scotia, see 971.6; for Prince Edward Island, see 971.7; for Newfoundland and Labrador, see 971.8
.501	Early history to 1763
.502	Period as British colonies, 1763–1867
.503	Period as provinces of Canada, 1867–
	For 1945 to present, see 971.504
.504	1945–
.51	*New Brunswick
.510 1	Early history to 1784
.510 2	Period as separate province, 1784–1867
.510 3	Period as a Province of Canada, 1867–
	For 1945 to present, see 971.5104
.510 4	1945–
.6	***Nova Scotia**

*Add as instructed under 930–990

.601	Early history to 1763
	Including Acadia
.602	Period as a British colony, 1763–1867
.603	Period as a Province of Canada, 1867–
	For 1945 to present, see 971.604
.604	1945–
.7	***Prince Edward Island**
.701	Early history to 1769
.702	Period as separate province, 1769–1873
.703	Period as a Province of Canada, 1873–
	For 1945 to present, see 971.704
.704	1945–
.8	***Newfoundland and Labrador, Saint Pierre and Miquelon**

Subdivisions are added for Newfoundland, Labrador, Saint Pierre and Miquelon together; for Newfoundland and Labrador together; for Newfoundland alone

---

> 971.801–971.804 Historical periods for Newfoundland and Labrador together, for Newfoundland alone

Class comprehensive works in 971.8

.801	Early history to 1855
.802	1855–1934
.803	Period of suspension of parliamentary government, 1934–1949
.804	Period as a Province of Canada, 1949–
.82	*Labrador
.820 1	Early history to 1763
.820 2	Period when claimed by Lower Canada (Quebec) and Newfoundland, 1763–1927
.820 3	Period as dependency of Newfoundland, 1927–1949
.820 4	Period as part of Newfoundland, 1949–
.88	†Saint Pierre and Miquelon
.9	***Northern territories**

*Add as instructed under 930–990

†Add as instructed under 930–990; however, do not add historical periods

.901–.903   Historical periods

> Add to base number 971.9 the numbers following 971.2 in 971.201–971.203, e.g., 1945 to present 971.903

972   Middle America   Mexico

SUMMARY

972.000 1–.000 9   **Standard subdivisions of Middle America**
.001–.009   **Standard subdivisions of Mexico**
.01–.08   **Historical periods of Mexico**
.8   **Central America**
.9   **West Indies (Antilles) and Bermuda**

.000 1–.000 8   Standard subdivisions of Middle America

> As modified under 930–990

.000 9   Historical periods; areas, regions, places in general; persons of Middle America

.000 901–.000 905   Historical periods

> Add to base number 972.0009 the numbers following —090 in notation 0901–0905 from Table 1, e.g., middle America during 20th century 972.000904

.000 91–.000 99   Areas, regions, places in general; persons

> As modified under 930–990

.001–.009   Standard subdivisions of Mexico

> As modified under 930–990

>   972.01–972.08   Historical periods of Mexico

Class comprehensive works in 972

.01   Early history to 1519

.016   Classical period, ca. 100–ca. 900

.017   Ca. 900–1325

> Class here period of Toltec empire, ca. 900–ca. 1200

.018   Aztec period, 1325–1519

.02   Conquest and colonial period, 1519–1810

.03   Revolutionary period and period of independence, 1810–1822

.04   Periods of first empire and republic, 1822–1845

Class here 19th century

For a part of 19th century not provided for here, see the part, e.g., period of second empire 972.07

.05   Period of war with United States, 1845–1848

(Option: Class here Mexican War; prefer 973.62)

.06   Period of reaction and reform, 1848–1861

.07   Period of European intervention, 1861–1867

Class here period of second empire, 1864–1867

.08   Period of Republic, 1867–

.081   1867–1917

.081 2   1867–1876

.081 4   Porfiriato, 1876–1910

Class here administrations of Porfirio Díaz, 1876–1880, 1884–1910

.081 6   Period of Mexican Revolution, 1910–1917

.082   1917–1964

Class here 20th century

For 1900–1910, see 972.0814; for 1910–1917, see 972.0816; for 1964–1999, see 972.083

.082 1   Administrations of Venustiano Carranza and Adolfo de la Huerta, 1917–1920

.082 2   Administration of Alvaro Obregón, 1920–1924

.082 3   Administration of Plutarco Elías Calles, 1924–1928

.082 4   Administrations of Emilio Portes Gil, Pascual Ortiz Rubio, Abelardo L. Rodríguez, 1928–1934

.082 42   Administration of Emilio Portes Gil, 1928–1930

.082 43   Administration of Pascual Ortiz Rubio, 1930–1932

.082 44   Administration of Abelardo L. Rodríguez, 1932–1934

.082 5   Administration of Lázaro Cárdenas, 1934–1940

.082 6   Administration of Manuel Avila Camacho, 1940–1946

.082 7   Administration of Miguel Alemán, 1946–1952

.082 8   Administration of Adolfo Ruiz Cortines, 1952–1958

.082 9   Administration of Adolfo López Mateos, 1958–1964

.083	1964–
.083 1	Administration of Gustavo Díaz Ordaz, 1964–1970
.083 2	Administration of Luis Echeverría, 1970–1976
.083 3	Administration of José López Portillo, 1976–1982
.083 4	Administration of Miguel de la Madrid Hurtado, 1982–1988
.083 5	Administration of Carlos Salinas de Gortari, 1988–1994
.083 6	Administration of Ernesto Zedillo Ponce de León, 1994–

> ### 972.8–972.9 Other parts of Middle America

Class comprehensive works in 972

.8 ***Central America**

.801	Early history to 1502
.802	Period of European discovery, exploration, conquest, 1502–1535
.803	Colonial period, 1535–1821
.804	1821–1899

Including period of United Provinces of Central America, 1823–1840

.805	1900–
.805 1	1900–1944

Class here 20th century

For 1944–1979, see 972.8052; for 1979–1999, see 972.8053

.805 2	1944–1979
.805 3	1979–1999
.805 4	2000–

.81 ***Guatemala**

.810 1	Early history to 1502
.810 16	Mayan period, ca. 300–ca. 900

Class here comprehensive works on Mayan period in Middle America

Class a specific aspect of the Mayan period not provided for here with the aspect, e.g., Mayan period from ca. 900 to 1325 in Mexico 972.6017

.810 2	Period of European discovery, exploration, conquest, 1502–1524
.810 3	Colonial period, 1524–1821

*Add as instructed under 930–990

.810 4	1821–1871
.810 42	1821–1839

> Class here period as a part of United Provinces of Central America, 1823–1839

.810 44	1839–1871

> Class here administration of Rafael Carrera, 1839–1865

.810 5	1871–
.810 51	1871–1931
.810 52	1931–1986

> Class here 20th century

> *For 1900–1931, see 972.81051; for 1986–1999, see 972.81053*

.810 53	1986–
.82	*Belize
.820 1	Early history to 1502
.820 2	Period of Spanish discovery and colonization, 1502–1638
.820 3	1638–1862

> Class here period of British involvement, 1638–1963

> *For period as a British colony, see 972.8204*

.820 4	Period as a British colony, 1862–1963

> Class here 20th century

> *For 1964–1999, see 972.8205*

.820 5	1964–
.83	*Honduras
.830 1	Early history to 1502
.830 2	Period of Spanish discovery, exploration, conquest, 1502–1542
.830 3	Colonial period, 1542–1821
.830 4	1821–1838

> Class here period as a part of United Provinces of Central America, 1823–1838

.830 5	1838–
.830 51	1838–1924

*Add as instructed under 930–990

.830 52	1924–1978
	Class here 20th century
	For 1900–1924, see 972.83051; for 1978–1999, see 972.83053
.830 53	1978–
.84	*El Salvador
.840 1	Early history to 1524
.840 2	Period of Spanish discovery, exploration, conquest, 1524–1542
.840 3	Colonial period, 1542–1821
.840 4	1821–1859
.840 42	1821–1839
	Class here period as a part of United Provinces of Central America, 1823–1839
.840 44	1839–1859
.840 5	1859–
.840 51	1859–1931
.840 52	1931–1979
	Class here 20th century
	For 1900–1931, see 972.84051; for 1979–1999, see 972.84053
.840 53	1979–
.85	*Nicaragua
.850 1	Early history to 1502
.850 2	Period of Spanish discovery, exploration, conquest, 1502–1527
.850 3	Colonial period, 1527–1821
.850 4	1821–1893
.850 42	1821–1838
	Class here period as a part of United Provinces of Central America, 1823–1838
.850 44	1838–1893
.850 5	1893–
.850 51	1893–1934
	Class here period of interventions by United States, 1909–1933

*Add as instructed under 930–990

.850 52	1934–1979
	Class here 20th century
	For 1900–1934, see 972.85051; for 1979–1990, see 972.85053; for 1990–1999, see 972.85054
.850 53	1979–1990
.850 54	1990–
.86	*Costa Rica
.860 1	Early history to 1502
.860 2	Period of Spanish discovery, exploration, conquest, 1502–1560
.860 3	Colonial period, 1560–1821
.860 4	1821–1948
.860 42	1821–1838
	Class here period as a part of United Provinces of Central America, 1823–1838
.860 44	1838–1948
.860 5	1948–
	Class here 20th century
	For 1900–1948, see 972.86044
.87	*Panama
.870 1	Early history to 1514
.870 11	Early history to 1501
.870 12	Period of Spanish discovery, exploration, conquest, 1501–1514
.870 2	Colonial period, 1514–1821
	Including period as a part of Viceroyalty of New Granada, 1739–1810
	Class comprehensive works on Viceroyalty of New Granada in 986.102
.870 3	Period as a part of Colombia, 1821–1903
.870 5	1903–
.870 51	1903–1977
.870 53	1977–

*Add as instructed under 930–990

.9	***West Indies (Antilles) and Bermuda**

Class here Caribbean Area

For a part of Caribbean Area not provided for here, see the part, e.g., Venezuela 987

.901	Early history to 1492
.902	Period of European discovery and early colonial period, 1492–1608
.903	1608–1801
.904	1801–1902
.905	1902–
.905 1	1902–1945
.905 2	1945–1999

Class here 20th century

For 1900–1902, see 972.904; for 1902–1945, see 972.9051

.905 3	2000–
.91	***Cuba**
.910 1	Early history to 1492
.910 2	Period of European discovery, exploration, conquest, 1492–1514
.910 3	1514–1763
.910 4	1763–1810
.910 5	1810–1899

For Spanish-American War, see 973.89

.910 6	1899–

Class here period of Republic, 1902 to present

.910 61	Period of American military occupation, 1899–1902
.910 62	1902–1933
.910 63	1933–1958
.910 64	Period of Fidel Castro, 1959–
.92	***Jamaica and Cayman Islands**

Subdivisions are added for Jamaica and Cayman Islands together, for Jamaica alone

---

> 972.920 1–972.920 6 Historical periods of Jamaica

Class comprehensive works in 972.92

*Add as instructed under 930–990

.920 1	Early history to 1494
.920 2	1494–1607
.920 3	1607–1832
.920 31	Last period of Spanish rule, 1607–1655
.920 32	1655–1692
	Including Great Earthquake, 1692
.920 33	1692–1782
.920 34	1782–1832
	Class here antislavery struggle and emancipation
.920 4	1832–1904
	Class here 19th century
	For 1801–1832, see 972.92034
.920 5	1904–1962
	Class here 20th century
	For 1901–1904, see 972.9204; for 1962–1999, see 972.9206
.920 6	Period of independence, 1962–
.921	†Cayman Islands
.93	*Dominican Republic
.930 1	Early history to 1492
.930 2	Period of European discovery and early colonial period, 1492–1608
.930 3	1608–1801
.930 4	1801–1902
.930 5	1902–
.930 52	1902–1930
.930 53	Period of Rafael Léonidas Trujillo Molina, 1930–1961
.930 54	1961–
.94	*Haiti
.940 1	Early history to 1492
.940 2	Period of Spanish rule, 1492–1625
.940 3	Period as a French colony, 1625–1804
.940 4	1804–1915

*Add as instructed under 930–990

†Add as instructed under 930–990; however, do not add historical periods

.940 5	Period of American occupation, 1915–1934
.940 6	1934–1957

Class here 20th century

For 1900–1915, see 972.8904; for 1915–1934, see 972.9405; for 1957–1999, see 972.9407

.940 7	1957–
.940 72	Periods of François Duvalier and Jean-Claude Duvalier, 1957–1986
.940 73	1986–
.95	*Puerto Rico
.950 1	Early history to 1493
.950 2	Period of European discovery and early colonial period, 1493–1602
.950 3	1602–1804
.950 4	1804–1899
.950 5	1900–
.950 52	1900–1952

Class here 20th century

For 1952–1999, see 972.95053

.950 53	Period of Commonwealth, 1952–
.96	†Bahama Islands
.97	†Leeward Islands

For Dominica, see 972.9841

.972	†Virgin Islands
.973	†Anguilla and Saint Kitts-Nevis
.974	†Antigua and Barbuda
.975	†Montserrat
.976	†Guadeloupe
.977	†Leeward Netherlands islands
.98	†Windward and other southern islands
.981	†Barbados
.982	†Martinique
.983	*Trinidad and Tobago

*Add as instructed under 930–990

†Add as instructed under 930–990; however, do not add historical periods

.983 01	Early history to 1498
.983 02	Spanish period, 1498–1797
.983 03	British period, 1797–1962

Including 20th century

For 1962–1999, see 972.98304

.983 04	Period of independence, 1962–
.984	†Windward Islands
.984 1	†Dominica
.984 3	†Saint Lucia
.984 4	†Saint Vincent and the Grenadines

For Carriacou, see 972.9845

.984 5	†Grenada and Carriacou
.986	†Netherlands islands

For Leeward Netherlands islands, see 972.977

.99	†Bermuda

973　United States

For specific states, see 974–979

SUMMARY

973.01–.09	Standard subdivisions
.1	Early history to 1607
.2	Colonial period, 1607–1775
.3	Periods of Revolution and Confederation, 1775–1789
.4	Constitutional period, 1789–1809
.5	1809–1845
.6	1845–1861
.7	Administration of Abraham Lincoln, 1861–1865　　Civil War
.8	Reconstruction period, 1865–1901
.9	1901–

.01–.09　Standard subdivisions

As modified under 930–990

(If optional notation 734–739 from Table 2 is chosen, use 973.01–973.09 for historical periods, and 973.001–973.009 for standard subdivisions)

.1　Early history to 1607

Add to base number 973.1 the numbers following 970.01 in 970.011–970.019, e.g., French explorations 973.18

.2　Colonial period, 1607–1775

†Add as instructed under 930–990; however, do not add historical periods

> 973.21–973.22 Period of early settlements, 1607–1643

Class comprehensive works in 973.21. Class a specific European settlement with the settlement in 974–975, e.g., settlement of New Plymouth Colony 974.48202, of Jamestown 975.5425101

.21 Period of Virginia settlements, 1607–1620

.22 Period of other early settlements, 1620–1643

Including Pequot War, 1636–1638

.23 1643–1664

.24 1664–1689

Including King Philip's War, 1675–1676

.25 1689–1732

Including King William's War (North American aspect of War of the League of Augsburg), 1688–1697; Queen Anne's War (North American aspects of War of the Spanish Succession), 1701–1714
(Option: Class North American aspects of War of the League of Augsburg, War of the Spanish Succession in 971.018)

Class comprehensive works on War of the League of Augsburg in 940.2525; class comprehensive works on War of the Spanish Succession in 940.2526

.26 Period of extension of English rule, 1732–1763

Including King George's War (North American aspects of War of the Austrian Succession), 1740–1748; French and Indian War (North American aspects of Seven Year's War), 1756–1763
(Option: Class North American aspects of War of the Austrian Succession in 971.018, class Seven Years' War in 971.0188)

Class comprehensive works on War of the Austrian Succession in 940.2532; class comprehensive works on Seven Years' War in 940.2534

.27 End of colonial period, 1763–1775

Including Pontiac's Conspiracy, 1763–1764
(Option: Class Pontiac's Conspiracy in 971.022)

Class events of 1763–1775 as causes of American Revolution in 973.311

.3 Periods of Revolution and Confederation, 1775–1789

.308 Kinds of persons during 1775–1789

Class here relation of kinds of persons to the Revolution [*formerly* 973.315]

.309 2 Persons

Class here personal narratives [*formerly* 973.38]

.31	Social, political, economic history
	For diplomatic history, see 973.32
.311	Causes
.311 1	Stamp Act, 1765–1766
.311 2	Commercial restrictions
	Including Navigation Acts, Townshend Acts, burning of the Gaspée, 1772
	For tax on tea, see 973.3115
.311 3	Quartering of troops and Boston Massacre, 1770
.311 4	Taxation and representation
.311 5	Tax on tea and Boston Tea Party, 1773
.311 6	Boston Port Bill, 1774
.312	Continental Congress
.313	Declaration of Independence, 1776
.314	Loyalists (Tories)
	Class settlement of Loyalists in Canada in 971.024
[.315]	Relation of kinds of persons to the Revolution
	Relocated to 973.308
.316	Results
	For Treaty of Peace, see 973.317
.317	Treaty of Peace (Versailles Treaty), 1783
.318	Period of confederation, 1783–1789

>   973.32–973.38   Aspects of American Revolution

Class comprehensive works in 973.3

.32	Diplomatic history
	Class here relations of United States with other nations
	Add to base number 973.32 the numbers following —4 in notation 41–49 from Table 2, e.g., relations with France 973.324
	For Treaty of Paris, see 973.317
.33	Operations
	For naval operations, see 973.35

.331	Operations of 1775
.331 1	Battles of Lexington and Concord, 1775
.331 2	Battle of Bunker Hill, 1775
.332	Operations of 1776–January 3, 1777
.333	Operations of 1777

Class Battle of Princeton in 973.332

For winter at Valley Forge, see 973.3341

.334	Operations of 1778
.334 1	Winter at Valley Forge, 1777–1778
.335	Operations of 1779
.336	Operations of 1780
.337	Operations of 1781
.338	Operations of 1782
.339	Operations of 1783
.34	Military units

Class here organization, history, rosters, service records

Class operations of military units in 973.33. Class units engaged in a special service with the service, e.g., privateering 973.35

For naval units, see 973.35; for rolls of honor, lists of dead, see 973.36

.341	British troops

For mercenary troops, see 973.342; for American native peoples as allies, see 973.343

.342	Mercenary troops
.343	American native peoples as allies of British
.344–.345	American troops

Add to base number 973.34 the numbers following —7 in notation 74–75 from Table 2, e.g., Pennsylvania troops 973.3448

.346	Auxiliary troops on American side

Including Polish, Spanish, Swedish

For French troops, see 973.347

.347	French troops

.35 Naval history

Including privateering

Class here operations, ships, units

.36 Celebrations, commemorations, memorials

Including rolls of honor, lists of dead

Class celebrations, commemorations, memorials of a specific event with the event, e.g., Battle of Bunker Hill 973.3312

.37 Prisoners of war; health and social services

.371 Prisoners of war

Including British prisons and prison ships, exchange of prisoners

For American prisons, see 973.372

.372 American prisons

.375 Medical services

For hospitals, see 973.376

.376 Hospitals

.38 Other topics of American Revolution

Including deserters, military life and customs, servicemen missing in action

Personal narratives relocated to 973.3092

.381 Treason

For treason of Benedict Arnold, see 973.382; for treason of Charles Lee, see 973.383

.382 Treason of Benedict Arnold

.383 Treason of Charles Lee

.385 American secret service and spies

Class here comprehensive works on secret service and spies

For British secret service and spies, see 973.386

.386 British secret service and spies

.388 Propaganda

.4 Constitutional period, 1789–1809

.41 Administration of George Washington, 1789–1797

For second term, see 973.43

.43 Second term of the administration of George Washington, 1793–1797

| .44 | Administration of John Adams, 1797–1801 |
| .46 | Administration of Thomas Jefferson, 1801–1809 |

> *For Tripolitan War, see 973.47; for second term, see 973.48*

| .47 | Tripolitan War, 1801–1805 |

(Option: Class in 961.023)

| .48 | Second term of the administration of Thomas Jefferson, 1805–1809 |
| **.5** | **1809–1845** |

Class here 19th century

Class events of 1809–1845 as causes of Civil War in 973.711

> *For a specific part of 19th century not provided for here, see the part, e.g.,*
> *Civil War 973.7*

| .51 | Administration of James Madison, 1809–1817 |

> *For War of 1812, see 973.52; for war with Algiers, see 973.53*

| .52 | War of 1812, 1812–1815 |

(Option: Class in 971.034)

| .520 92 | Persons |

Class here personal narratives [*formerly* 973.528]

| .521 | Social, political, economic history |

Including causes, results

> *For diplomatic history, see 973.522*

| .522 | Diplomatic history |

Relations of United States with other nations

| .523 | Operations |

> *For naval operations, see 973.525*

| .523 8 | Operations in the South |

> *For Battle of New Orleans, see 973.5239*

| .523 9 | Battle of New Orleans, 1815 |
| .524 | Military units |

Class here organization, history, rosters, service records

Class operations of military units in 973.523. Class units engaged in a special service with the service, e.g., privateering 973.525

> *For naval units, see 973.525; for rolls of honor, lists of dead, see*
> *973.526*

.524 1	British troops
.524 2	American native peoples as allies of the British
.524 4–.524 7	American troops

> Add to base number 973.524 the numbers following —7 in notation 74–77 from Table 2, e.g., Pennsylvania troops 973.52448

.525 Naval history

> Class here operations, ships, units
>
> Including privateering

.525 4	Battle of Lake Erie, 1813
.525 6	Battle of Lake Champlain, 1814

.526 Celebrations, commemorations, memorials

> Including rolls of honor, lists of dead
>
> Class celebrations, commemorations, memorials of a specific event with the event, e.g., Battle of Lake Erie 973.5254

.527 Prisoners of war; health and social services

> Including exchange of prisoners, prisoner-of-war camps

.527 5 Medical services

> Including hospitals

.528 Other topics of War of 1812

> Including deserters, military life and customs, servicemen missing in action
>
> Personal narratives relocated to 973.52092

.528 5 Secret service and spies

.53 War with Algiers, 1815

> (Option: Class in 961.023)

.54 Administration of James Monroe, 1817–1825

> Including First Seminole War, 1818; Missouri Compromise, 1820
>
> *See also 973.7113 for Missouri Compromise as a cause of Civil War*

.55 Administration of John Quincy Adams, 1825–1829

.56 Administration of Andrew Jackson, 1829–1837

> Including Black Hawk War, 1832
> (Option: Class Black Hawk War in 970.5)

.561 Nullification movement

.57	Administration of Martin Van Buren, 1837–1841

Including Second Seminole War, 1835–1842

.58	Administrations of William Henry Harrison and John Tyler, 1841–1845
.6	**1845–1861**

Class events of 1845–1861 as causes of Civil War in 973.711

.61	Administration of James Knox Polk, 1845–1849

Including Wilmot Proviso, 1847

For Mexican War, see 973.62

See also 973.7113 for Wilmot Proviso as a cause of Civil War

.62	Mexican War, 1845–1848

(Option: Class in 972.05)

.620 92	Persons

Class here personal narratives [*formerly* 973.628]

.621	Social, political, economic history

Including causes, results

For diplomatic history, see 973.622

.622	Diplomatic history

Relations of United States with other nations

.623	Operations

For naval operations, see 973.625

.624	Military units

Class here organization, history, rosters, service records

Class operations of military units in 973.623. Class units engaged in a special service with the service, e.g., naval operations 973.625

For naval units, see 973.625; for rolls of honor, lists of dead, see 973.626

.625	Naval history

Operations, ships, units

.626	Celebrations, commemorations, memorials

Including rolls of honor, lists of dead

Class celebrations, commemorations, memorials of a specific event with the event, e.g., capture of Chapultepec 973.623

.627	Prisoners of war; health and social services
	Including prisoner-of-war camps
.627 5	Medical services
	Including hospitals
.628	Other topics of Mexican War
	Including deserters; military life and customs; servicemen missing in action; unconventional warfare, propaganda
	Personal narratives relocated to 973.62092
.63	Administration of Zachary Taylor, 1849–1850
.64	Administration of Millard Fillmore, 1850–1853
	Including Compromise of 1850
	See also 973.7113 for Compromise of 1850 as a cause of Civil War
.66	Administration of Franklin Pierce, 1853–1857
.68	Administration of James Buchanan, 1857–1861
	For Dred Scott decision, see 973.7115; for John Brown's Raid, see 973.7116
.7	**Administration of Abraham Lincoln, 1861–1865 Civil War**

SUMMARY

973.701–.709	**Standard subdivisions**
.71	**Social, political, economic history**
.72	**Diplomatic history**
.73	**Operations**
.74	**Military units**
.75	**Naval history**
.76	**Celebrations, commemorations, memorials**
.77	**Prisoners of war; health and social services**
.78	**Other military topics and personal narratives**

.708	Civil War with respect to kinds of persons [*formerly* 973.715]
	Class southern Union sympathizers in 973.717; class northern Confederate sympathizers in 973.718
.709 2	Persons
	Do not use for personal narratives; class in 973.781–973.782
.71	Social, political, economic history
	For diplomatic history, see 973.72
.711	Causes
	For the South and secession, see 973.713

.711 2	Extension of slavery
.711 3	Wilmot Proviso, 1847, and compromises
	Including Missouri Compromise, 1820; Compromise of 1850
.711 4	Abolition movement
.711 5	Fugitive slaves
	Including underground railroad, Dred Scott decision
.711 6	John Brown's Raid, 1859
.712	Efforts to preserve or restore peace
	For compromises, see 973.7113
.713	The South and secession
	Confederate States of America in the war
.714	Results
	Including Emancipation Proclamation, 1863; establishment of Freedmen's Bureau, 1865
	Class a result as a specific event with the event, e.g., Reconstruction 973.8
[.715]	Civil War with respect to kinds of persons
	Relocated to 973.708
.717	Southern Union sympathizers
.718	Northern Confederate sympathizers
.72	Diplomatic history
.721	Relations of Confederacy with other nations
.722	Relations of Union with other nations
.73	Operations
	For naval operations, see 973.75
.730 1	Strategy
	Do not use for philosophy and theory; class in 973.73
.730 12	Union side
.730 13	Confederate side
.731	Opening phase, 1861–April, 1862
.732	May-August, 1862
.733	September, 1862–May, 1863

.733 6	Lee's invasion of Maryland, 1862
.734	June-August, 1863
.734 4	Siege and fall of Vicksburg, 1863
.734 9	Battle of Gettysburg, 1863
.735	September-December, 1863
.735 9	Chattanooga campaign, 1863
.736	January-May, 1864

For Atlanta Campaign, see 973.7371

.737	June-December, 1864
.737 1	Atlanta Campaign, 1864
.737 8	Sherman's March to the Sea and Savannah campaign, 1864
.738	1865
.74	Military units

Class here organization, history, rosters, service records

Class operations of military units in 973.73. Class units engaged in a special service with the service, e.g., privateering 973.75

For naval units, see 973.75; for rolls of honor, lists of dead, see 973.76

.741	Union troops

For state units, see 973.744–973.749

.741 5	Black troops
.742	Confederate troops

For state units, see 973.744–973.749

.744–.749	State units

Add to base number 973.74 the numbers following —7 in notation 74–79 from Table 2, e.g., Ohio troops 973.7471

.75	Naval history

Including operations, privateering, blockade running

.752	Battle of Monitor and Merrimac, 1862
.754	Battle of Kearsarge and Alabama, 1864
.757	Confederate Navy

Ships and units

.758	Union navy

Ships and units

.76	Celebrations, commemorations, memorials

Including rolls of honor, lists of dead

Class celebrations, commemorations, memorials of a specific event with the event, e.g., Battle of Antietam 973.7336

.77	Prisoners of war; health and social services
.771	Confederate prisoner-of-war camps

Including exchange of prisoners

Class here prisoners of war

> *For Union prisoner-of-war camps, see 973.772*

.772	Union prisoner-of-war camps
.775	Medical services

> *For hospitals, see 973.776*

.776	Hospitals
.777	Welfare work

Including United States Sanitary Commission

.778	Religious life and chaplain services
.78	Other military topics and personal narratives

Including deserters, servicemen missing in action

> 973.781–973.782   Personal narratives

Class comprehensive works in 973.78. Class personal narratives on a specific subject with the subject, e.g., on prisoner-of-war camps 973.771

.781	Personal narratives of individuals from Union side
.782	Personal narratives of individuals from Confederate side
.783	Military life and customs of Union side

Class here comprehensive works on military life and customs

> *For military life and customs of Confederate side, see 973.784*

.784	Military life and customs of Confederate side
.785	Union secret service and spies

Class here comprehensive works on secret service and spies

> *For Confederate secret service and spies, see 973.786*

.786	Confederate secret service and spies

.788	Propaganda
.8	**Reconstruction period, 1865–1901**
.81	Administration of Andrew Johnson, 1865–1869
.82	Administration of Ulysses Simpson Grant, 1869–1877
.83	Administration of Rutherford Birchard Hayes, 1877–1881
.84	Administrations of James Abram Garfield and Chester Alan Arthur, 1881–1885
.85	First administration of Grover Cleveland, 1885–1889
.86	Administration of Benjamin Harrison, 1889–1893
.87	Second administration of Grover Cleveland, 1893–1897
.88	Administration of William McKinley, 1897–1901

         For Spanish-American War, see 973.89

.89	Spanish-American War, 1898

         (Option: Class in 946.074)

.890 92	Persons

         Class here personal narratives [*formerly* 973.898]

.891	Social, political, economic history

         Including causes, results

         For diplomatic history, see 973.892

.892	Diplomatic history

         Relations of United States with other nations

.893	Operations

         For naval operations, see 973.895

.893 3	Cuban campaign, 1898
.893 5	Puerto Rican campaign, 1898
.893 7	Philippine campaign, 1898
.894	Military units

         Class here organization, history, rosters, service records

         Class operations of military units in 973.893. Class units engaged in a special service with the service, e.g., naval operations 973.895

         For naval units, see 973.895; for rolls of honor, lists of dead, see 973.896

.895	Naval history

Class here operations, ships, units

.896	Celebrations, commemorations, memorials

Including rolls of honor, lists of dead

Class celebrations, commemorations, memorials of a specific event with the event, e.g., Battle of Manila Bay 973.895

.897	Prisoners of war; health and social services
.897 5	Medical services

Including hospitals

.898	Other topics of Spanish-American War

Including deserters; military life and customs; servicemen missing in action; unconventional warfare, propaganda

Personal narratives relocated to 973.89092

.9	**1901–**
.91	1901–1953

Class here 20th century

For 1900–1901, see 973.88; for 1953–1999, see 973.92

.911	Administration of Theodore Roosevelt, 1901–1909
.912	Administration of William Howard Taft, 1909–1913
.913	Administration of Woodrow Wilson, 1913–1921
.914	Administration of Warren Gamaliel Harding, 1921–1923
.915	Administration of Calvin Coolidge, 1923–1929
.916	Administration of Herbert Clark Hoover, 1929–1933
.917	Administration of Franklin Delano Roosevelt, 1933–1945
.918	Administration of Harry S Truman, 1945–1953
.92	1953–
.921	Administration of Dwight David Eisenhower, 1953–1961
.922	Administration of John Fitzgerald Kennedy, 1961–1963
.923	Administration of Lyndon Baines Johnson, 1963–1969

Class here period of Vietnamese War, 1961–1975

For 1961–1963 period of Vietnamese War, see 973.922; for 1969–1974 period of Vietnamese War, see 973.924; for 1974–1975 period of Vietnamese War, see 973.925

.924	Administration of Richard Milhous Nixon, 1969–1974
.925	Administration of Gerald Rudolph Ford, 1974–1977
.926	Administration of Jimmy (James Earl) Carter, 1977–1981
.927	Administration of Ronald Reagan, 1981–1989
.928	Administration of George Bush, 1989–1993
.929	Administration of Bill Clinton, 1993–

> ## 974–979 Specific states of United States

Class comprehensive works in 973

For Hawaii, see 996.9

> ## 974–975 Northeastern and southeastern United States

Add to each subdivision identified by † as follows:

01	Early history to 1620
02	Colonial period, 1620 1776
03	1776–1865
04	1865–
041	1865–1918
042	1918–1945
043	1945–1999
	Class here 20th century
	For 1900–1918, see 041; for 1918–1945, see 042
044	2000–

Class comprehensive works in 974

974 *†Northeastern United States (New England and Middle Atlantic states)

.1	*†Maine
.2	*†New Hampshire
.3	*†Vermont
.4	*†Massachusetts
.5	*†Rhode Island
.6	*†Connecticut
.7	*†New York
.8	*†Pennsylvania

*Add as instructed under 930–990

†Add historical periods as instructed under 974–975

.9   *†New Jersey

975   *†**Southeastern United States (South Atlantic states)**

.1   *†Delaware

.2   *†Maryland

.3   *District of Columbia (Washington)

.301   Early history to 1799

.302   1800–1865

.303   1865–1933

.304   1933–

.304 1   1933–1999

> Class here 20th century
>
> *For 1900–1933, see 975.303*

.304 2   2000–

.4   *†West Virginia

.5   *†Virginia

.6   *†North Carolina

.7   *†South Carolina

.8   *†Georgia

.9   *Florida

.901   Early history to 1763

.902   English period, 1763–1783

.903   Spanish period, 1783–1821

.904   Territorial period, 1821–1845

.905   Early statehood period, 1845–1865

.906   1865–

.906 1   1865–1918

.906 2   1918–1945

.906 3   1945–1999

> Class here 20th century
>
> *For 1900–1918, see 975.9061; for 1918–1945, see 975.9062*

---

*Add as instructed under 930–990

†Add historical periods as instructed under 974–975

.906 4	2000–

976　*South central United States　Gulf Coast states

.01	Early history to 1700
.02	1700–1799
.03	1800–1865
.04	1865–
.041	1865–1918
.042	1918–1945
.043	1945–1999

> Class here 20th century
>
> *For 1900–1918, see 976.041; for 1918–1945, see 976.042*

.044	2000–

.1　*Alabama

.101	Early history to 1701
.102	French period, 1701–1763
.103	British period, 1763–1783
.104	Spanish and territorial periods, 1783–1817
.105	Territorial and early statehood periods, 1817–1865
.106	1865–
.106 1	1865–1918
.106 2	1918–1945
.106 3	1945–1999

> Class here 20th century
>
> *For 1900–1918, see 976.1061; for 1918–1945, see 976.1062*

.106 4	2000–

.2　*Mississippi

.201–.206	Historical periods

> Add to base number 976.2 the numbers following 976.1 in
> 976.101–976.106, e.g., British period 976.203

.3　*Louisiana

.301	Early history to 1718

*Add as instructed under 930–990

.302	French period, 1718–1763
.303	Spanish period, 1763–1803
.304	French and territorial periods, 1803–1812
.305	Early statehood period, 1812–1865
.306	1865–
.306 1	1865–1918
.306 2	1918–1945
.306 3	1945–1999

Class here 20th century

> For 1900–1918, see 976.3061; for 1918–1945, see 976.3062

.306 4	2000–

.4   *Texas

.401	Early history to 1680
.402	Spanish and French periods, 1680–1821
.403	Mexican period, 1821–1836
.404	Period of the Republic, 1836–1846
.405	Early statehood period, 1846–1865
.406	1865–
.406 1	1865–1918
.406 2	1918–1945
.406 3	1945–1999

Class here 20th century

> For 1900–1918, see 976.4061; for 1918–1945, see 976.4062

.406 4	2000–

.6   *Oklahoma

.601	Early history to 1682
.602	French and Spanish periods, 1682–1803
.603	Period of Indian Territory, 1803–1866
.604	Territorial and early statehood periods, 1866–1907
.605	1907–
.605 2	1907–1945

*Add as instructed under 930–990

.605 3	1945–1999
	Class here 20th century
	For 1900–1907, see 976.604; for 1907–1945, see 976.6052
.605 4	2000–

.7 *Arkansas

.701	Early history to 1686
.702	French and Spanish periods, 1686–1803
.703	Preterritorial and territorial periods, 1803–1836
.704	Early statehood period, 1836–1865
.705	1865–
.705 1	1865–1918
.705 2	1918–1945
.705 3	1945–1999
	Class here 20th century
	For 1900–1918, see 976.7051; for 1918–1945, see 976.7052
.705 4	2000–

.8 *Tennessee

.801	Early history to 1682
.802	French, Spanish, English periods, 1682–1769
.803	Early settlement and territorial periods, 1769–1796
	Including District of Washington, State of Franklin
.804	Early statehood period, 1796–1865
.805	1865–
.805 1	1865–1918
.805 2	1918–1945
.805 3	1945–1999
	Class here 20th century
	For 1900–1918, see 976.8051; for 1918–1945, see 976.8052
.805 4	2000–

.9 *Kentucky

.901	Early history to 1736

*Add as instructed under 930–990

.902	1736–1792

Including periods of French, British, Virginian control; Transylvania Colony

.903	Early statehood period, 1792–1865
.904	1865–
.904 1	1865–1918
.904 2	1918–1945
.904 3	1945–1999

Class here 20th century

> *For 1900–1918, see 976.9041; for 1918–1945, see 976.9042*

.904 4	2000–

977   *North central United States   Lake states

.01	Early history to 1787
.02	1787–1865
.03	1865–
.031	1865–1918
.032	1918–1945
.033	1945–1999

Class here 20th century

> *For 1900–1918, see 977.031; for 1918–1945, see 977.032*

.034	2000–

.1   *Ohio

.101	Early history to 1763
.102	British and early United States periods, 1763–1787
.103	Territorial and early statehood periods, 1787–1865
.104	1865–
.104 1	1865–1918
.104 2	1918–1945
.104 3	1945–1999

Class here 20th century

> *For 1900–1918, see 977.1041; for 1918–1945, see 977.1042*

*Add as instructed under 930–990

.104 4	2000–

.2 *Indiana

.201–.204	Historical periods

> Add to base number 977.2 the numbers following 977.1 in 977.101–977.104, e.g., territorial period 977.203

.3 *Illinois

.301–.304	Historical periods

> Add to base number 977.3 the numbers following 977.1 in 977.101–977.104, e.g., territorial period 977.303

.4 *Michigan

.401–.404	Historical periods

> Add to base number 977.4 the numbers following 977.1 in 977.101–977.104, e.g., territorial period 977.403

.5 *Wisconsin

.501–.504	Historical periods

> Add to base number 977.5 the numbers following 977.1 in 977.101–977.104, e.g., territorial period 977.503

.6 *Minnesota

.601	Early history to 1660
.602	French period, 1660–1783
.603	Preterritorial period, 1783–1849
.604	Territorial and early statehood periods, 1849–1900
.605	1900–
.605 1	1900–1918
.605 2	1918–1945
.605 3	1945–1999

> Class here 20th century
>
> *For 1900–1918, see 977.6051; for 1918–1945, see 977.6052*

.605 4	2000–

.7 *Iowa

.701	Early history to 1838
.702	Territorial and early statehood periods, 1838–1899

*Add as instructed under 930–990

.703	1900–
.703 1	1900–1918
.703 2	1918–1945
.703 3	1945–1999

> Class here 20th century
>
> *For 1900–1918, see 977.7031; for 1918–1945, see 977.7032*

.703 4	2000–

.8   *Missouri

.801	Early history to 1750
.802	French and Spanish periods, 1750–1803
.803	Territorial and early statehood periods, 1803–1899
.804	1900–
.804 1	1900–1918
.804 2	1918–1945
.804 3	1945–1999

> Class here 20th century
>
> *For 1900–1918, see 977.8041; for 1918–1945, see 977.8042*

.804 4	2000–

978   *Western United States

.01	Early history to 1799
.02	1800–1899
.03	1900–
.031	1900–1918
.032	1918–1945
.033	1945–1999

> Class here 20th century
>
> *For 1900–1918, see 978.031; for 1918–1945, see 978.032*

.034	2000–

.1   *Kansas

.101	Early history to 1803
.102	Territorial period, 1803–1861

*Add as instructed under 930–990

.103	Statehood period, 1861–
.103 1	1861–1918
.103 2	1918–1945
.103 3	1945–1999

Class here 20th century

> For 1900–1918, see 978.1031; for 1918–1945, see 978.1032

.103 4	2000–
.2	***Nebraska**
.201	Early history to 1854
.202	Territorial period, 1854–1867
.203	Statehood period, 1867–
.203 1	1867–1918
.203 2	1918–1945
.203 3	1945–1999

Class here 20th century

> For 1900–1918, see 978.2031; for 1918–1945, see 978.2032

.203 4	2000–
.3	***South Dakota**
.301	Early history to 1861
.302	Territorial period, 1861–1889
.303	Statehood period, 1889–
.303 1	1889–1918
.303 2	1918–1945
.303 3	1945–1999

Class here 20th century

> For 1900–1918, see 978.3031; for 1918–1945, see 978.3032

.303 4	2000–
.4	***North Dakota**
.401–.403	Historical periods

Add to base number 978.4 the numbers following 978.3 in 978.301–978.303, e.g., territorial period 978.402

.6   ***Montana**

*Add as instructed under 930–990

.601	Early history to 1864
.602	Territorial period, 1864–1889
.603	Statehood period, 1889–
.603 1	1889–1918
.603 2	1918–1945
.603 3	1945–1999

Class here 20th century

For 1900–1918, see 978.6031; for 1918–1945, see 978.6032

.603 4	2000–
.7	***Wyoming**
.701	Early history to 1868
.702	Territorial period, 1868–1890
.703	Statehood period, 1890–
.703 1	1890–1918
.703 2	1918–1945
.703 3	1945–1999

Class here 20th century

For 1900–1918, see 978.7031; for 1918–1945, see 978.7032

.703 4	2000–
.8	***Colorado**
.801	Early history to 1803
.802	Acquisition and territorial periods, 1803–1876
.803	Statehood period, 1876–
.803 1	1876–1918
.803 2	1918–1945
.803 3	1945–1999

Class here 20th century

For 1900–1918, see 978.8031; for 1918–1945, see 978.8032

.803 4	2000–
.9	***New Mexico**
.901	Early history to 1598

*Add as instructed under 930–990

.902	Spanish period, 1598–1821
.903	Mexican period, 1821–1848
.904	Territorial period, 1848–1912
.905	Statehood period, 1912–
.905 2	1912–1945
.905 3	1945–1999

            Class here 20th century

                For 1900–1912, see 978.904; for 1912–1945, see 978.9052

.905 4	2000–

979   *Great Basin and Pacific Slope region of United States Pacific Coast states

.01–.03	Historical periods

            Add to base number 979 the numbers following 978 in 978.01–978.03, e.g., 1900 to present 979.03

.1   *Arizona

.101–.105	Historical periods

            Add to base number 979.1 the numbers following 978.9 in 978.901–978.905, e.g., territorial period 979.104

.2   *Utah

.201	Early history to 1848
.202	Territorial period, 1848–1896
.203	Statehood period, 1896–
.203 1	1896–1918
.203 2	1918–1945
.203 3	1945–1999

            Class here 20th century

                For 1900–1918, see 979.2031; for 1918–1945, see 979.2032

.203 4	2000–

.3   *Nevada

.301	Early history to 1861
.302	Territorial and early statehood periods, 1861–1899
.303	1900–

*Add as instructed under 930–990

.303 1	1900–1918
.303 2	1918–1945
.303 3	1945–1999

Class here 20th century

For 1900–1918, see 979.3031; for 1918–1945, see 979.3032

.303 4	2000–

.4 ***California**

.401	Early history to 1769
.402	Spanish period, 1769–1822
.403	Mexican period, 1822–1848
.404	Territorial and early statehood periods, 1848–1899
.405	1900–
.405 1	1900–1918
.405 2	1918–1945
.405 3	1945–1999

Class here 20th century

For 1900–1918, see 979.4051; for 1918–1945, see 979.4052

.405 4	2000–

.5 ***Oregon**

.501	Early history to 1778
.502	Spanish and British periods, 1778–1819
.503	Preterritorial and territorial periods, 1819–1859
.504	Statehood period, 1859–
.504 1	1859–1918
.504 2	1918–1945
.504 3	1945–1999

Class here 20th century

For 1900–1918, see 979.5041; for 1918–1945, see 979.5042

.504 4	2000–

.6 ***Idaho**

.601	Early history to 1863

*Add as instructed under 930–990

.602		Territorial period, 1863–1890
.603		Statehood period, 1890–
.603 1		1890–1918
.603 2		1918–1945
.603 3		1945–1999

Class here 20th century

> For 1900–1918, see 979.6031; for 1918–1945, see 979.6032

.603 4		2000–
.7	***Washington**	
.701		Early history to 1818
.702		British and preterritorial periods, 1818–1853
.703		Territorial period, 1853–1889
.704		Statehood period, 1889–
.704 1		1889–1918
.704 2		1918–1945
.704 3		1945–1999

Class here 20th century

> For 1900–1918, see 979.7041; for 1918–1945, see 979.7042

.704 4		2000–
.8	***Alaska**	
.801		Early history to 1799
.802		Russian period, 1799–1867
.803		Preterritorial period, 1867–1912
.804		Territorial period, 1912–1959

Class here 20th century

> For 1900–1912, see 979.803; for 1959–1999, see 979.8051

.805		Statehood period, 1959–
.805 1		1959–1999
.805 2		2000–

980 General history of South America

Class here Latin America

> For Middle America, see 972

*Add as instructed under 930–990

SUMMARY

.001–.003   Standard subdivisions

.004   Racial, ethnic, national groups

> Add to base number 980.004 notation 03–99 from Table 5, e.g., general history and civilization of South American native peoples in South America 980.00498
>> (Option: Class South American native peoples in South America in 980.1; class specific native peoples in 980.3)
>
> Class prehispanic history and civilization of South American native peoples in a specific place with the place, without using notation 00498, e.g., Incas before 1519 985.019

.005–.009   Standard subdivisions

> As modified under 930–990

> 980.01–980.04 Historical periods

> Class comprehensive works in 980

.01   Early history to 1806

.012   Earliest history to 1498

.013   Period of European discovery, exploration, colonization, 1498–1806

.02   Period of struggles for independence, 1806–1830

.03   1830–1999

.031   1830–1899

> Class here 19th century
>
> *For 1801–1806, see 980.013; for 1806–1830, see 980.02*

.032   1900–1918

.033	1918–1949

Class here 20th century

For a specific part of 20th century not provided for here, see the part, e.g., 1950–1959 980.035

.035	1950–1959
.036	1960–1969
.037	1970–1979
.038	1980–1989
.039	1990–1999
.04	2000–

(.1)   South American native peoples (Indians)

(Optional number; prefer 980.00498)

Class special topics in 980.3–980.5

(.3)   Specific native peoples

(Optional number; prefer 981–989 with use of subdivision 00498 from table under 930–990, e.g., Quechua in Potosí department of Bolivia 984.1400498323)

Arrange alphabetically by name of people

Class government relations with specific native peoples in 980.5

(.4)   Native peoples in specific places in South America

(Optional number; prefer 981–989 with use of subdivision 00498 from table under 930–990, e.g., native peoples in Brazil 981.00498)

Add to base number 980.4 the numbers following —8 in notation 81–89 from Table 2, e.g., native peoples in Brazil 980.41

Class specific native peoples in specific places in 980.3; class government relations in specific places in 980.5

(.5)   Government relations with native South Americans

(Optional number; prefer 323.1198 for comprehensive works; a specific subject with the subject, e.g., conquest of Incas by Pizarro 985.02, relation to state in Chile 323.1198083)

>   **981–989   Countries and localities**

Class comprehensive works in 980. Class a specific native people in a specific place with the place in 981–989 with use of subdivision 00498 from table under 930–990, e.g., Quechua in Potosí department of Bolivia 984.1400498323
    (Option: Class South American native peoples in specific places in South America in 980.4)

981   *Brazil

.01   Early history to 1500

[.012]   Prehispanic period to 1500

                    Number discontinued; class in 981.01

[.013]   Period of European explorations, 1500–1533

                    Relocated to 981.031

[.02]   1533–1549

                    Relocated to 981.032

.03   Colonial period, 1500–1822

.031   Period of European explorations, 1500–1533 [*formerly* 981.013]

.032   Period of hereditary captaincies, 1533–1762

                    Including 1533–1549 [*formerly* 981.02]

.033   1762–1822

.04   Period of Empire, 1822–1889

                    For Paraguayan War, see 989.205

.05   Period of First Republic, 1889–1930

.06   Period of Second Republic, 1930–

                    Class here 20th century

                    For 1901–1930, see 981.05

.061   Period of Getúlio Vargas, 1930–1954

                    Including administrations of José Finol Linhares and Eurico Gaspar Dutra, 1945–1951

.062   1954–1964

                    1964–1967 relocated to 981.063

.063   Period of military presidents, 1964–1985

                    Including 1964–1967 [*formerly* 981.062]

                    Administration of José Sarney, 1985–1990, relocated to 981.064

.064   1985–

                    Including administration of José Sarney, 1985–1990 [*formerly* 981.063]; administrations of Fernando Affonso Collor de Mello, Itamar Franco, Fernando Henrique Cardoso, 1990–

982   *Argentina

*Add as instructed under 930–990

.01   Early history to 1516

.02   Period of European discovery, conquest, colonization, 1516–1810

.022   Period of European discovery and conquest, 1516–1580

.023   Colonial period, 1580–1810

> *For period of viceroyalty of La Plata, 1776–1810, see 982.024*

.024   Period of viceroyalty of La Plata, 1776–1810

.03   Period of struggle for independence, 1810–1829

.04   1829–1861

Class here 19th century

> *For 1801–1810, see 982.024; for 1810–1829, see 982.03; for 1861–1900, see 982.05*

.05   1861–1910

> *For Paraguayan War, see 989.205*

.06   1910–

.061   1910–1946

.062   First administration of Juan Domingo Perón, 1946–1955

.063   1955–1973

.064   1973–

Including second administration of Juan Domingo Perón, 1973–1974; administration of Isabel Perón, 1974–1976

983   *Chile

.01   Early history to 1535

.02   Period of European discovery and conquest, 1535–1560

.03   Colonial period, 1560–1810

.04   Period of early republics, 1810–1861

Class here 19th century

> *For period of autocratic republic, 1830–1861, see 983.05. For a specific part of 19th century not provided for here, see the part, e.g., 1879–1883 983.0616*

.05   Period of autocratic republic, 1830–1861

.06   Period of later republics, 1861–

.061   Period of liberal republic, 1861–1891

*Add as instructed under 930–990

.061 6	‡War of the Pacific, 1879–1883
	(Option: Class in 984.045)
.062	Revolution of 1891
.063	Period of parliamentary republic, 1891–1925
.064	1925–1973

Class here 20th century

> For 1901–1925, see 983.063; for 1973–1990, see 983.065; for 1990–1999, see 983.066

.064 1	1925–1932
.064 2	1932–1946
.064 3	1946–1958
.064 4	Administration of Jorge Alessandri, 1958–1964
.064 5	Administration of Eduardo Frei Montalva, 1964–1970
.064 6	Administration of Salvador Allende Gossens, 1970–1973
.065	Period of military rule, 1973–1990
.066	1990–

984   *Bolivia

.01	Early history to 1532
.02	Period of European discovery and conquest, 1532–1559
.03	Colonial period, 1559–1809
.04	1809–1899
.041	Period of struggle for independence, 1809–1825
.042	Period of formation of the Republic, 1825–1831
.044	Administration of Andrés Santa Cruz, 1831–1839

Including Peru-Bolivian Confederation, 1836–1839

| .045 | 1839–1883 |

(Option: Class here War of the Pacific; prefer 983.0616)

| .046 | Period of conservative republic, 1883–1899 |
| .05 | 1899– |

*Add as instructed under 930–990

‡Add as instructed under 940–990

.051	1899–1952
	Class here 20th century
	For 1952–1999, see 984.052
	(Option: Class here Chaco War; prefer 989.20716)
.052	1952–
	Including revolution of 1952

985   *Peru

| .01 | Early history to 1519 |
| .019 | Period of Inca (Inka) empire, ca. 1438–1519 |

For a part of Inca empire not provided for here, see the part, e.g., Inca empire in Bolivia 984.01

.02	Period of European discovery and conquest, 1519–1555
	(Option: Class conquest in 980.5)
.03	Colonial period, 1555–1808
.04	Period of struggle for independence, 1808–1824
.05	1824–1867
	Class here 19th century
	Including Peru-Bolivian Confederation, 1836–1839

For a specific part of 19th century not provided for here, see the part, e.g., 1867–1883 985.061

| .06 | 1867– |
| .061 | 1867–1883 |

For War of the Pacific, see 983.0616

.062	Period of reconstruction, 1883–1895
.063	1895–
.063 1	1895–1933
.063 2	1933–1968
.063 3	1968–

986   *Colombia and Ecuador

| .1 | *Colombia |
| .101 | Early history to 1550 |

*Add as instructed under 930–990

.102	Colonial period, 1550–1810

Including periods as Viceroyalty of New Granada, 1718–1724 and 1740–1810

Class here comprehensive works on Viceroyalty of New Granada

> *For Panama as part of Viceroyalty of New Granada, see 972.8702; for Ecuador as part of Viceroyalty of New Granada, see 986.602; for Venezuela as part of Viceroyalty of New Granada, see 987.03*

.103	Period of struggle for independence, 1810–1819
.104	Period of Gran Colombia, 1819–1832

Class here comprehensive works on Gran Colombia

> *For Panama as a part of Gran Colombia, see 972.8703; for Ecuador as part of Gran Colombia, see 986.604; for Venezuela as part of Gran Colombia, see 987.05*

.105	1832–1863
.105 2	Period of Republic of New Granada, 1832–1858

Class here comprehensive works on Republic of New Granada

> *For Panama as part of Republic of New Granada, see 972.8703*

.105 3	Period of Granadine Confederation, 1858–1863

Class here comprehensive works on Granadine Confederation

> *For Panama as part of Granadine Confederation, see 972.8703*

.106	1863–
.106 1	Period of United States of Colombia, 1863–1886

Class here comprehensive works on United States of Colombia

> *For Panama as part of United States of Colombia, see 972.8703*

.106 2	Period of Republic of Colombia, 1886–

> *For Panama as part of Republic of Colombia, see 972.8703; for Colombian history from 1930 to present, see 986.1063*

.106 3	1930–

Class here 20th century

> *For 1901–1930, see 986.1062*

.106 31	Period of liberal domination, 1930–1946
.106 32	1946–1958
.106 33	Period of National Front, 1958–1974
.106 34	1974–1991

.106 35	1991–
.6	***Ecuador**
.601	Early history to 1562
.602	Colonial period, 1562–1810
	Including period as part of Viceroyalty of New Granada, 1740–1810
.603	Period of struggle for independence, 1810–1822
.604	Period as part of Gran Colombia, 1822–1830
	Class here Quito Presidency
.605	1830–1859
	Including period of formation of Republic
.606	1860–1895
.607	1896–
.607 1	1896–1925
.607 2	1925–1948
.607 3	1948–1960
.607 4	1960–

987 *Venezuela

.01	Early history to 1498
.02	Period of discovery and conquest, 1498–1528
.03	Colonial period, 1528–1810
	Including period as part of Viceroyalty of New Granada, 1740–1810
.04	Period of struggle for independence, 1810–1821
.05	Period as part of Gran Colombia, 1821–1830
.06	Period of Republic, 1830–
.061	1830–1864
.062	1864–1899
	Class here period of Antonio Guzmán Blanco, 1870–1888
.063	1899–
.063 1	1899–1935
.063 12	Period of Cipriano Castro, 1899–1908
.063 13	Period of Juan Vicente Gómez, 1908–1935

*Add as instructed under 930–990

.063 2	1935–1959
.063 3	1959–

988   *Guiana

.01	Early history to 1815
.02	1815–1945
.03	1945–

Class here 20th century

For 1901–1945, see 988.02

.1   *Guyana

.101	Early history to 1815
.102	1815–1945
.103	1945–

Class here 20th century

For 1901–1945, see 988.102

.103 1	1945–1966
.103 2	1966–

.2   *French Guiana (Guyane)

.3   *Surinam (Suriname)

.301	Early history to 1815
.302	1815–1945
.303	1945–

Class here 20th century

For 1901–1945, see 988.302

.303 1	1945–1975
.303 2	1975–

989   Paraguay and Uruguay

.2   *Paraguay

.201	Early history to 1524
.202	Period of European discovery, exploration, conquest, 1524–1537
.203	Colonial period, 1537–1811
.204	Period of struggle for independence, 1811–1814

*Add as instructed under 930–990

.205	Period of dictatorship, 1814–1870
	Including Paraguayan War (War of the Triple Alliance), 1865–1870
.206	1870–1902
.207	1902–
.207 1	1902–1940
.207 16	‡Chaco War, 1933–1935
	(Option: Class in 984.051)
.207 2	1940–1958
.207 3	1958–
.5	***Uruguay**
.501	Early history to 1516
.502	Period of European discovery and conquest, 1516–1724
.503	Colonial period, 1724–1811
.504	Period of struggle for independence, 1811–1830
.505	Period of Republic, 1830–
	For Paraguayan War, see 989.205; for 1886 to present, see 989.506
.506	1886–
.506 1	1886–1917
.506 2	1917–1933
.506 3	1933–1951
.506 4	1951–1966
.506 5	1966–1973
.506 6	1973–1985
.506 7	1985–

990 General history of other parts of world, of extraterrestrial worlds   Pacific Ocean islands

.01–.09	Standard subdivisions of Pacific Ocean islands
	As modified under 930–990

[991–992][Unassigned]

Most recently used in Edition 17

---

*Add as instructed under 930–990

‡Add as instructed under 940–990

993   *New Zealand

.01   Early history to 1840

> Including history of Maoris before European settlement, of European settlers

.02   Colonial period, 1840–1908

.021   Period as a Crown colony, 1840–1853

> Including New Zealand Wars of 1843–1847

.022   Period of provincial governments, 1853–1876

> Class here comprehensive works on New Zealand Wars
>
> *For New Zealand Wars of 1843–1847, see 993.021*

.023   Period of centralized government, 1876–1908

.03   Dominion period, 1908–

.031   1908–1918

.032   1918–1945

.035   1945–1969

.037   1970–

994   *Australia

.01   Early history to 1788

.02   Period of settlement and growth, 1788–1851

.03   Period of development of self government, 1851–1901

.031   Period of gold discovery and consolidation, 1851–1891

.032   1891–1901

.04   Period of Commonwealth, 1901–

> Class here 20th century
>
> *For 1945–1966, see 994.05; for 1966–1999, see 994.06; for 2000 and beyond, see 994.07*

.041   1901–1922

.042   1922–1945

> Including first prime ministership of Robert Gordon Menzies, 1939–1941

.05   1945–1966

> Class here second prime ministership of Robert Gordon Menzies, 1949–1966

*Add as instructed under 930–990

.06	1966–1999
.061	1966–1972
.062	1972–1975
.063	1976–1983
.064	1983–1991
.065	1991–1999
.07	2000–

995   †Melanesia   New Guinea

Class here Oceania

Class Polynesia in 996

> ### 995.1–995.7 New Guinea

Class comprehensive works in 995

.1   *Irian Jaya

.101–.104   Historical periods

Add to base number 995.1 the numbers following 959.8 in
959.801–959.804, e.g., period of administration of Sukarno 995.1035

.3   *Papua New Guinea   New Guinea region

*For Papuan region, see 995.4; for Highlands region, see 995.6; for
Momase region, see 995.7; for Bismarck Archipelago, see 995.8; for North
Solomons Province, see 995.92*

.301   Early history to 1884

.302   1884–1942

Class here 20th century

*For 1942–1945, see 995.303; for 1945–1975, see 995.304; for
1975–1999, see 995.305*

.302 1   1884–1921

Class here German New Guinea

.302 2   1921–1942

Class here period as Territory of New Guinea, 1921–1949

For 1942–1945, see 995.303; for 1945–1949, see 995.304

.303   Period of World War II, 1942–1945

---

*Add as instructed under 930–990

†Add as instructed under 930–990; however, do not add historical periods

.304	1945–1975

        Class here Territory of Papua and New Guinea, 1949–1975

.305	Period of independence, 1975–

.4   ***Papuan region**

.401	Early history to 1884
.402	1884–1942

        Class here 20th century

           For 1942–1945, see 995.403; for 1945–1975, see 995.404; for 1975–1999, see 995.405

.402 1	Period as British New Guinea, 1884–1906
.402 2	1906–1942

        Class here period as Territory of Papua, 1906–1949

           For 1942–1945, see 995.403; for 1945–1949, see 995.404

.403	Period of World War II, 1942–1945
.404	1945–1975

        Class here Papuan region as a part of Territory of Papua and New Guinea, 1949–1975

.405	Period of independence, 1975–

.6   ***Highlands region**

.601–.605	Historical periods

        Add to base number 995.6 the numbers following 995.3 in 995.301–995.305, e.g., period of World War II 995.603

.7   ***Momase (Northern coastal) region**

.701–.705	Historical periods

        Add to base number 995.7 the numbers following 995.3 in 995.301–995.305, e.g., period of World War II 995.703

.8   ***Bismarck Archipelago**

.801–.805	Historical periods

        Add to base number 995.8 the numbers following 995.3 in 995.301–995.305, e.g., period of World War II 995.803

.9   **†Other parts of Melanesia**

.92	*North Solomons Province

*Add as instructed under 930–990

†Add as instructed under 930–990; however, do not add historical periods

.920 1–.920 5   Historical periods

> Add to base number 995.92 the numbers following 995.3 in 995.301–995.305, e.g., period of World War II 995.9203

.93   †Solomon Islands

.95   †Vanuatu

.97   †New Caledonia

996   Other parts of Pacific   Polynesia

.001–.009   Standard subdivisions of Polynesia

> As modified under 930–990

.1   **†Southwest central Pacific, and isolated islands of southeast Pacific**

.11   †Fiji

.12   †Tonga (Friendly Islands)

.13   †American Samoa

.14   †Western Samoa

.15   †Tokelau (Union Islands)

.16   †Wallis and Futuna Islands

.18   †Isolated islands of southeast Pacific

.2   **†South central Pacific Ocean islands**

.3   **†Southeast central Pacific Ocean islands**

> *For isolated islands of southeast Pacific, see 996.18*

.4   **†Line Islands (Equatorial Islands)**

.5   **†West central Pacific Ocean islands (Micronesia)   Trust Territory of the Pacific Islands**

.6   **†Federated States of Micronesia and Republic of Palau**

.7   **†Mariana Islands**

.8   **†Islands of eastern Micronesia**

.81   †Kiribati

.82   †Tuvalu

.83   †Marshall Islands

.85   †Nauru (Pleasant Island)

.9   **North central Pacific islands   Hawaii**

†Add as instructed under 930–990; however, do not add historical periods

.900 01–.900 08   Standard subdivisions of north central Pacific islands

                         As modified under 930–990

.900 09   Historical periods; areas, regions, places in general; persons of north central Pacific islands

.900 090 1–.900 090 5   Historical periods

                         Add to base number 996.90009 the numbers following —090 in notation 0901–0905 from Table 1, e.g., north central Pacific islands during 20th century 996.9000904

.900 091–.900 099   Areas, regions, places in general; persons

                         As modified under 930–990

.900 1–.900 9   Standard subdivisions of Hawaii

                         As modified under 930–990

>   996.902–996.904 Historical periods of Hawaii

                  Class comprehensive works in 996.9

.902   Early history to 1898

.902 7   Period of kingdom, 1810–1893

.902 8   Period of republic, 1893–1898

.903   Territorial period, 1898–1959

                      Class here 20th century

                          For 1959–1999, see 996.9041

.904   Statehood period, 1959–

.904 1   1959–1999

.904 2   2000–

.99   †Outlying islands

997   †Atlantic Ocean islands

For each specific island or group of islands not provided for here, see the island or group of islands, e.g., Azores 946.99

.1   †Falkland Islands, South Georgia and South Sandwich Islands, Bouvet Island

.11   *Falkland Islands (Islas Malvinas)

.110 1   Early history to 1832

                      Including French, British, Spanish, Argentine presence

---

*Add as instructed under 930–990

†Add as instructed under 930–990; however, do not add historical periods

.110 2	British period, 1832–	
.110 24	‡Falkland Islands War, 1982	

.3 **†Saint Helena and dependencies**

998 †Arctic islands and Antarctica

.2 **†Greenland**

999 Extraterrestrial worlds

Class here extraterrestrial civilization, extraterrestrial intelligence, SETI (search for extraterrestrial intelligence)

Do not add from table under 930–990

---

†Add as instructed under 930–990; however, do not add historical periods

‡Add as instructed under 940–990

The 21st edition of the Dewey Decimal Classification was designed by Lisa Hanifan of Albany, New York. Edition 21 was generated from an online database. Database design, technical support, and programming for this edition were provided by John Finni and Kurt Lanza from Inforonics, Inc. of Littleton, Massachusetts. Composition was done in Times Roman and Helvetica under the supervision of Inforonics, Inc. and Word Management, Inc. of Albany, New York. The book was printed and bound by Hamilton Printing Company of Rensselaer, New York.